AF251826

KATSUYA IWAMOTO
EMBODY DESIGN

デザインはスタイリングではない。
表層を整えることに意味はない。
ただ美しい空間をつくるのなら、僕じゃなくてもいい。
僕の仕事は、まだ目には見えない目的を、
五感と頭脳で感じ取って具現化すること、
デザインで、人を幸せにすることだ。

Design is not styling.

There is no meaning in merely arranging a surface.

If it is simply to create a beautiful space, someone other than I could do it.

Incorporating the five senses and the mind to actualize

an idea that is not yet visible to the eye…

my job is to make people happy through designs.

人を幸せにするデザイン

15年前、26才でEMBODY DESIGN ASSOCIATIONを立ち上げた。
それまで丹青社という会社でミュージアムデザインを手掛けていた僕は、今だから打ち明けるが、
実は商空間を手掛けた経験はほぼゼロに等しかった。
それでも、僕の仕事は「ここ」にあると強く信じていたし、その自信があった。
一体その根拠と自信はどこから来たのかと、あきれられることも多いのだが、それはこうだ。
「ミュージアムには、老若男女も国籍も問わない、まさに多様な人が訪れる。そこでは、皆が展示内容を理解することができ、
かつ小難しい歴史や文明や科学を楽しく、興味深く感じることができなくてはならない。
その為に必要な思考的、技術的ノウハウは、絶対にどの分野のデザインにおいても繋がっているはずだ・・・」
根拠は、これだけである。あそこで僕は、「色んな人の立場に立って多角的にモノゴトを見る」感覚、
「社会に本当に必要なものだけを創らなくてはいけない」という使命感をからだ全体で感じていた。
もともと、商空間デザインの部署への配属を約束して丹青社に入社したところ、ミュージアムデザインの部署に配属され、
不本意の極みのようなところから始まった数年間だったが、
そこから得た経験は、まぎれもなく今の僕の揺るぎない大切な土台となっている。

エンバディ デザイン

事務所名に使っている「EMBODY」は、「目的を具現化する」という意味で、
これは僕のデザインという概念の土台となる言葉である。
そして、その「目的」とは、デザインしたモノやコトが、人と人、人とコト、個人と社会、個人と内面の自己等を結び、
幸せのきっかけを生み出すことだと考えている。そのために、デザインは美しく表層を整えるだけでは意味がないのだ。
様々な既存条件と未来にあるべき姿を、丁寧に結びあわせて構築・デザインすることで、
出会いやコミュニケーションを生み出し、人に愛され、そこでの時間軸を常にプラスに変換して行くような空間になると考える。
それを僕は今までも目指して来て、これからも目指して行く。
初めて本の出版の話をいただいて、心に決めたことは、その戦いの軌跡を「僕の言葉で伝えよう」ということだ。
つたない表現方法かもしれないが、これが今のEMBODY DESIGNと僕の姿だ。
僕たちには、まだまだ進化の余地があることを伝えるのだ、と強がっておく。

Designs Making People Happy

Fifteen years ago, at age 26, I established EMBODY DESIGN ASSOCIATION,

and although I am able to make a confession now, I had practically no experience in commercial space design

as all the experience I had acquired until then was in museum design at a company known as Tanseisha Co., Ltd.

Nevertheless, with great conviction I believed my job was right here.

But where did this conviction come from and what was it based on?

Although many things amazed me along the way, this is how it was. "All sorts of people, from many walks of life, age,

gender and nationality visit museums. Museums are there for visitors to grasp an understanding of the exhibits

and to enjoy and be intrigued by the slightly complex topics of history, civilization and science.

For this reason I believe that the essential conceptual and technical knowledge are linked together in all fields of design."

My foundation in design stemmed from there. It was there that I felt deep within myself my mission in life

to look at things differently and from the perspective of others and create only what is needed by society.

When I first entered Tanseisha I was originally promised a position in the commercial space department

however was placed in museum design, and although for many years I felt disappointed,

the experience I gained there has given me the solid foundation I have today.

EMBODY DESIGN

EMBODY, meaning to give concrete form to an idea,

is a term representing the foundational concept of my designs and the name we have chosen for our office.

I believe that this idea will create an opportunity for happiness and what we design to bind people to people,

people to happenings and bond together individuals and society and individuals to their inner-self.

For this reason there is no meaning in merely creating a beautiful surface.

Through construction and design that combines a variety of existing aspects with ideal future designs,

I believe we can bring people together, generate communication and create a space that people can admire

and in which time is appreciated. This is what I have always aimed for and what I will continue to aspire to.

The first time I received an offer to publish my book I decided that I would convey the road fought with my own words.

Although perhaps clumsily expressed, it represents me and EMBODY DESIGN at present.

In conclusion, I would like to strongly express that we still have plenty of room left for development.

INDEX

draw out the beauty of mental

connect the minds

privacy

a comfortable dream place

reversal idea

openness pride

clearness

veiled in sense of beauty

design of relationship

内面の美しさを引き出す

心を結ぶ

開放感 プライド

美意識

関係性のデザイン

憧れの心地よい居場所

美音

転換

居場所

HAIR SALON

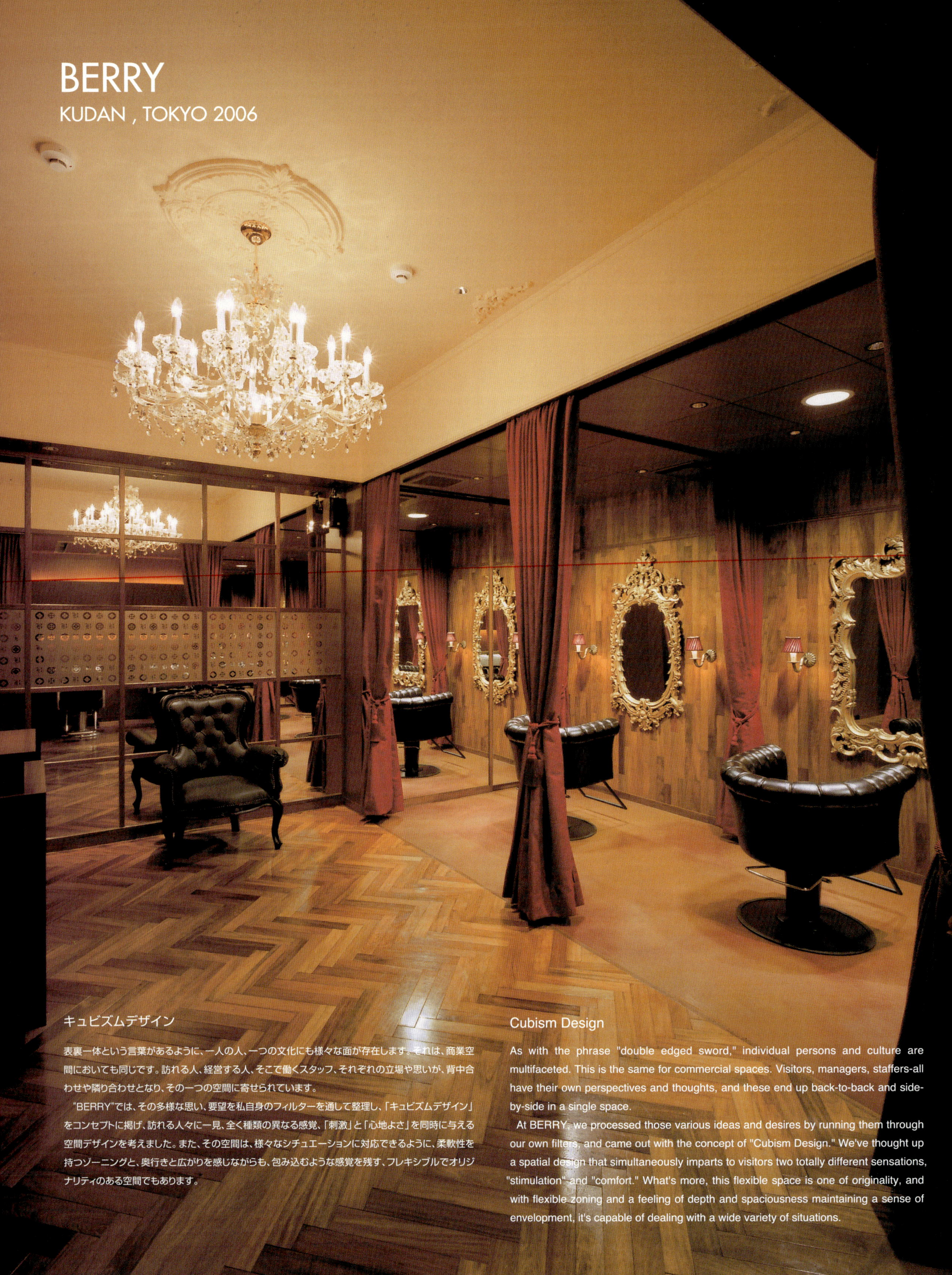

BERRY
KUDAN , TOKYO 2006

キュビズムデザイン

表裏一体という言葉があるように、一人の人、一つの文化にも様々な面が存在します。それは、商業空間においても同じです。訪れる人、経営する人、そこで働くスタッフ、それぞれの立場や思いが、背中合わせや隣り合わせとなり、その一つの空間に寄せられています。

　"BERRY"では、その多様な思い、要望を私自身のフィルターを通して整理し、「キュビズムデザイン」をコンセプトに掲げ、訪れる人々に一見、全く種類の異なる感覚、「刺激」と「心地よさ」を同時に与える空間デザインを考えました。また、その空間は、様々なシチュエーションに対応できるように、柔軟性を持つゾーニングと、奥行きと広がりを感じながらも、包み込むような感覚を残す、フレキシブルでオリジナリティのある空間でもあります。

Cubism Design

As with the phrase "double edged sword," individual persons and culture are multifaceted. This is the same for commercial spaces. Visitors, managers, staffers-all have their own perspectives and thoughts, and these end up back-to-back and side-by-side in a single space.

　At BERRY, we processed those various ideas and desires by running them through our own filters, and came out with the concept of "Cubism Design." We've thought up a spatial design that simultaneously imparts to visitors two totally different sensations, "stimulation" and "comfort." What's more, this flexible space is one of originality, and with flexible zoning and a feeling of depth and spaciousness maintaining a sense of envelopment, it's capable of dealing with a wide variety of situations.

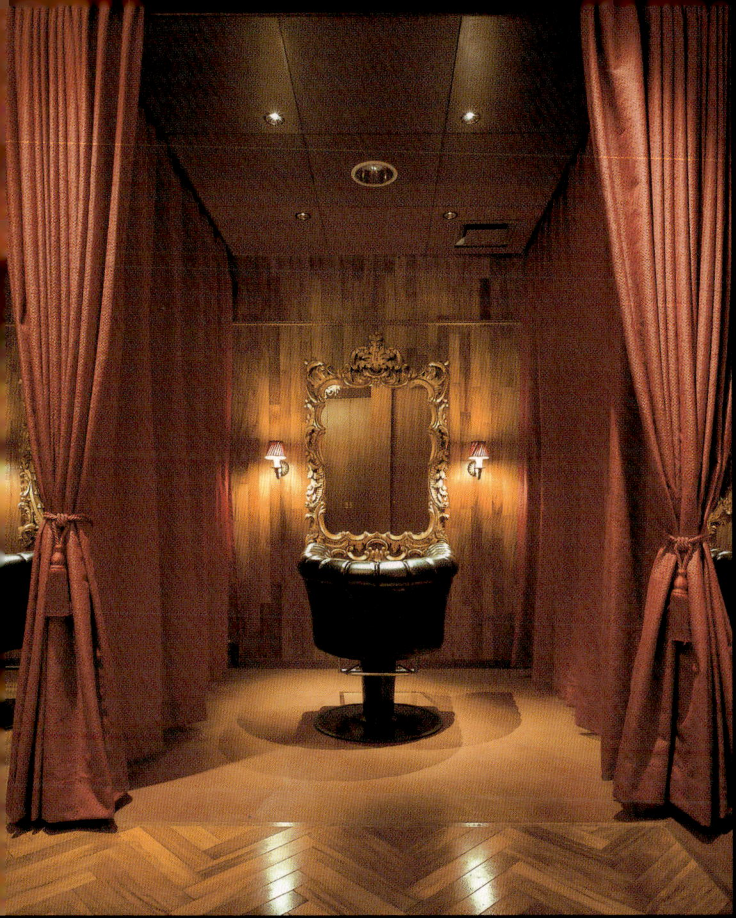

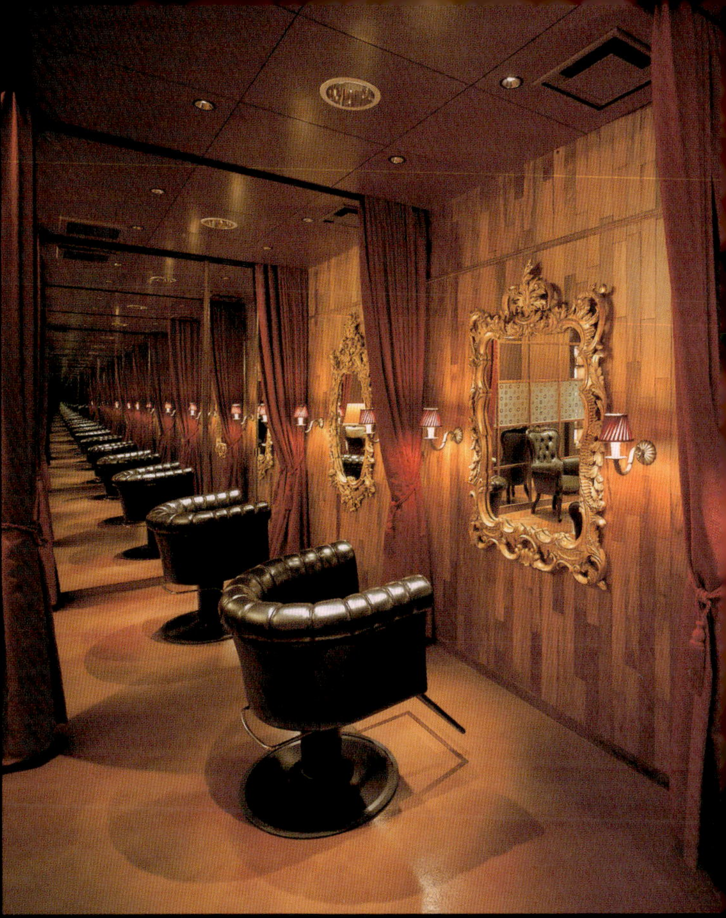

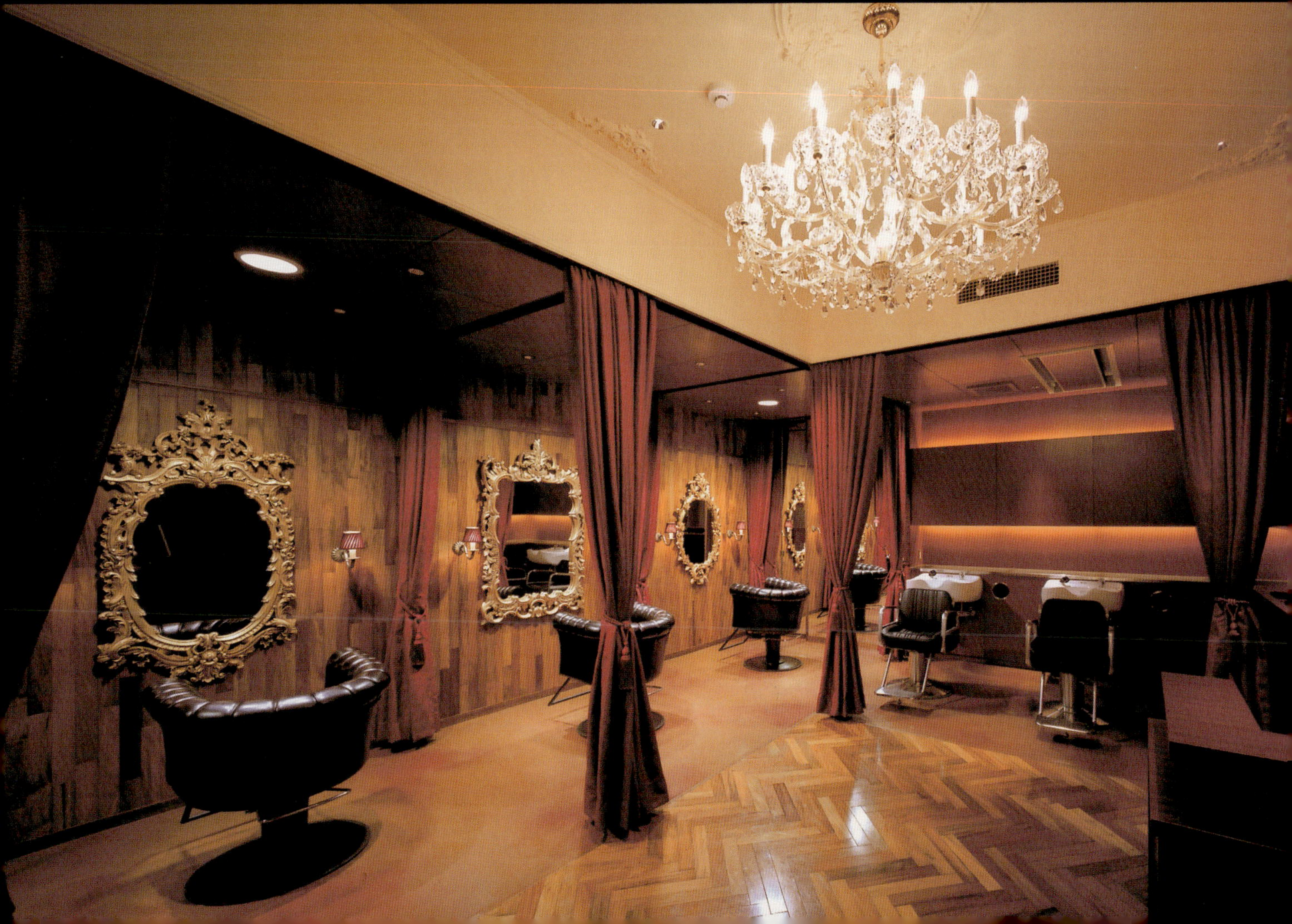

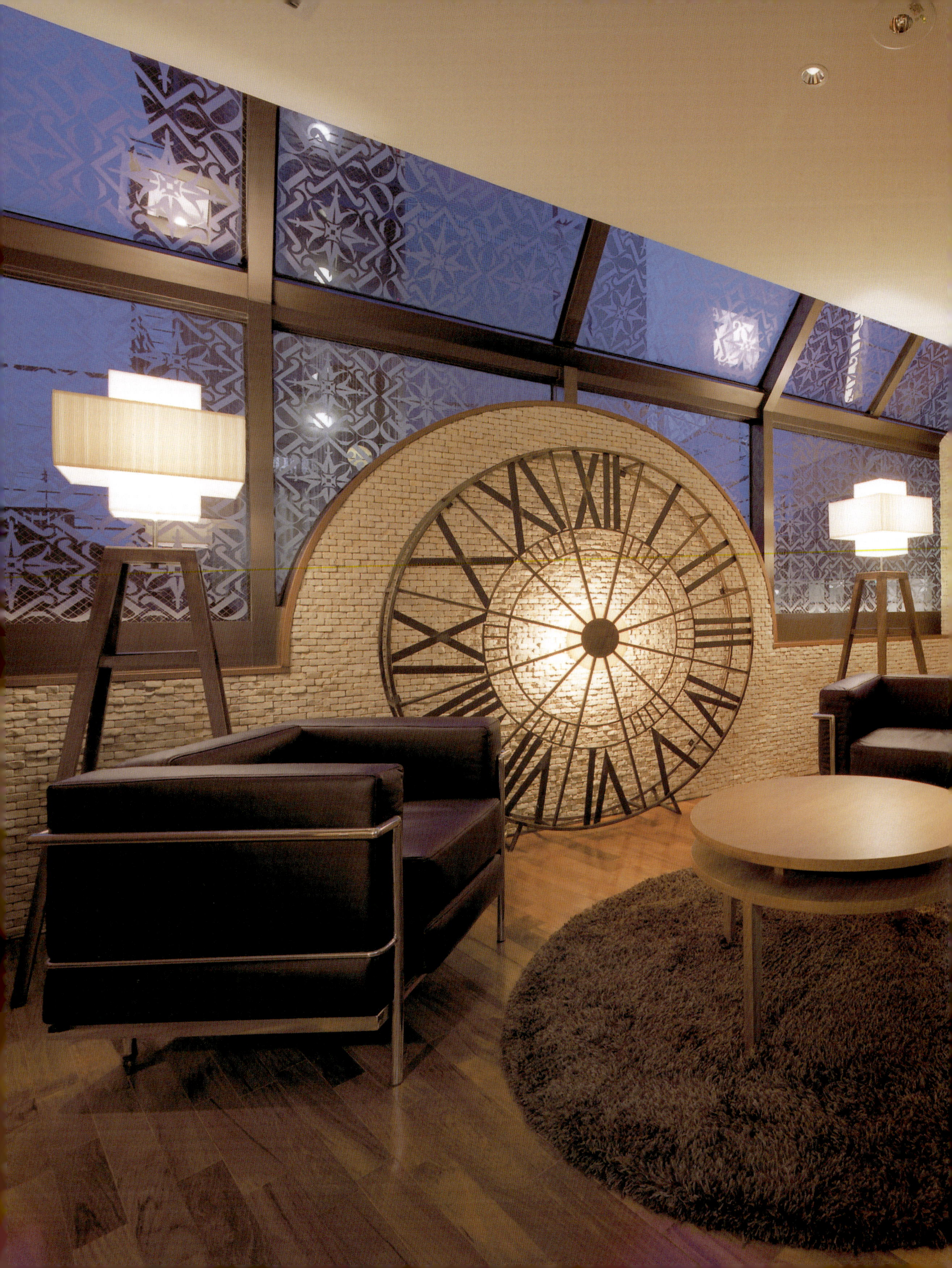

DONFUN
MOTOAZABU , TOKYO 2006

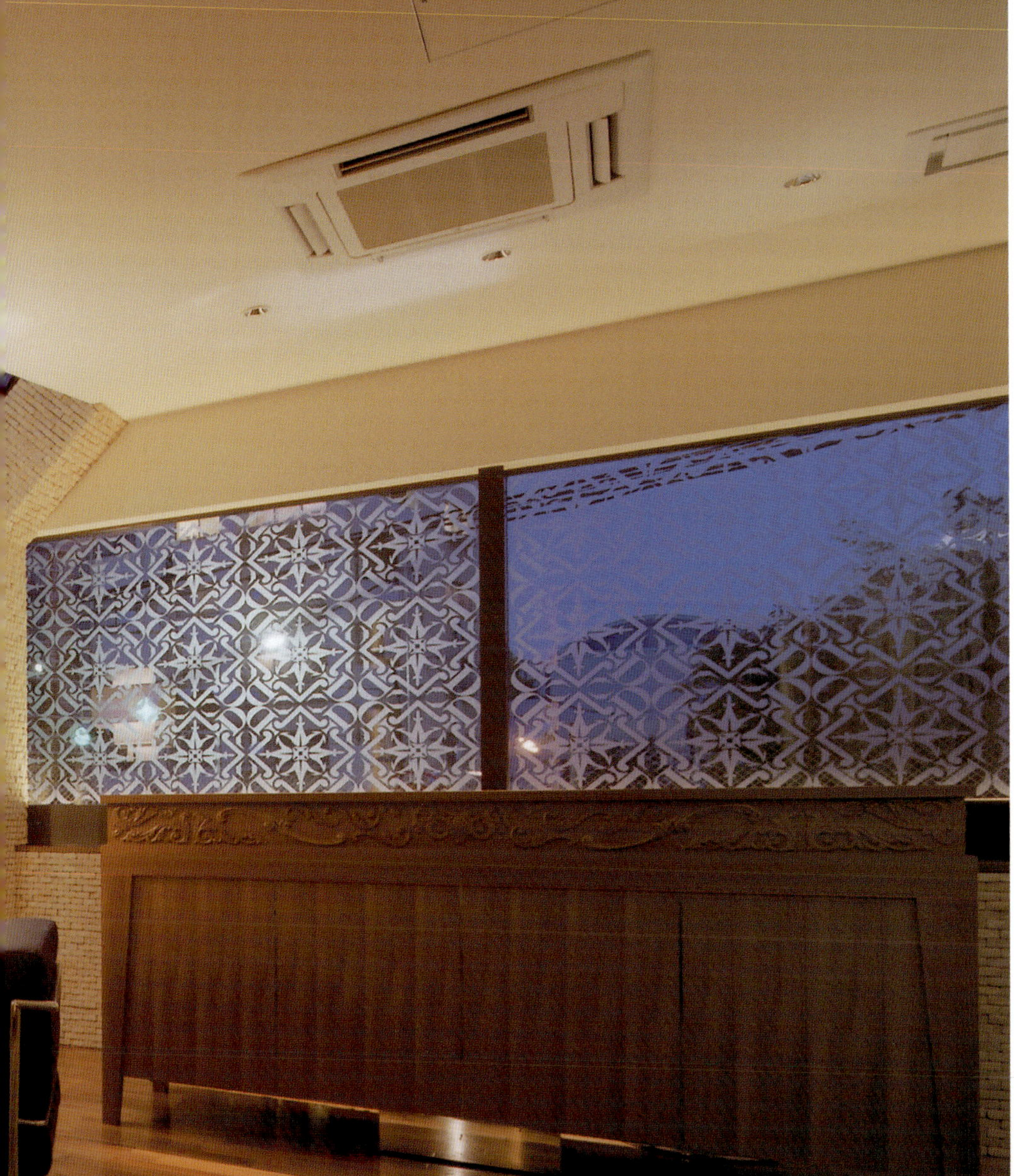

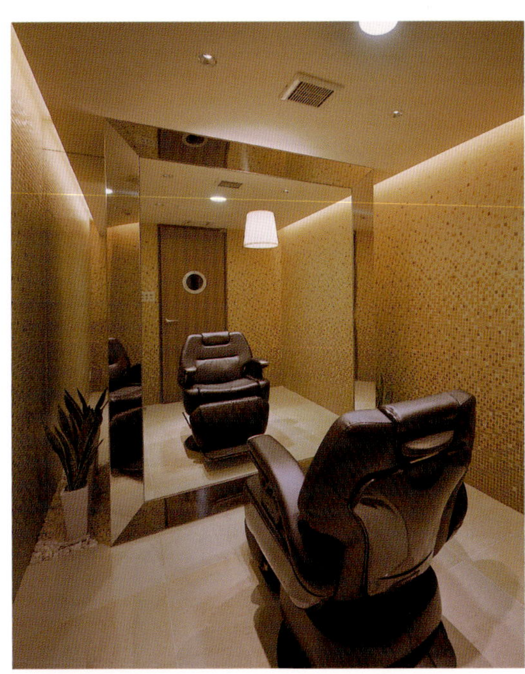

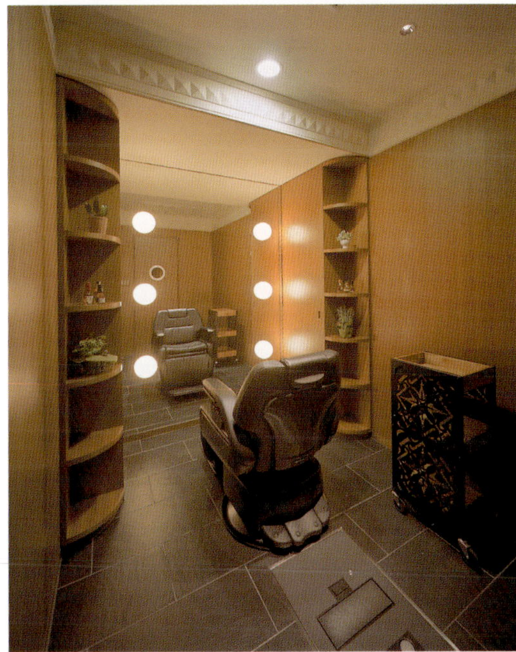

ファーストクラスへようこそ

世の中をリードする人々は、日々戦略を立て、具現化していくという多忙な毎日を送っていることでしょう。そんな人たちには、時に心を落ち着かせ、頭の中を整理するための特別な時間が必要ではないでしょうか。

"DON FUN"は、そんな選ばれし男たちのために、生まれました。

「オーセンティック　モダン」をコンセプトに構成した空間は、完全な個室を用意して、訪れるセレブリティ達が心地よく、贅沢な時間を過ごせるように配慮しました。また、身だしなみを整えるためだけではなく、ゆったりと本来の自分を見つけることができるような、そんな空気が流れる特別なサロンです。

Welcome to First Class!

Every day the leaders of the world must come up with strategies and make things happen, and so every day they are extremely busy. For these people, a special interlude is no doubt needed where they can allow their minds to relax and compose themselves.

DON FUN was created with just that sort of elite man in mind.

The space is constructed around the concept of "authentic modern"-and we've thought ahead--preparing totally private rooms where visiting celebrities can while away the time in pleasant luxury. Indeed, this is a very special salon with an atmosphere where not only can one primp and preen--but also seek the true self in comfort.

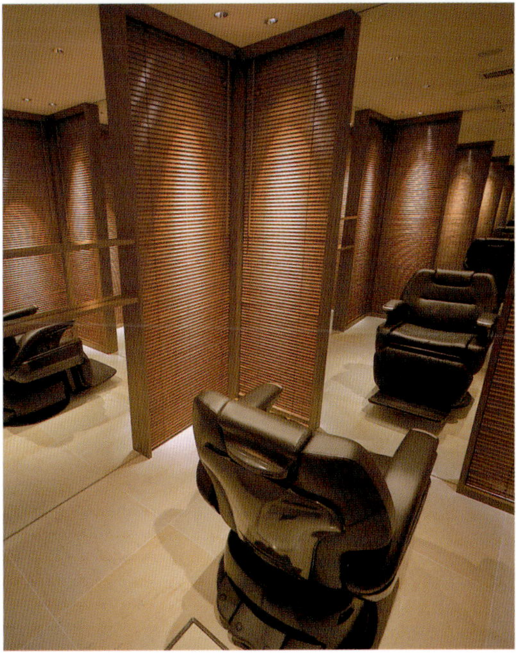

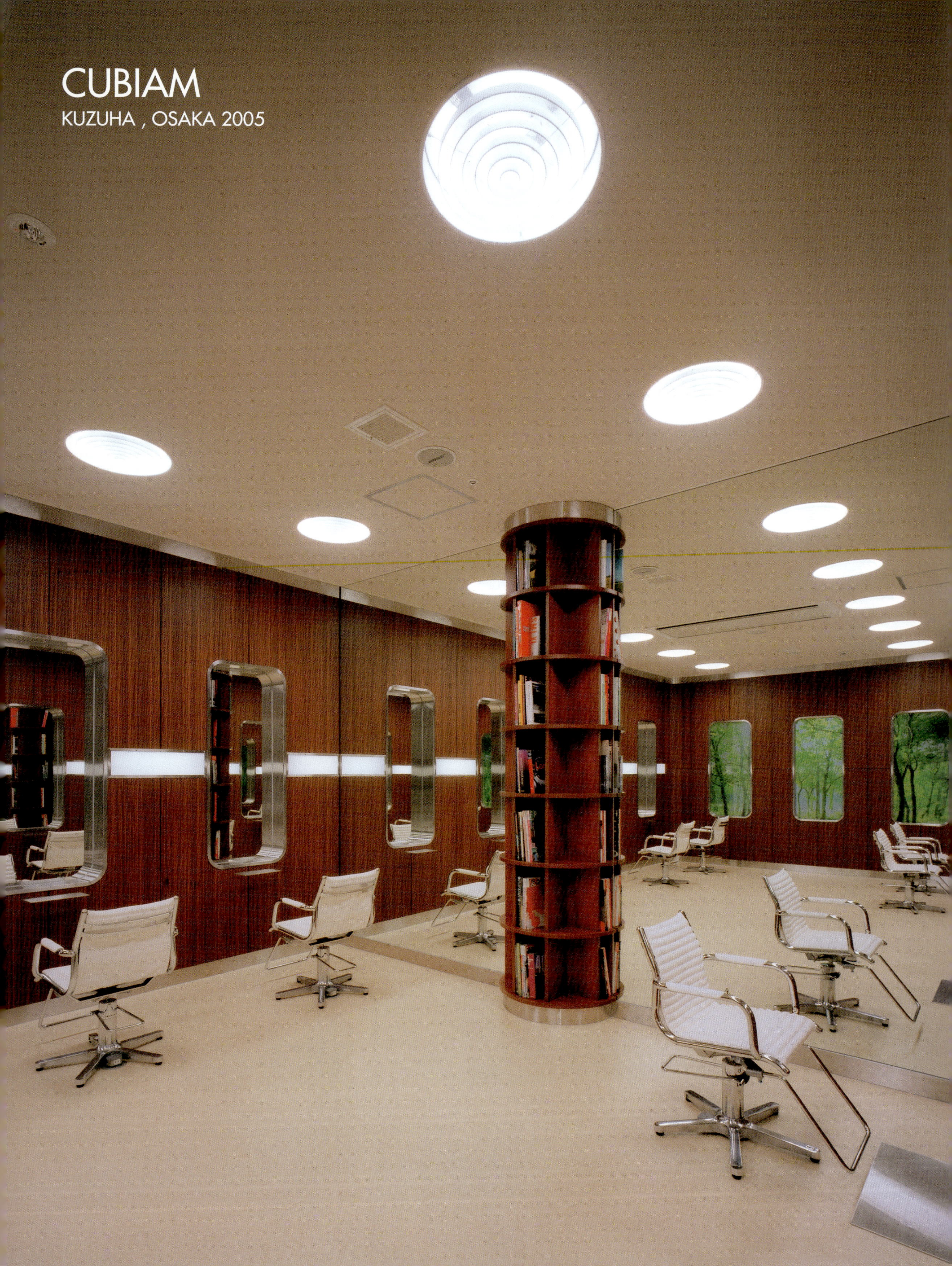

CUBIAM
KUZUHA , OSAKA 2005

手の届く幸せ

"CUBIAM"は、楠葉駅に隣接する大型複合施設の4階フロアでの計画で、このフロアは、クリニック・エステ・ヘアサロンで構成され、楠葉周辺で暮らす人々と日常を共有し、健康美をサポートすることを目的としている。

そのフロアにおいて、ここ"CUBIAM"は、「憧れの心地よい居場所」をコンセプトに、訪れる人があわただしい日常からエスケープして、少しだけ上質な時間を過ごせるスイッチとなるような空間をイメージしながらデザインした。

そして、訪れる人々にとってだけの心地よさを追求するのではなく、街にとって、またこの施設にとっての"CUBIAM"の役割や位置付けも意識してカタチにしていった。様々な層のお客様に、訪れてみたいと思っていただける、上品でありながら開放感のある空間が具現化できたと思う。

Happiness you can reach

CUBIAM is a design on the 4th floor of the large complex located adjacent to Kuzuha Station. The 4th floor of this facility consists of clinics, beauty salons, and hair salons, sharing everyday life with the people that live around Kuzuha, and supporting their health and beauty.

In designing CUBIAM, my concept was for a "familiar and comfortable place" that would act as a switch, allowing people to escape from frantic everyday life and spend a little quality time.

In forming the CUBIAM concept I didn't just pursue the comfort of those that would visit, but I also tried to retain a consciousness of the role and position of CUBIAM within this facility, and also within the local community. I believe that I was able to create a space that, while having a feel of elegance, also gives a sense of freedom and release, so that all different classes of customers are encouraged to come inside and see.

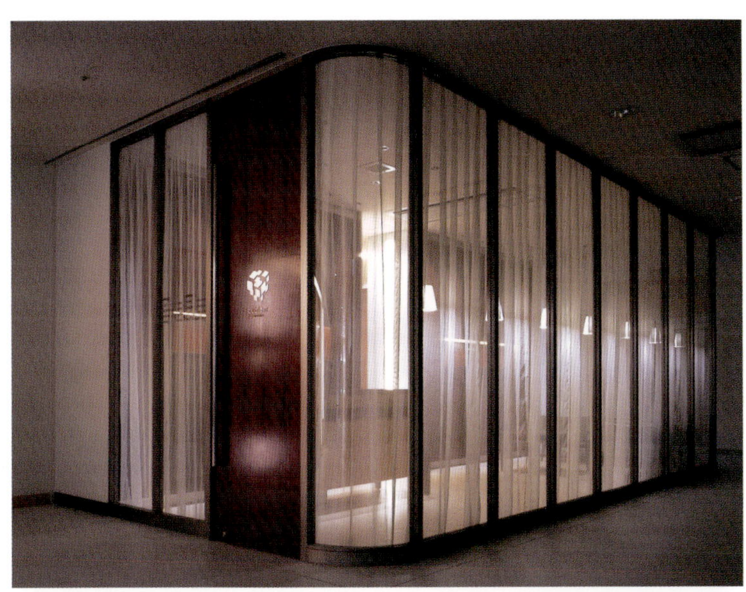

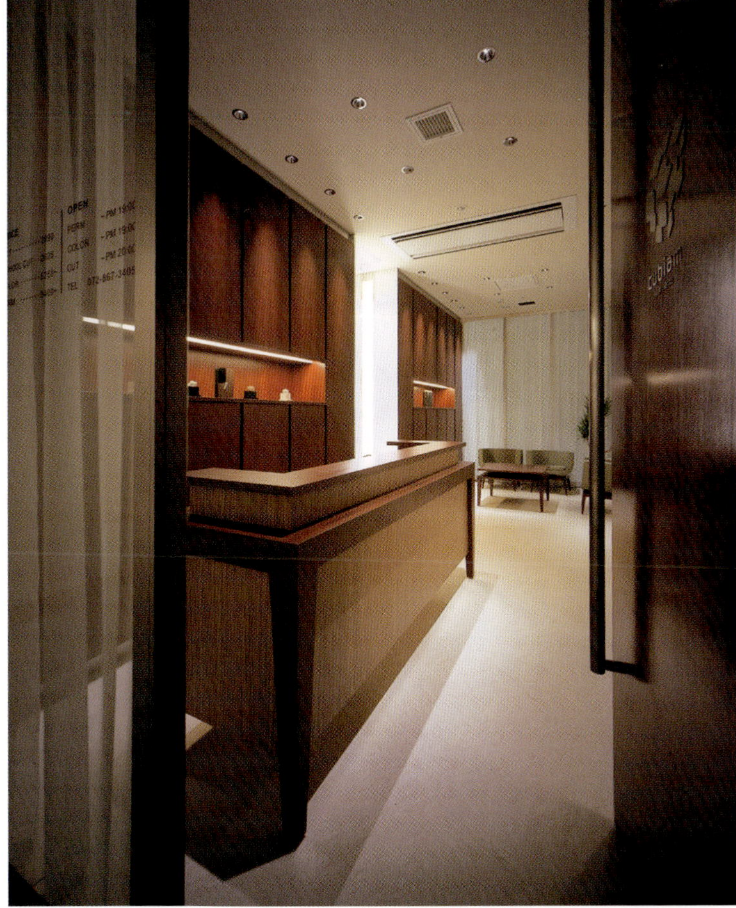

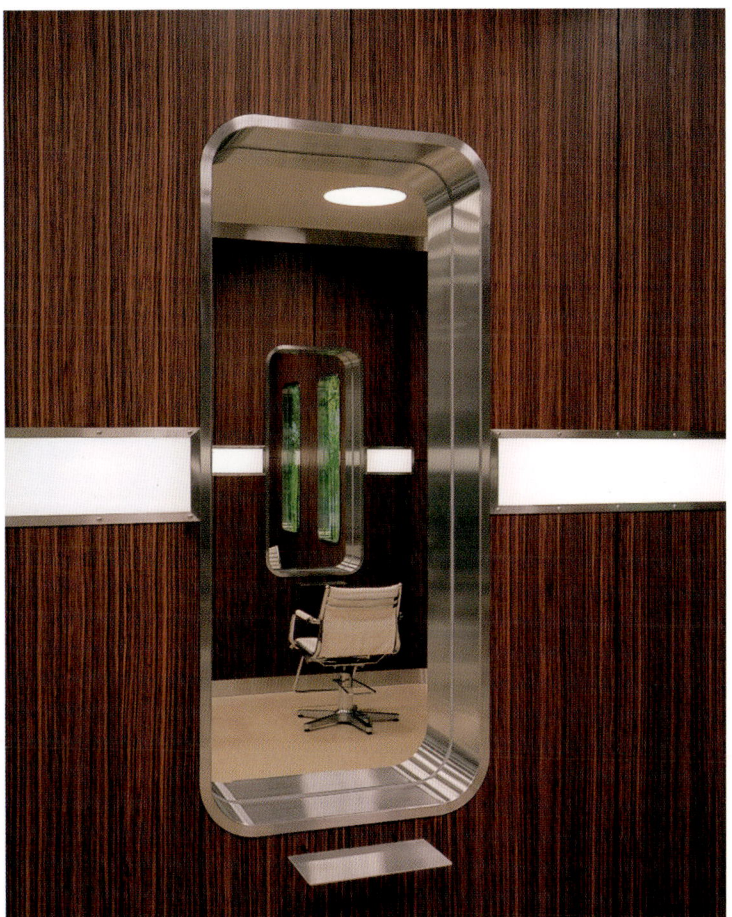

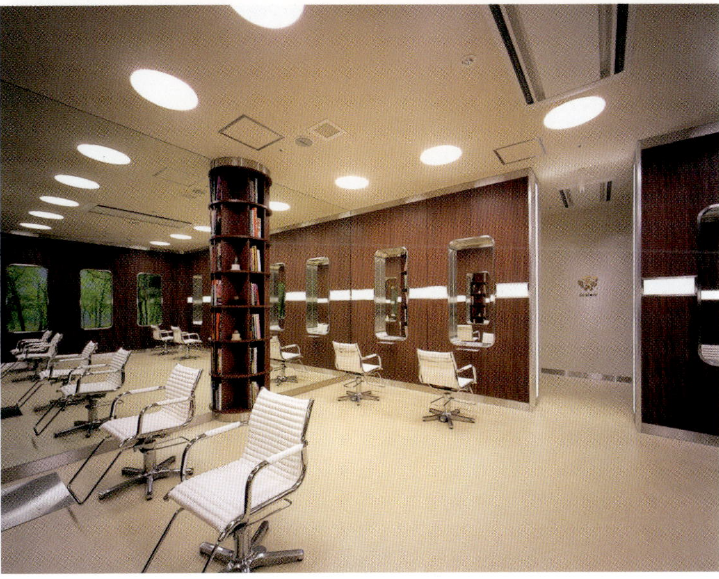

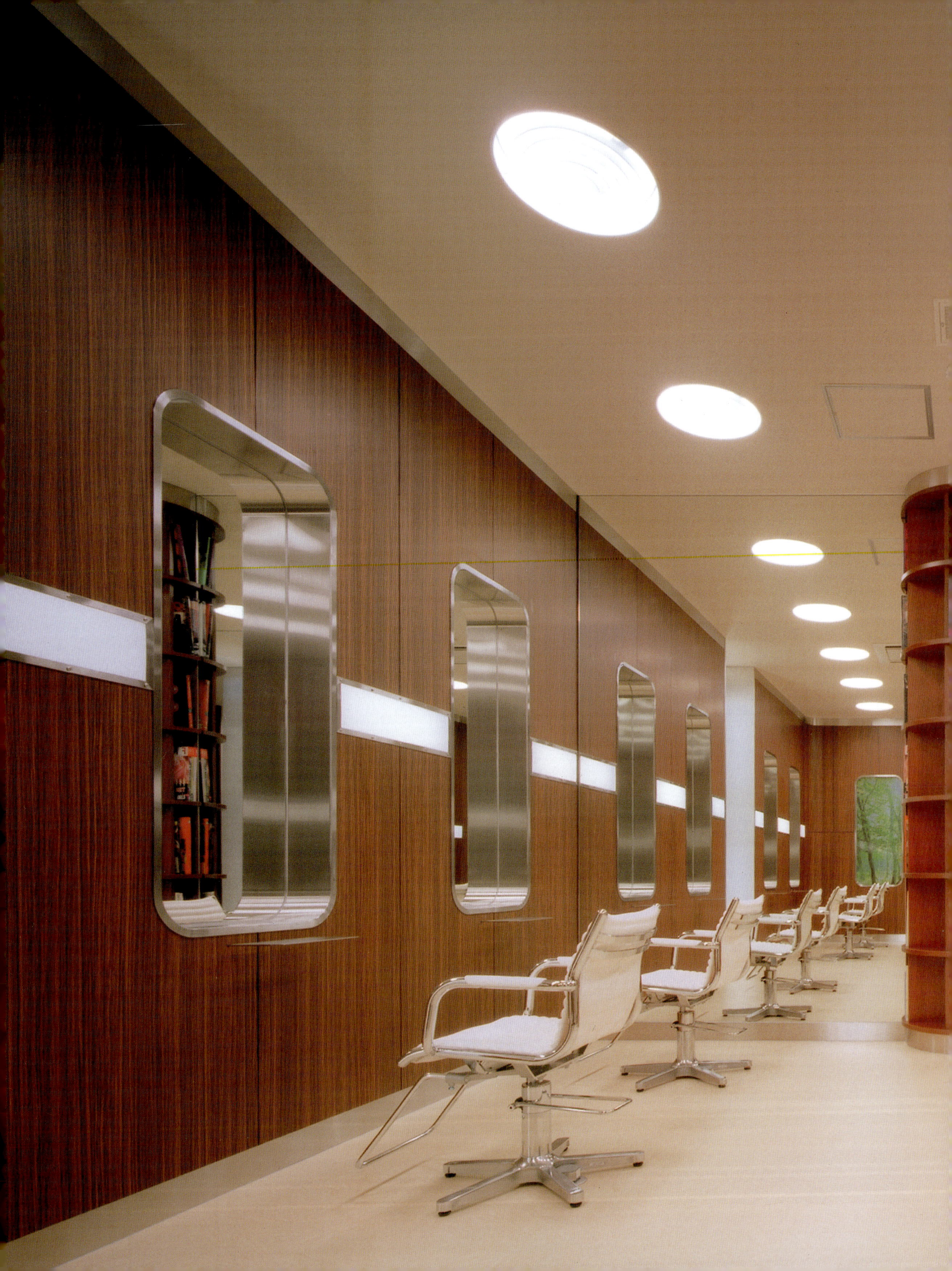

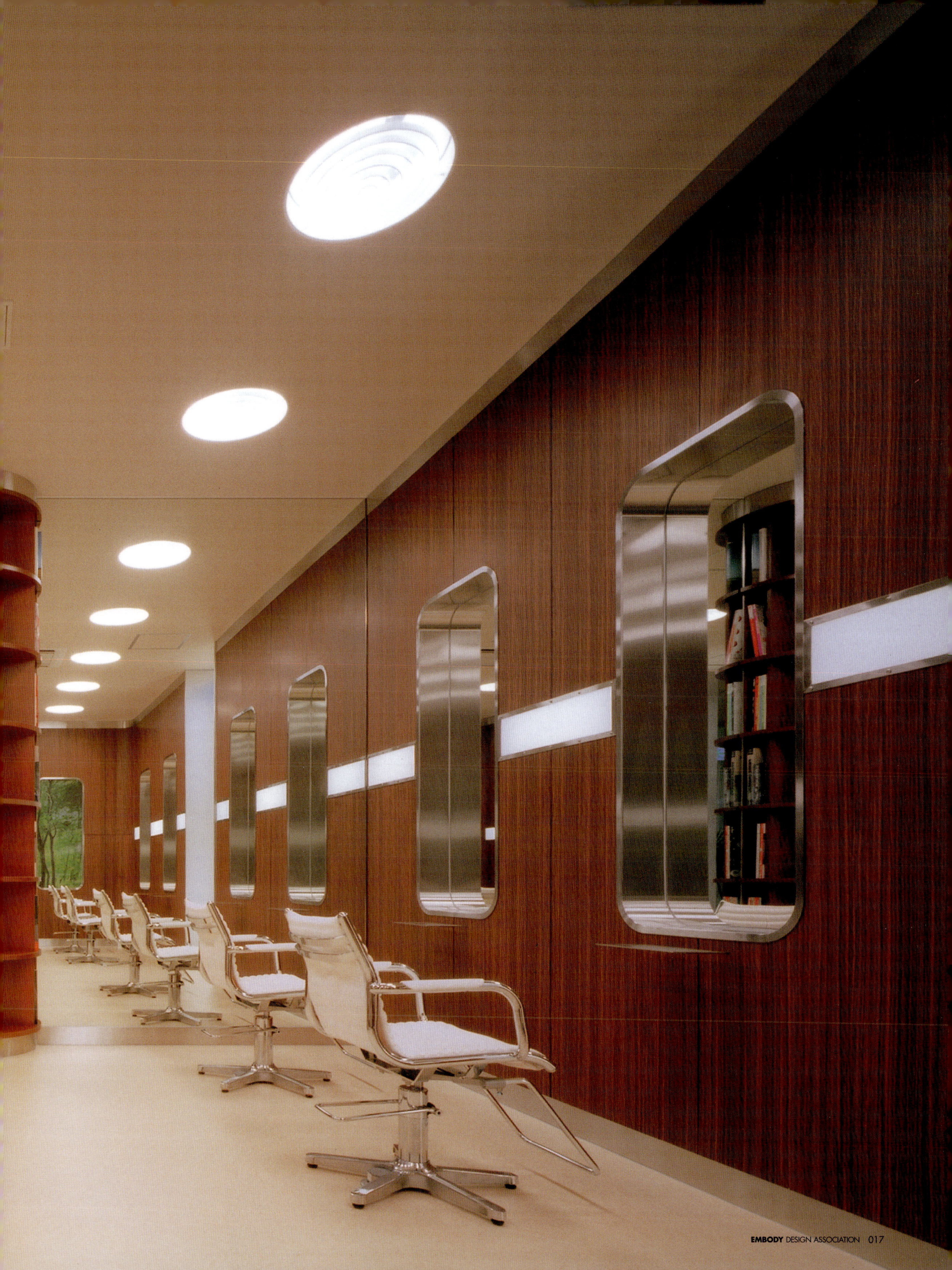

M-CLUB
KISAICHO , SAITAMA 2005

アジアン エレガンス

なぜ日本人は、オリエンタルな空間に心和むのでしょう。

　それは、アジアという土壌で今日まで日本人の中に脈々と受け継がれてきた、プリミティブな感性や感覚を潜在的に満たしてくれるからではないでしょうか。

　ここ、"M-CLUB"では、その心の奥の欲求を満たす空間を「アジアン エレガンス」をテーマに、表層的なカタチにとらわれず、アジアに暮す私たちの根底に流れる美意識やきめ細やかな心づかいを追求し、具現化しました。"M-CLUB"はこの探究心を土台に、ここで時と歴史を重ね、お客様にとって唯一の存在価値を築き上げて行くのです。

Asian Elegance

Why is it that Japanese people feel at peace in an oriental atmosphere?

　Perhaps this is because it subconsciously satisfies the primitive sensitivities and sensations that have been passed down, unbroken, to the Japanese people that live today in the land of Asia.

　At M-CLUB, I used as my concept, an atmosphere of "Asian elegance" that would satisfy these deepest desires. I pursued and expressed, without giving way to superficialities, the sense of beauty and delicate thoughtfulness that is fundamental to us, the people of Asia. With this sense of curiosity as its cornerstone, M-CLUB's atmosphere is rich in time and history, and it will gradually earn a unique place and meaning for existence in the hearts of its customers.

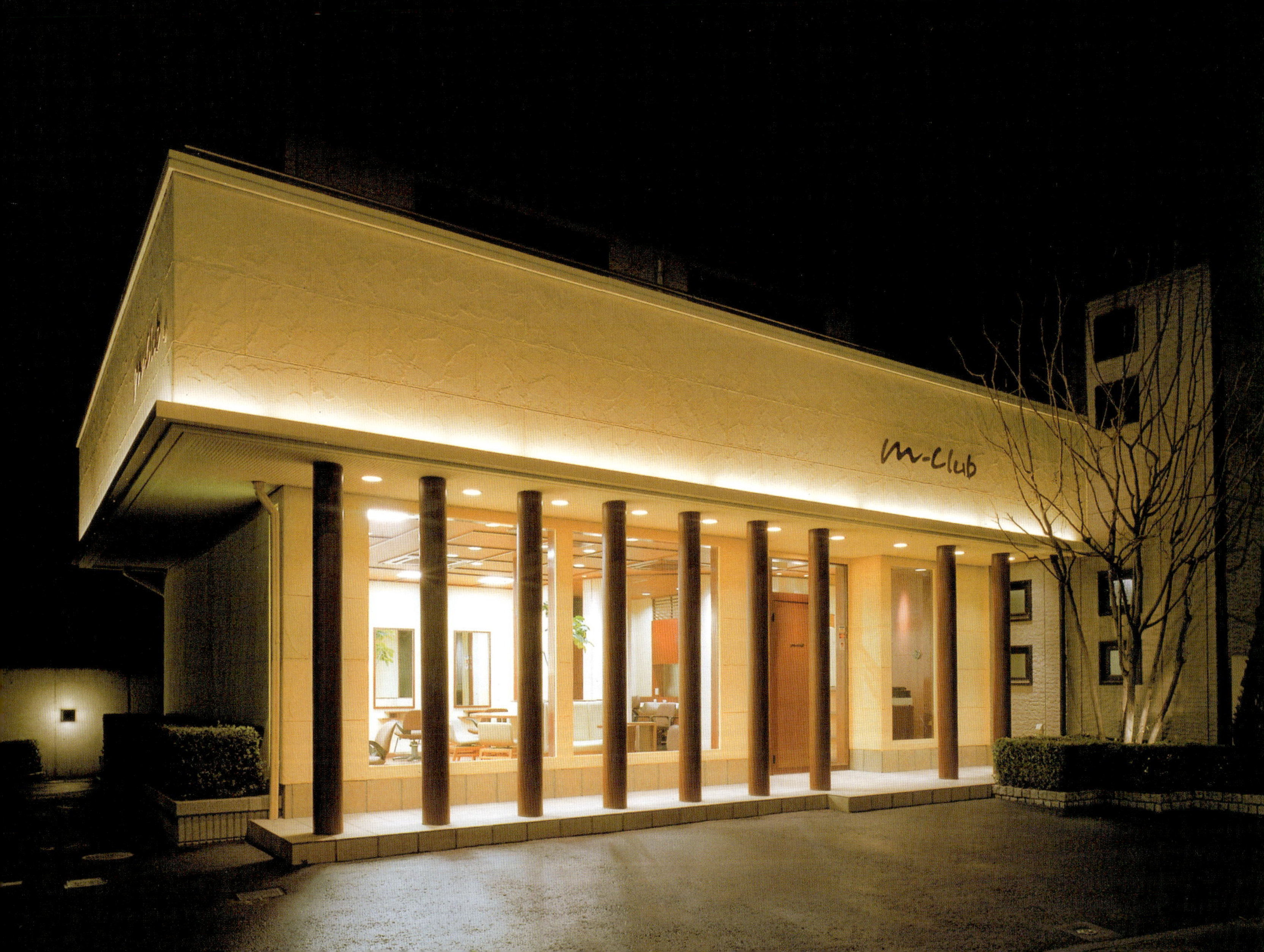

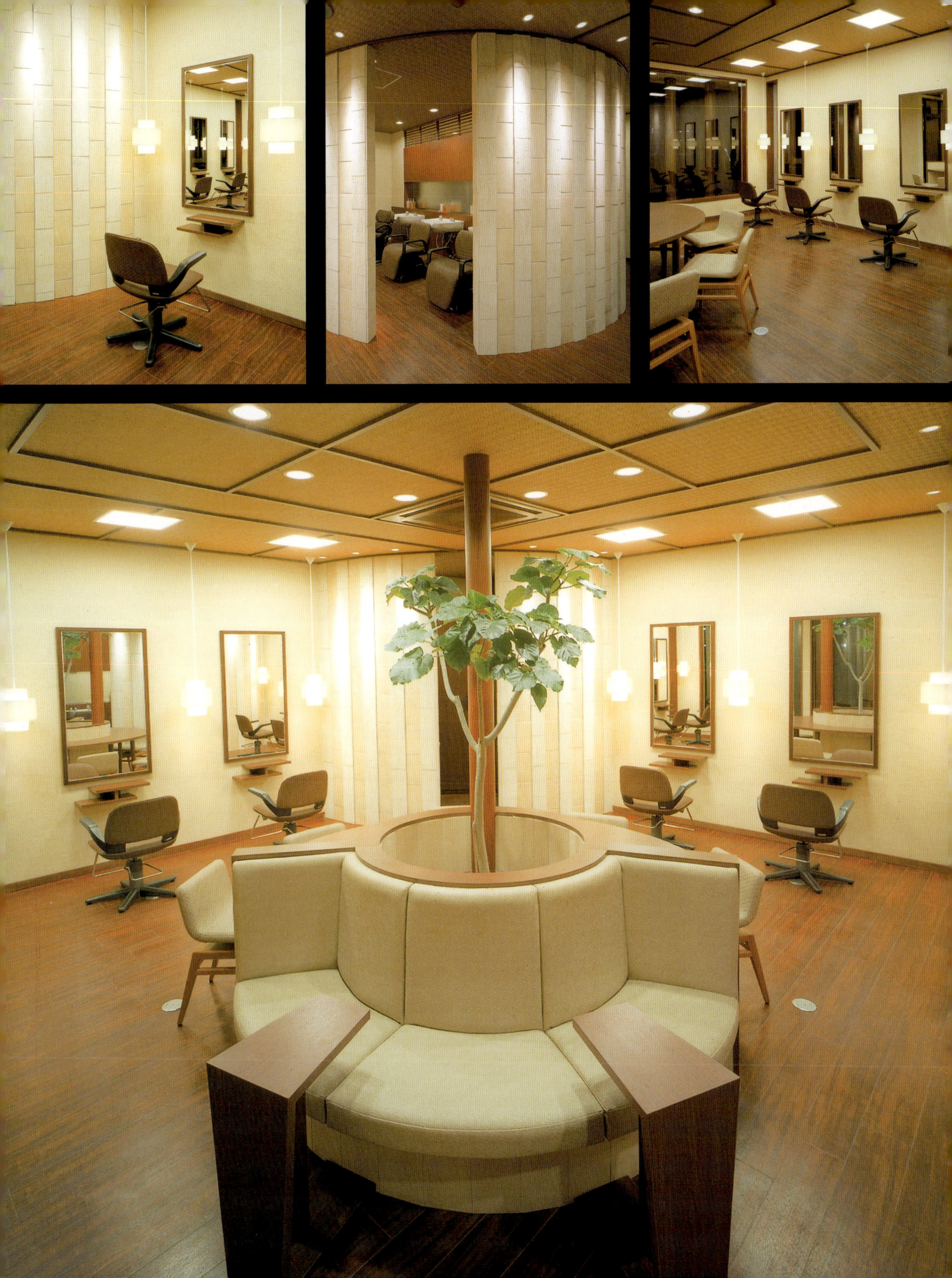

TIP TOP ikebukuro west
IKEBUKURO , TOKYO 2004

不変的な価値

"TIP TOP"というヘアサロンのデザインにあたって、私は、"TIP TOP"全体のブランディング、出店エリアの立地環境、ターゲット、そしてヘアサロンに欠かせない時代性を踏まえて、各店舗に合ったデザインコンセプトを立案し、チェーン店としてのオリジナリティを追求してきました。

その中で池袋という街は、都会の「光と陰」、「裏と表」等、全てを吸収し増殖していくように私の目には映ります。日常と非日常が交錯するこの街で、消費されずに永遠に愛され続けるような不変的価値のある空間を提供したい。そんな思いから、今も女性を惹き付けてはなさない、ユーロアルチザンの繊細なアイアンワークをヒントに「フェミニンスチール」をこの空間のコンセプトとしました。池袋の喧噪の中、ここでは流行を追うのではなく、訪れる女性が心地よく美意識に包まれて過ごす、穏やかな時間がいつも静かに流れています。

Enduring value

In planning the TIP TOP hair salons, I adhered to the branding of TIP TOP as a whole, and gave due consideration to store site environments, target demographics, and also to a sense of the era, or contemporaneity, which is an essential part of a hair salon. I developed individual design concepts to suit each store, and pursued a feeling of originality throughout the chain of stores.

Ikebukuro to me, comes across as a town that grows and multiplies by absorbing everything, "light and shadow," "the visible and the hidden." In this town where the everyday is entangled with the extraordinary, I want to create a space that will not be consumed, but enduringly loved; a space that has an everlasting value. With that in mind, I used "feminine steel" as the concept for this space. This concept is reminiscent of the delicate ironwork of European artisans, and aims to continuously captivate and charm the imaginations of women. The store does not attempt to stand out among the clamor of Ikebukuro, but instead allows the women that visit to be pleasantly engulfed in a sense of beauty. It is a place where quiet times flow with tranquility.

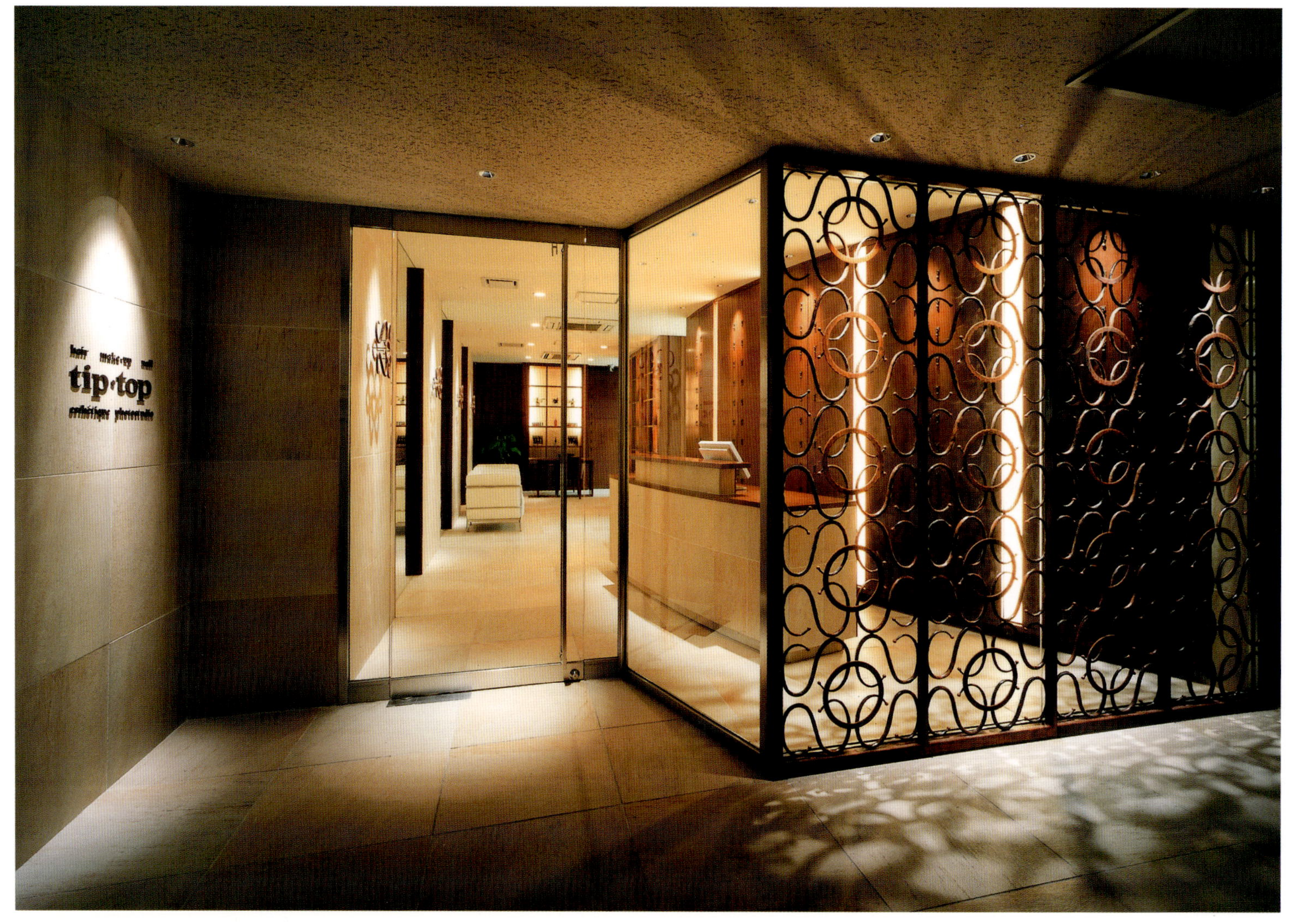

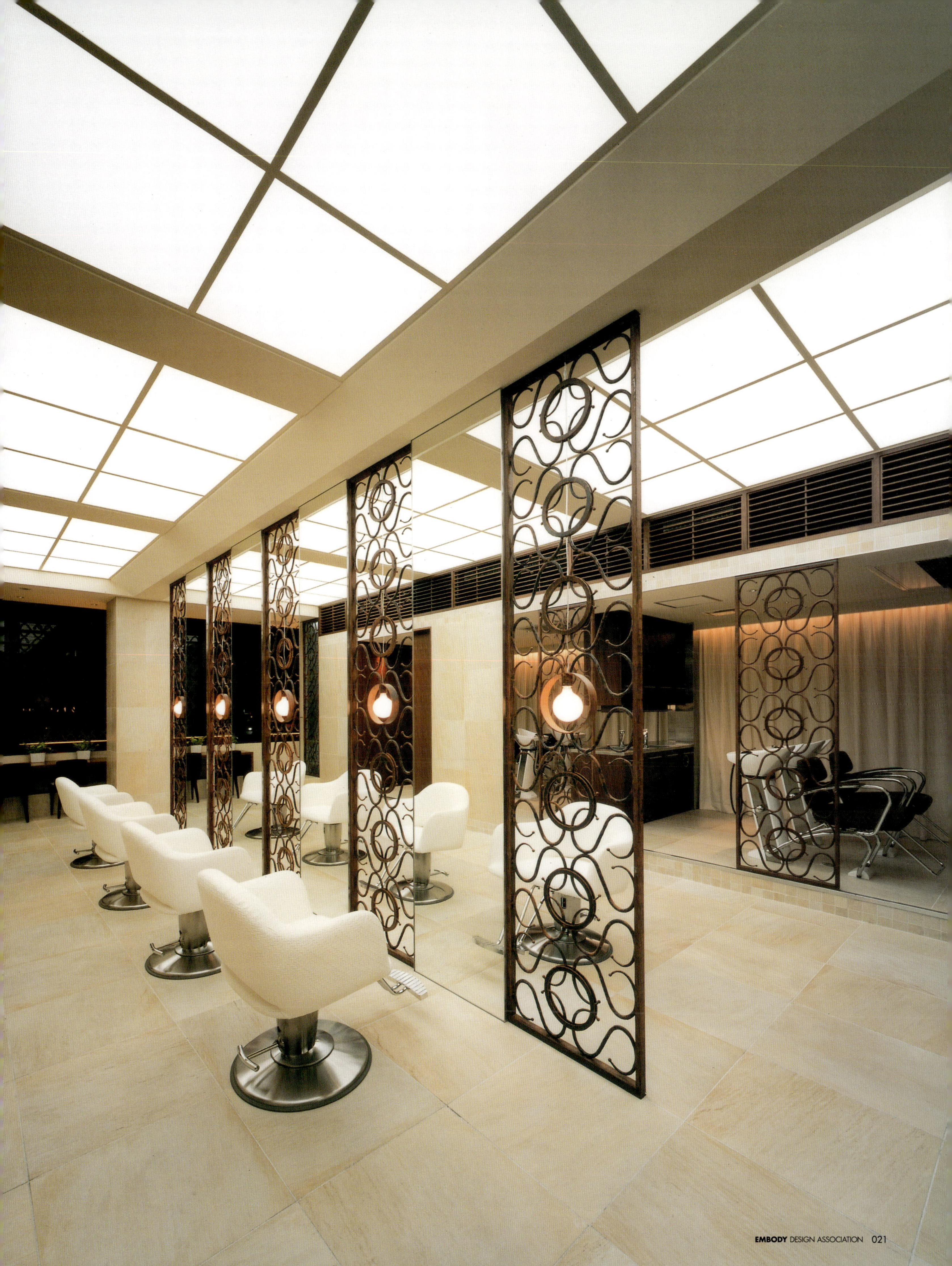

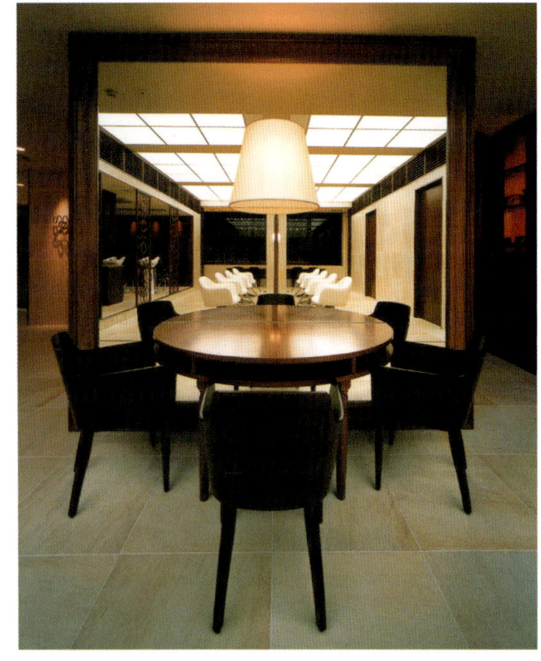

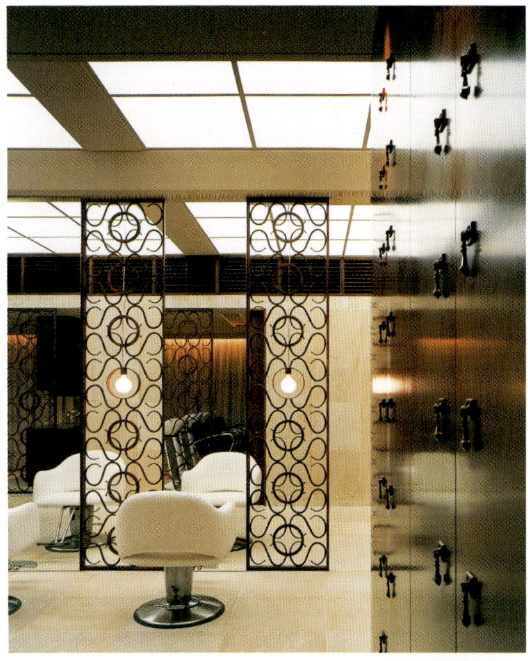

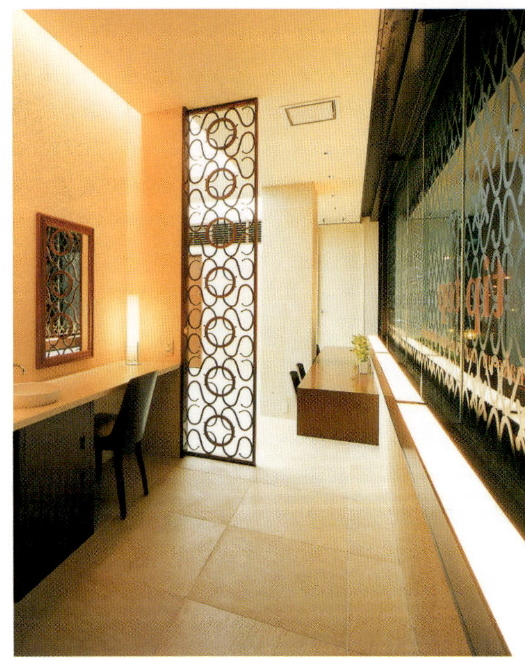

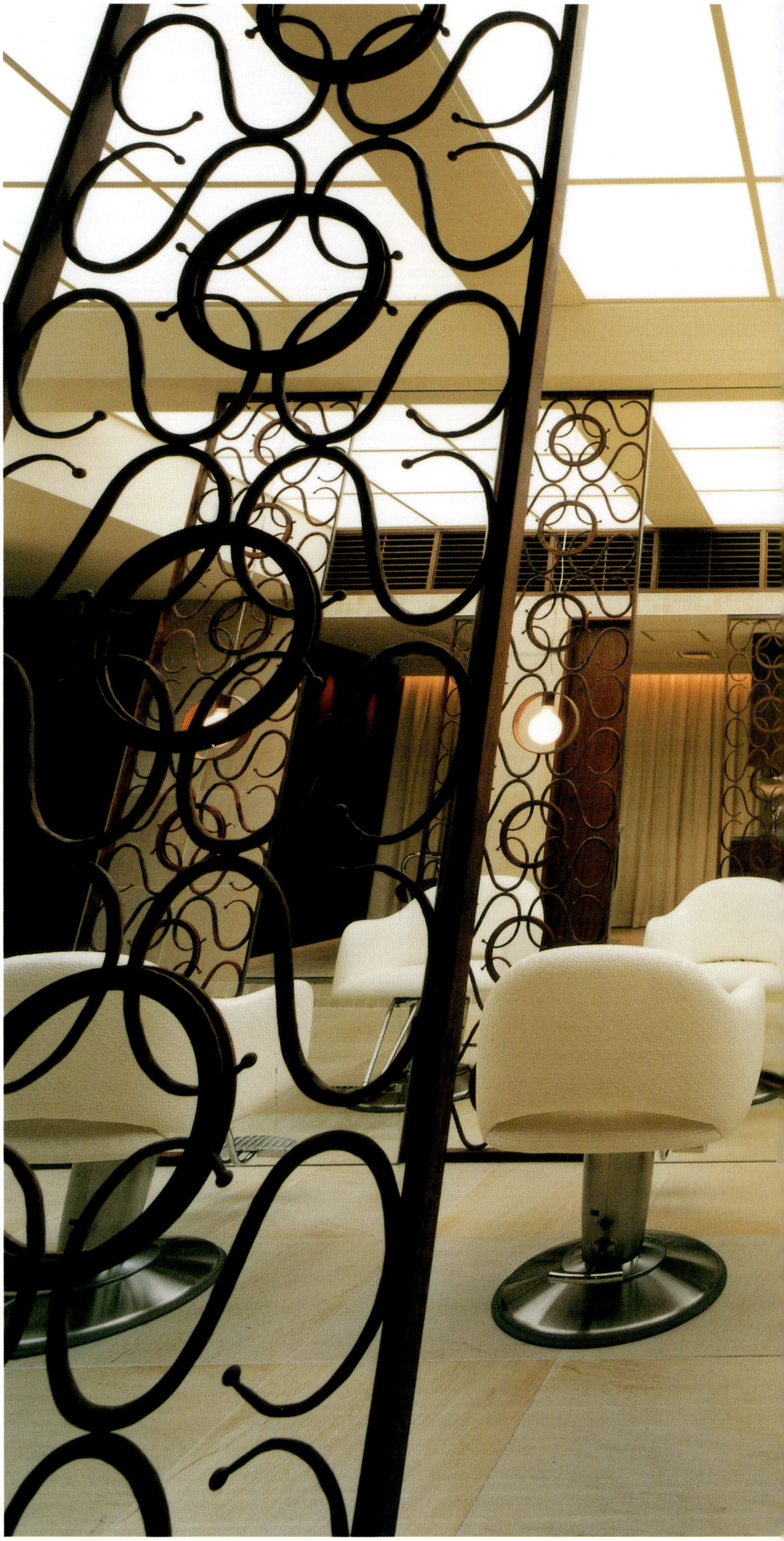

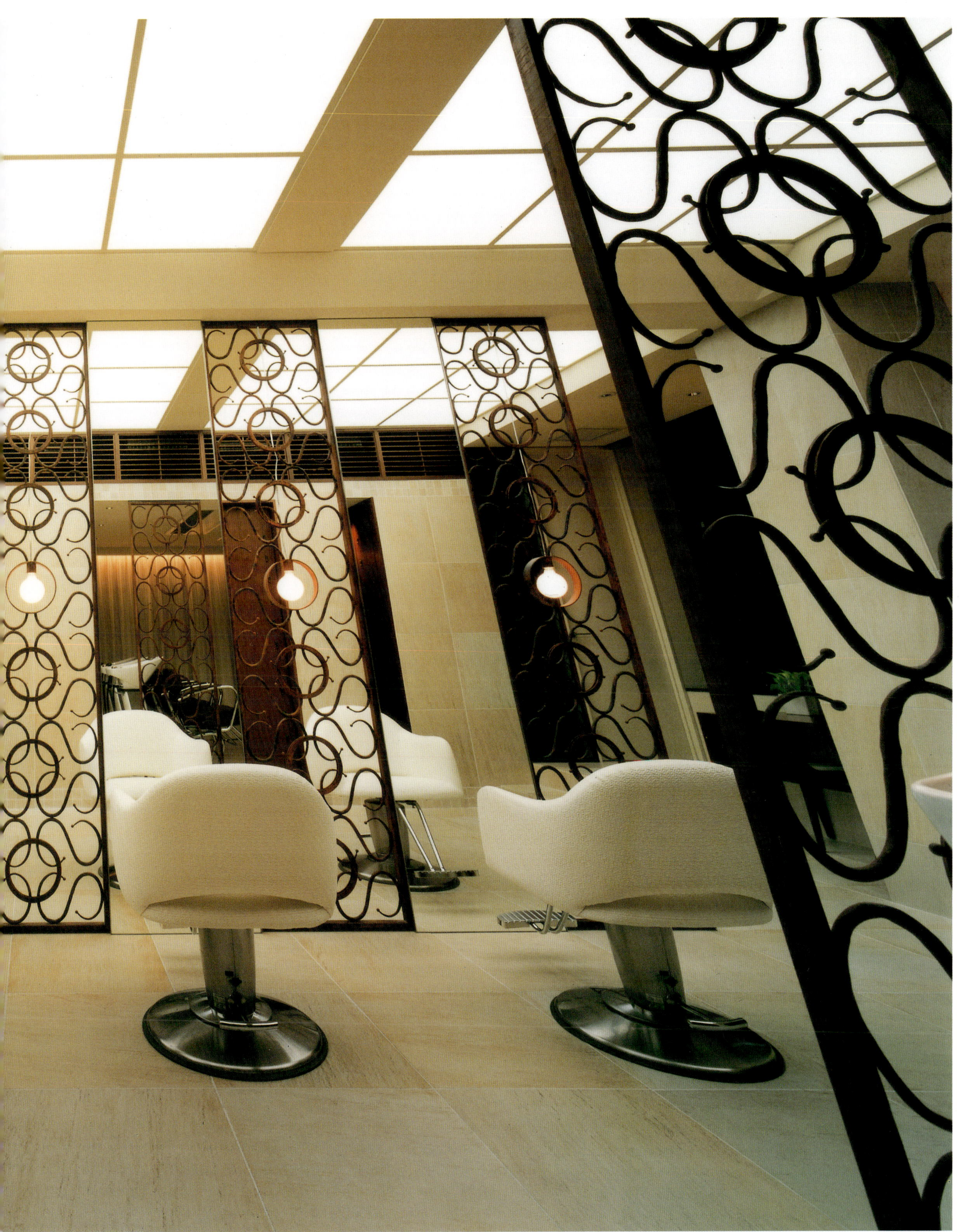

SHARE

MINAMISENBA , OSAKA 2003

発想の転換

オーナーと見たその場所は、ヘアサロンとしては決して恵まれた環境とは言えない所にあった。その場所とは、オフィスビルの4階にあり、入口に辿り着くのも容易ではない上に、ミラーを多用するヘアサロンとしては西日が強く差し込む空間だった。

　通常、ヘアサロンでは空間を広く使うためにミラー面を壁面や窓面に配置するのが基本とされているが、"SHARE"では訪れる人とスタイリストとの関係性を整理し発想を逆転させ、窓を背にミラーを設置した。すると、それはパーテーションとなり、ウエイティングからは、視線を遮るだけでなく、大きなブックラックとして機能する。また街行く人に、ここがヘアサロンであることをうったえかけるシャンデリアグラフィックで窓面を飾った。

　出来るだけデメリットをメリットに転換できるよう心掛け、様々な関係性をデザインすることで、"SHARE"はヘアサロンにとって欠かせない要素が、バランスよく美しいハーモニーを奏でる空間となった。

Reversal of ideas

The location that I went to see with the owner could not really be called the best place for a hair salon. That place was on the 4th floor of an office building, and not only was finding your way to the entrance not easy, but considering that hair salons use several mirrors, the space was also subject to fairly strong sun from the west.

Usually, the basics of putting together a hair salon are that mirrors are placed against the walls or windows to keep the usable space as wide as possible. However, at SHARE, I readjusted the relationship between the stylist and the people that visit, reversing conventional ideas by positioning the mirrors so that they faced inwards. Doing this made them act as partitions, that not only blocked the view from the waiting area, but that also acted as large book racks. The windows were adorned with large chandelier graphics to appeal to the people getting around town that the place is a hair salon.

By endeavoring to convert disadvantages into advantages as much as possible, and actively designing the various interrelationships, SHARE was turned into a space where the essential elements of a hair salon are woven together in beautiful and balanced harmony.

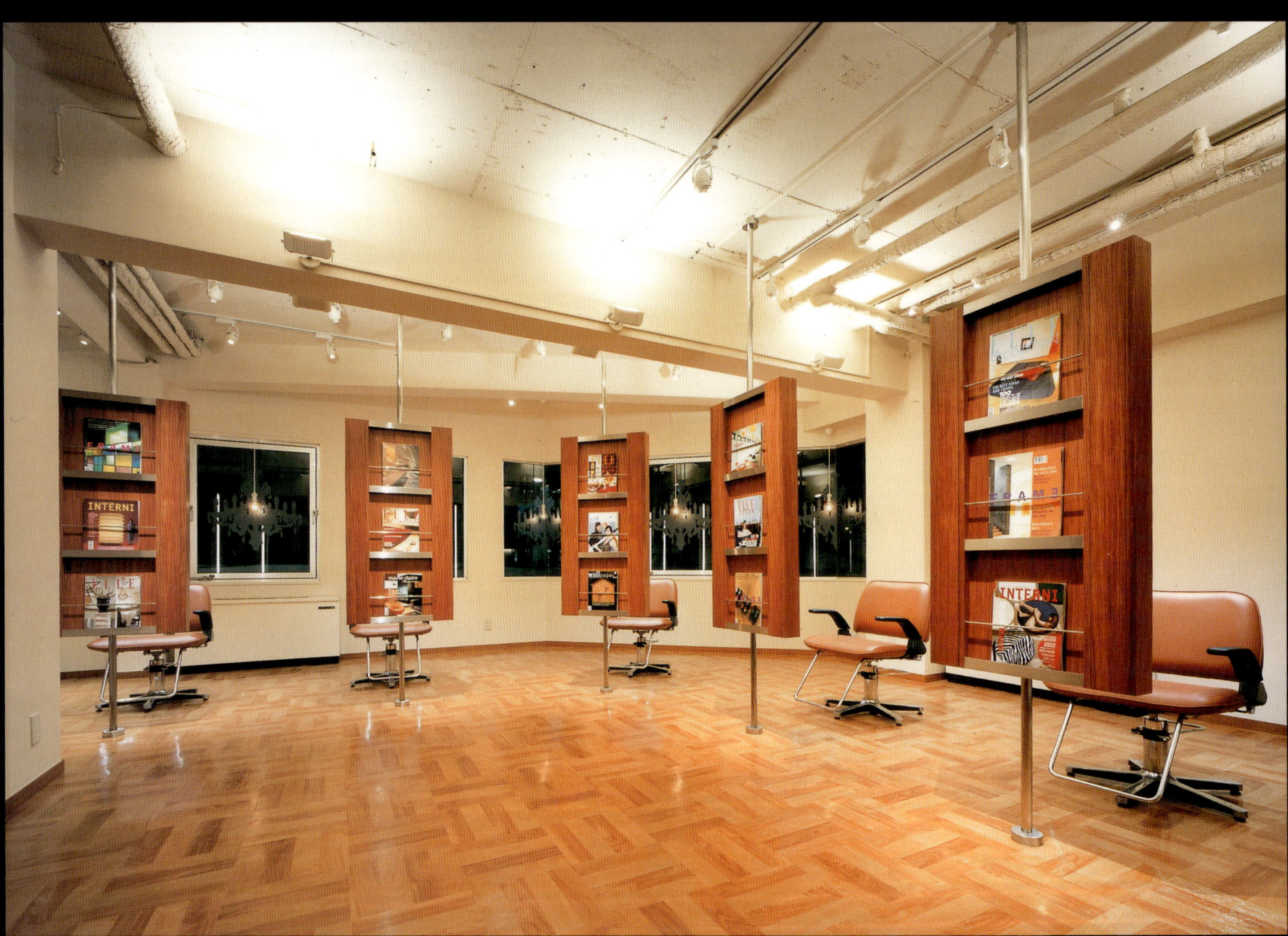

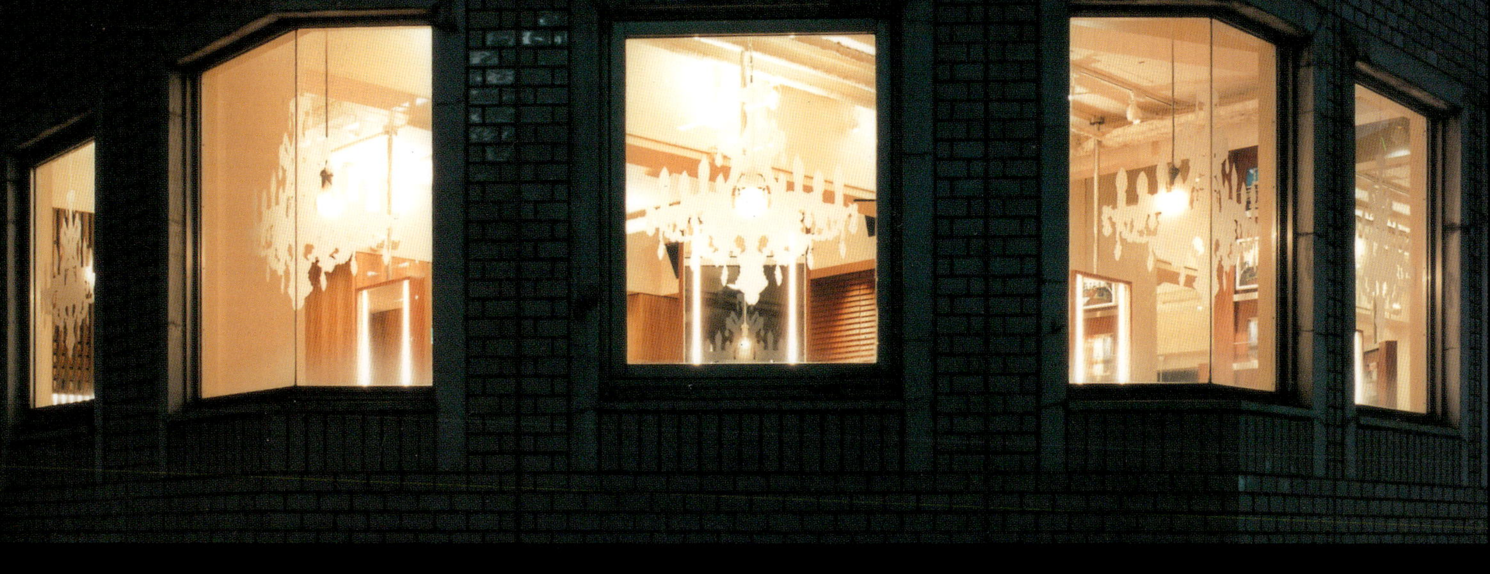

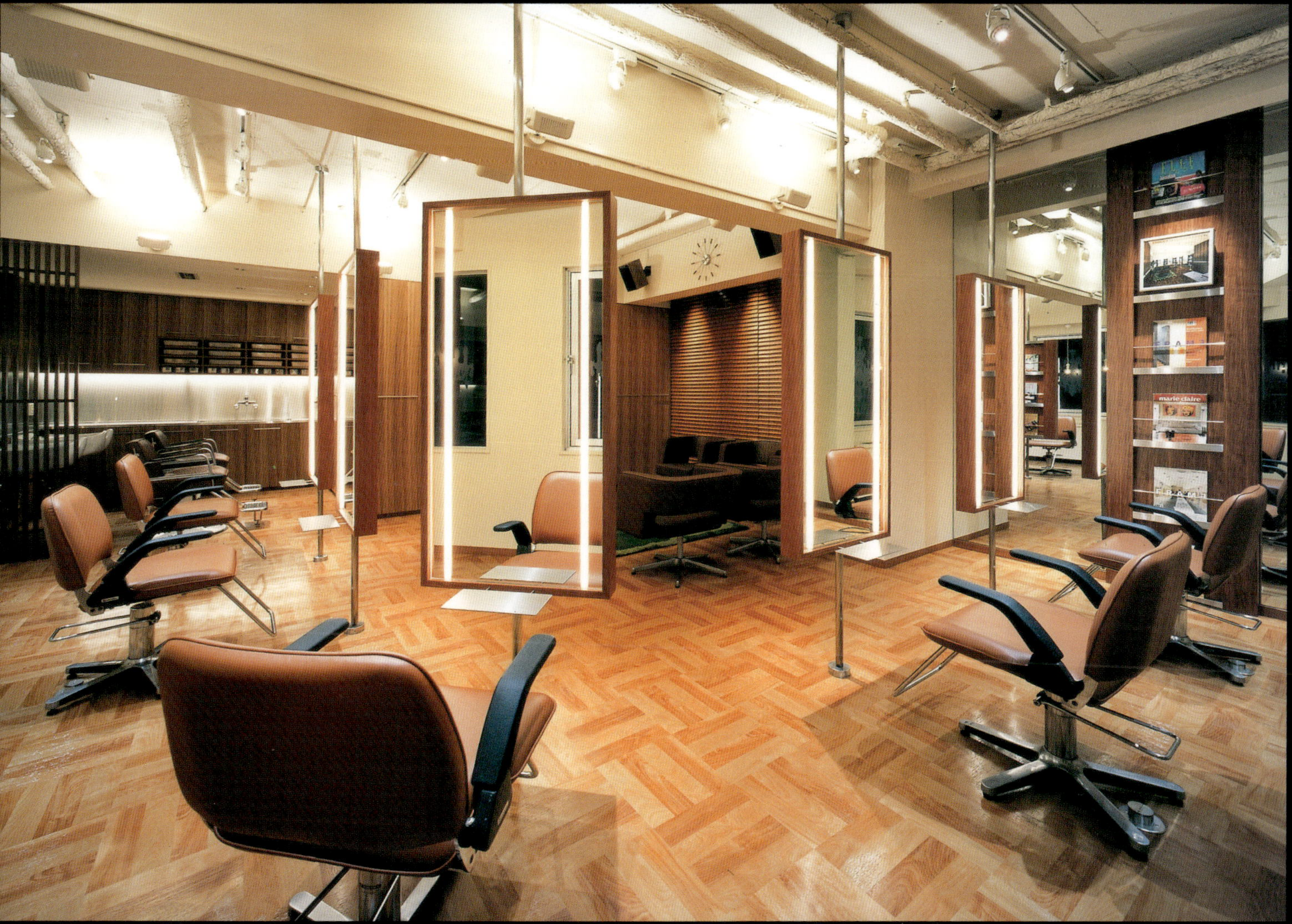

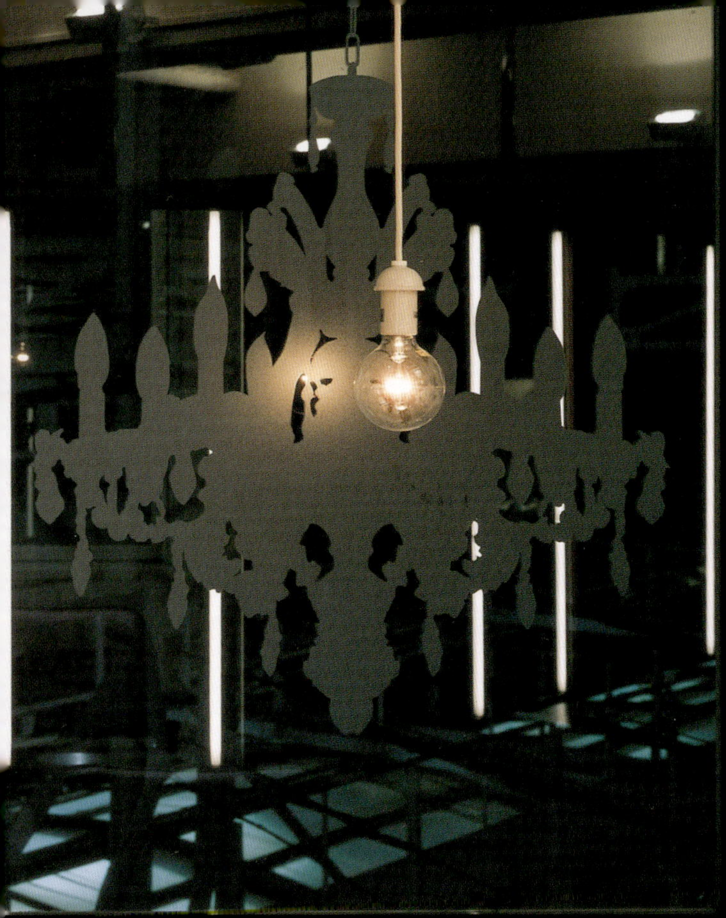

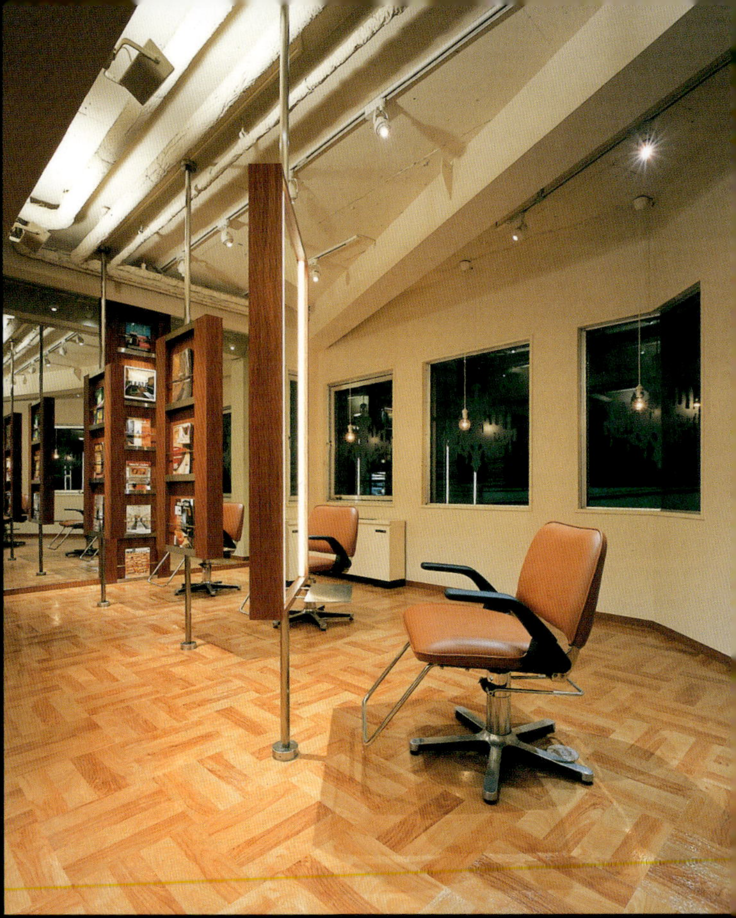

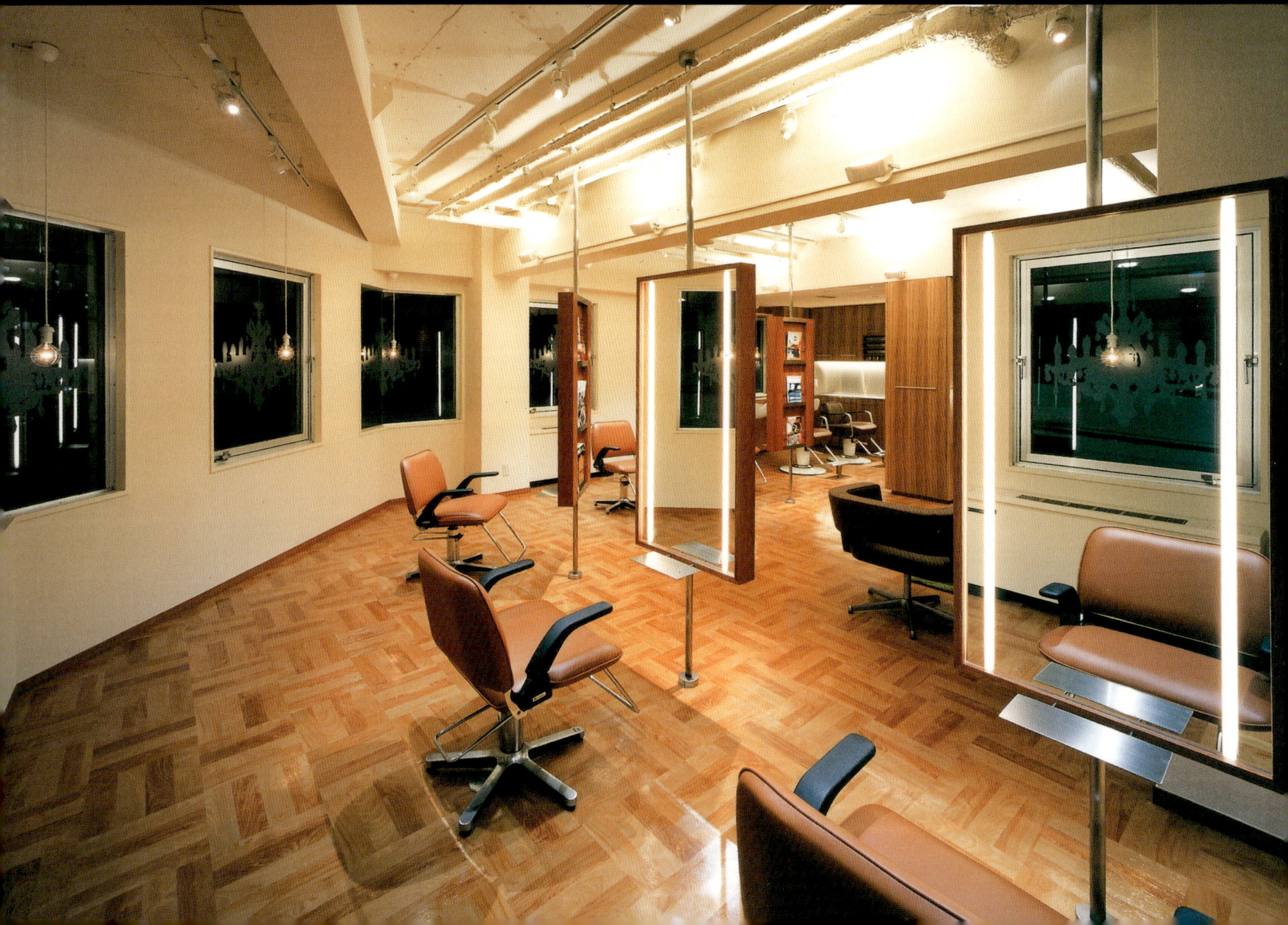

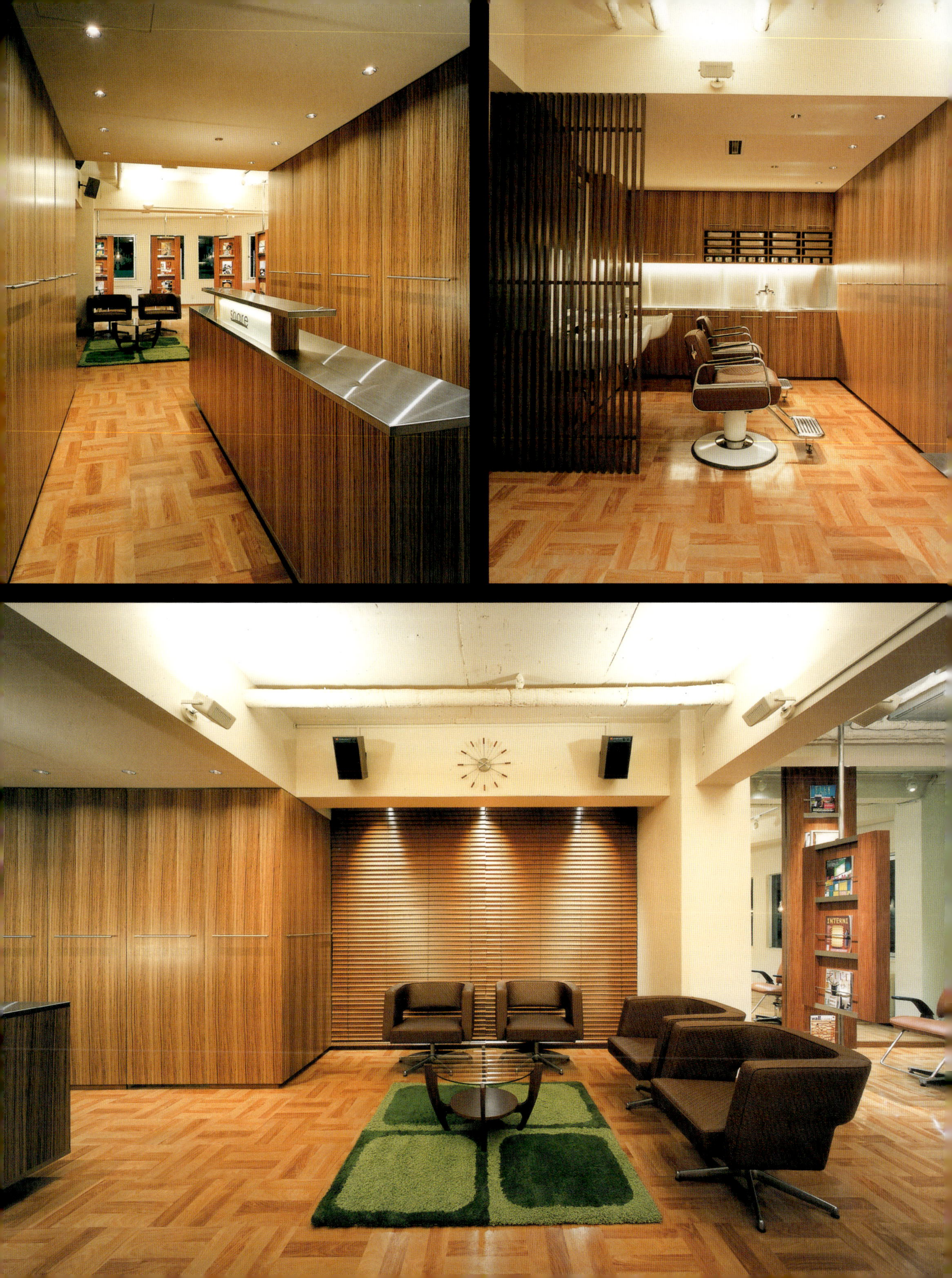

TIP TOP mejiro
MEJIRO , TOKYO 2003

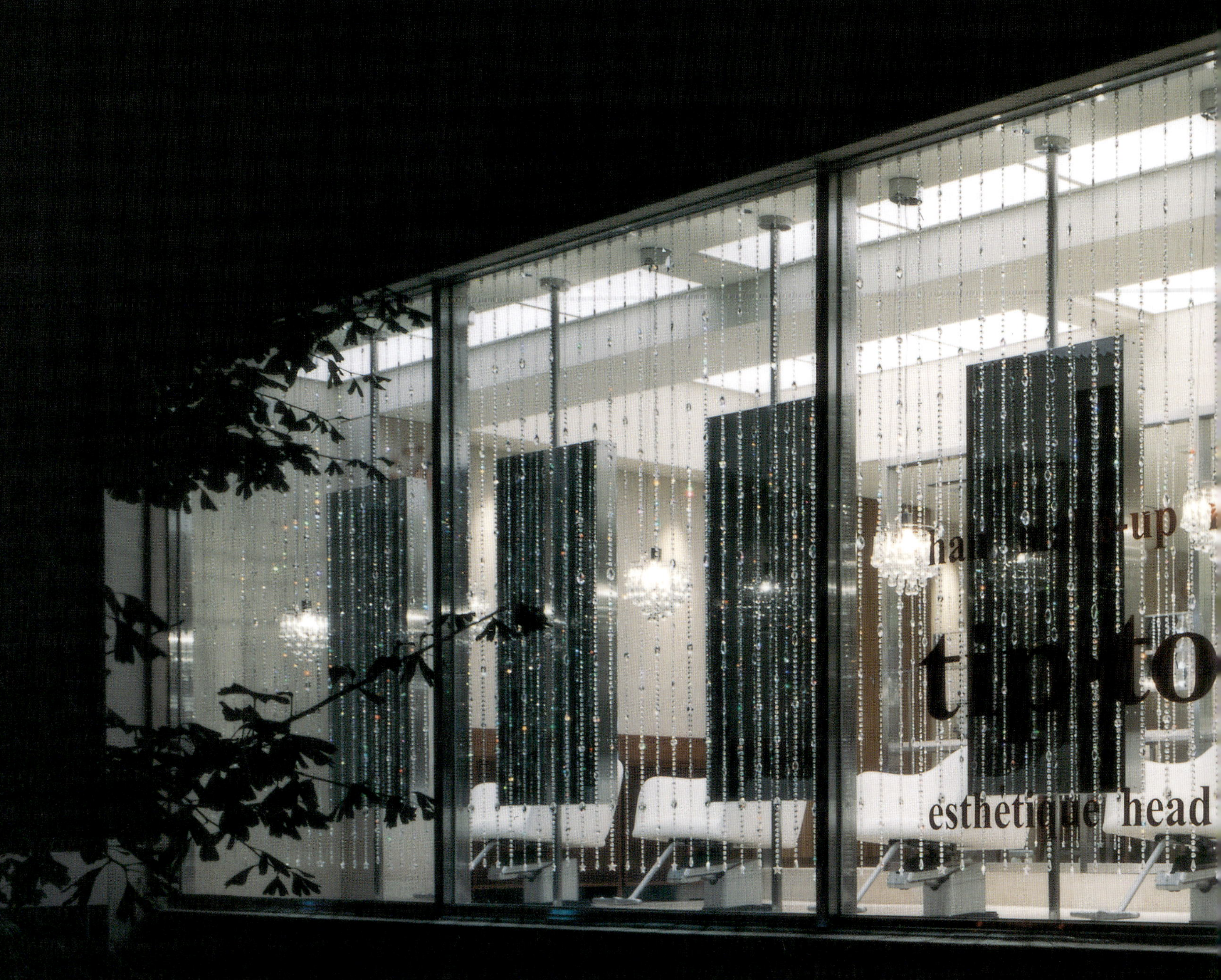

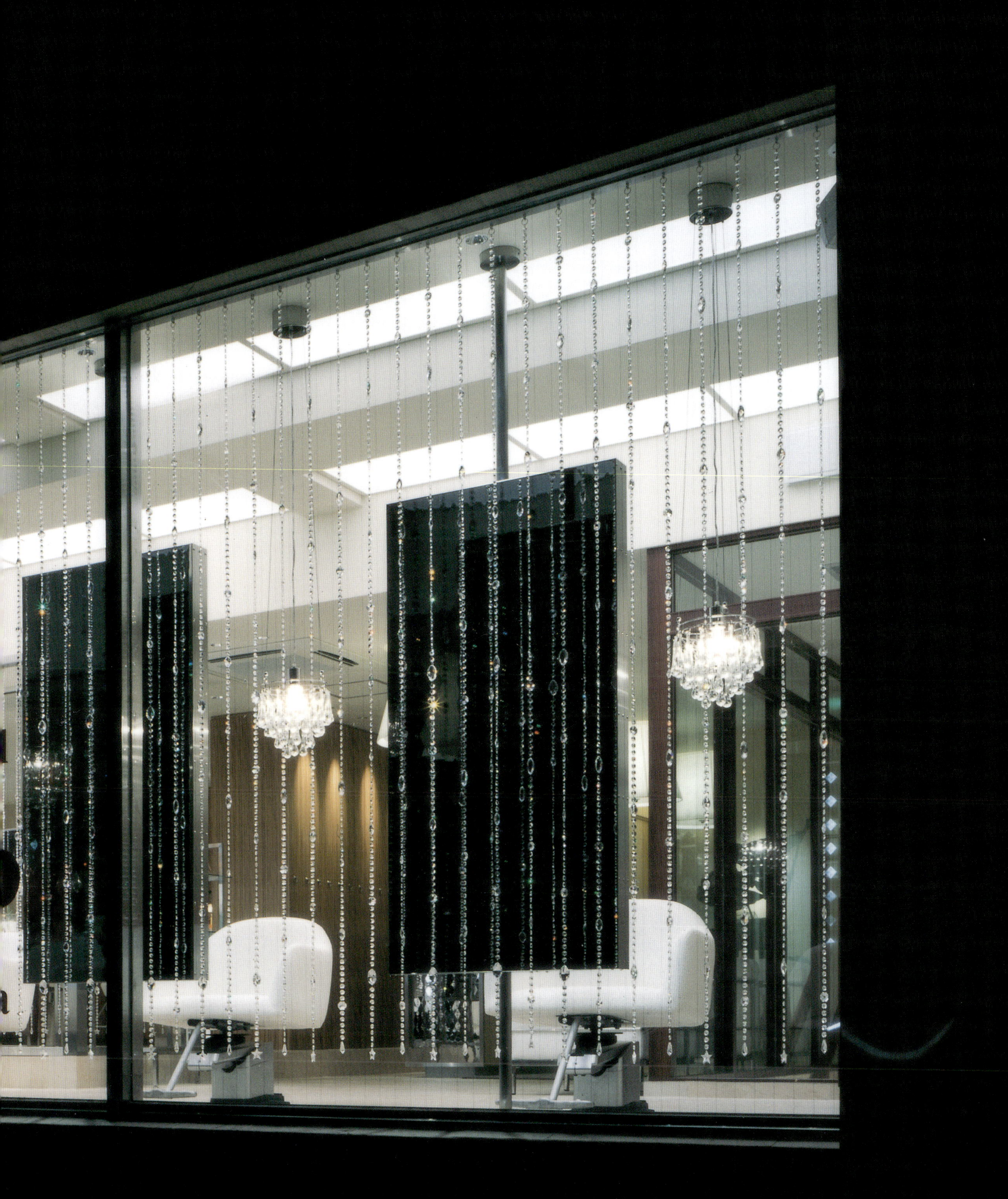

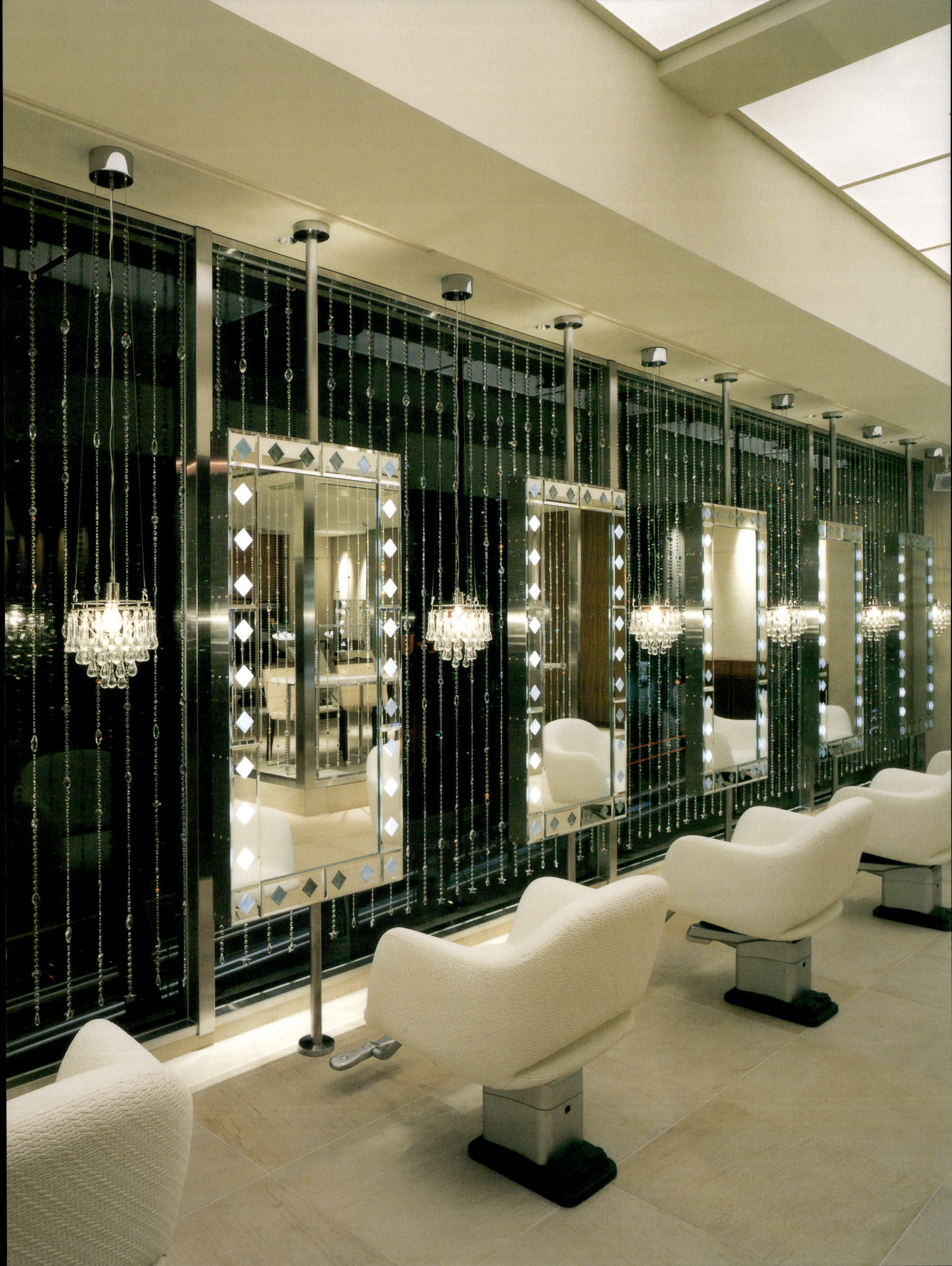

建築や空間デザインの世界でも、コンセプトがなく、表面を繕っただけの外観の美しさだけで
は人を魅了することは出来ません。女性の美しさもまた、外見だけではなく内面からかもし
出されるものに左右されるといっても過言ではないと思います。
　"TIP　TOP　mejiro"では、立地環境とニーズを踏まえ「透明感のある、真なる美しさ」を
デザインコンセプトに、訪れる人に永遠の美しさを予感させる空間を目指しました。透き通っ
たクリアな美しさをスワロフスキーとのコラボレーションによって表現し、表面的な美しさだ
けではなく、女性が内に秘める少女のように純粋で無垢な、美に対する憧れを引き出す空間
ができたのではないかと思います。

Crystal beauty

In architectural as well as spacial design, you cannot expect to capture
people's fascination with an exterior beauty created by simply tidying up the
outside surfaces. It is also no exaggeration to say that female beauty does
not rest just on appearance, but that it is affected by what comes from within.
　Given the requirements and site environment at TIP TOP mejiro, I used a
design concept of "true and crystalline beauty," and aimed to create a space
that would give the people that visited it a sense of beauty that might be
everlasting. I expressed this elegantly translucent and clear beauty through a
collaboration with Swarovski, and I think that an atmosphere that brings out
not only a woman's external beauty, but also her deepest desires with respect
to beauty, like those of her inner child, pure and innocent, has been created.

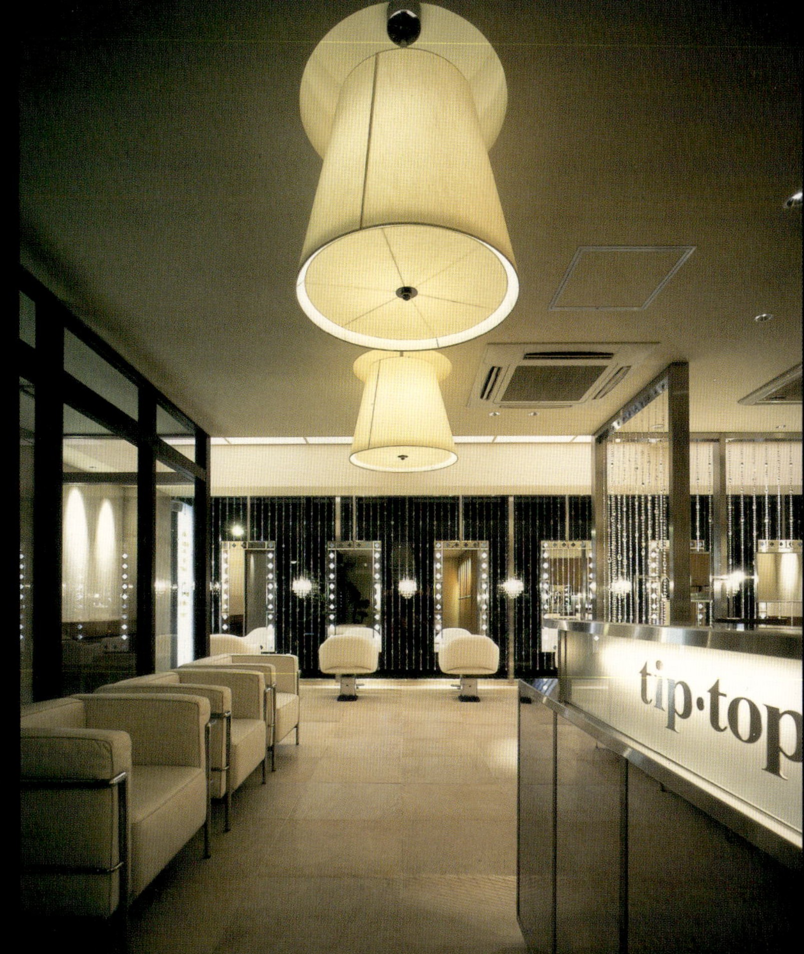

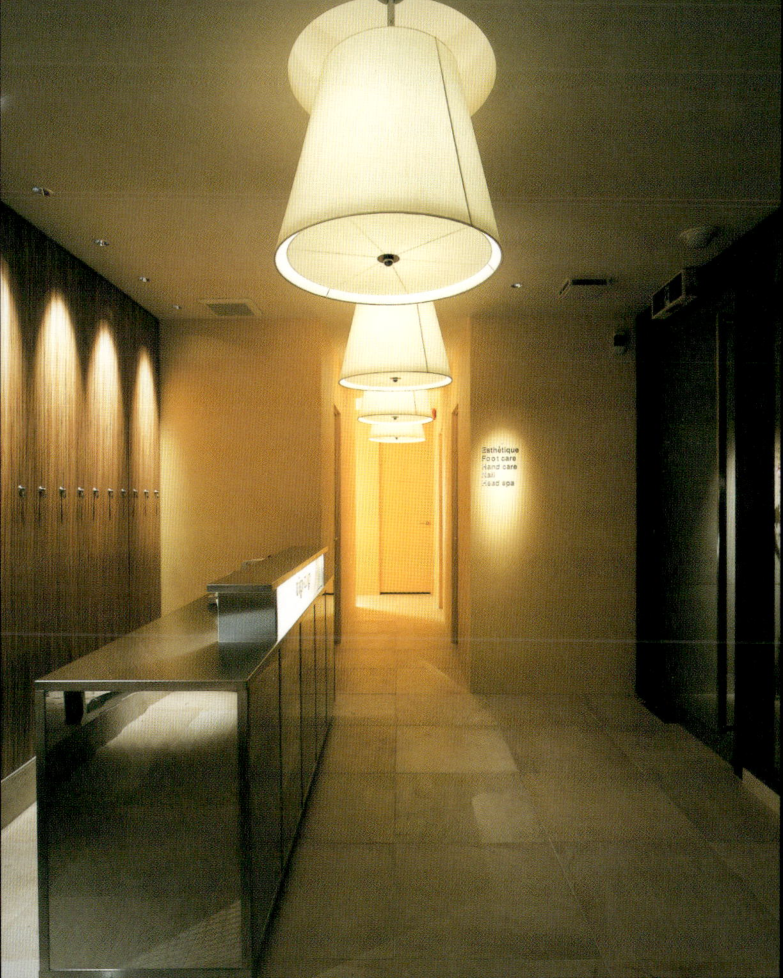

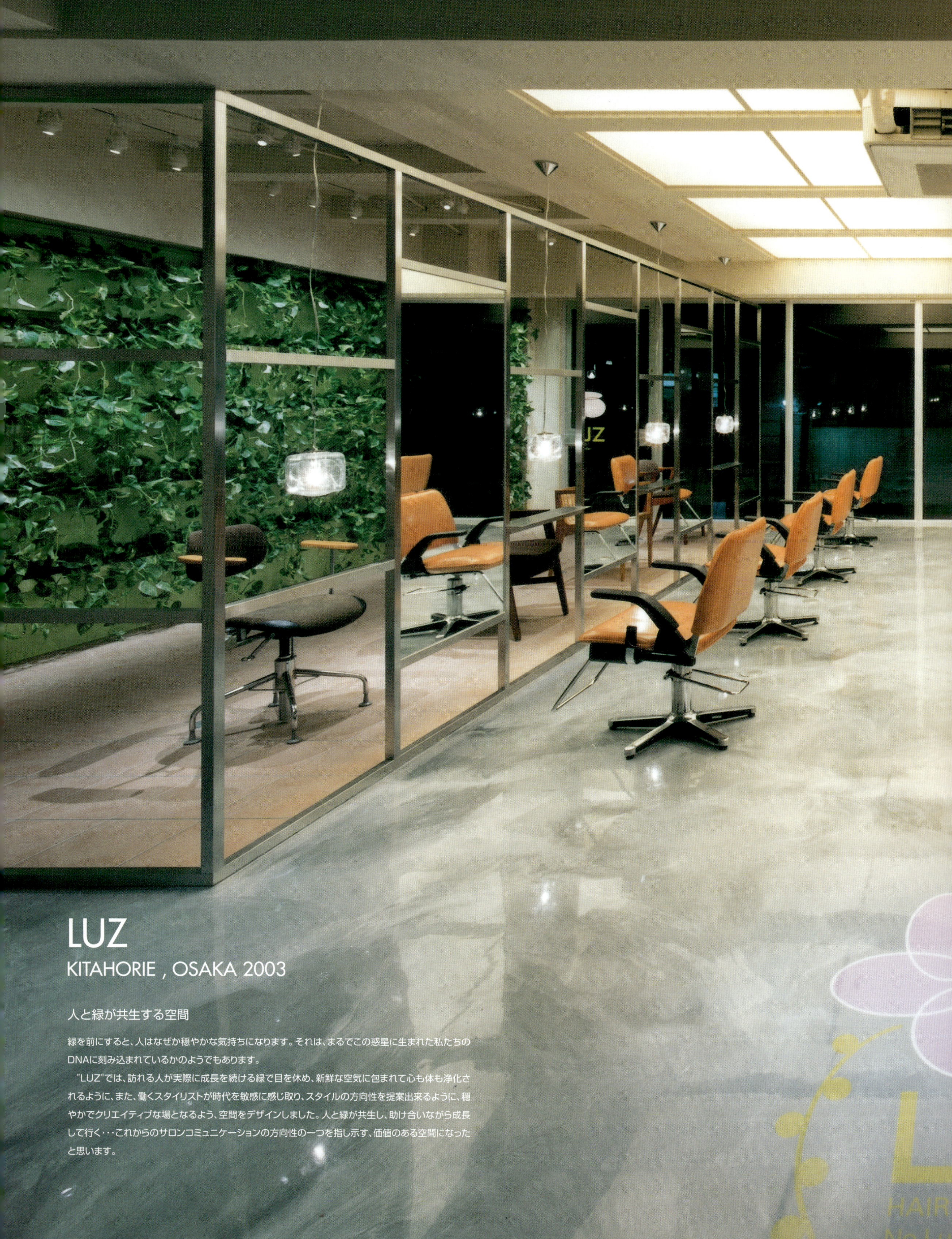

LUZ
KITAHORIE , OSAKA 2003

人と緑が共生する空間

緑を前にすると、人はなぜか穏やかな気持ちになります。それは、まるでこの惑星に生まれた私たちの
DNAに刻み込まれているかのようでもあります。
　"LUZ"では、訪れる人が実際に成長を続ける緑で目を休め、新鮮な空気に包まれて心も体も浄化さ
れるように、また、働くスタイリストが時代を敏感に感じ取り、スタイルの方向性を提案出来るように、穏
やかでクリエイティブな場となるよう、空間をデザインしました。人と緑が共生し、助け合いながら成長
して行く・・・これからのサロンコミュニケーションの方向性の一つを指し示す、価値のある空間になった
と思います。

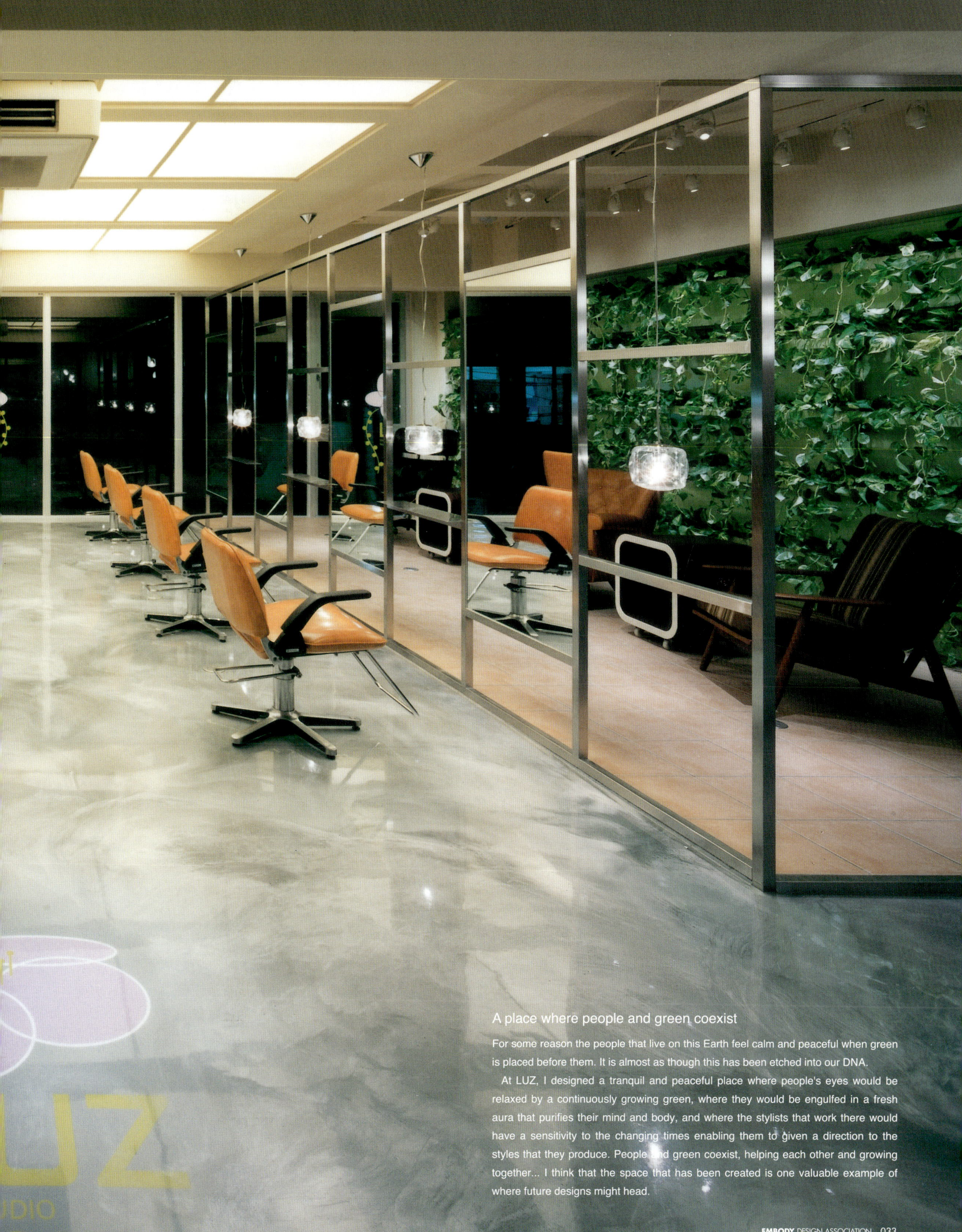

A place where people and green coexist

For some reason the people that live on this Earth feel calm and peaceful when green is placed before them. It is almost as though this has been etched into our DNA.

At LUZ, I designed a tranquil and peaceful place where people's eyes would be relaxed by a continuously growing green, where they would be engulfed in a fresh aura that purifies their mind and body, and where the stylists that work there would have a sensitivity to the changing times enabling them to given a direction to the styles that they produce. People and green coexist, helping each other and growing together... I think that the space that has been created is one valuable example of where future designs might head.

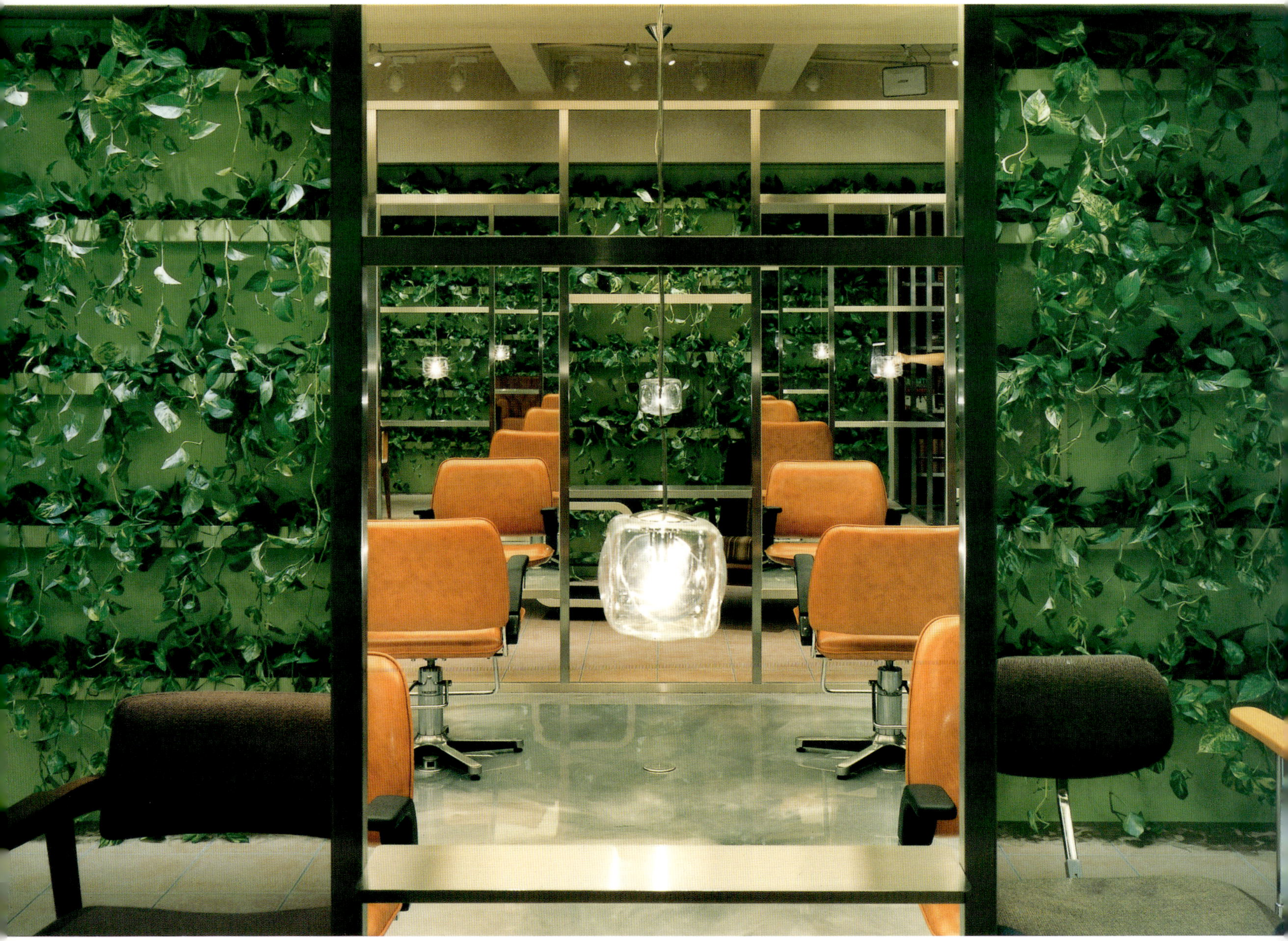

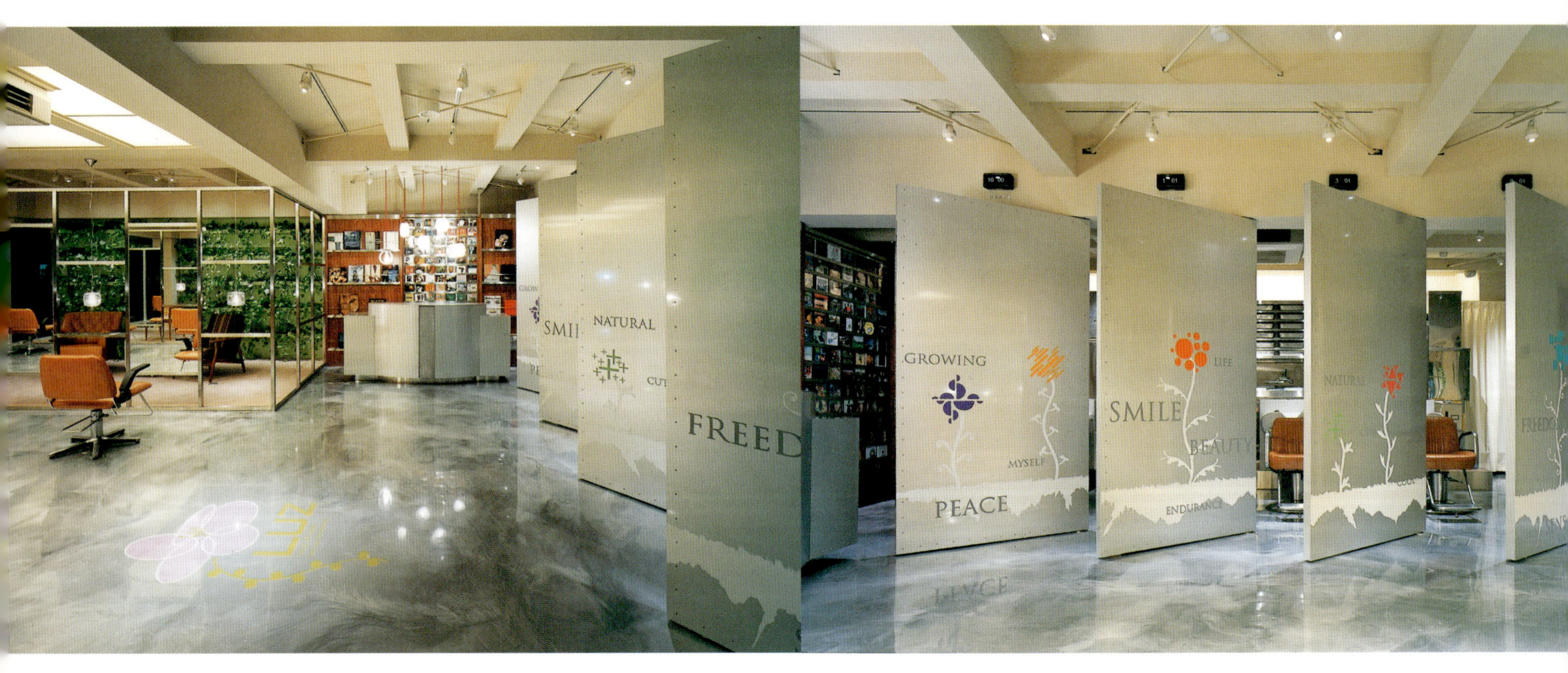
SMILE
NATURAL
CUT
FREED
PEACE
GROWING
MYSELF
LIFE
SMILE
BEAUTY
NATURAL
ENDURANCE
FREE
PEACE

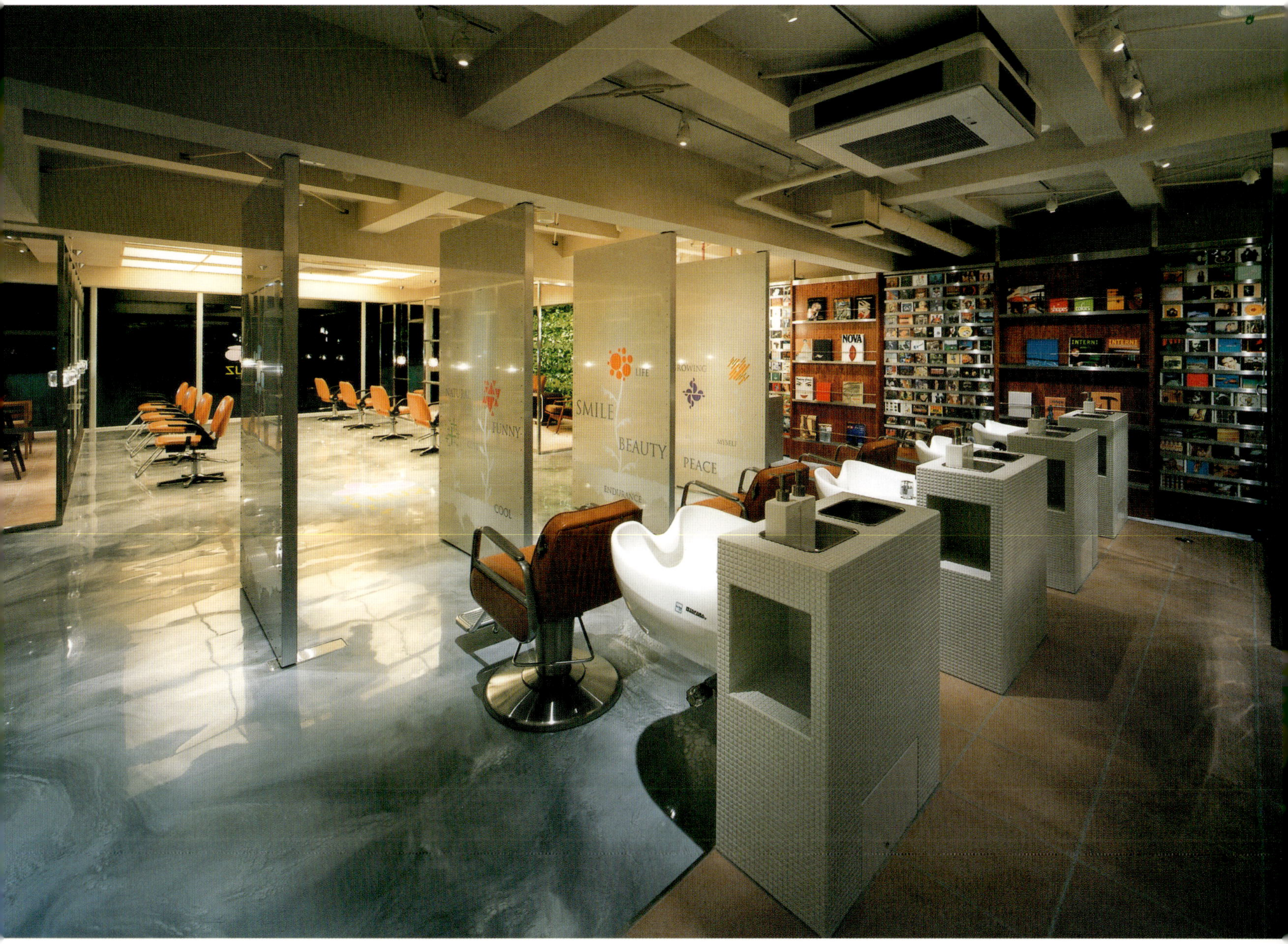

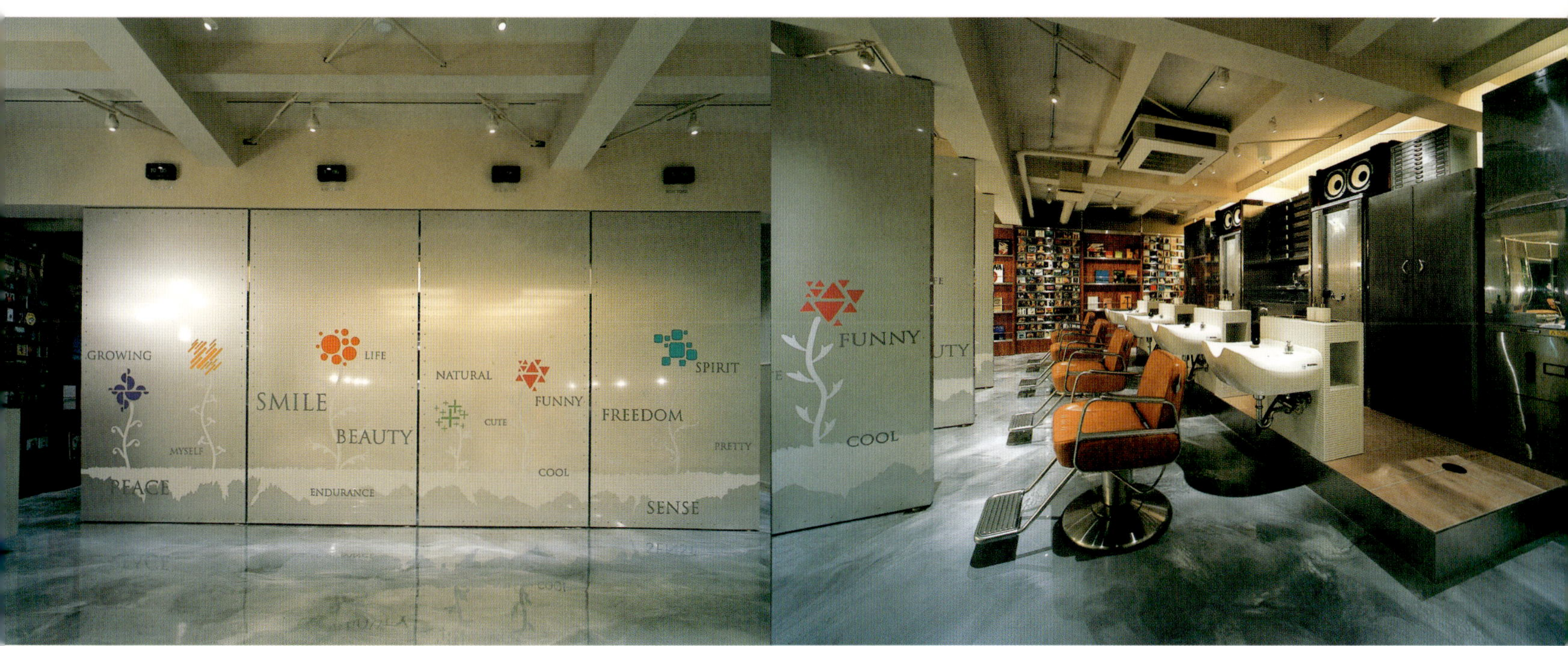
GROWING
LIFE
SMILE
NATURAL
BEAUTY
MYSELF
CUTE
FUNNY
SPIRIT
FREEDOM
FUNNY
PEACE
ENDURANCE
COOL
PRETTY
COOL
SENSE

TIP TOP tsutsujigaoka
TSUTSUJIGAOKA , TOKYO 2002

ジャパニーズ　コンテンポラリー

高度経済成長期と呼ばれた時代に、日本人はそれまで大切にしてきたモノやコトを見失ってしまったように感じます。"TIP TOP tsutsujigaoka"では、「和」本来の意味を、現代に生きる私というフィルターを通して見つめ直して、「ジャパニーズコンテンポラリー」をコンセプトに、日本人としてのプリミティブな感性で空間を構成しました。

　そして、複数のお客様が多種多様な目的を持って訪れるサロンにおいて、人と人、人と自然が共生するために生まれた、日本の建築文化を構成する要素の一つである、「しきり」を空間のメインテーマとしました。その「しきり」を私なりに昇華させ、目に映るだけではない、感じ取ることの出来る和の空気を具現化しました。

Japanese contemporary

During what is commonly known as Japan's era of high economic growth, I feel that the Japanese people lost sight of the things that had until that point been of great importance to them. At TIP TOP tsutsujigaoka, I used "Japanese contemporary" as my design concept, re-examining the traditional meaning of the Japanese concept of "wa," or peace and harmony, by filtering it through my own contemporary eyes. Holding close to my own identity and pride as a Japanese, I constructed the space with a sort of primitive sensitivity.

Partitions that were created for coexistence with nature have long been one of the basic elements of Japanese architectural culture. Here, I have created my own interpretation of these divisions in the context of a salon; a place that welcomes many and various customers with diverse expectations. I think that I have created a space where they are not just visible, but where they can be felt, also.

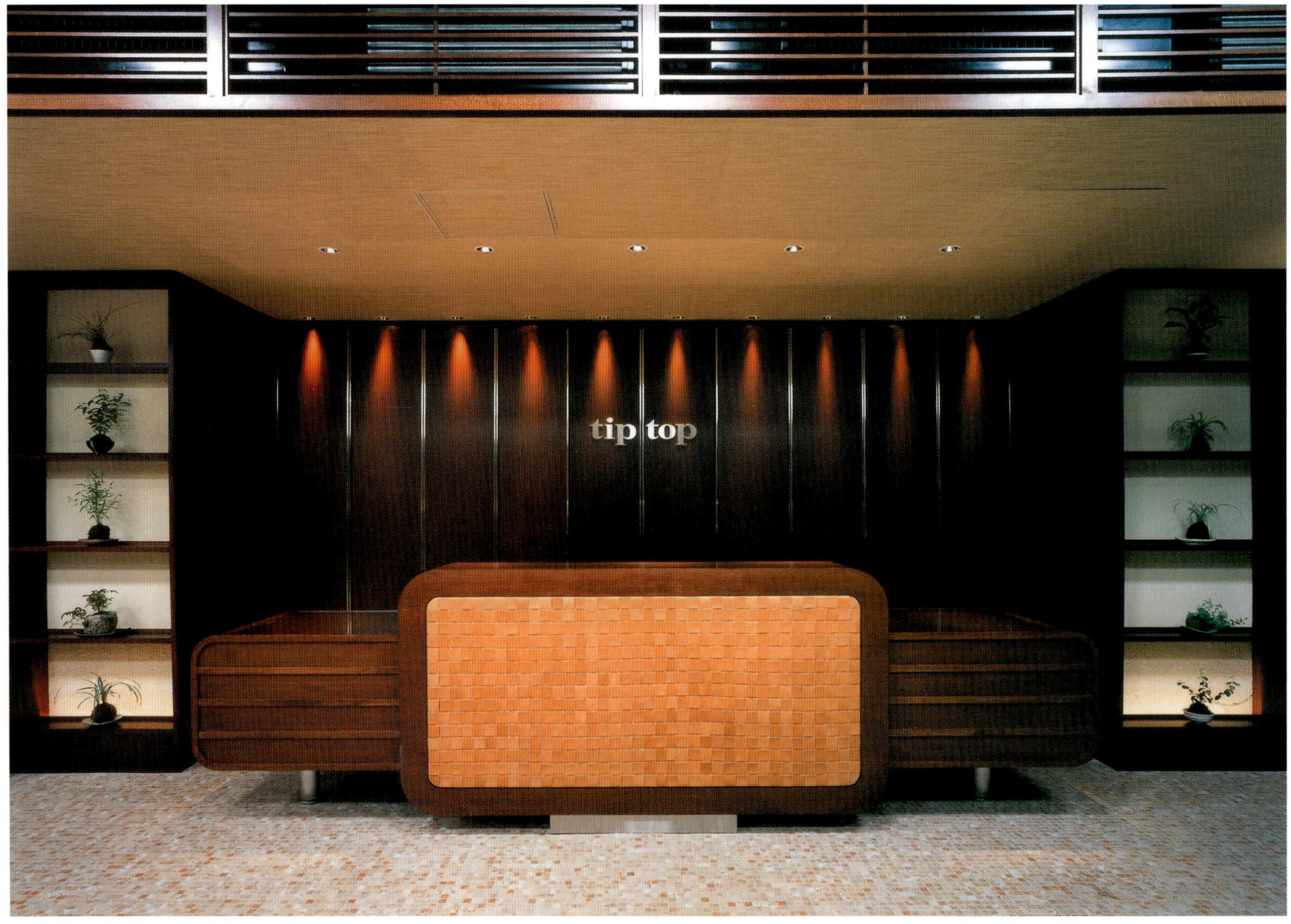

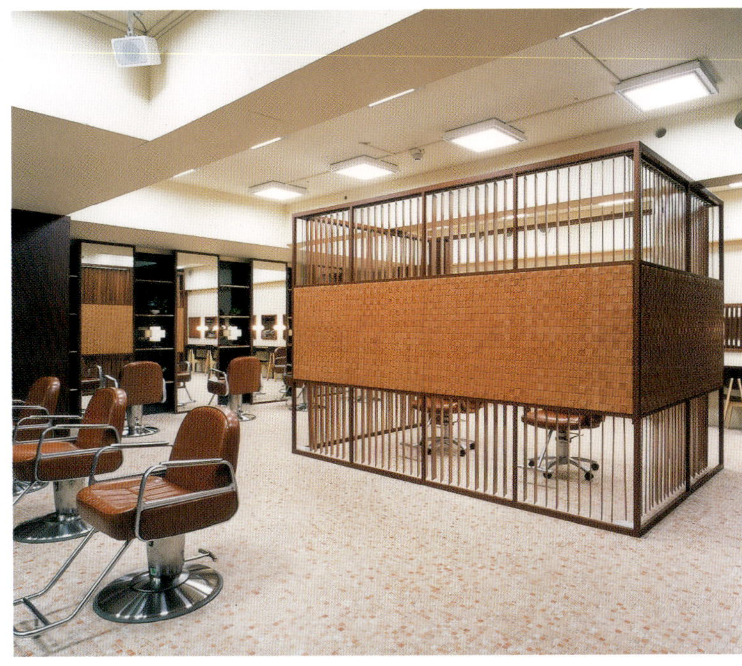

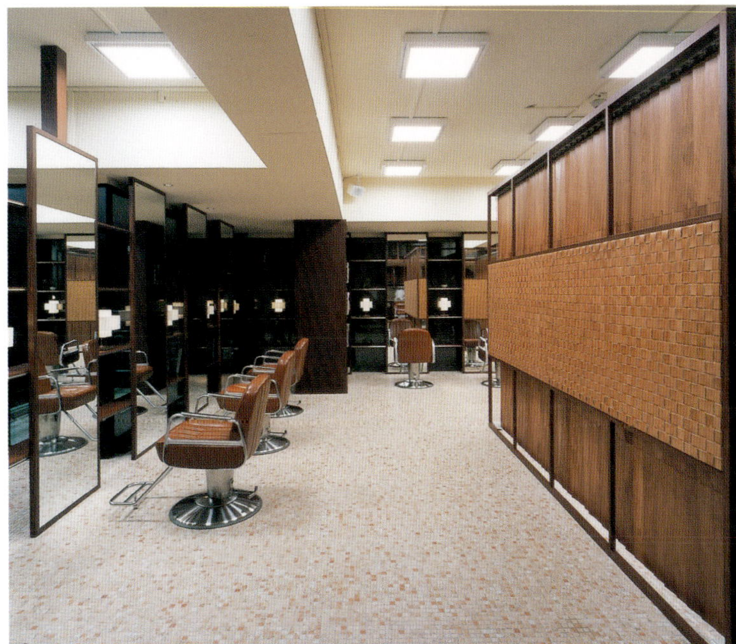

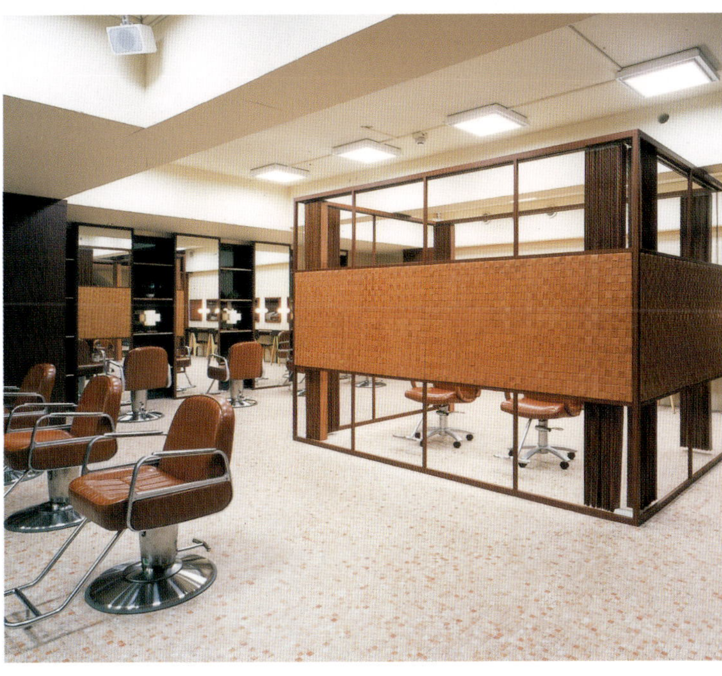

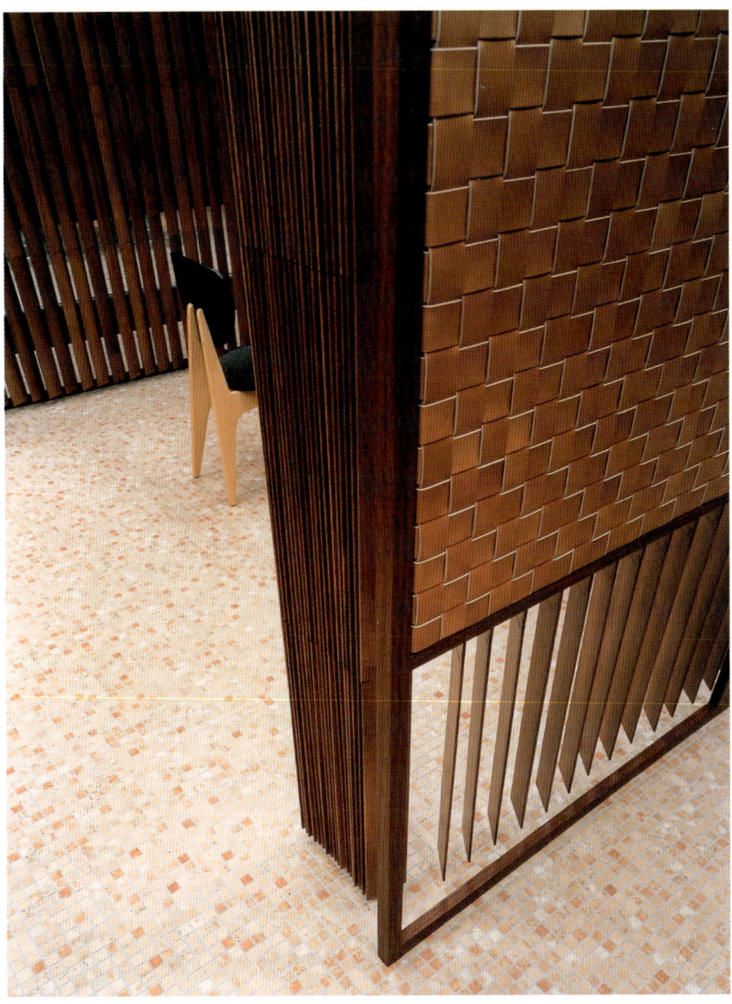

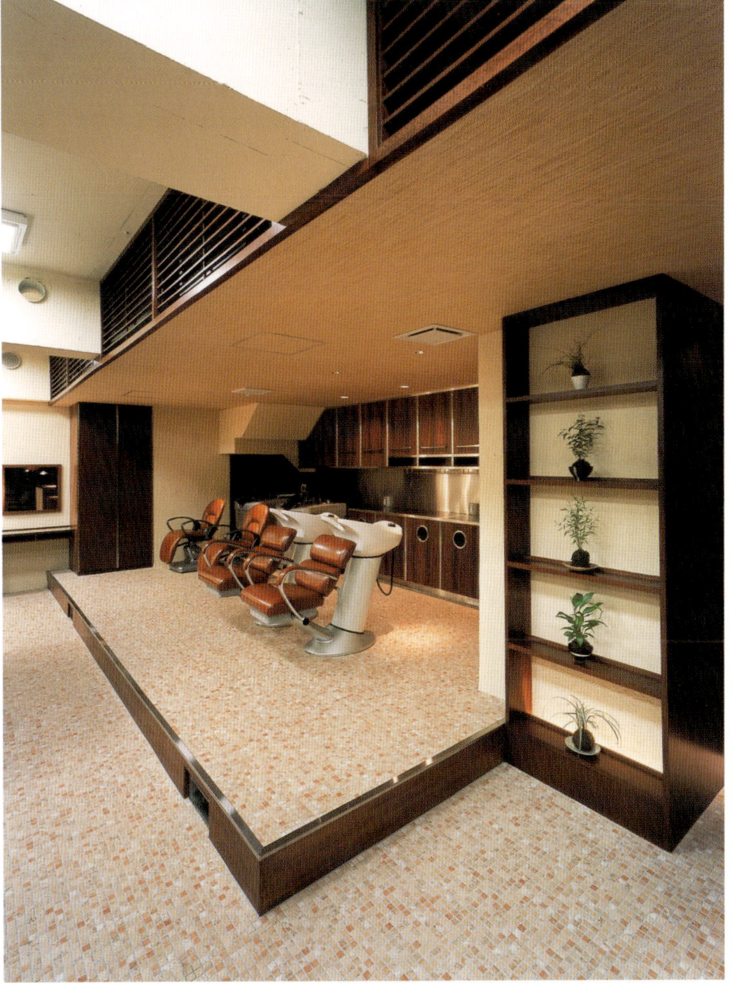

JOUR DOUX
KUZUHA , OSAKA 2002

時代が求める日常と非日常の境界

"JOUR DOUX"は銀行跡という今の時代を象徴する建物をリノベーションしたプロジェクトです。銀行という機能をはたすのためにつくられた建物は、どこか冷たく無機質なもので、まず私は、この建物にヘアサロンとしての新たな命を吹き込むことをイメージして、プランに取り組みました。

立地や地域性によってヘアサロンの業態は異なりますが、"JOUR DOUX"はヘア・ネイル・カフェ・スパの4つの分野から美に焦点を当てており、お客様の多様な要望や目的に対応できる空間を目指しています。

店名である「JOUR DOUX（やわらかな太陽の光）」からもイメージできるように、お客様の緊張をときほぐす開放的かつ日常的な空気感と、ドラマチックなゾーニングからうまれる、非日常的なシーンが交錯するようにデザインしました。

The boundry between the ordinary and unusual demanded by today's society

JOUR DOUX is a project that involves the reinnovation of a building that is characteristic of the modern era, one in which the remains of many banking businesses can be found. Buildings that were constructed to function as banks are somehow chillingly barren and inorganic, and my first step in working on this plan was to visualize how the new life of a hair salon could be breathed into this place.

The form and structure of hair salons does depend on local and site characteristics. However, JOUR DOUX aims to be a place that is able to satisfy the various desires of individual customers, with a focus on beauty in its four functions as a spa, a hair salon, a nail boutique, and a cafe.

I designed the space to blend a relaxing, everyday atmosphere that releases customers from their anxieties, as you can imagine given the title "JOUR DOUX (gentle sunlight)," with non-everyday settings created through dramatic zoning.

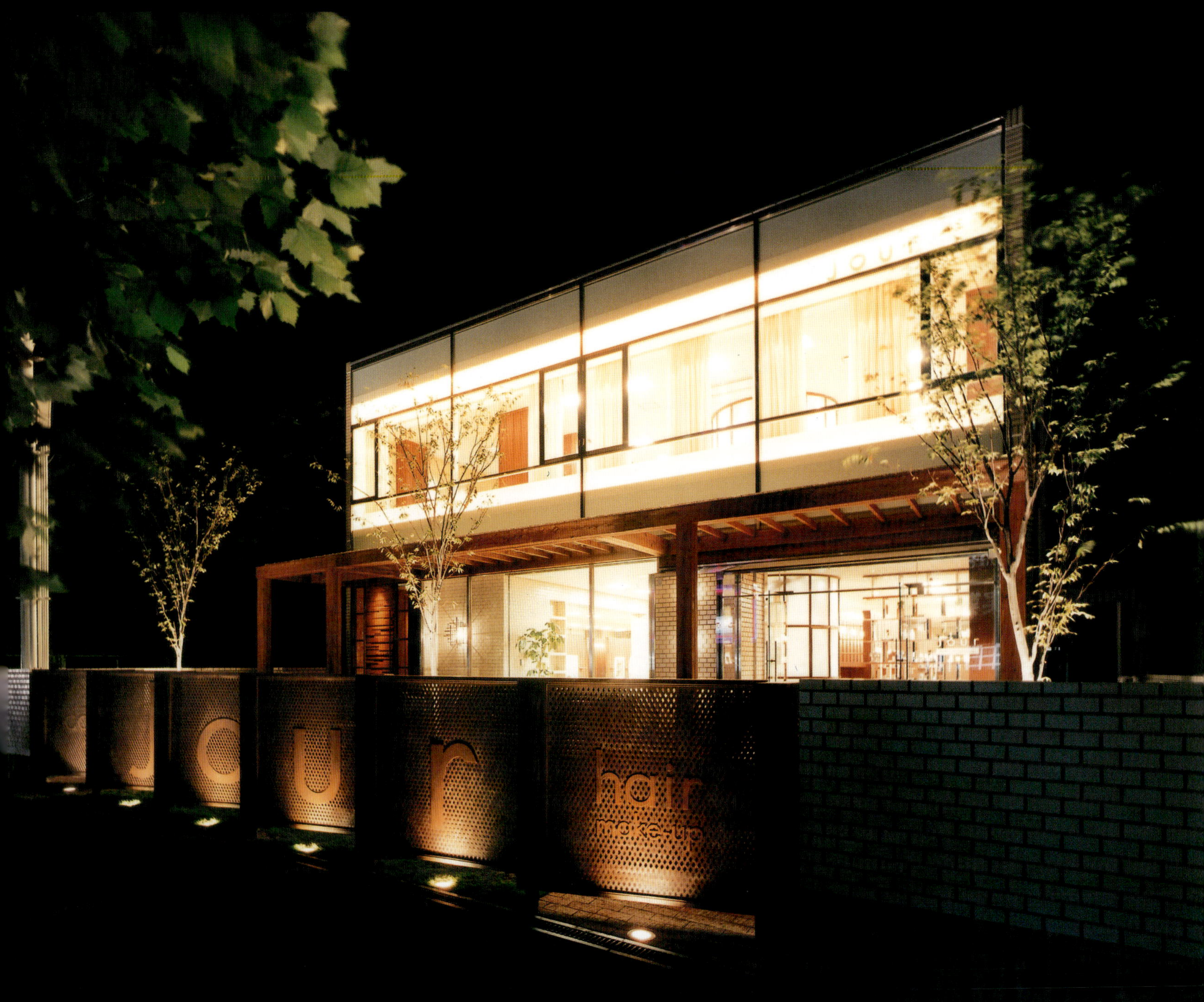

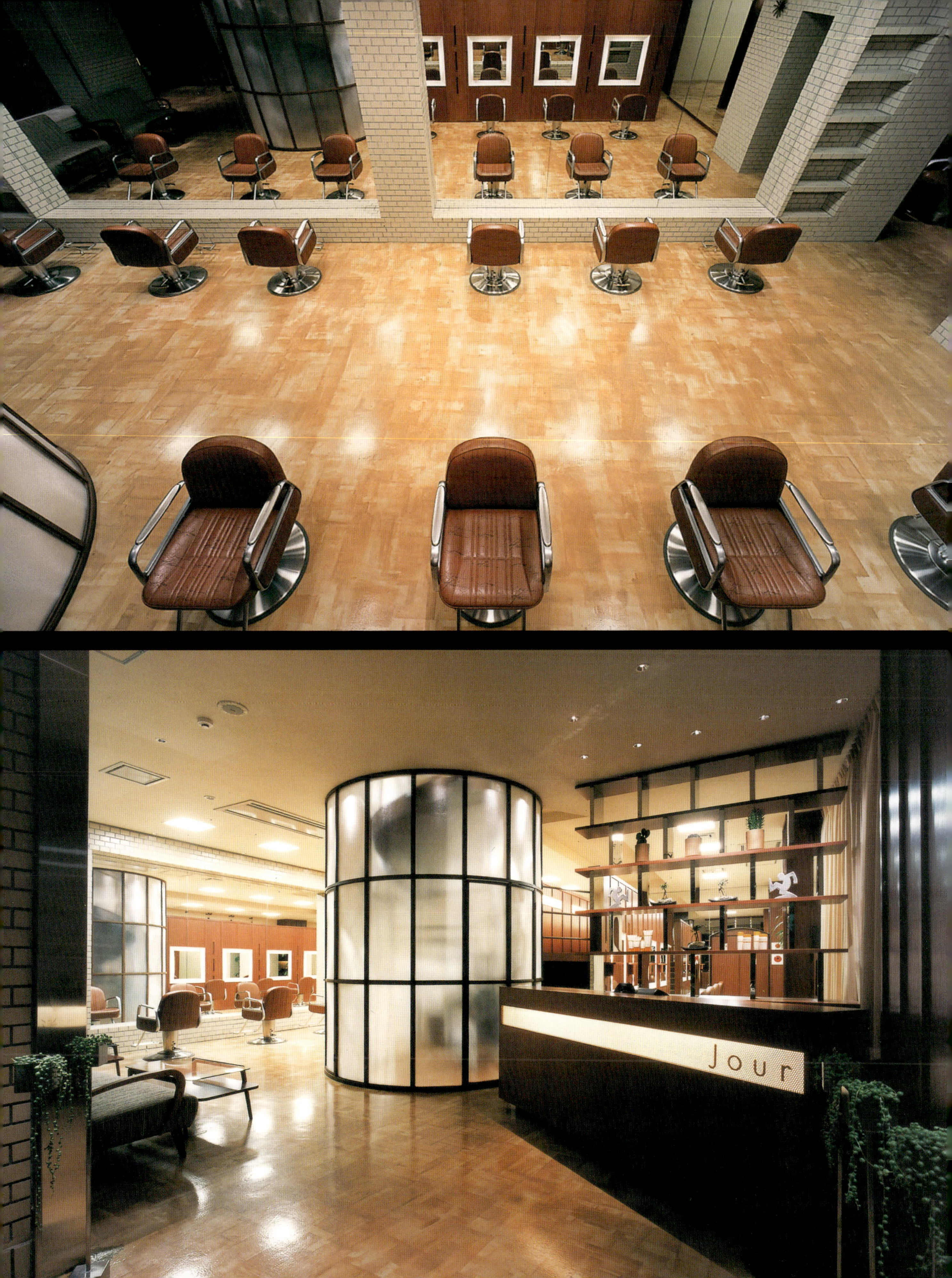
Jour

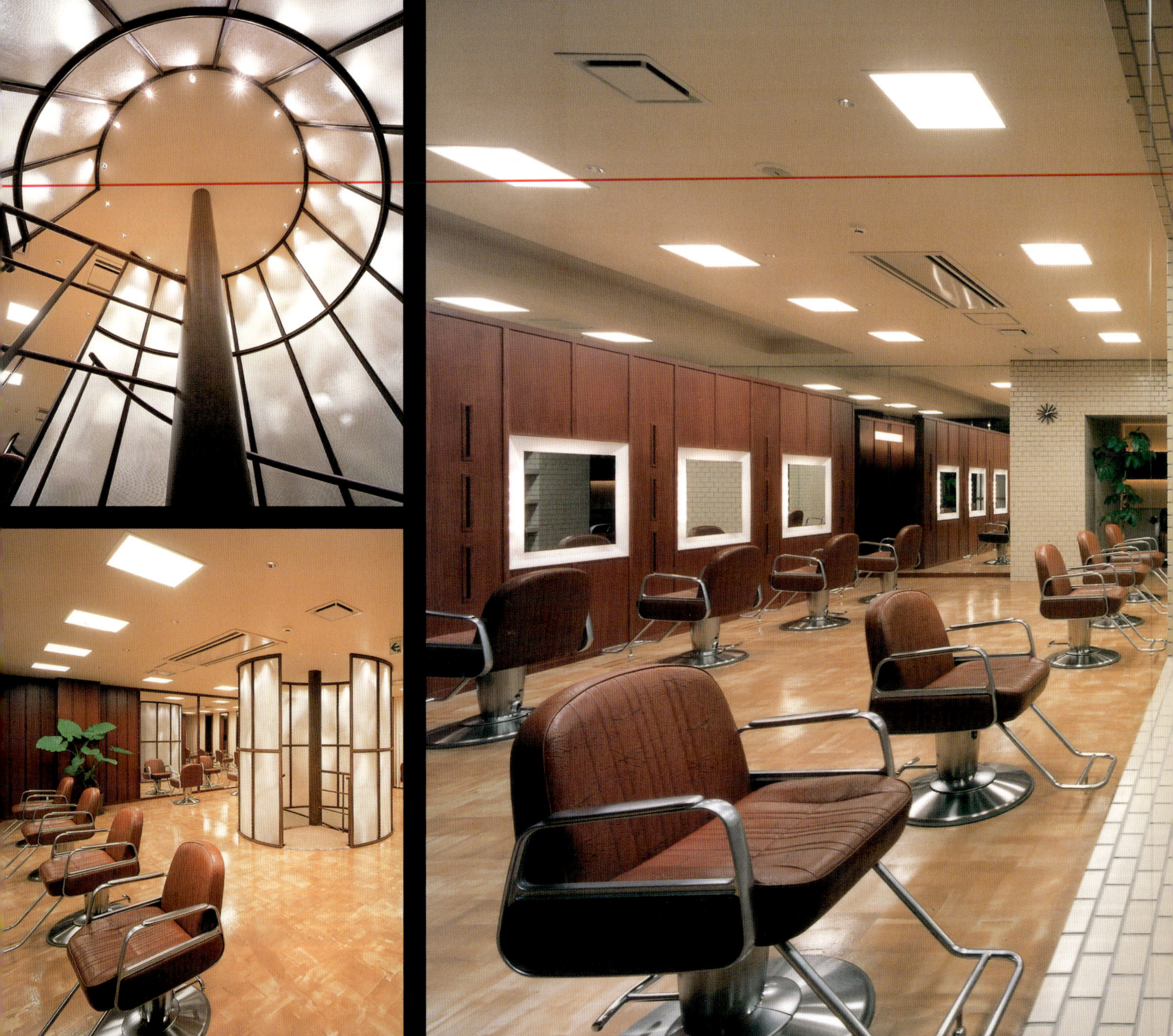

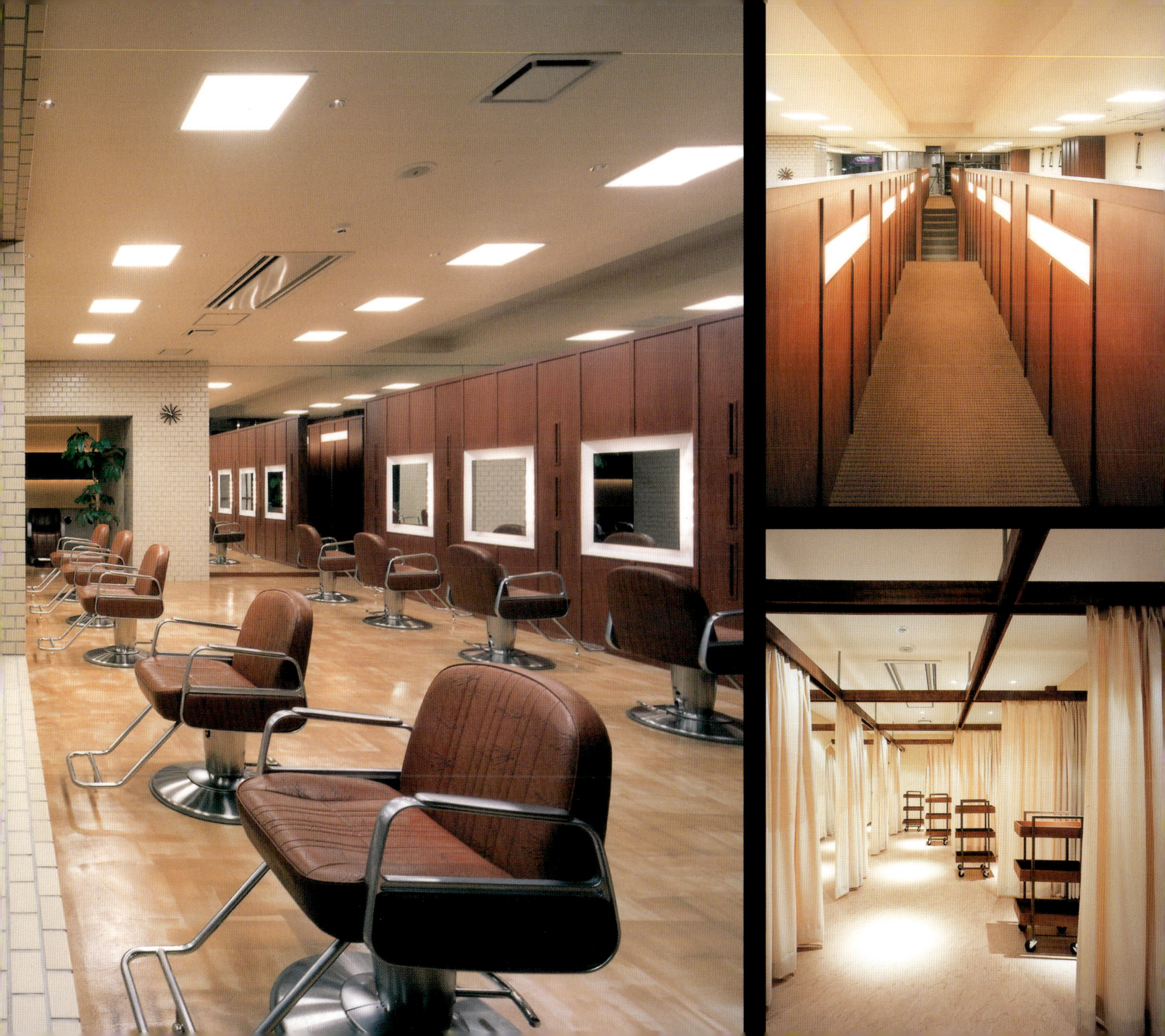

TIP TOP machida
MACHIDA , TOKYO 2002

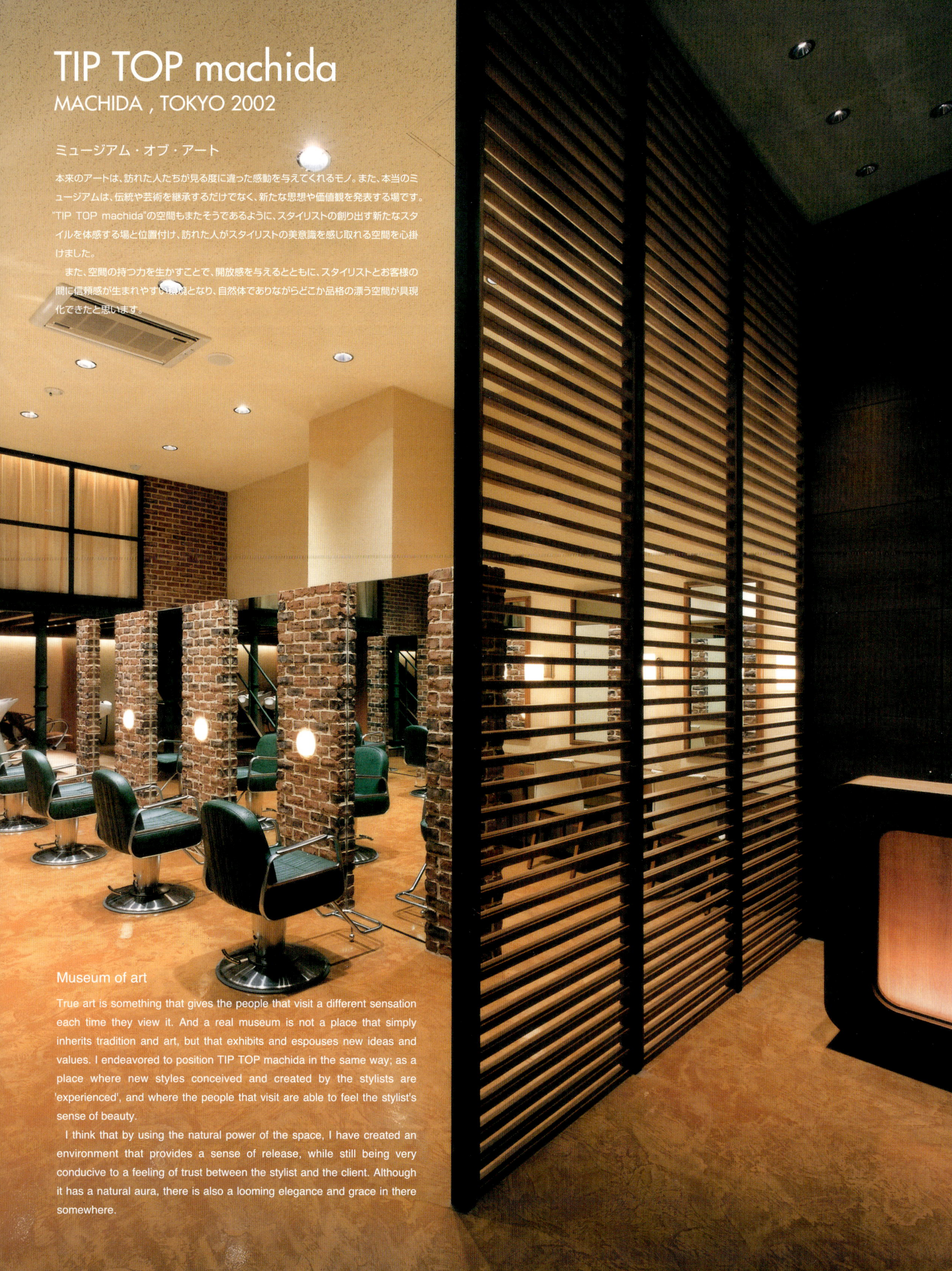

ミュージアム・オブ・アート

本来のアートは、訪れた人たちが見る度に違った感動を与えてくれるモノ。また、本当のミュージアムは、伝統や芸術を継承するだけでなく、新たな思想や価値観を発表する場です。"TIP TOP machida"の空間もまたそうであるように、スタイリストの創り出す新たなスタイルを体感する場と位置付け、訪れた人がスタイリストの美意識を感じ取れる空間を心掛けました。

また、空間の持つ力を生かすことで、開放感を与えるとともに、スタイリストとお客様の間に信頼感が生まれやすい環境となり、自然体でありながらどこか品格の漂う空間が具現化できたと思います。

Museum of art

True art is something that gives the people that visit a different sensation each time they view it. And a real museum is not a place that simply inherits tradition and art, but that exhibits and espouses new ideas and values. I endeavored to position TIP TOP machida in the same way; as a place where new styles conceived and created by the stylists are 'experienced', and where the people that visit are able to feel the stylist's sense of beauty.

I think that by using the natural power of the space, I have created an environment that provides a sense of release, while still being very conducive to a feeling of trust between the stylist and the client. Although it has a natural aura, there is also a looming elegance and grace in there somewhere.

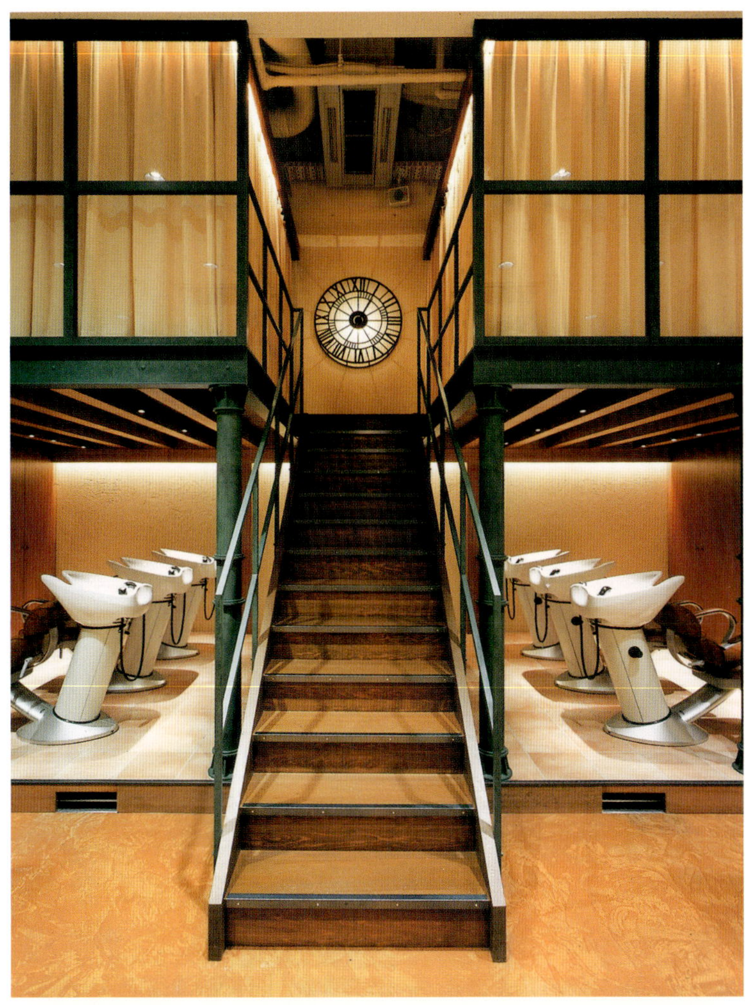
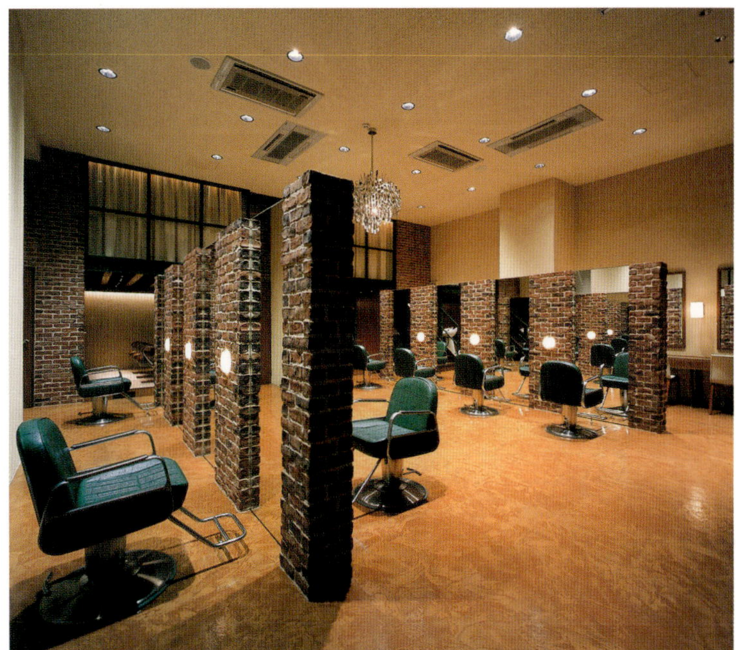
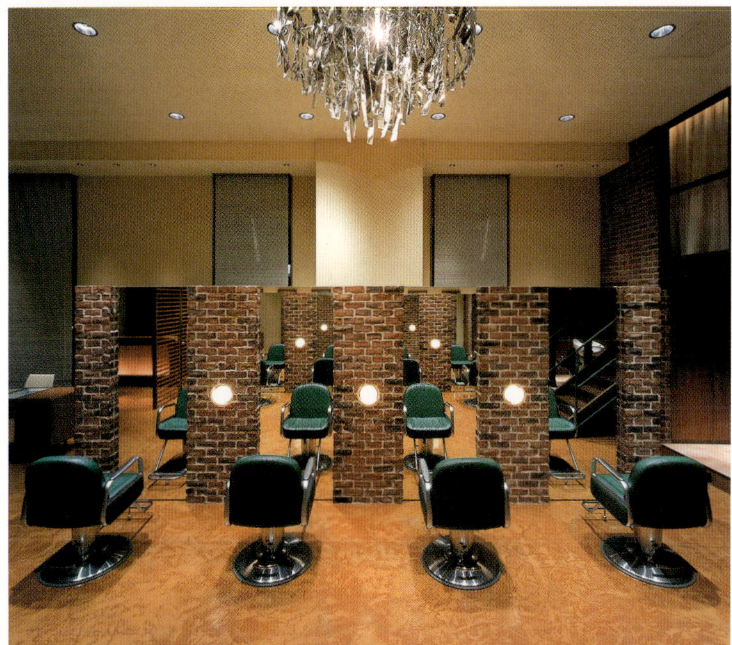
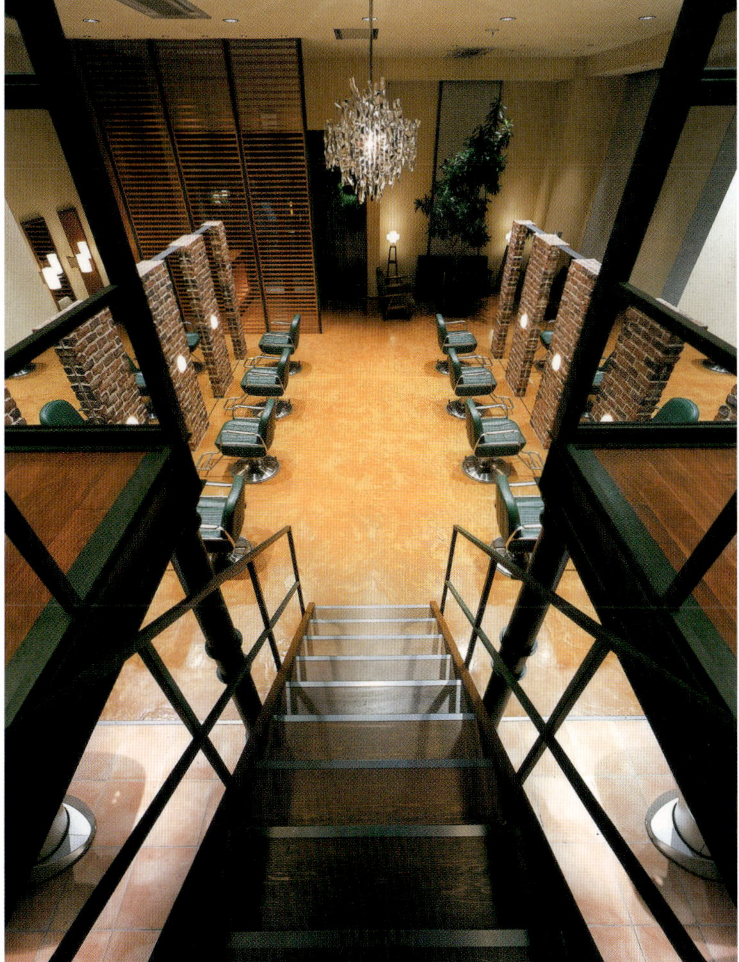
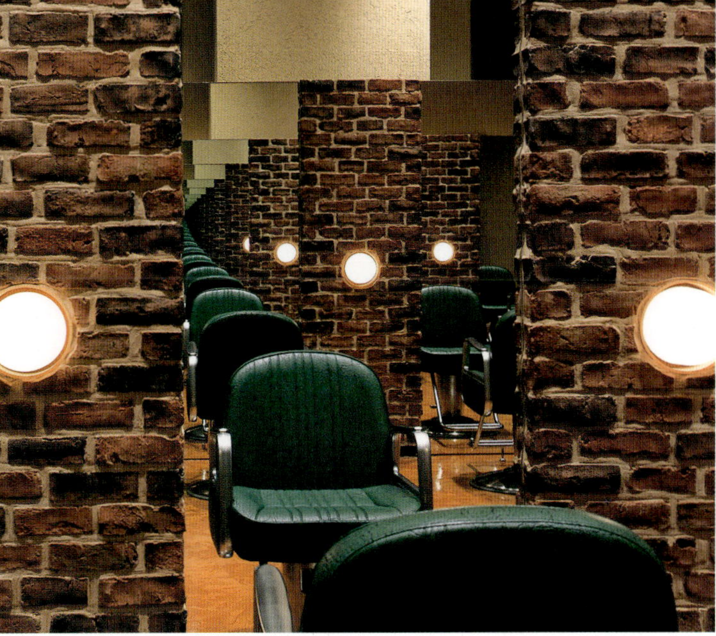

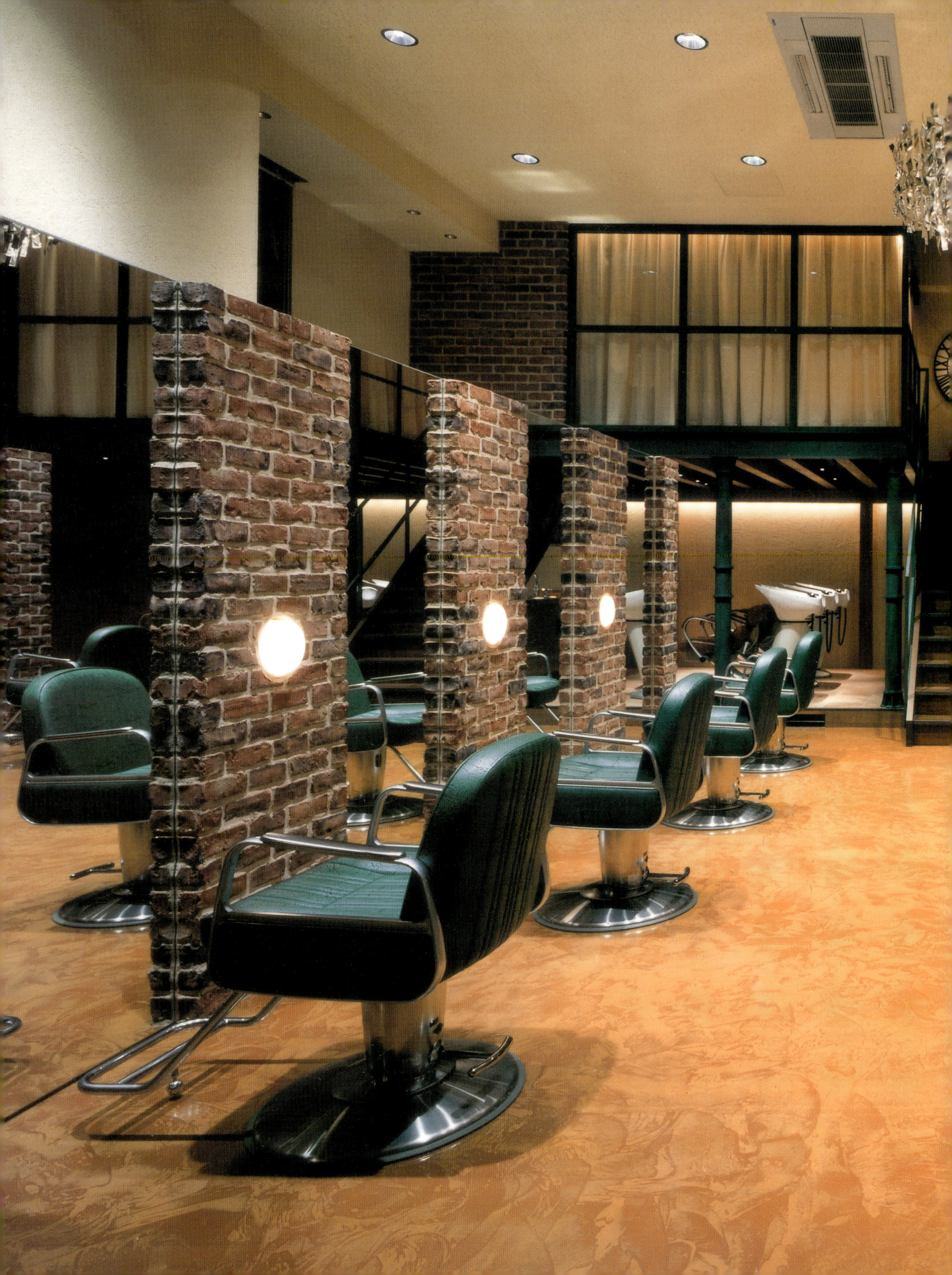

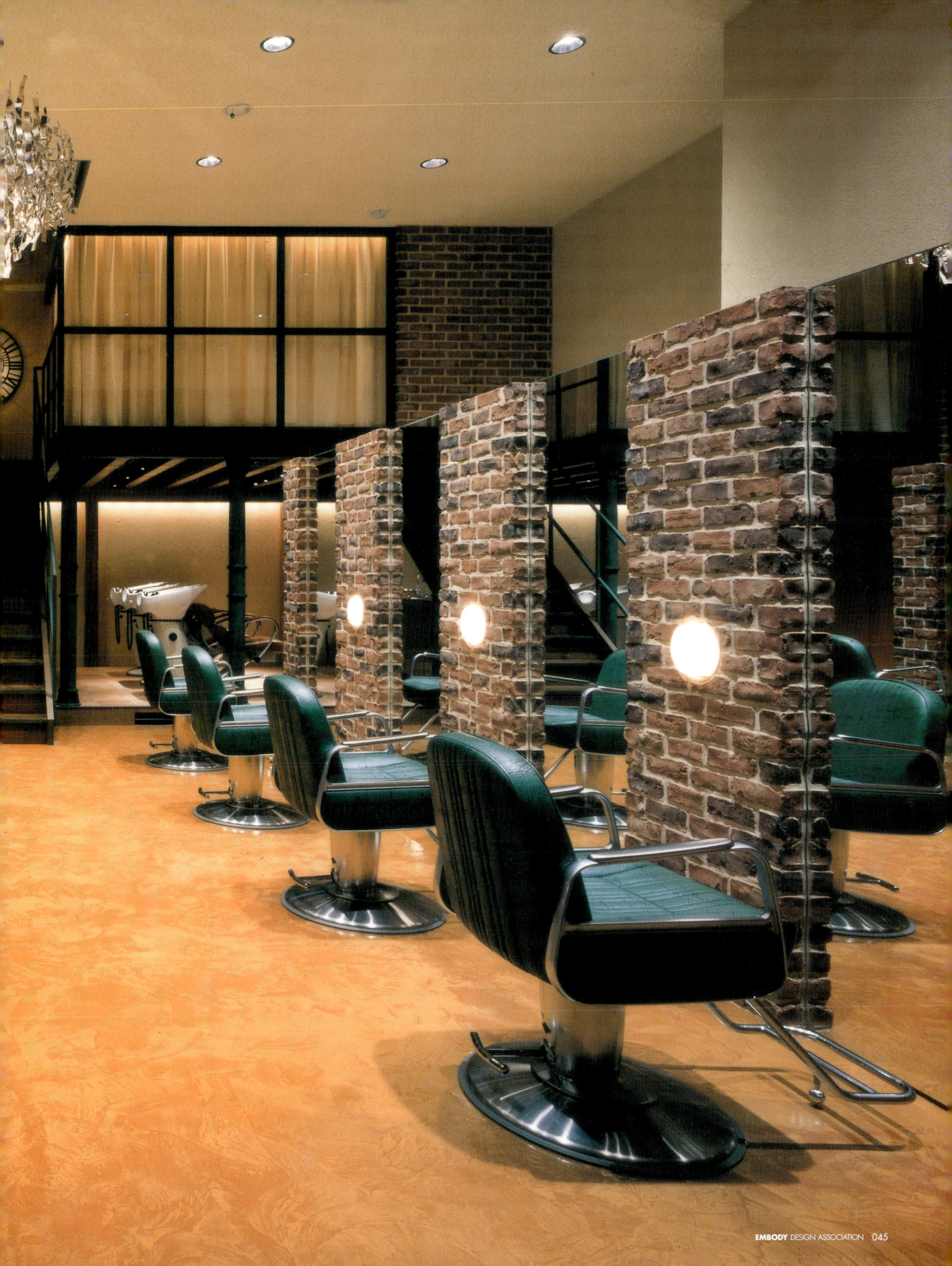

DEUX UN
SHINSAIBASHI , OSAKA 2001

人と人を結ぶデザイン

訪れた人が椅子に腰かけ、スタイリストがその人のための扉を開ける･･･。
そこには訪れた人とスタイリストだけの特別な空間があらわれる･･･。
腰かけた人だけを照らす明かりがともり、扉は回りの人々の視線を遮るパーテーションとなり、スピーカーからはその人のための音楽が流れる･･･。
回りを気にせず会話も楽しむ･･･。
　人と人の心を結ぶ、たしかなモノ、　日本人が一番大切にしていたコトがここにはあります。

A design that binds people together

The client sits down, and the stylist opens up a doorway especially for them...
Within lies a place that exists exclusively for the client and stylist.
The lights illuminate only the person seated in the chair, the doorway becomes a partition that secludes them from the view of others, and music especially for the client flows from the speakers...
 They enjoy conversation without being concerned with their surroundings.
Here there exists something real that binds people's hearts together...
Here there exists what Japanese people have always held dearest...

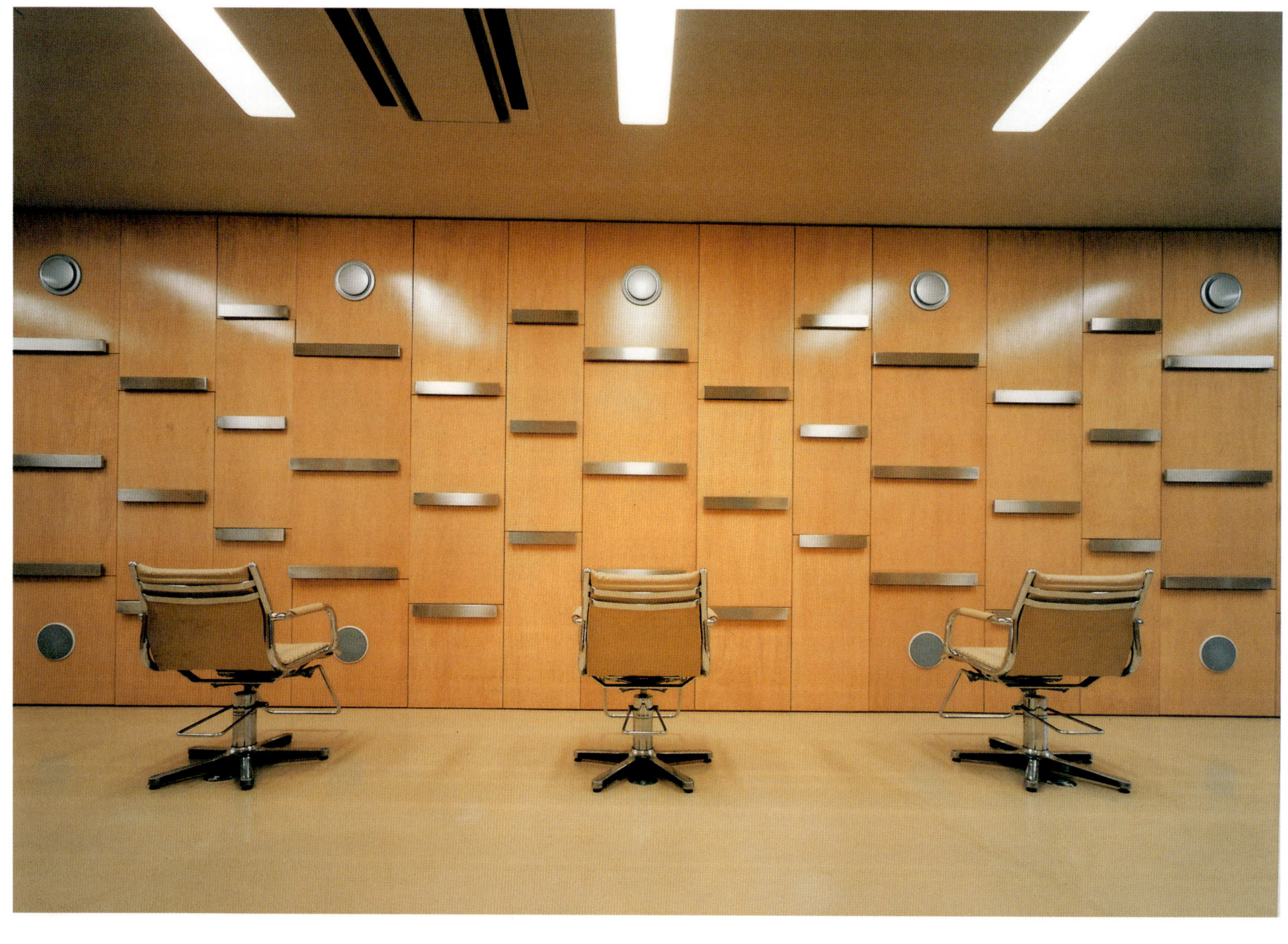

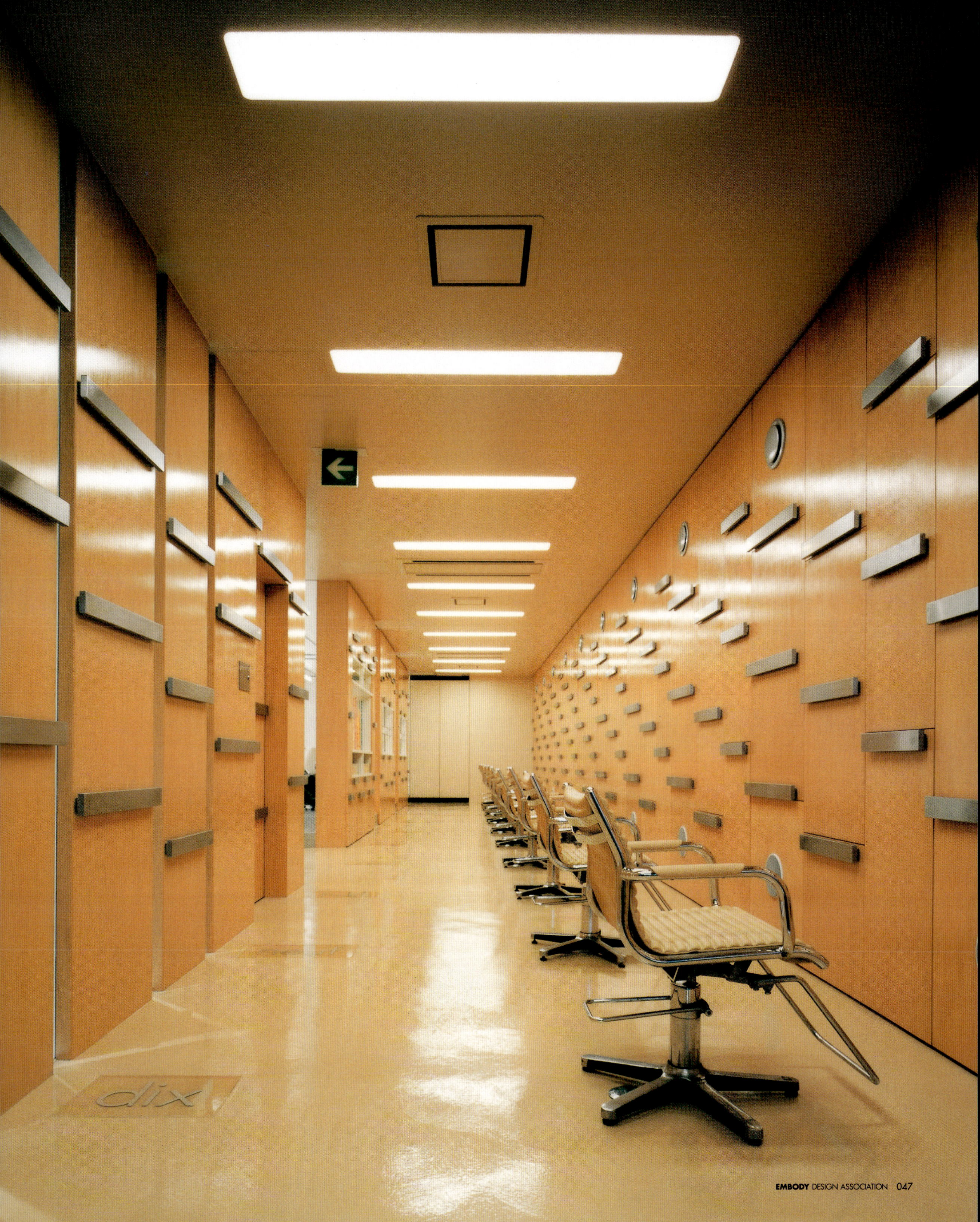

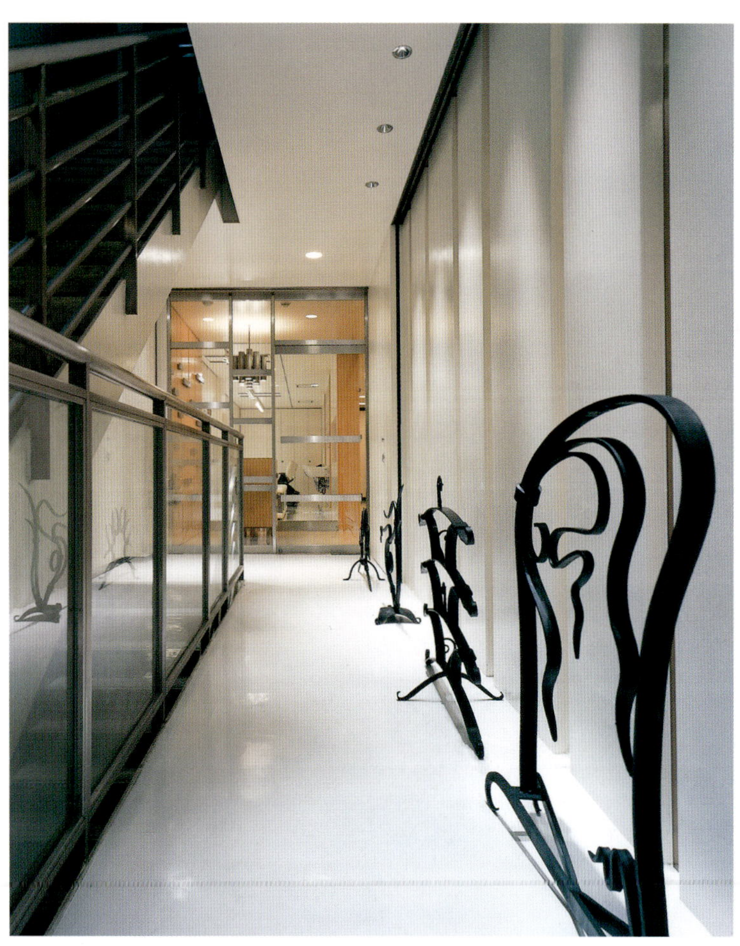
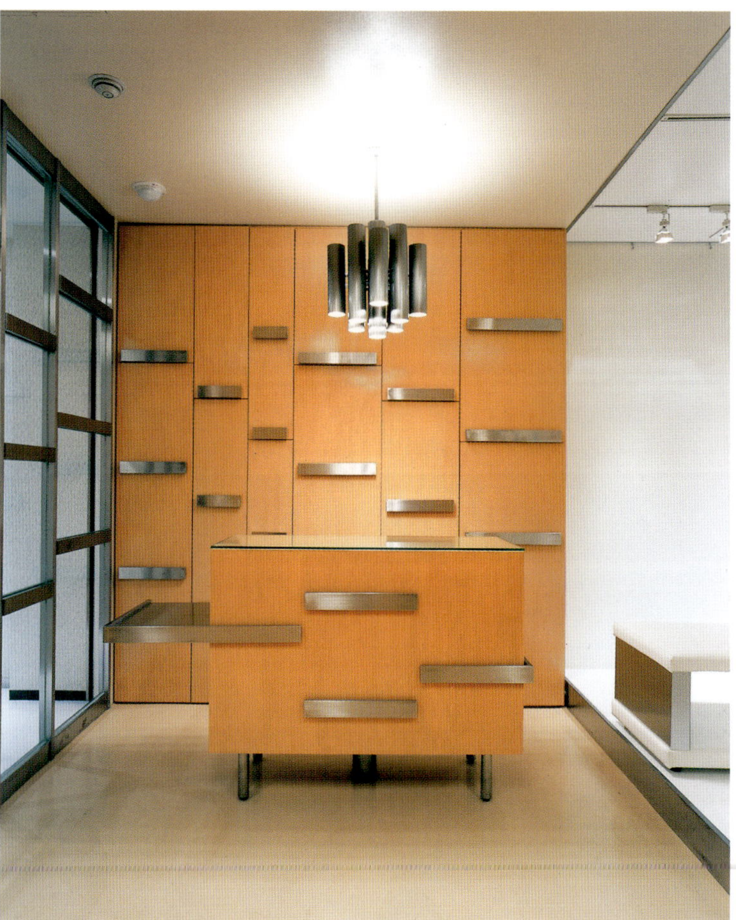

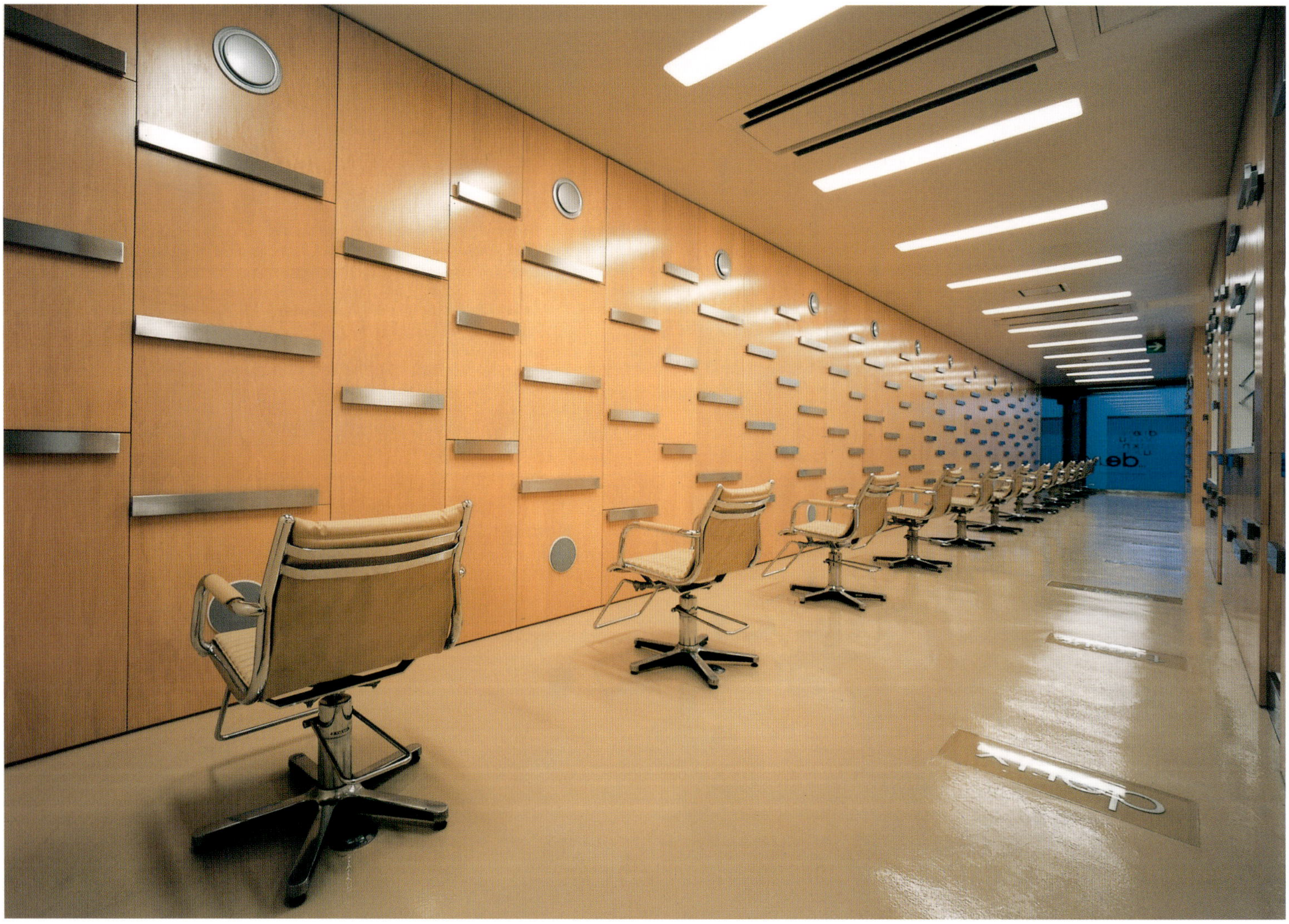

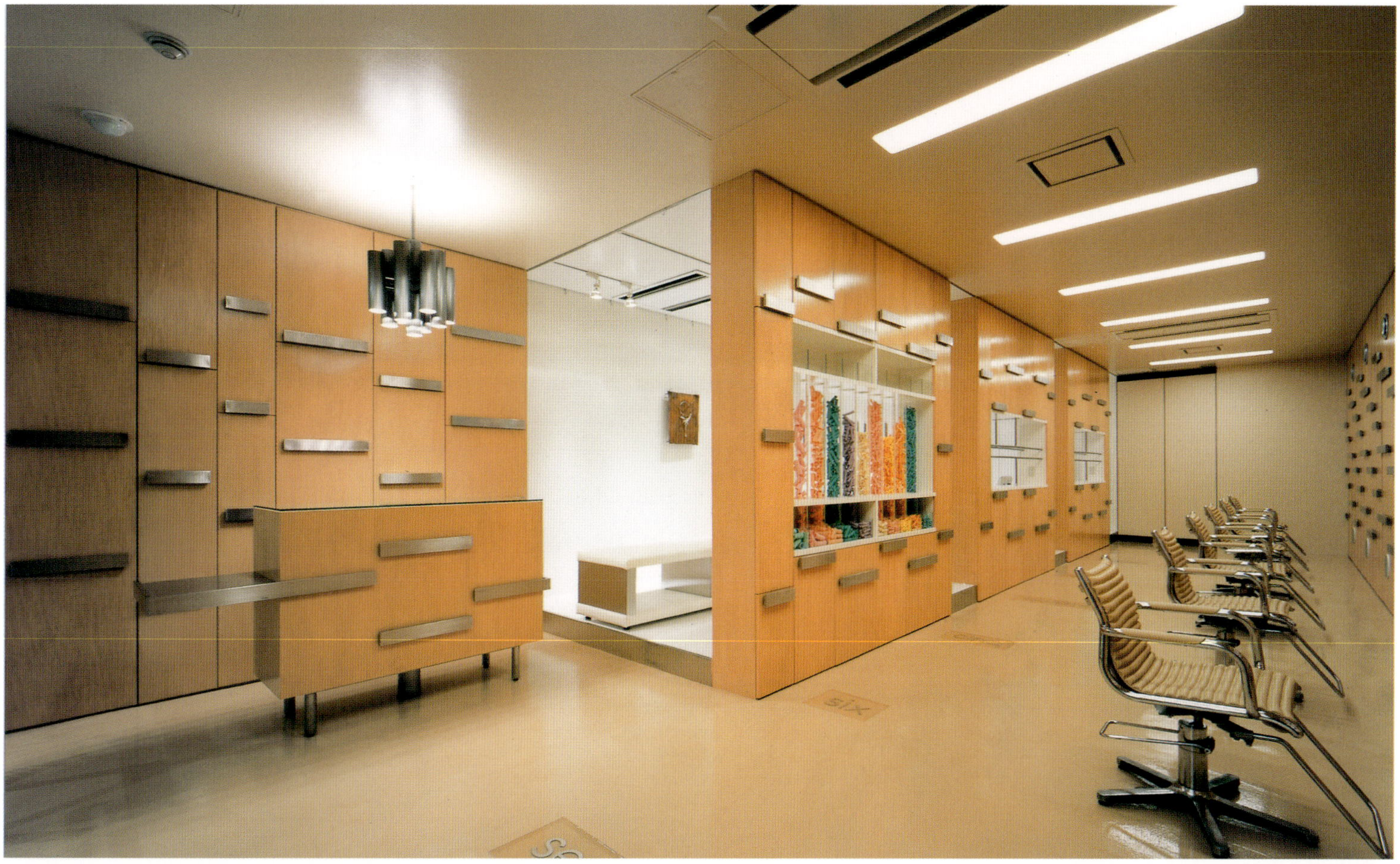

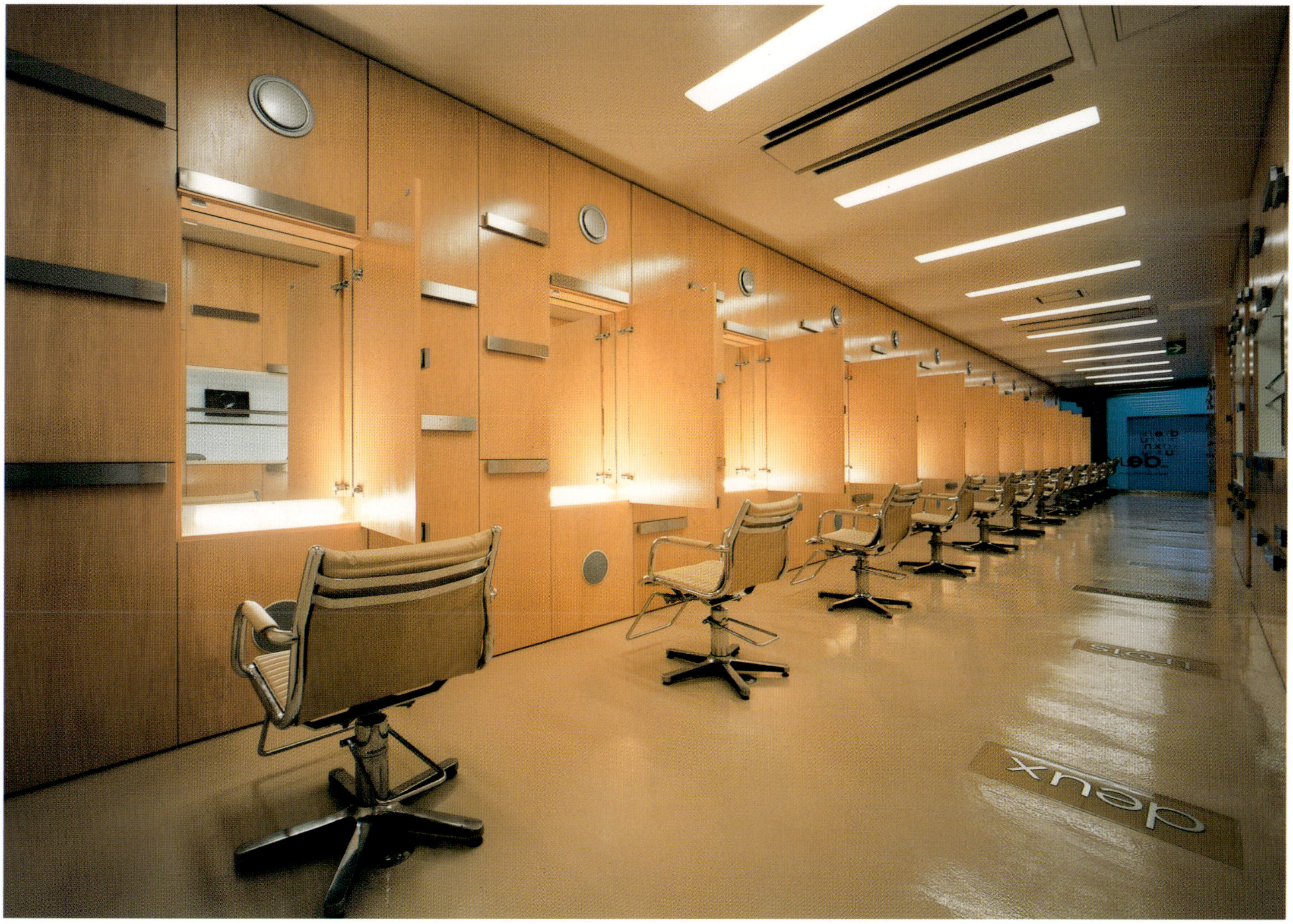

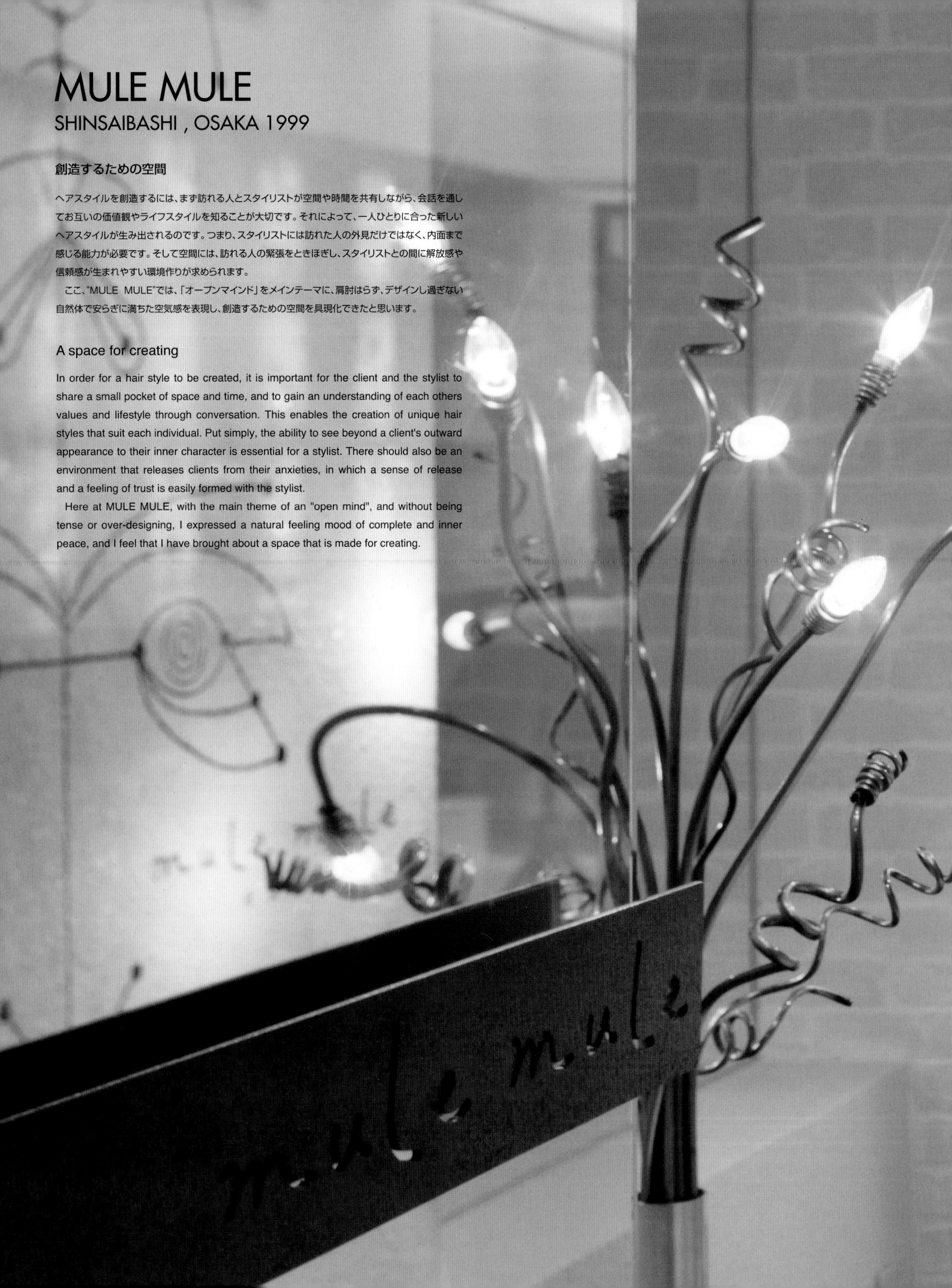

MULE MULE
SHINSAIBASHI , OSAKA 1999

創造するための空間

ヘアスタイルを創造するには、まず訪れる人とスタイリストが空間や時間を共有しながら、会話を通してお互いの価値観やライフスタイルを知ることが大切です。それによって、一人ひとりに合った新しいヘアスタイルが生み出されるのです。つまり、スタイリストには訪れた人の外見だけではなく、内面まで感じる能力が必要です。そして空間には、訪れる人の緊張をときほぐし、スタイリストとの間に解放感や信頼感が生まれやすい環境作りが求められます。

　ここ、"MULE MULE"では、「オープンマインド」をメインテーマに、肩肘はらず、デザインし過ぎない自然体で安らぎに満ちた空気感を表現し、創造するための空間を具現化できたと思います。

A space for creating

In order for a hair style to be created, it is important for the client and the stylist to share a small pocket of space and time, and to gain an understanding of each others values and lifestyle through conversation. This enables the creation of unique hair styles that suit each individual. Put simply, the ability to see beyond a client's outward appearance to their inner character is essential for a stylist. There should also be an environment that releases clients from their anxieties, in which a sense of release and a feeling of trust is easily formed with the stylist.

　Here at MULE MULE, with the main theme of an "open mind", and without being tense or over-designing, I expressed a natural feeling mood of complete and inner peace, and I feel that I have brought about a space that is made for creating.

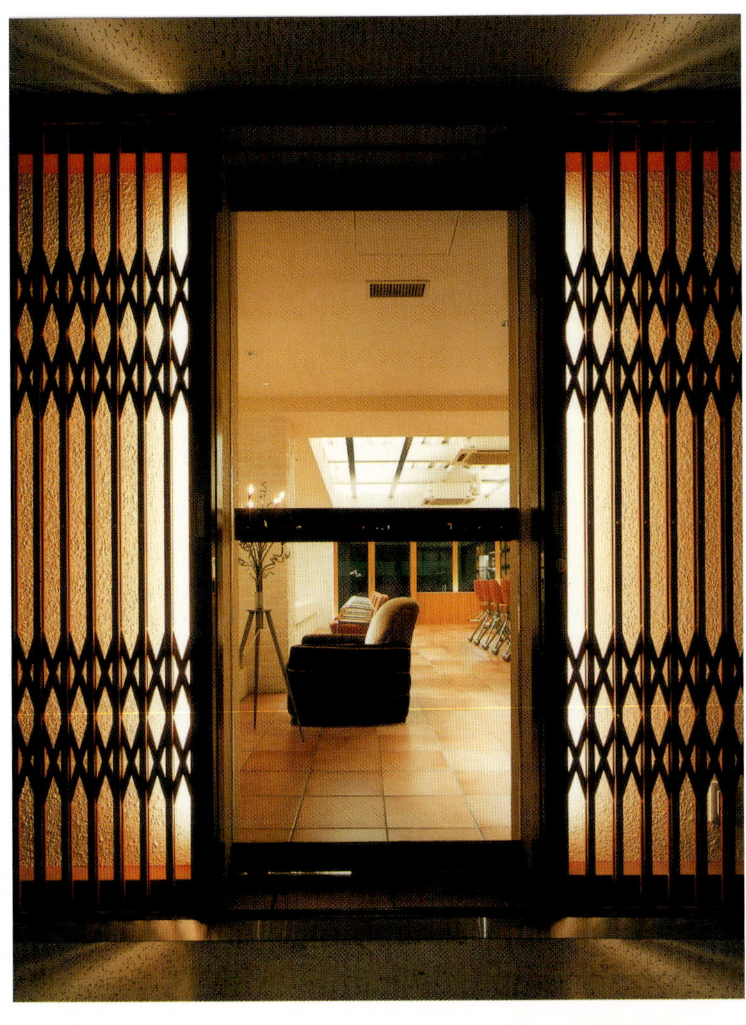
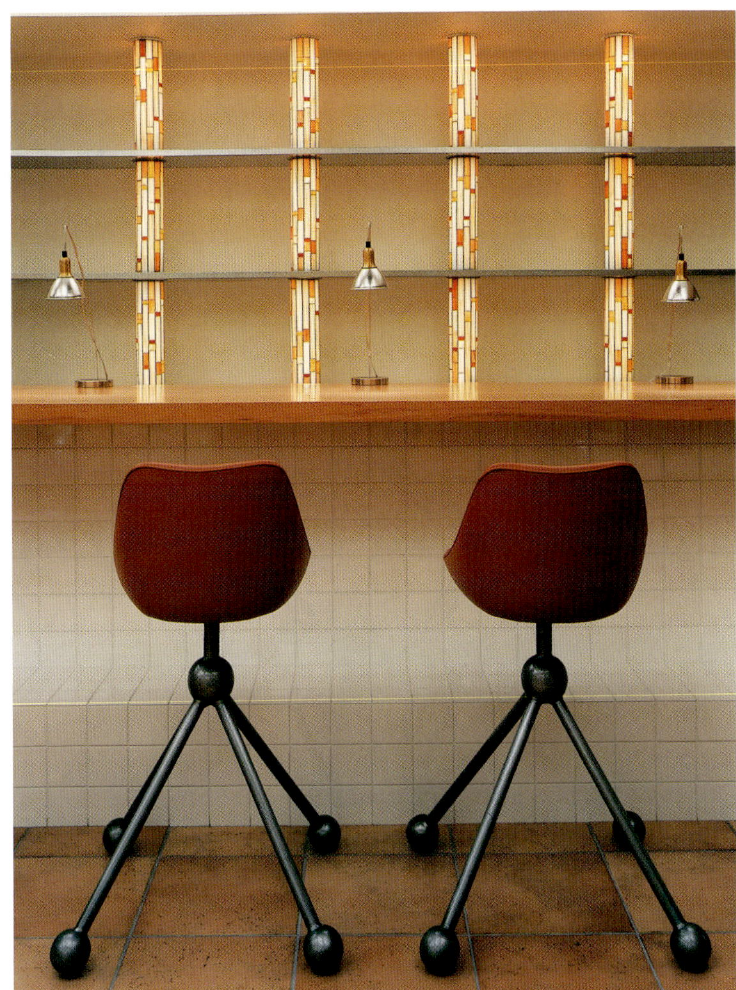
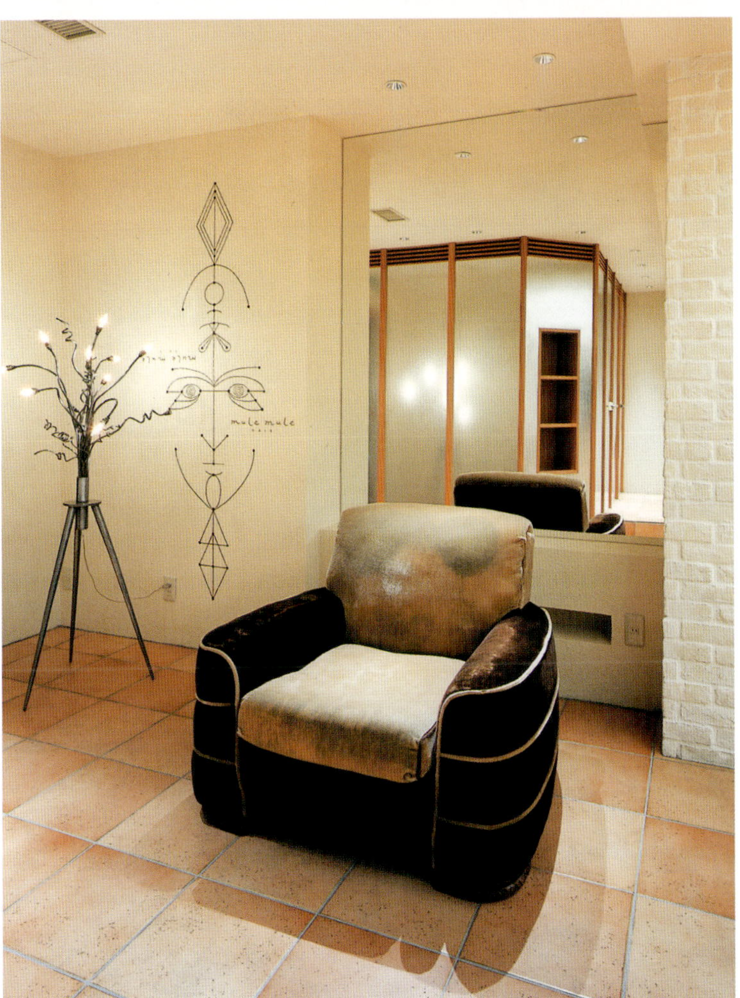
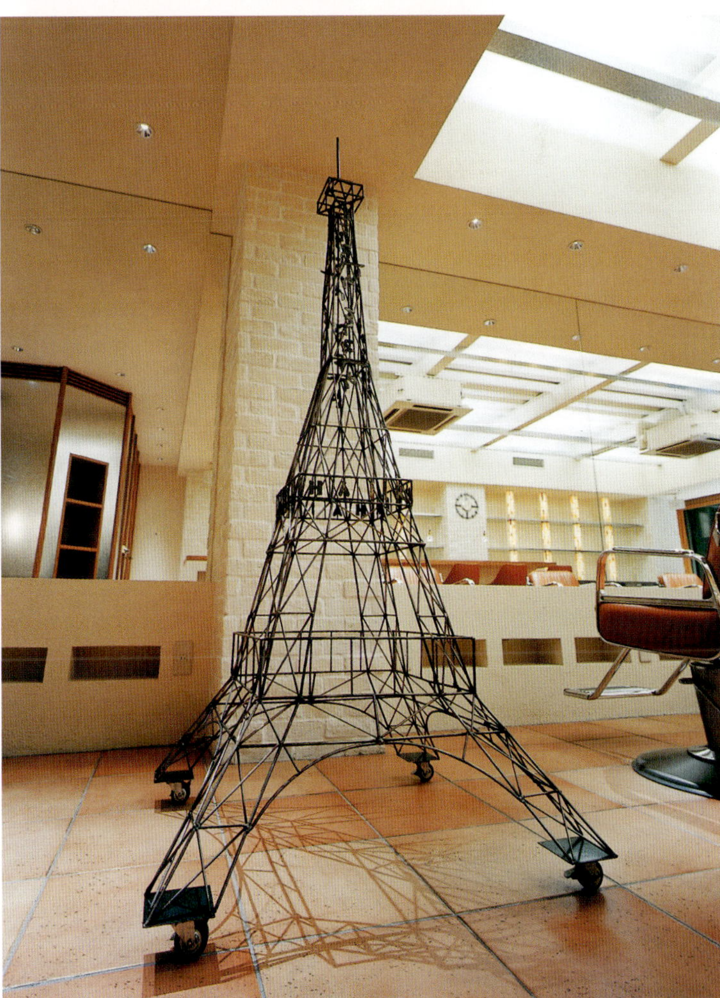

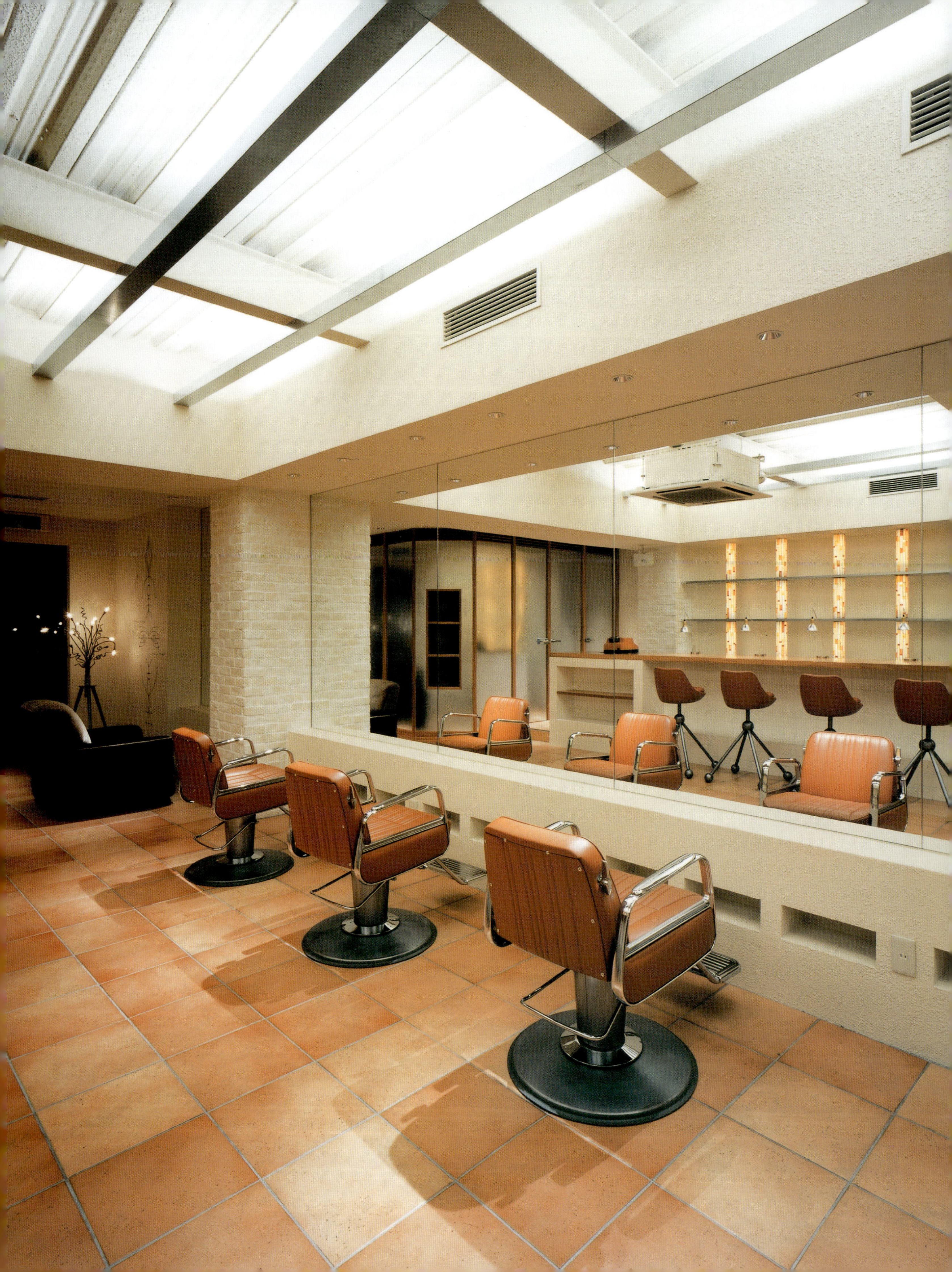

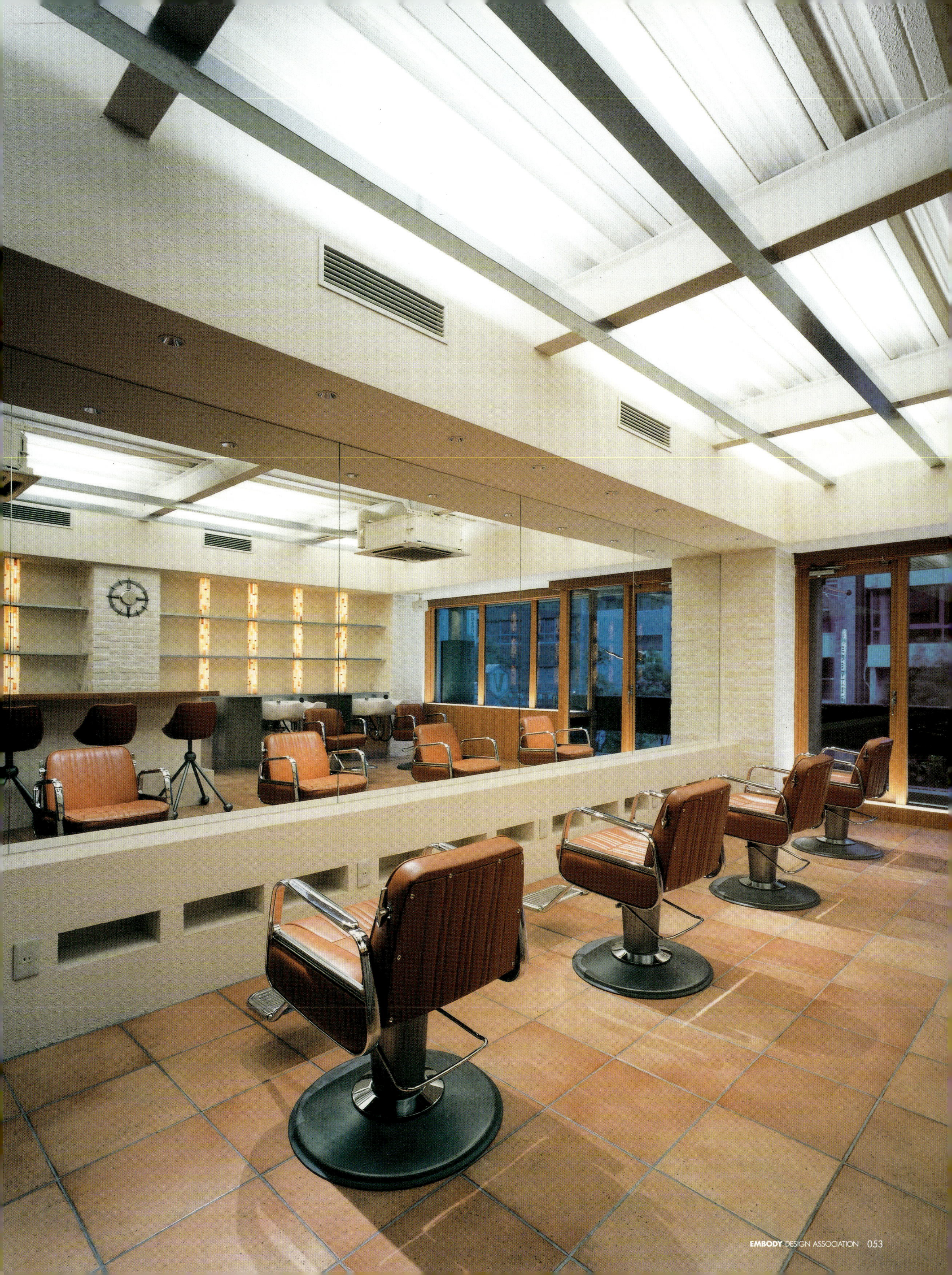

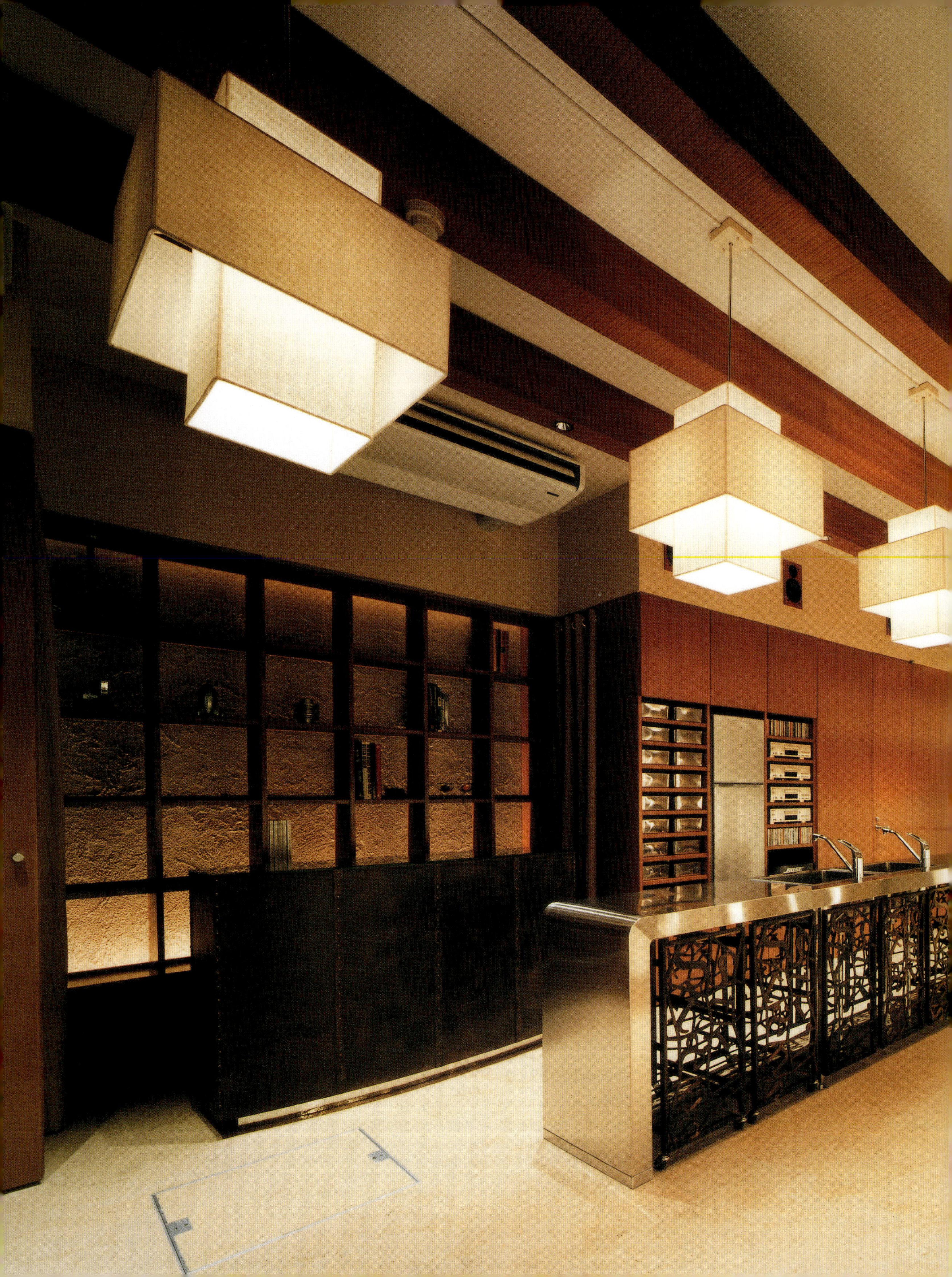

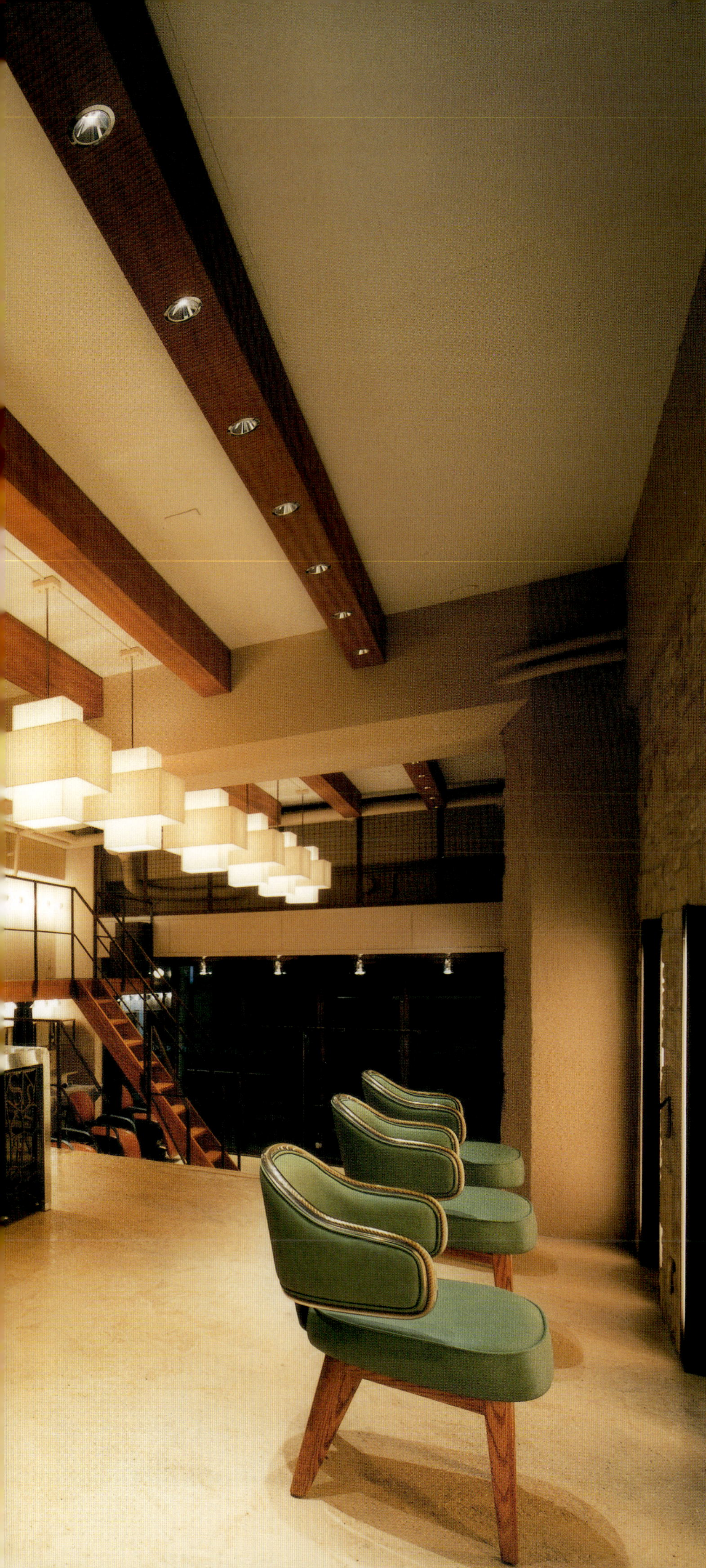

STIL STAENS
KITAHORIE , OSAKA 2000

空間の力を引き出すデザイン

表も裏も通りに面した見え過ぎる立地環境と、路面のレベルの違いで
1メートルの高低差が生じる空間。ヘアサロンとしては一つ間違える
とデメリットになってしまう部分をメリットに転換し、立地環境や空間
がもともと持っている力を最大限に引きだせる、日本的なデザインを
心掛けました。

　ヘアサロンという業態のため、スタイリングやマテリアルは西洋的
であっても、そこに息づく精神性はどこか日本を感じ取れる、時代に風
化されないジャパニーズモダンな空間になったと思います。

A design to bring out the space's natural power

The site is too plainly visible from outside, facing roads to
the front and back, and there is 1 meter change in
elevation due to the differing street levels. One false step
with respect to certain aspects of the site can turn them
into drawbacks for a hair salon, so I made a real effort to
turn these into advantages, while giving maximum effect
to the natural power of the space and the site
environment to create a particularly Japanese style
design.

　Although the styling and materials used are western in
nature, by virtue of the fact that it is a hair salon business,
there is a lingering Japanese spirituality there somewhere,
and I believe that I have created a "Japanese modern"
type feel that is still somehow timeless and unaffected by
the era.

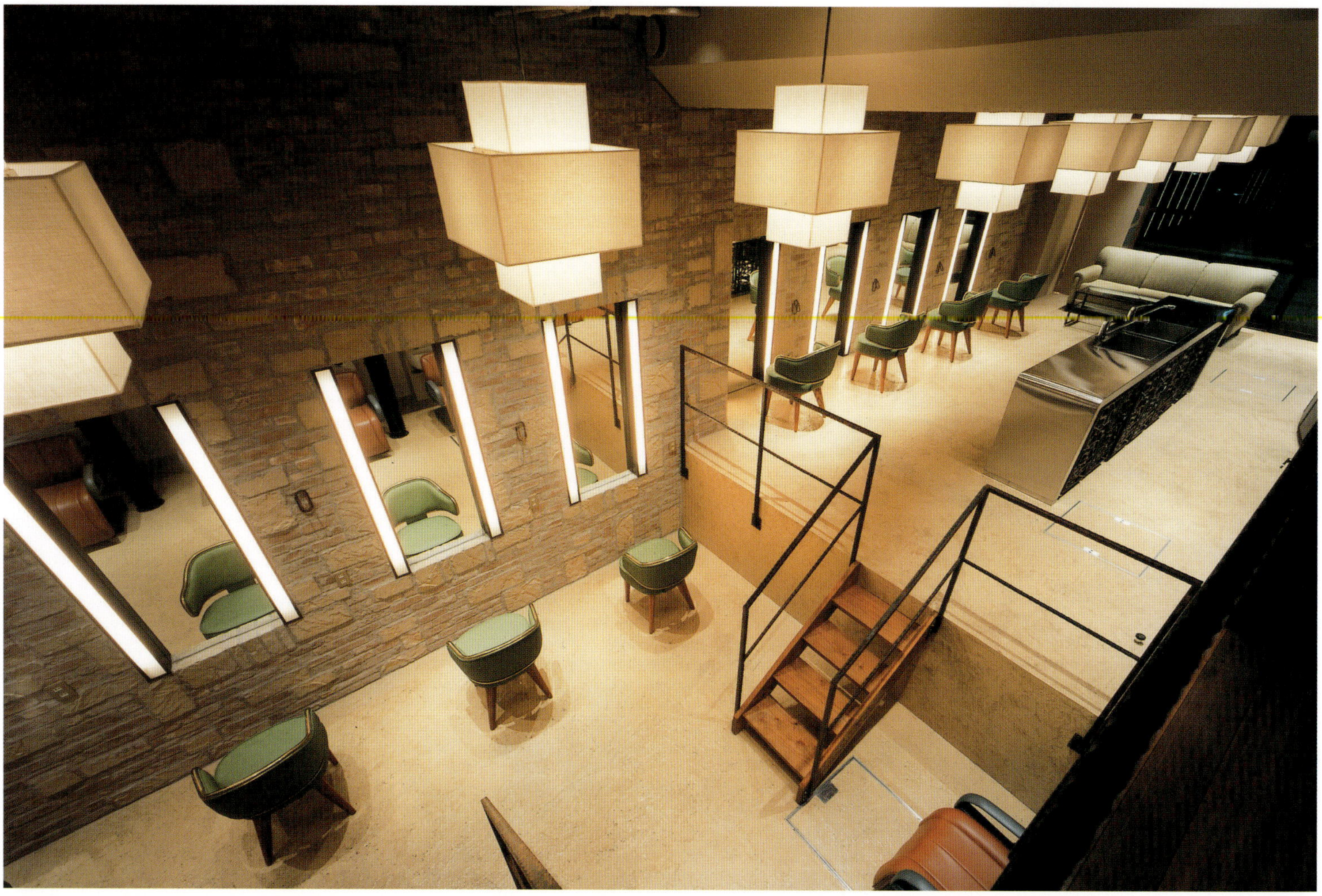

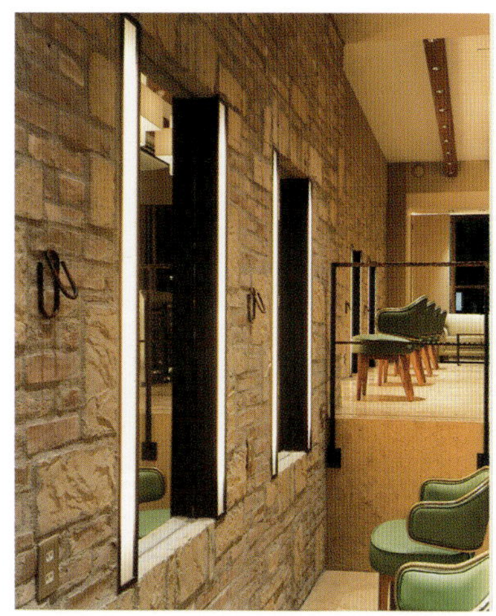
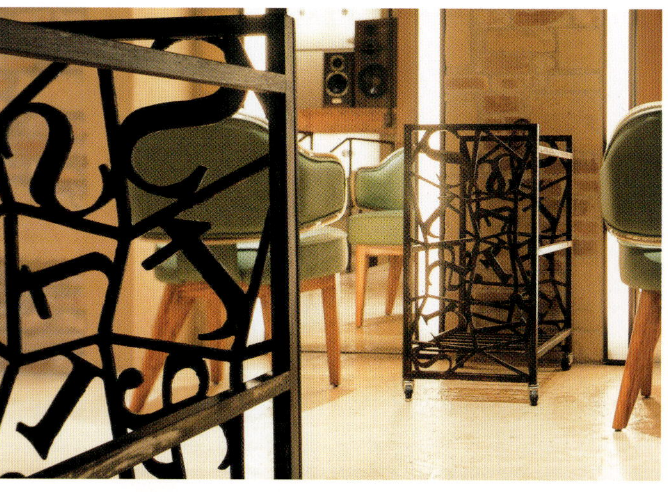
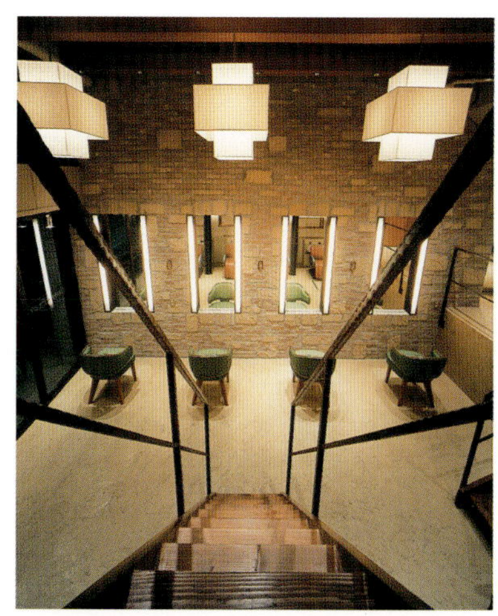
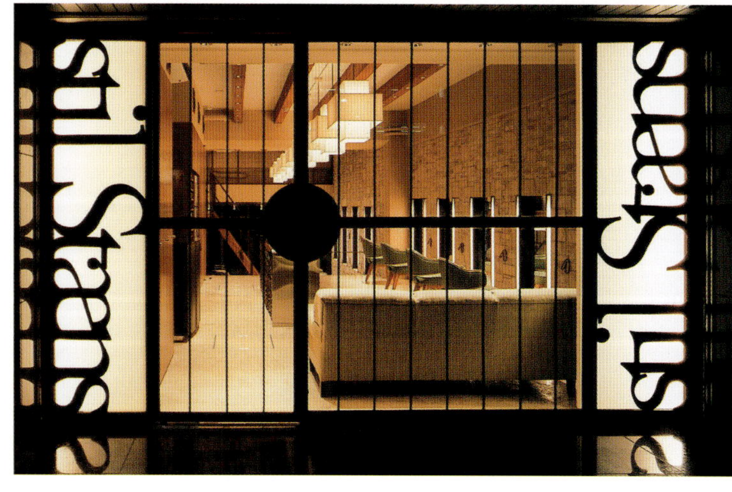
stil Straes
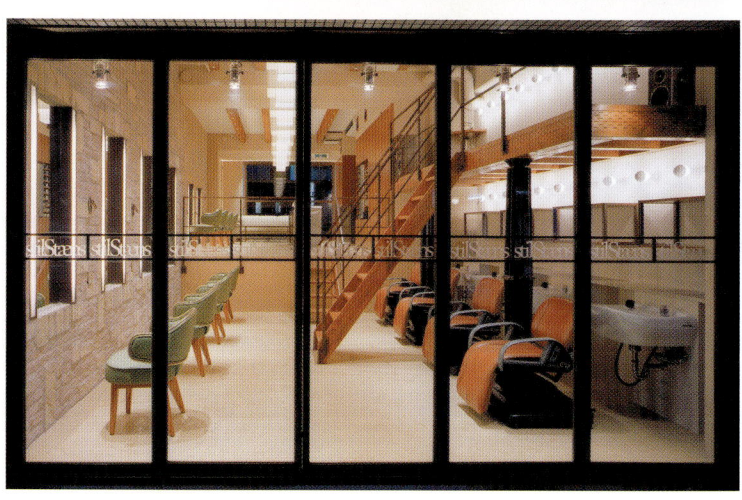

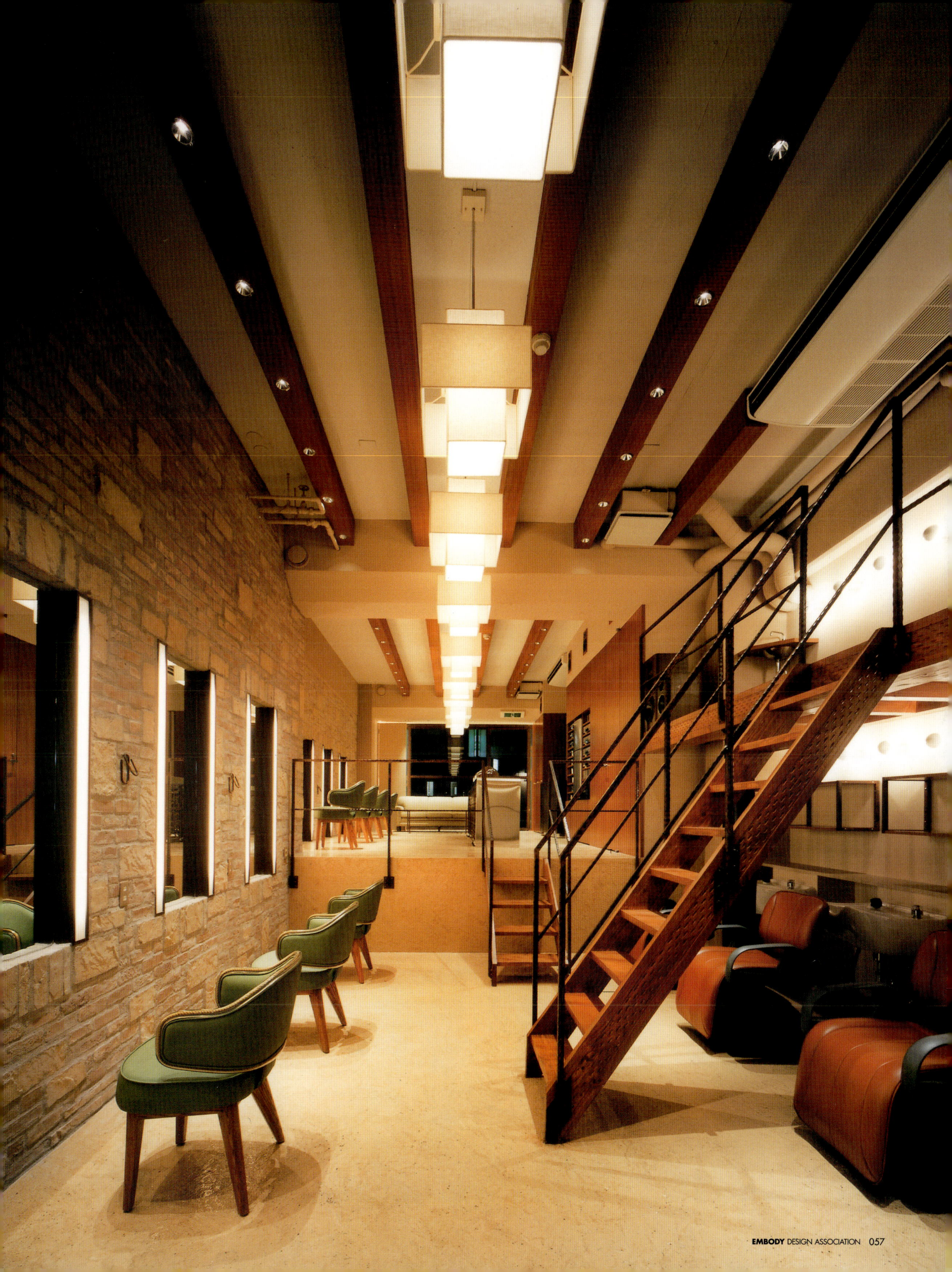

BLUE BEAR FACTORY
KAWACHINAGANO , OSAKA 1998

光の魔法

"BLUE BEAR FACTORY"は南海電車と近鉄電車が交わる、河内長野駅から3〜4分の所にあります。立地条件はとてもよいとは言えませんが、流行に最も敏感な10代から20代前半をメインターゲットにしたい、という若きオーナーのやる気と自信は本物です。その心意気に後押しされながら、どこか次元の違う、人によっては新しく人によってはなつかしい空間をイメージし、アクリルという透明感のある素材を、「光」という魔法の調味料で様々な味付けをすることで、目的とした空間が具現化できたと思います。

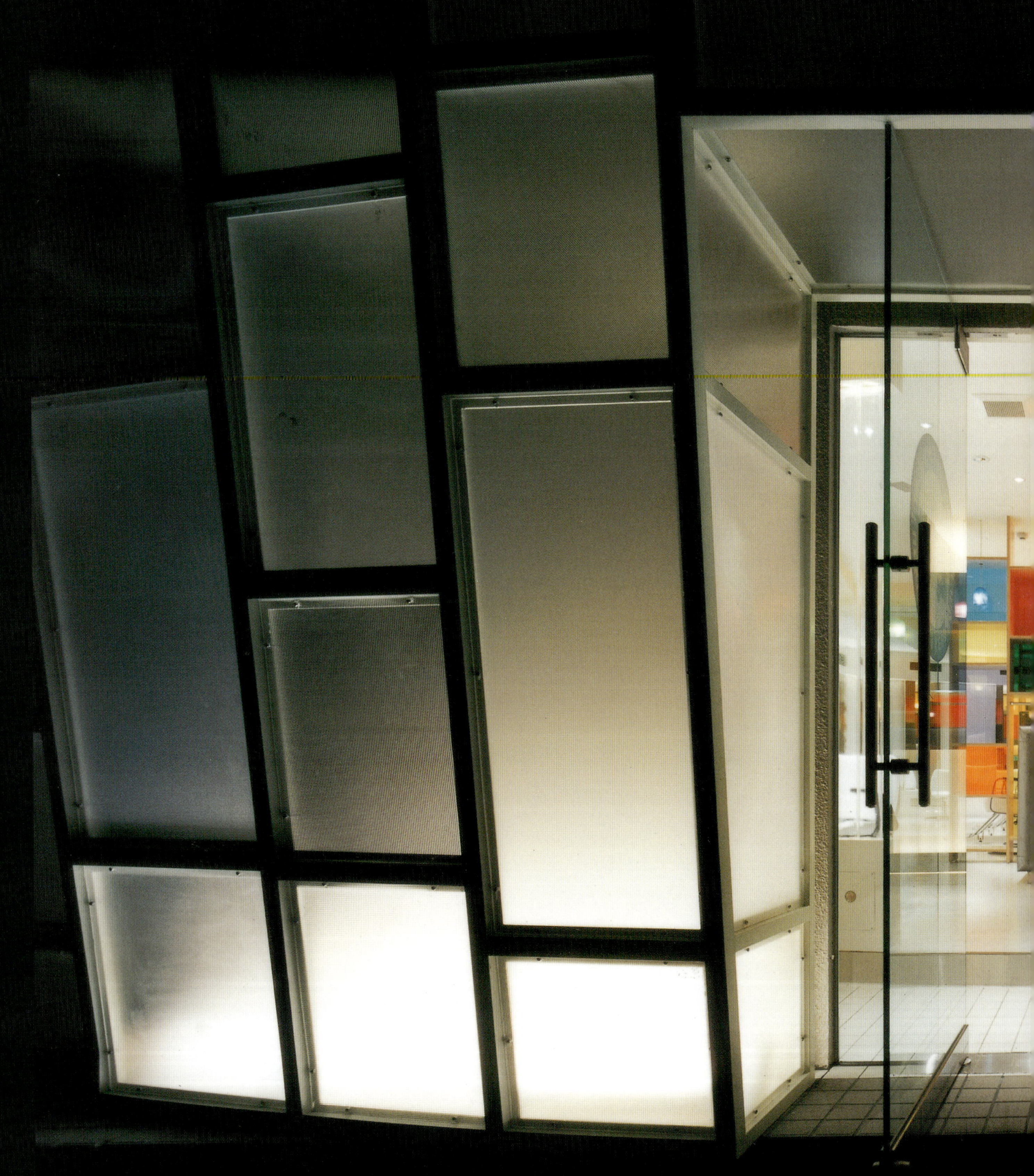

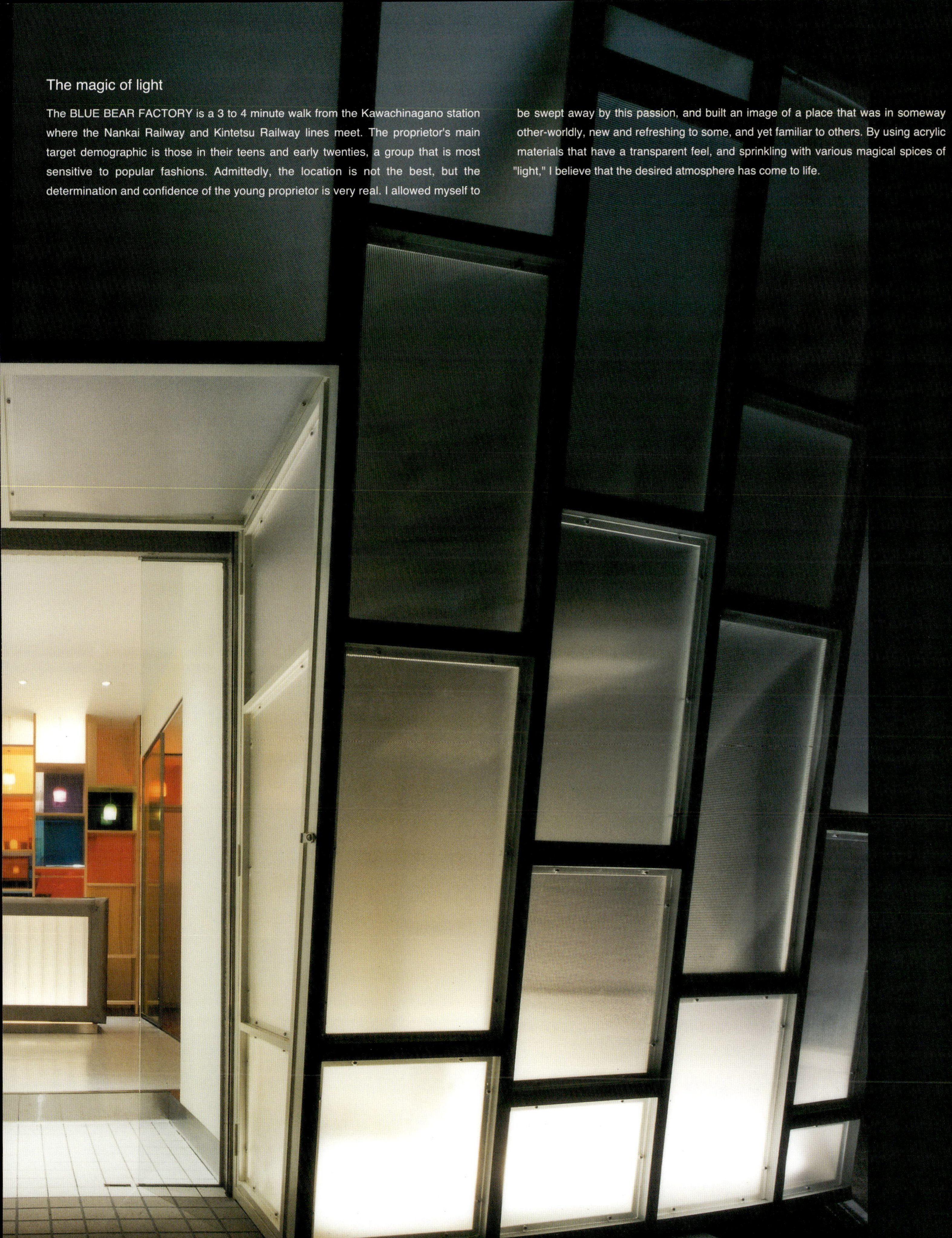

The magic of light

The BLUE BEAR FACTORY is a 3 to 4 minute walk from the Kawachinagano station where the Nankai Railway and Kintetsu Railway lines meet. The proprietor's main target demographic is those in their teens and early twenties, a group that is most sensitive to popular fashions. Admittedly, the location is not the best, but the determination and confidence of the young proprietor is very real. I allowed myself to be swept away by this passion, and built an image of a place that was in someway other-worldly, new and refreshing to some, and yet familiar to others. By using acrylic materials that have a transparent feel, and sprinkling with various magical spices of "light," I believe that the desired atmosphere has come to life.

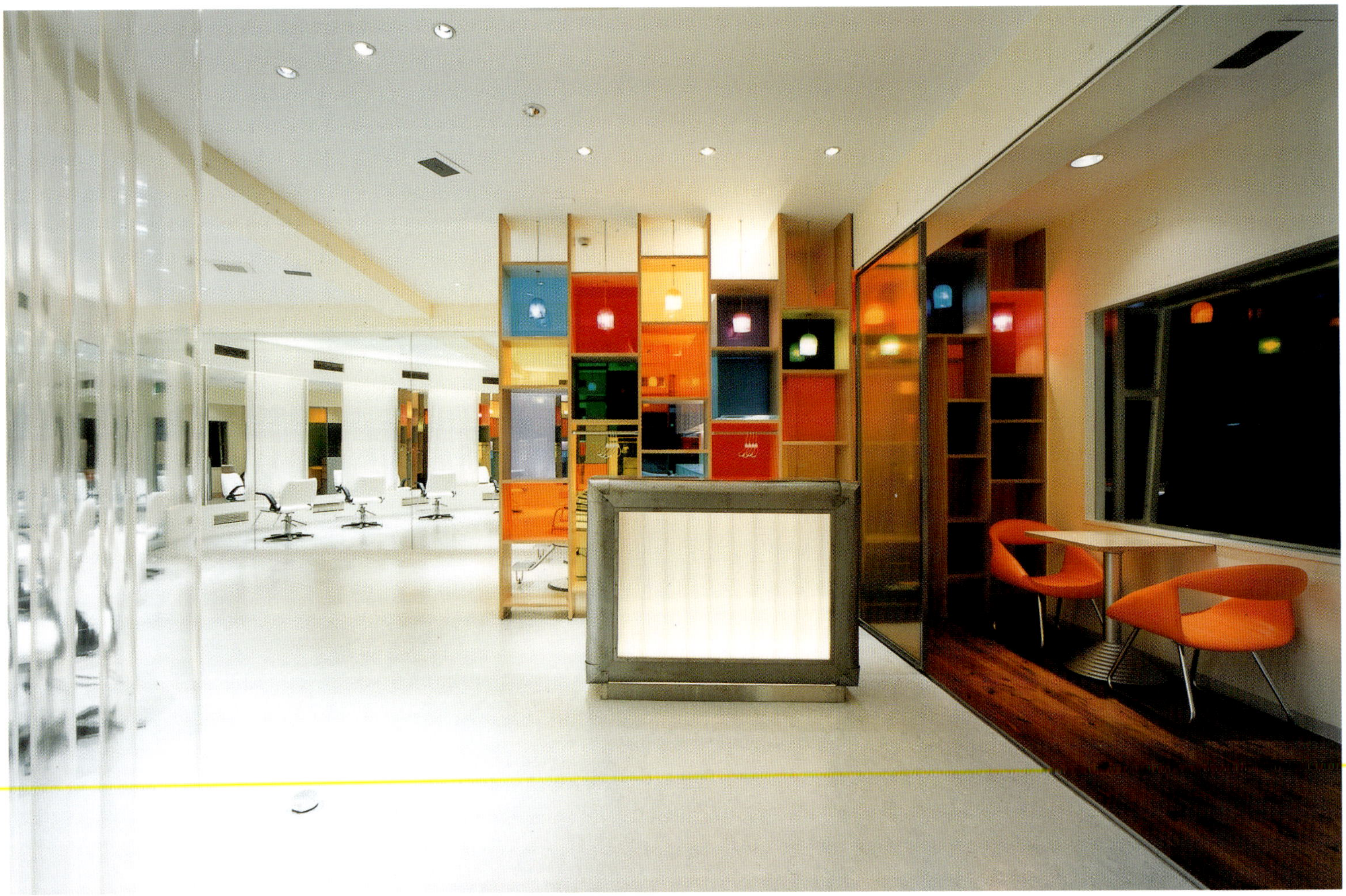

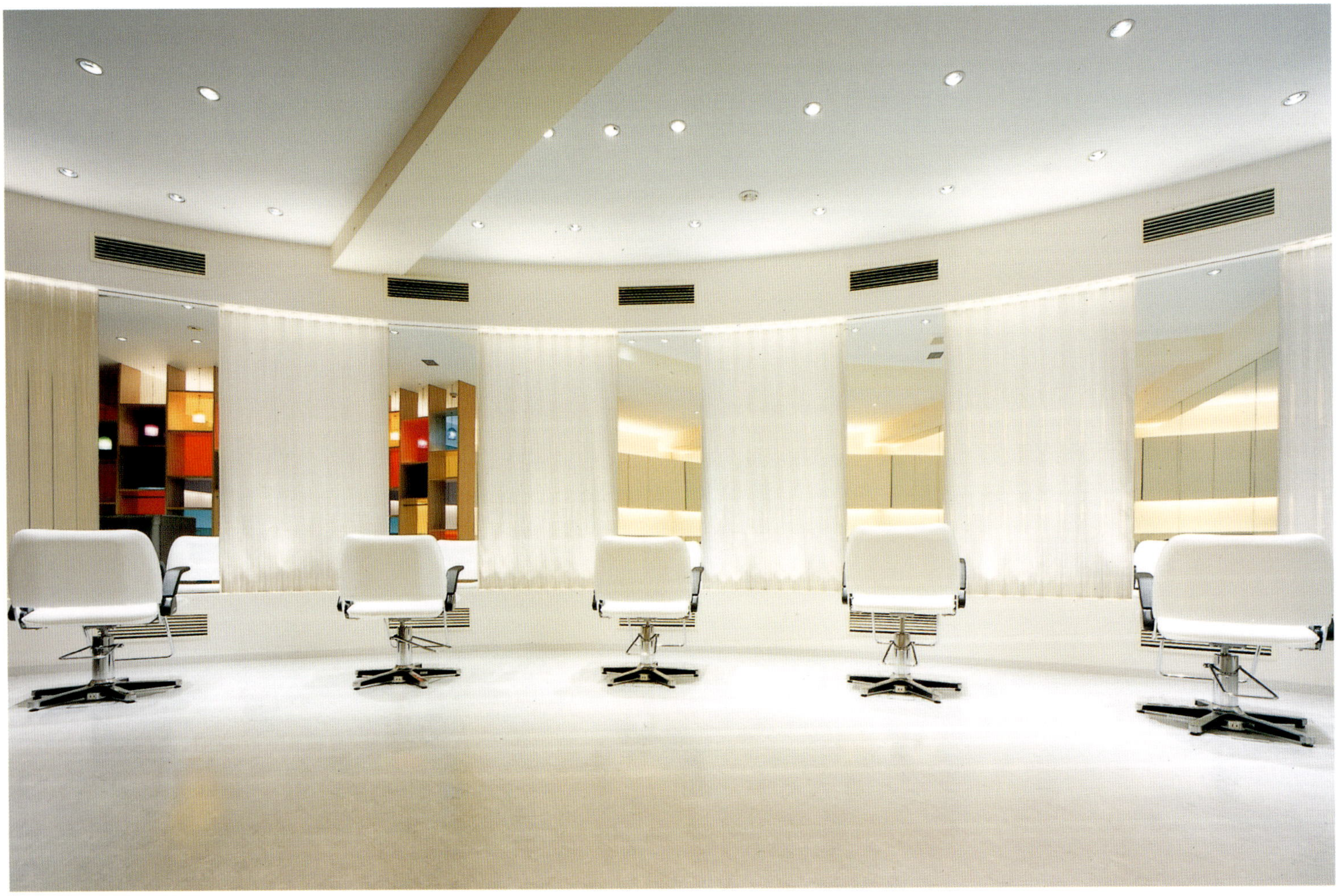

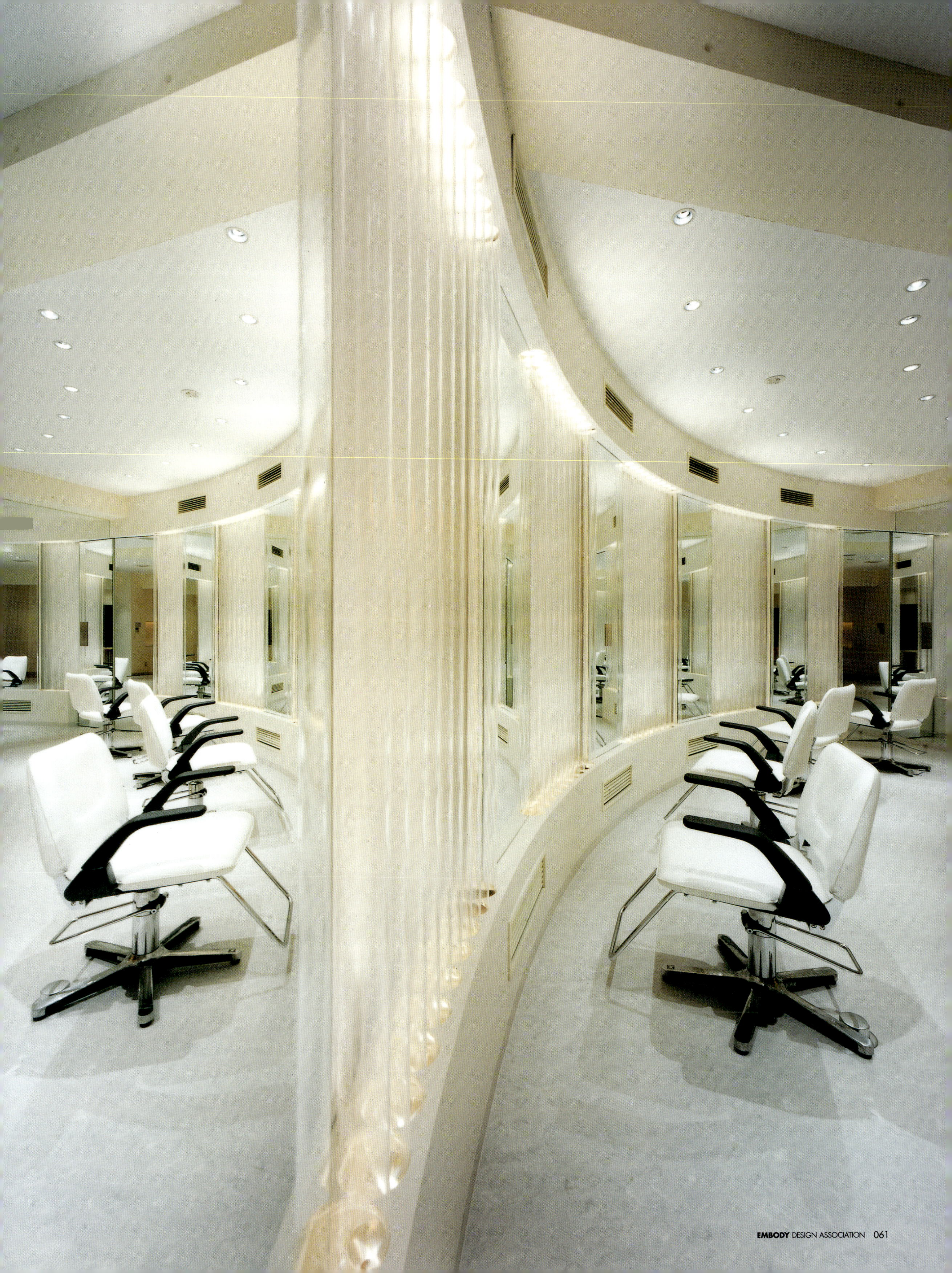

CAPELLI

SHINSAIBASHI , OSAKA 1996

人を美しく見せる空間

"CAPELLI"は美を求めて訪れる人々に、洗練された美意識やスタイル、そして誰もが持つ内面的な美を引き出し、提案するお店です。

「美との出会いの場」をテーマに、訪れる人とスタイリストとの間で繰り広げられるであろう様々な情景を想定し、映画のワンシーンを取るように、その背景となる空間を一つ一つ大切に考えました。

また、空間全体に浮遊感を創出することで、ミラーに映り込む世界は、訪れた人とヘアスタイリストだけが美しく浮かび上がる、特別な空間です。あくまで主役は人と人であり、その主役を美しく見せるために、脇役である空間はよりミニマムな表現で主役を引き立てるものとしました。

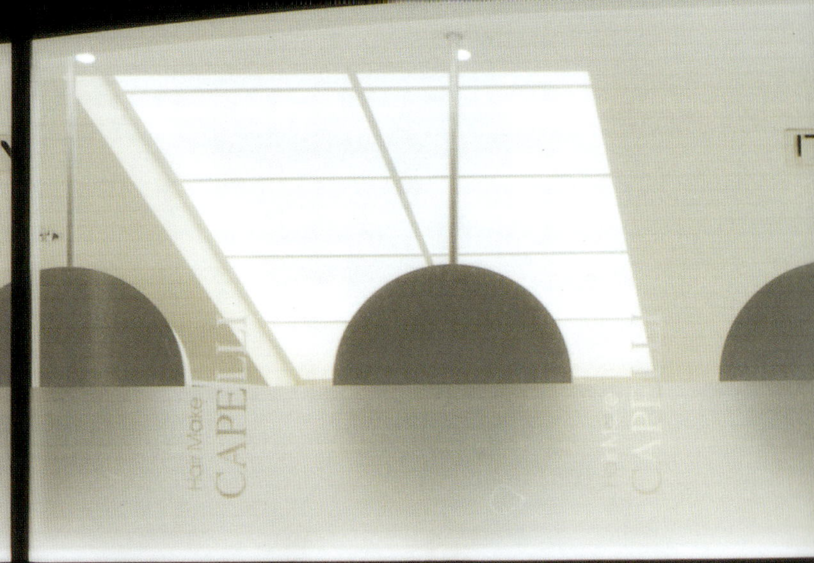

A place where people always appear beautiful

For people that visit seeking it, CAPELLI offers a sophisticated sense of beauty and style, and draws out the inner beauty that lies within all of us.

"A setting where beauty is encountered" was taken as the theme here. I imagined the myriad scenes that might take place between the client and stylist, and like the filming of one complete scene for a movie, I composed a backdrop that would have a special significance for each individual shot.

By giving the overall space a buoyant sort of feel, a unique atmosphere is formed in which the client and the stylist sort of float, in a beautiful way, out of the reflection of the world on the other side of the mirror. The people are the stars of the scene, and the space can be thought of as performing a supporting role. To make the stars stand out, and to show them as beautiful, I used fairly minimal expression with respect to the space itself.

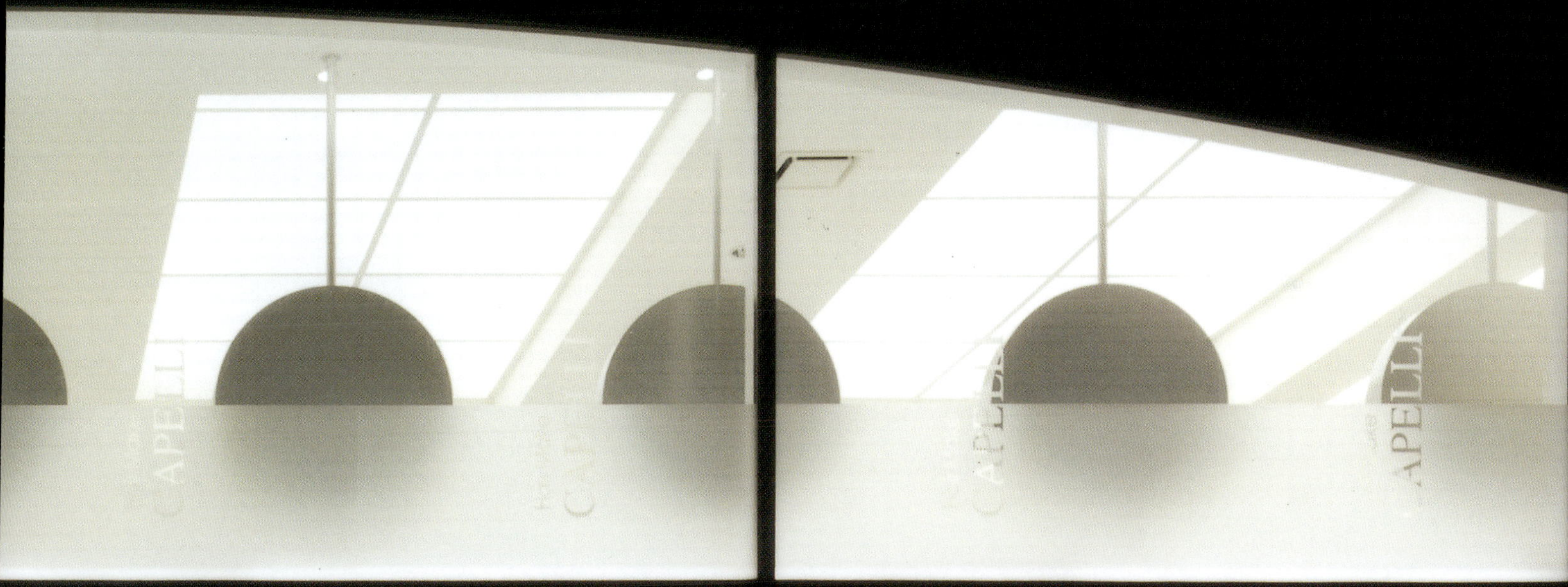

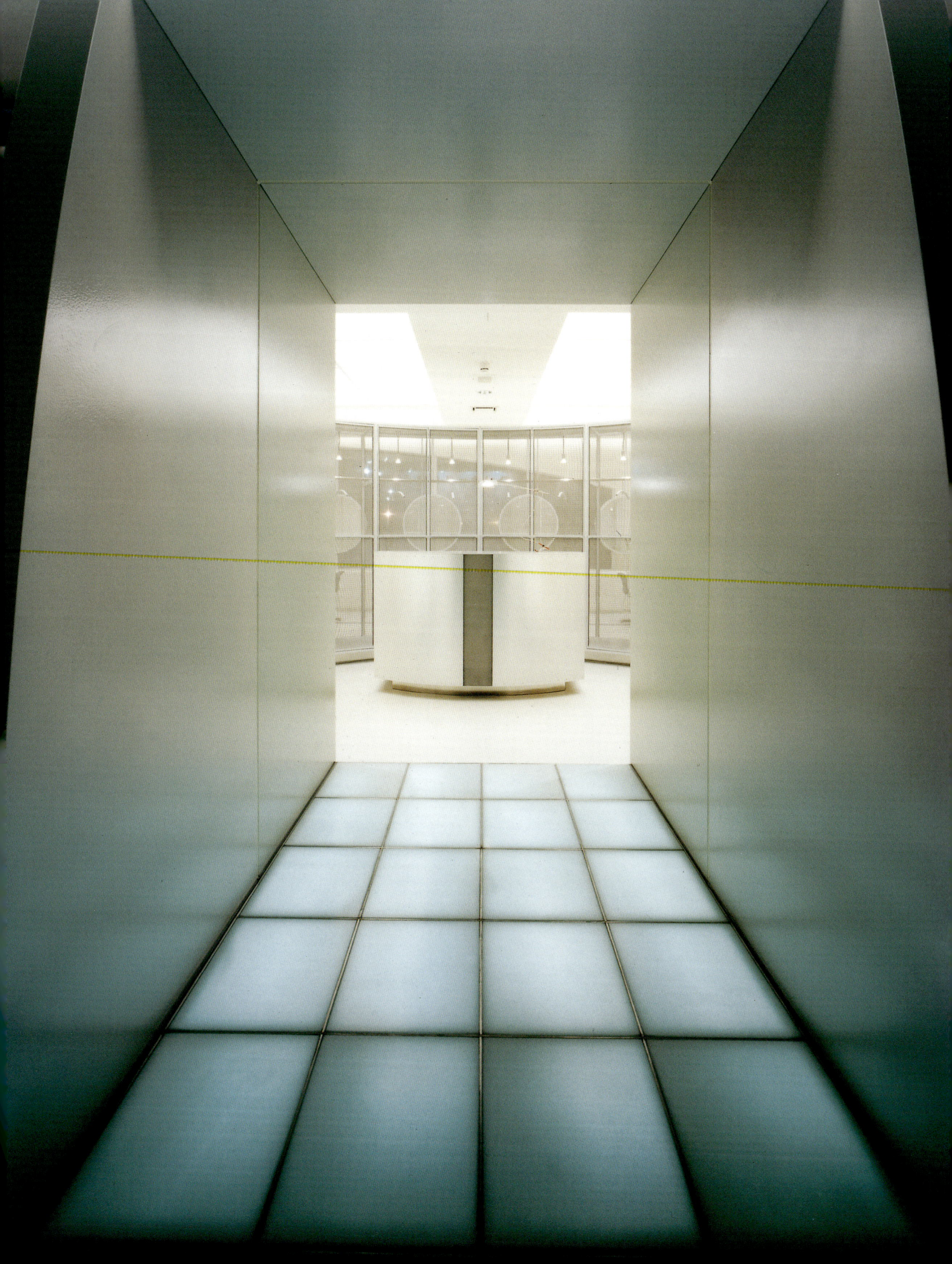

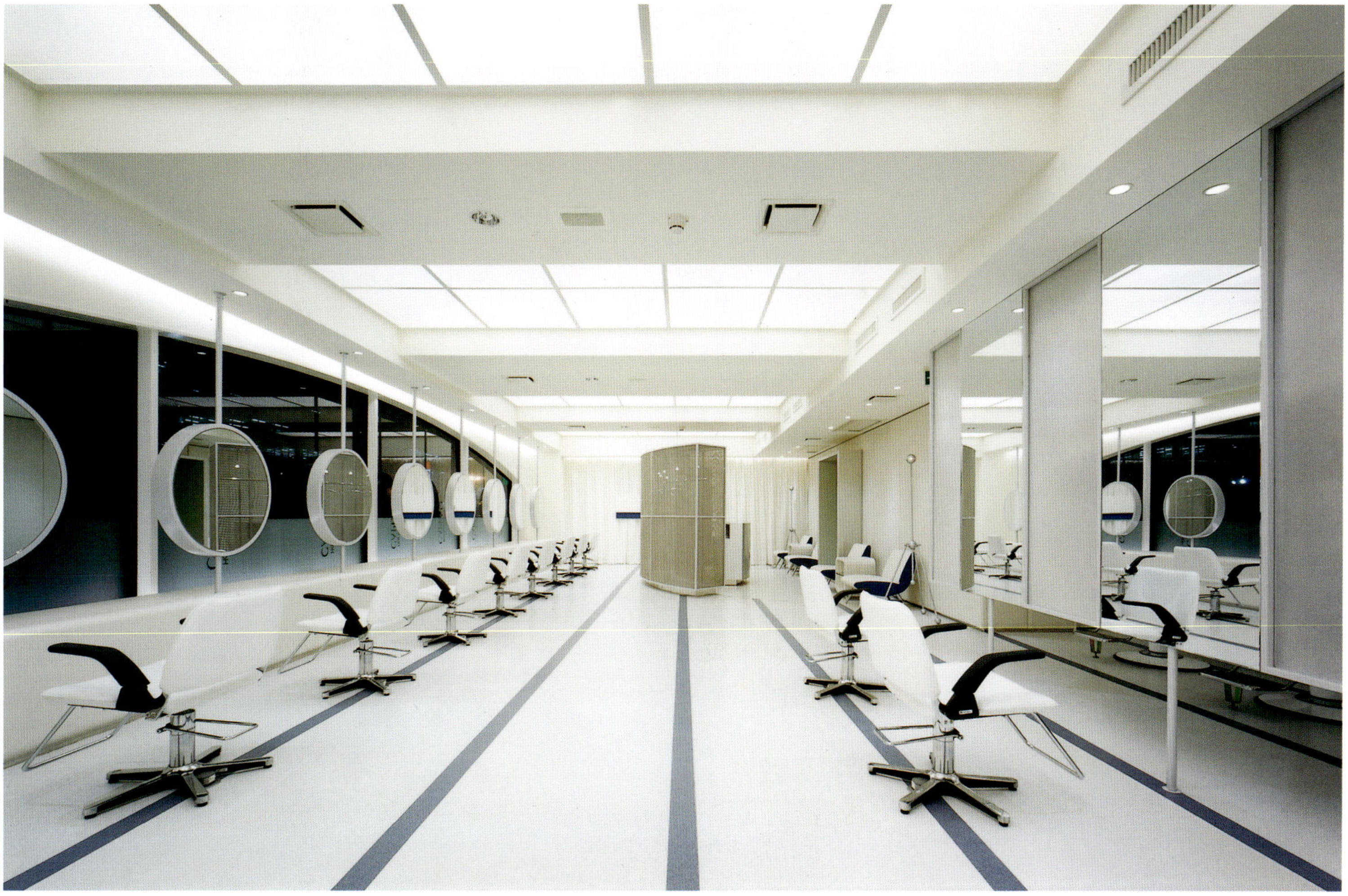

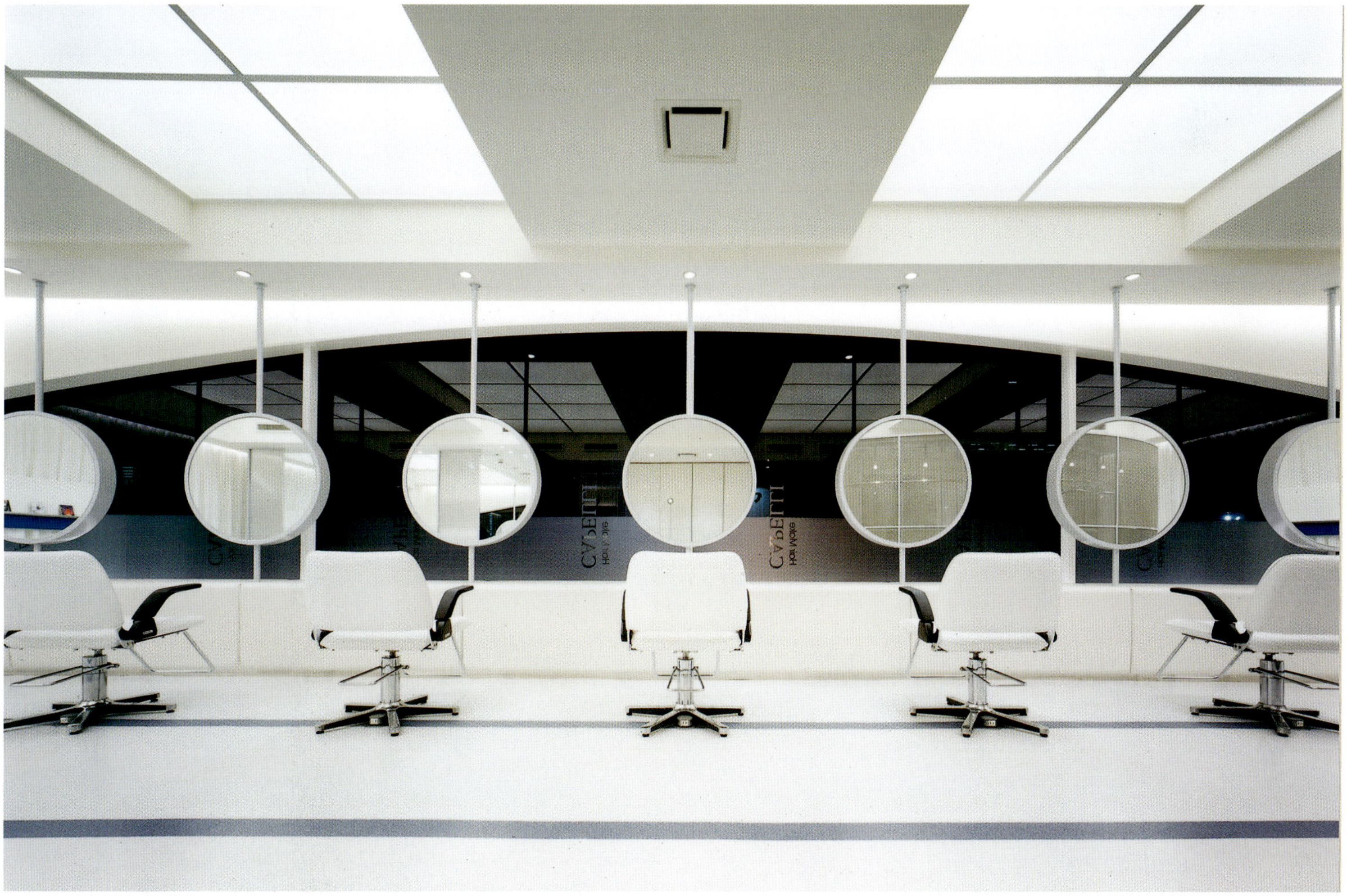

神　美　間　存在　礼儀　役割　価値

もてなし

再生と創造

精神性

伝統

空間の役割

不変的な

唯一の心

礼儀や作法

primitive

traditional beauty

role of space

courtesy and politeness

hospitality

the only value for existing

aesthetics

JAPANESE DINING

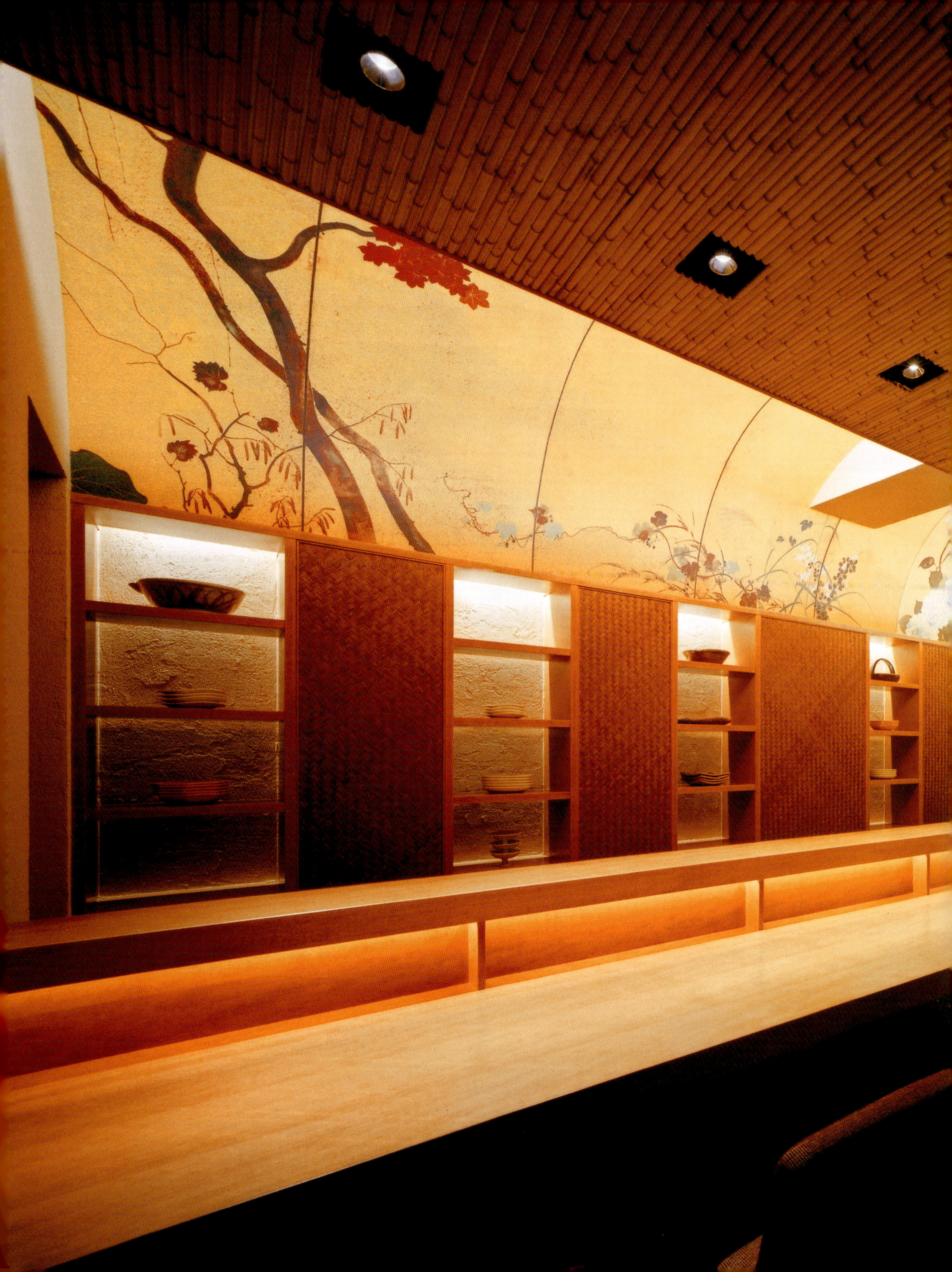

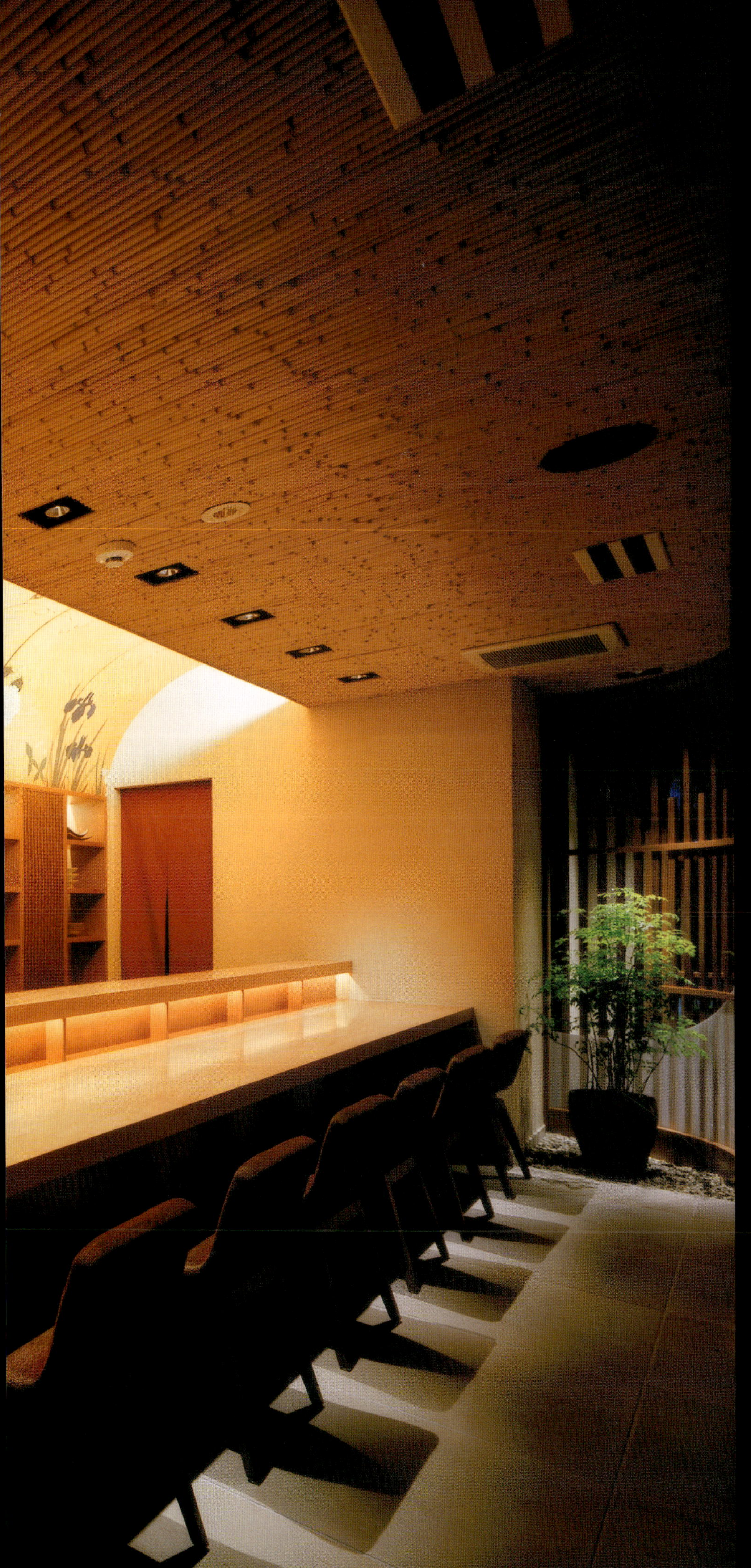

TAKENAWA
KITASHINCHI , OSAKA 2005

もてなしの空間

西日本を代表する繁華街、大阪・北新地に位置する「旬菜割烹 闌」。旬の食材を生かした本格的な日本料理で、舌のこえた熟年層をも魅了するために計画された。

　"闌"をデザインするにあたり心掛けたことは、訪れるであろうセレブレティたちのプライバシーを守り、静かにゆっくりと料理を味わっていただける空間づくりだった。それは「個室感」という曖昧なアプローチではなく、お客様同士が顔をささないように視線に配慮し、一部屋一部屋の「個室」をデザインしていくこと。日本文化の中で、私たちの先人たちが作り上げてきた「人をもてなす気持ち」をお手本にして、現代の「客間」を具現化した。

A place of hospitality and service

TAKENAWA is situated in Kitashinchi, Osaka, the bustling commercial and entertainment icon of western Japan. Utilizing seasonal ingredients to produce real, authentic Japanese cuisine, the restaurant aims to please the palettes of older folk as well.

　In designing TAKENAWA, I endeavored to construct a space that would maintain the privacy of the celebrities likely to visit, and in which cuisine could be quietly and leisurely savored. Eschewing the vague sort of 'private room style' approach, I designed each private room individually, giving consideration to the guests' lines of sight and being careful to ensure that people would not be in each others' faces. I used the Japanese cultural concepts that our forebears created regarding hospitality and service as a reference, and created a modern customer service area.

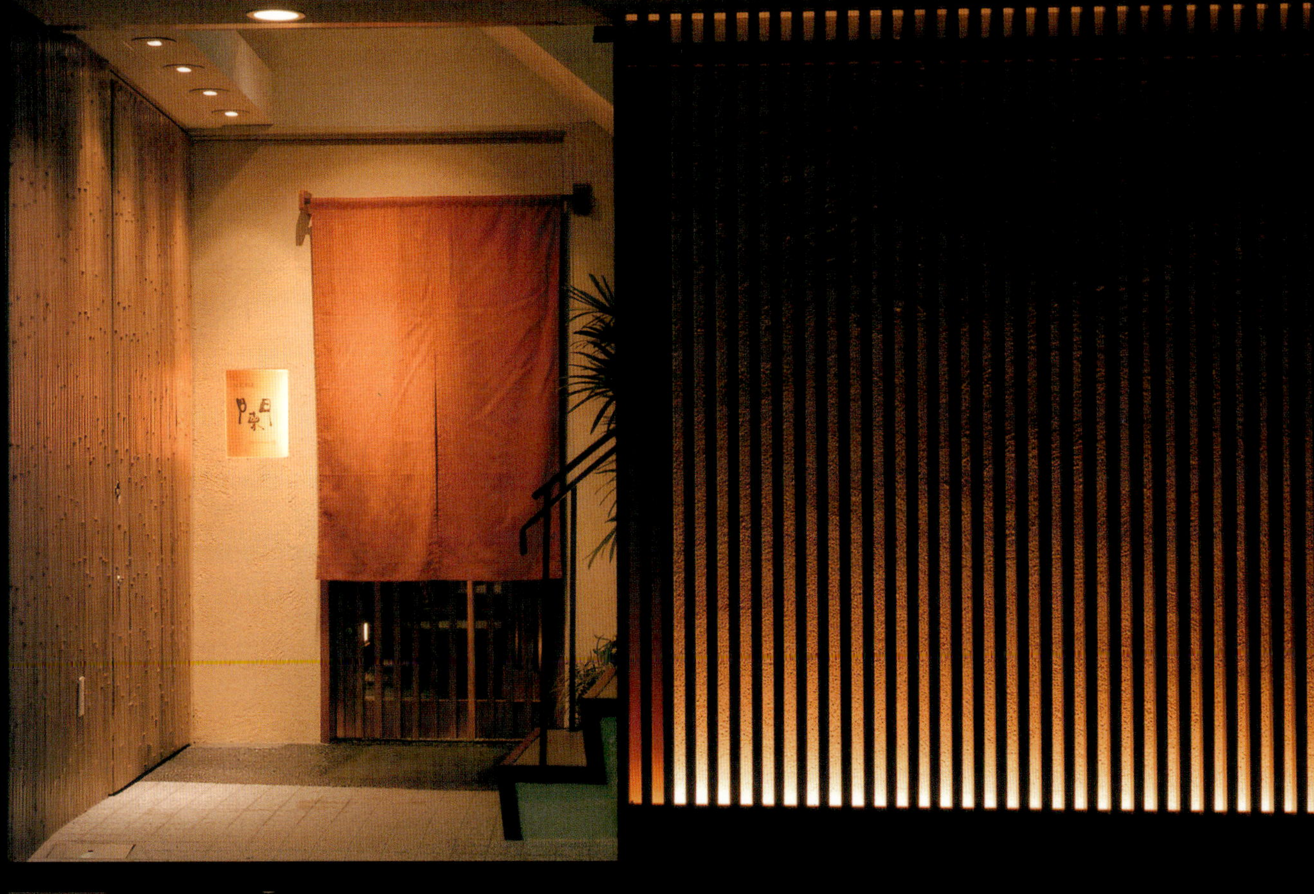
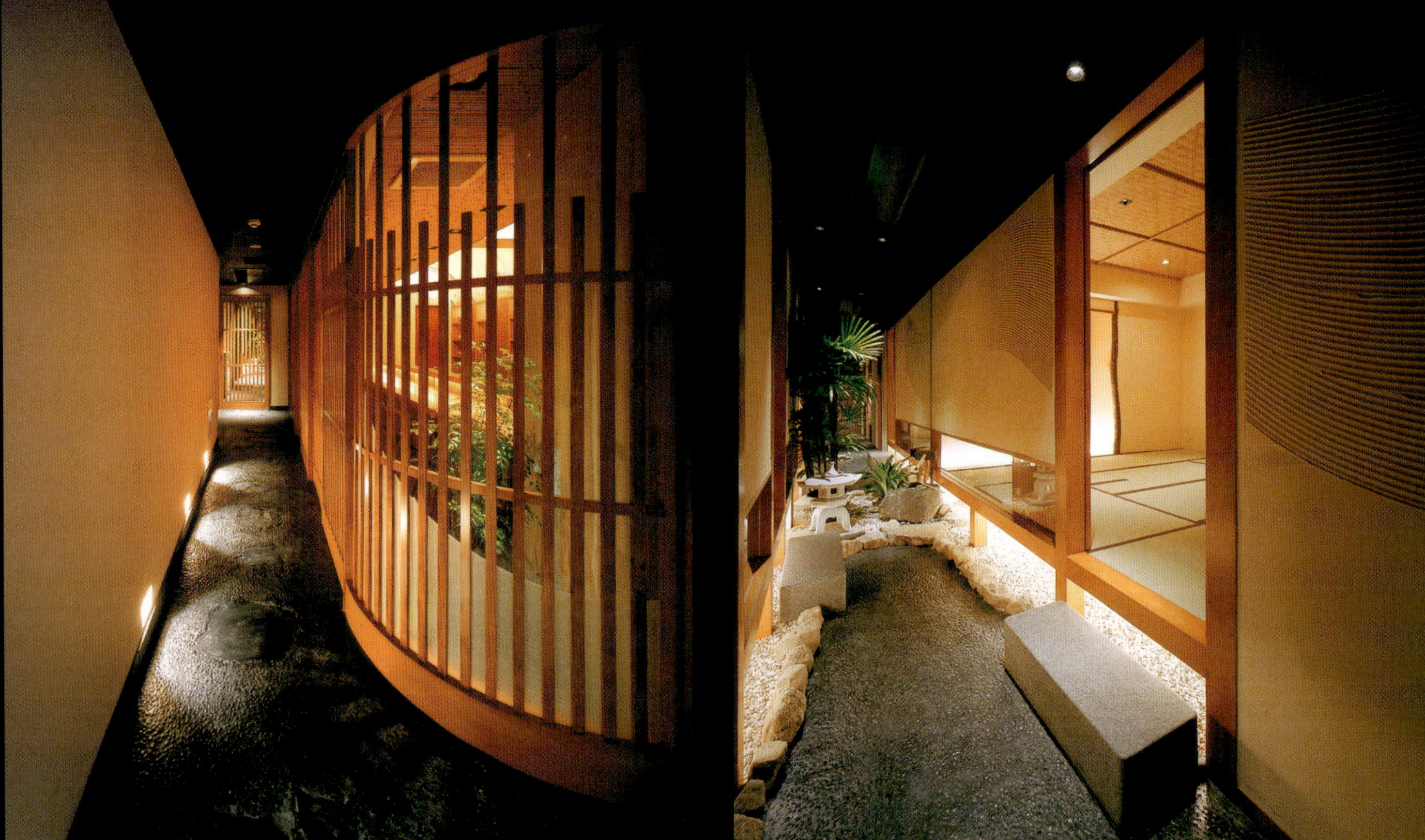

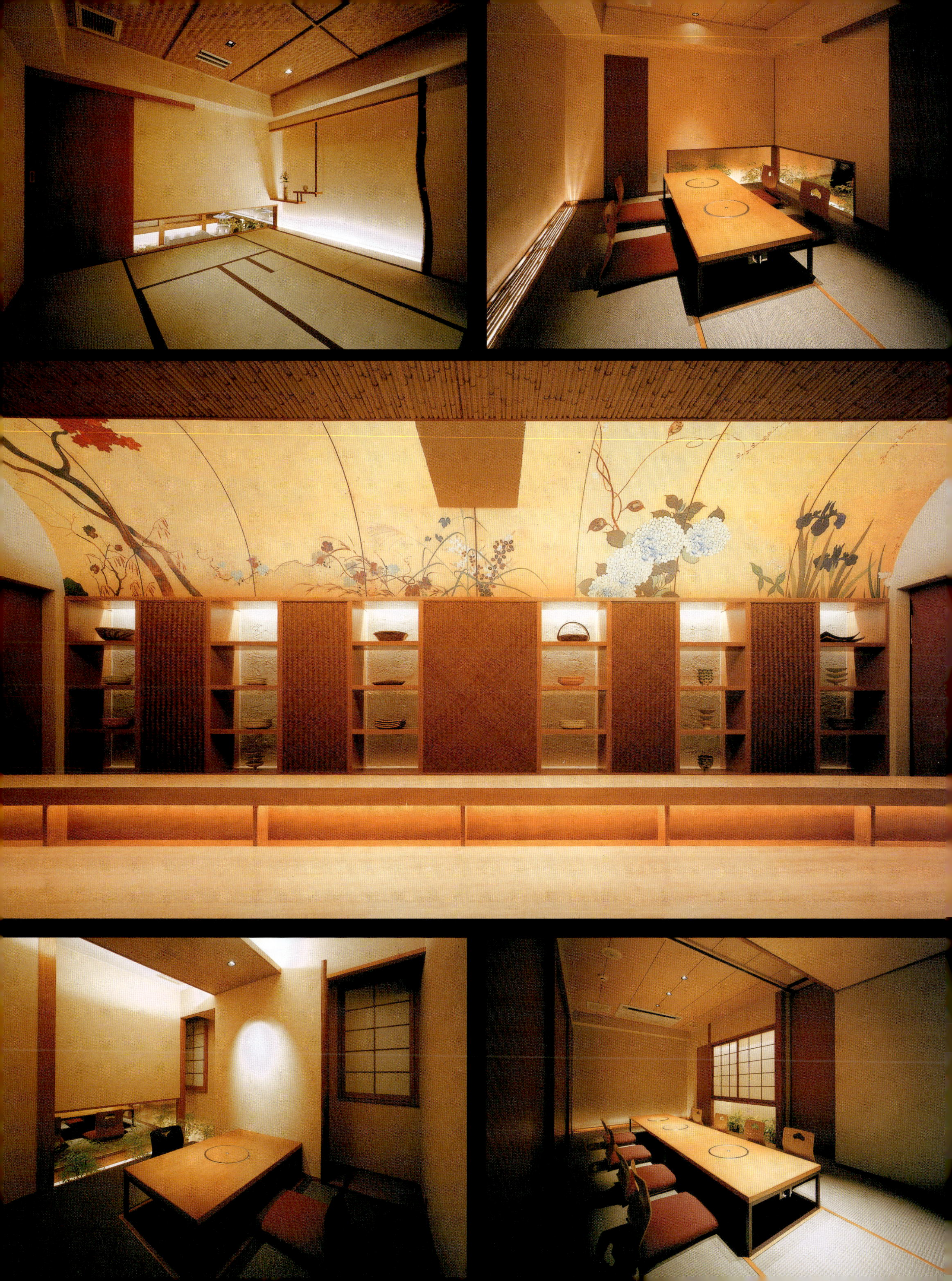

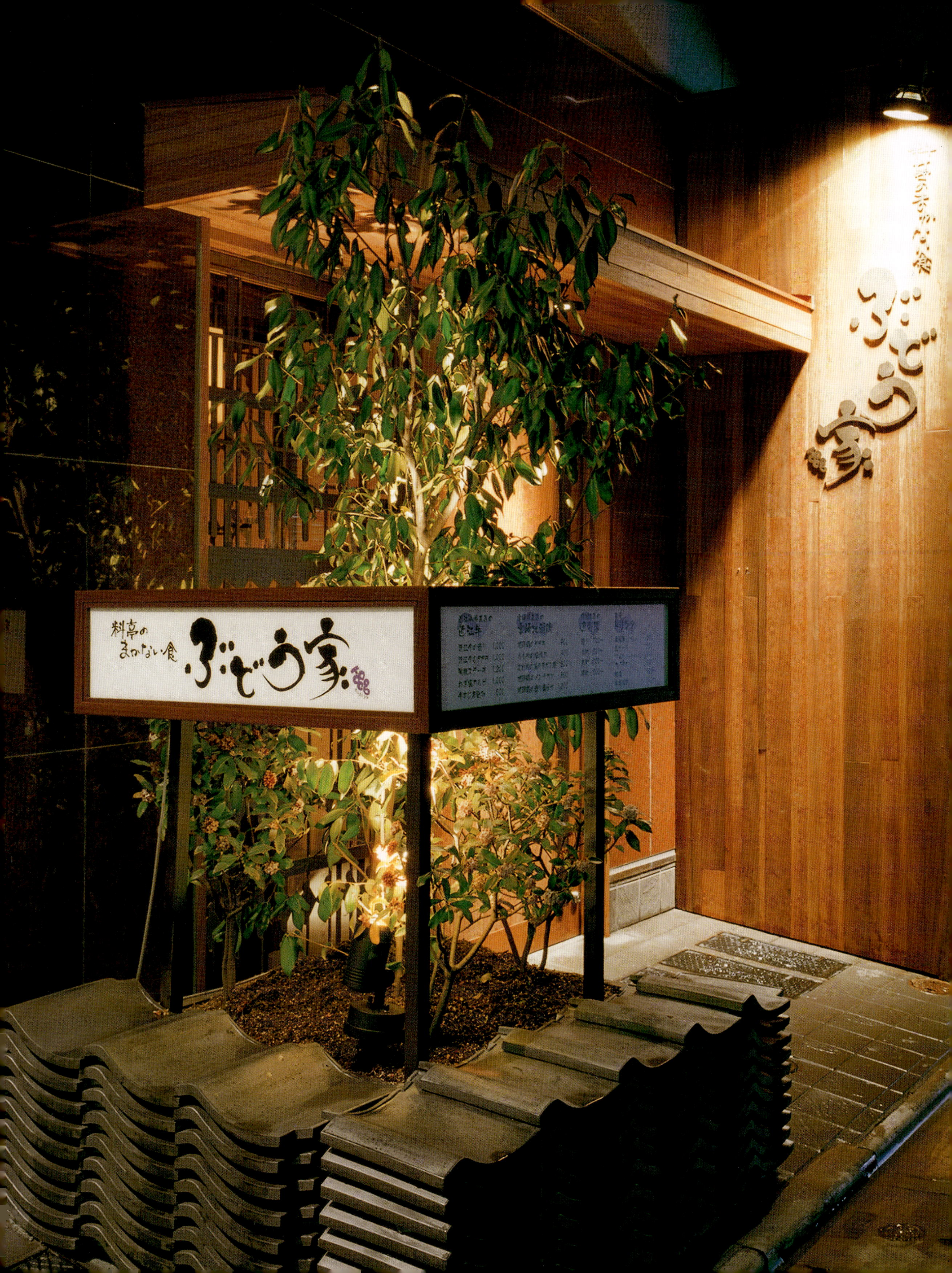
料亭の
まかない食
ぶどう家
ぶどう家

BUDOYA
SHINBASHI , TOKYO 2005

素直なカタチと空気感

"ぶどう家"は、料亭のまかない料理をテーマに、新橋のサラリーマンやOLが本格料亭の味を、リーズナブルに味わえるお店です。

　空間もオーナーが持つ男っぽさと、人なつっこさがにじみ出るような、温かみのある空間を目指しました。客席を仕切りつつも、やわらかく結ぶためのパーテーションは、鉄工所から出る廃材を幾重も重ねて透過性を加減しながら荒っぽさの中に繊細さを折り込みました。限られた空間を最大限に活かすことを心掛け、狭さをにぎわいに変えて、奇をてらうのではなく、訪れる人の「日常に溶け込む空間」を具現化することが出来たと思います。

Unpretentious mood and style

The idea at BUDOYA is to provide the type of meals that are commonly prepared for staff in the kitchens of traditional high-class Japanese restaurants. This allows the office workers of Shinbashi to taste authentic Japanese cuisine at a reasonable price.

I aimed to create an atmosphere which would bring out the owner's natural masculinity and warmth. The partitions that divide, while at the same time softly enveloping the seats, are made of scraps from an ironworks. The multi-layered constructions suggest permeability, and I have woven a delicacy into the rough appearance. I endeavored to optimize the limited space, converting narrowness into liveliness. I think that I have created a place that does not come across as too formal, but that melts into become part of the individual's everyday life.

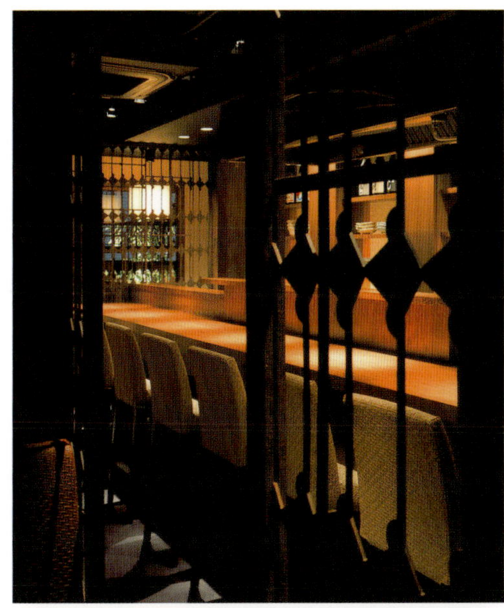

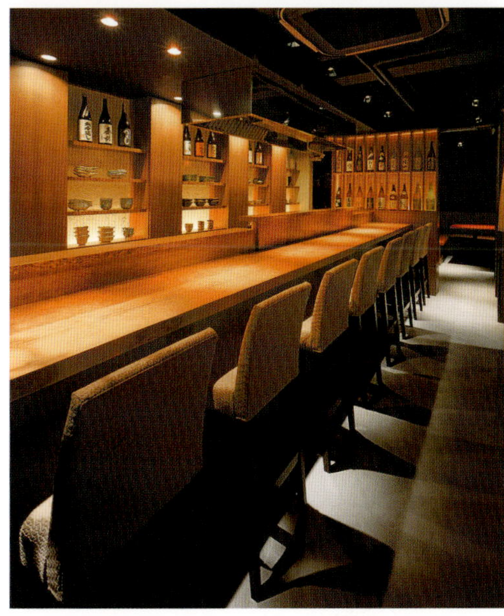

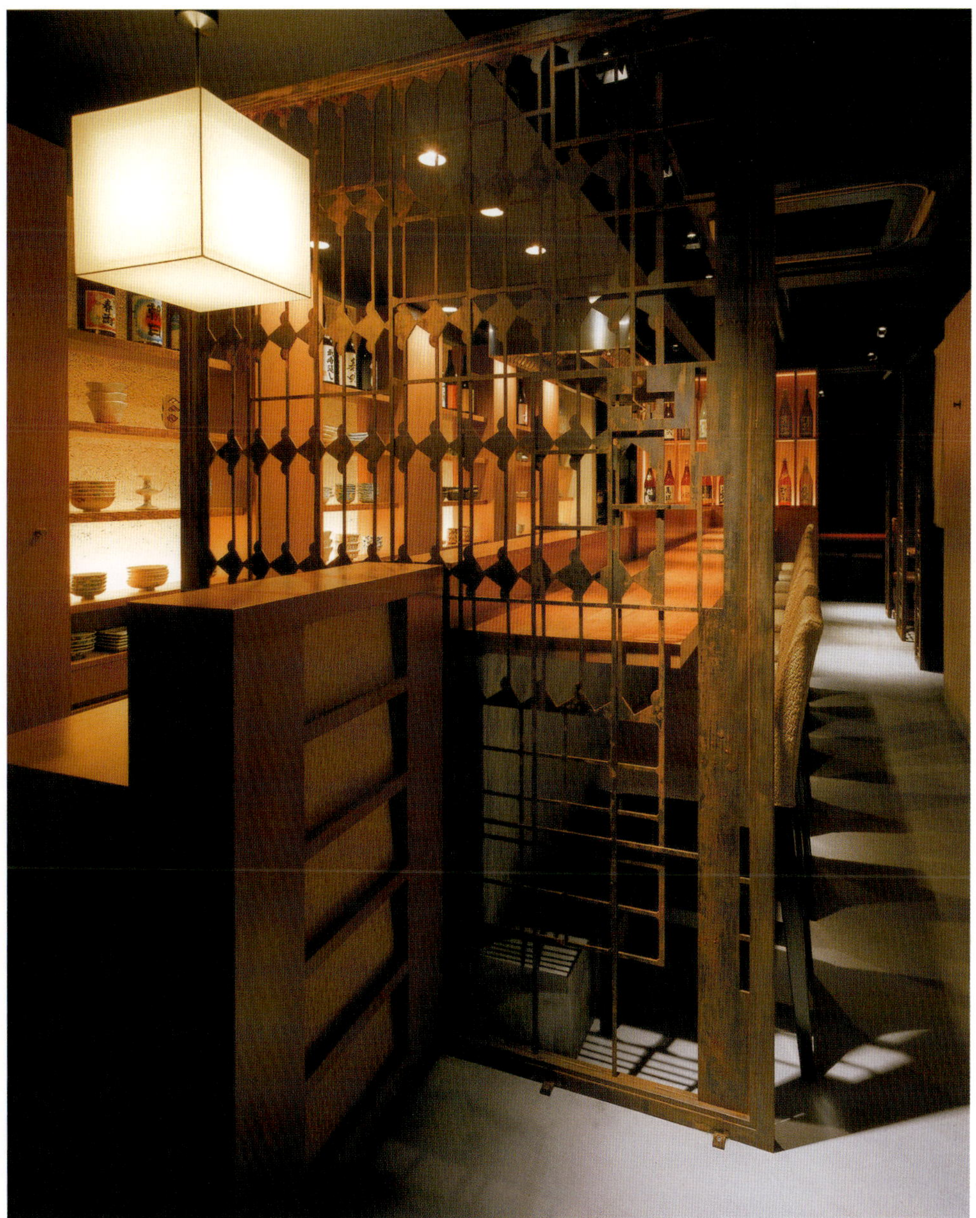

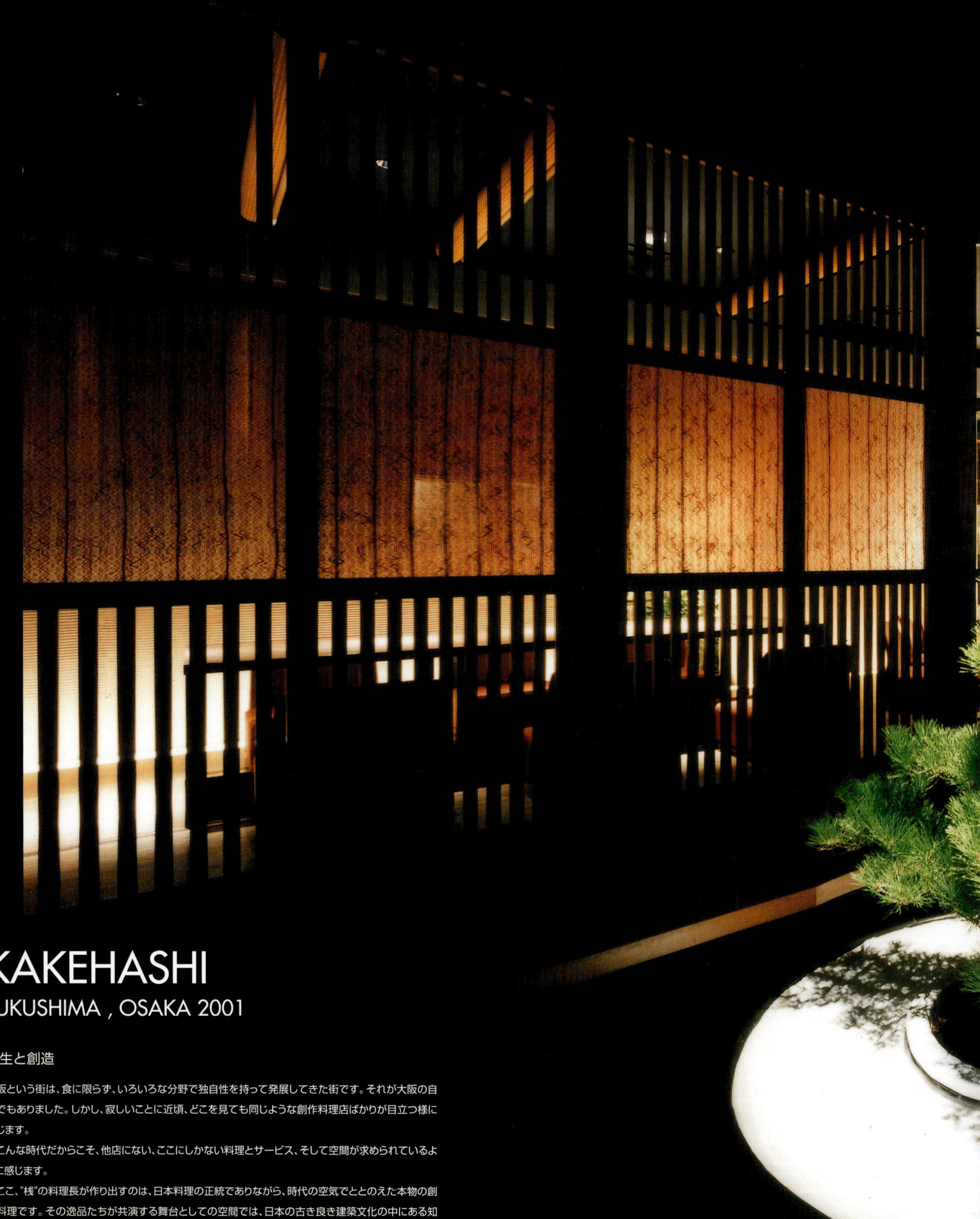

KAKEHASHI
FUKUSHIMA , OSAKA 2001

再生と創造

大阪という街は、食に限らず、いろいろな分野で独自性を持って発展してきた街です。それが大阪の自慢でもありました。しかし、寂しいことに近頃、どこを見ても同じような創作料理店ばかりが目立つ様に感じます。

　こんな時代だからこそ、他店にない、ここにしかない料理とサービス、そして空間が求められているように感じます。

　ここ、"桟"の料理長が作り出すのは、日本料理の正統でありながら、時代の空気でととのえた本物の創作料理です。その逸品たちが共演する舞台としての空間では、日本の古き良き建築文化の中にある知恵や工夫を伝承しながらも、ここにしかない新たな空間構築を試みてみようと、「目に映らないしきり（水平なしきりを組み合わせることで、限られた空間に奥行きと広さを生み出す）」を用い、日本文化の再生と創造を表現しました。

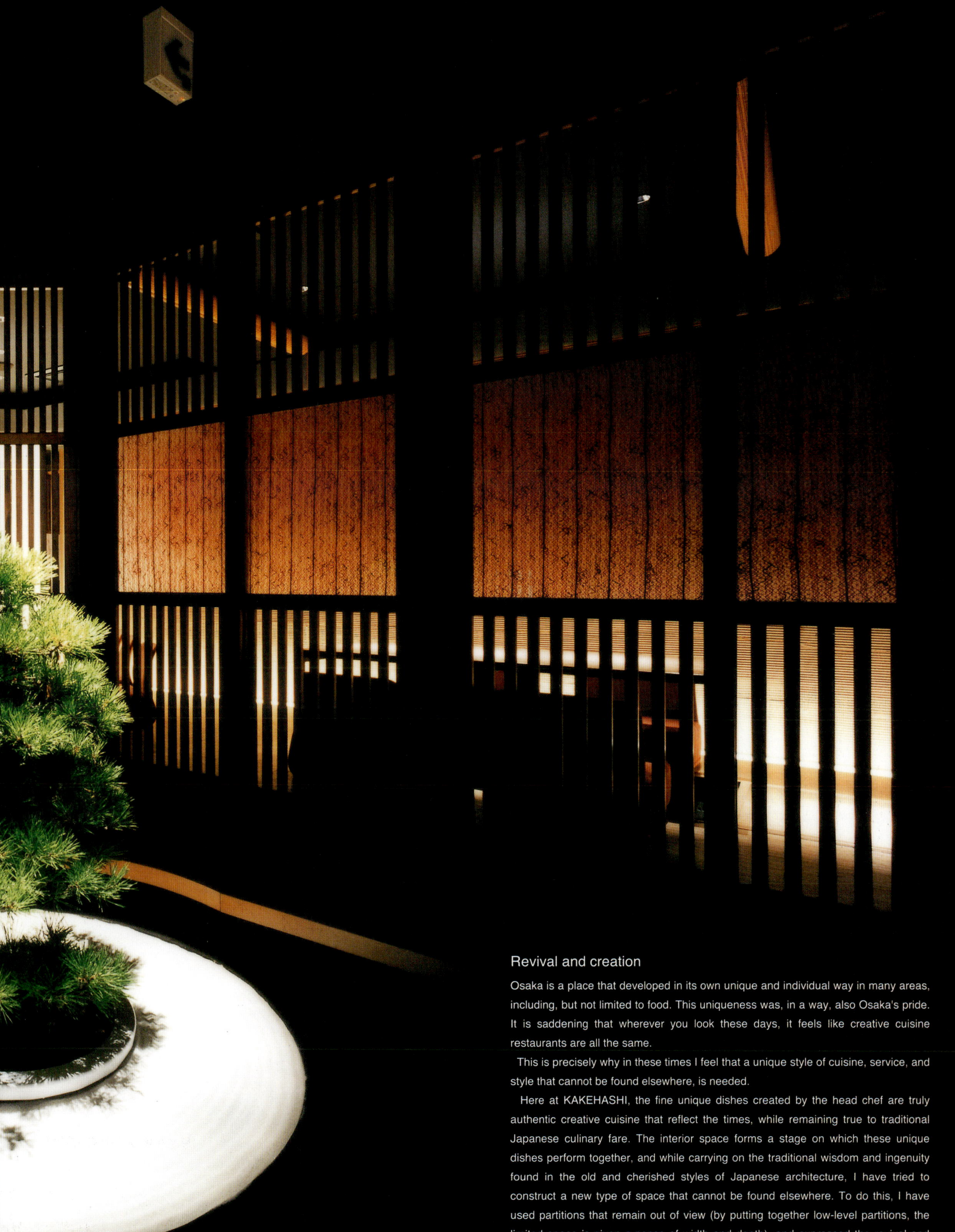

Revival and creation

Osaka is a place that developed in its own unique and individual way in many areas, including, but not limited to food. This uniqueness was, in a way, also Osaka's pride. It is saddening that wherever you look these days, it feels like creative cuisine restaurants are all the same.

This is precisely why in these times I feel that a unique style of cuisine, service, and style that cannot be found elsewhere, is needed.

Here at KAKEHASHI, the fine unique dishes created by the head chef are truly authentic creative cuisine that reflect the times, while remaining true to traditional Japanese culinary fare. The interior space forms a stage on which these unique dishes perform together, and while carrying on the traditional wisdom and ingenuity found in the old and cherished styles of Japanese architecture, I have tried to construct a new type of space that cannot be found elsewhere. To do this, I have used partitions that remain out of view (by putting together low-level partitions, the limited space is given a sense of width and depth), and expressed the revival and creation of Japanese culture.

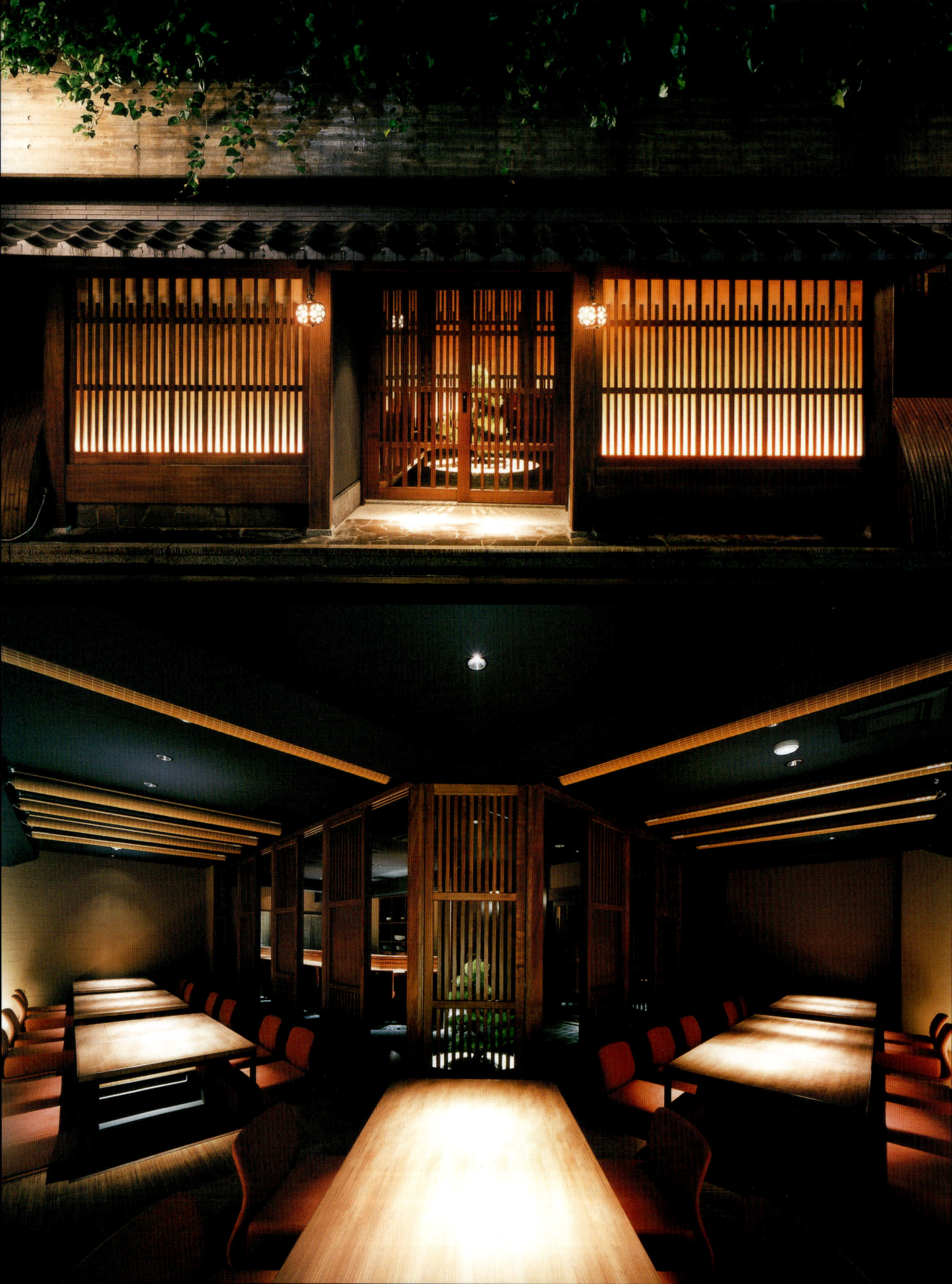

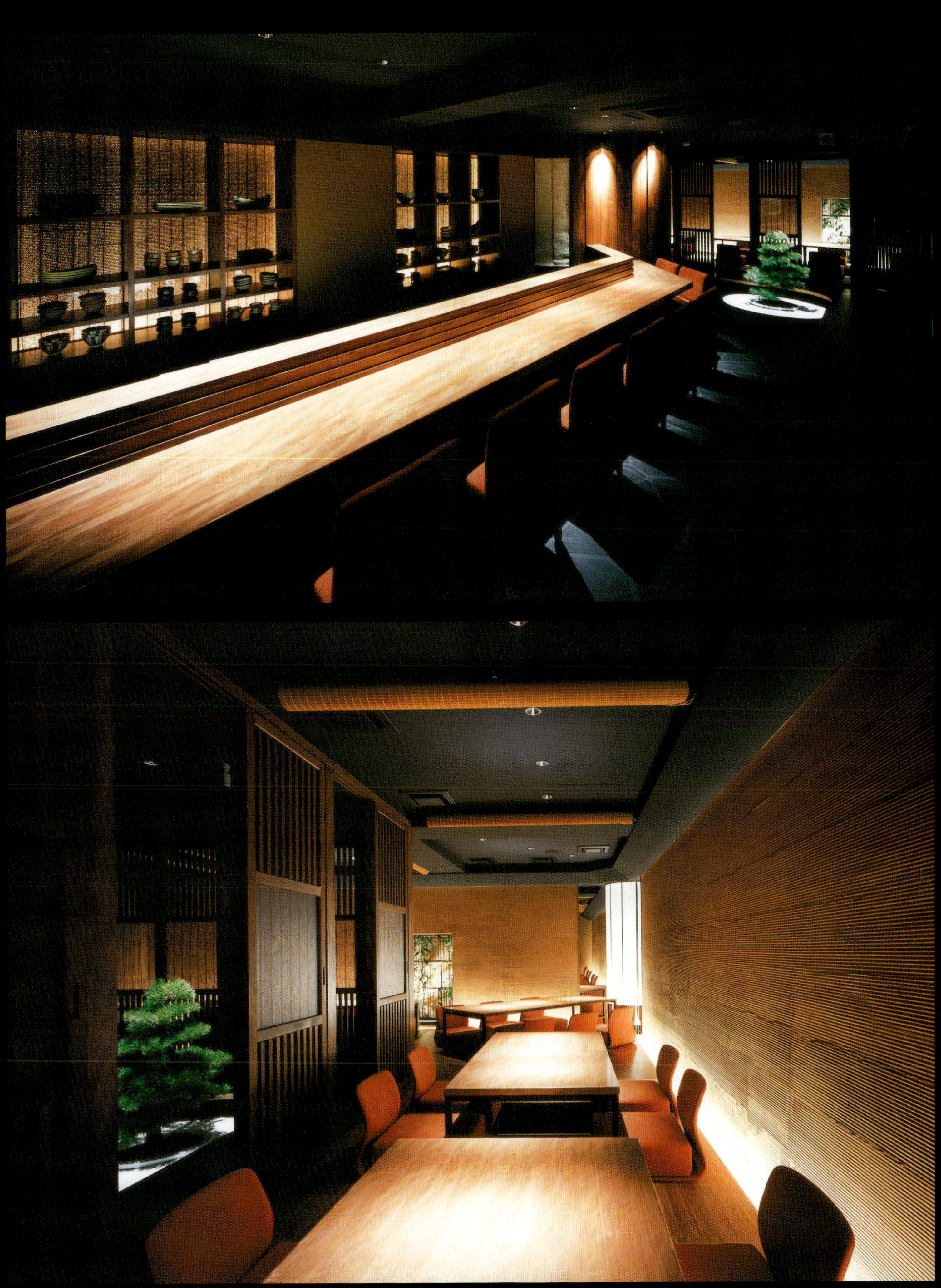

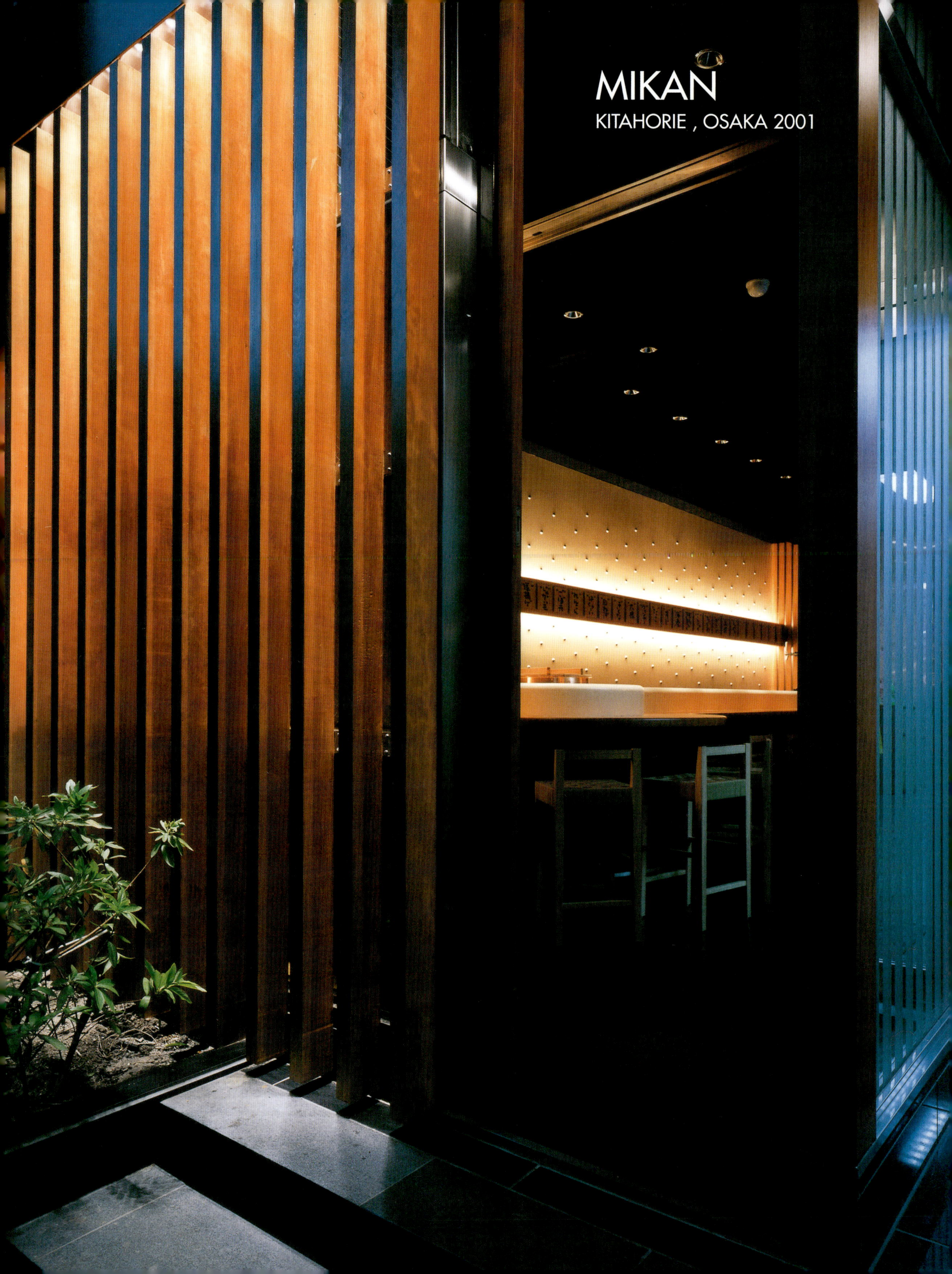

MIKAN
KITAHORIE , OSAKA 2001

こたつで"みかん"

"みかん"は北堀江の四ツ橋筋に面した、ビジネスマンとフリーターが混在し日々豹変し続ける街にあります。リーズナブルでありながら、美味しい料理を提供できる業態を目指して生まれたのが、この"おでん・根菜食堂 みかん"です。

　子供の頃に見たスタンドバーのような立ち呑み感覚をイメージしながら、また、どこか懐かしい昭和40年代の日本の空気感を意識し、空間を構成しました。こたつでほっこりみかんを食べているような、日常的であたたかな空間に仕上がったと思います。

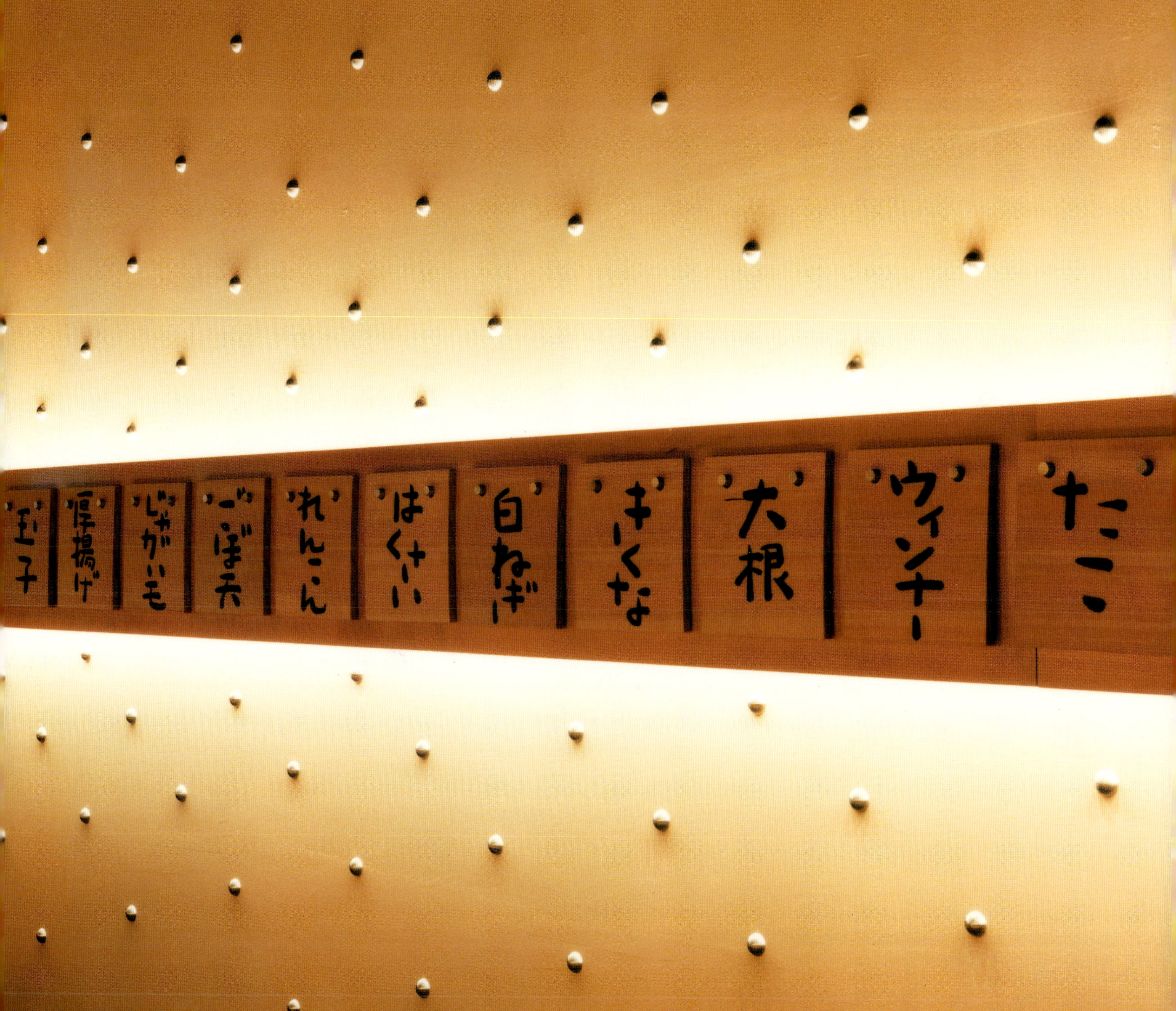

Mikan at a kotatsu

MIKAN was created in an ever changing, ever adapting area of Kitahorie facing the Yotsubashisuji main road; an area full of a mixture of businessmen and habitual part-timers. MIKAN was born with the aim of being an establishment that provides delicious food at a reasonable price.

When constructing the space, I imagined a type of standing drinking arrangement found in the small single-bar establishments that I remember as a child, and I also tried to stay conscious of the nostalgic feel of 1960s Japan.

I think I've created an everyday feeling, like that of sitting casually at a kotatsu* to eat a Japanese mikan**.

* Kotatsu: A typically Japanese type of living room, or family dining table. They are just high enough for one to sit at cross-legged, with legs underneath the table. There is commonly a heater located on the underside of the table, and this is used in winter months together with a blanket draped over the sides of the table to hold the heat in and keep the legs and feet warm.

** Mikan: Commonly called an orange tangerine, or Japanese mikan. It is a sweet citrus fruit that is quite similar to a tangerine.

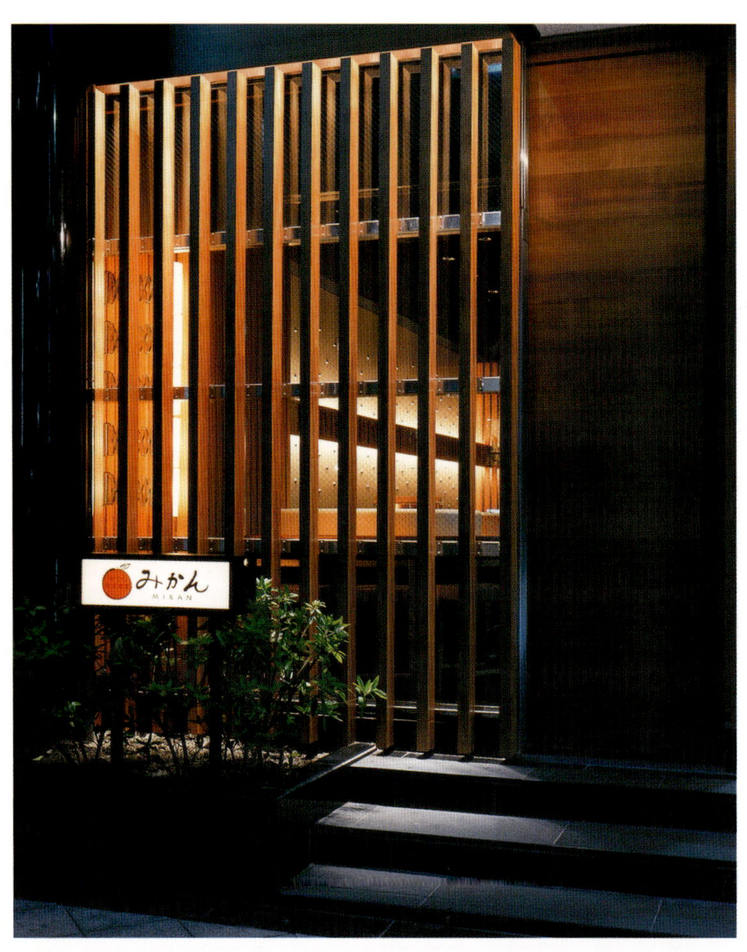
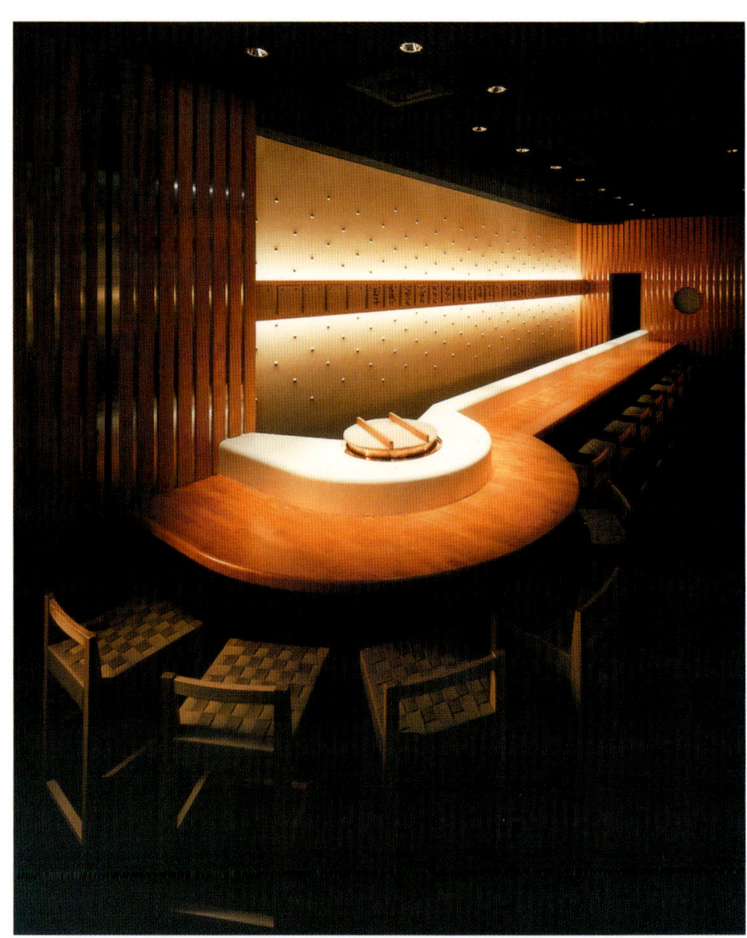

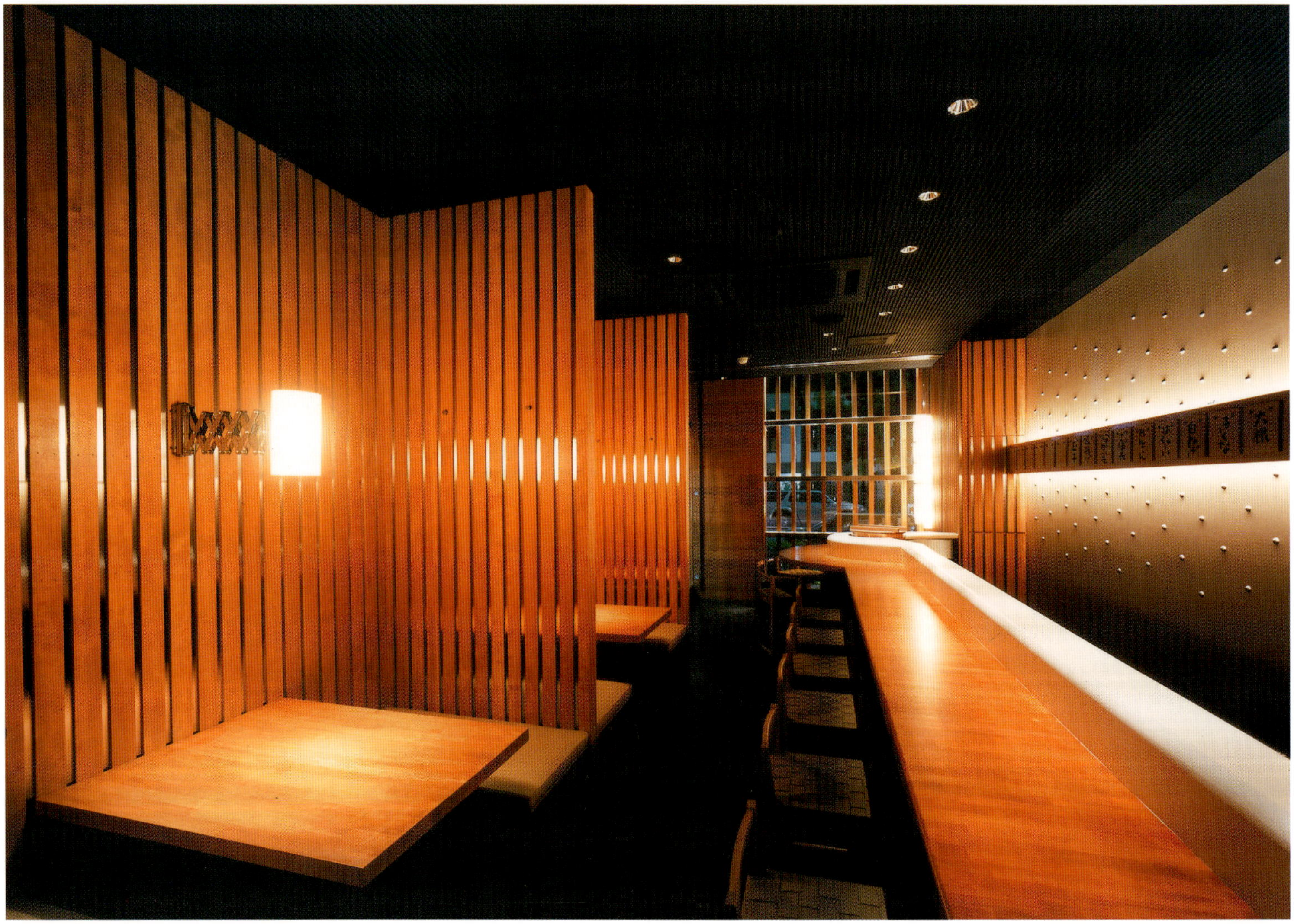

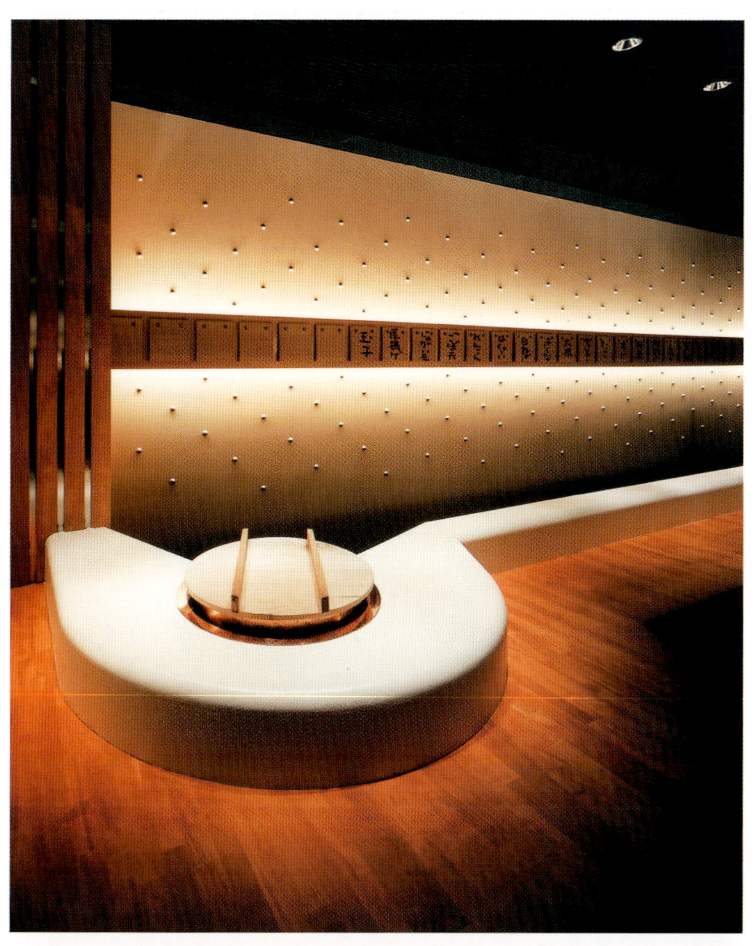
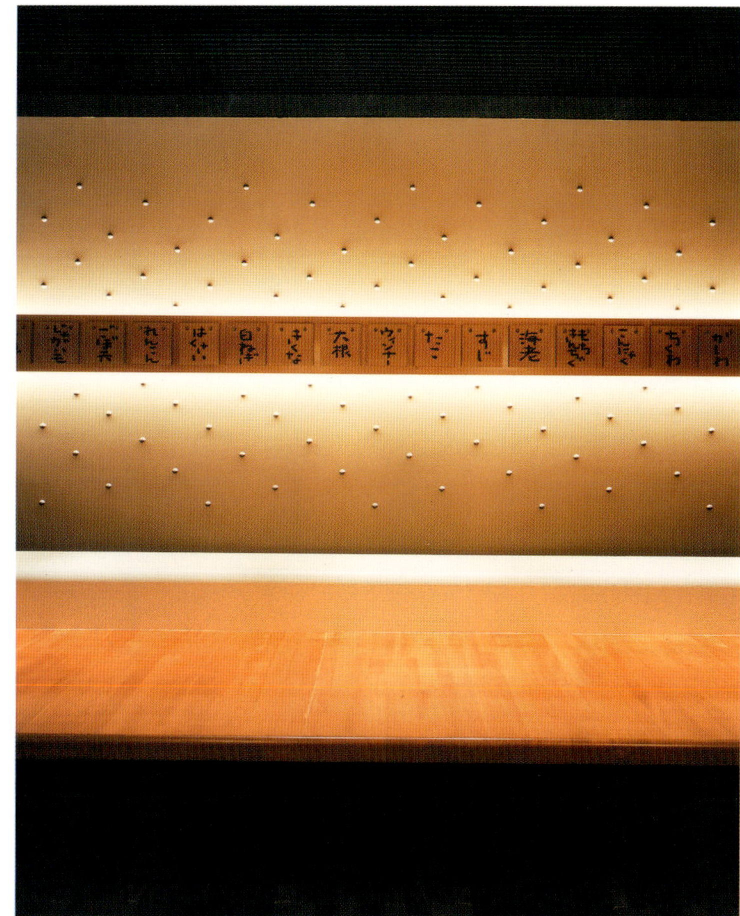

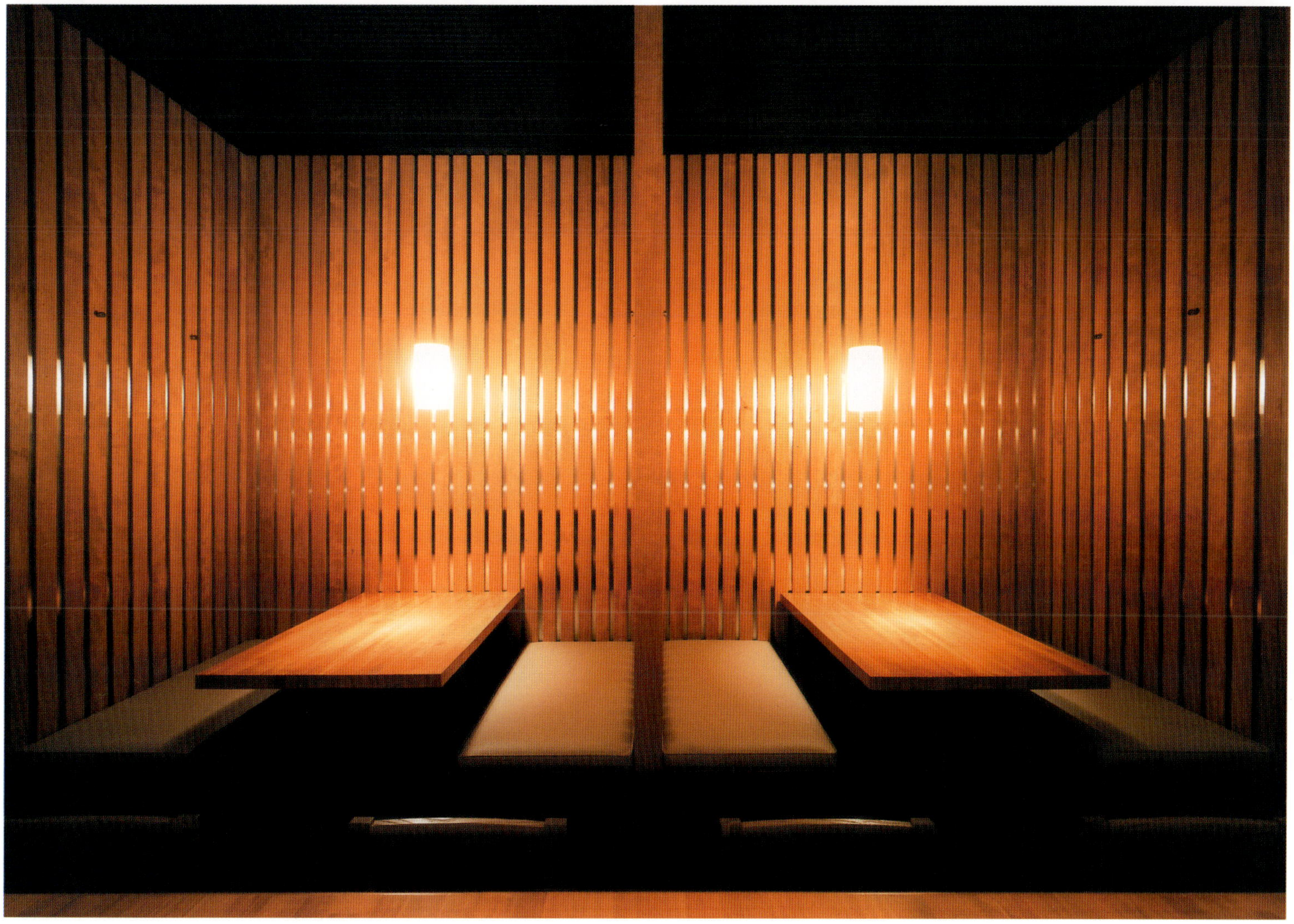

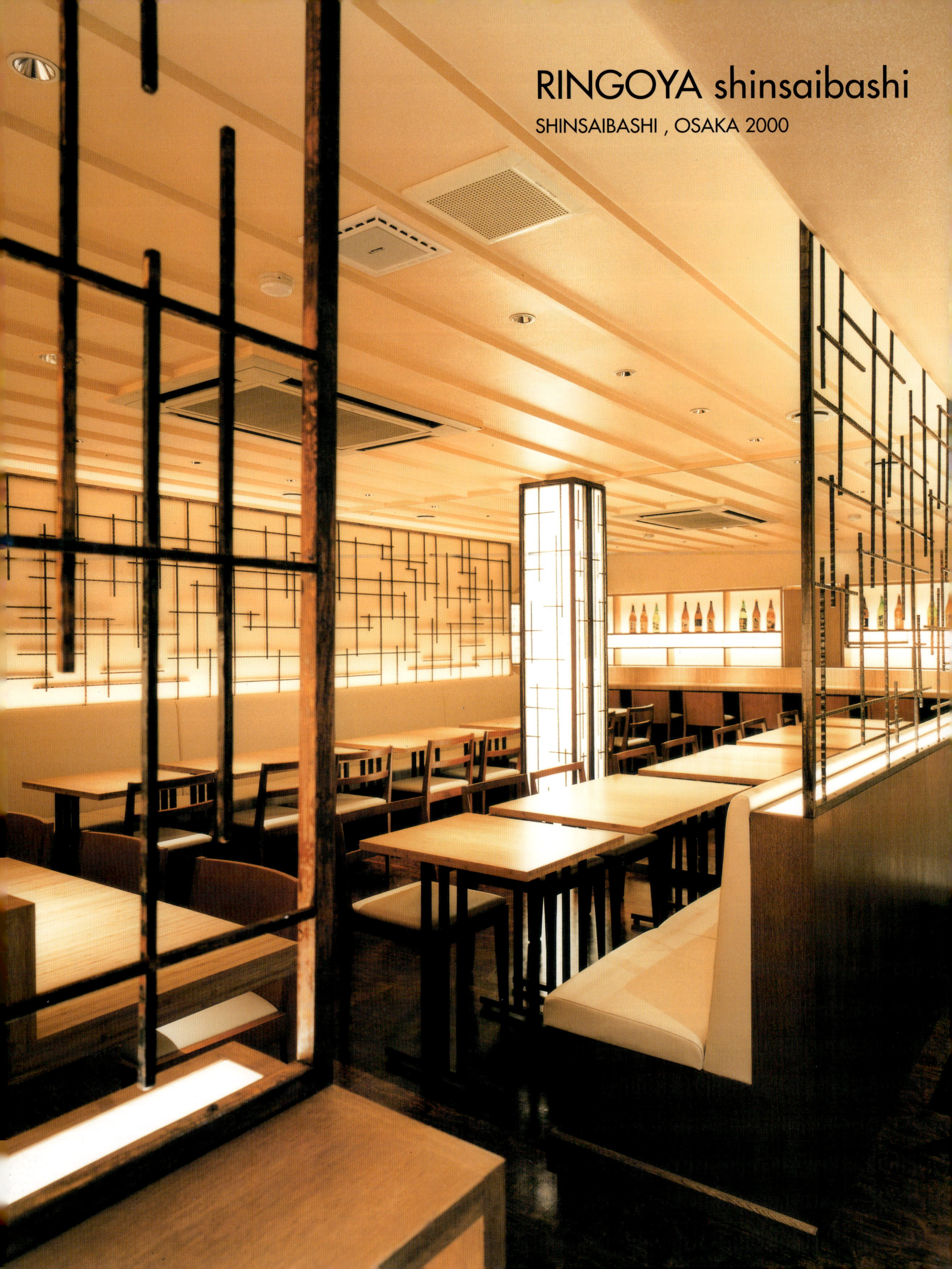

RINGOYA shinsaibashi
SHINSAIBASHI , OSAKA 2000

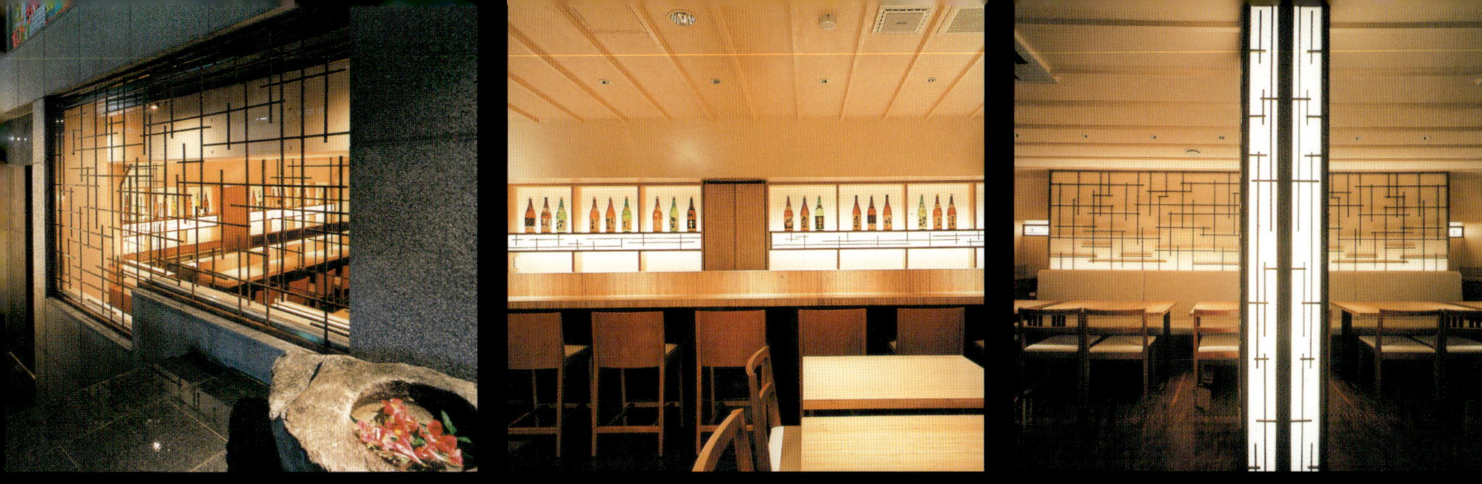

鍛造格子越しに現れる風景

大阪、心斎橋の日航ホテルの北側の通りを西へ1分程歩くと、"りんご家"の看板のあかりが目に入ってきます。そして丹念に鍛造でつくられた格子が幾重にも重なりあう、そのお店が現れます。お出迎えは手水鉢。格子越しに店内のにぎわいを感じながら階段を降りて店内へ・・・。

と、イメージしながら、空間そのものにできる限りの柔軟性と機能性を持たせることにより、狭さというデメリットをにぎわいというメリットに転換するよう、デザインしました。

また、鍛造格子にもそれぞれ役割を与えています。「光を受けて空間を広げる格子」。「光を放ち、空間を優しく包み込む格子」。鍛造格子がそれぞれの役割を果たすことで最初のイメージを具現化できました。さまざまなモノやヒトが混在するこのアメリカ村で、小さいけれど存在感のあるお店が"りんご家"です。

A view beyond the steel forged lattice

If you walk 1 minute to the west on the road to the northern side of the Hotel Nikko Osaka, in Shinsaibashi, the light of the RINGOYA sign soon comes into view. There appears the elaborately forged, multiple layered lattice of RINGOYA. You're greeting by a traditional stone hand-wash basin. You sense the activity in the restaurant below as you descend the stairs beyond the lattice... This was the image that I had as I designed, attempting to convert narrowness into liveliness by giving the space as much flexibility and functionality as possible.

Each forged lattice was given a task: Some to capture light and open up space. Some to release light, and gently envelope space. My original idea was brought to life as each lattice performed its individual role. Although only a small part of America Mura, a vibrant commercial area of Osaka that is home to myriad people and all sorts of material things, I think that a good little shop with a real presence has been created.

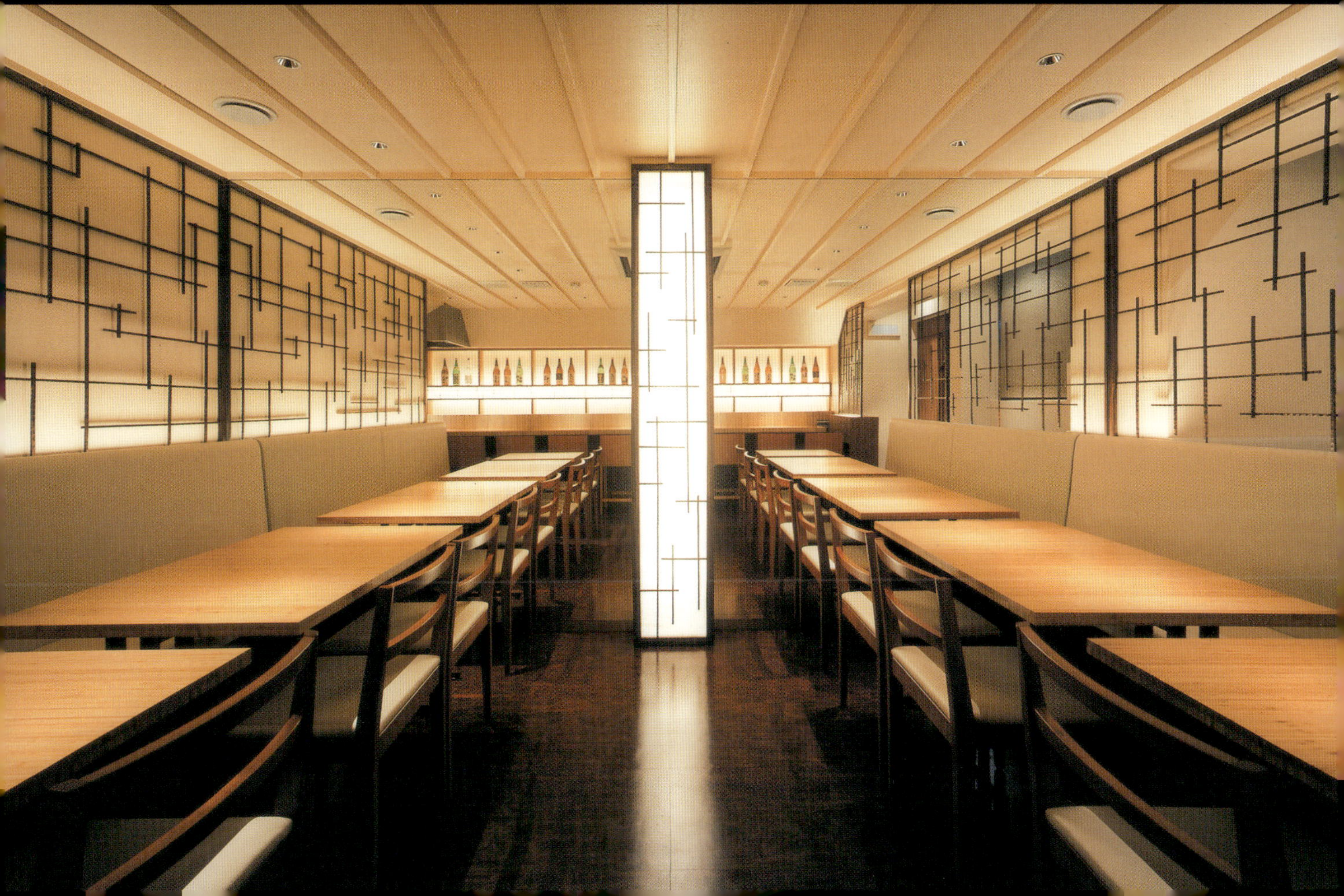

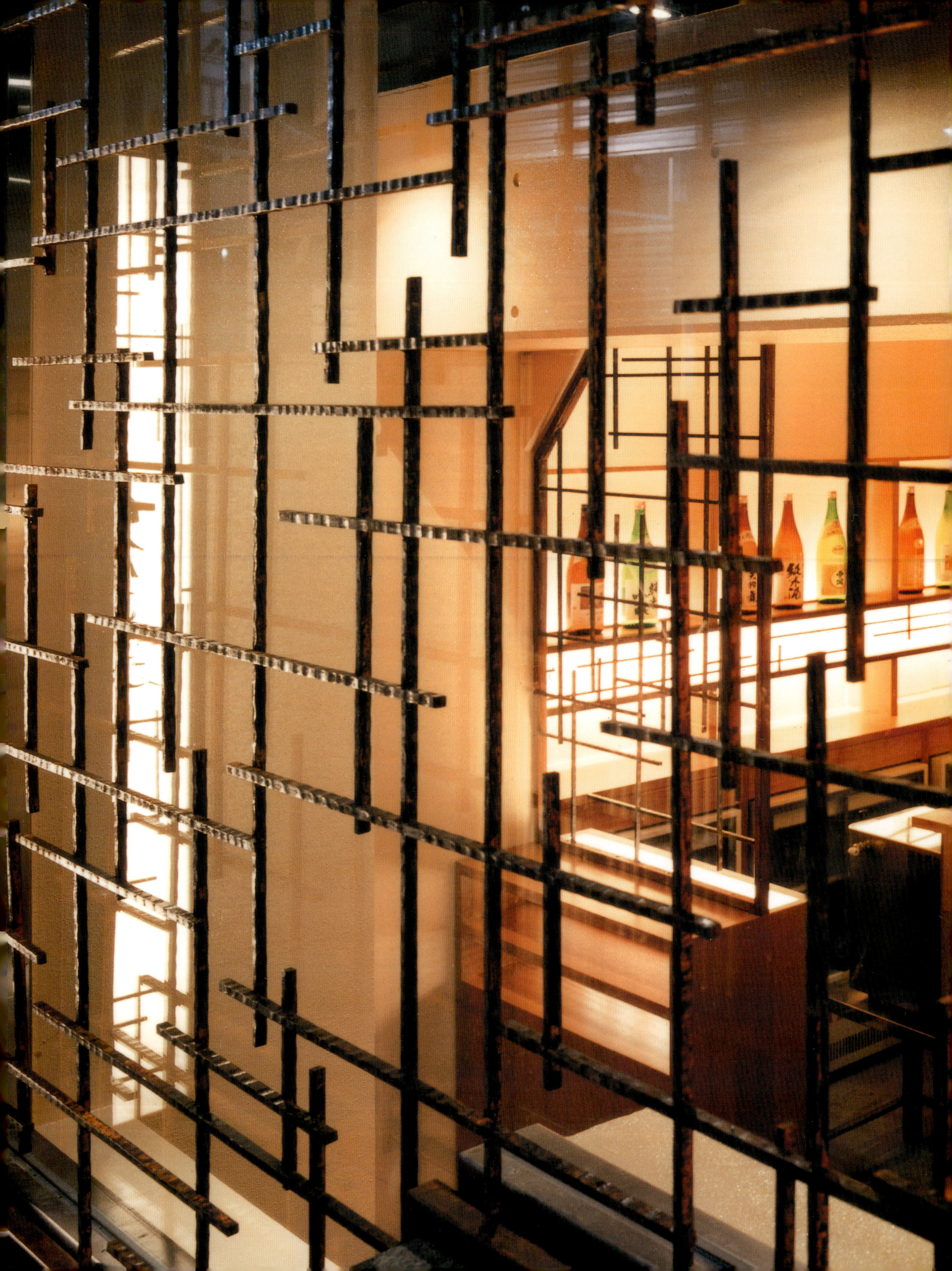

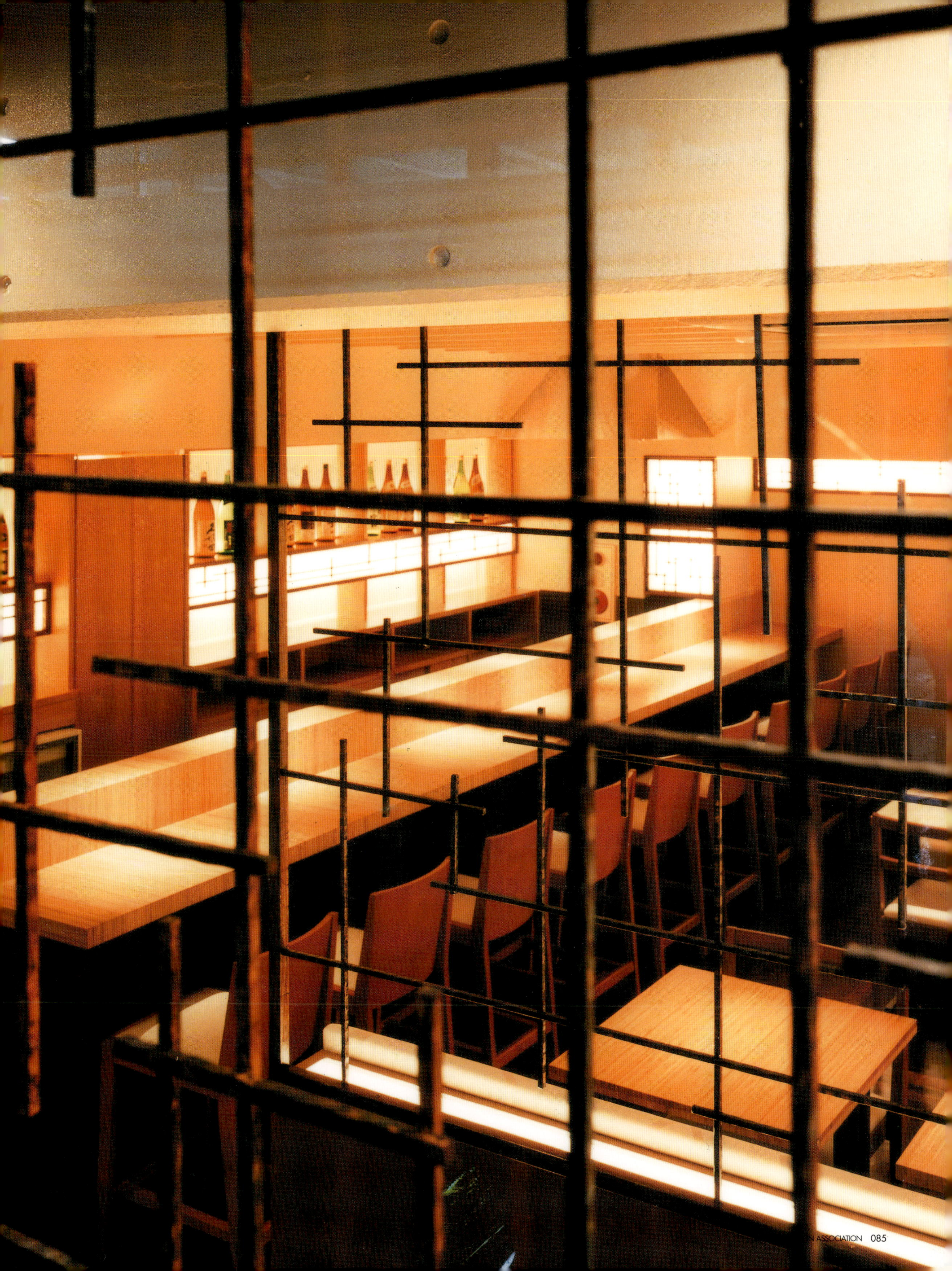

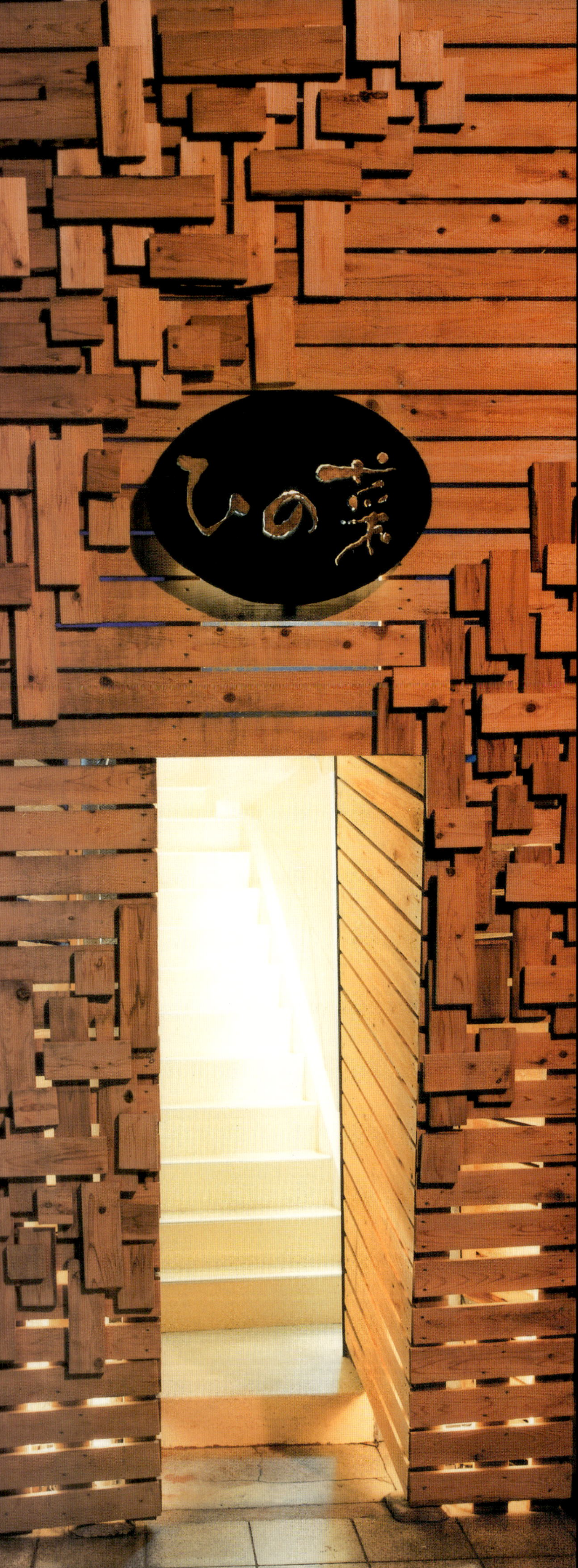

HINONA
MINAMIHORIE , OSAKA 2000

親しみのあるデザイン

ダイニングにとって、ファサードは最も大切な要素の一つだと言えます。まして路面から店内を望め
ない、2階のお店にとっては生命線とも言えるでしょう。
　"ひの菜"はまさにその2階での計画であり、そのままでは上がりづらく冷たい感じがする階段を、
明かりと素朴な素材を使って、あたたかく気軽にのぞいてもらえるようなファサードを考えました。

A design that feels familiar

It might be said that a most important element for dining establishments is the
facade. It might also be said that the facade is a vital for second floor
establishments, the interiors of which cannot be clearly seen from street level.
　HINONA exists in just that type of second floor space. In planning the facade, I
thought about making the stairs, which present an uninviting and difficult climb to the
second floor, into a warm and inviting area that would encourage people to casually
glance inside. I designed the facade to incorporate light, and to be constructed of
simple materials, and I think that by giving it a sort of hand made feel that the
restaurant has become a cozy and friendly place from the entrance inwards.

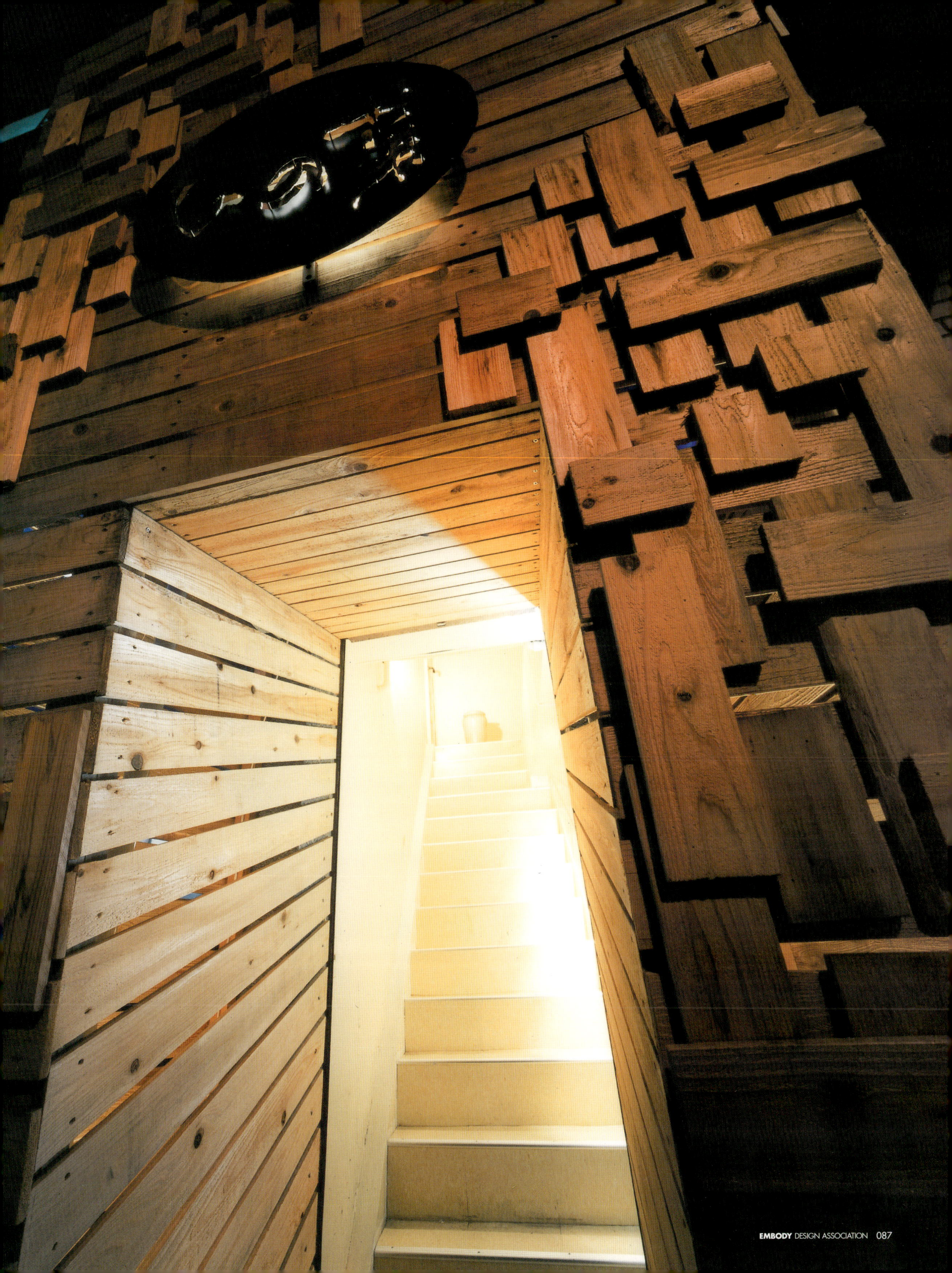

NANAYA
SHINSAIBASHI , OSAKA 1998

小さな空間から生まれる和み

"ななや"では、オーナーの熱いスピリッツを感じ受け、ゆっくり料理を味わい、酒をたのしみ、話がはずむ、そしていつの間にか気持ちよく酔っているような、このうえなく居心地のよいお店をイメージしながら、空間を構成していきました。

　客が店を選ぶ時はちょっとドキドキさせて、店の前でガラス越しに店内のにぎわいを感じさせる。スタッフの接客は、礼儀正しく親しみやすく。カウンターの手触りはこんな質感で、隣の客との距離感はこれぐらいが和む。カウンター越しに見えるバック棚の光は品よく主張し過ぎないように。人と人の視線はこんな関係が落ち着く。もちろん料理は、ほどよいタイミングで出てきてほしい。お客様の色で溢れる空間だから、色彩はひかえめに。テーブル席の空気感はこんな感じが盛り上がる。光はそっとやさしく包み込むように・・・。

　33才だった「私が行きたい小料理屋」をつくらせていただきました。

Contentment born of a snug little space

When composing the space, I imagined being uplifted by the proprietor's warm spirit, casually savoring the food, enjoying sake, and indulging in lively banter, and before long being pleasantly inebriated in a shop that could not be any more comfortable.

Customers feel a little anticipation when deciding whether to come in or not, and they can feel the liveliness beyond the window as they glance in from outside. Staff are warm and friendly, and perfectly well mannered. The feel of the counter under your hand, and the sense of distance between you and the customer sitting next to is just right to give that feeling of contentment. The illumination of the back shelf on the other side of the counter is not over-emphasized, giving a refined feel. The human atmosphere is relaxed and comforting as peoples' gazes interact. Of course, you want the food to be presented with just the right timing. The space overflows with the vibrance of the customers, so colors are used moderately. The mood at the table seats is just right to create that festive feel. Lighting delicately enfolds the space...

I created "the little restaurant that I wanted to visit" when I was 33.

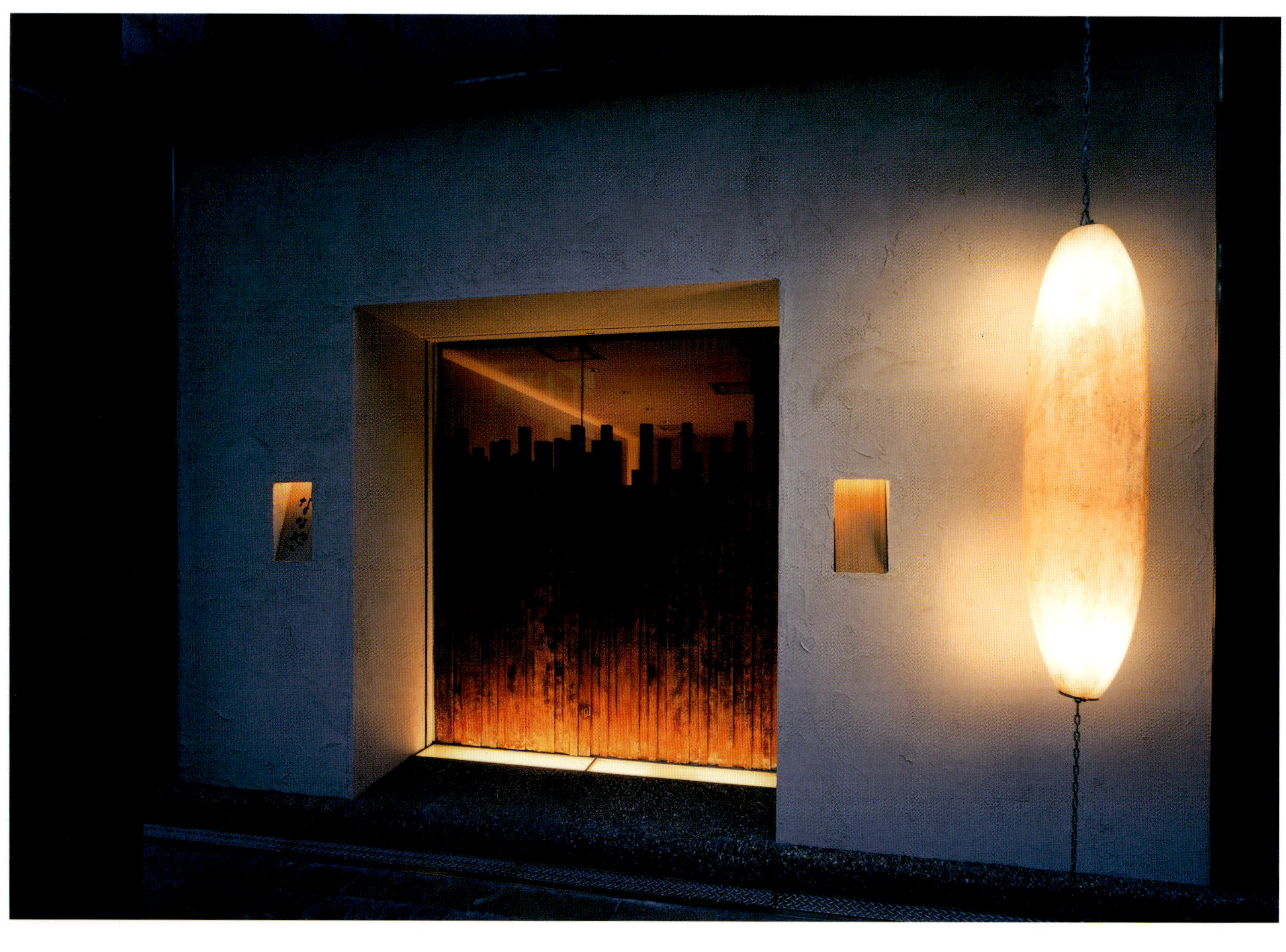

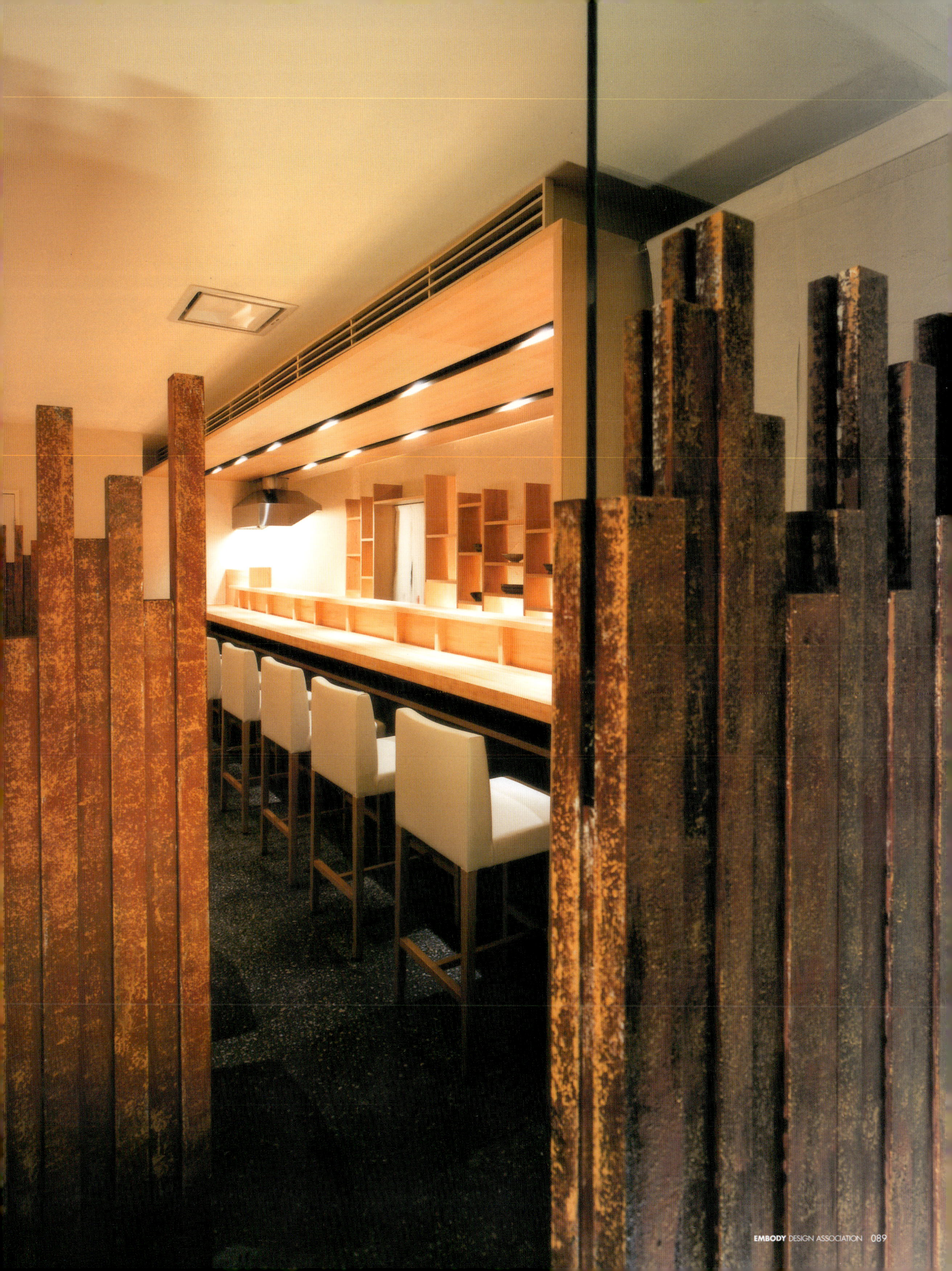

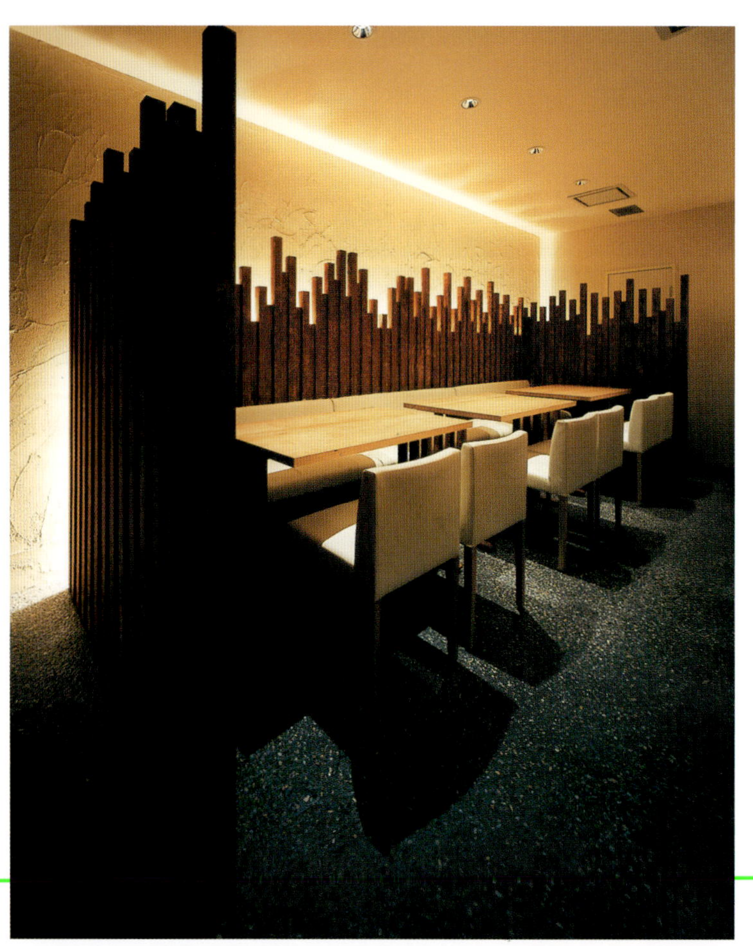
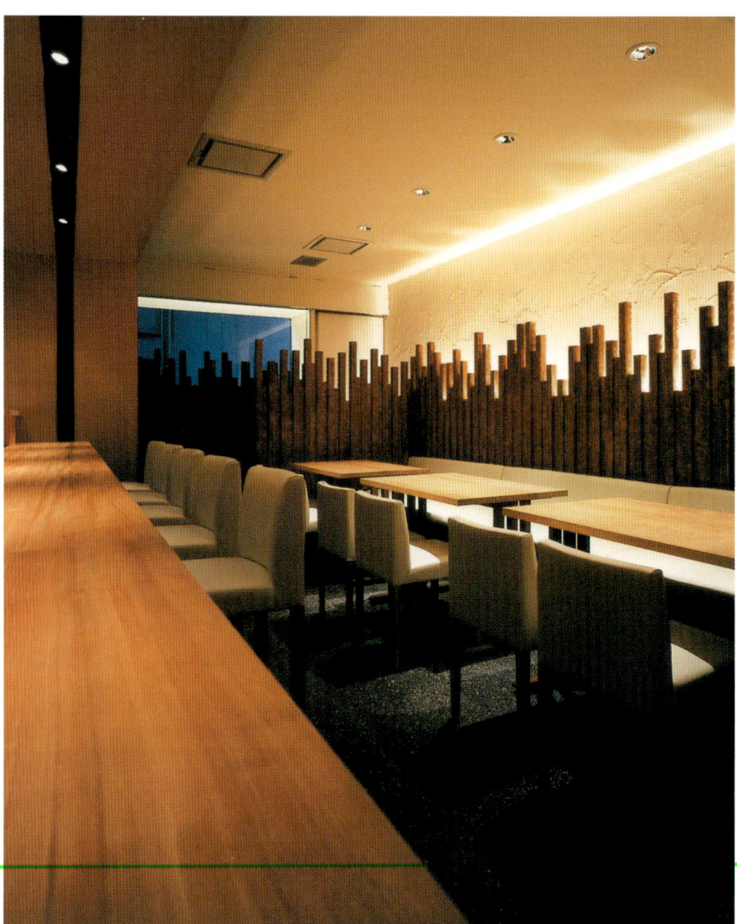

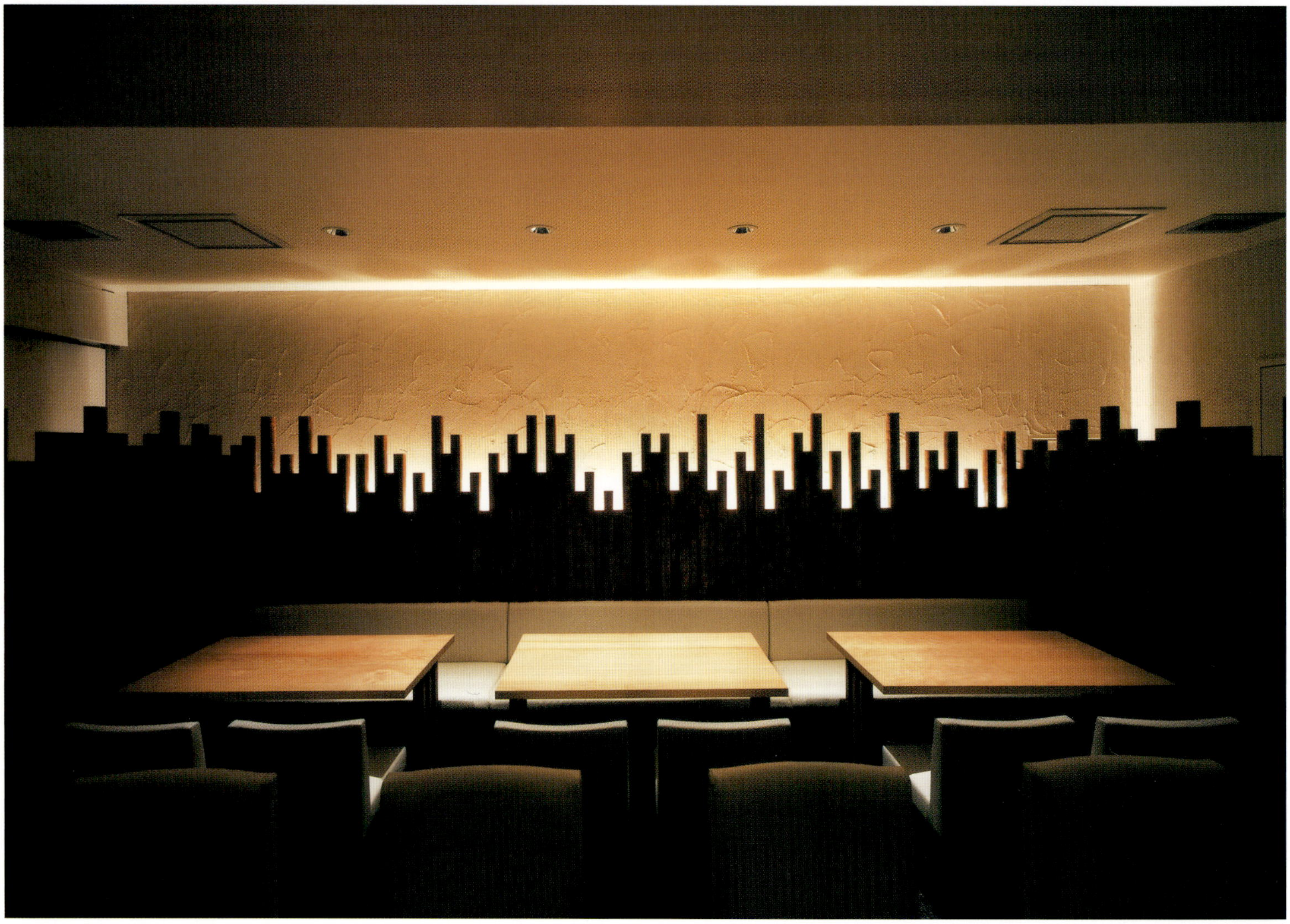

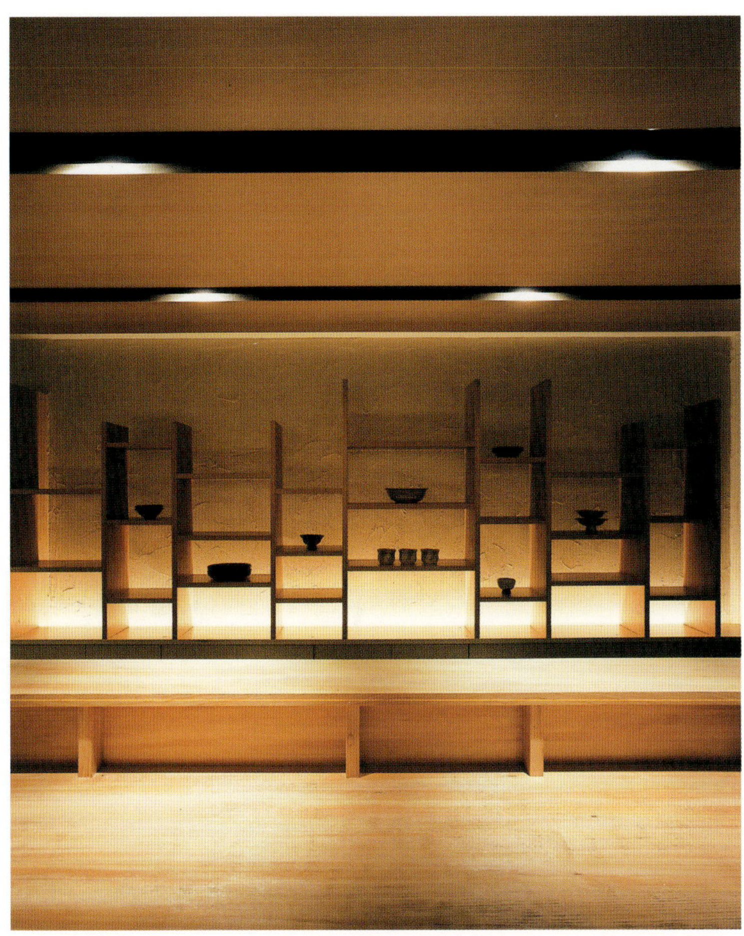 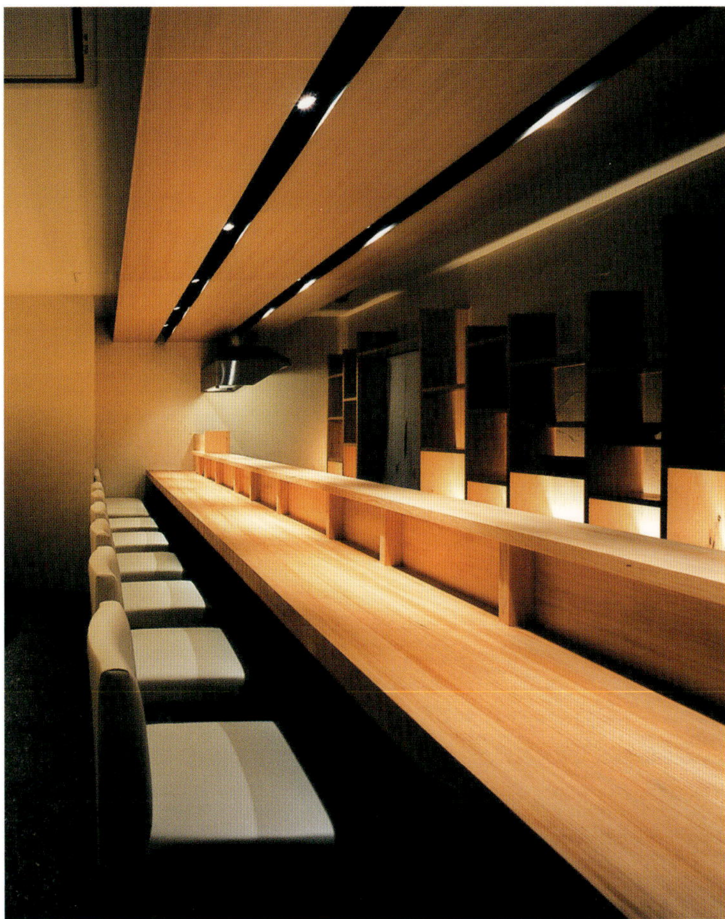

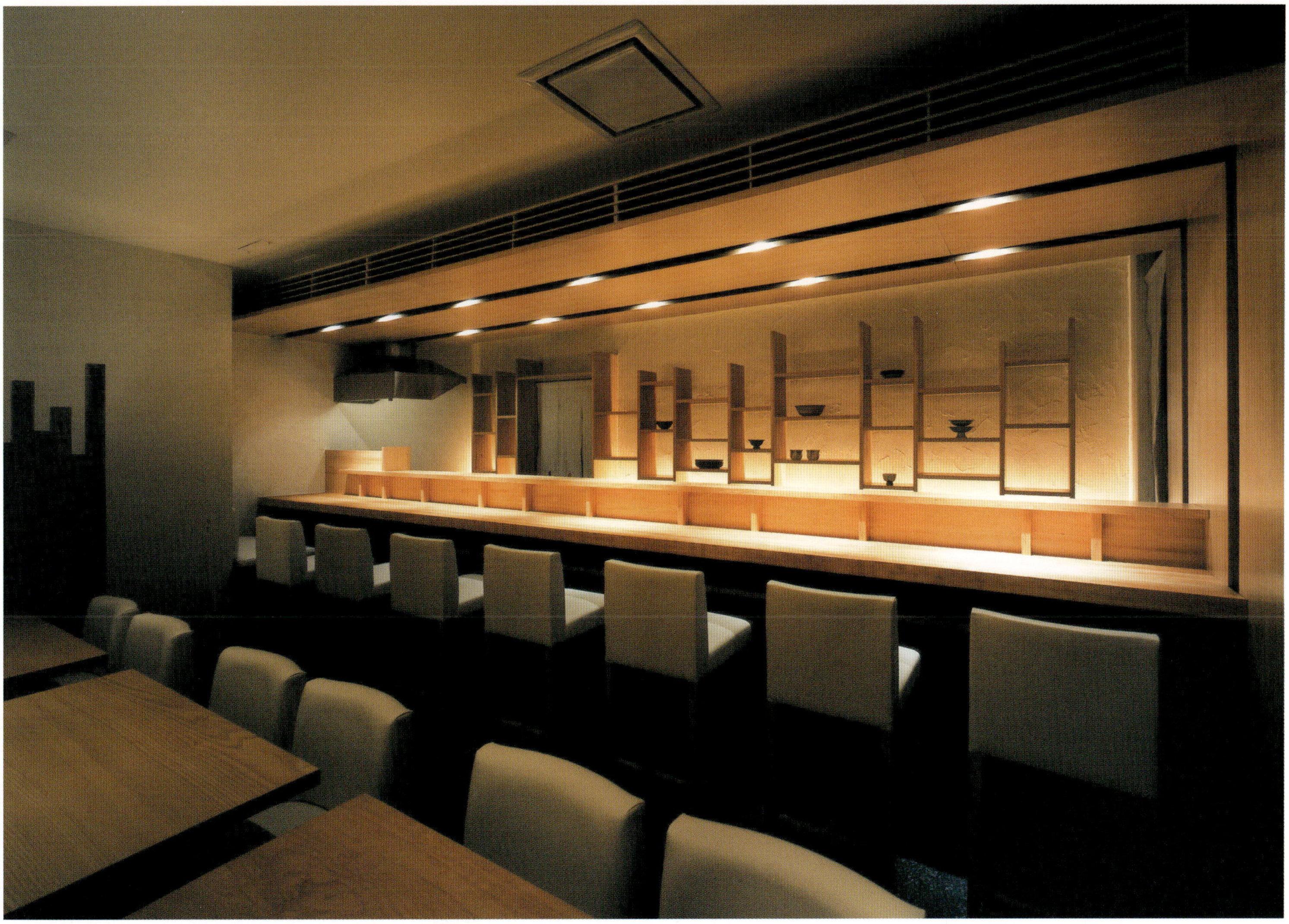

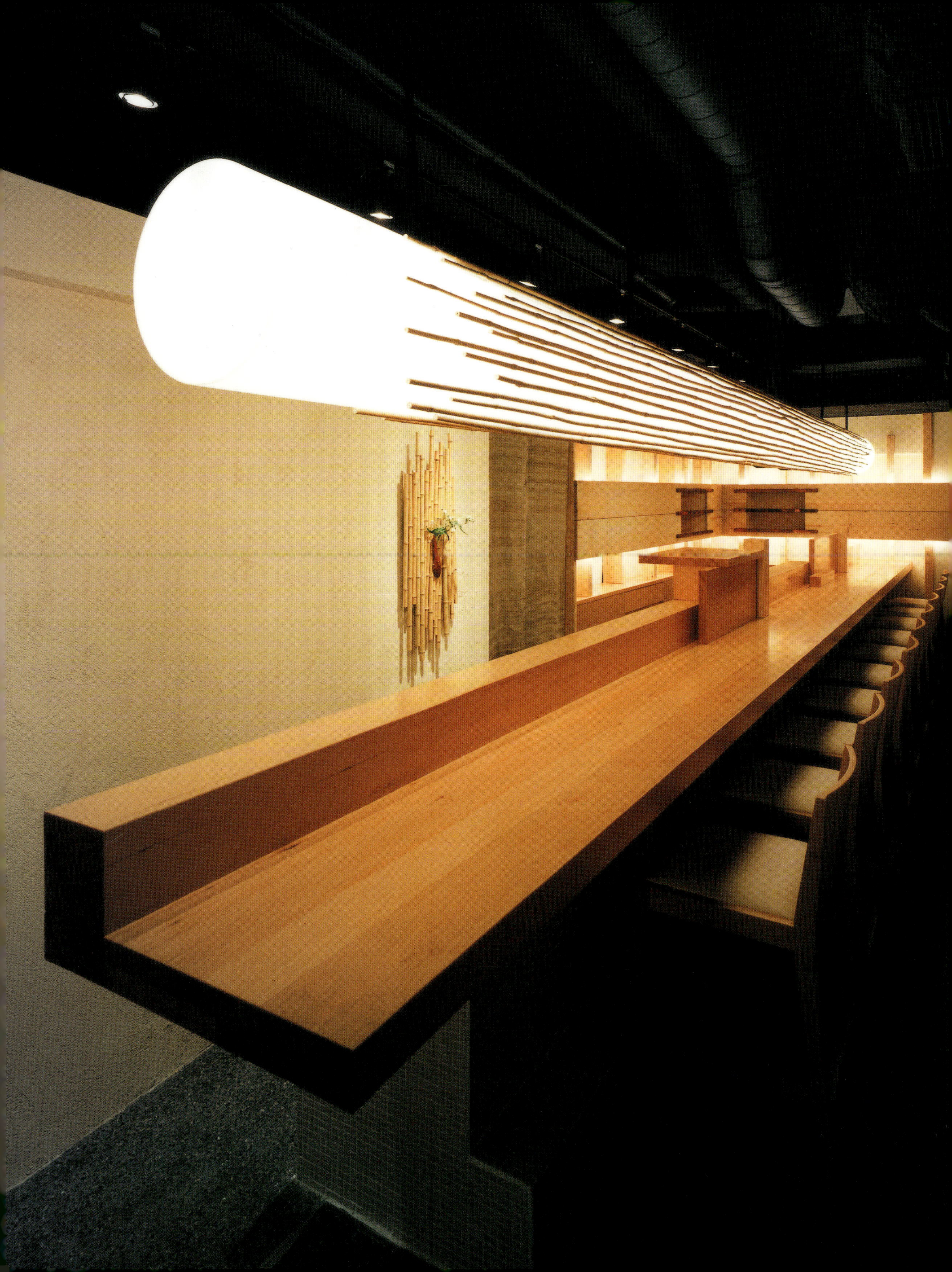

RINGOYA honmachi
HONMACHI , OSAKA 1997

心に映る美学

古くから日本では、造形だけではなく目に見えないもの、例えば礼儀や言葉、生き方にも美の心が息づいています。私は日本人として、その日本文化をしっかり自分の中に取り込み、自分のモノにした上で現代の消費社会と向かい合うことが大切だと思っています。ここ、"りんご家 本町" では、オーナーのお店に対する熱い思いをゾーニングやディテールに宿し、訪れる人の目には映らなくとも感じることのできる「おもてなしの心」を具現化できたと思います。

Aesthetics of the soul

The soul of of true beauty has long been alive in Japan, not just in materially crafted things, but also in manners, speech, and way of living. I believe that as a Japanese, it is important to fully take in the Japanese culture, and to face the modern consumer society with it as part of you. At RINGOYA honmachi, the proprietor's passionate ideas were born out in the zoning and detail, and I believe that I have brought out a "hospitable heart," that although unseen, can be felt by those that visit.

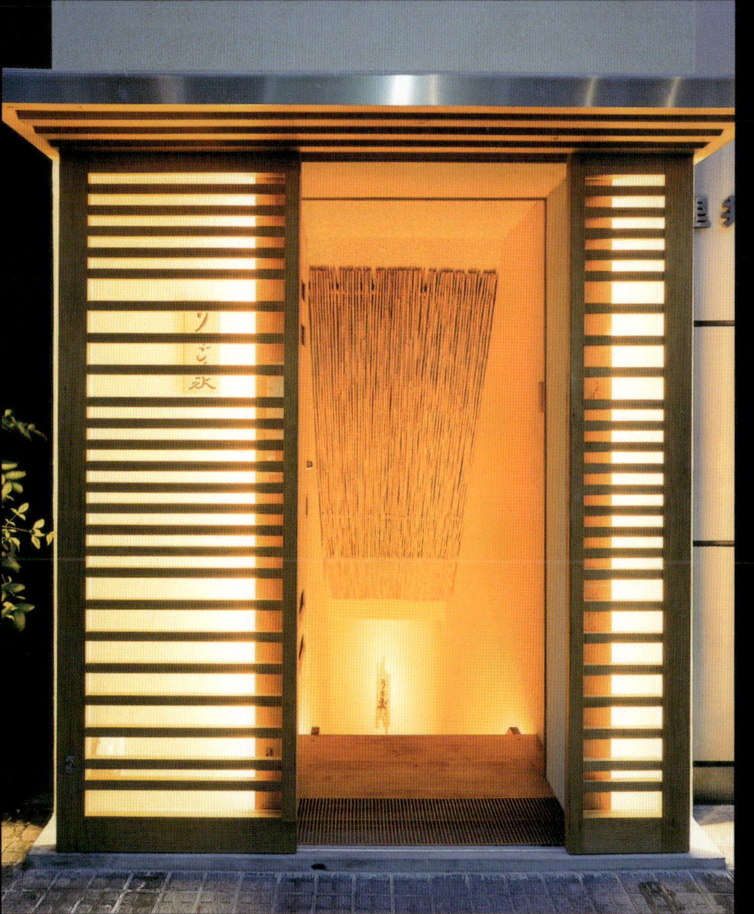

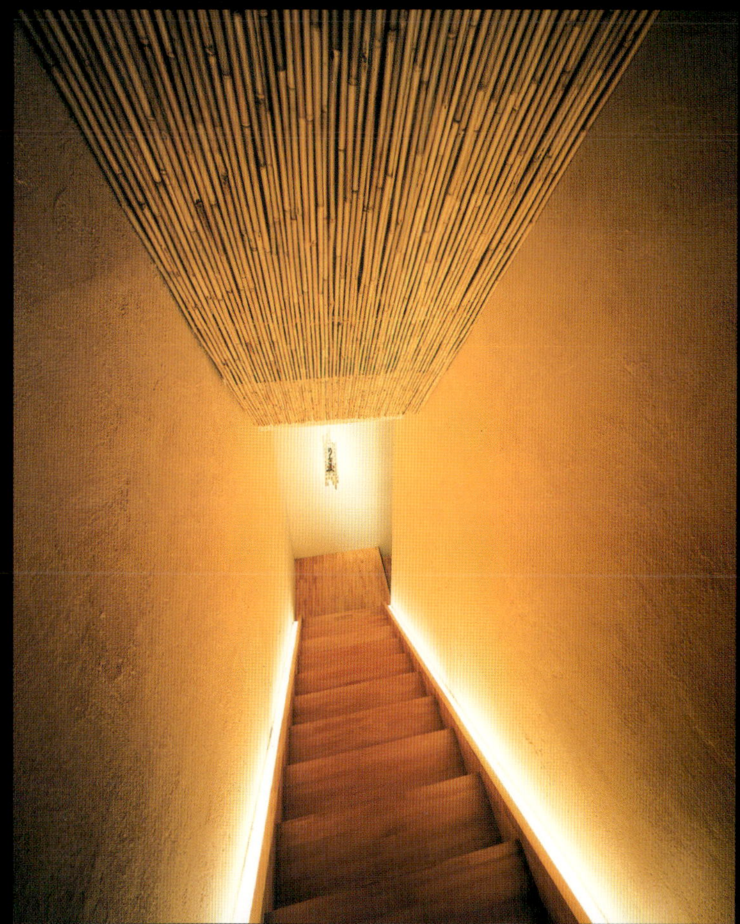

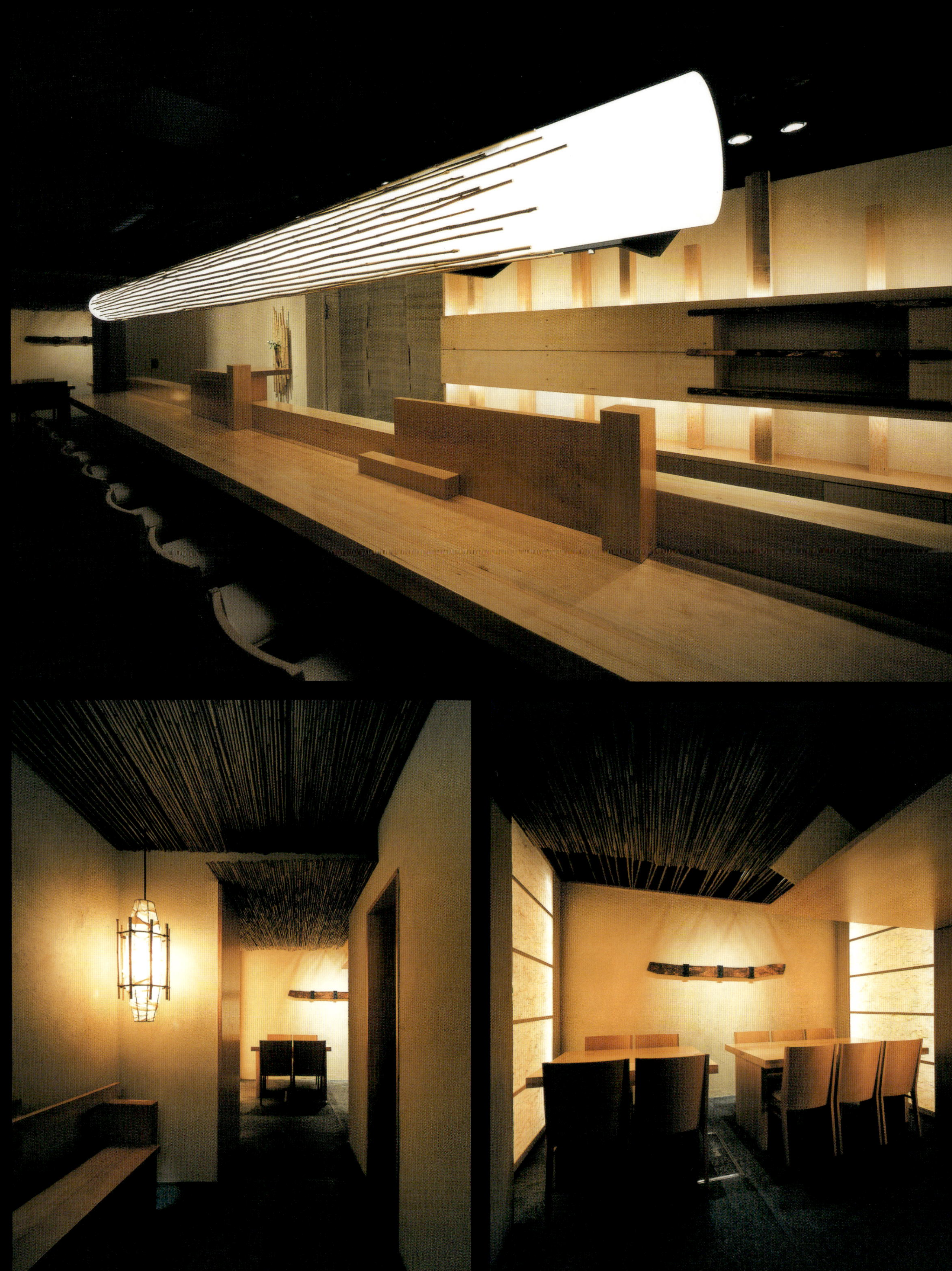

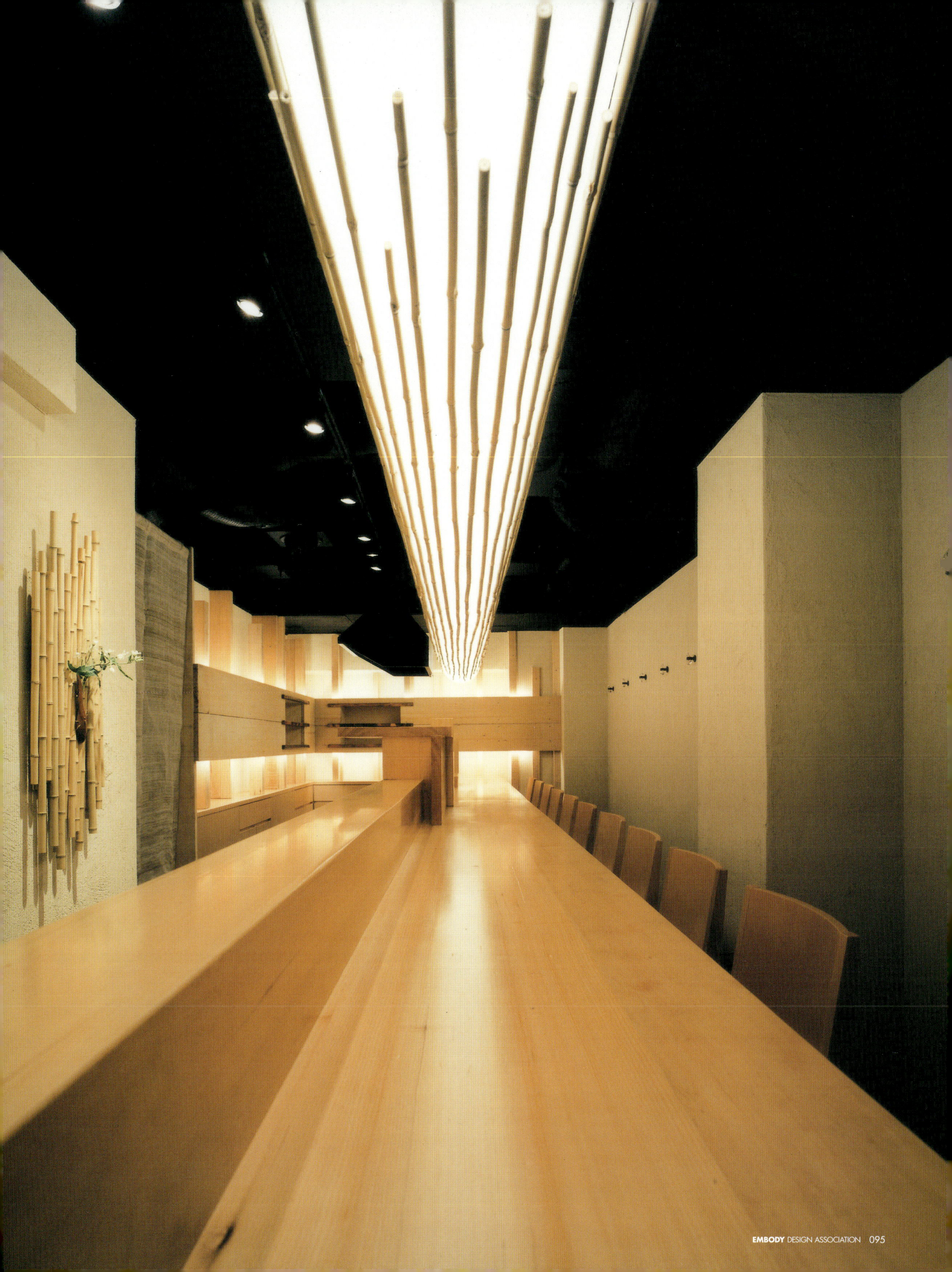

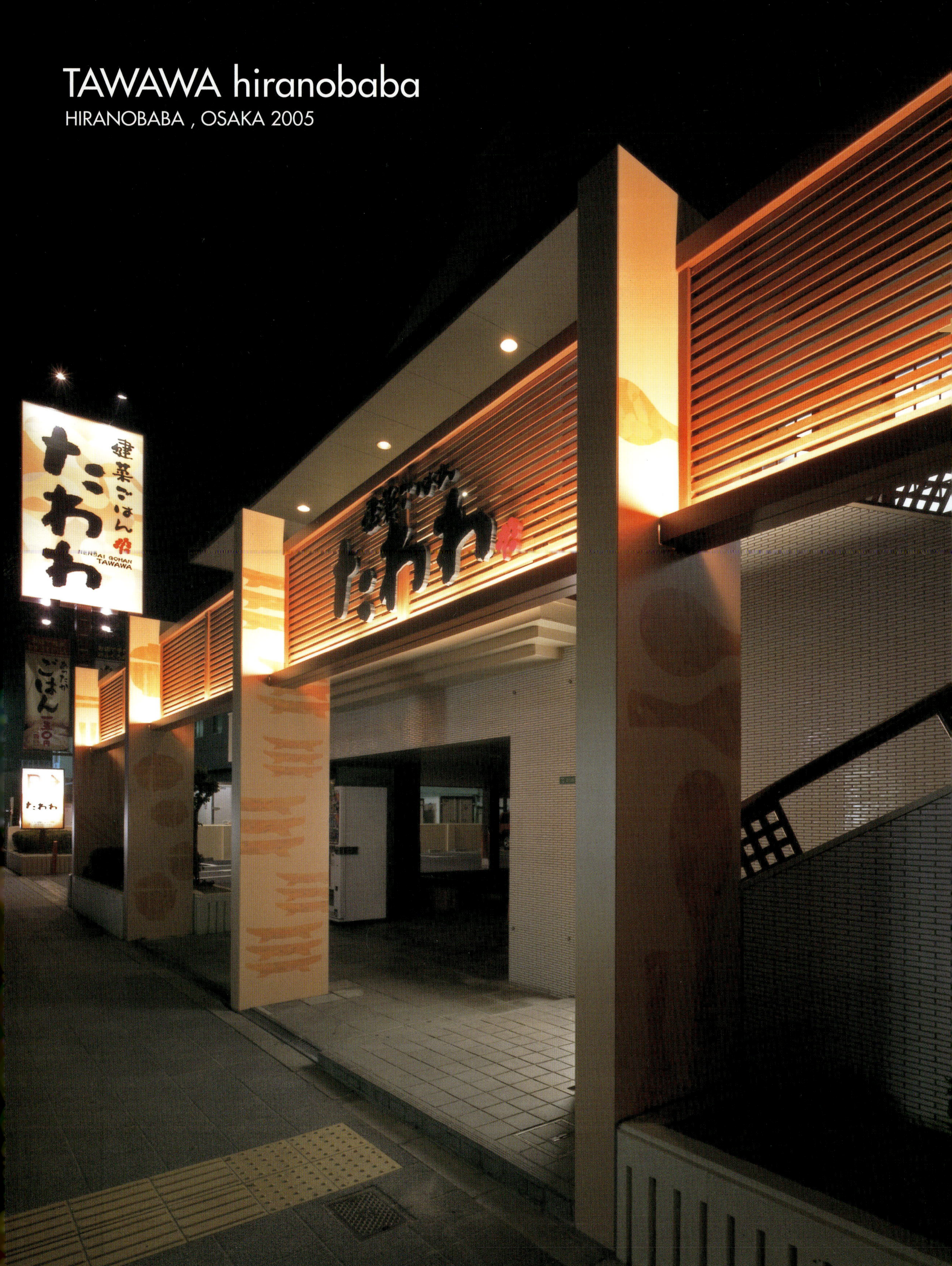

TAWAWA hiranobaba
HIRANOBABA , OSAKA 2005

子供の頃、バイキングと聞くだけで、ワクワクしたものです。しかし、カフェテリア形式のお店を選択する時、安さ、速さという経済的な理由は当然ですが、私たちは、それだけでお店選びをしているでしょうか。多様化の進む日本の食文化の中で、今後求められるスタイルとは、「健康」をキーワードに自分にあった食事を、食べたい分だけ選ぶ楽しみのようなものではないでしょうか。

　"健菜ごはん　たわわ"の空間をデザインするにあたり、思い描いたのは、そんな小さな楽しみや幸せがたくさんつまった「食するための心地よい場」です。

The fun of choosing! The satisfaction of eating!

When I was a child, the mere mention of "all-you-can-eat" got me excited. Customers that select a cafeteria style restaurant are most definitely economically motivated by the fact that they are quick and cheap, but is that all they consider in choosing a restaurant? With increasing diversity in Japan's culinary culture, perhaps people will begin demanding a healthy style that allows them the fun of eating the food that suits them, in the amount that is right for them. When designing TAWAWA, I pictured a "comfortable place made for eating," full of these sorts of small joys and delights.

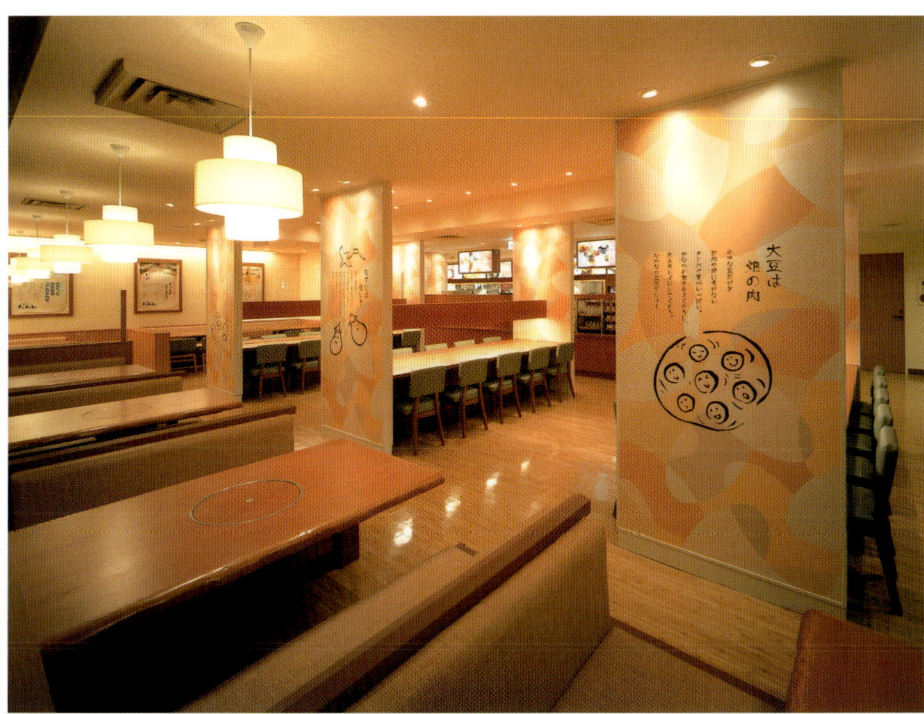

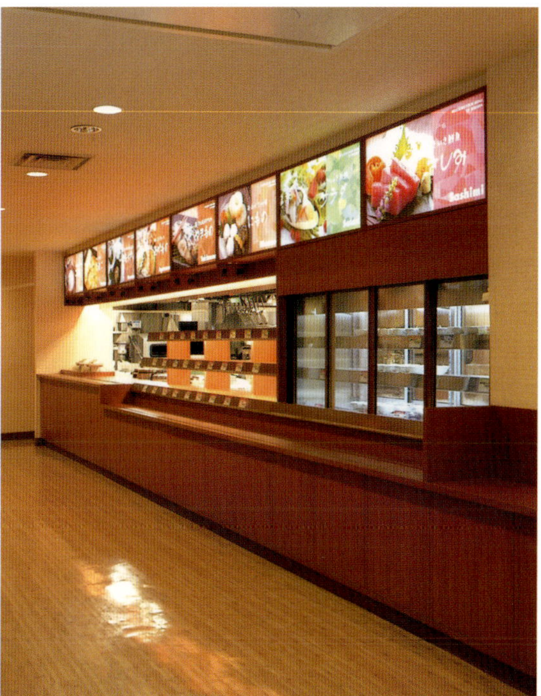

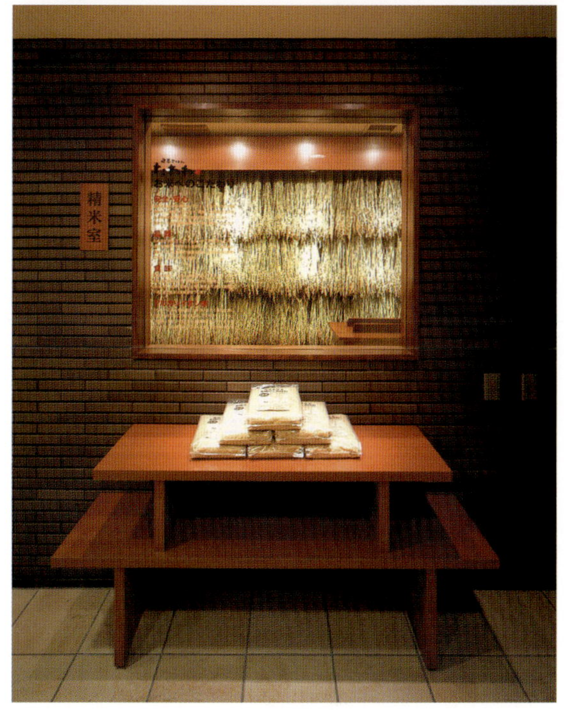

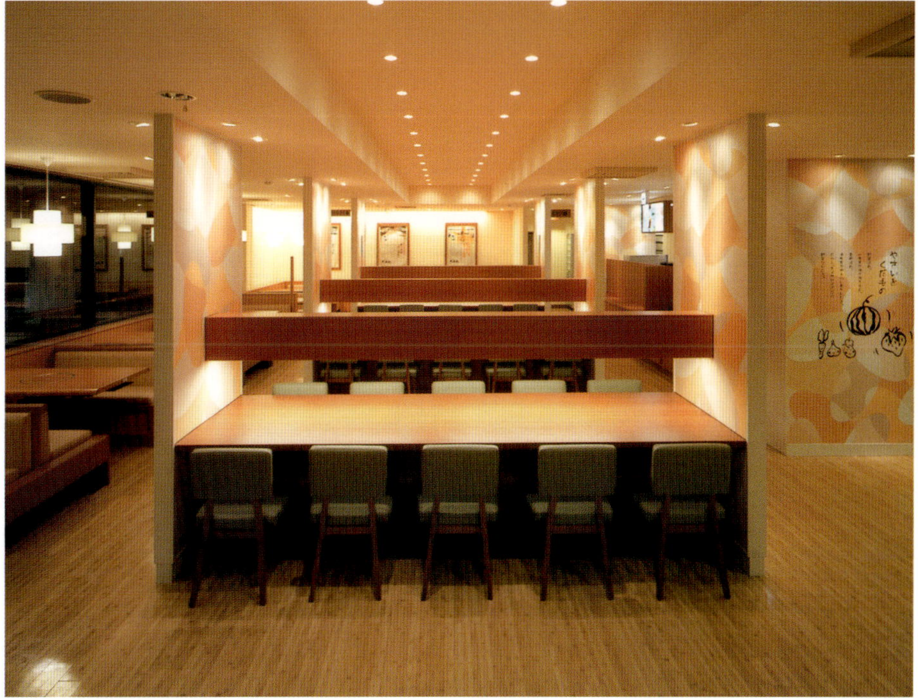

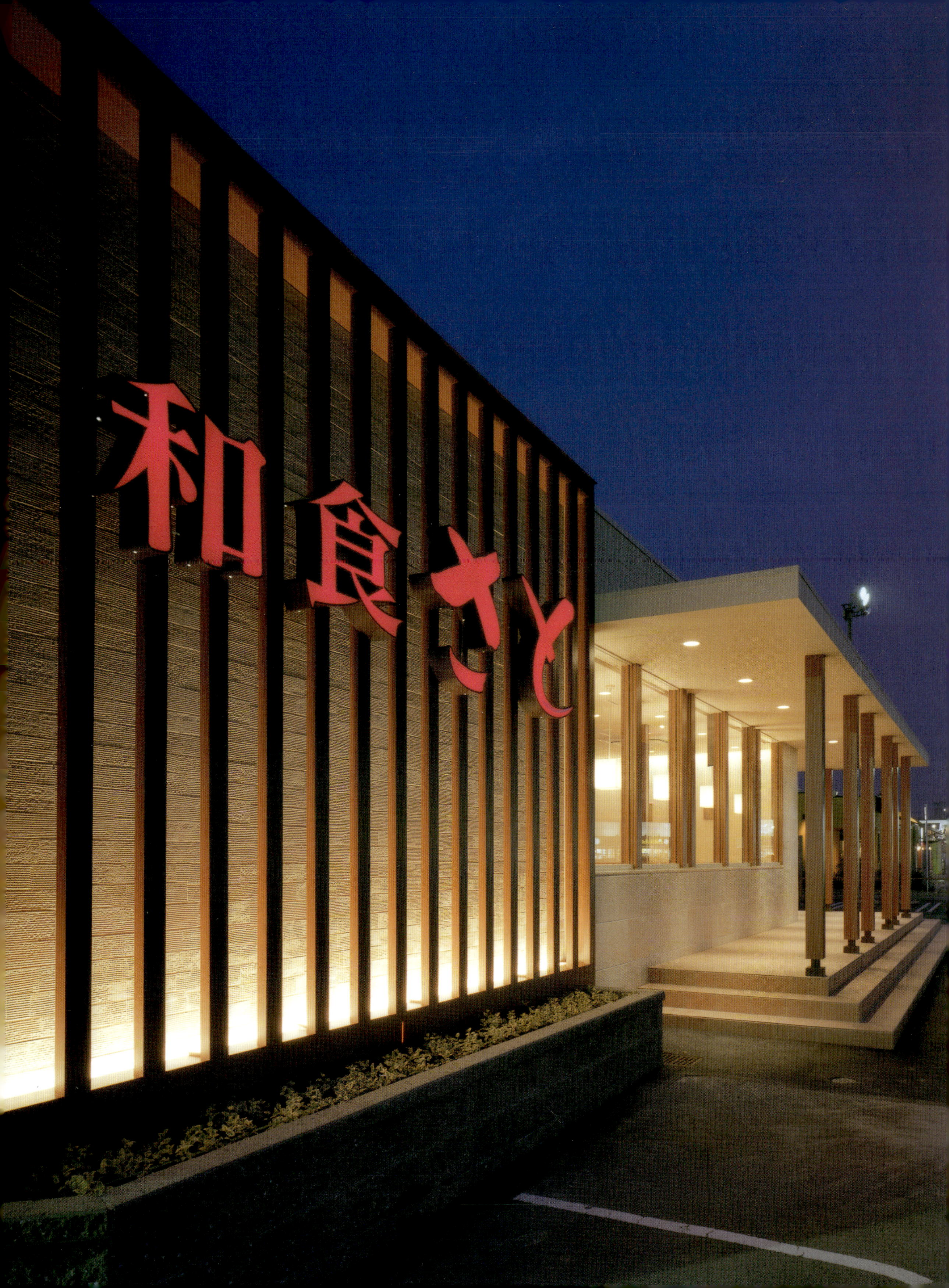
和食さと

SATO yatomi
YATOMI , AICHI 2004

ジャパニーズ プリミティブ

チェーン化された、和食ビジネスの店舗空間に必要なものは、合理性を追求したアメリカ的発想のファーストフードの考え方ではなく、また、ヨーロッパ的なスローフードの考え方でもないと思います。
　私は、「和食」は「環食」であり、「輪食」なのではないかと思うのです。命の源となる食べ物を、親しい人たちと共に輪になって囲み、自然の環の中で暮らしに感謝しながら「いただきます」の心を毎日感じさせてくれる時間、それが私たち日本人の食だと考えています。そんな時間を提供するために必要なのは、メニュー、サービス、空間の調和を大切にした、あたたかで、穏やかな、なごみの空間だと考えます。

Japanese primitive

The in-store atmosphere needed by Japanese cuisine businesses that have begun opening up chains of stores is not the American invented fast-food style that pursues rationalized business operations, nor is it the European style of slow-food.

Instead, I believe that it is a place of harmony and contentment made for eating Japanese cuisine, with effort made to create harmony between the menu, the service, and the atmosphere. It should be a place that reflects the true traditional meaning of the Japanese concept of "wa," or peace and harmony, based on the very primitive sources of Japanese ideology that are borne out in the Japanese view of the natural world.

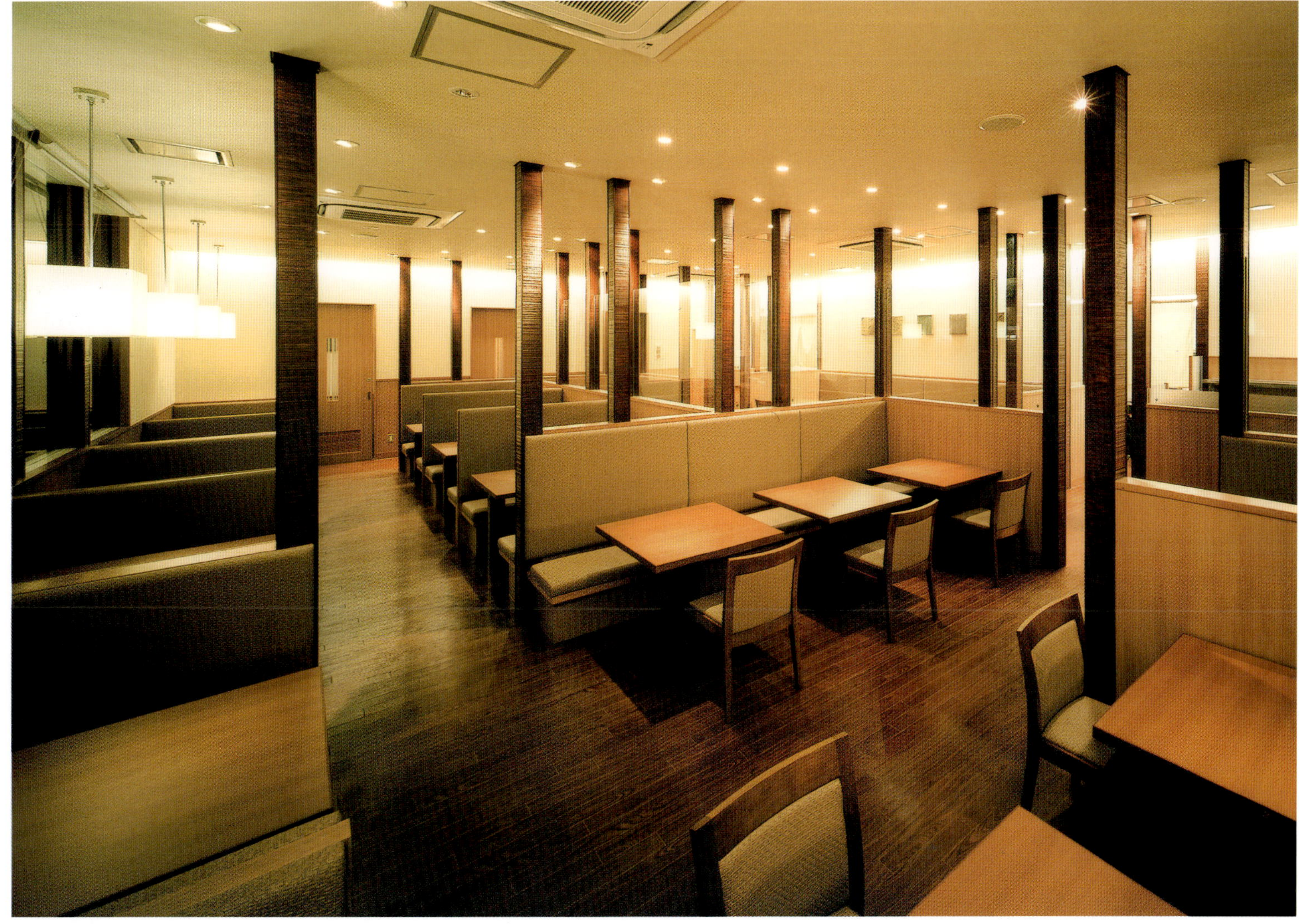

SATO hamamatsu
HAMAMATSU , SHIZUOKA 2004

未来を切り開く鍵

90年代、レストランビジネス界では海外のスタイルや時代のムード、サービスをアレンジした「何々風」の業態や空間が横行しました。時代が移り、お客様も世界中の様々なサービスや空間を体験し、目も舌もこえてきている今、お店にとって一番必要なモノは、訪れる人たちの欲求を満たすことのできるオリジナリティだと思います。

　"さと"では、和食ファミリーレストランのさきがけとしての、「らしさ」や「ならでは」のプライドとこだわりを具体的なカタチにし、表現しました。

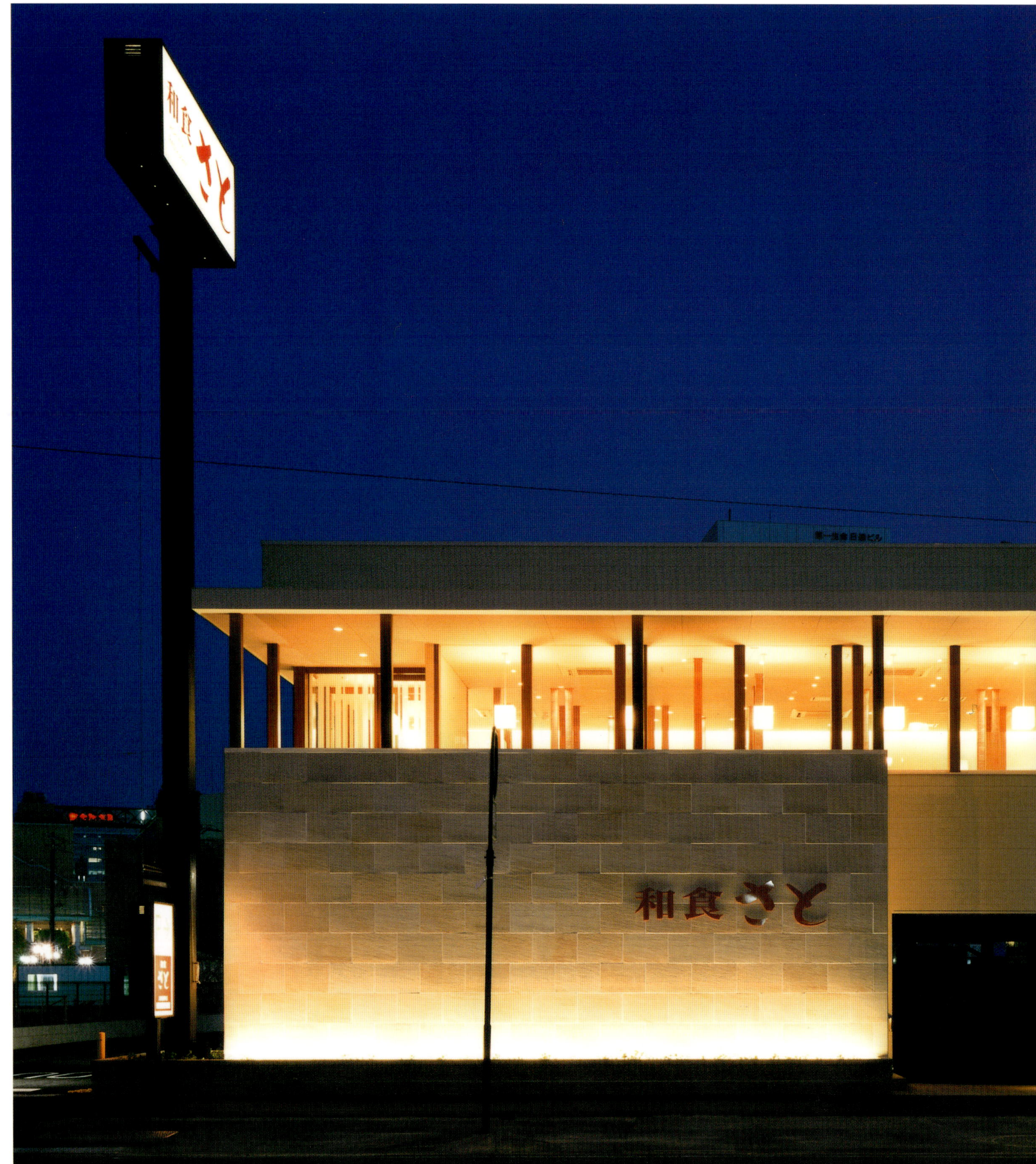

The key to the future

The restaurant business of the 90s was proliferated by all sorts of restaurants and shop spaces that brought together the styles, moods, and service from overseas. Times have changed, customers have experienced the various styles and atmospheres from around the world, and they are now beginning to see beyond this and demand something more. I think that the most important thing for shops in this environment is the requisite originality to satisfy the desires of customers.

I expressed the unique elements of SATO as a forward moving Japanese family restaurant, giving form to its unique pride and meticulousness.

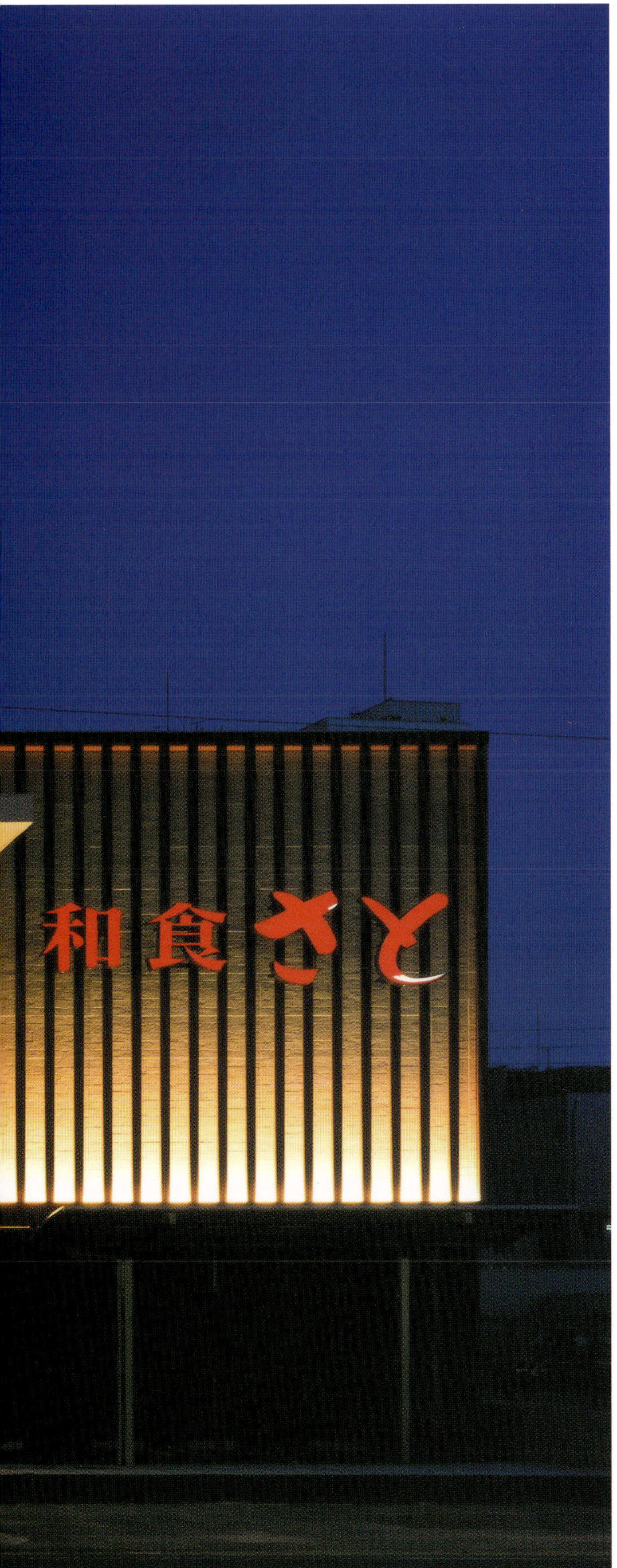

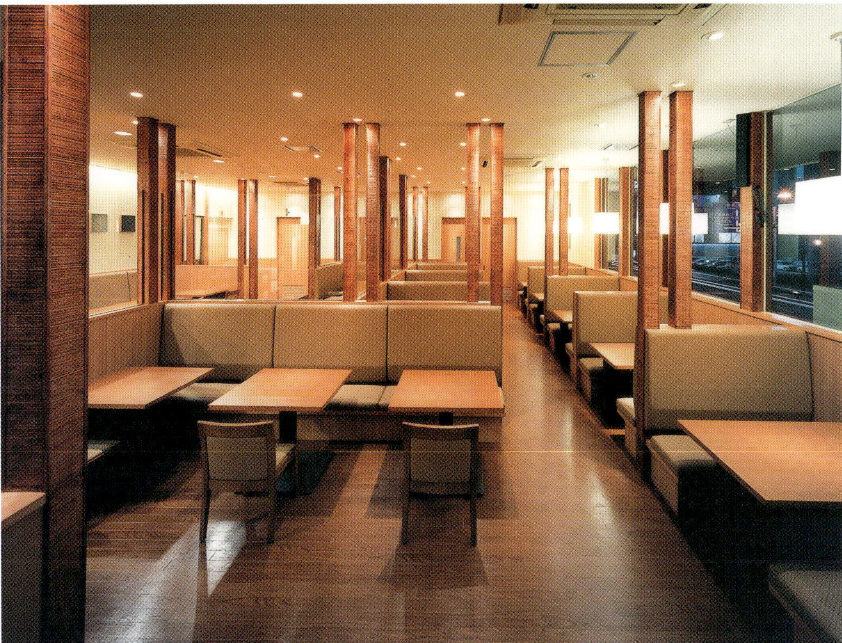

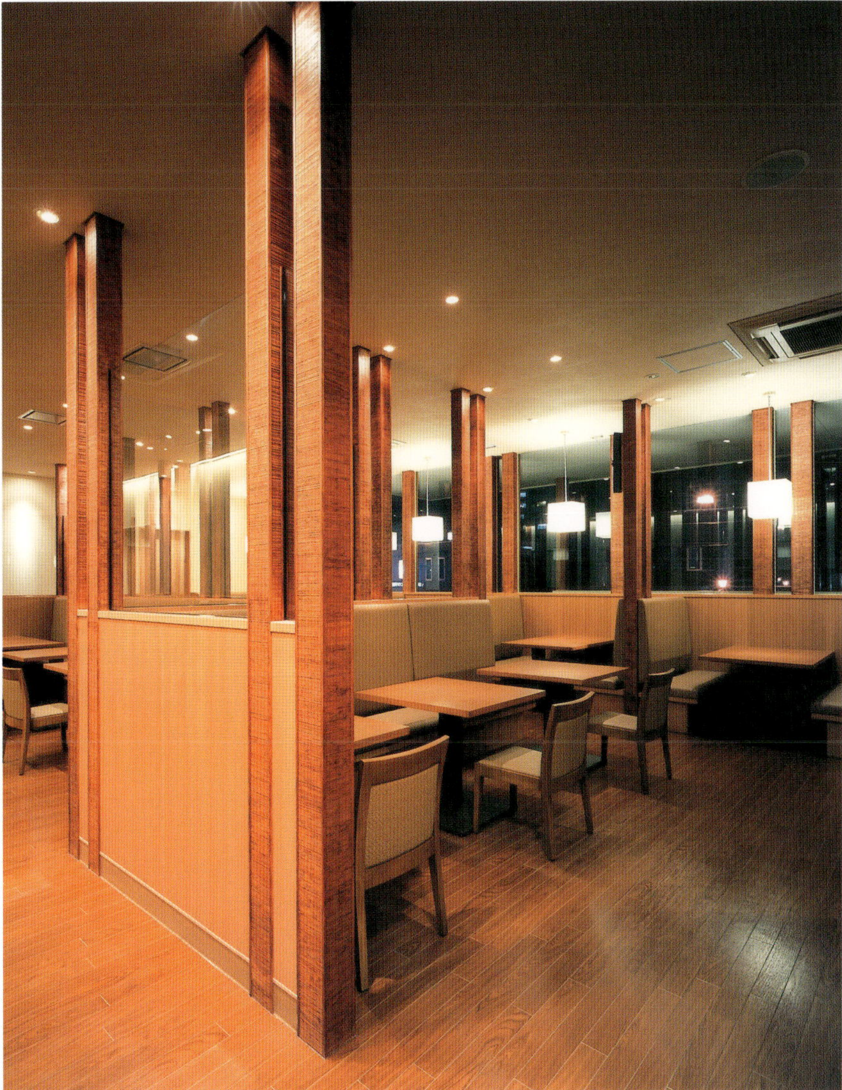

harmony

brightness

感　素材　sense　of material

華やかさ　mind　inquiring

space for the grown ups

アイデンティティー　大人の空間

バランス　探　究心　identity

時代と　革新

tradition and

共有　common　space

balance　時代　ハーモニー　性

innovation

する空間

sense of times

素材感

sense material

brightness

アイデンティティー

identity

感

時代

inquiring mind

華やかさ

時代 と革新 共有する

空間 間

時代性

sense of

探究

ハーモニー

バランス 心

harmony balance

common space

tradition and innovation

RESTAURANT

HARDEN TIGHTEN
AZABUJYUBAN , TOKYO 2006

伝統と革新

大都会の持つ華やかな煌めきと、人の温かみを感じる下町が交差するこの街に、エッジの効いた人たち
だけではなく、地元の人たちに日常的に使われ、愛されるようなお店を目指しました。

　そのために、この立地が欲するニーズも踏まえて、「伝統と革新」を空間コンセプトに、チャイニーズ
モチーフを大切に守りながら、目的とする様々なシーンに溶け込むようなデザインを心掛けています。

　自分のための時間を創り出し、その時間を存分に楽しむ大人たちが集う空間の一つのカタチです。

Tradition and Innovation

This is a neighborhood where the color and sparkle of a great city and the human warmth of a downtown area overlap, and we aimed here to create a spot which would not only be used by those at the forefront, but which would also be used and loved by locals on a daily basis.

For this purpose, based on the requirements of this location, with the spatial concepts of tradition and innovation and while carefully maintaining a Chinese motif, the design aims at the objective of blending-in a wide variety of ambiences.

This is one incarnation of a space where grownups gather who are capable of making time for themselves and enjoying it.

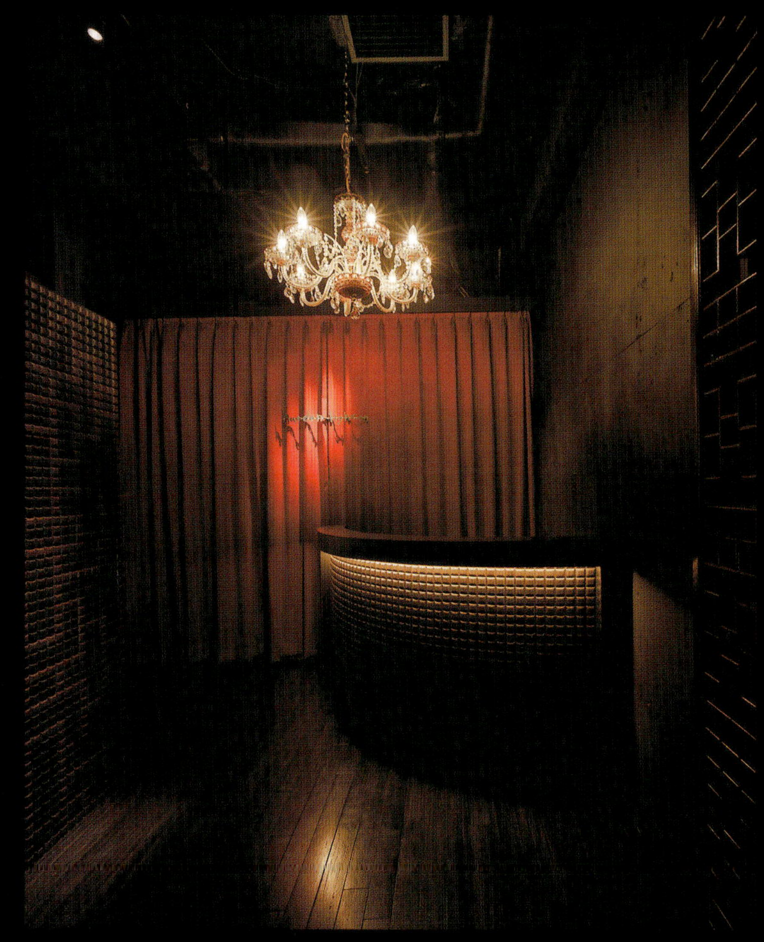

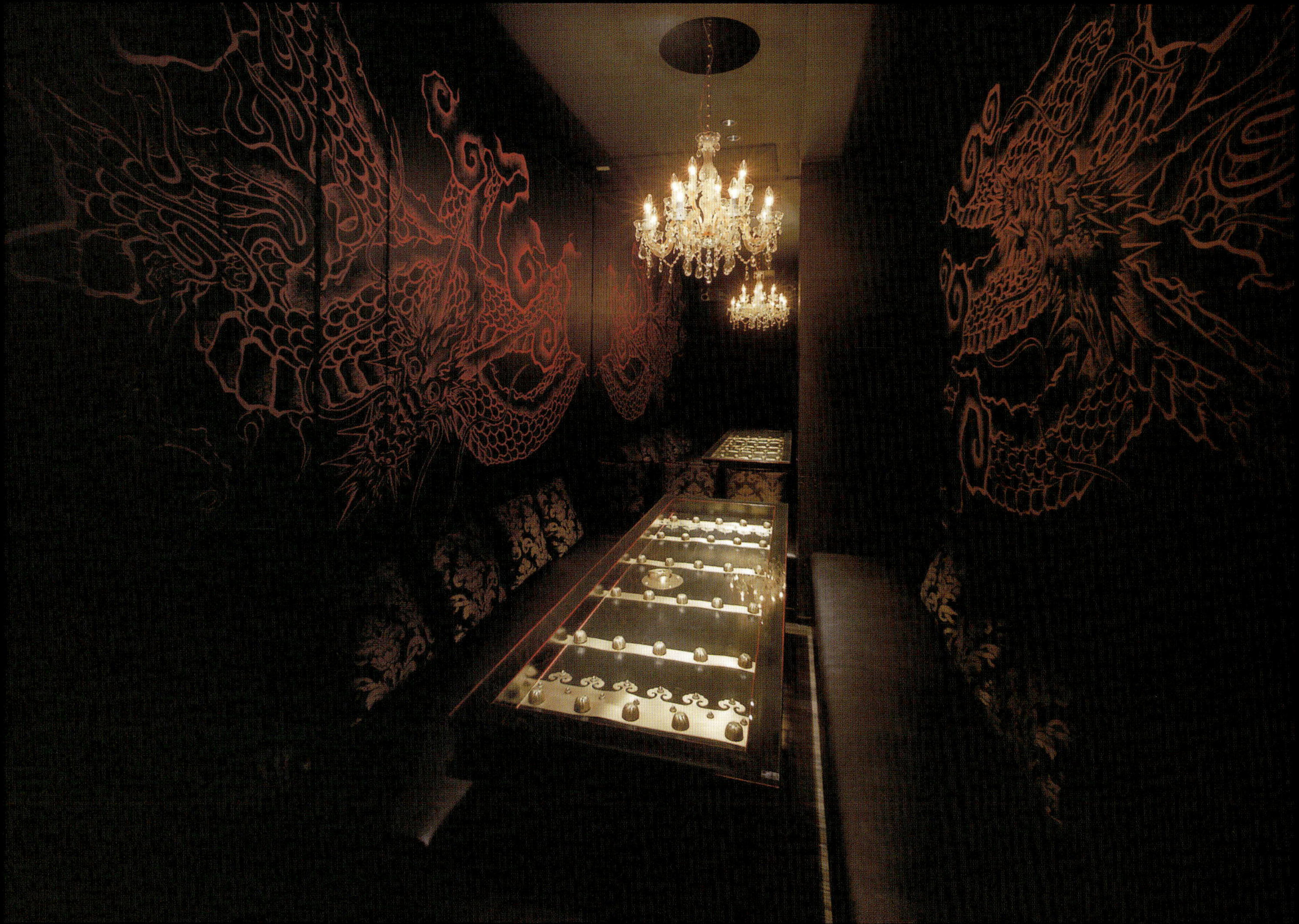

伝統と革新

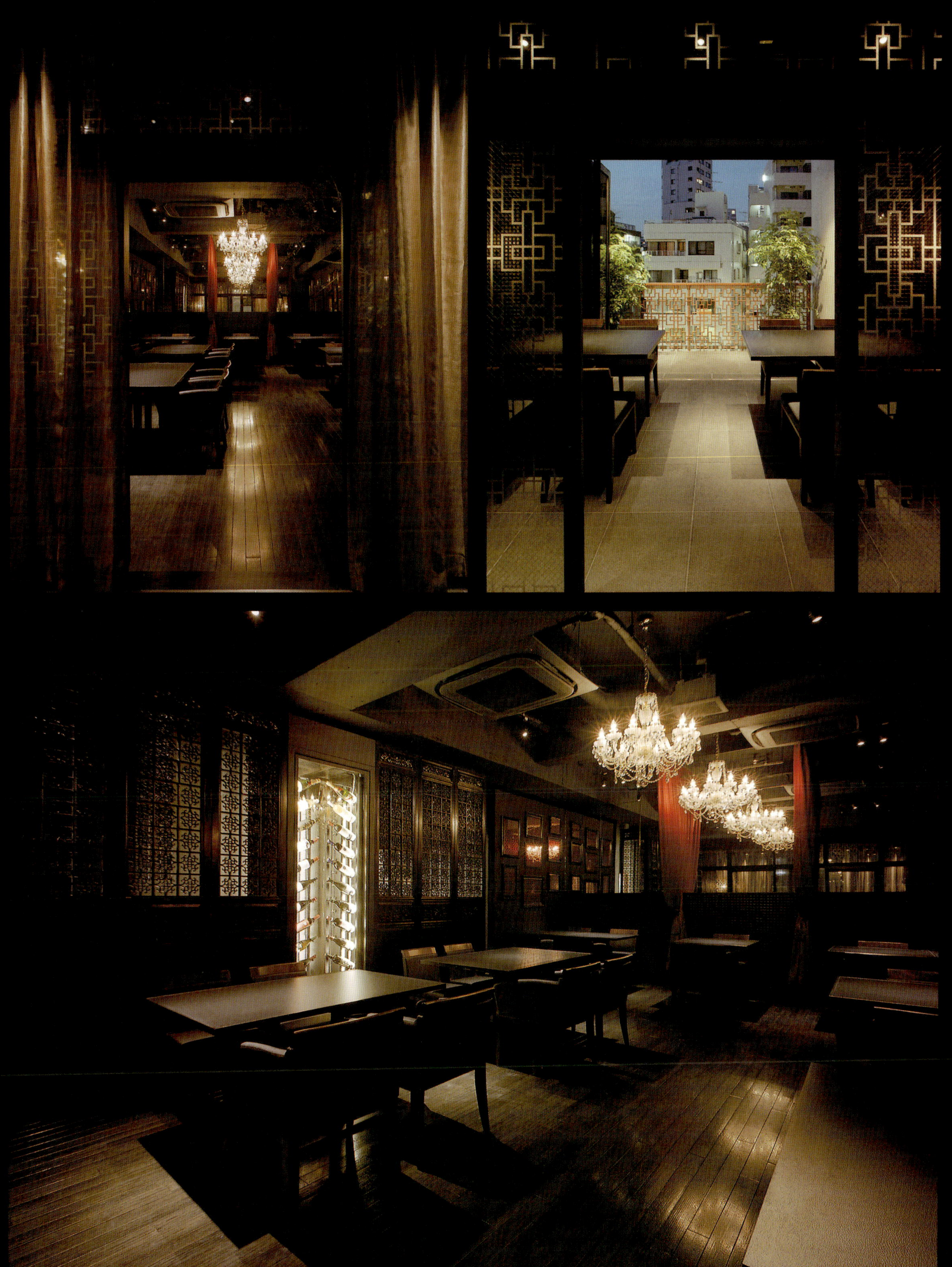

BON SOLEIL
KITASHINCHI , OSAKA 2004

鉄に新たな命を吹き込む

様々な人が行き交う街、大阪、北新地。この街で南仏料理をベースにし、訪れる人々のシーンや食に対する、多様な欲求を満たすために"BON SOLEIL"は計画されました。

　かつて、ホテルで腕を振るったオーナーシェフがつくり出す料理は、南仏料理ならではの素材を生かしきる、家庭的で素朴な味がウリです。そんな"BON SOLEIL"のデザインでは、ここで出される料理をヒントにして、空間を構成するマテリアルの「力」を存分に引き出すよう心掛けました。例えば、厚い鉄板から切り落とされた、不要部分の「くず鉄」を集めて、コラージュしたパーテーションなど。素材の特性と魅力を最大限に生かす空間は、"BON SOLEIL"の料理と共に、やさしく心地よい時間を用意して、訪れる人を招き入れます。

Breathing New Life into Steel

A city bustling with people-Osaka's Kita Shinchi-and in this city, based on the cuisine of southern France, BON SOLEIL was planned to satisfy a wide range of guest desires for ambience and food.

For the food created by the owner-chef, who formerly honed his skills to the utmost in a hotel kitchen, the sales point is the feel of home-cooking and simple flavors, with full use made of ingredients particular to the cuisine of southern France.

At BON SOLEIL, taking off from the kind of cuisine served here, the design aims at bringing out the strengths of the materials used in constructing the space. For example, thick steel plate is sheared off, and the left-over scraps are assembled into collages on the partitions. A space that brings out the special qualities and charm of the materials to the fullest extent, BON SOLEIL beckons to visitors with its food and promise of a gentle and pleasant interlude.

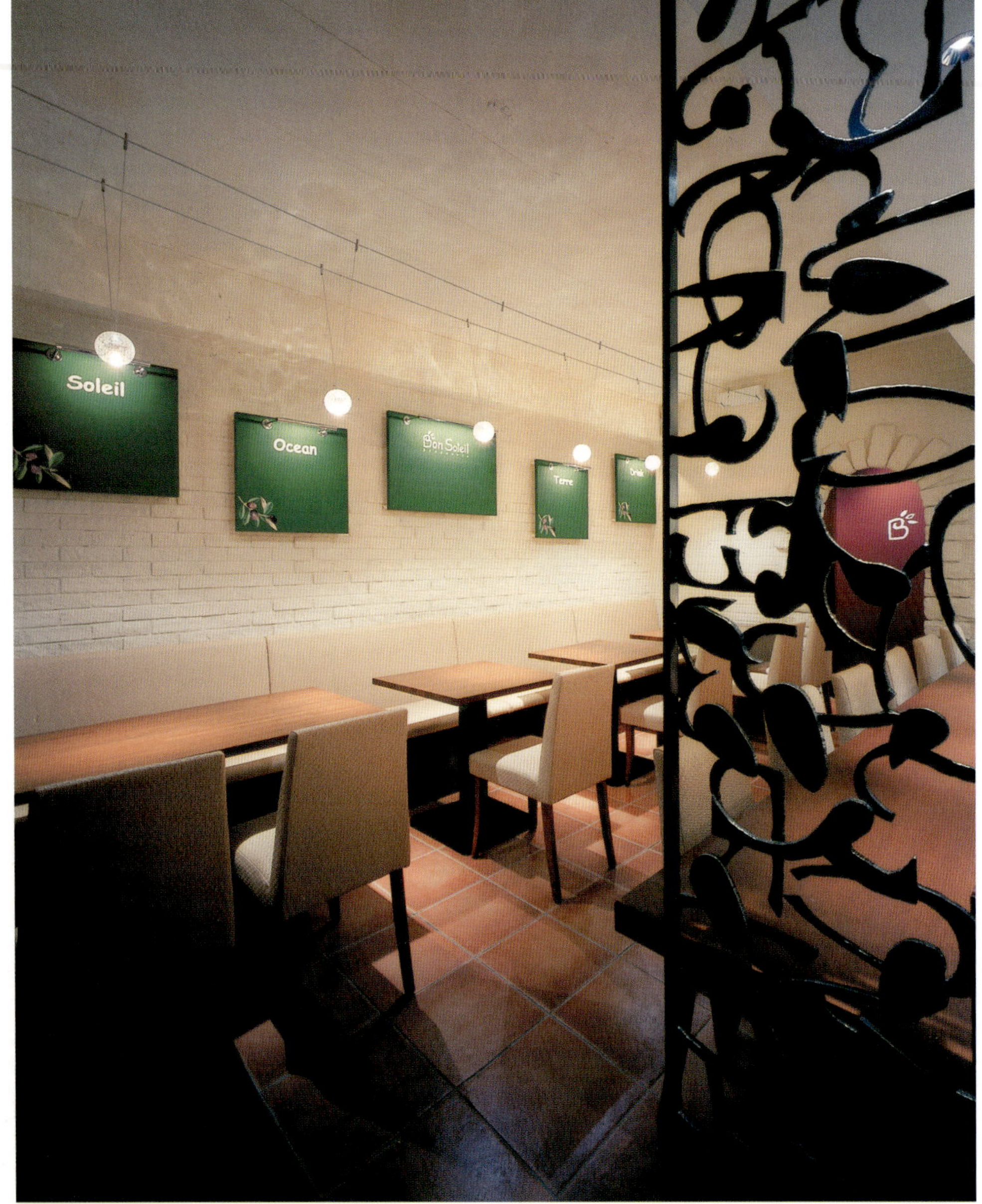

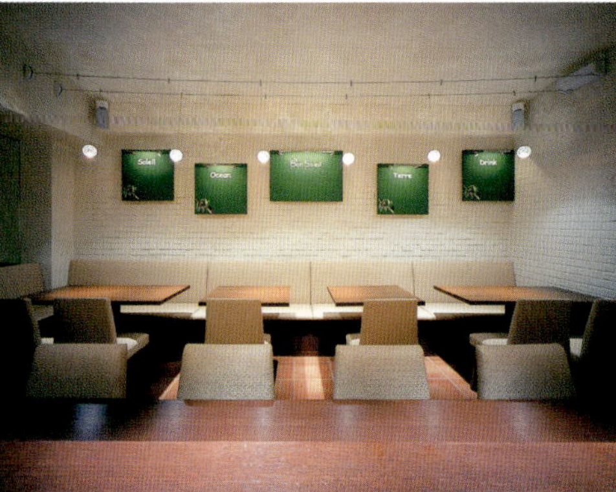

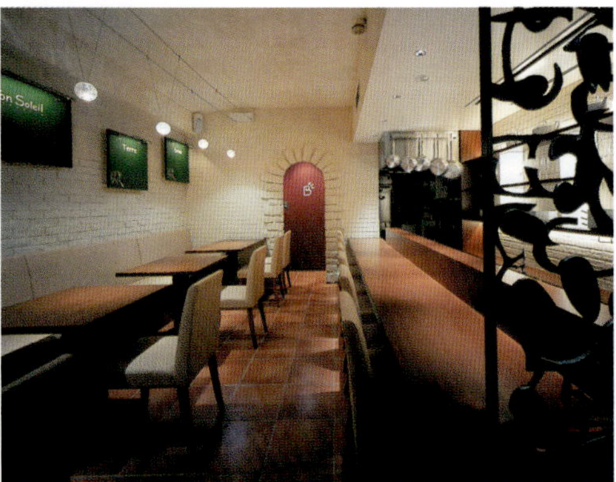

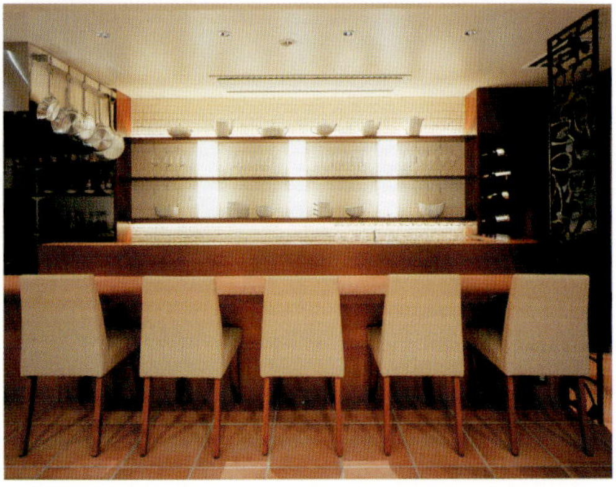

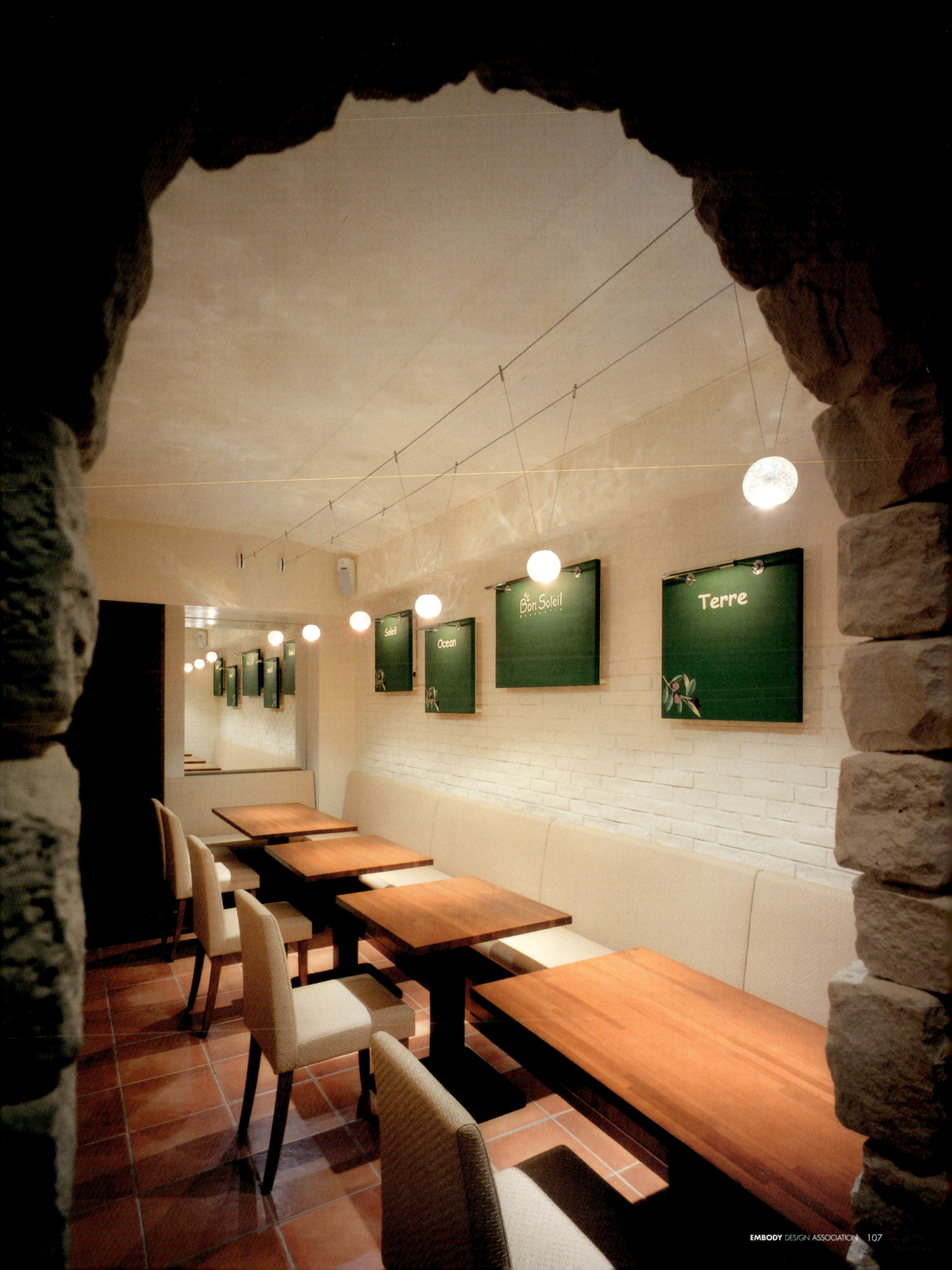
Bon Soleil
Terre
Ocean
Soleil

LA CENA
KITASHINCHI , OSAKA 2002

真心と美味しいワイン

"LA CENA"はきめ細かい心遣いで、丹念につくり出される一串一串と、それに相性の良い厳選されたワインで、心ゆくまで食を楽しんで欲しいというオーナーの思いから生まれました。

そのため、「もてなしの心、和の精神」と、「洋の味の伝統」を有機的に結び付けることのできる空間デザインを目指しました。主役である串の揚げ場を中心に、カウンター席を配置することで、お客様は次に出てくる串への期待感をふくらまし、シェフは食の進み具合をカウンターの端から端まで常に感じ取ることが出来ます。また、ワインに似合う、やわらかな曲線を用いたアイアンワークで空間を緩やかに仕切って、食の空間への歓迎の意を込めています。

Wine of Honesty and Fine Flavor

LA CENA was born out of the owner's desire to have guests enjoy dining to the fullest--with intricately detailed kebabs created in total meticulousness together with strictly-chosen wines of perfect compatibility.

For this purpose, the design aims at creating a space where the "Japanese spirit of hospitality" can be brought together organically with the "Western taste tradition." Centering on the kebab grill, the counter seats are arranged so that customer anticipation builds for the next kebab to be served, and meanwhile the chef is able to gauge at all times the progress of the meal--from one end of the counter to the other. With the delicately curving lines of ironwork as a divider, it's a dining space filled with a welcoming spirit.

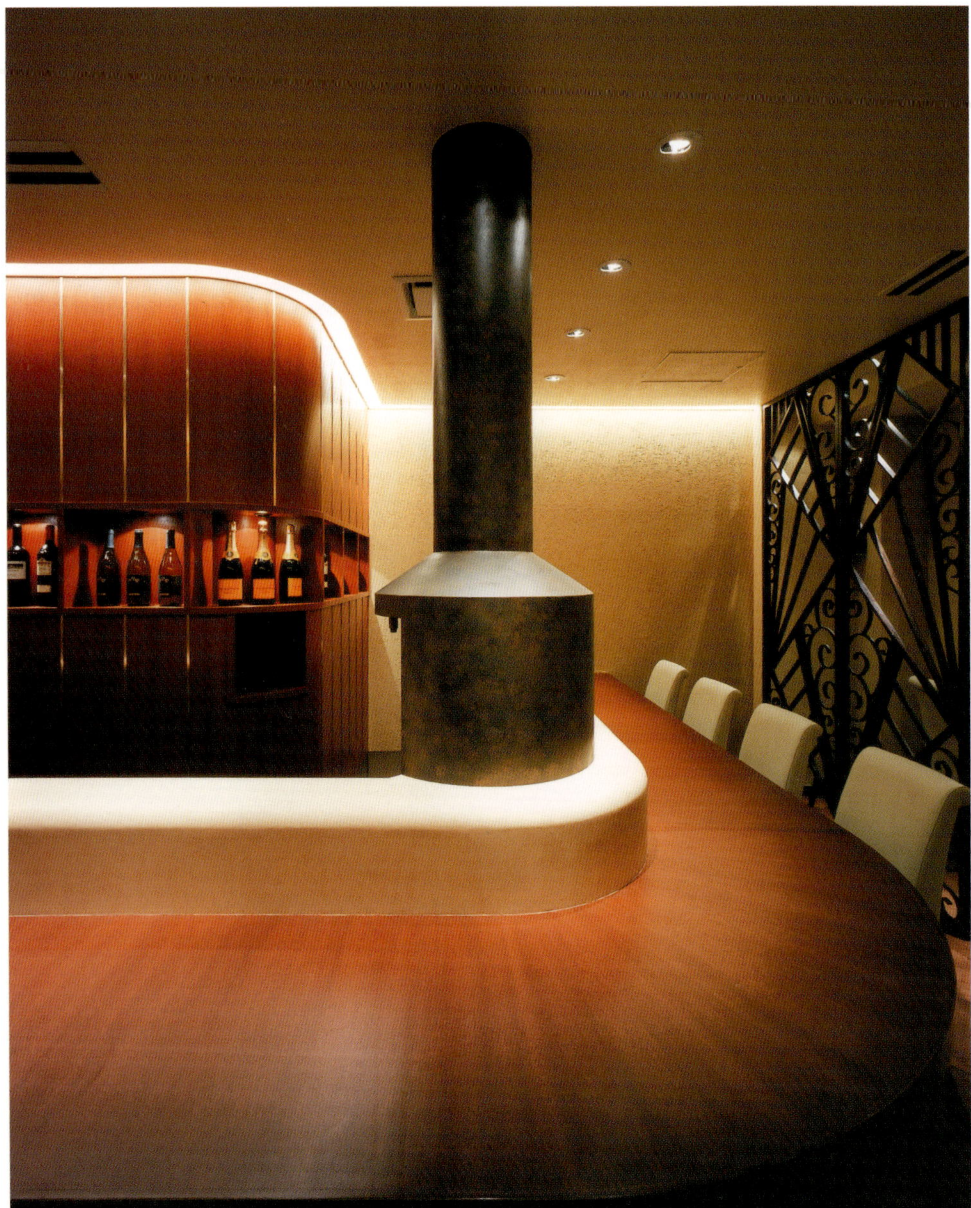
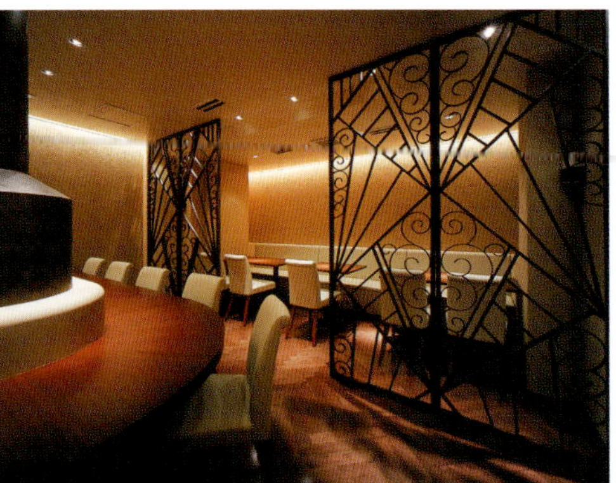
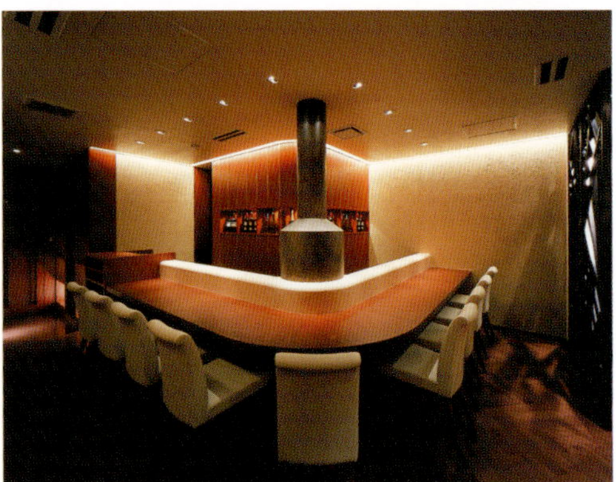
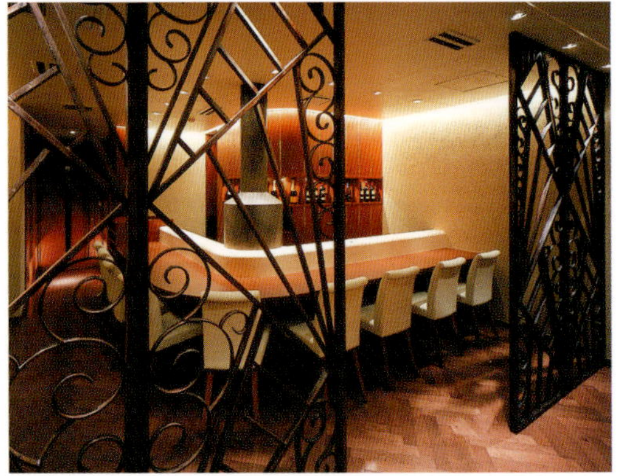

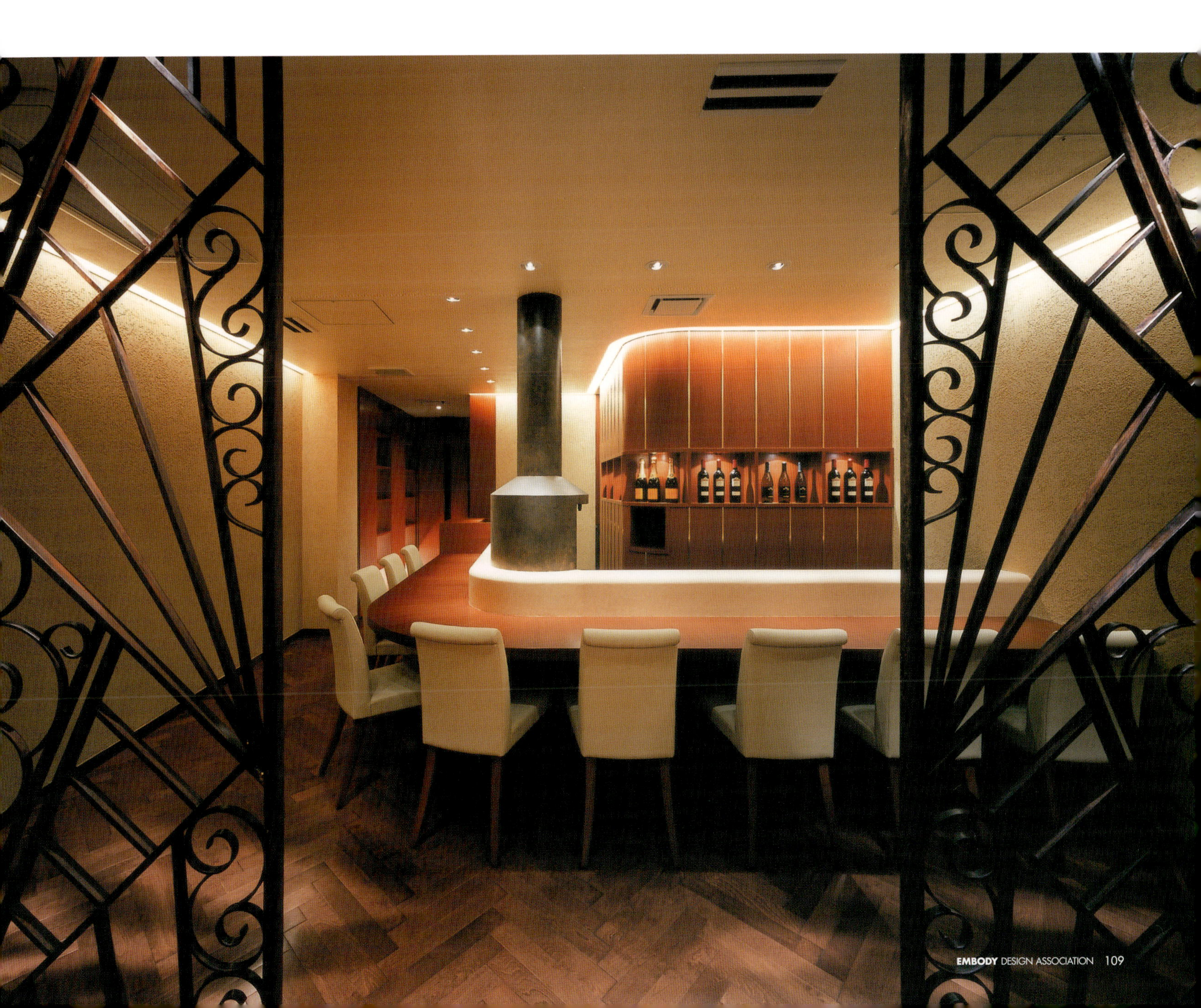

FORTUNE COOKIES
KITASHINCHI , OSAKA 2000

からだとこころにおいしい空間

大阪の北新地は料亭や高級クラブが立ち並ぶ、大人の街でしたが、地下鉄が開通したこともあり、自分の財布で飲み食いをする仕事帰りの若者の姿も多く見かけられるようになりました。

　そんな彼らを奇をてらわず、迎えるのは、立ち上がる湯気と食欲をそそる香り、目を楽しませる新鮮な食材、そして中華鍋の力強く活気ある音や、素材を活かした味付け、備長炭で焼き上げた香ばしさ。ここには「こころとからだを満たす食を楽しむ空間」があります。

　"FORTUNE COOKIES"は医食同源・五味五性という中国の知恵を生かしてつくり出される、からだにおいしい料理を、心地よい空間でゆったり味わってもらう、今までの北新地にはなかった、こころにもおいしい店です。

A place that satisfies both heart and body

Osaka's Kitashinchi, lined with traditional high-class Japanese dining establishments and classy clubs, was a place for mature adult entertainment, but the opening of a subway has also brought with it a large number of younger people, each with their own wallet, seeking food and drink on their way home from work.

They are warmly greeted by rising steam and aromas to excite the appetite, beautiful fresh ingredients, the powerful and vigorous sounds of Chinese woks, well seasoned food, the savory smell of charcoal grills... This is a place that fulfills both heart and body, a place for enjoying food.

The cuisine on offer follows the traditional Chinese wisdom that food and medicine share a common origin, and utilizes the distinct characteristics of each of the five elemental flavors of Chinese cooking. A unique type of establishment thus far not seen in Kitashinchi, FORTURNE COOKIES allows patrons to enjoy tasty food that satisfies the physical body in a leisurely and comfortable atmosphere, and also provides spiritual satisfaction for the heart.

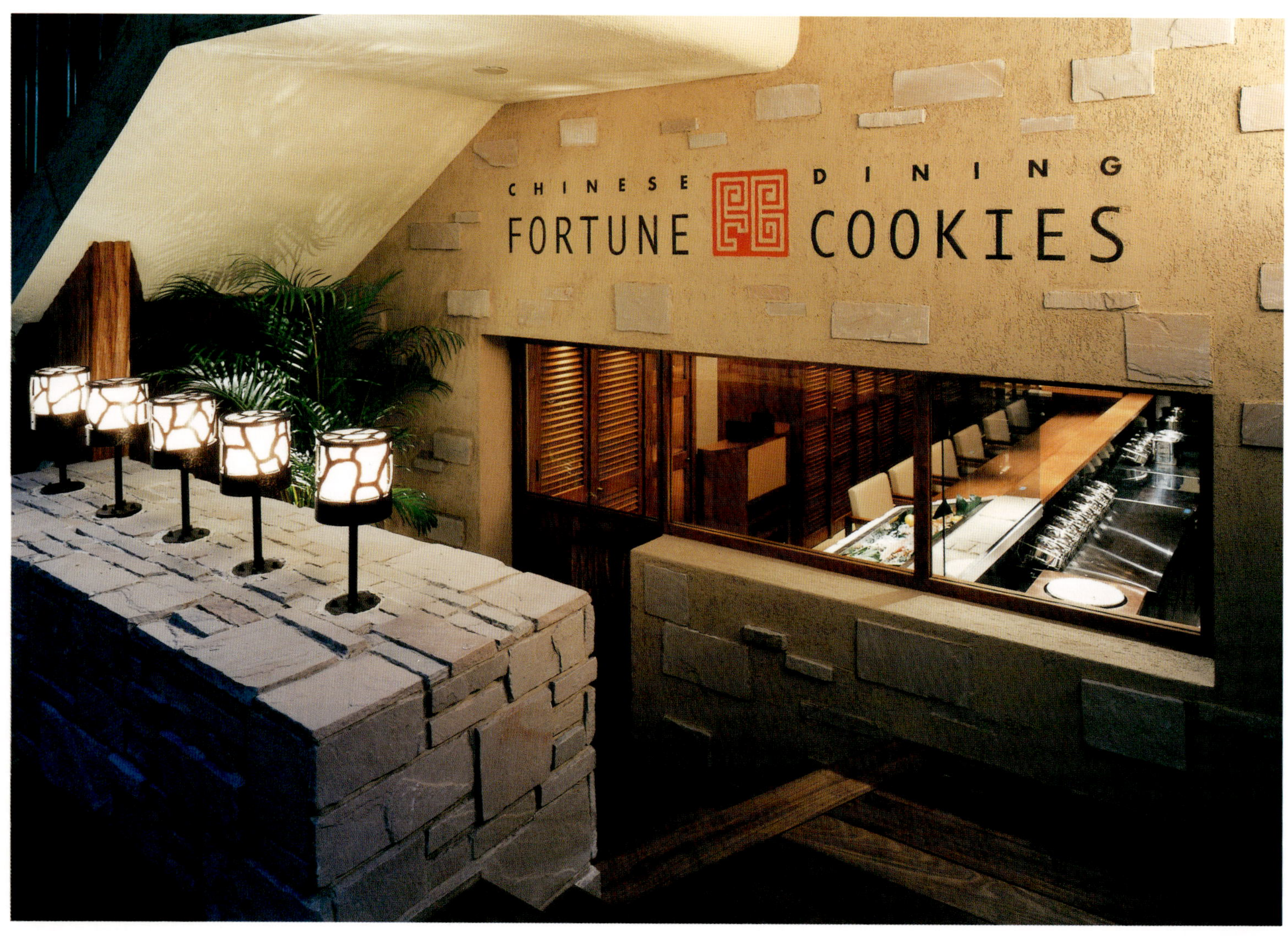

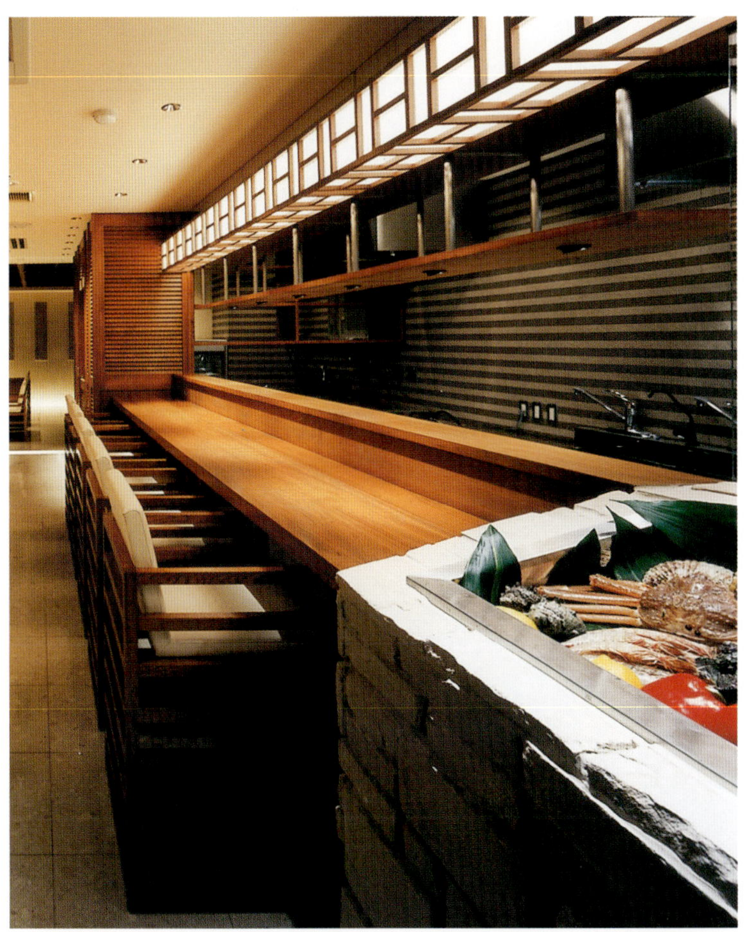
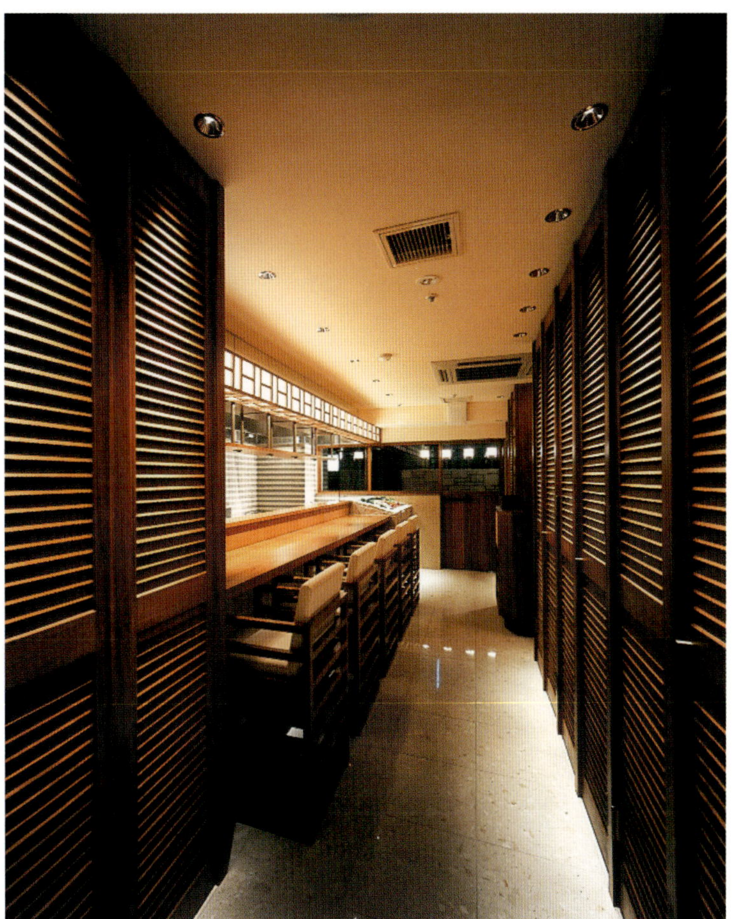

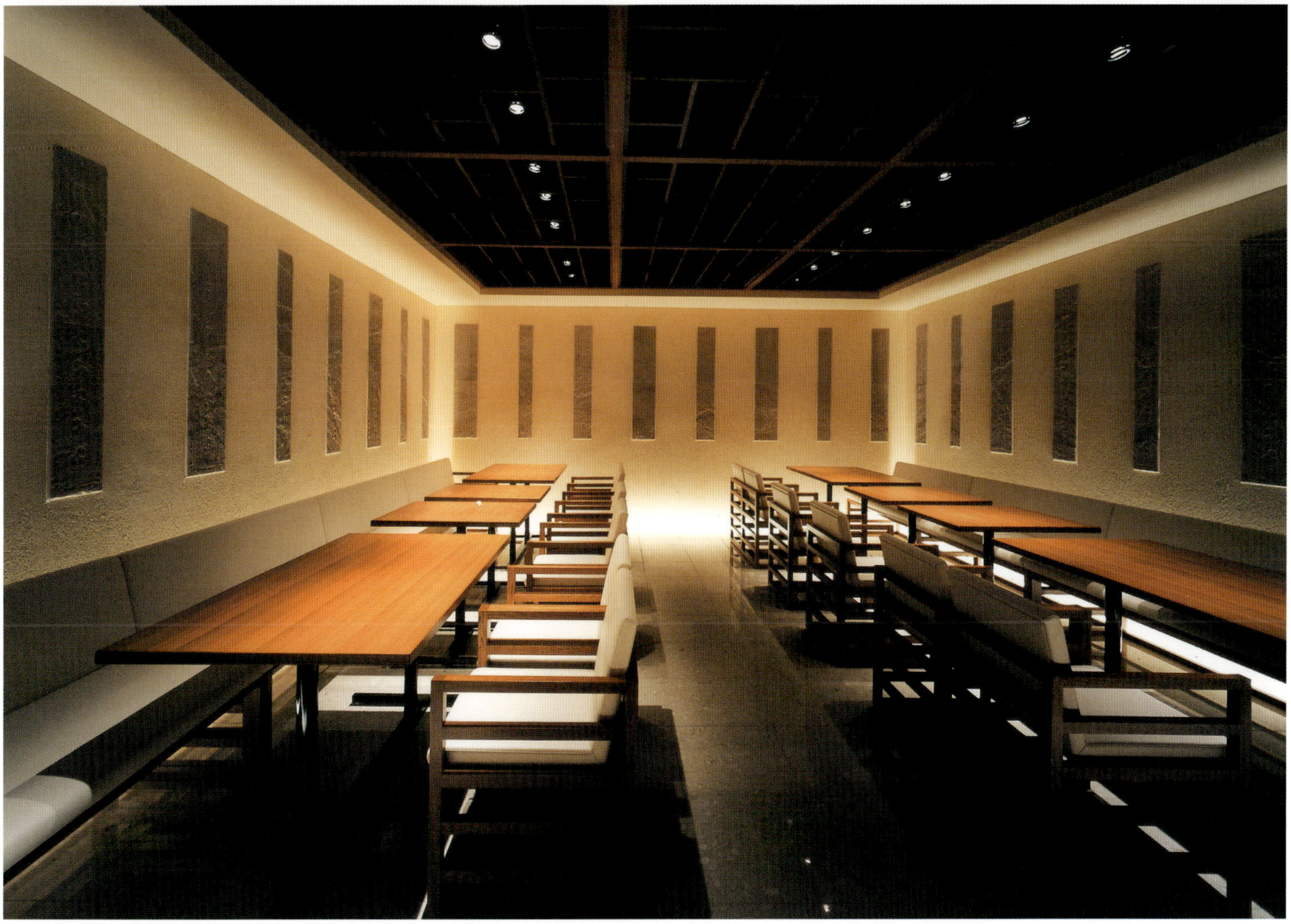

暮らしの中のワイン

ワインが日本人の日常の暮らしの中に入り込み始めた頃、「ワインとお箸」をコンセプトに、訪れる人の日常に溶け込むことのできる、自然体で落ち着きのある食空間を目指してデザインしたのが"AVRIL SIX"です。

　食する場として、ここ"AVRIL SIX"に流れる「時」を味わい、「食」を楽しみ、訪れた人が空間を着こなすことが出来るよう、奇をてらわず気軽に立ち寄れる、飽きのこないデザインを具現化できたと思います。

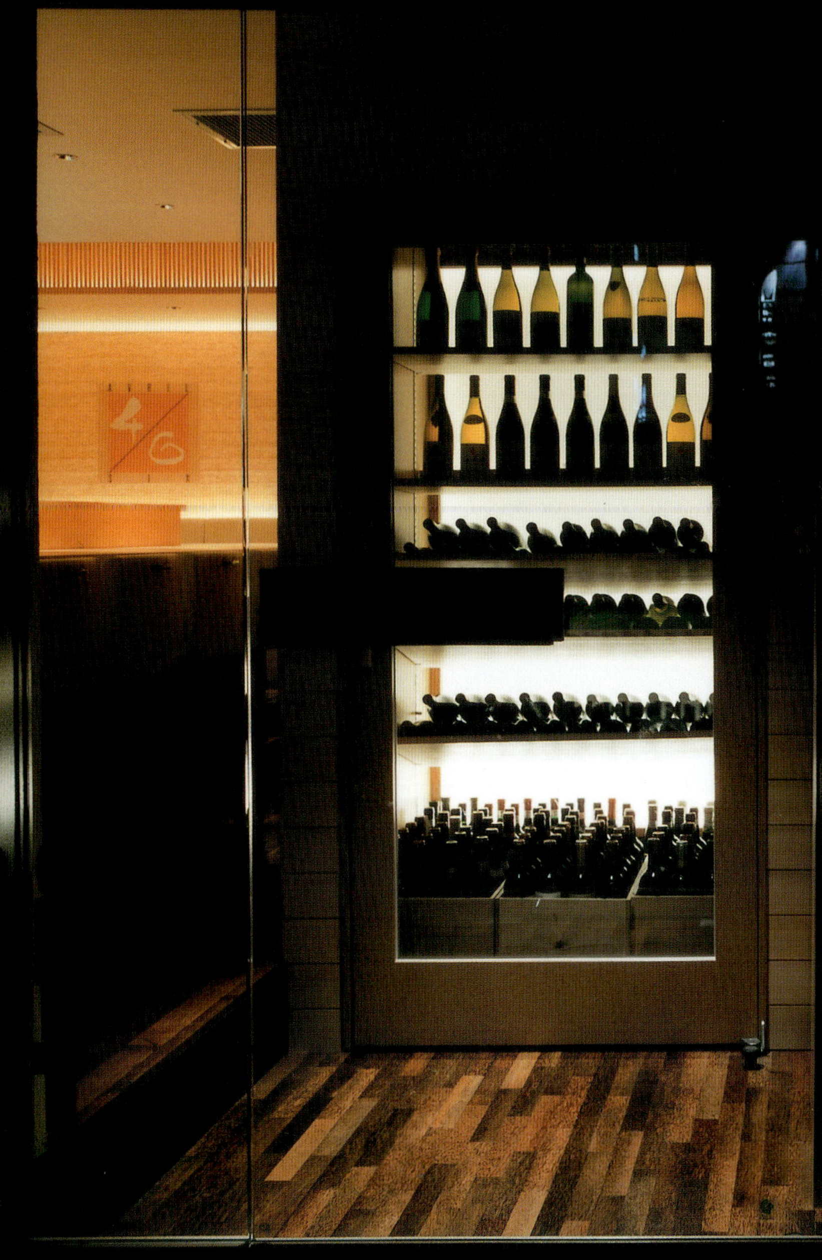

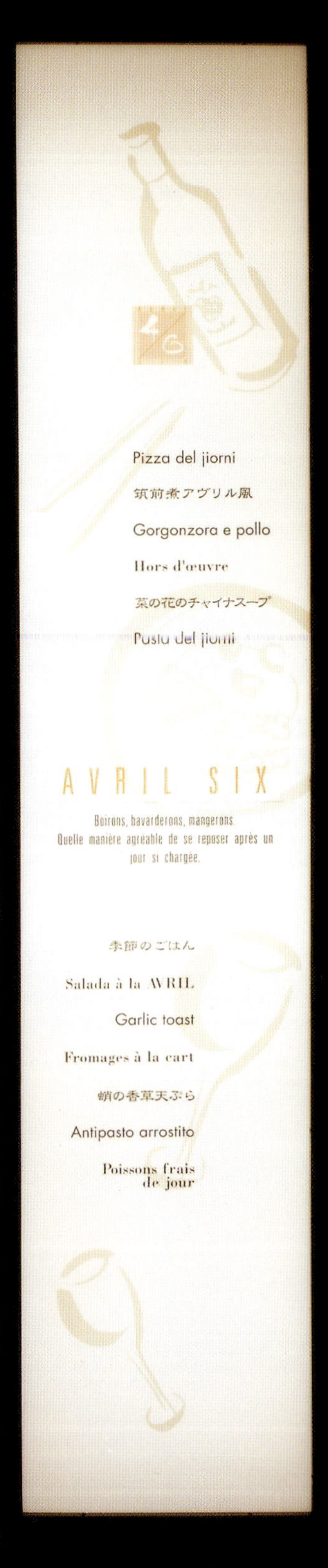

Wine in Daily Life

When wine first began to enter the Japanese lifestyle, it was able blend into the everyday life of the visitor under the concept of "wine and chopsticks." AVRIL SIX was designed aiming at being a natural dining space with a relaxing feeling capable of blending into the visitor's everyday life.

　In this design, rather than something eccentric, we believe that we were able to embody something that never becomes tiresome to visitors and that allows them to casually drop in-a space where they can fit in perfectly, to savor the moment and enjoy the food, AVRIL SIX.

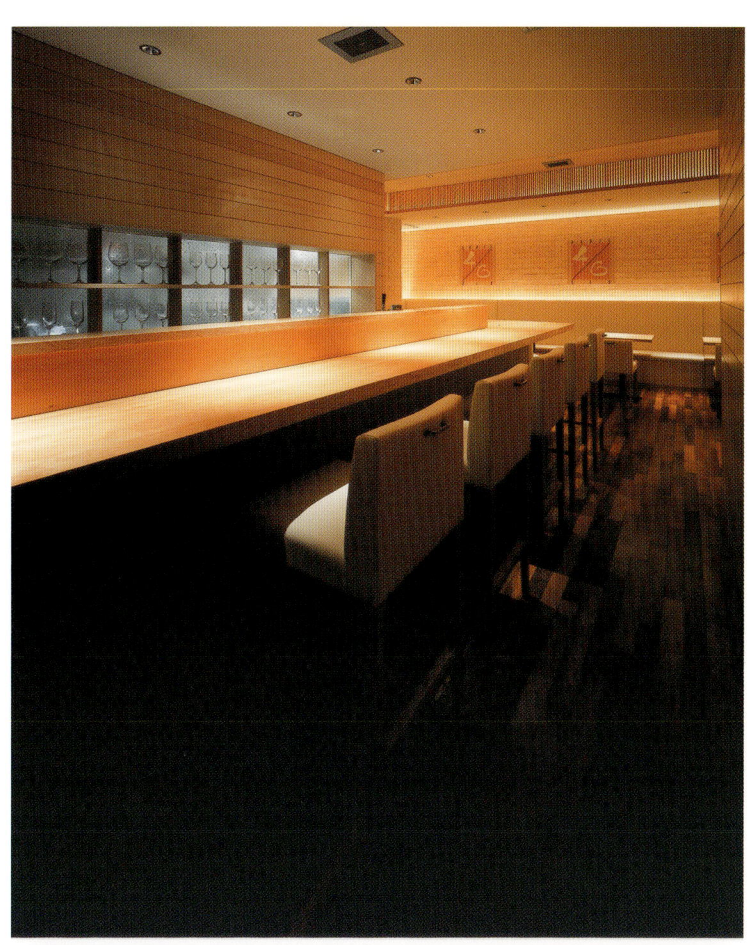

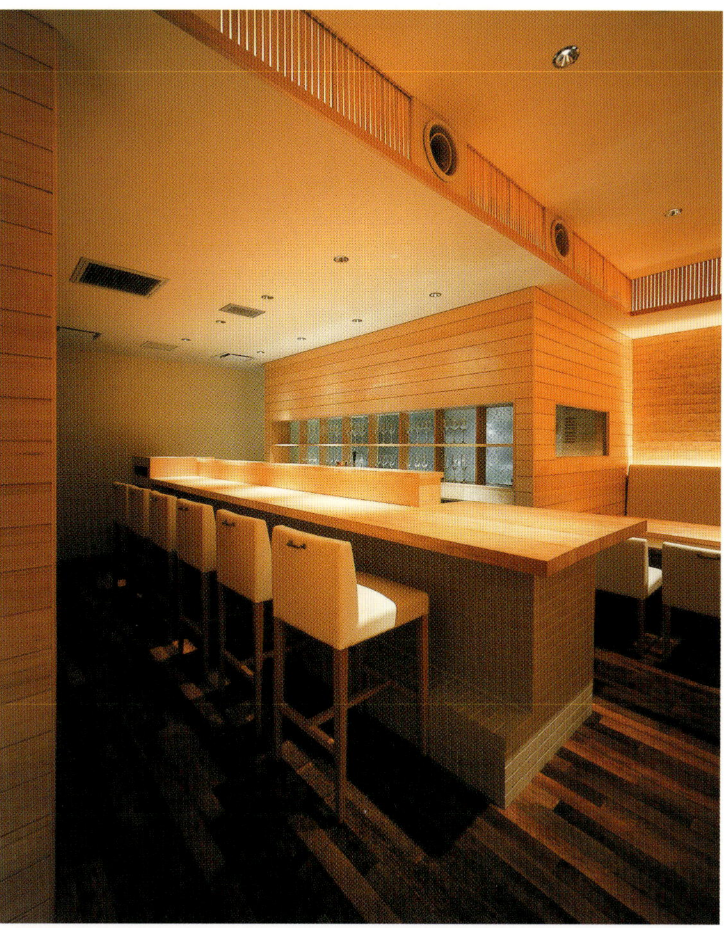

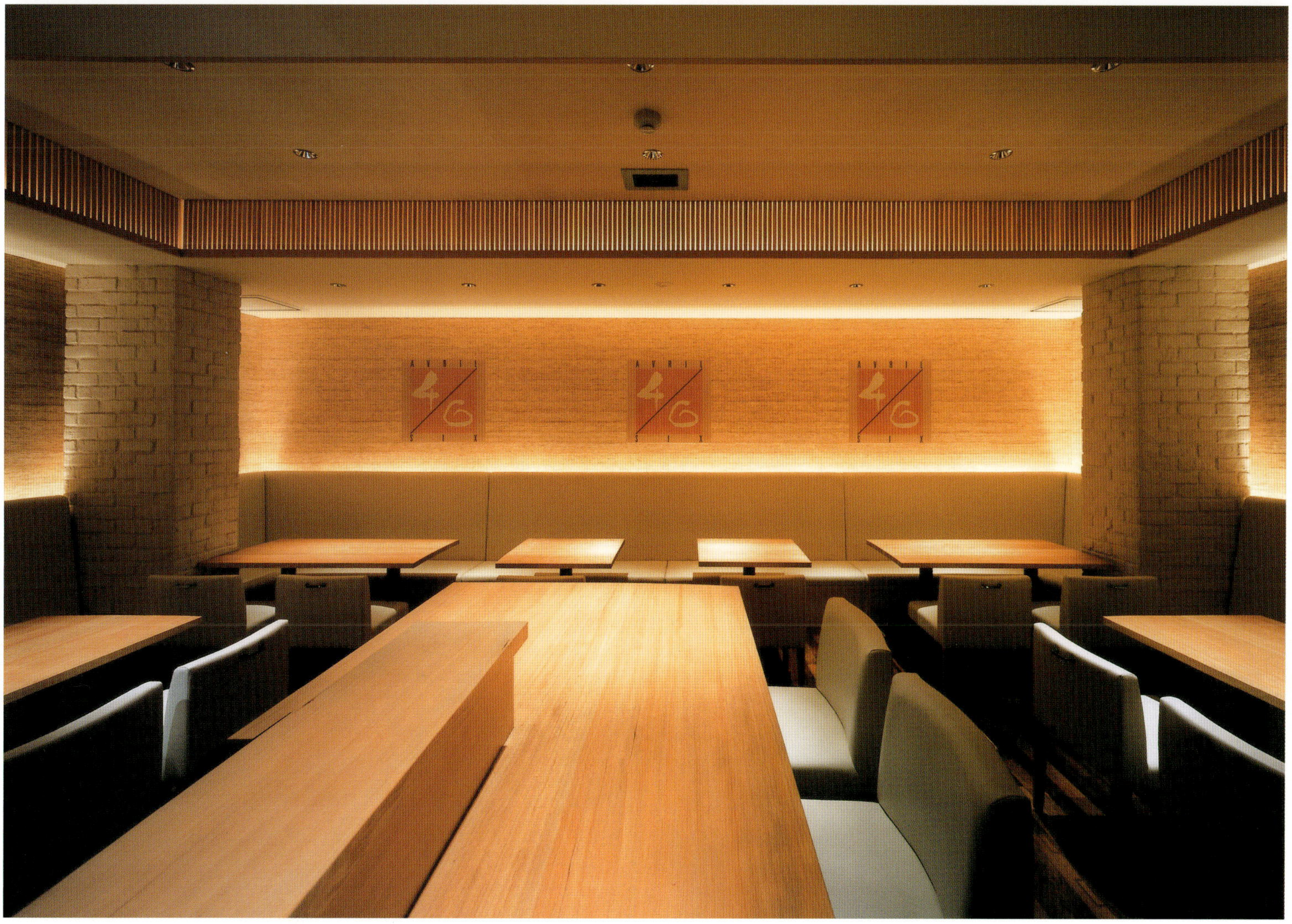

IRORIYA neyagawa
NEYAGAWA , OSAKA 1998

アジアン モダニティ

"炭火焼肉工房いろり屋 寝屋川店"は大阪と京都を結ぶ、国道18号線沿いに位置する典型的な郊外型ロードサイド店です。「もっとおいしく」をテーマに、そして「炭火」をキーワードに、名産地から届く厳選された素材を適材適所に使用した、多彩な料理を創造しています。

　食に対する探究心の結晶である料理を、どんな雰囲気の中で、おいしく食べてもらうかを考え、決して空間が邪魔しないようつとめると共に、日本料理を含めた広い意味でのアジア料理を優しく包み込む、懐の深い「アジアンモダン」の空間を具現化しました。

Asian Modernity

IRORIYA neyagawa (Charcoal Korean Bar-be-Cue Shop) is located along Rt. 18, which links Osaka and Kyoto--a typical roadside shop. With a theme of "more delicious" and with "charcoal flame" as keywords, a varied cuisine has been created using strictly-selected ingredients in the most suitable ways from famous areas of production.

Thinking about the optimum atmosphere for food, we set out to determine the most delicious ways to eat, and we strove to ensure that the space should never interfere in this. The result was an Asian Modern space, embodied with the capacity to gently encompass Asian cuisine in the broad sense--including Japanese cuisine.

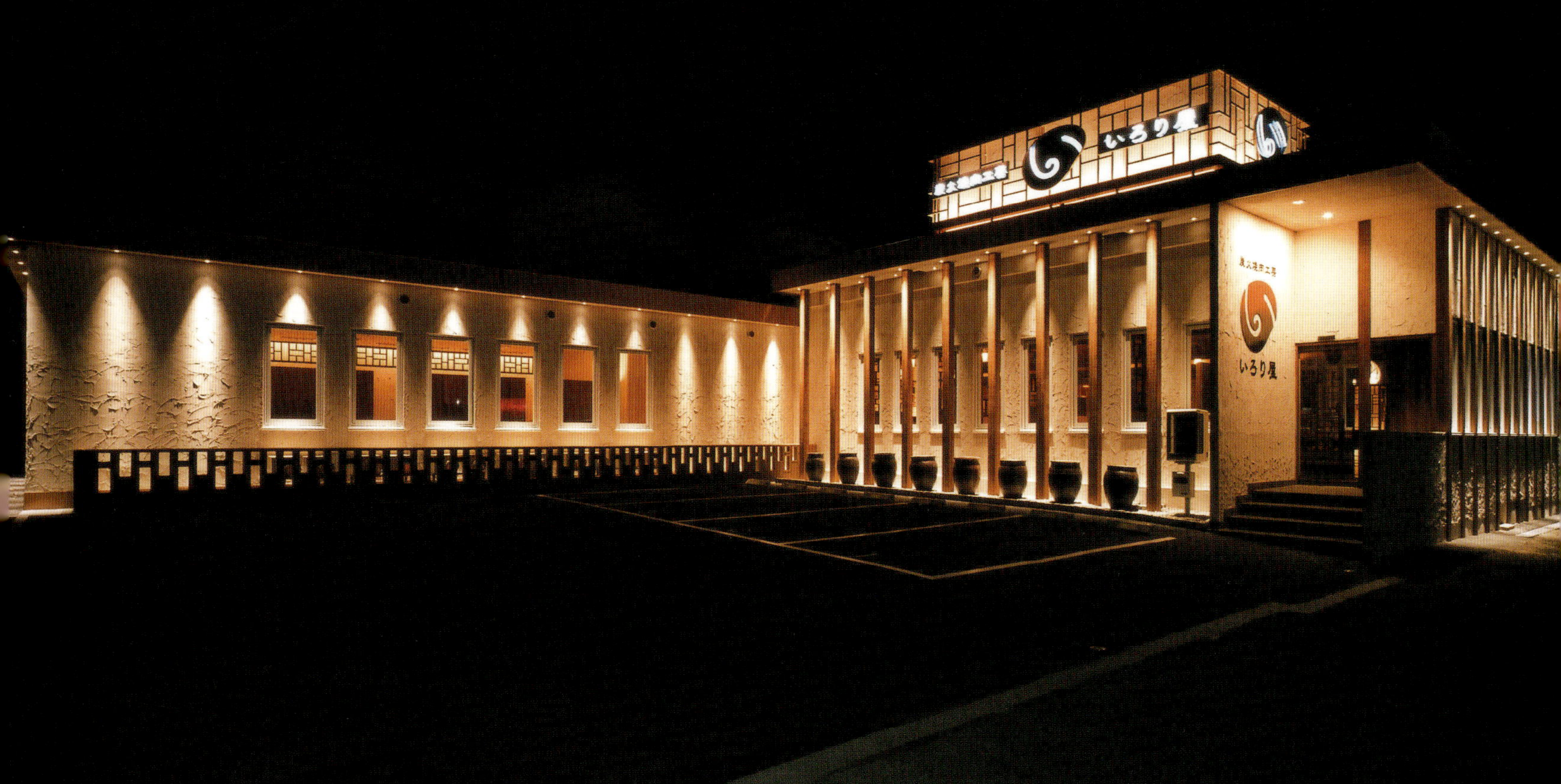

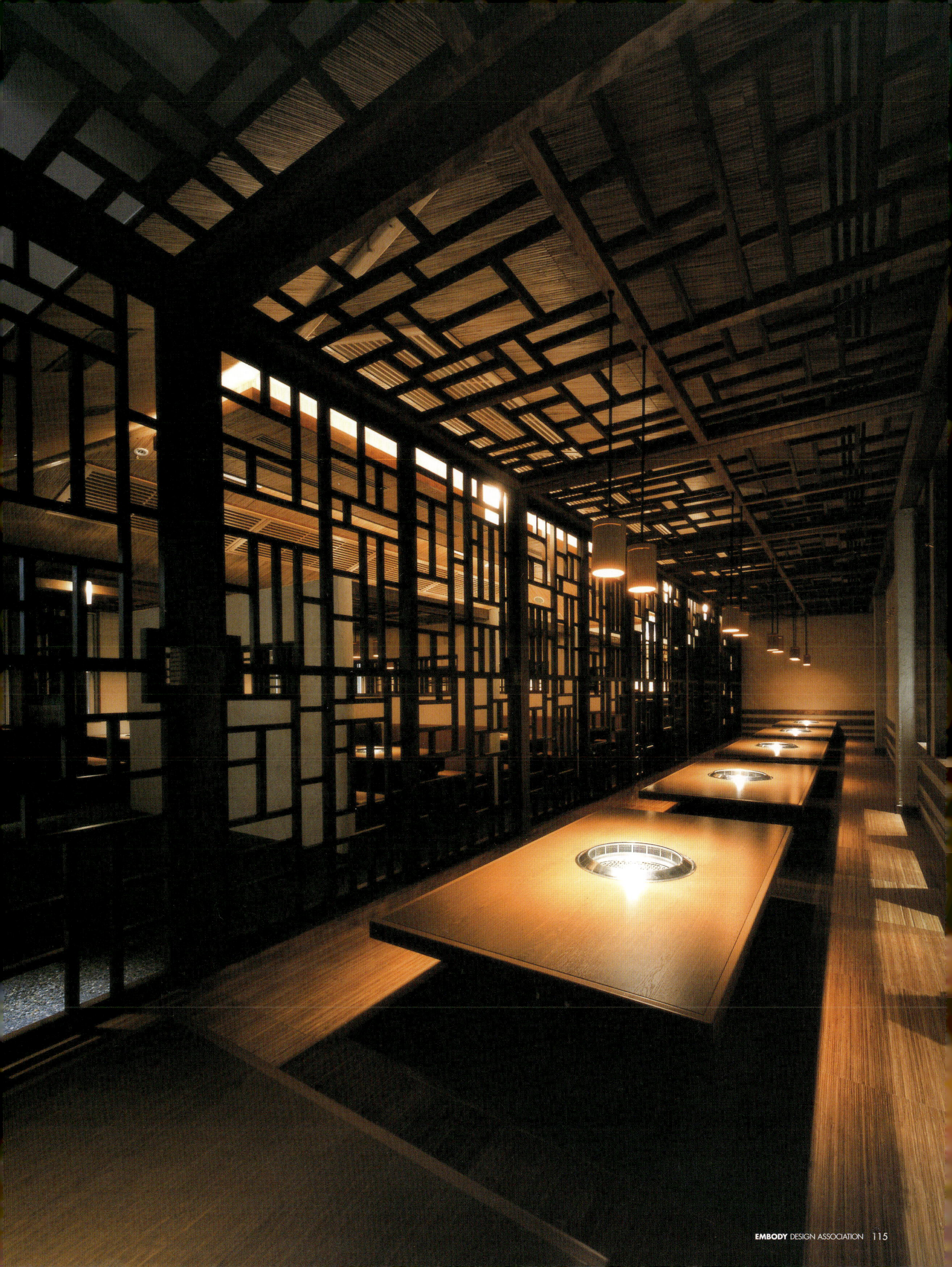

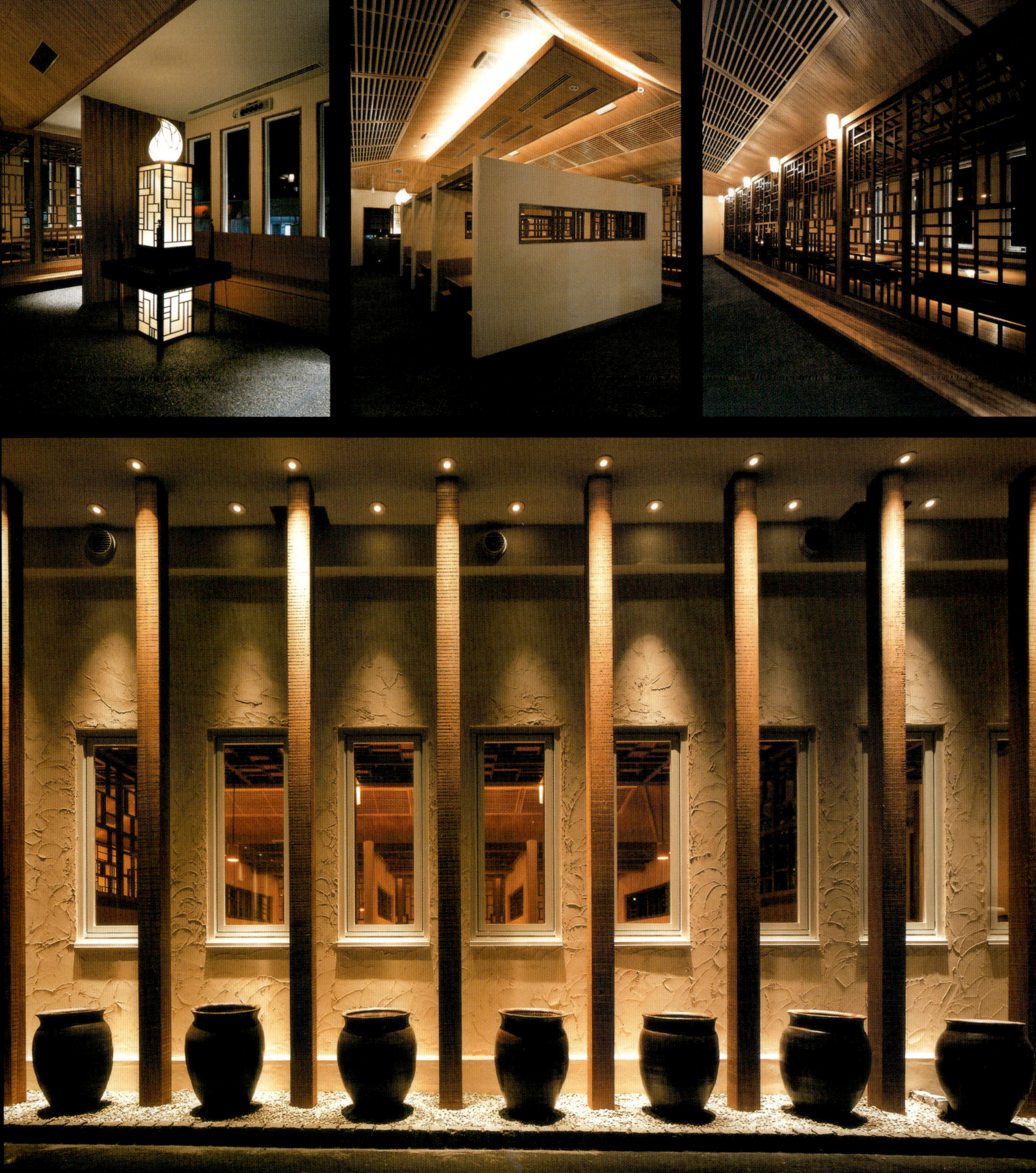

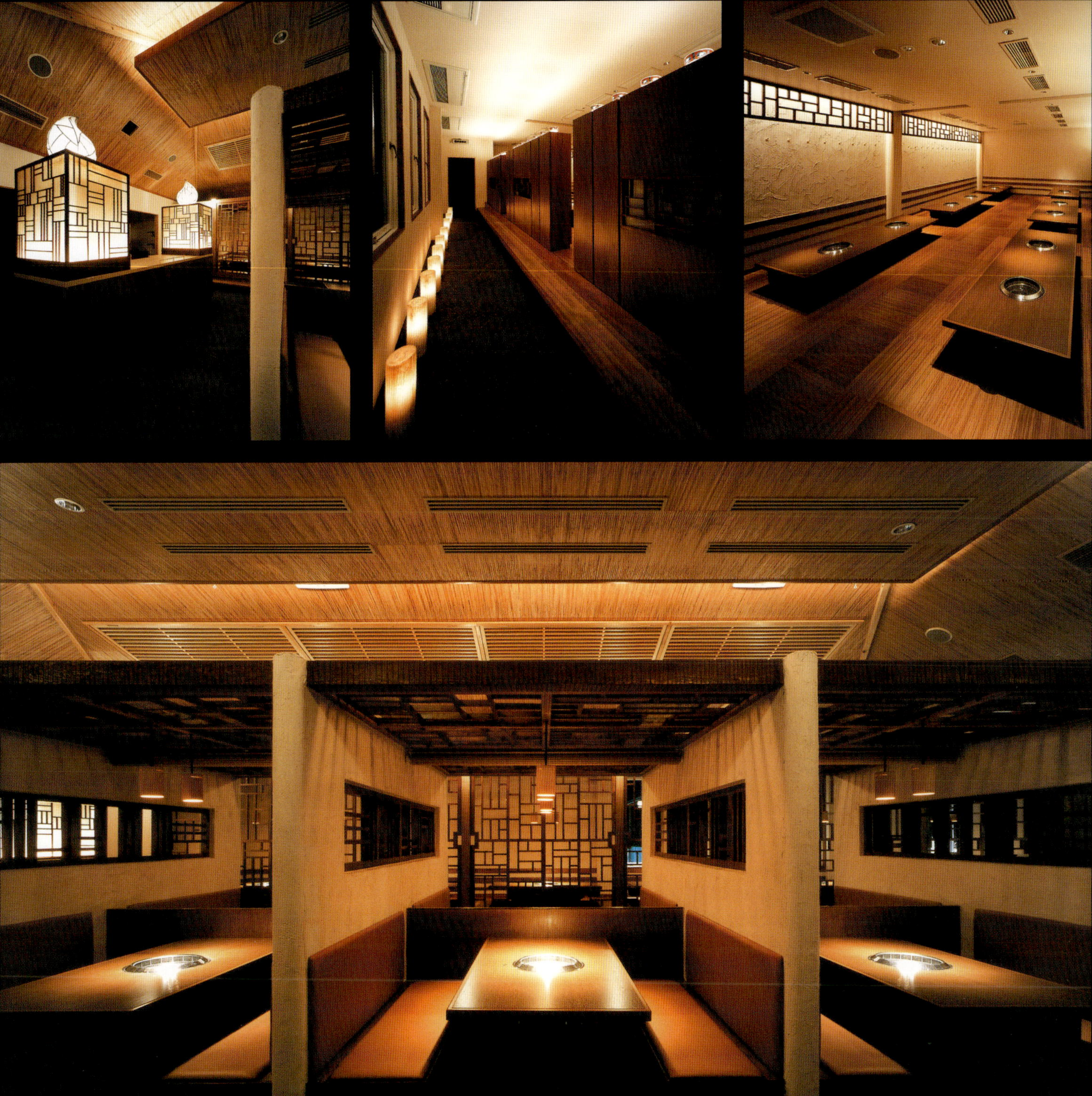

IRORIYA kadoma

KADOMA , OSAKA 1995

共有する間

"炭火焼肉工房いろり屋 門真"は大阪の古川橋に位置します。この辺りは、大手メーカーの工場が立ち並ぶ地域であり、大阪市内で働く人々のベッドタウンでもあります。また、ファミリーレストラン化された焼肉店から、名店と呼ばれる店までライバル店が多くひしめき合う地域でもあります。

　そんな地域性と時代の微妙な変化に対応し、厳選されたお肉をリーズナブルな価格で提供する回転性の高いお店、そして"いろり屋"ならではの食に対するこだわりを随所に感じられる空間を目指しました。人と人が限られた空間を「共有」しながらも食する場としての「間」を保つことのできる空間を具現化するために、人の意識だけを遮り、「間」をつくり出す簾の引き戸や、空間を「共有」しながらも、圧迫感を与えない竹の吊り天井など、日本の伝統的な素材を用いて、いろり屋のこだわりを「間」と「共有」というカタチで表現できたのではないかと思います。

Spaces to share

IRORIYA kadoma is a Japanese charcoal fired barbecue restaurant situated in Osaka's Furukawabashi. This is an area lined by the factories of large manufacturers, and is also a dormitory suburb for many people that work in Osaka city. It is also an area characterized by vigorous competition between rival restaurants, from Japanese barbecue establishments that have morphed into family restaurants, to some well renowned establishments.

Paying attention to these regional characteristics and the subtle ways in which times are changing, I aimed to create a high-turnover style restaurant that provides carefully selected barbecue meats at reasonable prices, and an atmosphere in which IRORIYA's unique philosophy with regards to food would be felt all around. In order to achieve an atmosphere in which people would share the limited space, but also one in which the room required in an eatery would be preserved, I used traditional Japanese materials, such as sliding bamboo screens that create spaces and make people less conscious of those around them, and a suspended bamboo ceiling that dispels any oppressive, closed in sort of sensation. I think that I have expressed IRORIYA's unique dining philosophy through the main themes of spaces and sharing.

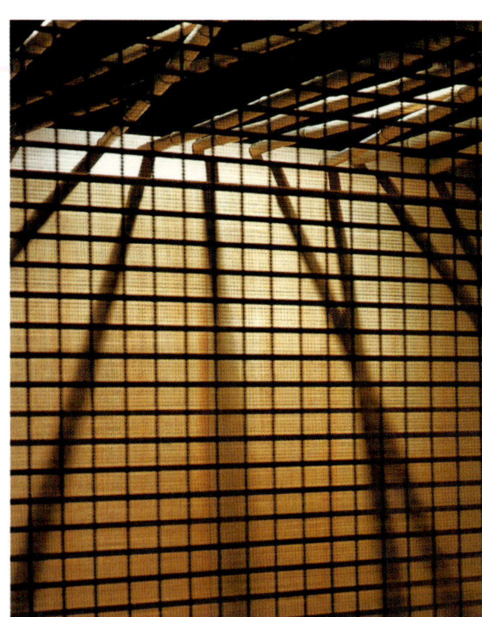

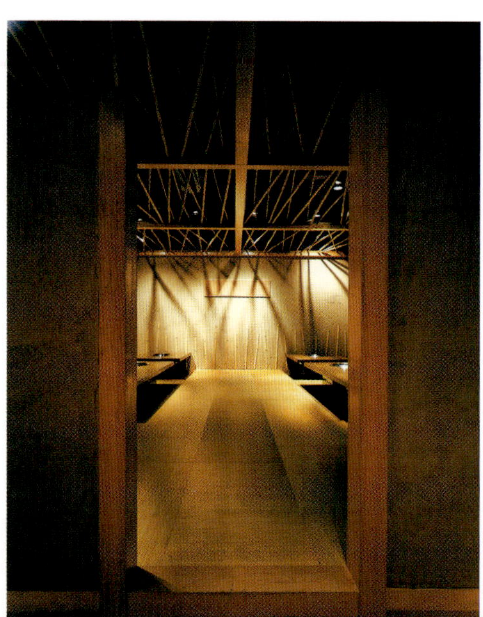

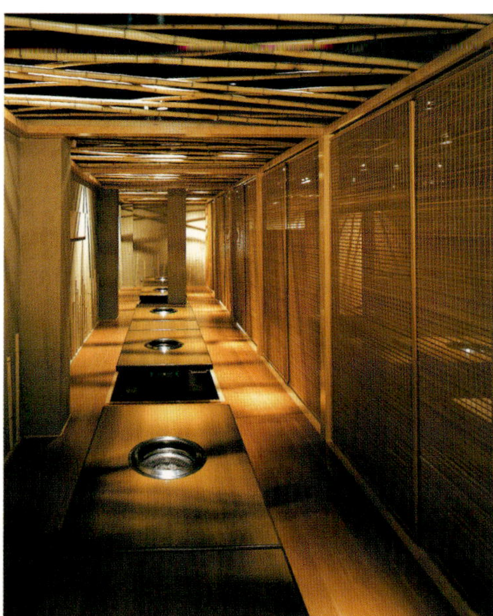

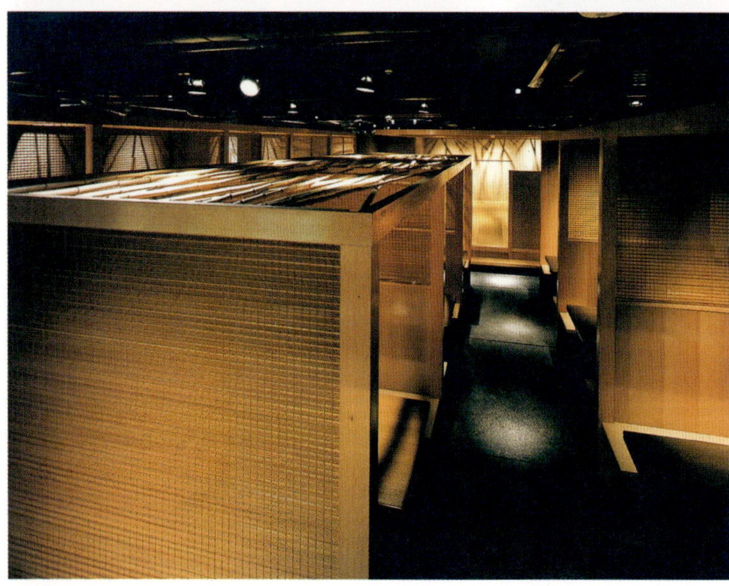

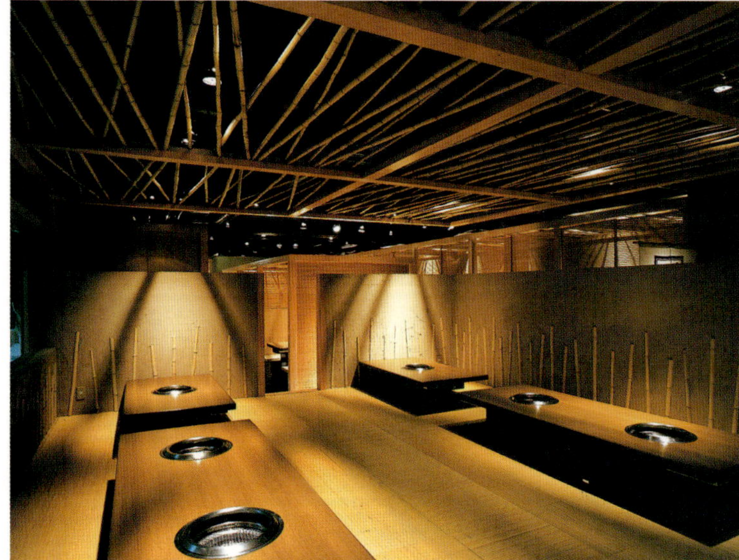

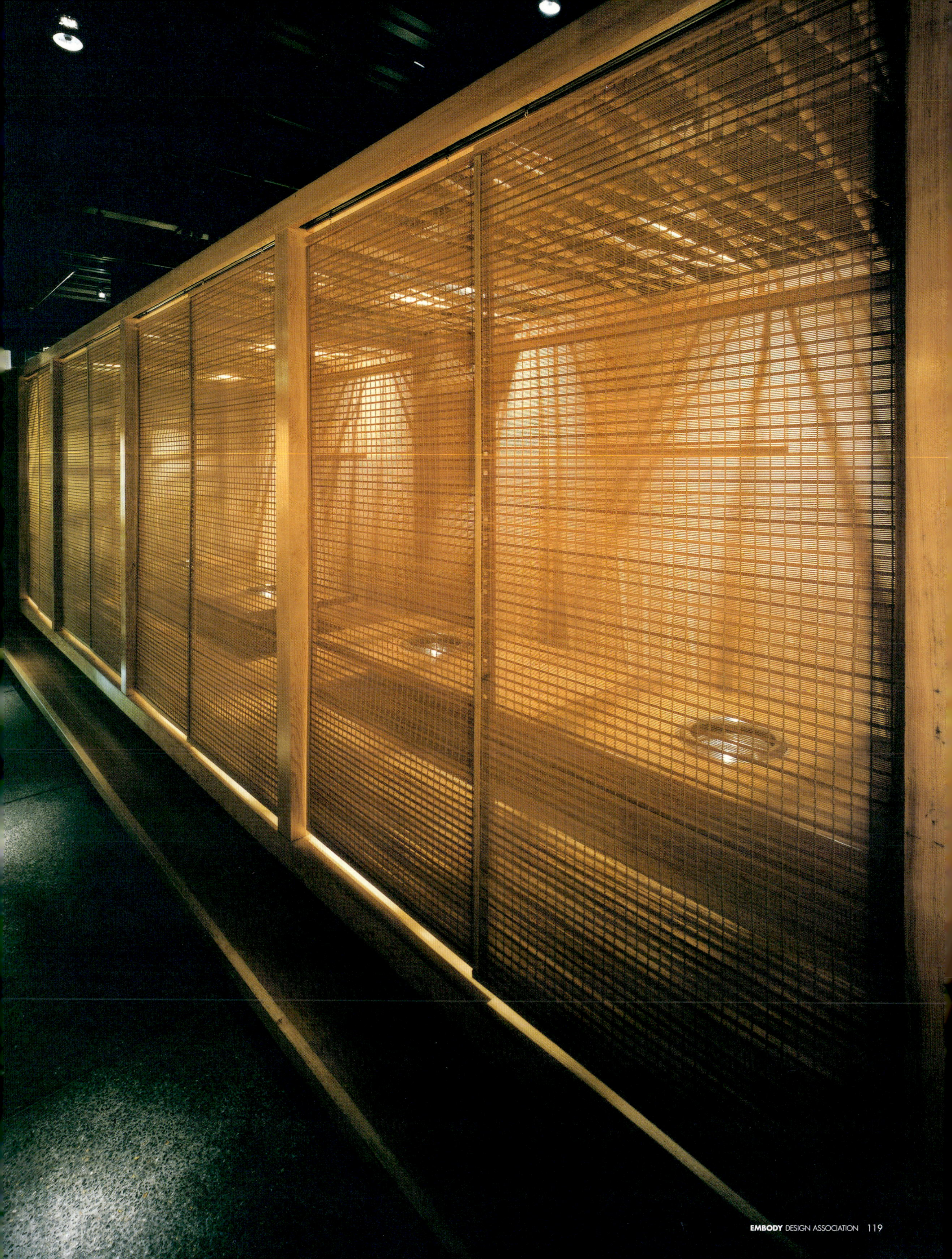

非日常的 高揚感 解放 日常から いざなう する 空間

AMUSEMENT

AIR
SENNICHIMAE , OSAKA 2006

心踊る場所

空港という場所には特別な時間と空気が流れているように感じませんか？
そこは、いつ訪れても、胸が踊る非日常的な高揚感に包まれているようです。
きっとそれは、空港には単なる交通要所としての魅力だけではなく、集まる人々の夢やパワーがいっぱい詰まっているからではないでしょうか。
　そんな「エアーターミナル」をテーマに、"AIR"は、訪れる人々を日常から解放する場として、それぞれの夢や目的地へといざなえるような空間をデザインしました。

A Space for the Heart to Dance

Don't you get the feeling that an airport is the sort of place where there's a special flow of time and a special air? No matter when you visit, an airport is a place where you feel immersed in a dance of extraordinary elation. Surely this is rooted in the fact that the airport's charm is not in being a mere traffic hub, but because it's fully infused with the dreams and power of the people assembled there, isn't it?

　We designed AIR on such an air terminal theme as a place where visitors can be liberated from their daily lives, a space where we can guide visitors to their own dreams and destinations.

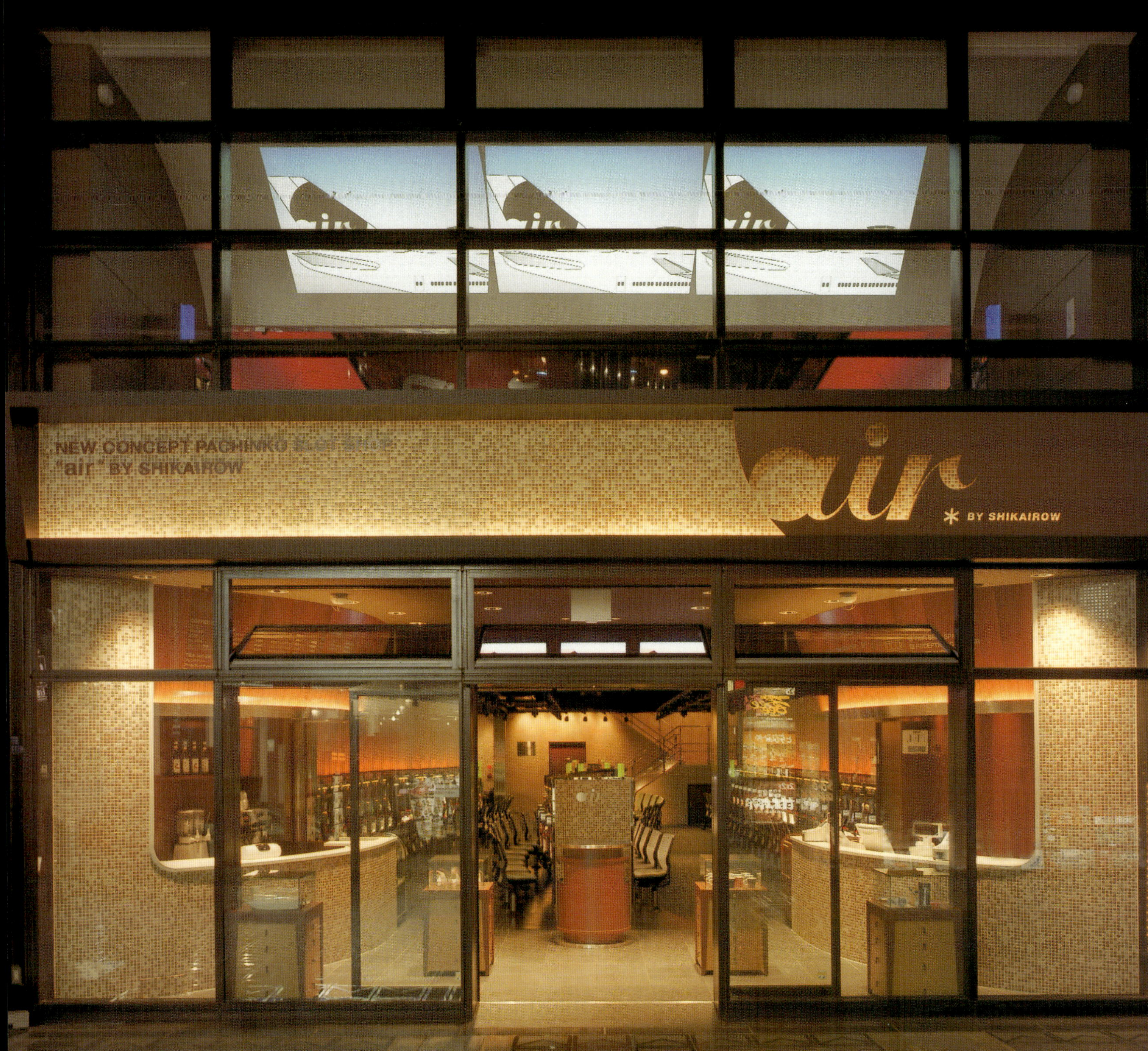

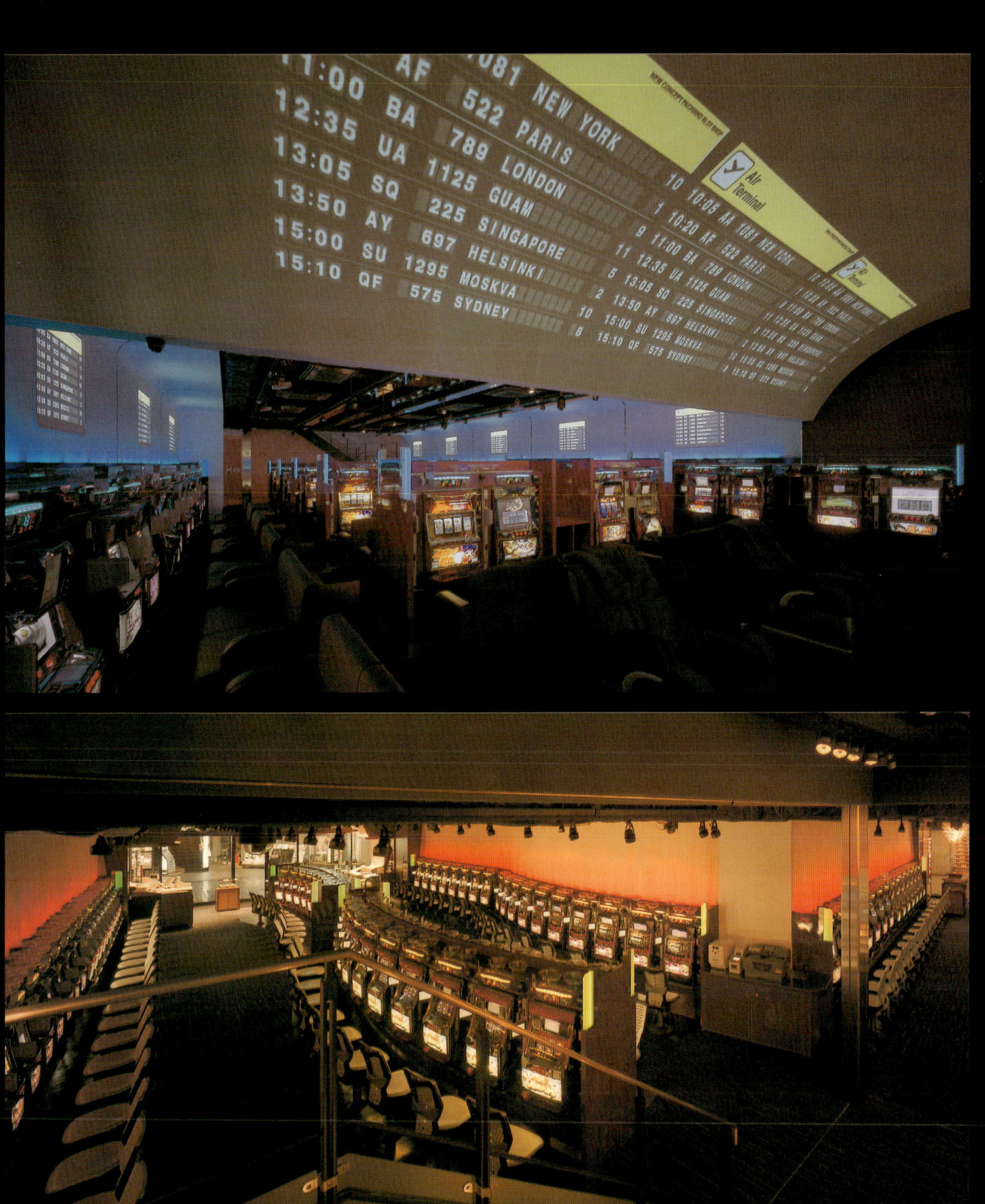
11:00 AF 1081 NEW YORK
12:35 BA   522 PARIS
13:05 UA   789 LONDON
13:50 SQ 1125 GUAM
15:00 AY   225 SINGAPORE
15:10 SU   697 HELSINKI
       QF 1295 MOSKVA
            575 SYDNEY
Air Terminal

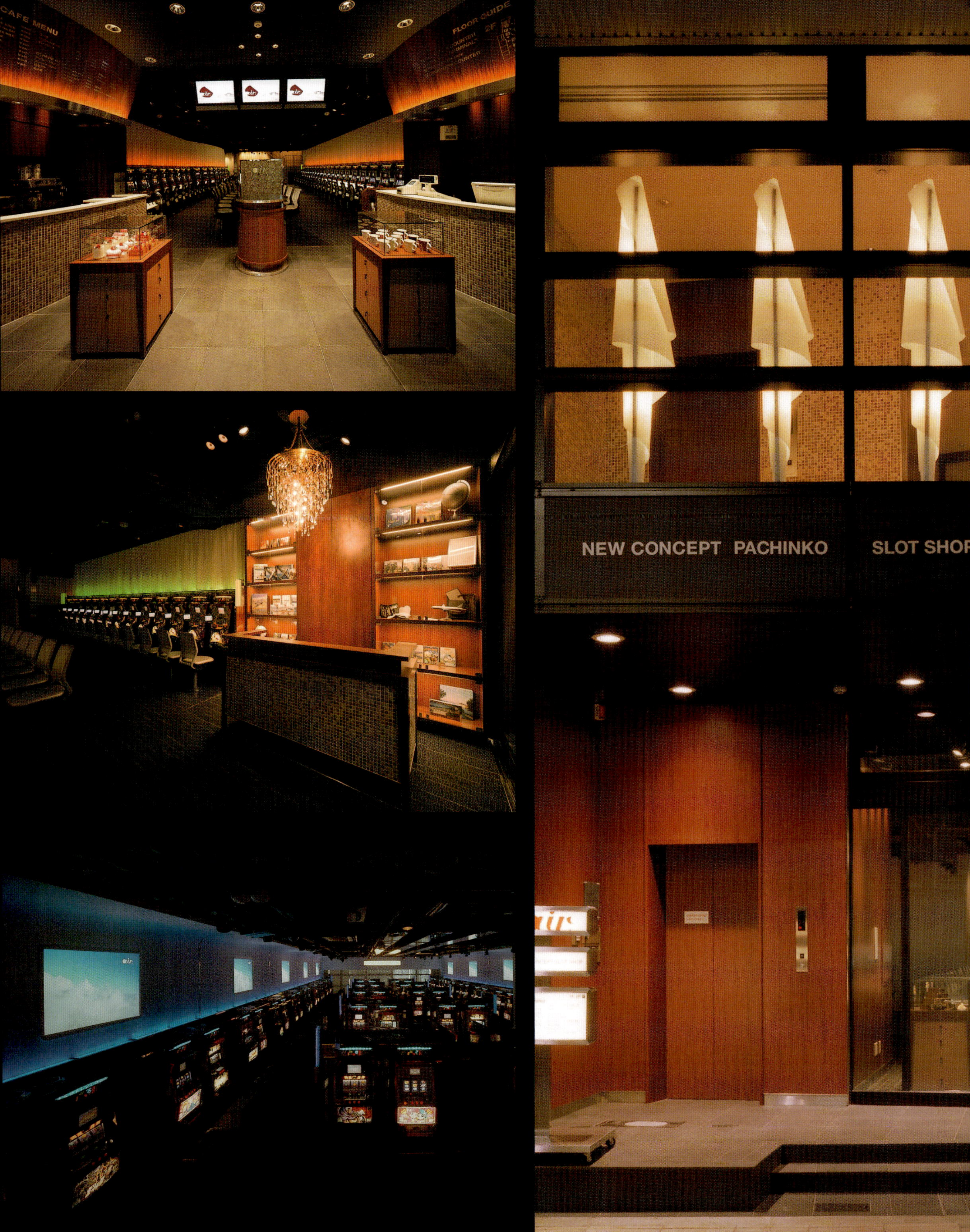
NEW CONCEPT PACHINKO   SLOT SHOP

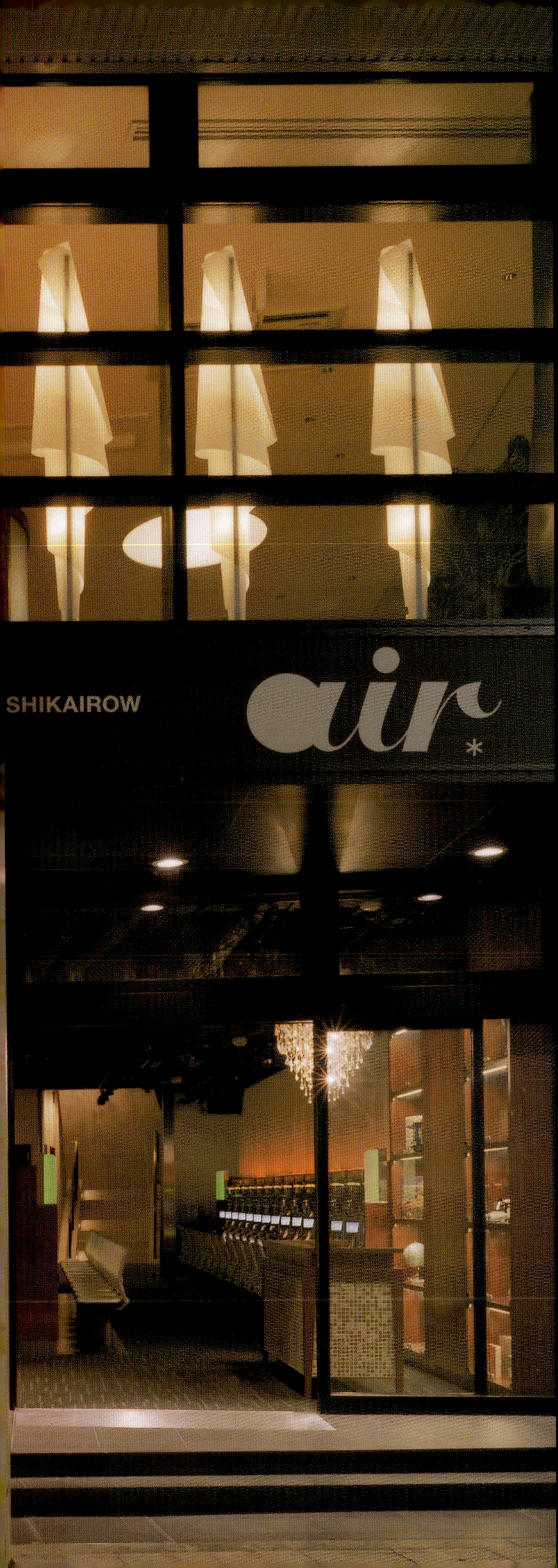

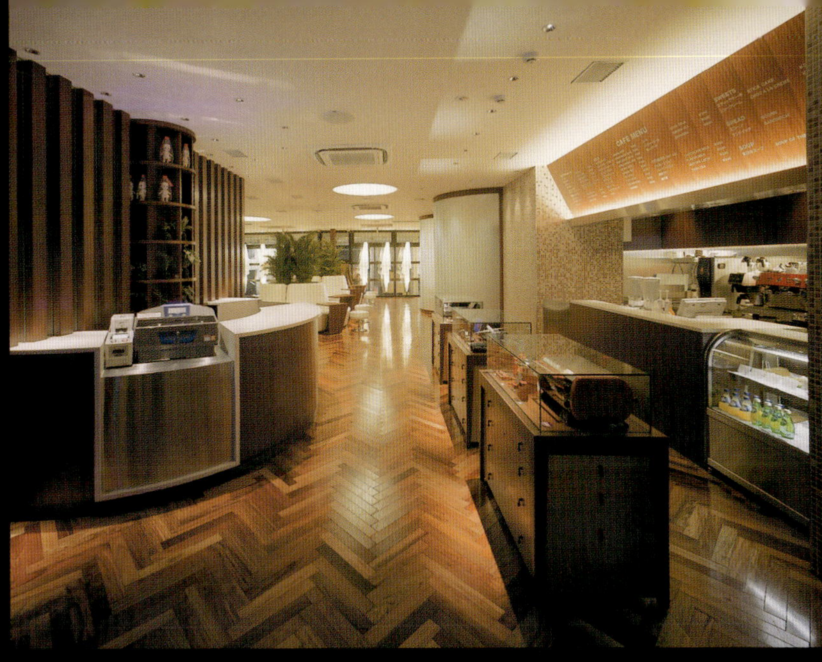

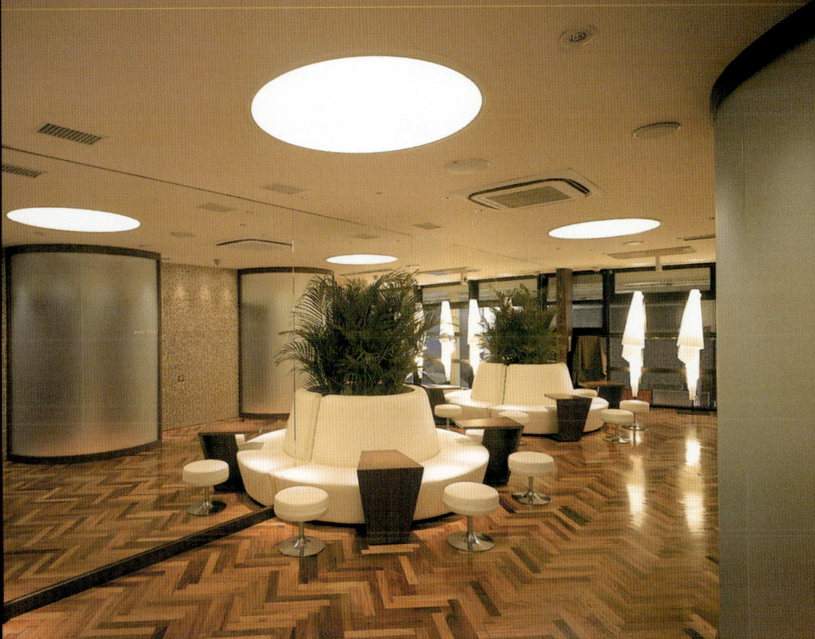

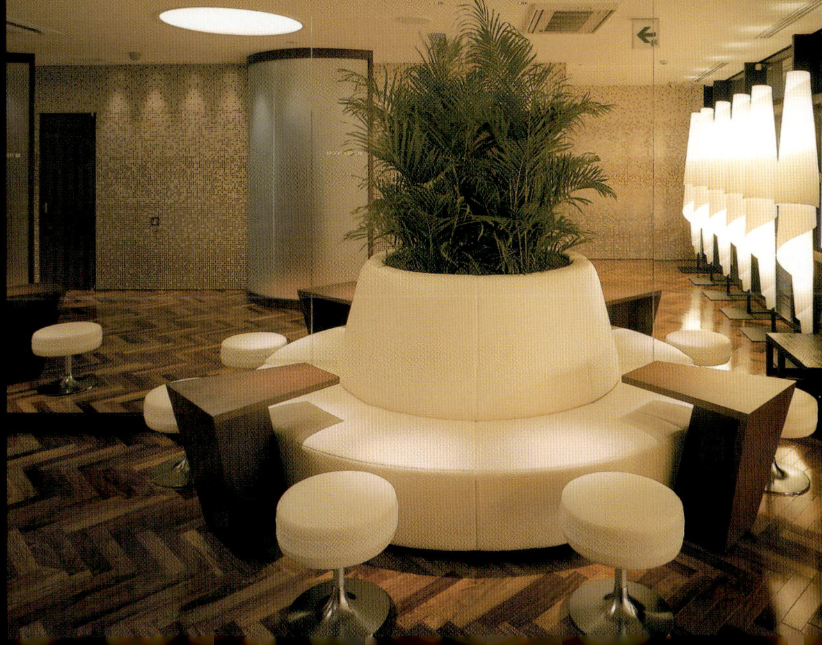

SHIKAIROW
air

construction of relationship 丹

関係性を構築する

not weeding out by time

時間軸に淘汰されない

keep the space from filling up

間 を残す デザイン

atmosphere of high quality

上質な 空気

念 care with

connect the 繋ぐ society and people

人と街を

人と人を 結ぶ ...man and the other

オーセンティック authentic

借景 flexibility

natural scenery

柔軟性 around it

念 care
with
connect the 繋く society and people
人と街を
人と人を 結ぶ connect
a man and the other
オーセンティック authentic
借景 flexibility
natural scenery
柔軟性 around it

CAFE.BAR

high quality
品質する atmosphere of

keep the space 間 from filling up
out by time 時間 not weeding
時間軸で 関係性を構築する
relationship
construction of

ROMI'S BAR
KITASHINCHI , OSAKA 2003

オーセンティック

"ROMI'S BAR"は商業ビルの地下1階に計画され、最初に訪れたその場は、全く光の入らない、闇を連想する空間だった。デザインするにあたり、ここで目指したのは、一見デメリットと感じられる部分をメリットに転換し、訪れる人も、もてなす人も、誰もが居心地良く和むことのできる空間である。

そして「空間という造形」を創るのではなく、「オーセンティック」をコンセプトに、ここに集う人々の上質な空気感がプラスされて、完成するように空間に少しの「間」を残すデザインを具現化した。私は、「オーセンティック－本物」というものは、時間軸に淘汰されず、時間軸をプラスに変換していく力を持つものだと思うのだ。

Authentic

ROMI'S BAR was planned out in the first basement floor of a business building, a space that sees absolutely no outside light and is very suggestive of darkness. My aim in designing this space was to turn what at first glance seemed to be a drawback into a positive feature, creating a space where anyone, hosts and visitors alike, would feel peaceful and welcome. Rather than trying to build a constructed space, I have instead created a design that leaves some of the space untouched as it were, so that the refined aura of those that gather here augments and completes the atmosphere.

I believe that authentic means that something is not weathered by, but rather that it has a strength that grows with the passage of time.

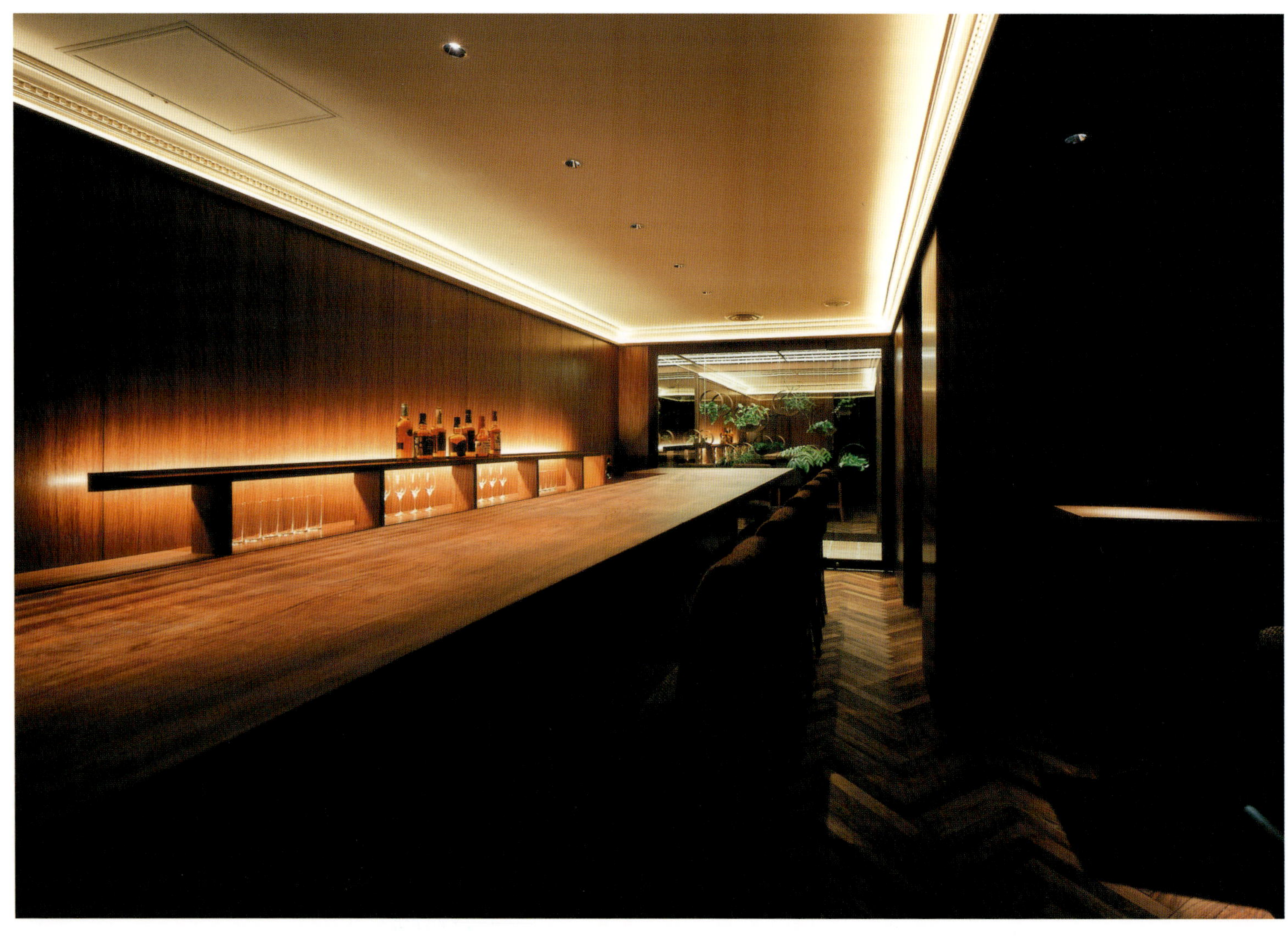

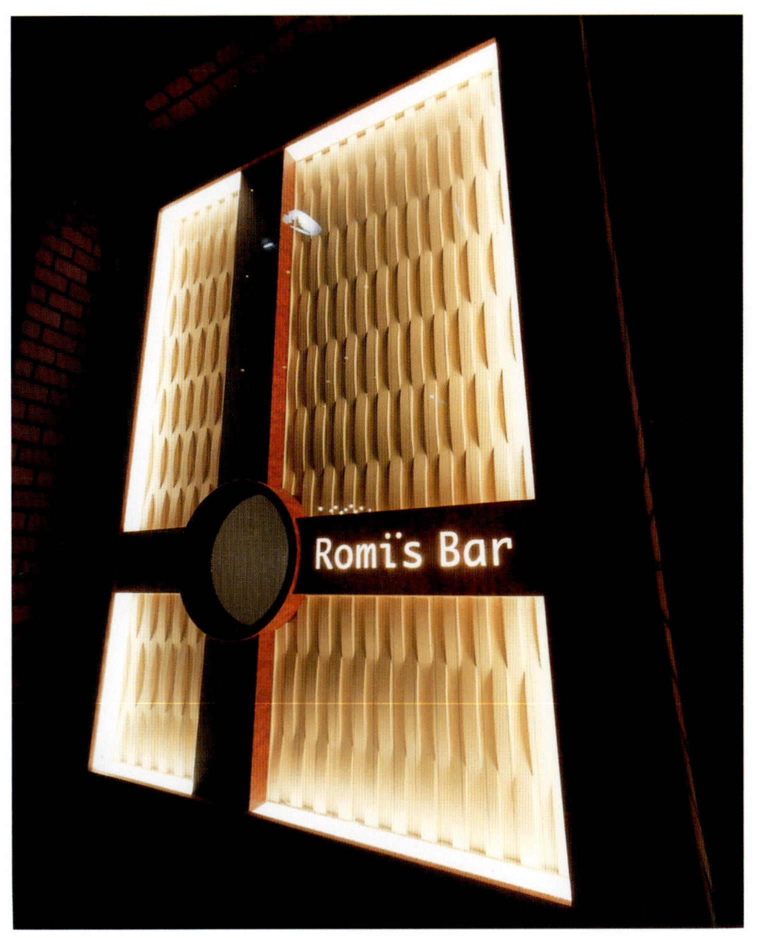

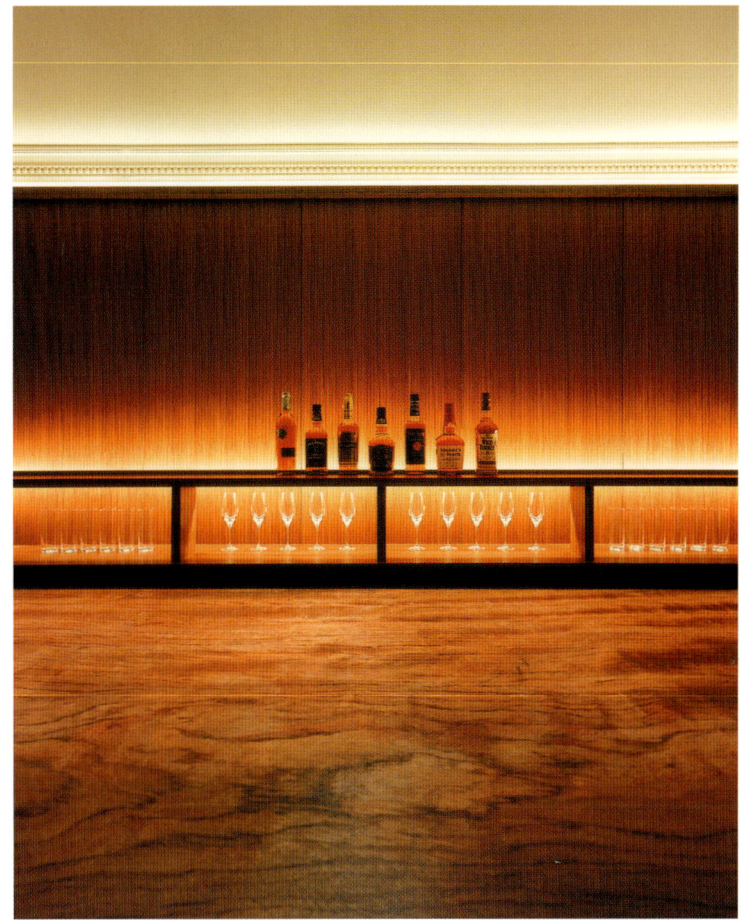

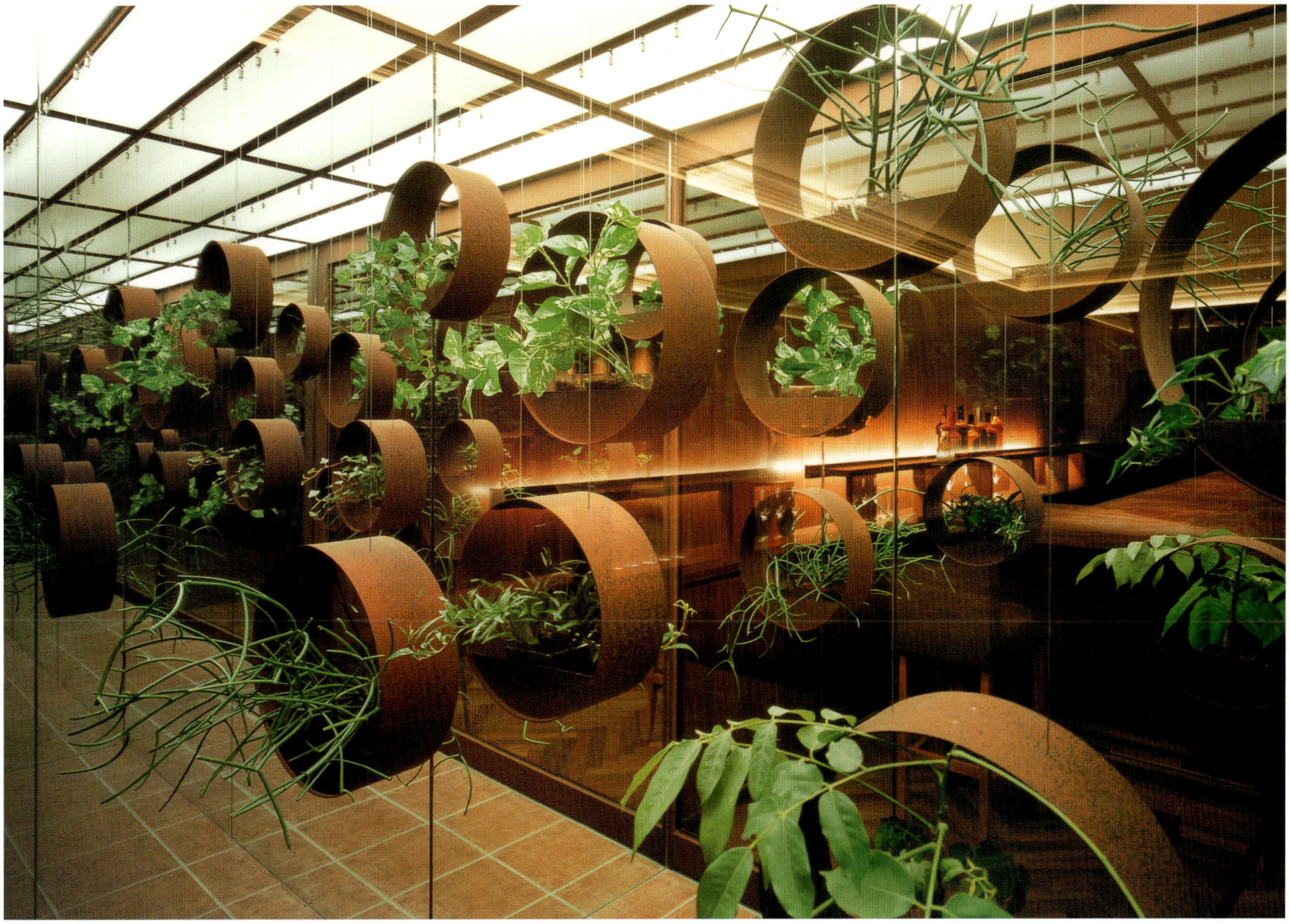

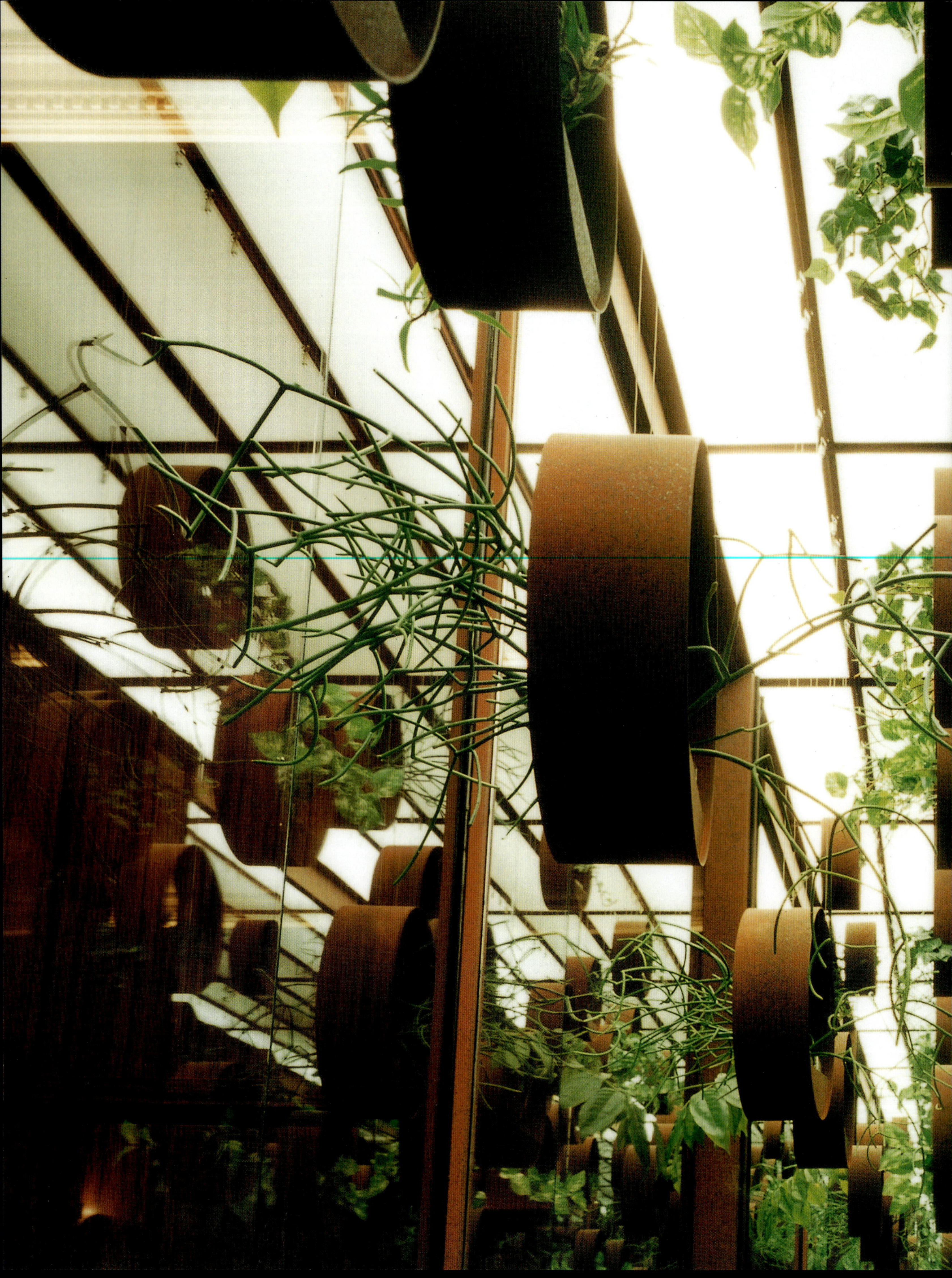

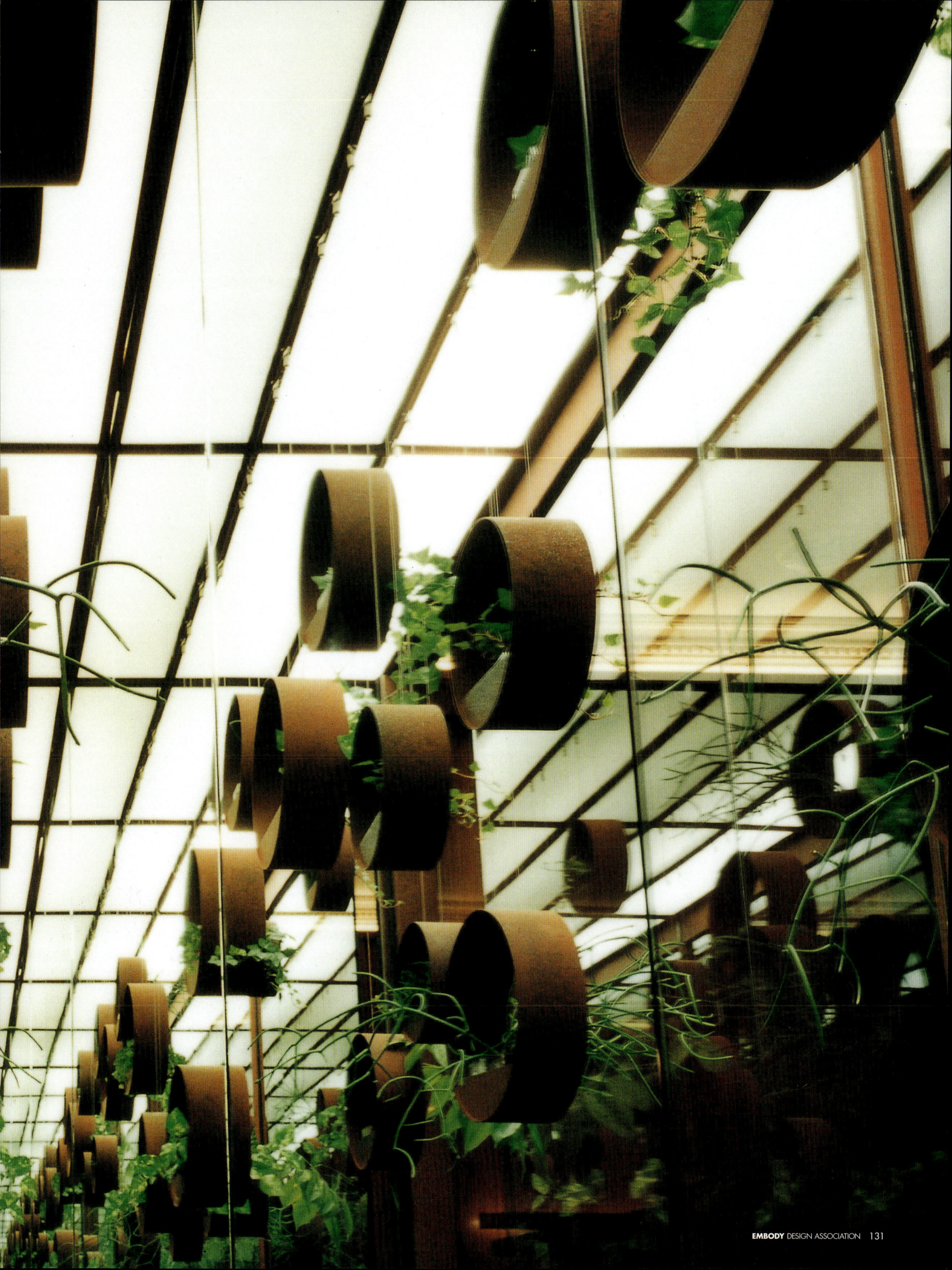

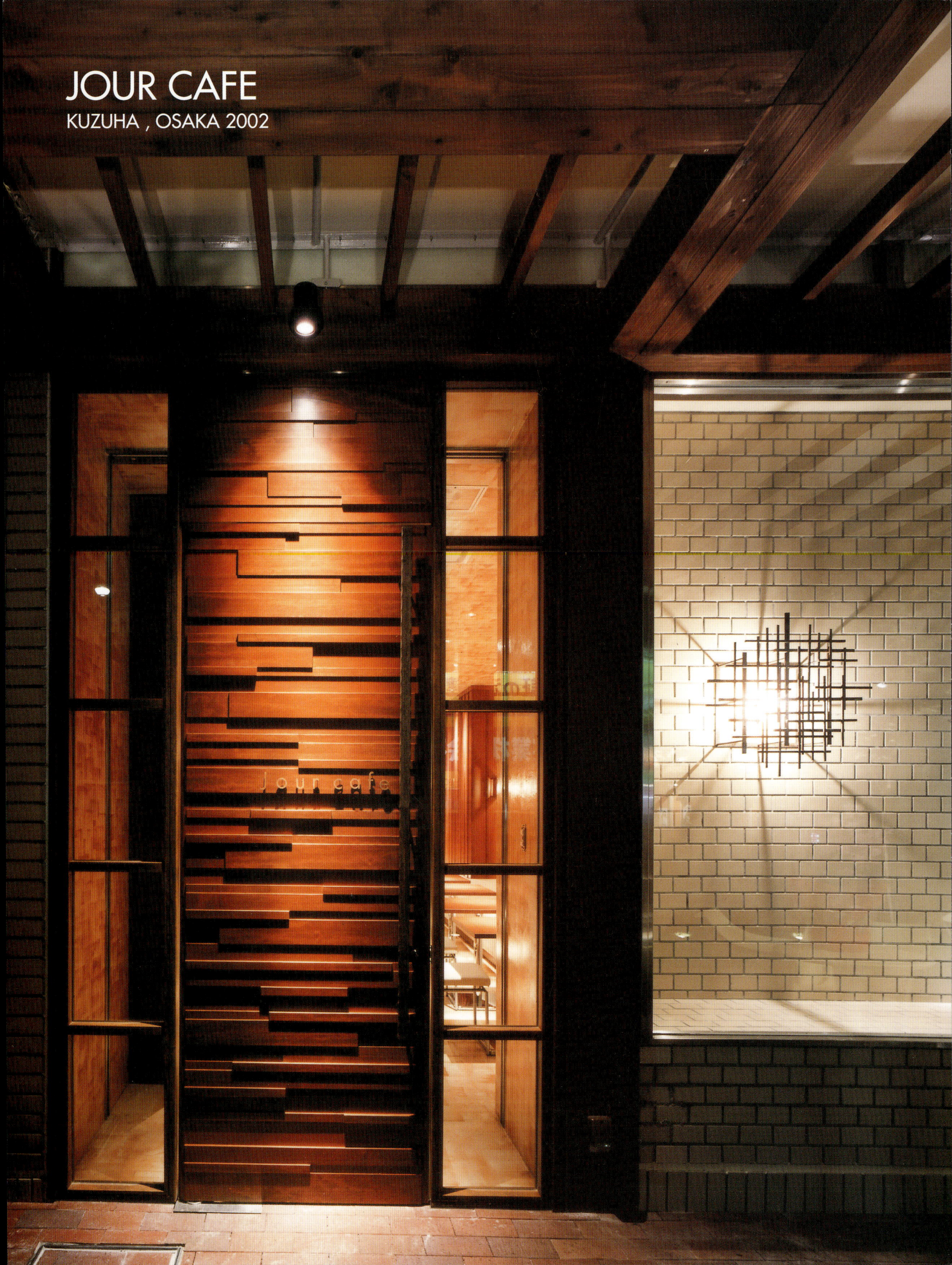
JOUR CAFE
KUZUHA , OSAKA 2002
Jour cafe

"JOUR CAFE"はヘアーサロンに併設されたカフェ。

　ここは間口が狭く、ウナギの寝床のような空間で、人と人、人とモノ、モノとモノの「距離感」、そして、来店者のニーズに対応できる「柔軟性」を大切に、既存のカタチを活かしたゾーニングを心掛けました。

　また素材は、床・壁・天井に、時を重ねるごとに味わい深さを増すスタッコで、丹念にパターンを描き出し、特種樹脂で仕上げることで、朽ちる美しさを持つ、時の流れを味方に付けた空間に仕上げています。

Designing the Beauty in Decay

JOUR CAFE was set up as an annex to a hair salon.

　The frontage is narrow here, just a sliver of a space, and we aimed at a zoning that would bring to life the existing shape with a sense of distance between man-to-man, man-to-thing and thing-to-thing, and then made a priority of meeting the needs of customers with flexibility.

　In addition, as for the materials, stucco, which accumulates a deep patina, was used on floors, walls and ceilings, and a pattern carefully worked in, topped with a special vinyl finish, and the space has a lustre that shows the beauty in decay, favored by the passage of time.

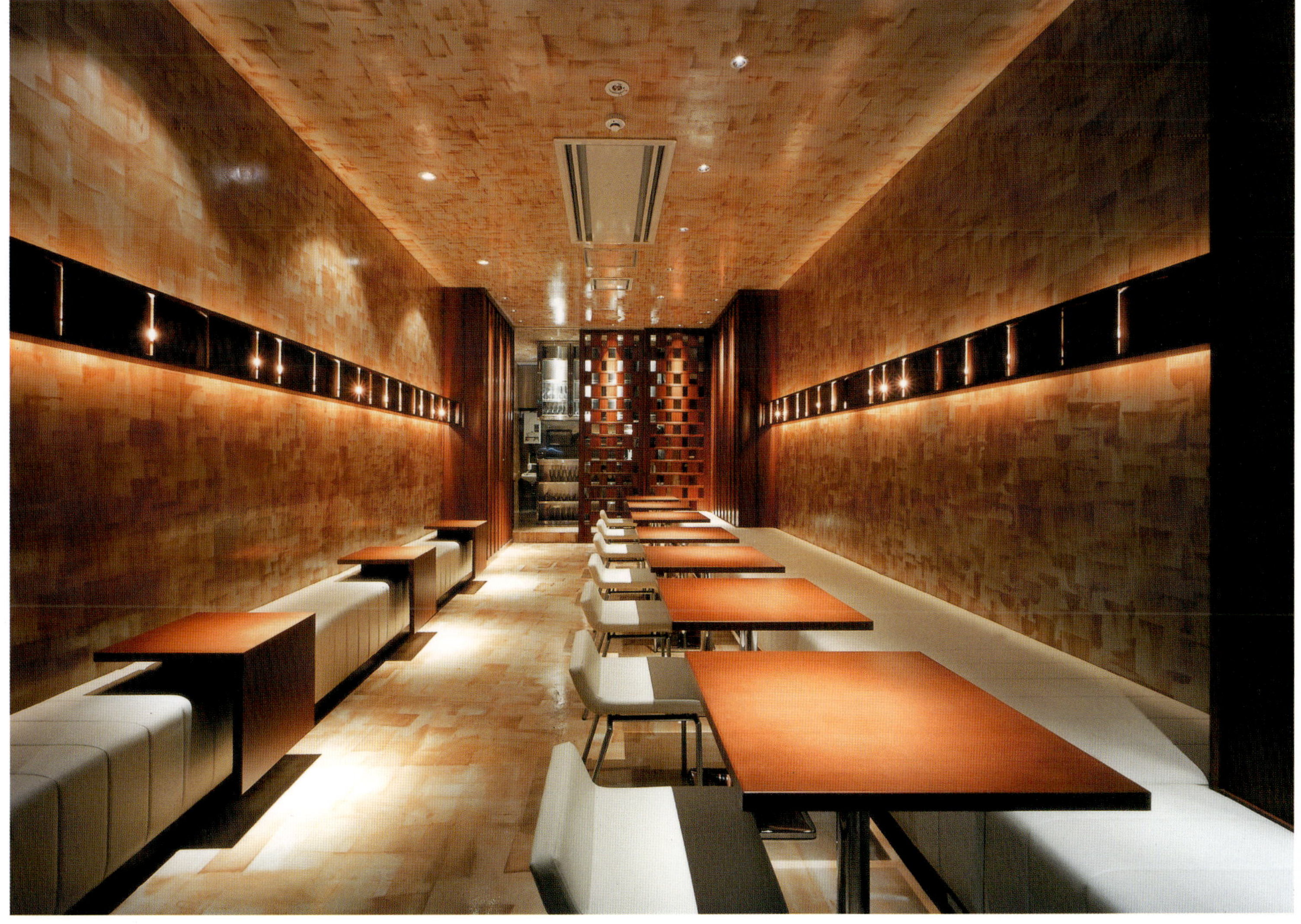

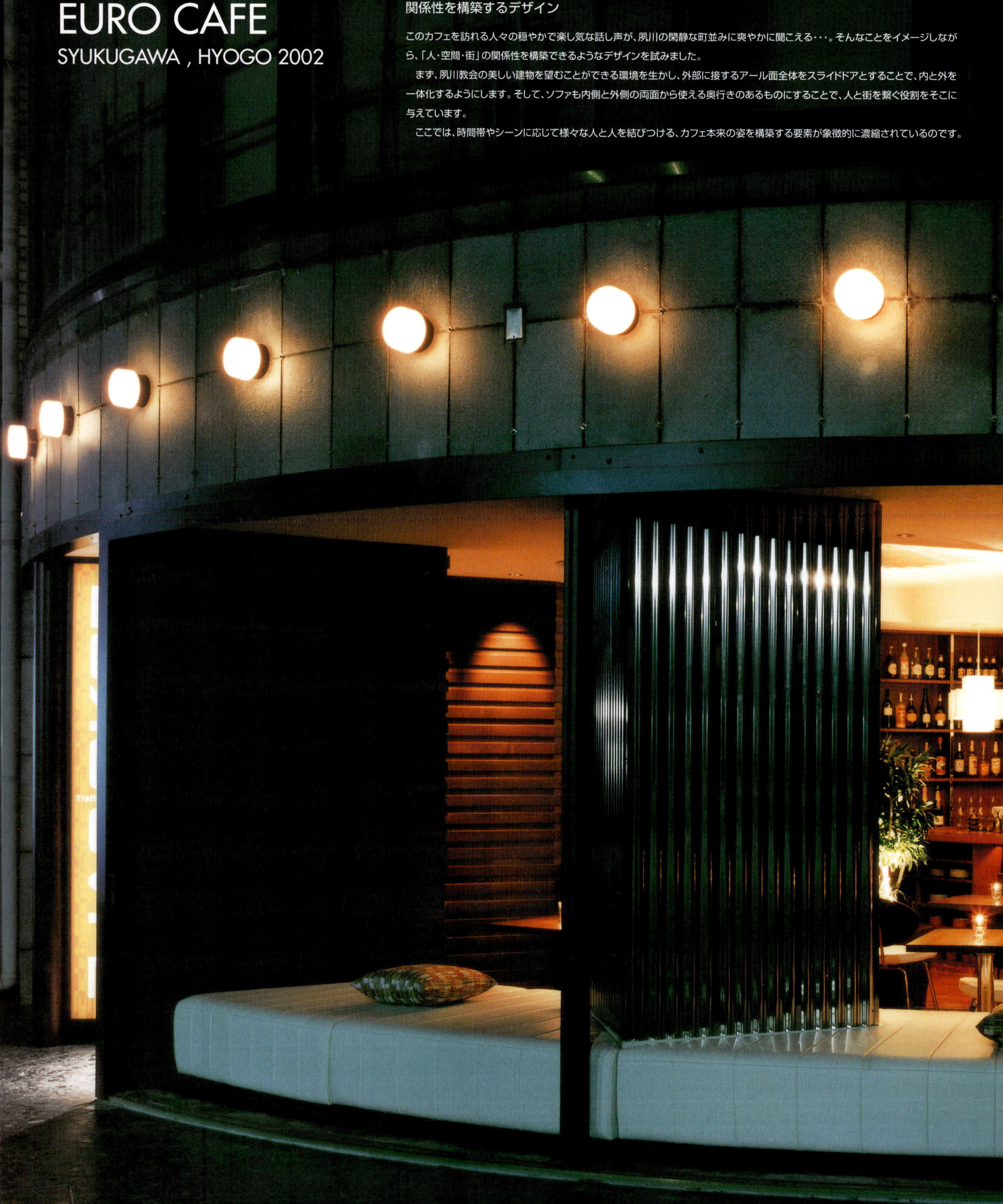

EURO CAFE
SYUKUGAWA , HYOGO 2002

関係性を構築するデザイン

このカフェを訪れる人々の穏やかで楽し気な話し声が、夙川の閑静な町並みに爽やかに聞こえる・・・。そんなことをイメージしながら、「人・空間・街」の関係性を構築できるようなデザインを試みました。

　まず、夙川教会の美しい建物を望むことができる環境を生かし、外部に接するアール面全体をスライドドアとすることで、内と外を一体化するようにします。そして、ソファも内側と外側の両面から使える奥行きのあるものにすることで、人と街を繋ぐ役割をそこに与えています。

　ここでは、時間帯やシーンに応じて様々な人と人を結びつける、カフェ本来の姿を構築する要素が象徴的に濃縮されているのです。

A Design that Builds Connectedness

The mild spirit of enjoyment of the voices of visitors conversing at a cafe, in the streetscape of a quiet neighborhood in Shukugawa-it sounds so cool and refreshing! With this sort of thing in mind, we aimed at a design that enhances the connectedness of "people, space and city."

First, taking advantage of an environment in which the beautiful building of the Shukugawa Church can be viewed by making use of sliding doors on an entire curving wall, which interfaces with the outdoors, outside and inside were unified. Then, employing a massive sofa that can used both from inside and outside, a role of bringing together people and neighborhood is given.

Here is a symbolic concentration of the factors that constitute the original form of the cafe, a place to connect a variety of people depending on the time slot and situation.

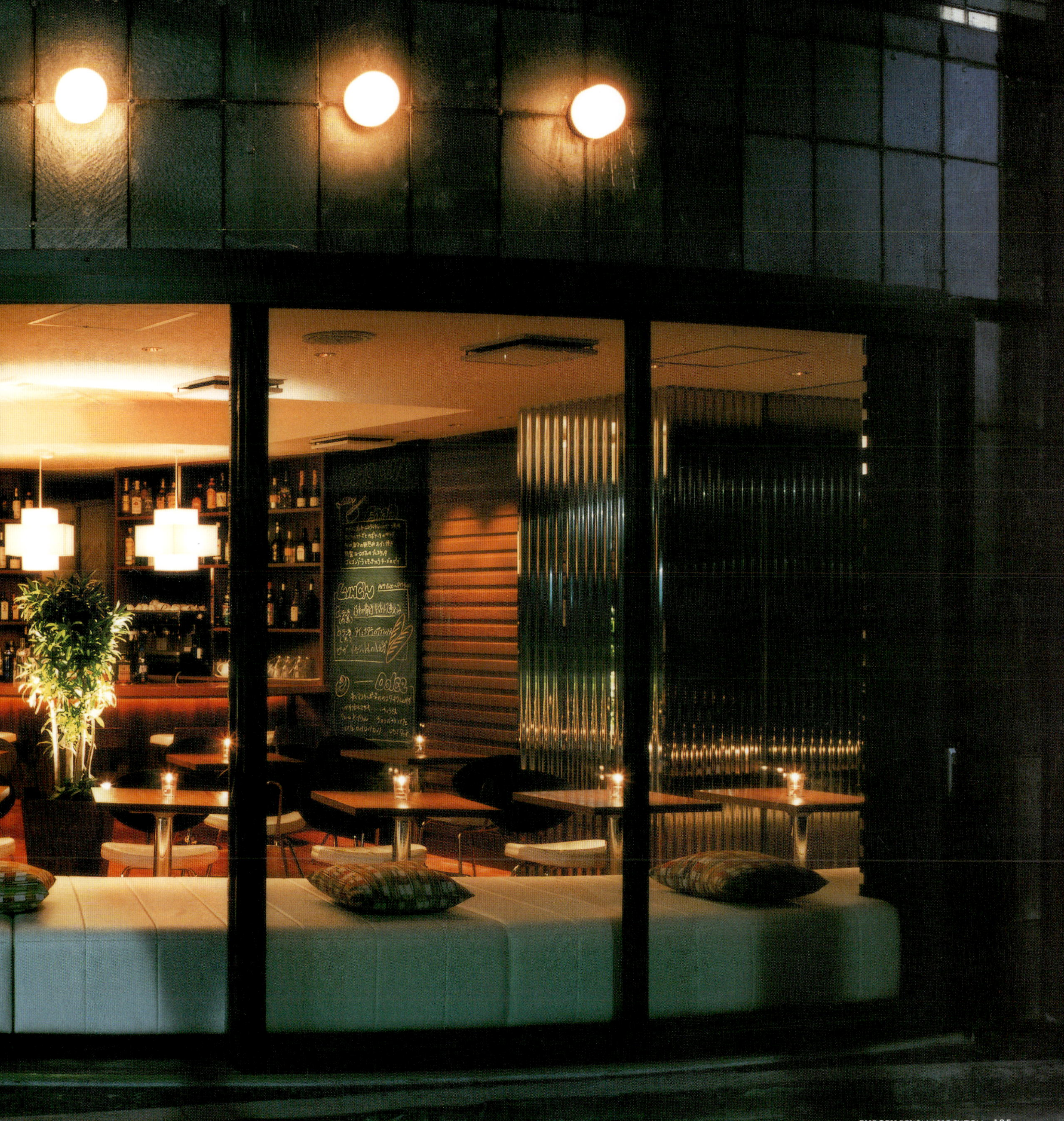

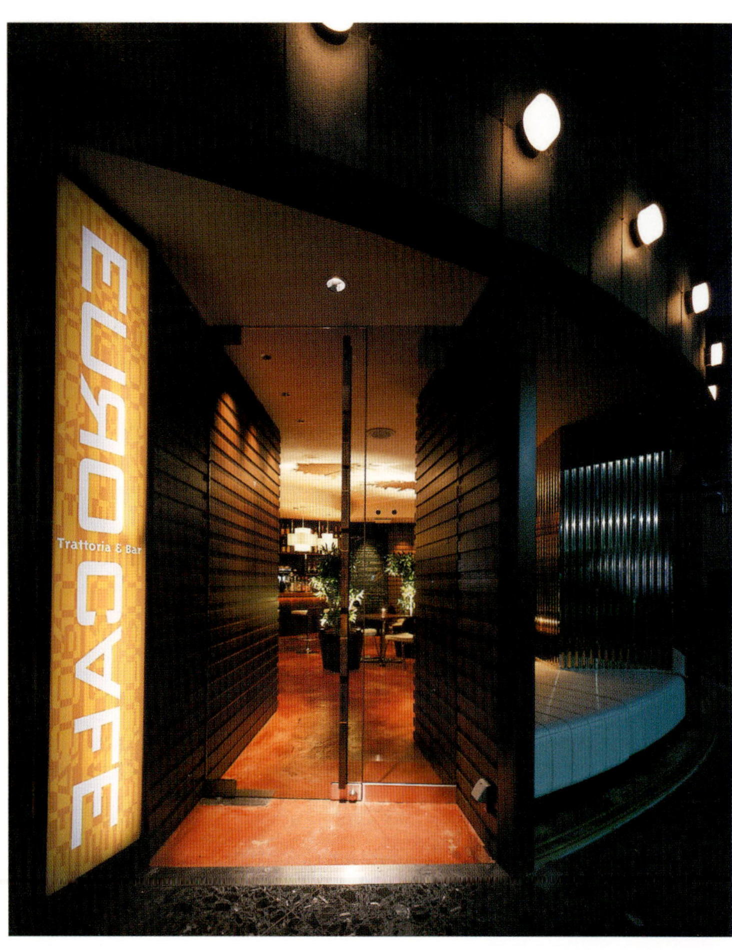

EURO CAFE
Trattoria & Bar

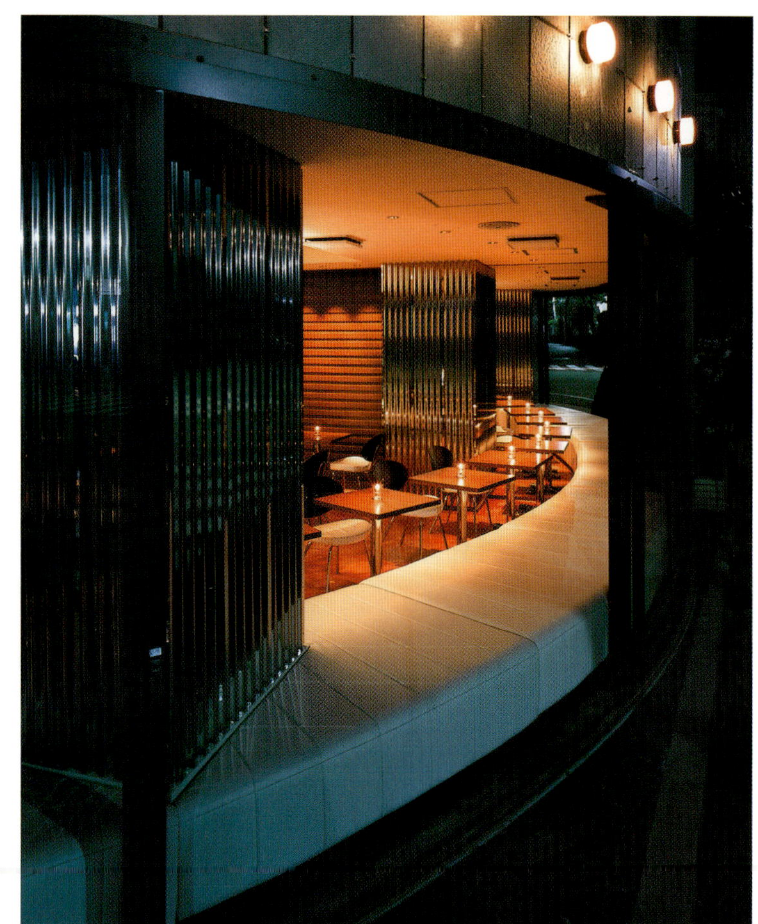

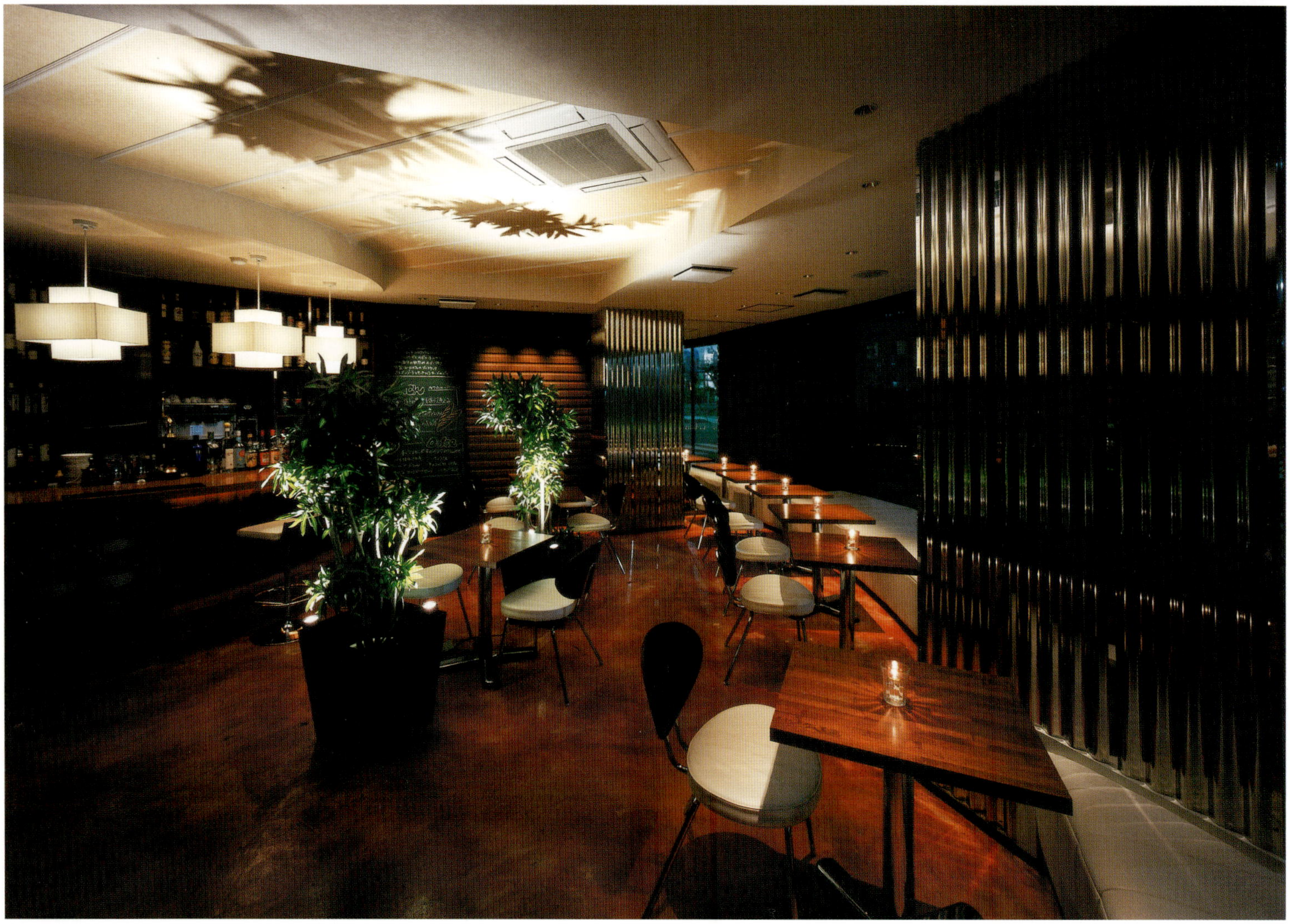

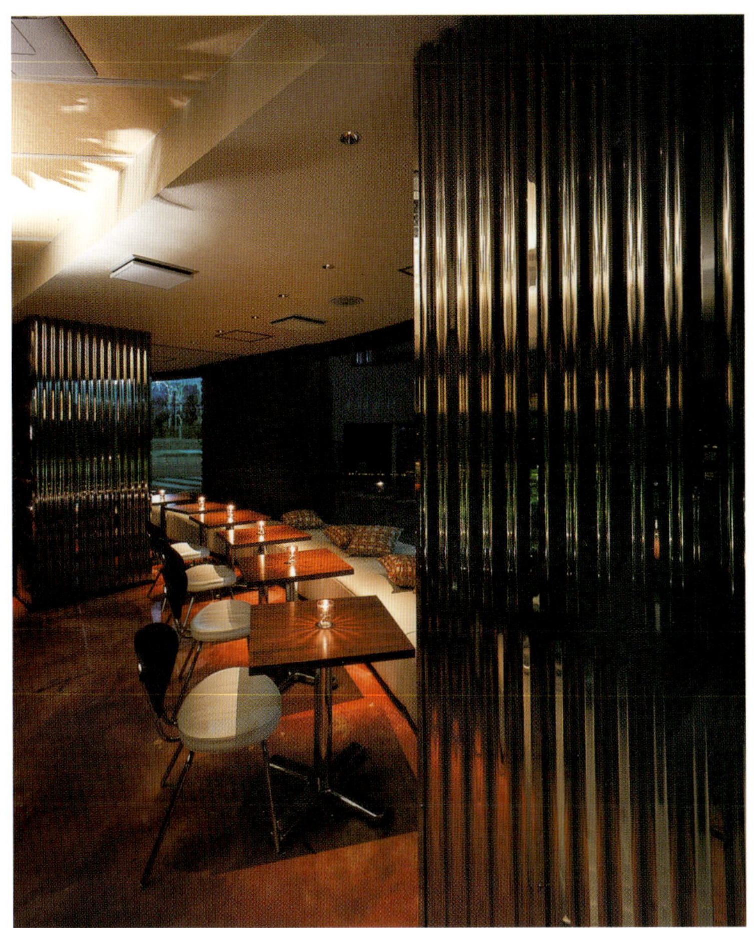

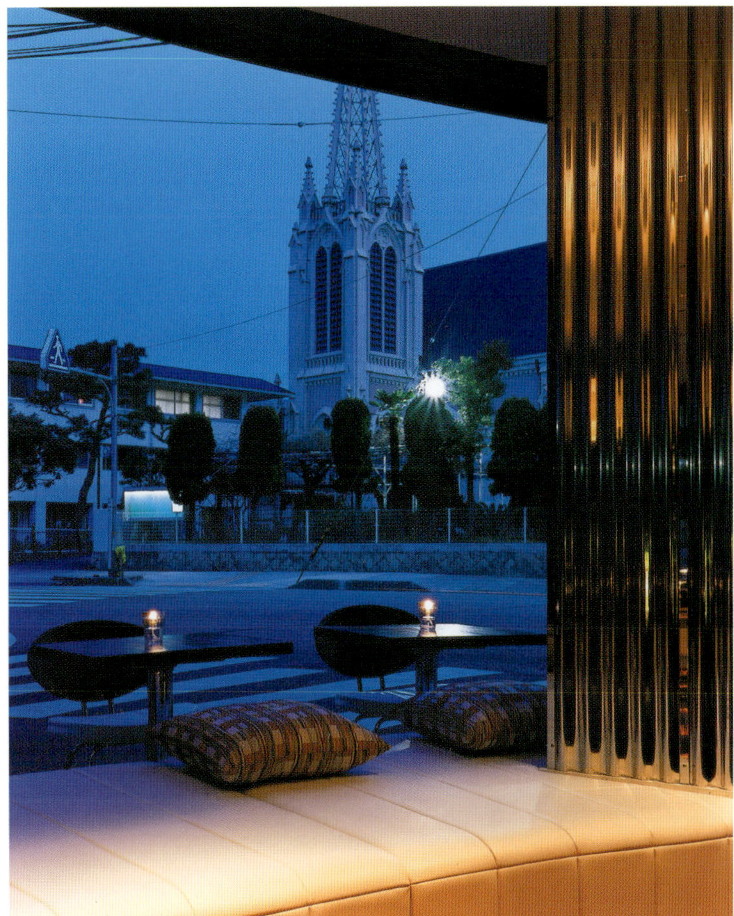

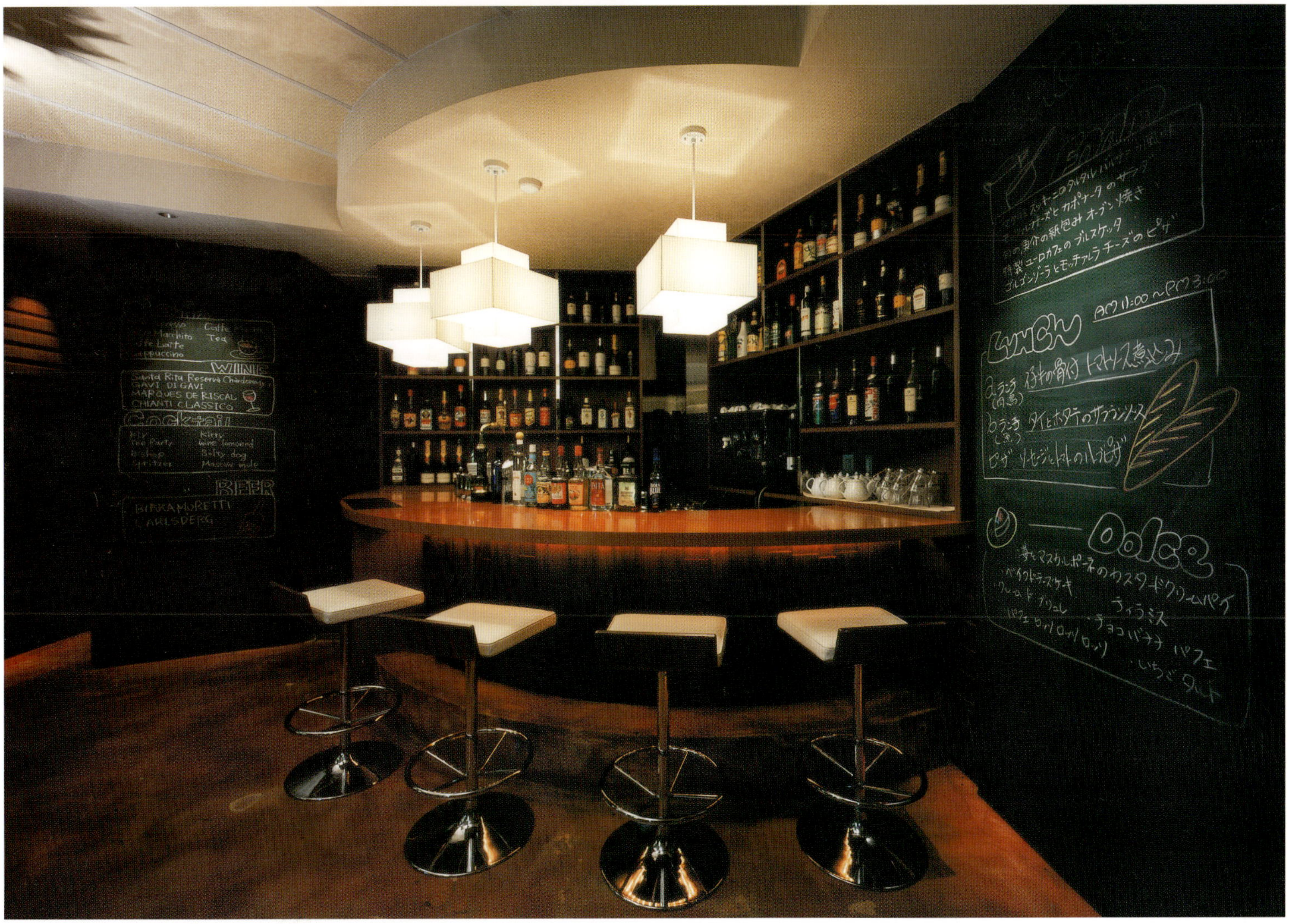

curiosity

history 好

culture 歷史

glamour 文化 色

voluptuous 色

龍 色 民

border between ordinary and extraordinary

日常と非日常の境界

ma / space, interval, pause, timing

間

temptation 誘惑

two sides of the same coin

兩面

originality 独創性

originality

temptation

two sides of the same coin

ma

/space/interval, pause, timing

border between ordinary and extraordinary

voluptuous

glamour

curiosity

history

culture

CLUB

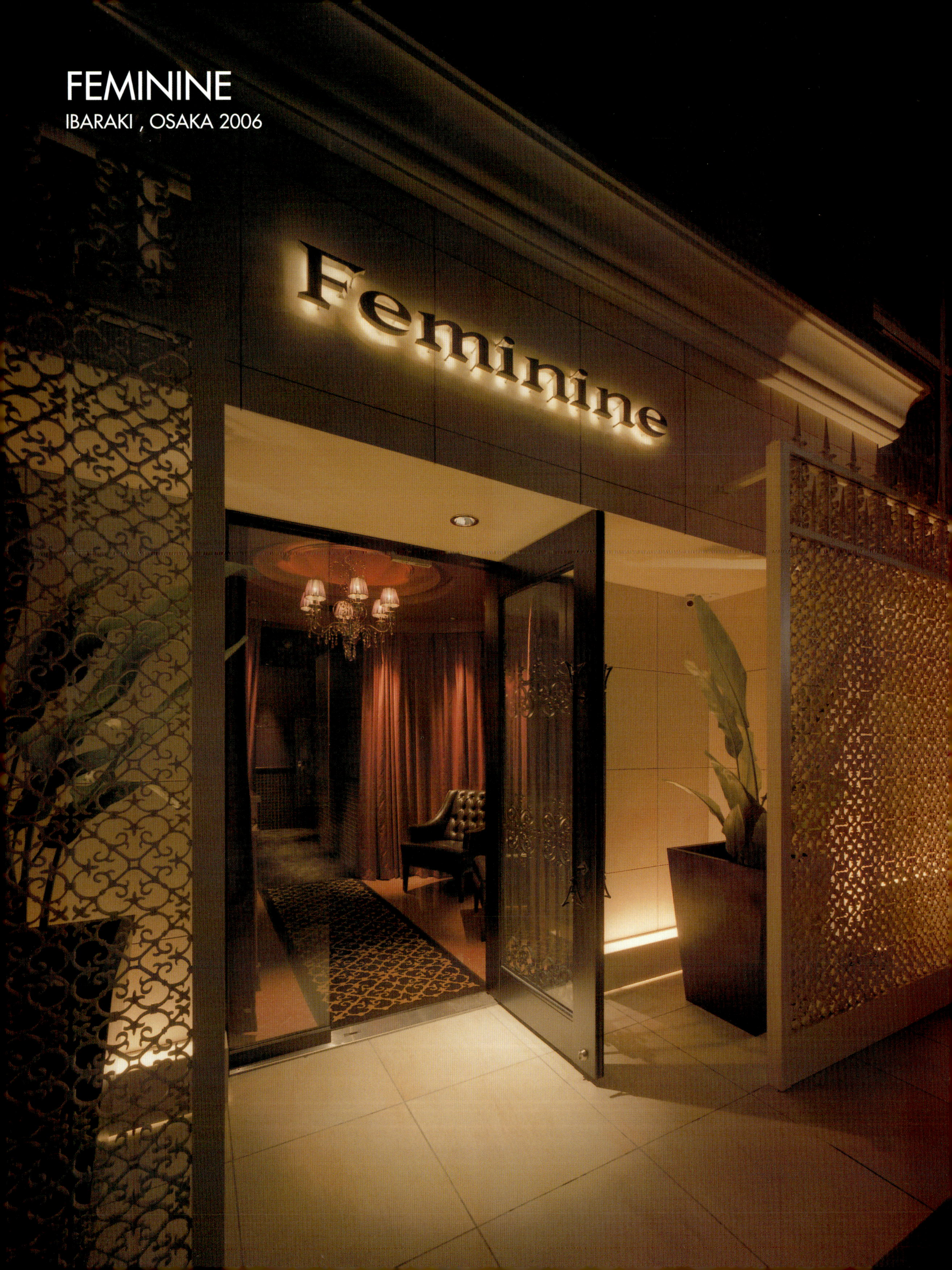

FEMININE
IBARAKI , OSAKA 2006

心と空間のネガとポジ

ファサードは、丹念に組み上げられた白いアルミフレームで、清楚さと知性を持つ「品格」を表し、インテリアは黒い空間に赤いアルミフレームを浮き上がらせて、好奇心と高揚感を与える「情熱」を表現しています。

　ファサードとインテリアが、訪れる人々のそれぞれ「外」と「内」にリンクして、ネガとポジを映し出すようなデザインを試みました。

Heart and Space, Negative and Positive

The façade is composed of carefully assembled white aluminum frames, which express the dignity of tidiness and intelligence, and inside the black interior float red aluminum frames, expressing a passion that imparts curiosity and exaltation.

　The design aims at reflecting the negative and positive, through linkage for visitors of the outside and inside by the façade and interior.

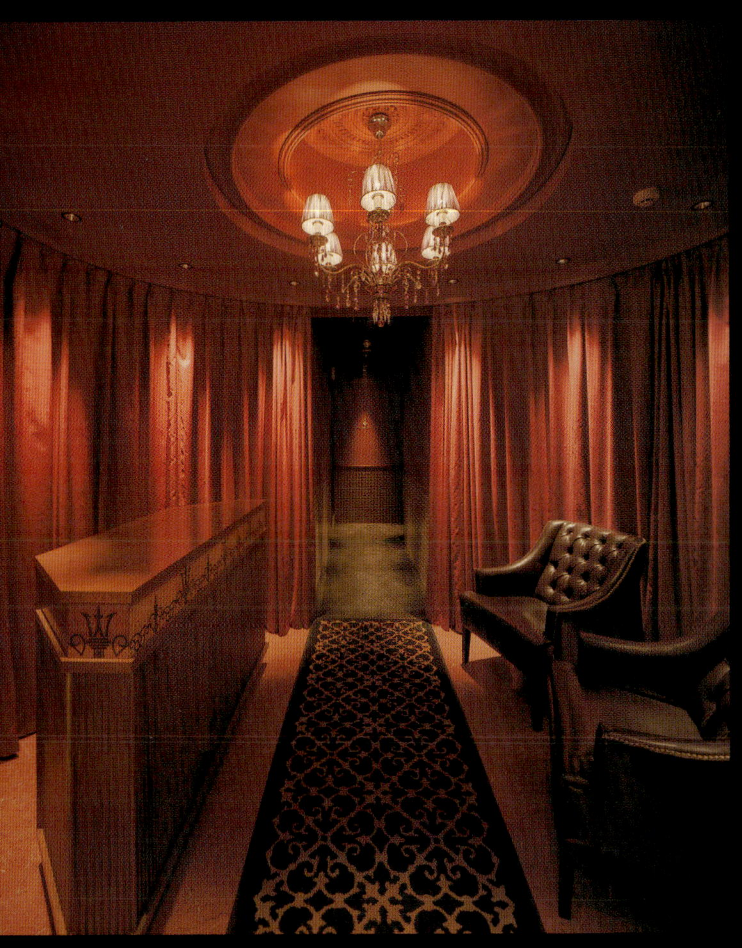

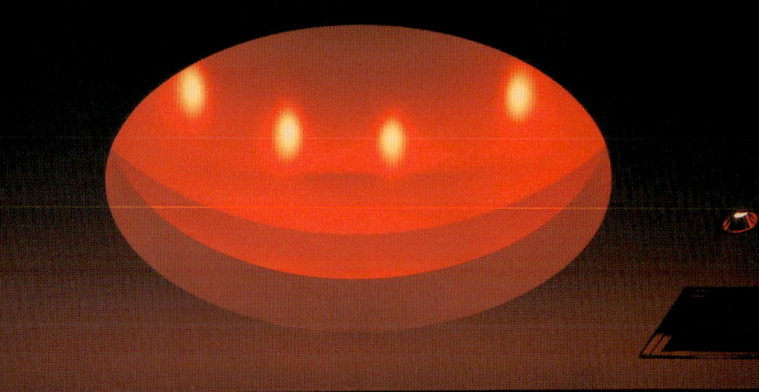

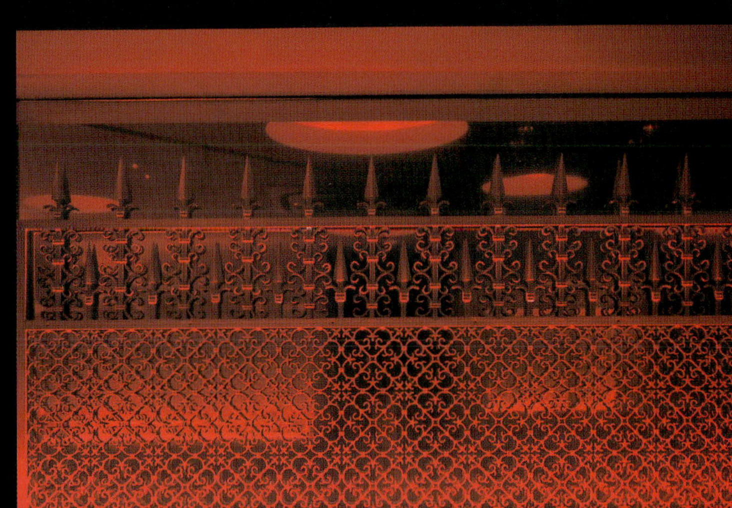

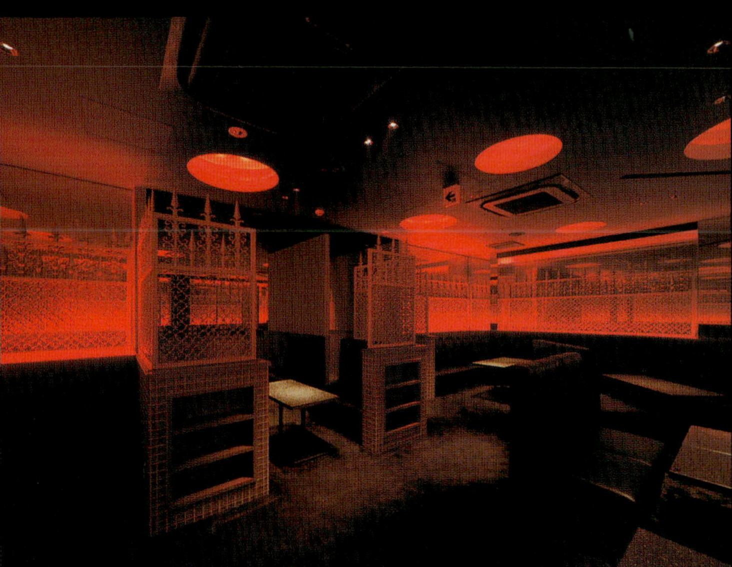

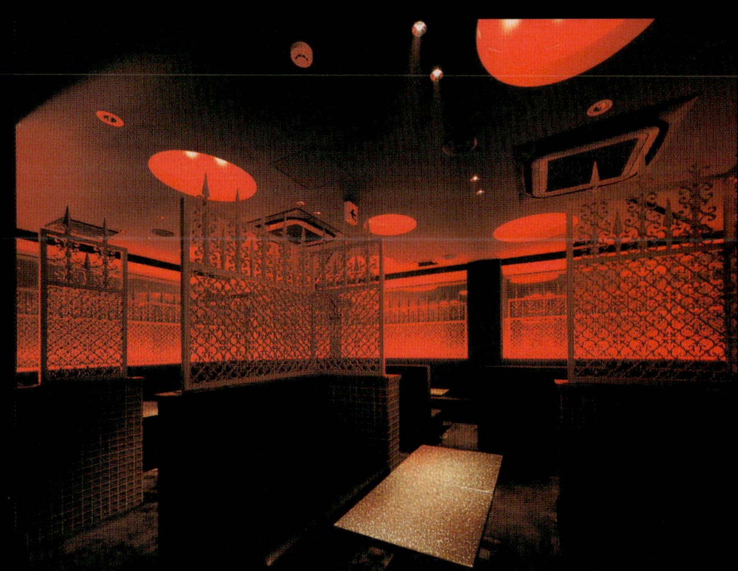

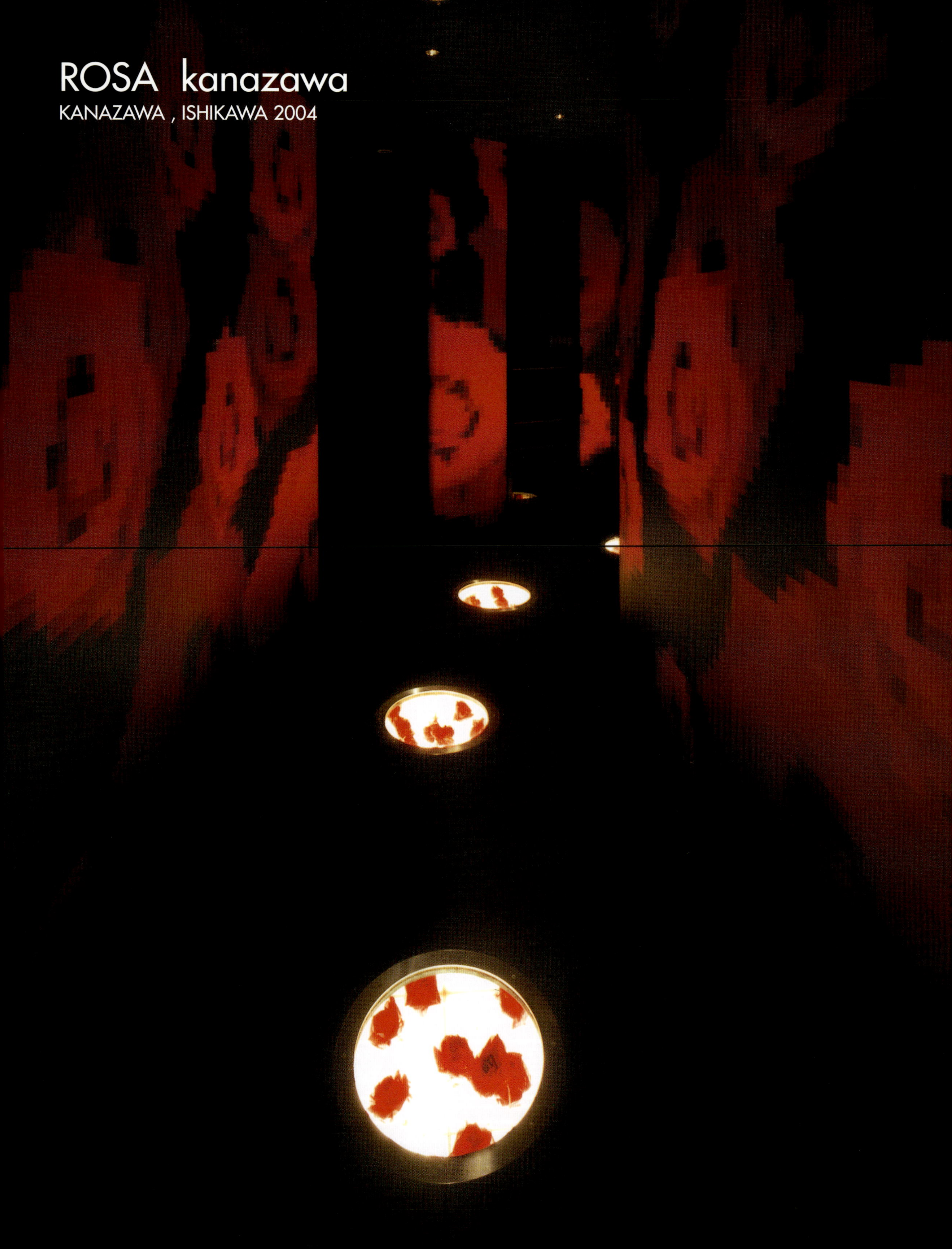

ROSA kanazawa
KANAZAWA , ISHIKAWA 2004

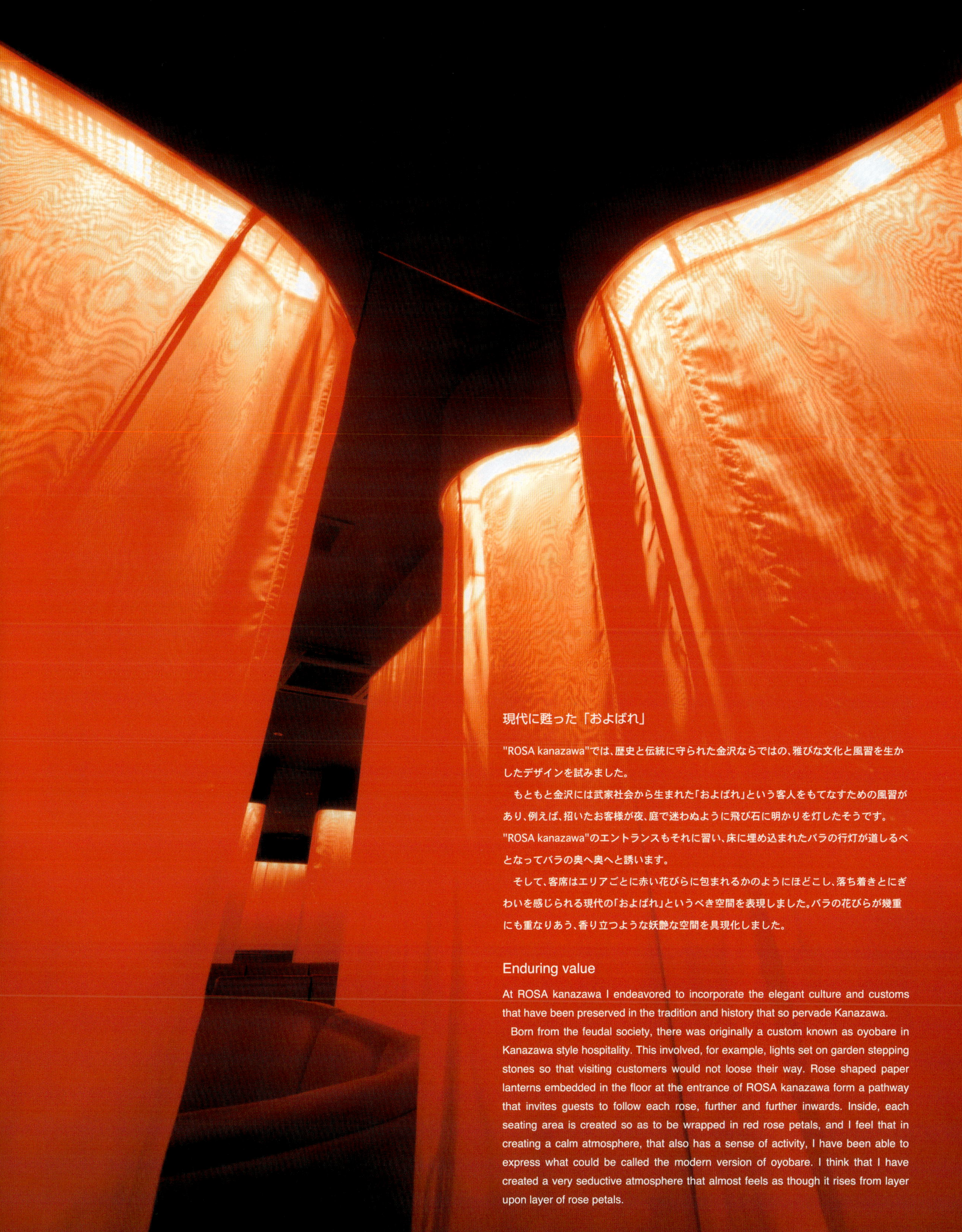

現代に甦った「およばれ」

"ROSA kanazawa"では、歴史と伝統に守られた金沢ならではの、雅びな文化と風習を生かしたデザインを試みました。

　もともと金沢には武家社会から生まれた「およばれ」という客人をもてなすための風習があり、例えば、招いたお客様が夜、庭で迷わぬように飛び石に明かりを灯したそうです。"ROSA kanazawa"のエントランスもそれに習い、床に埋め込まれたバラの行灯が道しるべとなってバラの奥へ奥へと誘います。

　そして、客席はエリアごとに赤い花びらに包まれるかのようにほどこし、落ち着きとにぎわいを感じられる現代の「およばれ」というべき空間を表現しました。バラの花びらが幾重にも重なりあう、香り立つような妖艶な空間を具現化しました。

Enduring value

At ROSA kanazawa I endeavored to incorporate the elegant culture and customs that have been preserved in the tradition and history that so pervade Kanazawa.

Born from the feudal society, there was originally a custom known as oyobare in Kanazawa style hospitality. This involved, for example, lights set on garden stepping stones so that visiting customers would not loose their way. Rose shaped paper lanterns embedded in the floor at the entrance of ROSA kanazawa form a pathway that invites guests to follow each rose, further and further inwards. Inside, each seating area is created so as to be wrapped in red rose petals, and I feel that in creating a calm atmosphere, that also has a sense of activity, I have been able to express what could be called the modern version of oyobare. I think that I have created a very seductive atmosphere that almost feels as though it rises from layer upon layer of rose petals.

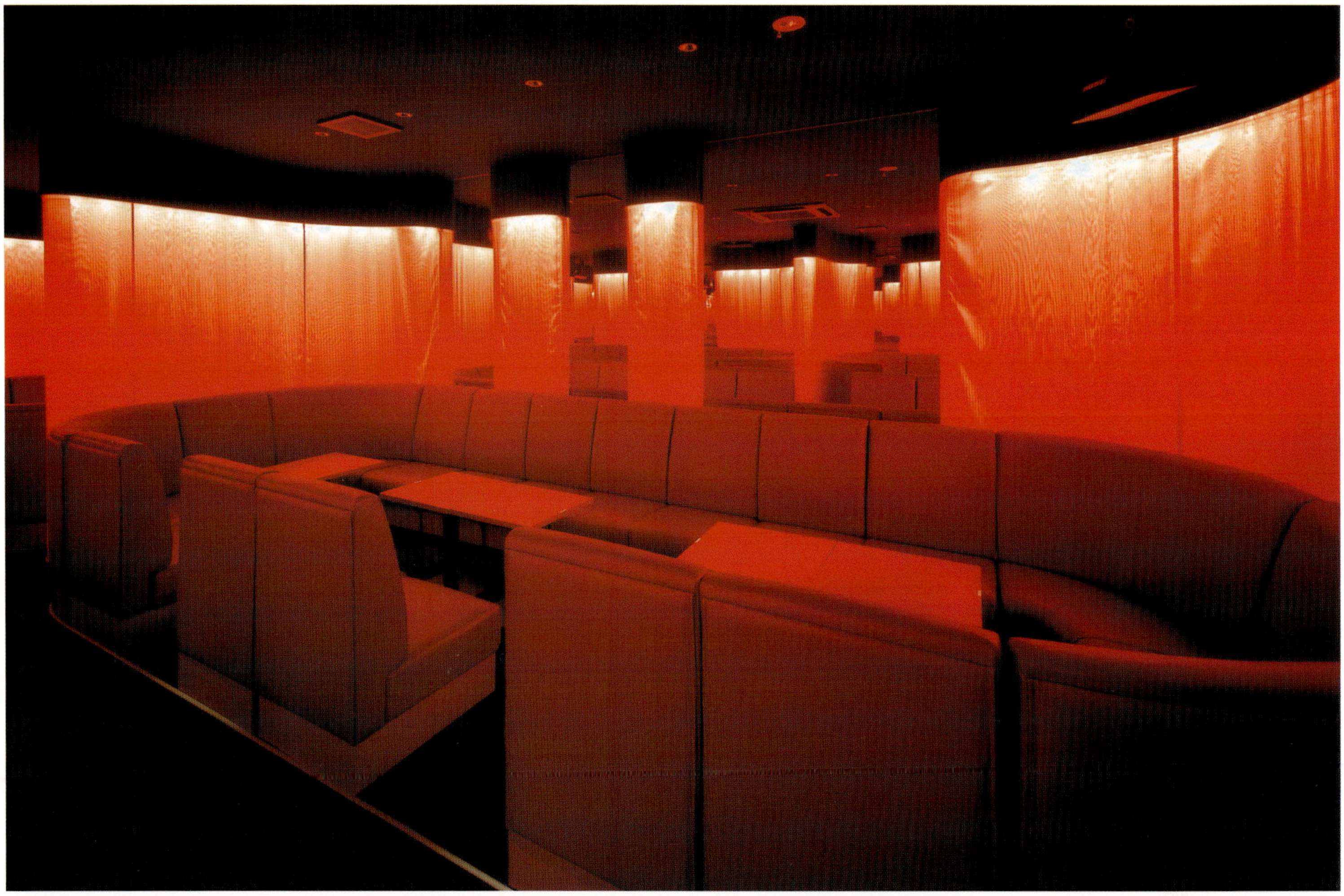

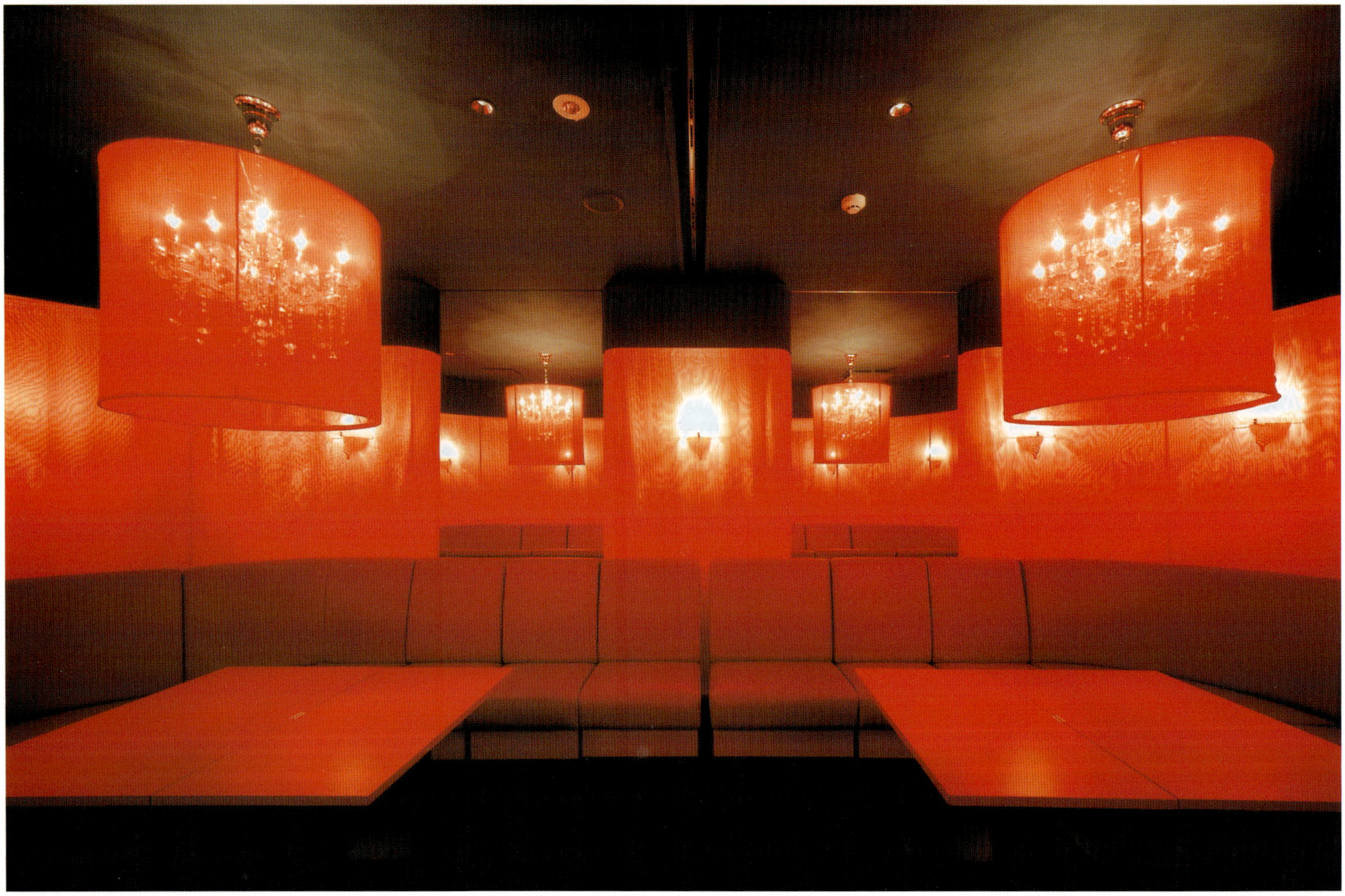

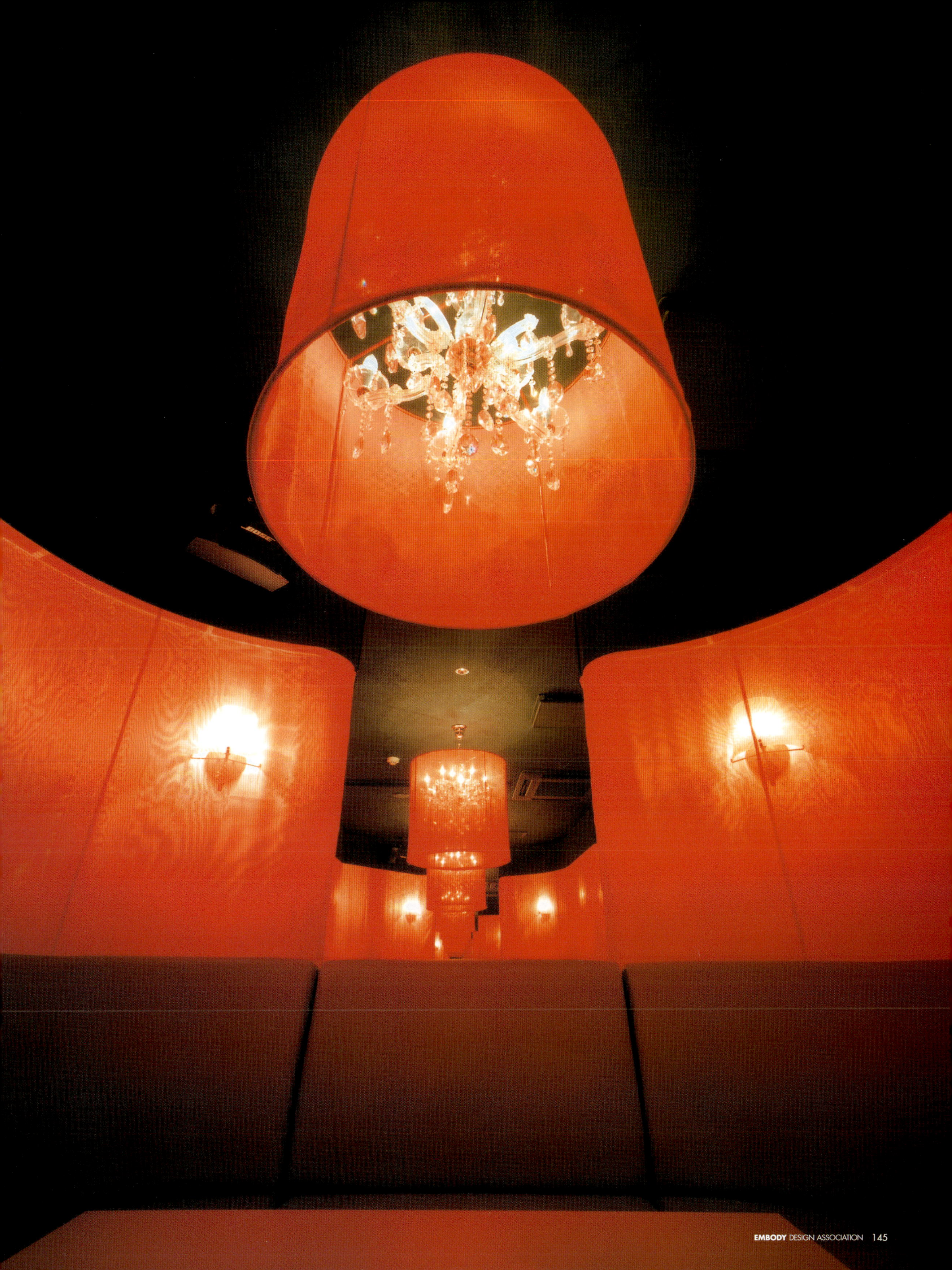

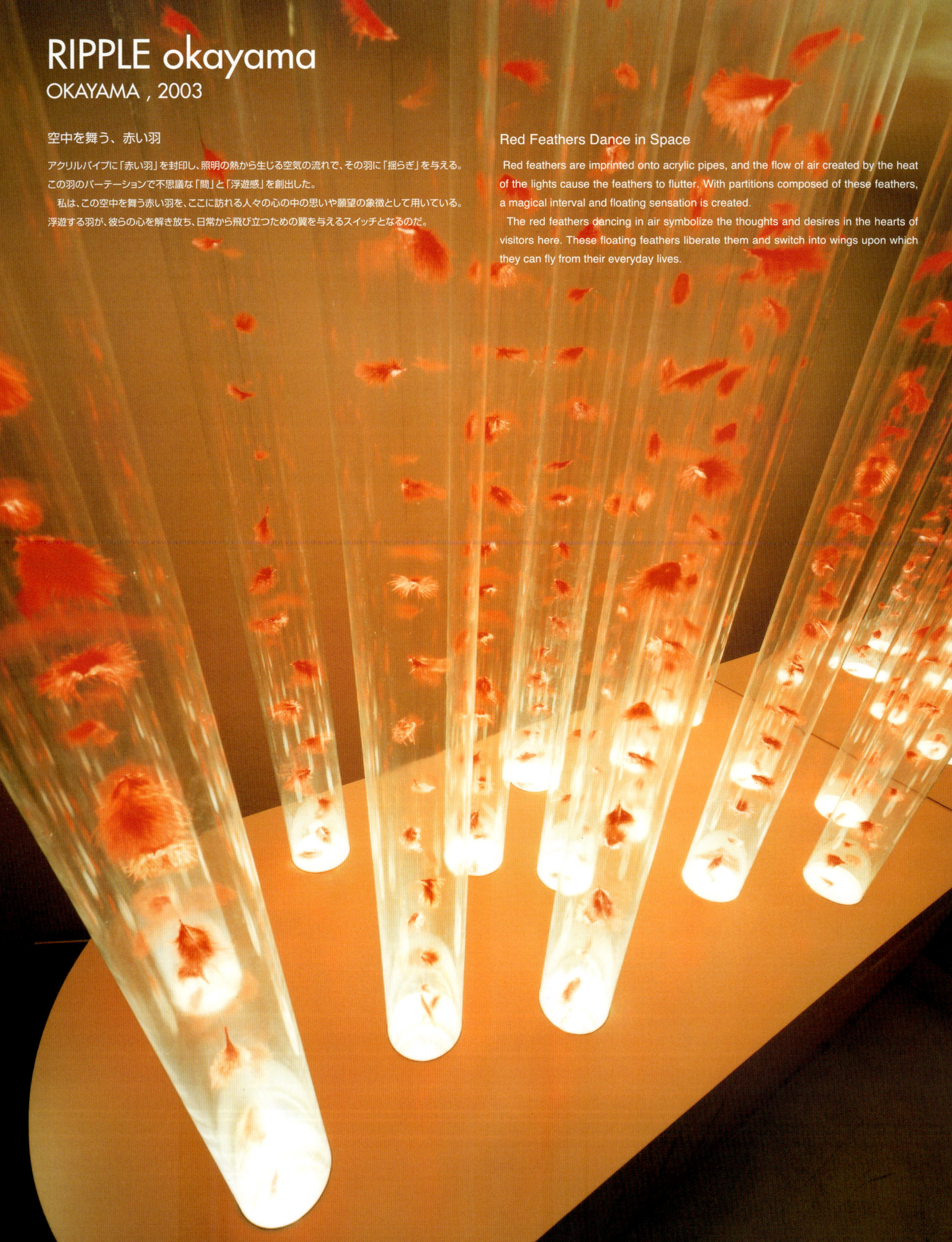

RIPPLE okayama
OKAYAMA , 2003

空中を舞う、赤い羽

アクリルパイプに「赤い羽」を封印し、照明の熱から生じる空気の流れで、その羽に「揺らぎ」を与える。
この羽のパーテーションで不思議な「間」と「浮遊感」を創出した。

　私は、この空中を舞う赤い羽を、ここに訪れる人々の心の中の思いや願望の象徴として用いている。
浮遊する羽が、彼らの心を解き放ち、日常から飛び立つための翼を与えるスイッチとなるのだ。

Red Feathers Dance in Space

 Red feathers are imprinted onto acrylic pipes, and the flow of air created by the heat
of the lights cause the feathers to flutter. With partitions composed of these feathers,
a magical interval and floating sensation is created.

 The red feathers dancing in air symbolize the thoughts and desires in the hearts of
visitors here. These floating feathers liberate them and switch into wings upon which
they can fly from their everyday lives.

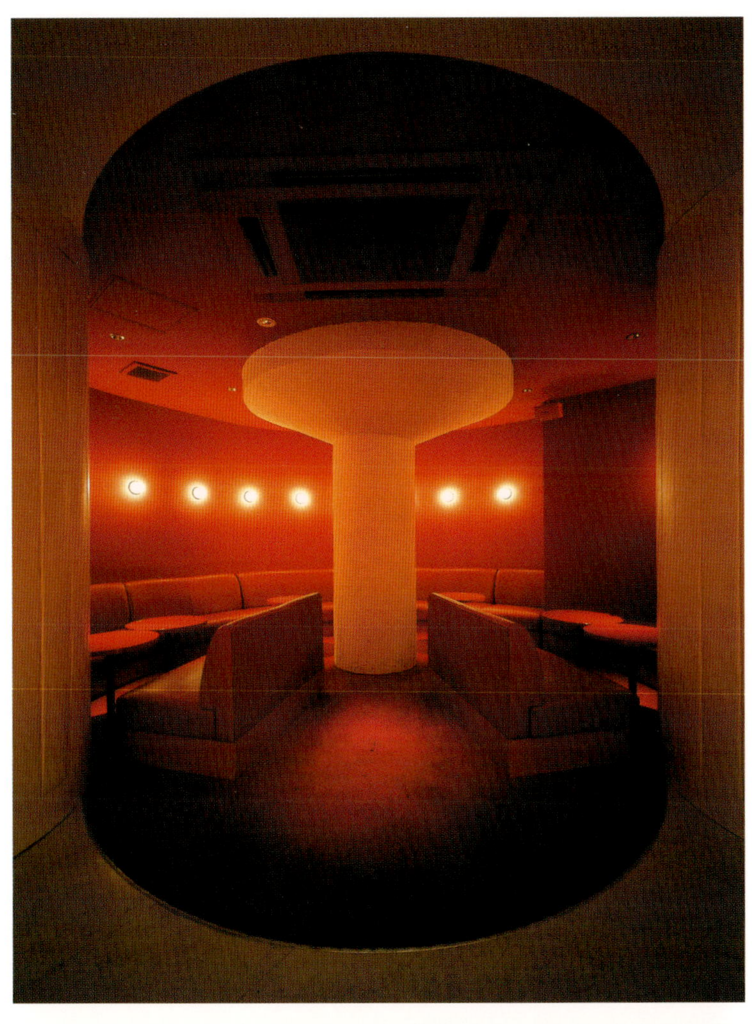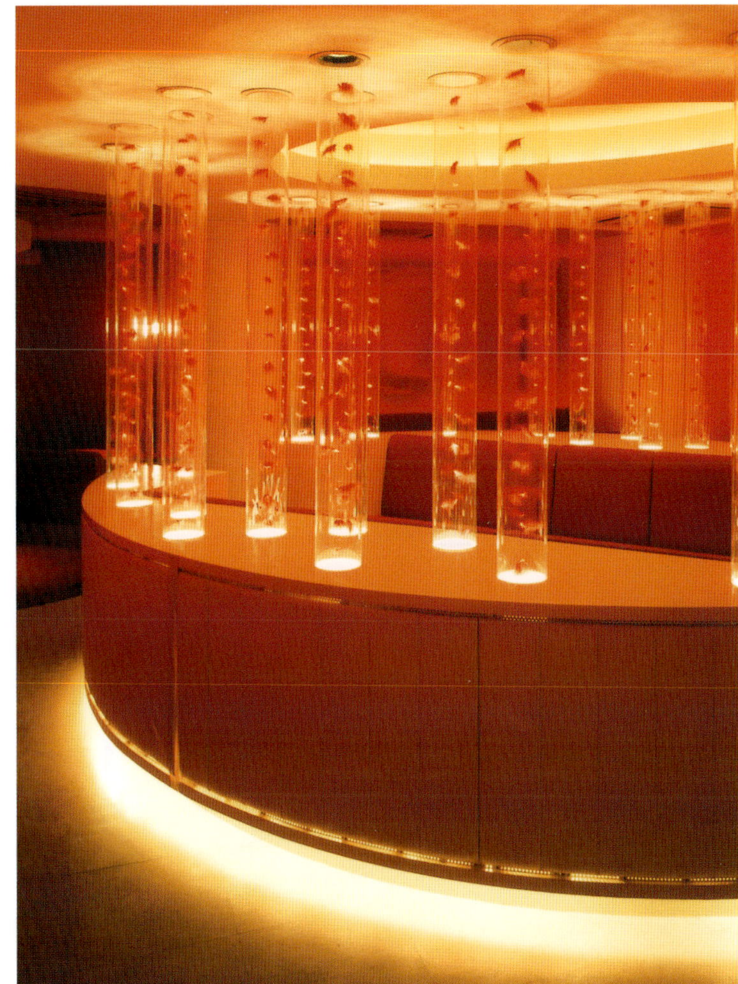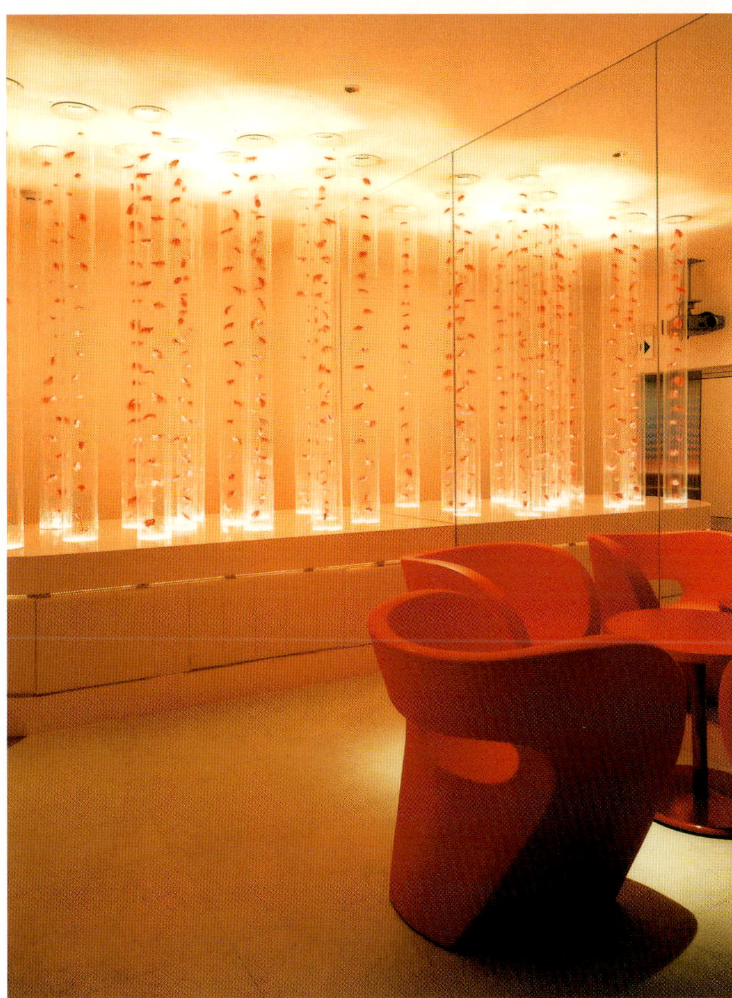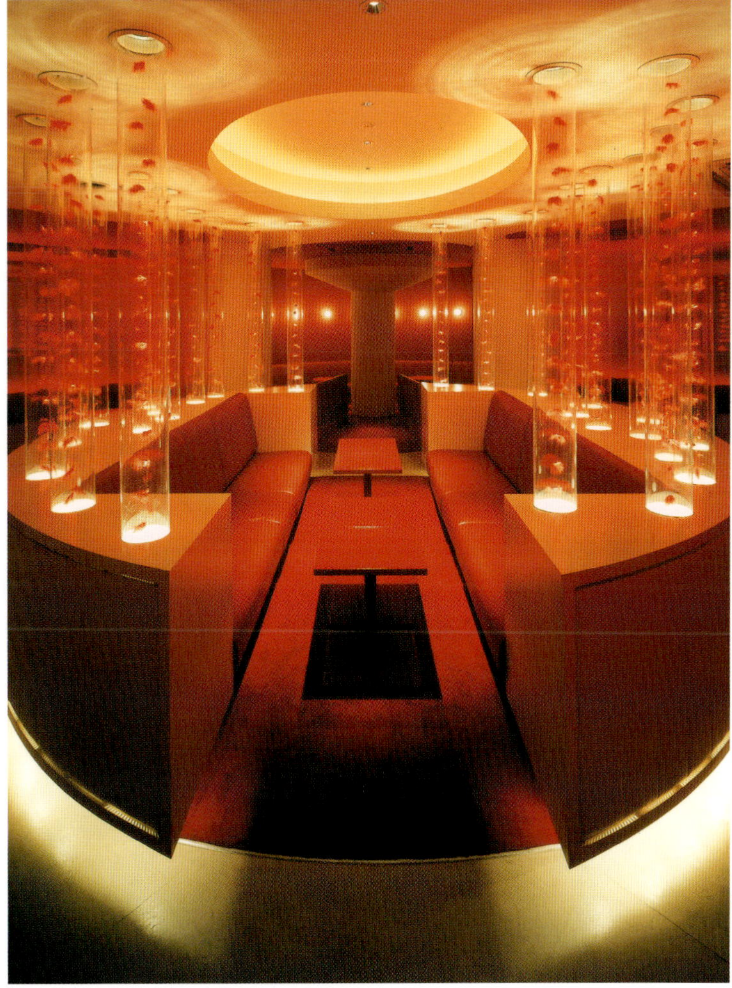

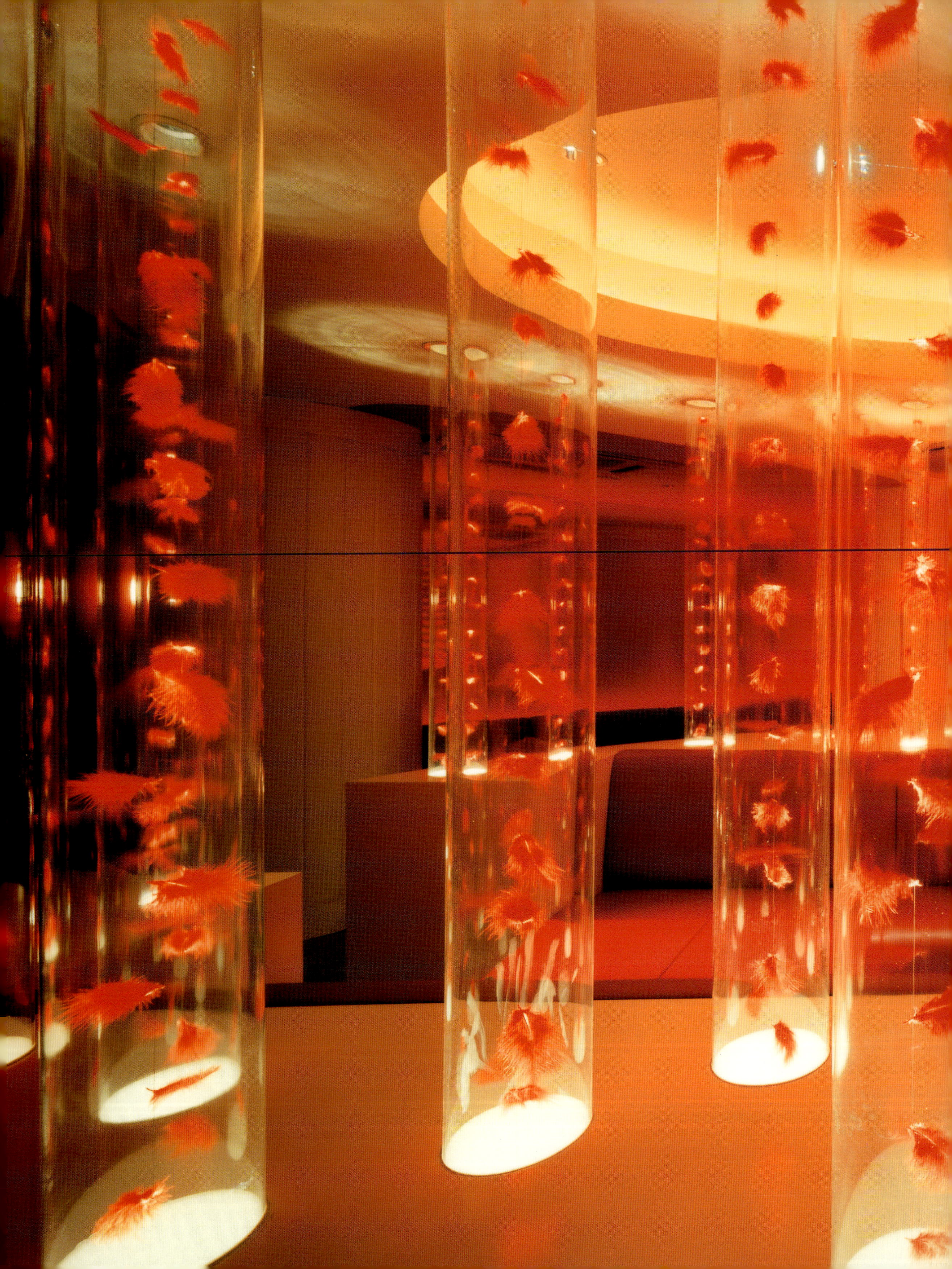

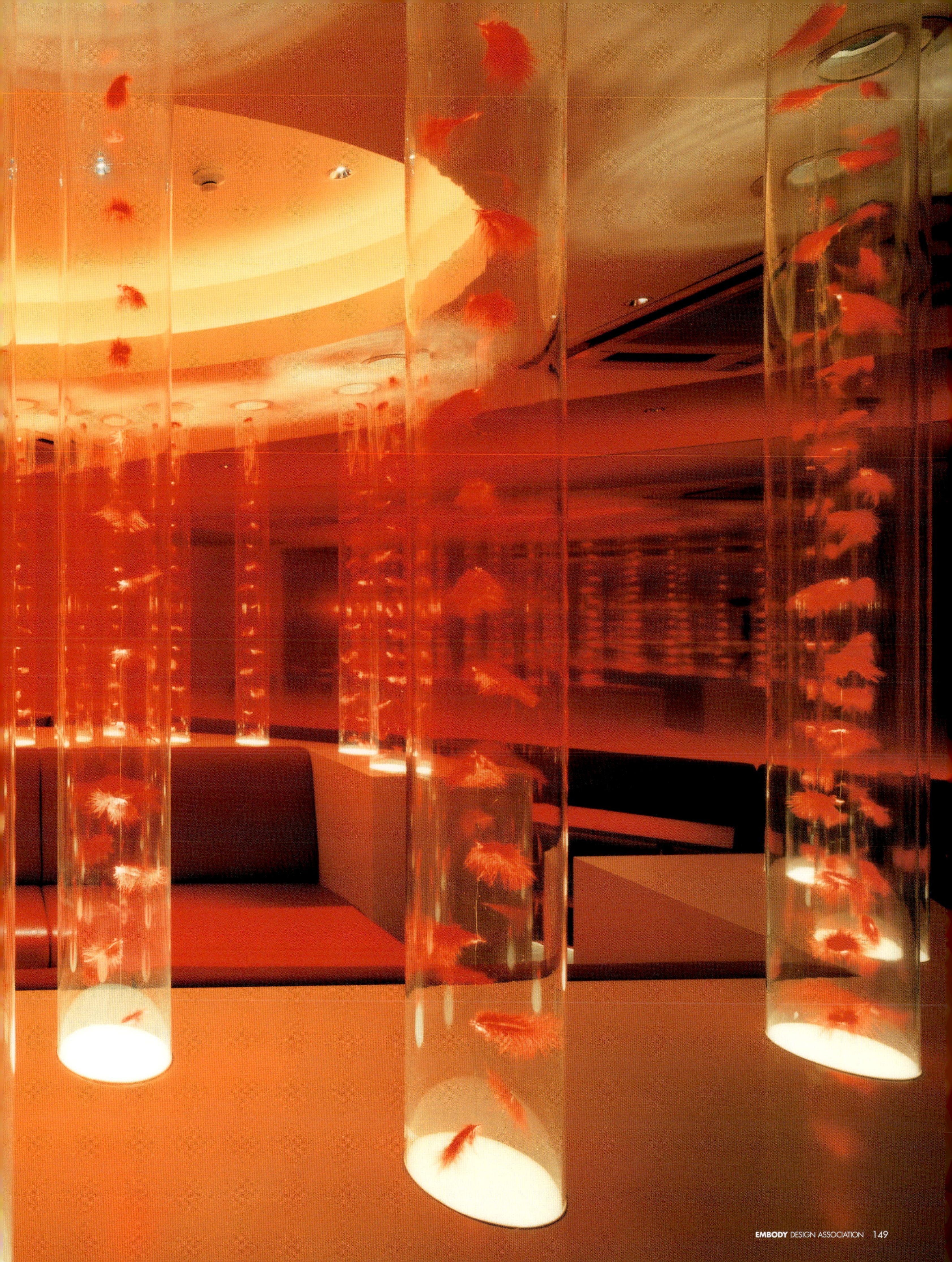

ROSA kobe
KOBE , HYOGO 2002

華と香りに包まれて

「甘い蜜の香りに誘われて蝶が花に群がるように、男たちが"ROSA"にひしめく。」ここで繰り広げられるであろう、そんなシーンを想像しながら、空間全体を大きな一輪のバラをイメージしてデザインした。

　いびつで使いにくいスペースを逆手にとったゾーニングと、発光するファブリックを用いて、光に包まれる心地よさと、妖艶で色気のある空間を創り出した。

Temptation of Rosa

Like a swarm of butterflies enticed by the aroma of sweet floral nectar, men are drawn to ROSA. With an image of the scenes that will unfold here, the entire space was designed in the image of a huge rose.

　Using zoning that turns the distorted and hard-to-use space to advantage, along with light-emitting fabric, and, bathing it in light, a comfortable space of voluptuousness and seductiveness is created.

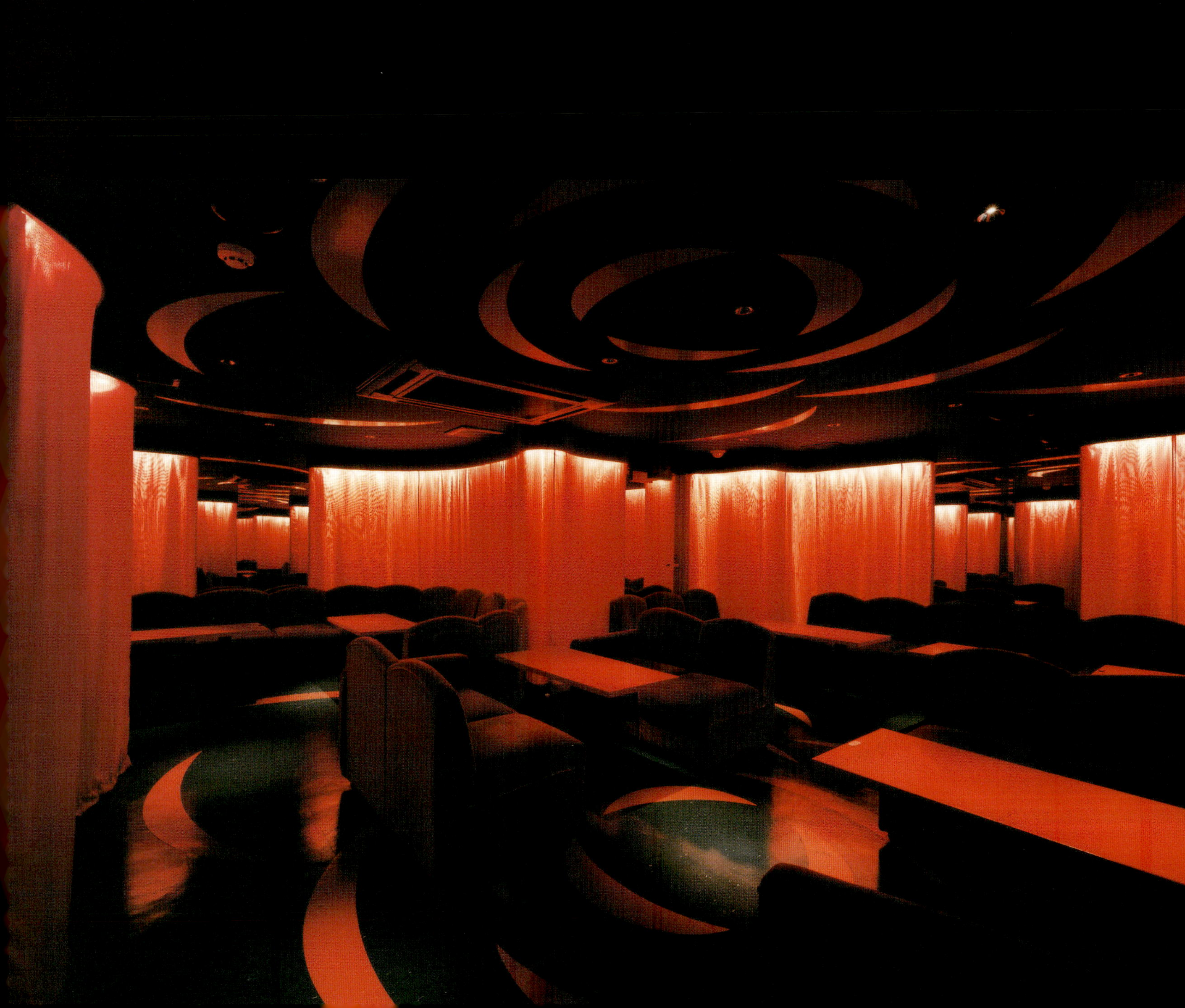

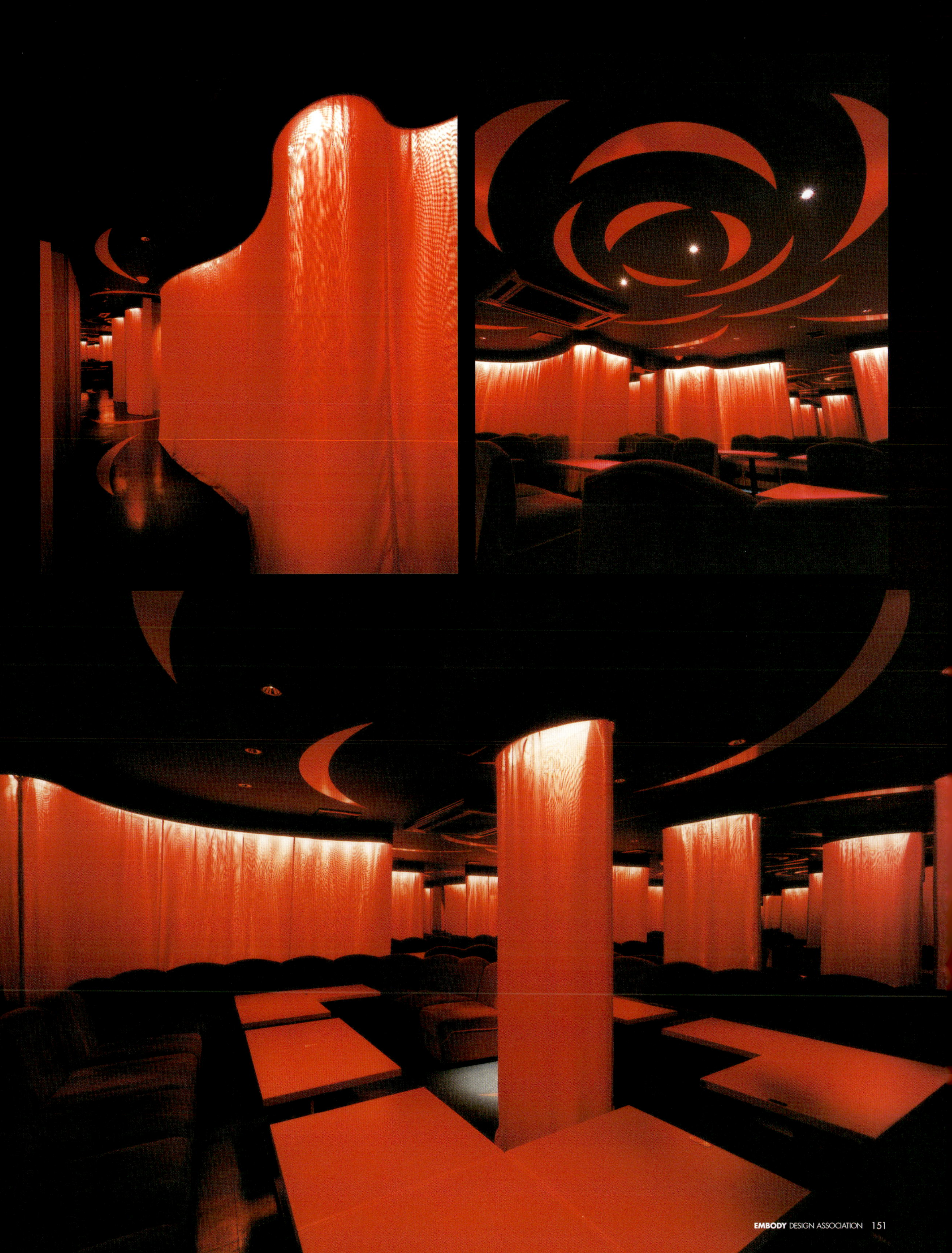

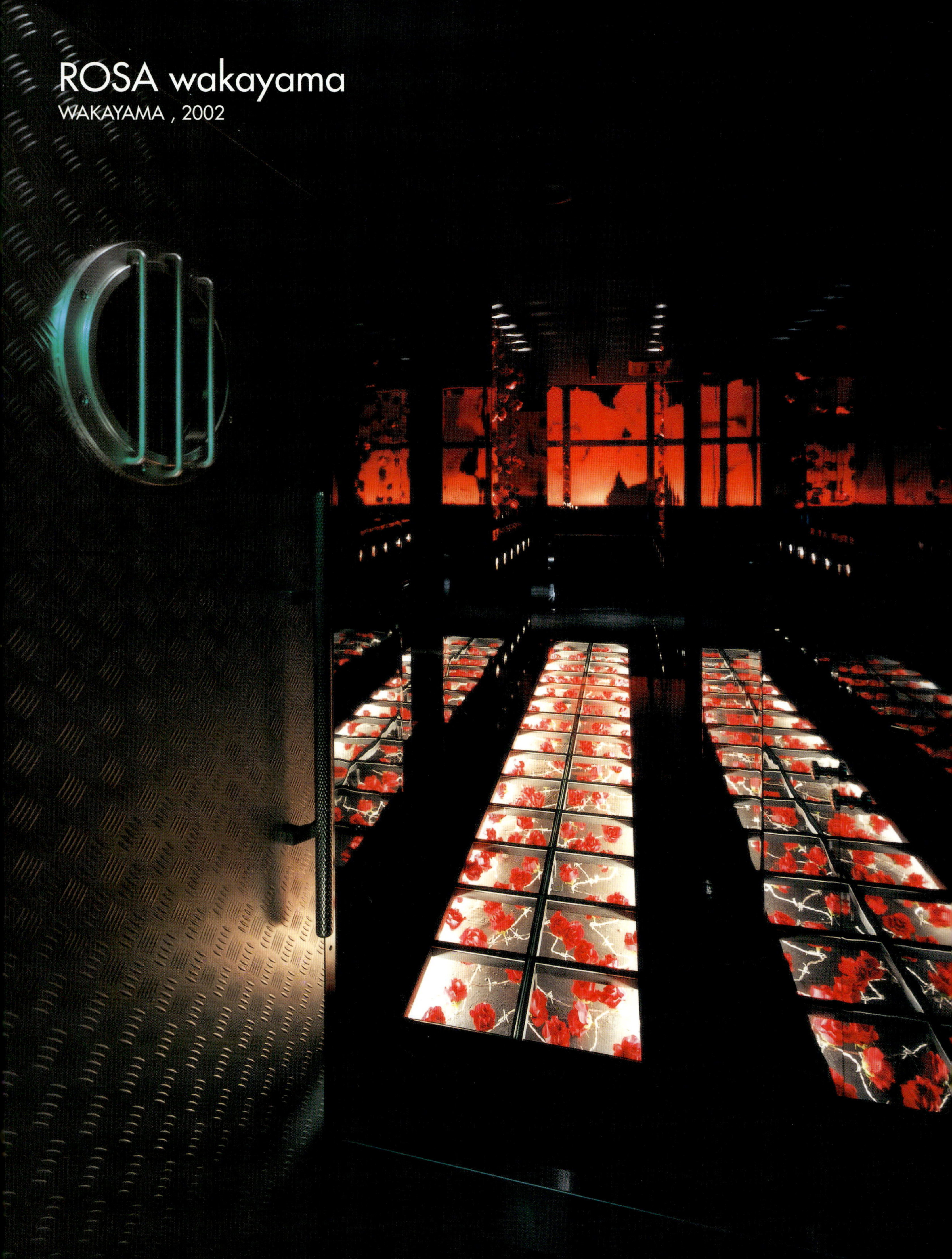

ROSA wakayama
WAKAYAMA , 2002

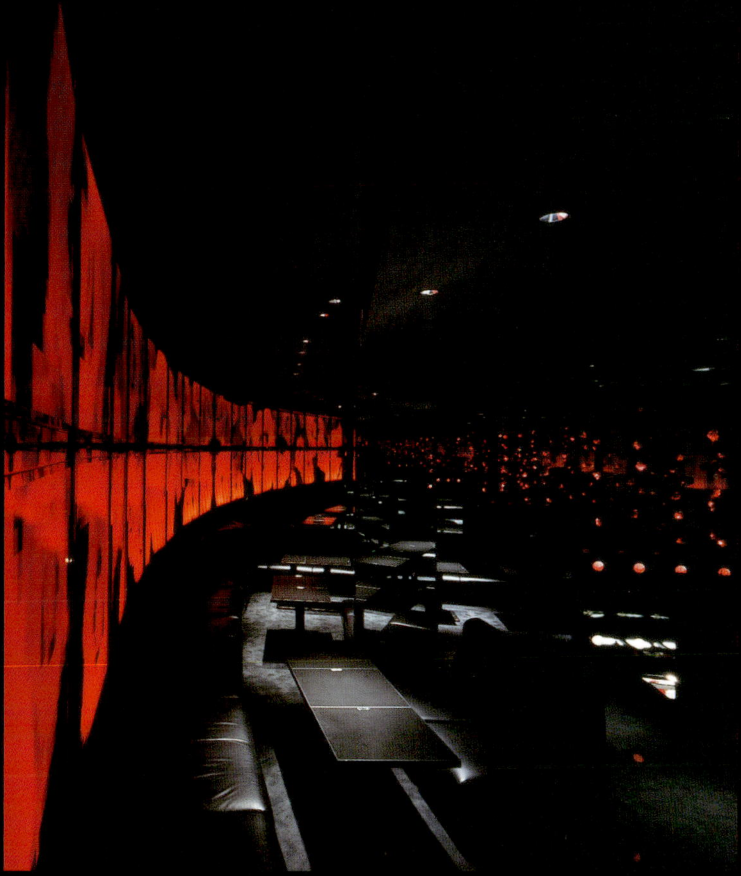

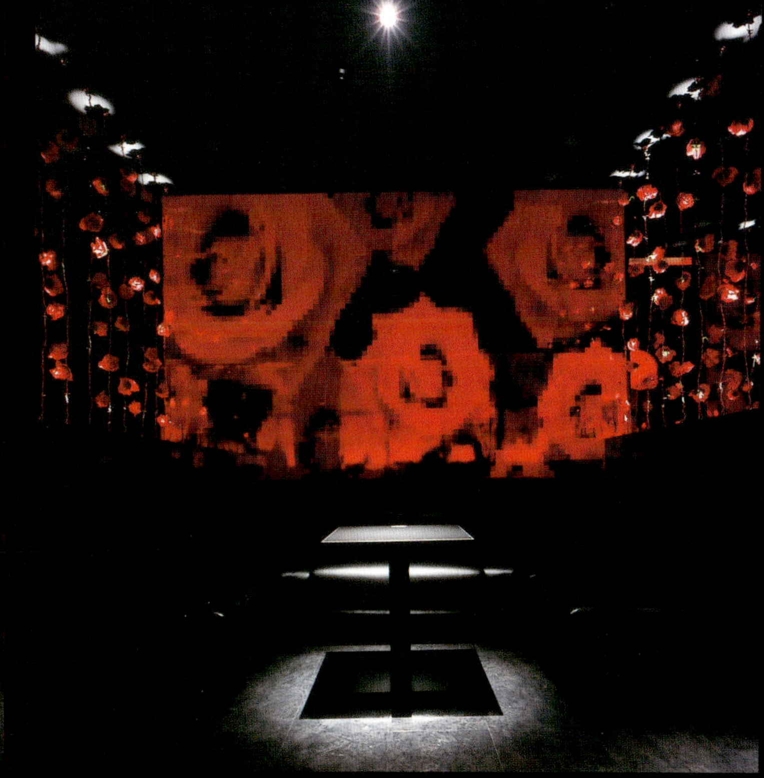

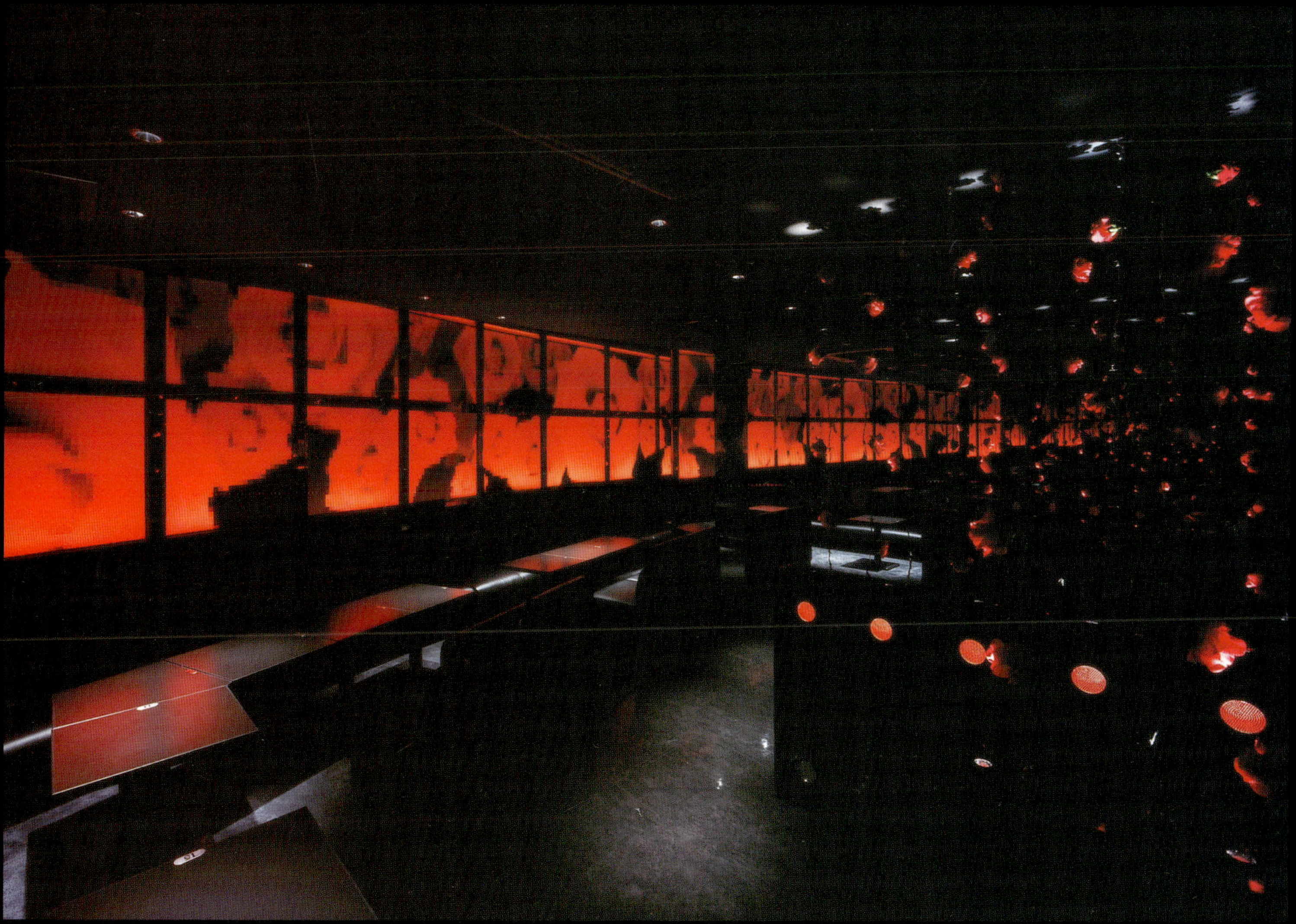

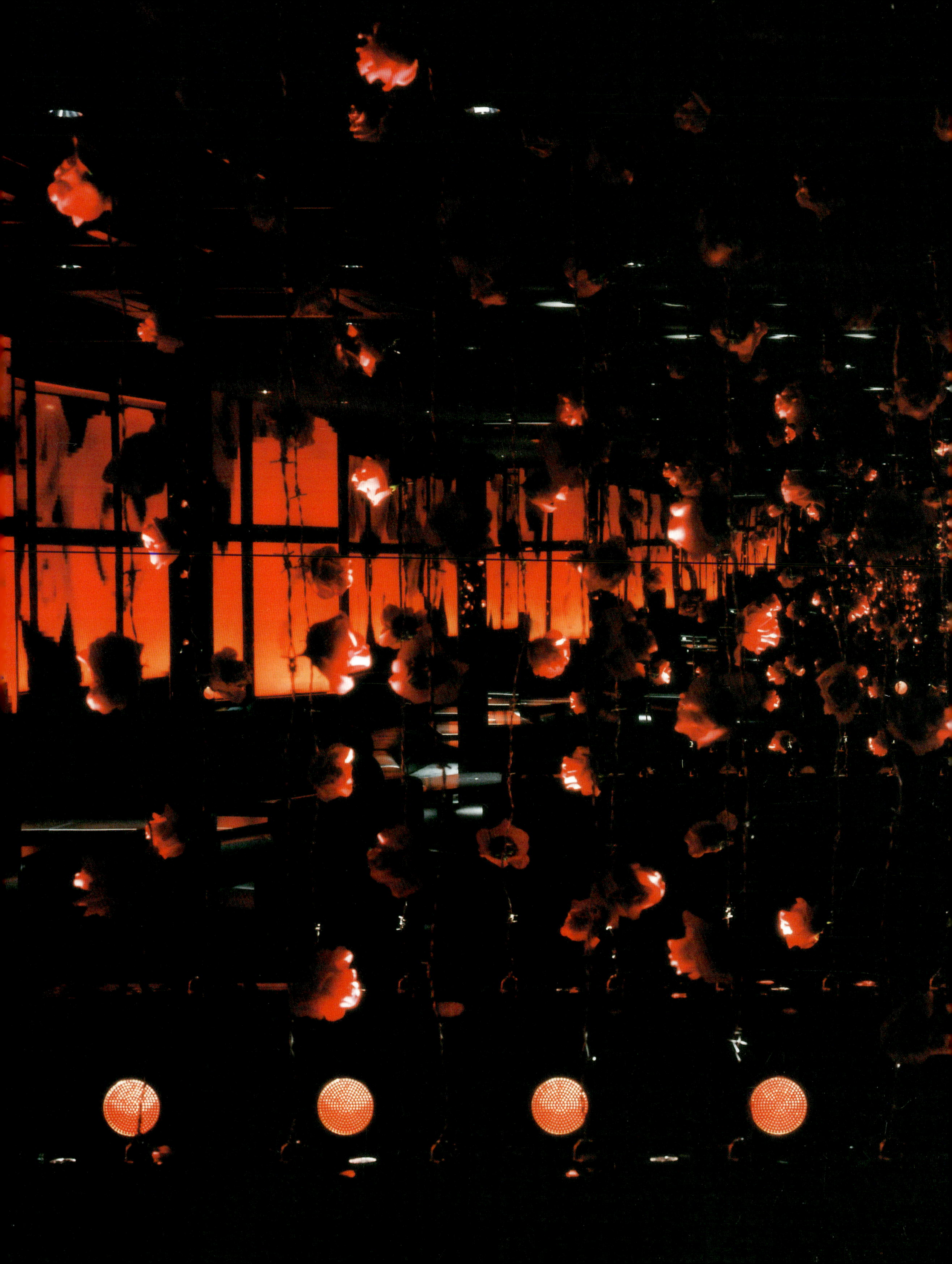

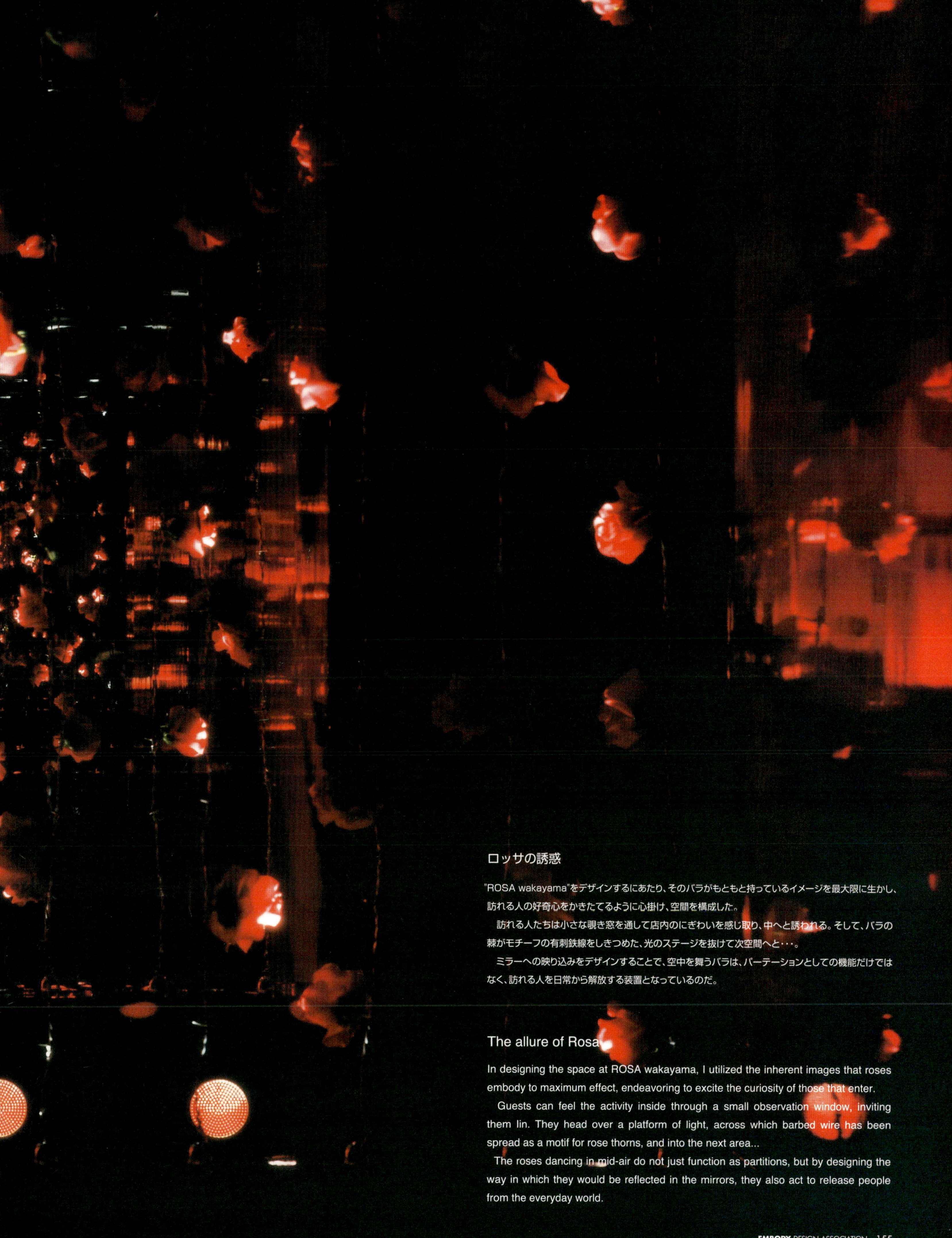

ロッサの誘惑

"ROSA wakayama"をデザインするにあたり、そのバラがもともと持っているイメージを最大限に生かし、訪れる人の好奇心をかきたてるように心掛け、空間を構成した。

　訪れる人たちは小さな覗き窓を通して店内のにぎわいを感じ取り、中へと誘われる。そして、バラの棘がモチーフの有刺鉄線をしきつめた、光のステージを抜けて次空間へと・・・。

　ミラーへの映り込みをデザインすることで、空中を舞うバラは、パーテーションとしての機能だけではなく、訪れる人を日常から解放する装置となっているのだ。

The allure of Rosa

In designing the space at ROSA wakayama, I utilized the inherent images that roses embody to maximum effect, endeavoring to excite the curiosity of those that enter.

Guests can feel the activity inside through a small observation window, inviting them Iin. They head over a platform of light, across which barbed wire has been spread as a motif for rose thorns, and into the next area...

The roses dancing in mid-air do not just function as partitions, but by designing the way in which they would be reflected in the mirrors, they also act to release people from the everyday world.

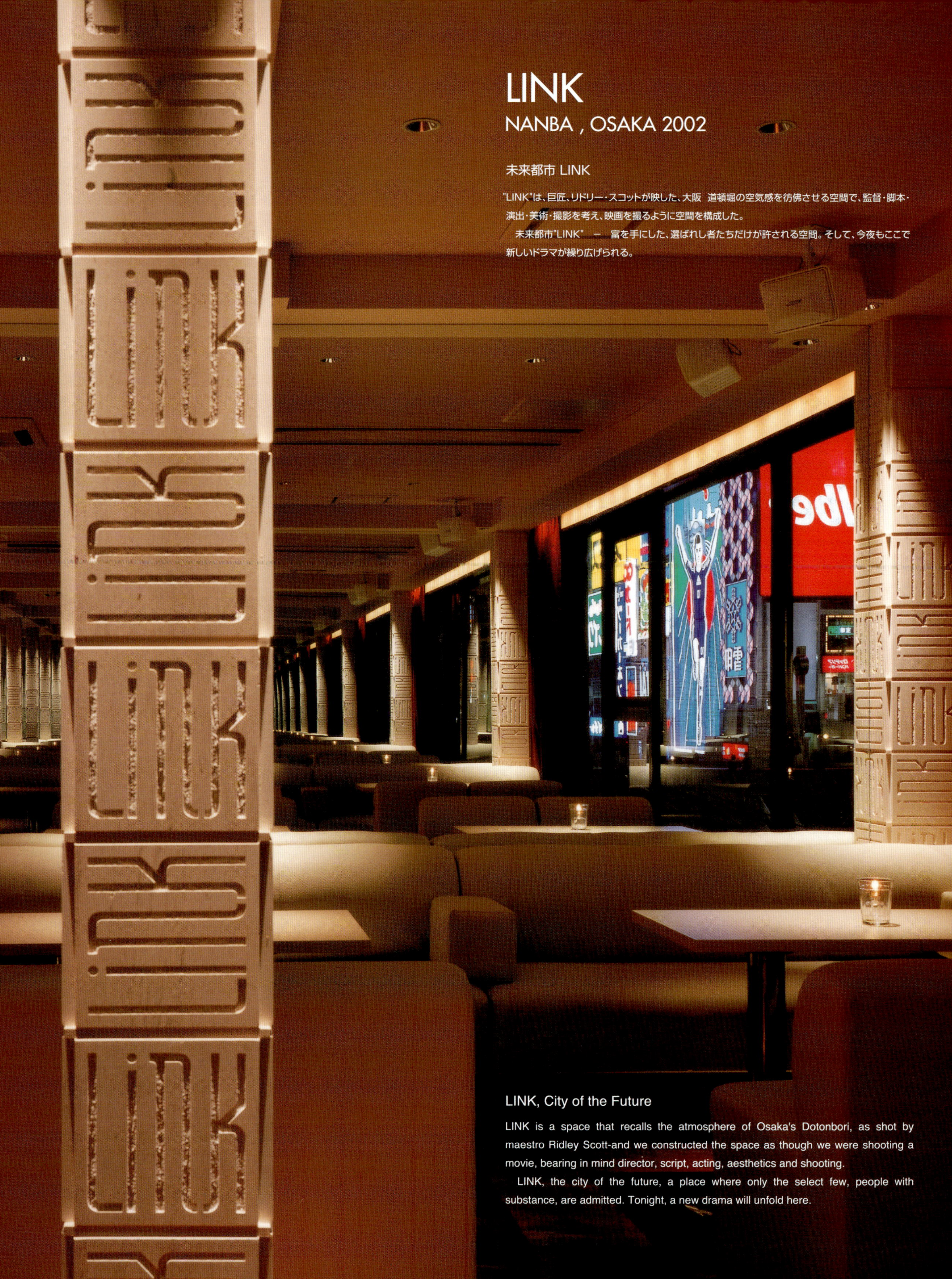

LINK
NANBA , OSAKA 2002

未来都市 LINK

"LINK"は、巨匠、リドリー・スコットが映した、大阪 道頓堀の空気感を彷彿させる空間で、監督・脚本・演出・美術・撮影を考え、映画を撮るように空間を構成した。
　未来都市"LINK" ― 富を手にした、選ばれし者たちだけが許される空間。そして、今夜もここで新しいドラマが繰り広げられる。

LINK, City of the Future

LINK is a space that recalls the atmosphere of Osaka's Dotonbori, as shot by maestro Ridley Scott-and we constructed the space as though we were shooting a movie, bearing in mind director, script, acting, aesthetics and shooting.
　LINK, the city of the future, a place where only the select few, people with substance, are admitted. Tonight, a new drama will unfold here.

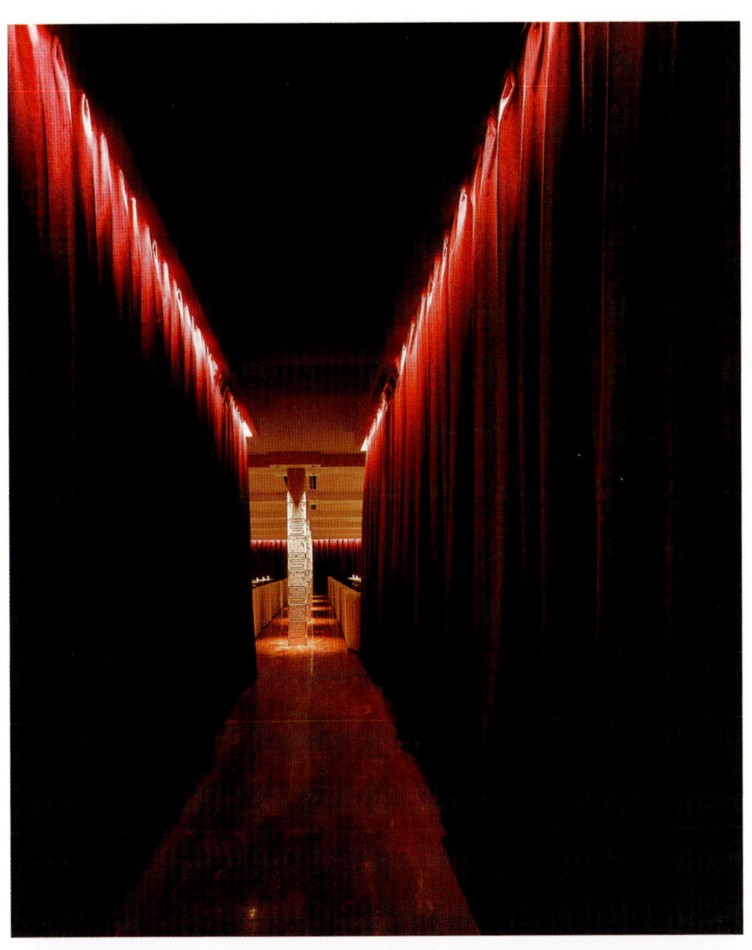
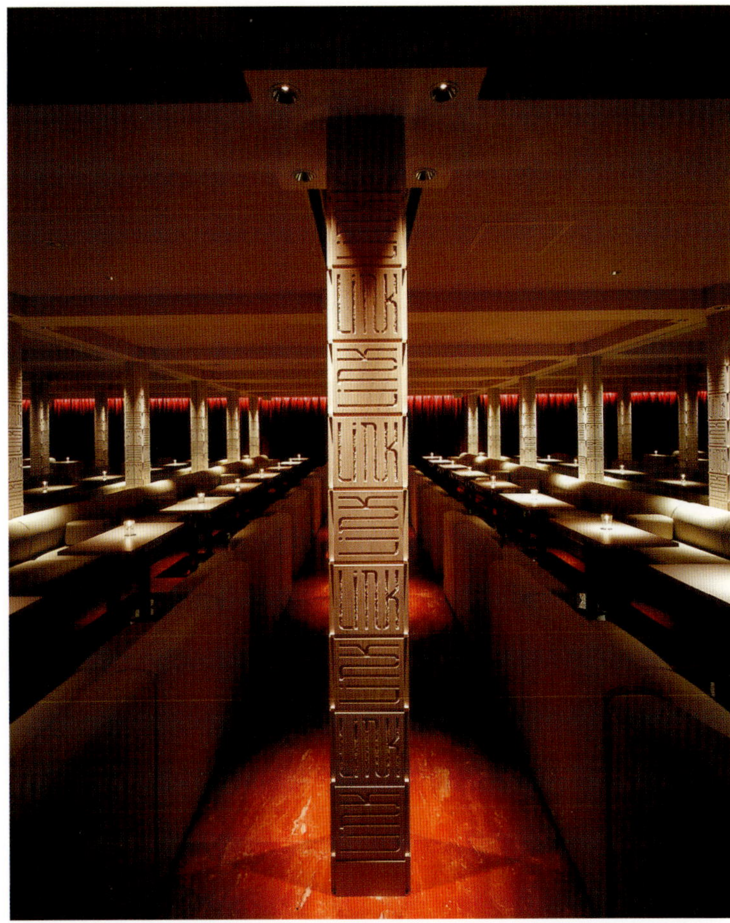

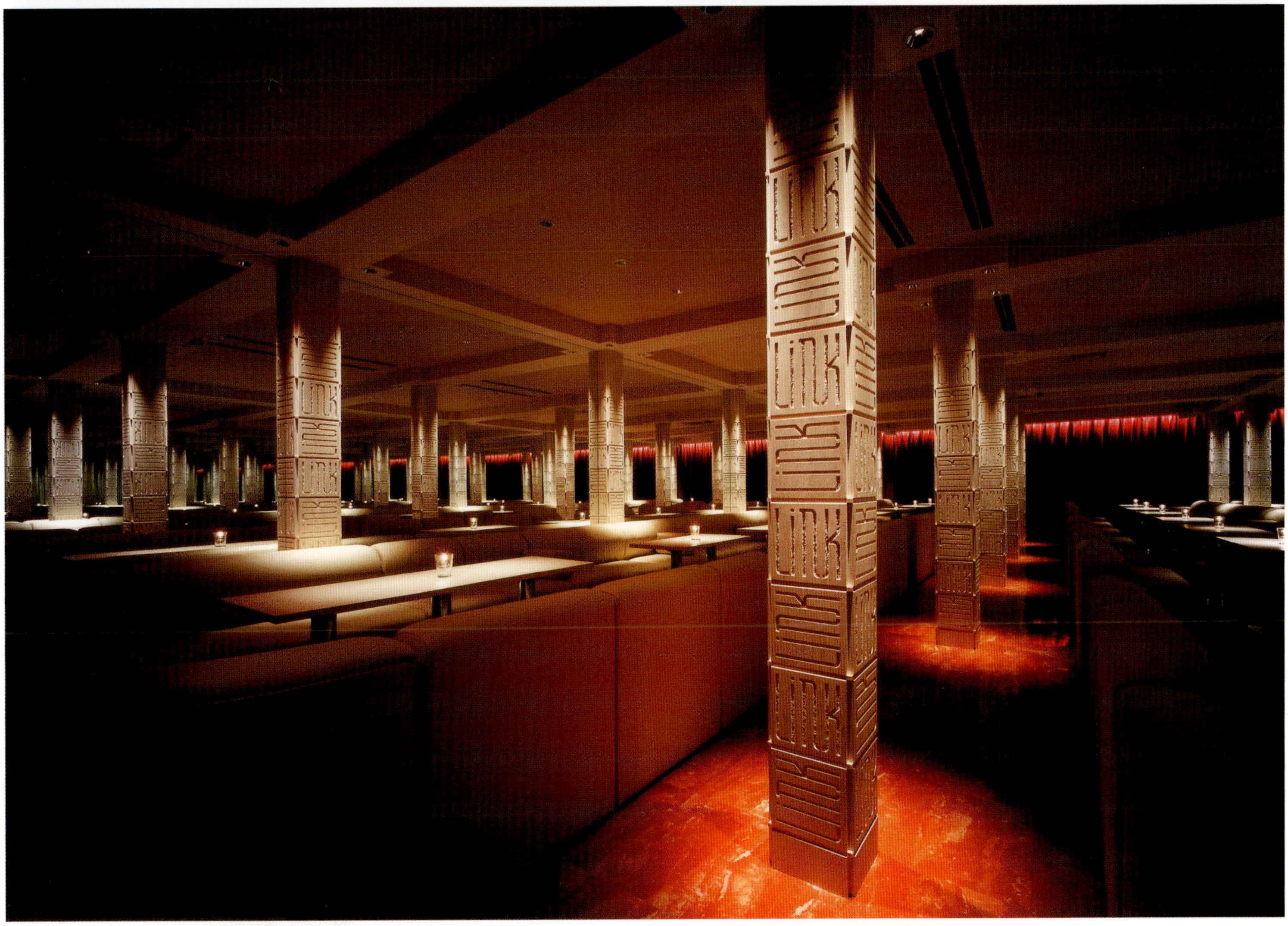

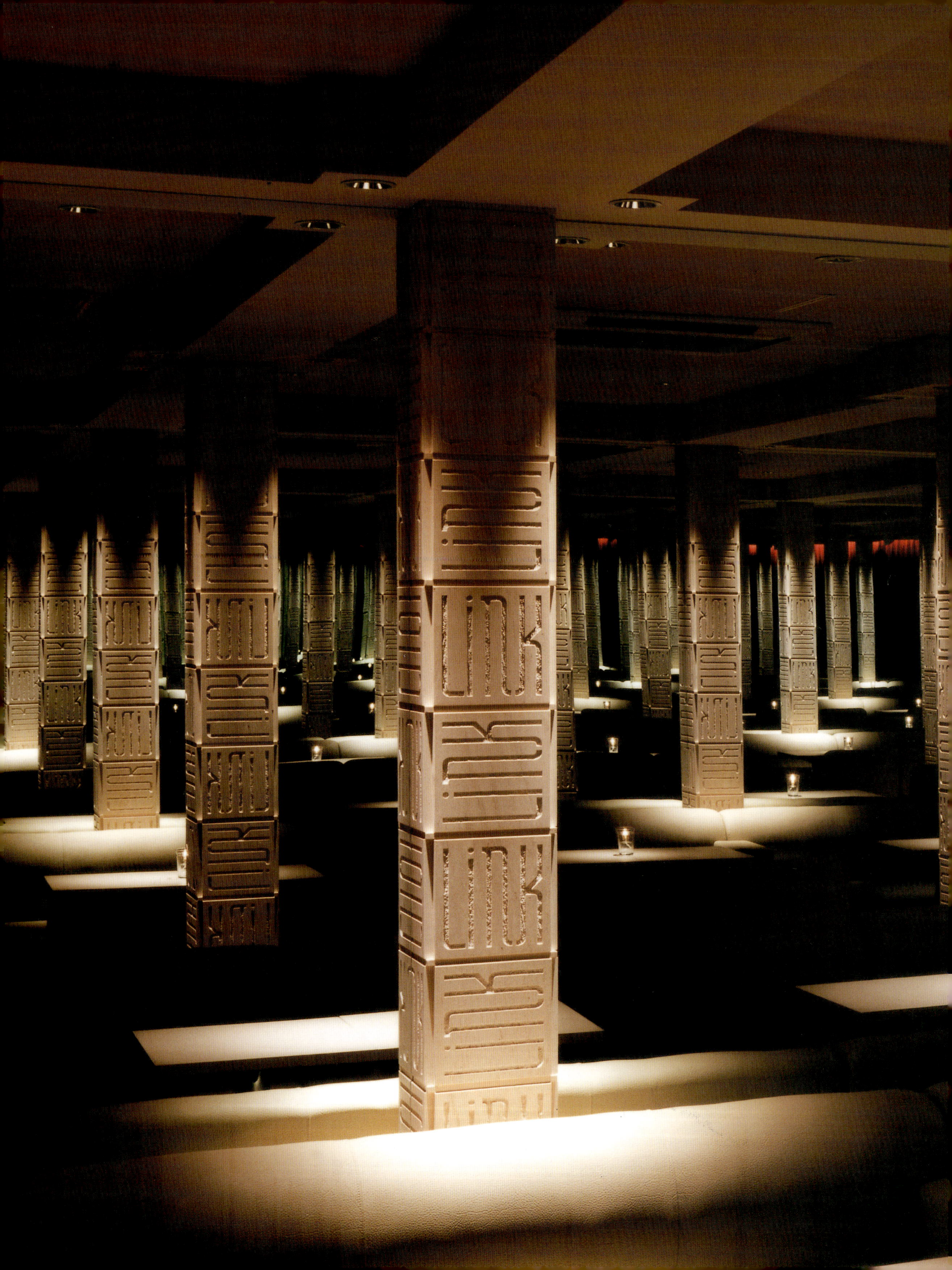

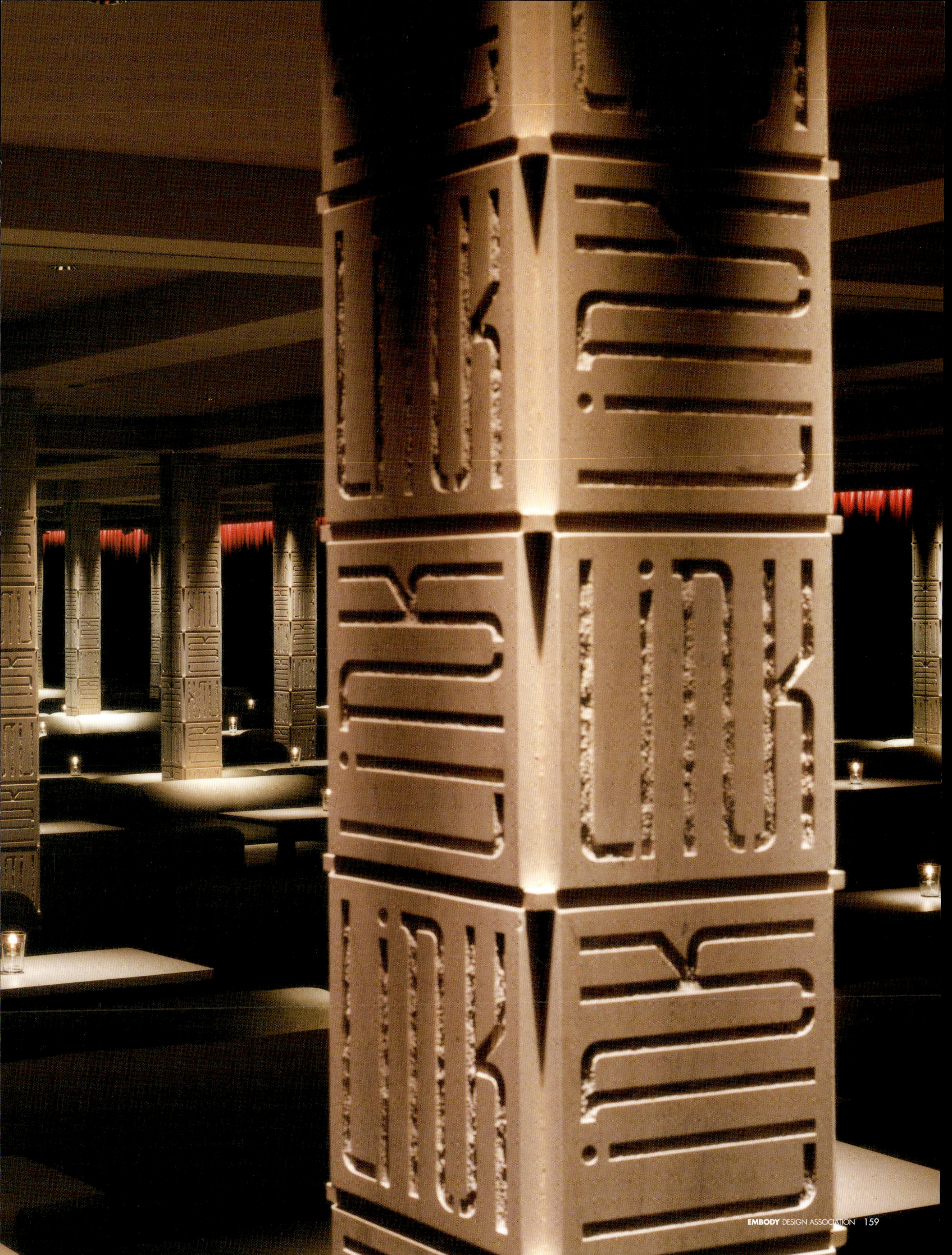

CLUB GALAXY
KITASHINCHI , OSAKA 2001

大人のクラブ活動

日本には、学校では教えてくれない、人や社会についての色々なことを教えてくれる街があります。それが、東の銀座、西の北新地という街です。次世代を握る選ばれし若者たちに、時には常識やエチケットだけでなく、人の大きさや奥行きまで考えさせてくれる街です。

　"CLUB GALAXY"では、日本の独自文化と言えるクラブの伝統を守っていくために、会話を楽しみ、夢を真剣に語れる「場」をイメージし、訪れる人のプライバシーを大切にした空間を構築しました。

Club Activities for Adults

In Japan, there are areas that teach various things about people and society not taught in schools: in the East, "Ginza", and, in the West, "Kita Shinchi." For the elite young people chosen to lead the next era, this is an area that also leads the them think about the greatness of people and their capacity, and not just about common sense things and politesse.

 The club tradition, which could be said to be a culture unique to Japan, is in good hands at CLUB GALAXY. Imagining a place where people can enjoy the thrill of conversation and talk about their dreams in earnest, a space that respects visitors' privacy was constructed.

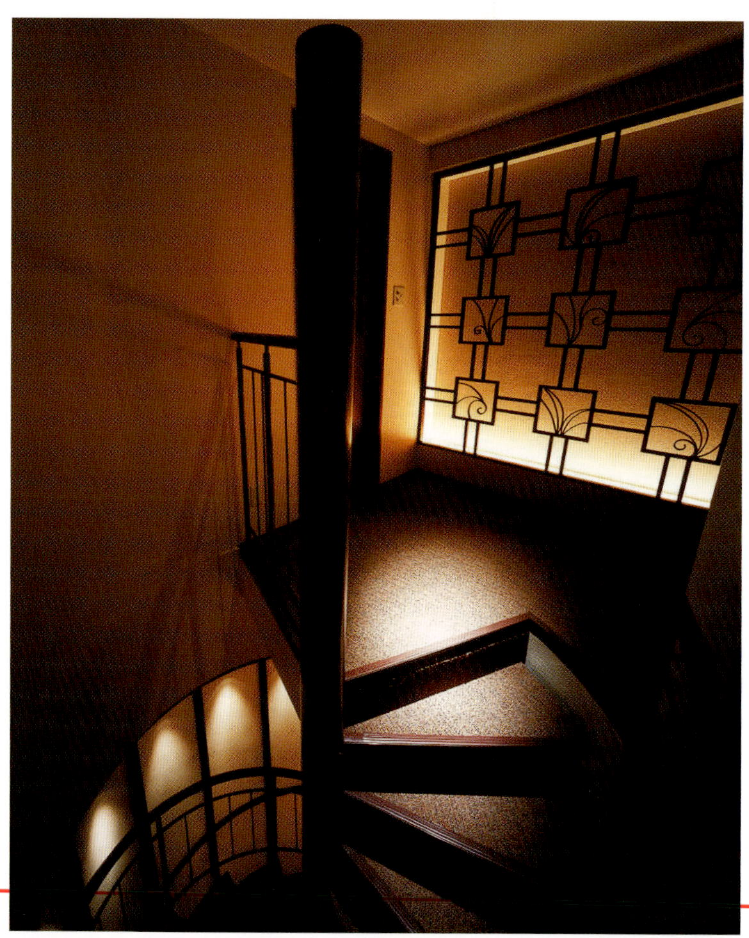

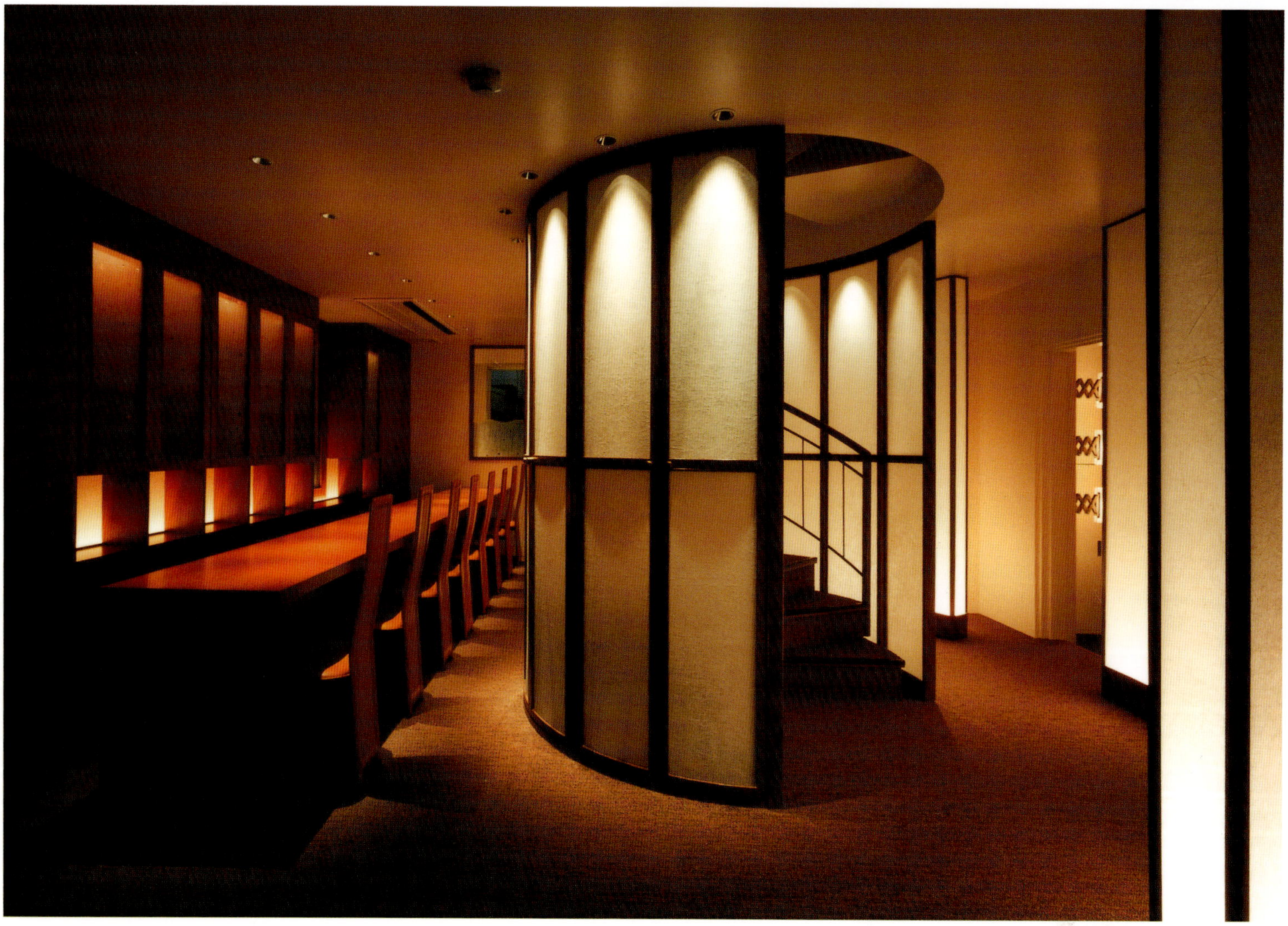

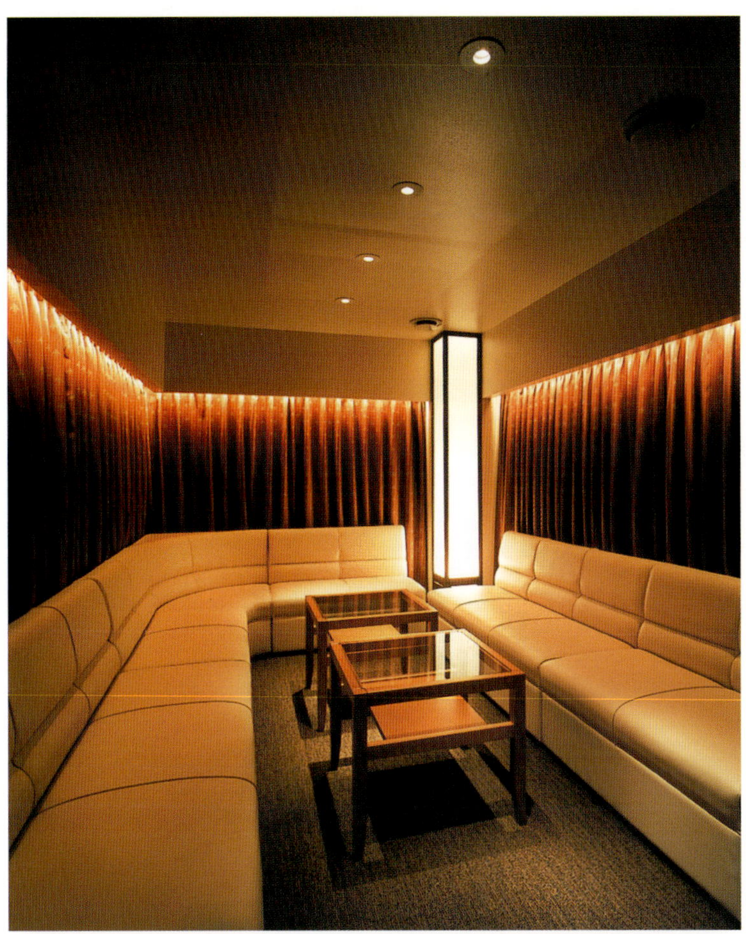

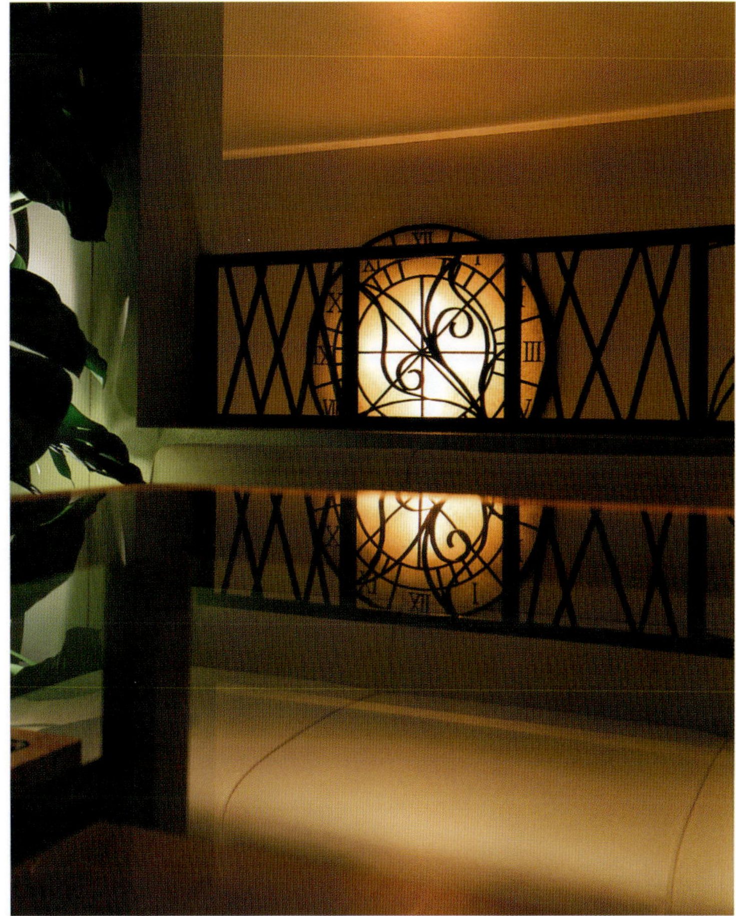

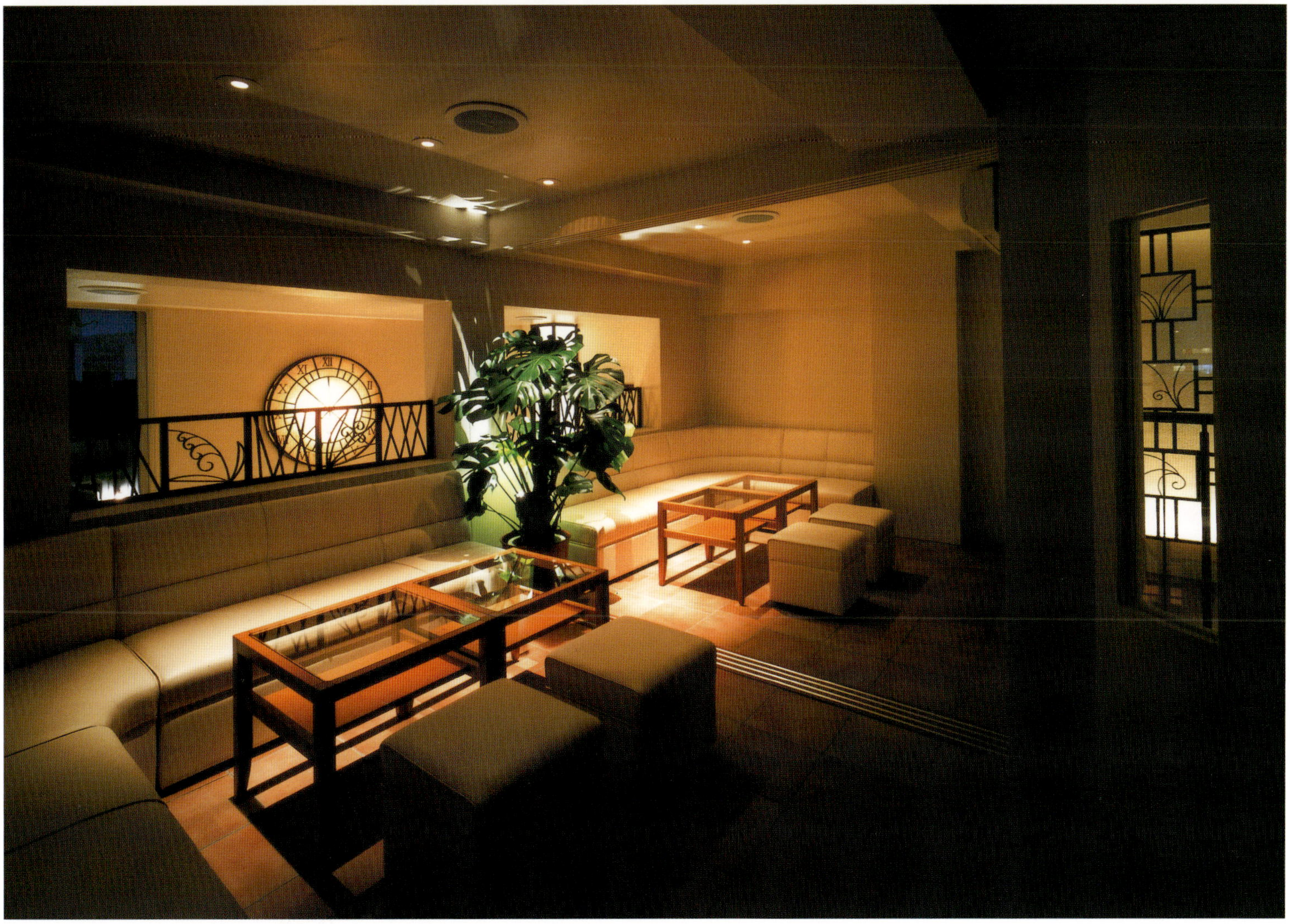

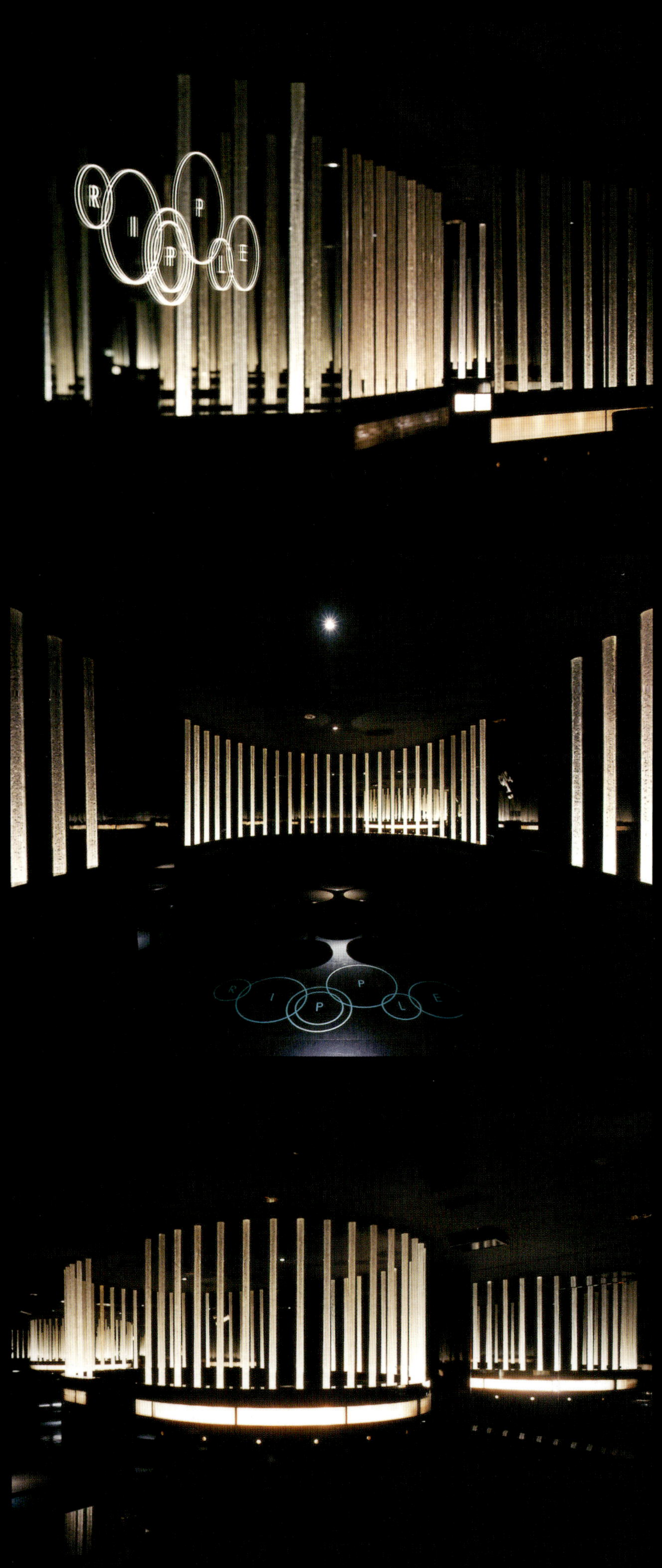

RIPPLE
HIRANO , OSAKA 2000

光の迷宮

"RIPPLE"は、クラブならではの色気のある空気感を大切に、光を用いて空間を構成した。ここでデザインした、「光のパーテーション」には三つの目的を持たせた。

一つ目は、主役である女性が美しく浮き上がるように低いポジションからのライティングを心掛け、「あかり」としての役割。

二つ目は空間として境界や領域を示し、人と人の関係性をデザインして、そこに「間」を創り出す役割。

三つ目は訪れる人の好奇心をかき立てながら、次空間へ・・・次空間へと誘うように、様々な角度を与えたミラーに映り込む、被写体としての役割。

この三つの目的を具現化したことで訪れた人々が心ときめく「光の迷宮」が生まれた。

Labyrinth of light

At RIPPLE, utilizing light to construct the space, I worked to create an alluring and enticing mood, something that is essential for a club. The partitions of light that I designed have three roles.

Firstly, they function as lighting, and I endeavored to get this to come from a low position to beautifully illuminate the most important guests, the women, making them the center of attention.

Their second role is to create spaces by defining boundaries and zones, and designing the interrelationships between people and those around them.

Their third role is as photographic subjects reflected and displayed in mirrors on various angles. They are designed to pique the curiosity of those that enter, enticing them into the next space... and the next.

By achieving this third role, I feel that a labyrinth of light that will capture the hearts of those that visit has successfully been created.

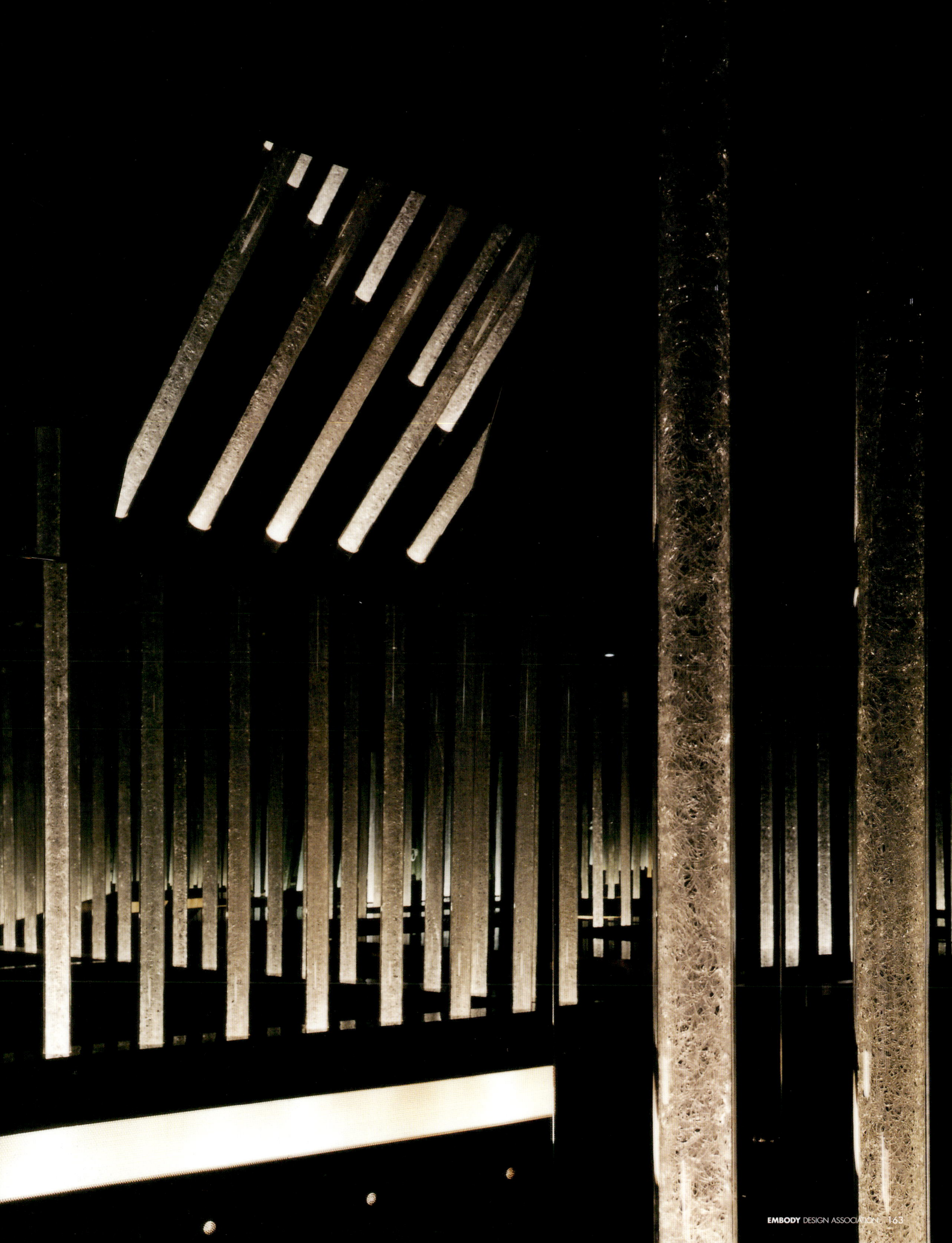

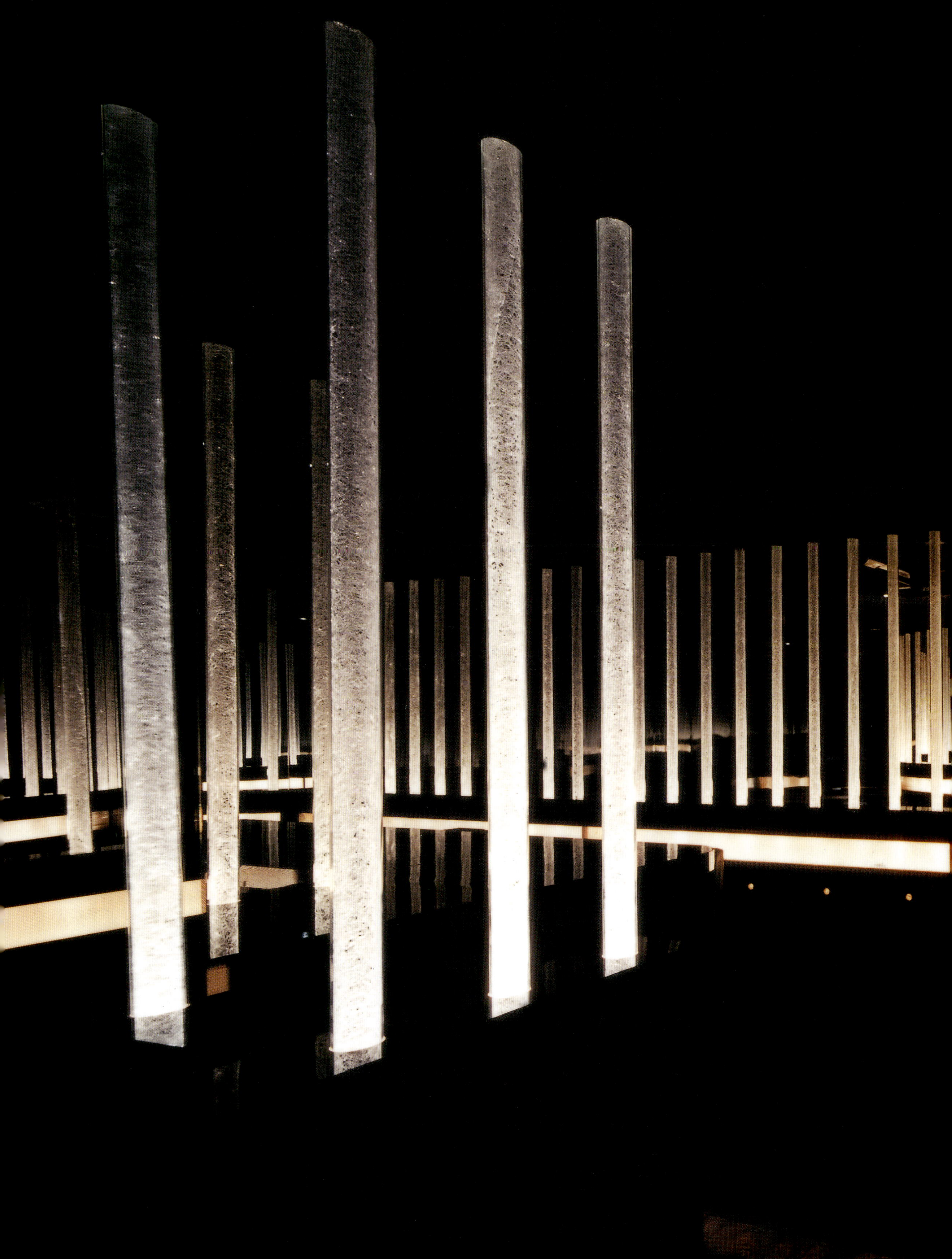

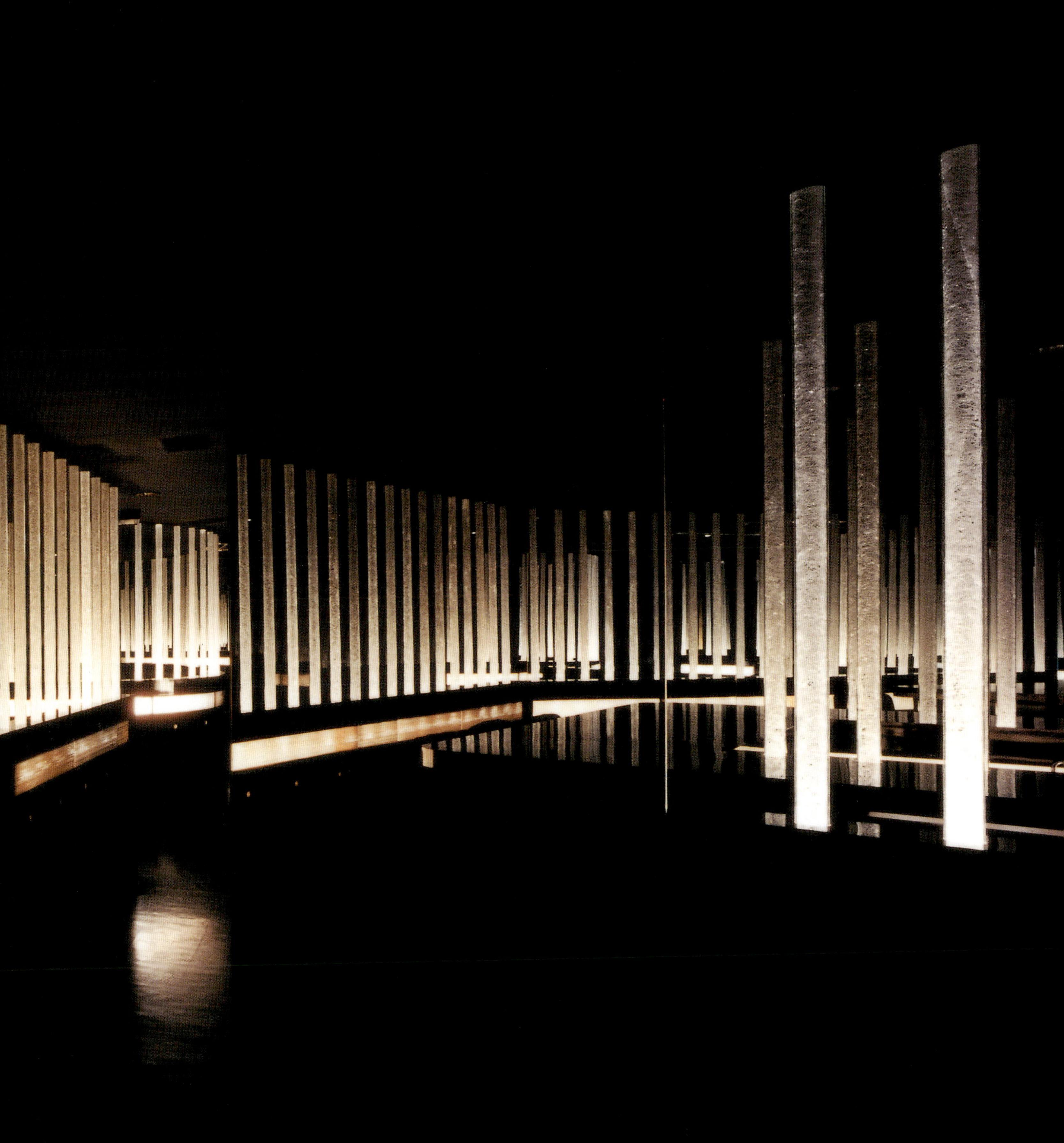

ライフスタイルをデザインする
心地よい暮らし
幸せの種
新たな伝統
列ら
文化
ブランディングデザイン
コミュニケーション
記号化
ビジネスをデザインする
漂う空気をデザインする
pleasant life
lifestyle
Japan
tradition
new
a seed of happiness
design the
future of
branding design
symbolization
communication
business
design the atmosphere

幸せの種

心地よい暮らし

ライフスタイルをデザインする

新たな伝統

列ら 文化

ブランディングデザイン

記号化

コミュニケーション

ビジネスをデザインする

漂う空気をデザインする

SHOP

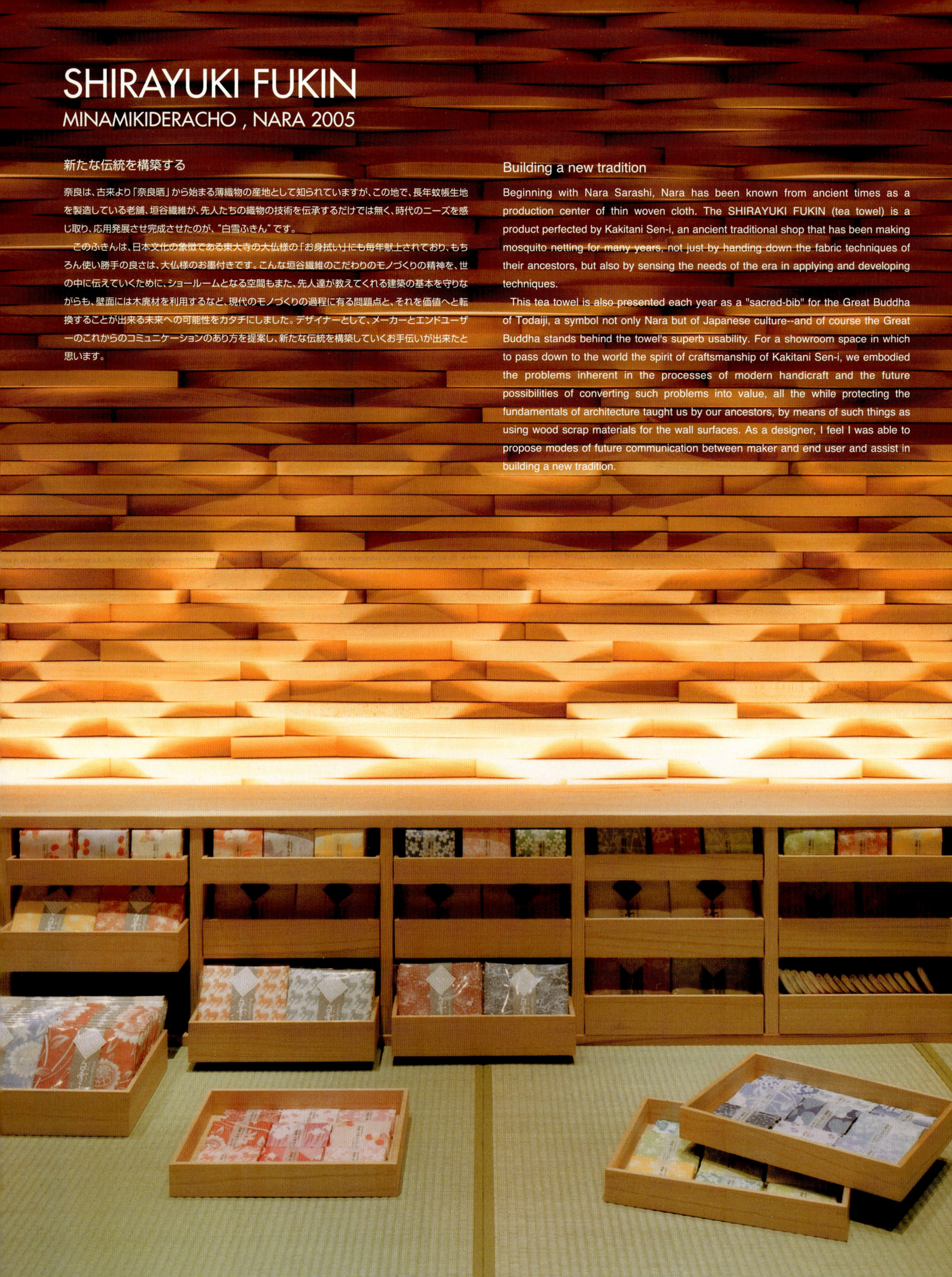

SHIRAYUKI FUKIN
MINAMIKIDERACHO , NARA 2005

新たな伝統を構築する

奈良は、古来より「奈良晒」から始まる薄織物の産地として知られていますが、この地で、長年蚊帳生地を製造している老舗、垣谷繊維が、先人たちの織物の技術を伝承するだけでは無く、時代のニーズを感じ取り、応用発展させ完成させたのが、"白雪ふきん"です。

このふきんは、日本文化の象徴である東大寺の大仏様の「お身拭い」にも毎年献上されており、もちろん使い勝手の良さは、大仏様のお墨付きです。こんな垣谷繊維のこだわりのモノづくりの精神を、世の中に伝えていくために、ショールームとなる空間もまた、先人達が教えてくれる建築の基本を守りながらも、壁面には木廃材を利用するなど、現代のモノづくりの過程に有る問題点と、それを価値へと転換することが出来る未来への可能性をカタチにしました。デザイナーとして、メーカーとエンドユーザーのこれからのコミュニケーションのあり方を提案し、新たな伝統を構築していくお手伝いが出来たと思います。

Building a new tradition

Beginning with Nara Sarashi, Nara has been known from ancient times as a production center of thin woven cloth. The SHIRAYUKI FUKIN (tea towel) is a product perfected by Kakitani Sen-i, an ancient traditional shop that has been making mosquito netting for many years, not just by handing down the fabric techniques of their ancestors, but also by sensing the needs of the era in applying and developing techniques.

This tea towel is also presented each year as a "sacred-bib" for the Great Buddha of Todaiji, a symbol not only Nara but of Japanese culture--and of course the Great Buddha stands behind the towel's superb usability. For a showroom space in which to pass down to the world the spirit of craftsmanship of Kakitani Sen-i, we embodied the problems inherent in the processes of modern handicraft and the future possibilities of converting such problems into value, all the while protecting the fundamentals of architecture taught us by our ancestors, by means of such things as using wood scrap materials for the wall surfaces. As a designer, I feel I was able to propose modes of future communication between maker and end user and assist in building a new tradition.

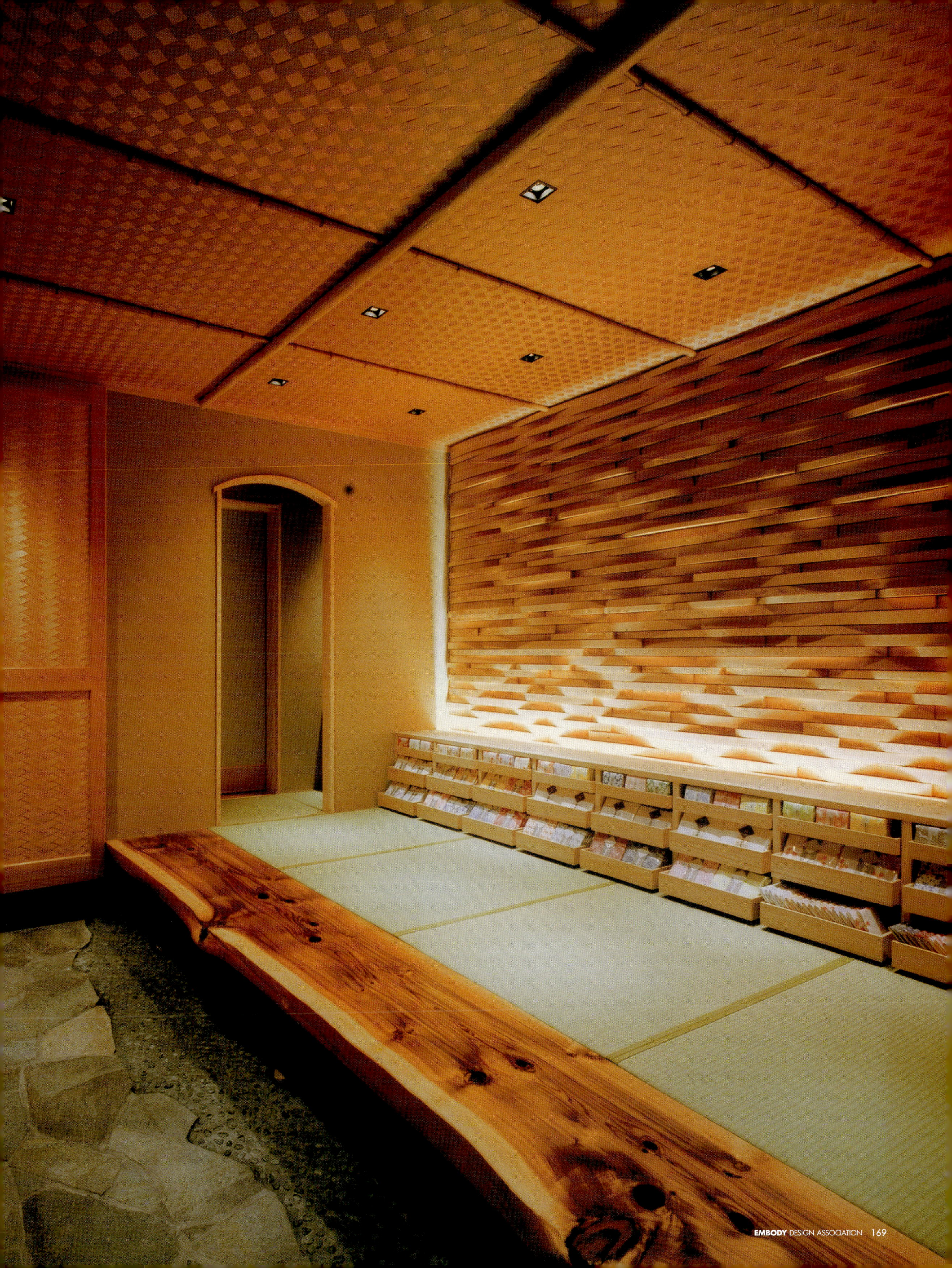

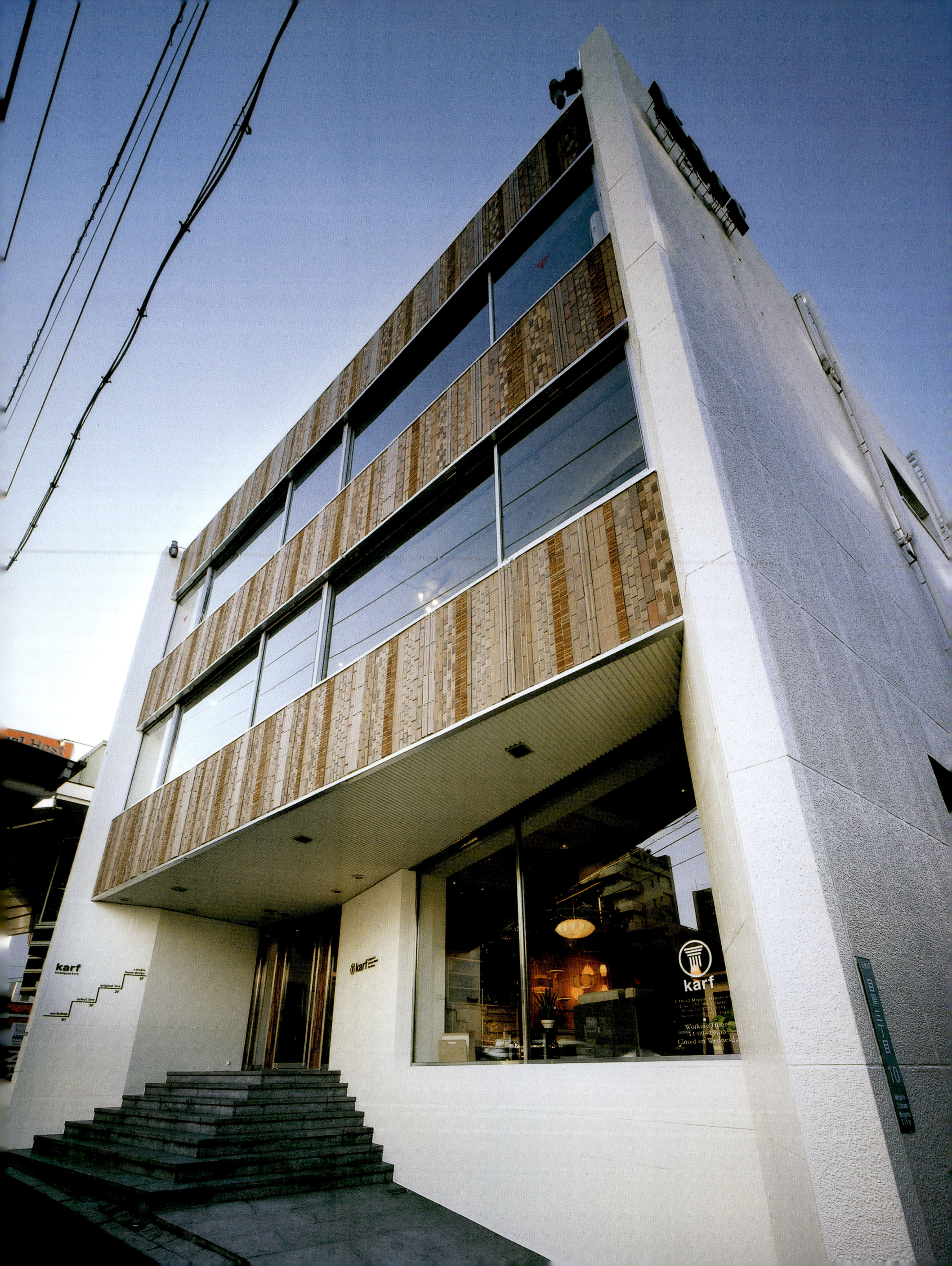

KARF
MEGURO, TOKYO 2004

ライフスタイルをデザインする

ほんの些細な出来事で、幸せを感じることがあります。

たった一つの椅子が幸せの種となり、それまでの暮らしを変えてしまうことだってあります。

　"KARF"をデザインする際に心に描いたのは、素材感（マテリアルがもともと持っている特性を生かし、引き出すこと）と普遍性（トレンドに踊らされない、変わらぬ価値を見出し引き出すこと）をキーワードに、訪れる人々の暮らしに幸せの種を届けることができるようなデザインです。ただ家具を売るためだけの空間ではなく、ここから生まれる「心地よい暮らし」を感じてもらえる空間を目指しました。

Designing lifestyles

Sometimes the most trivial things make you happy.

A single chair can completely change your life.

In designing KARF, I visualized a place where those that visit could find this type of happiness.

I used material sensibility (bringing out and utilizing the natural characteristics of the materials) and universality (discerning and revealing the constant values that remain unaffected by trends) as keywords, and designed with the aim of revealing the charm of the materials used, giving it shape and form so that customers would be able to utilize it as part of their lifestyle. I think that I have created a space that isn't just for selling furniture, but a place that gives people a real sense of the 'comfortable living' that could be born from here.

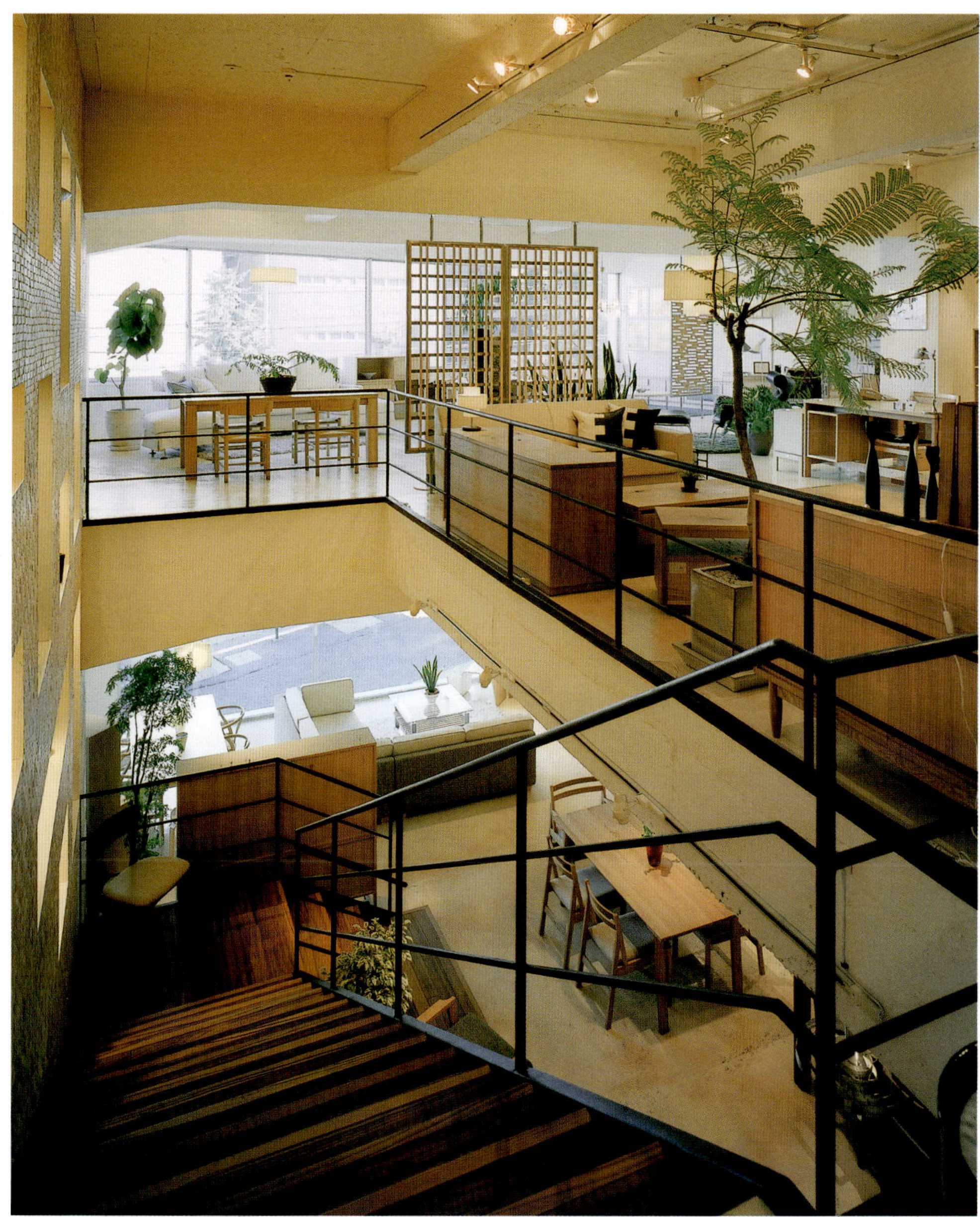

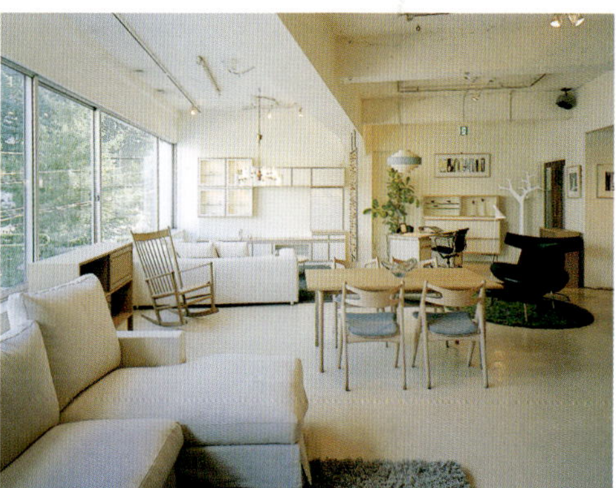

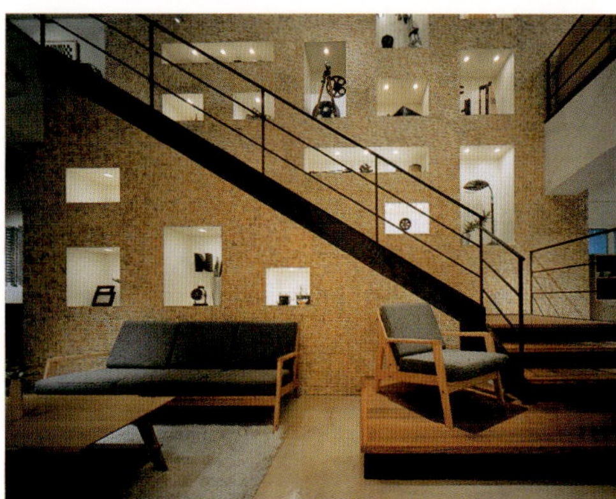

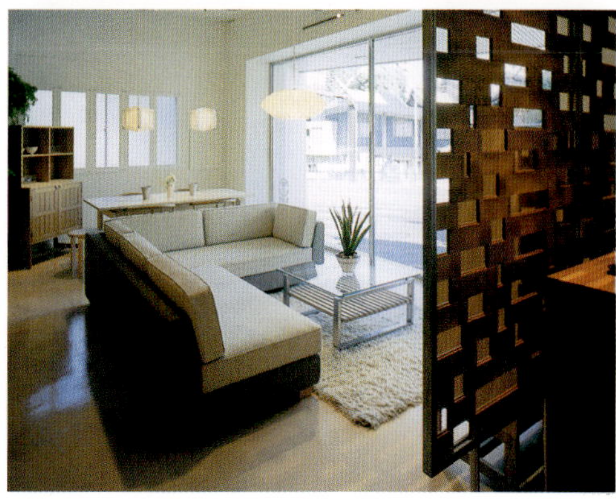

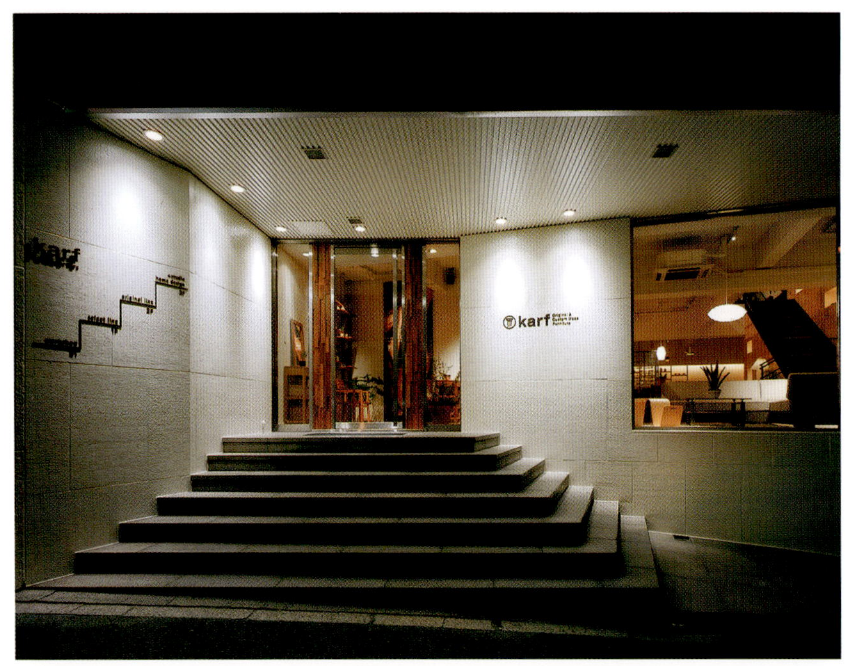

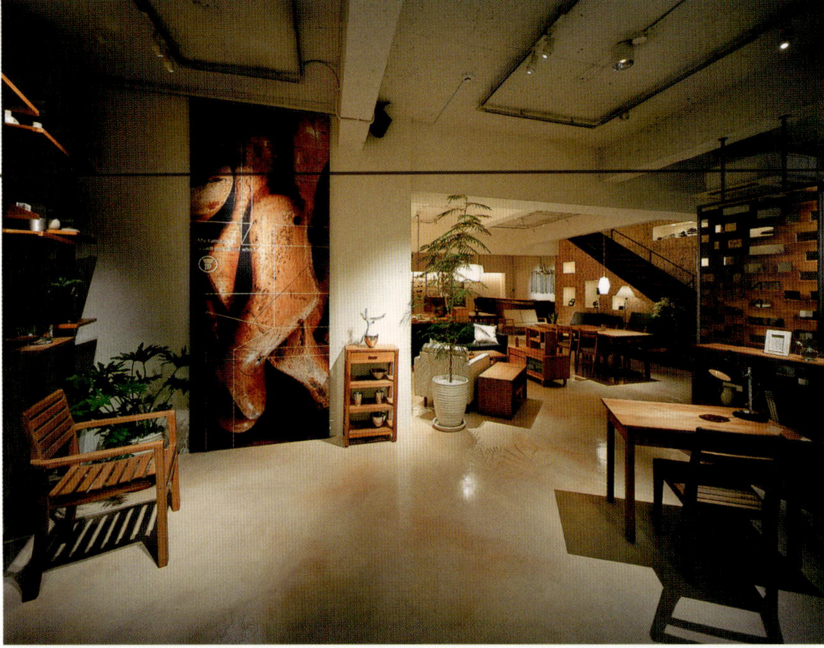

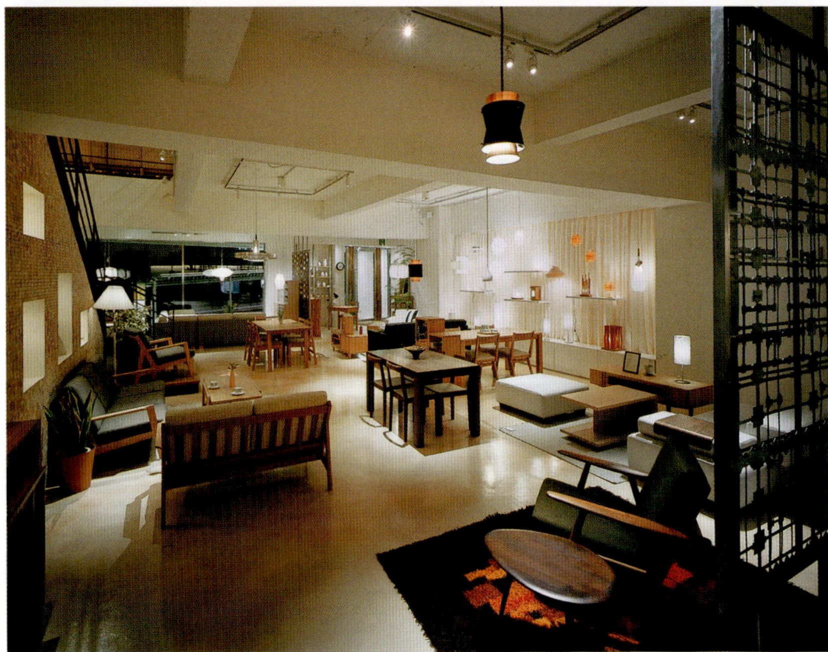

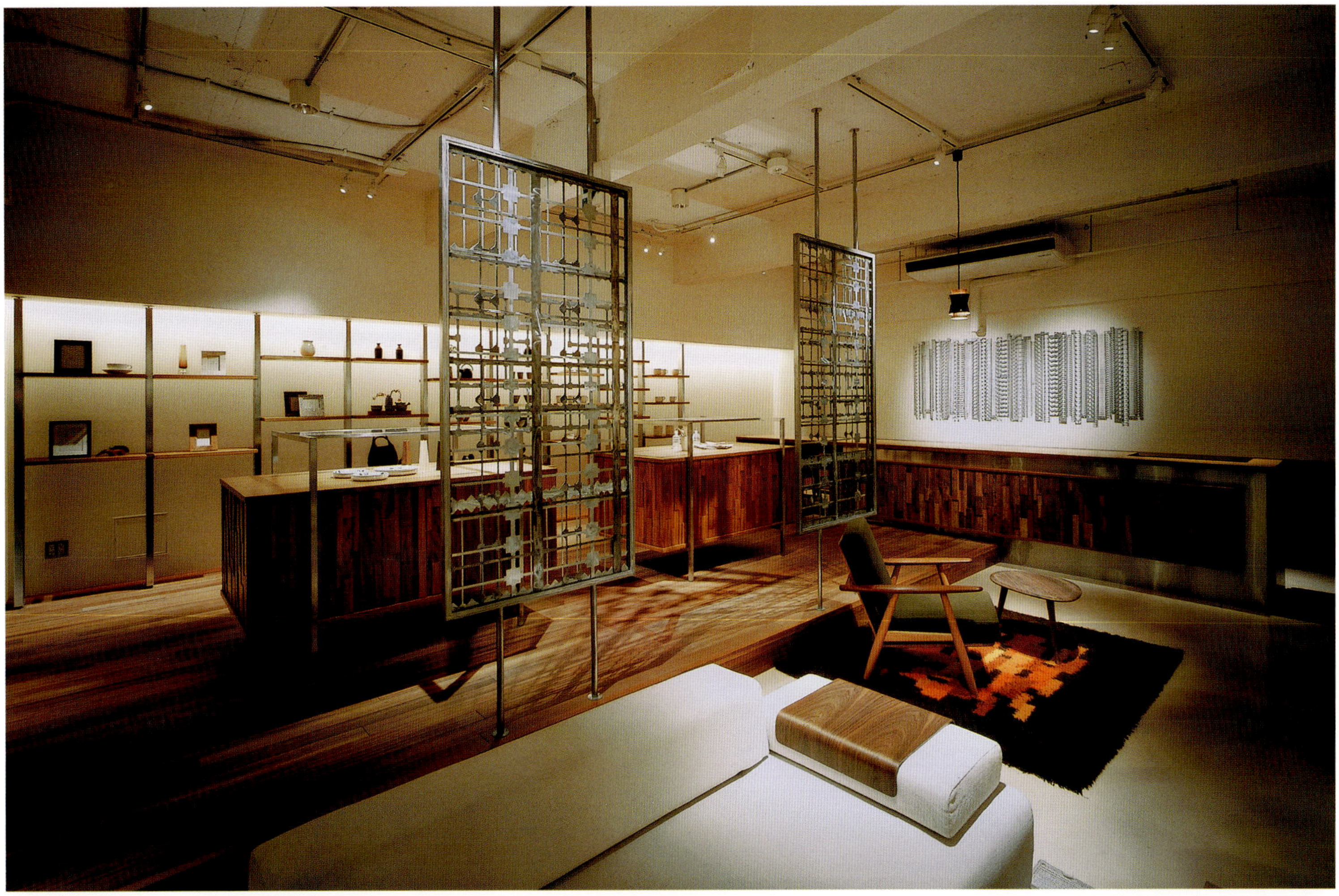

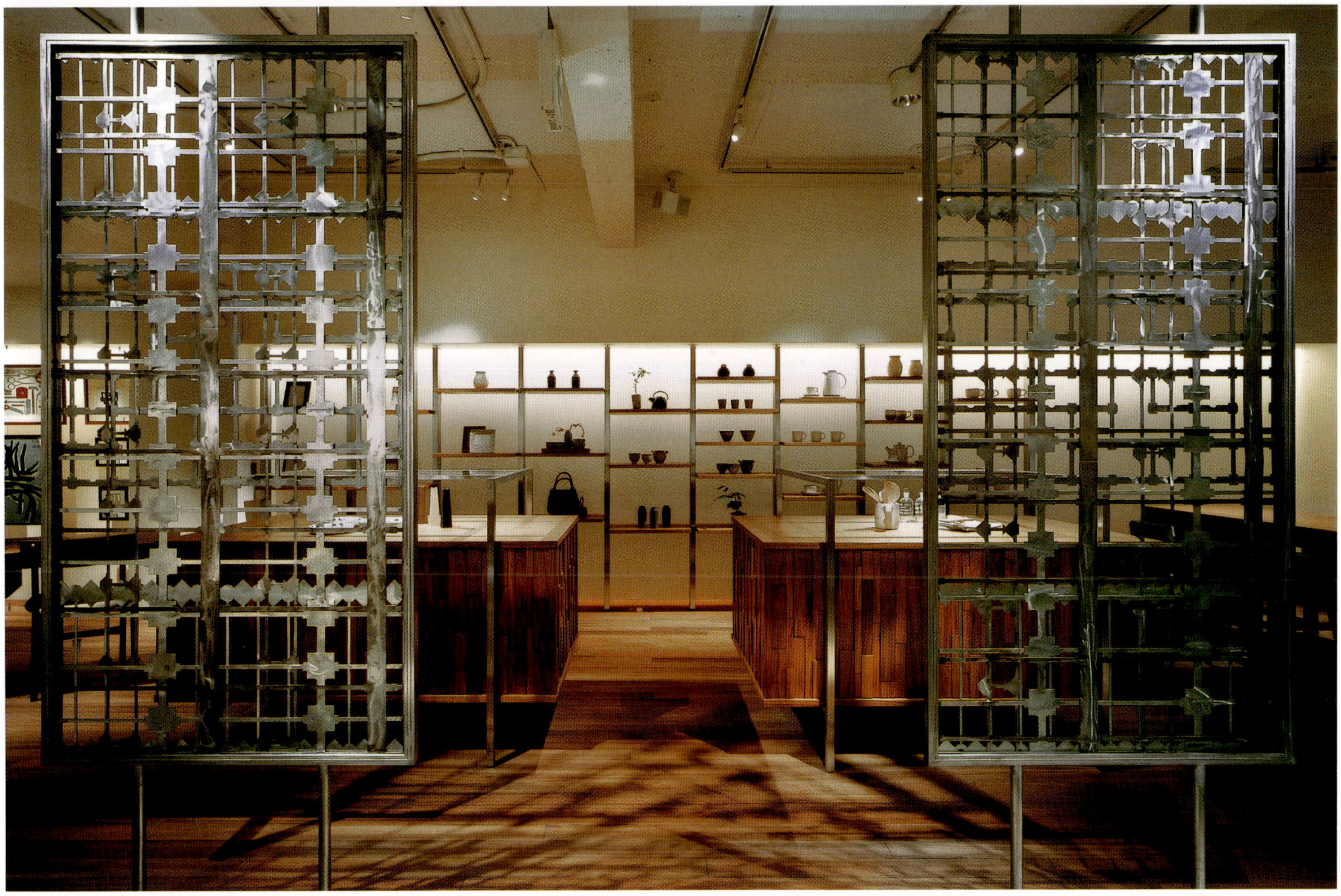

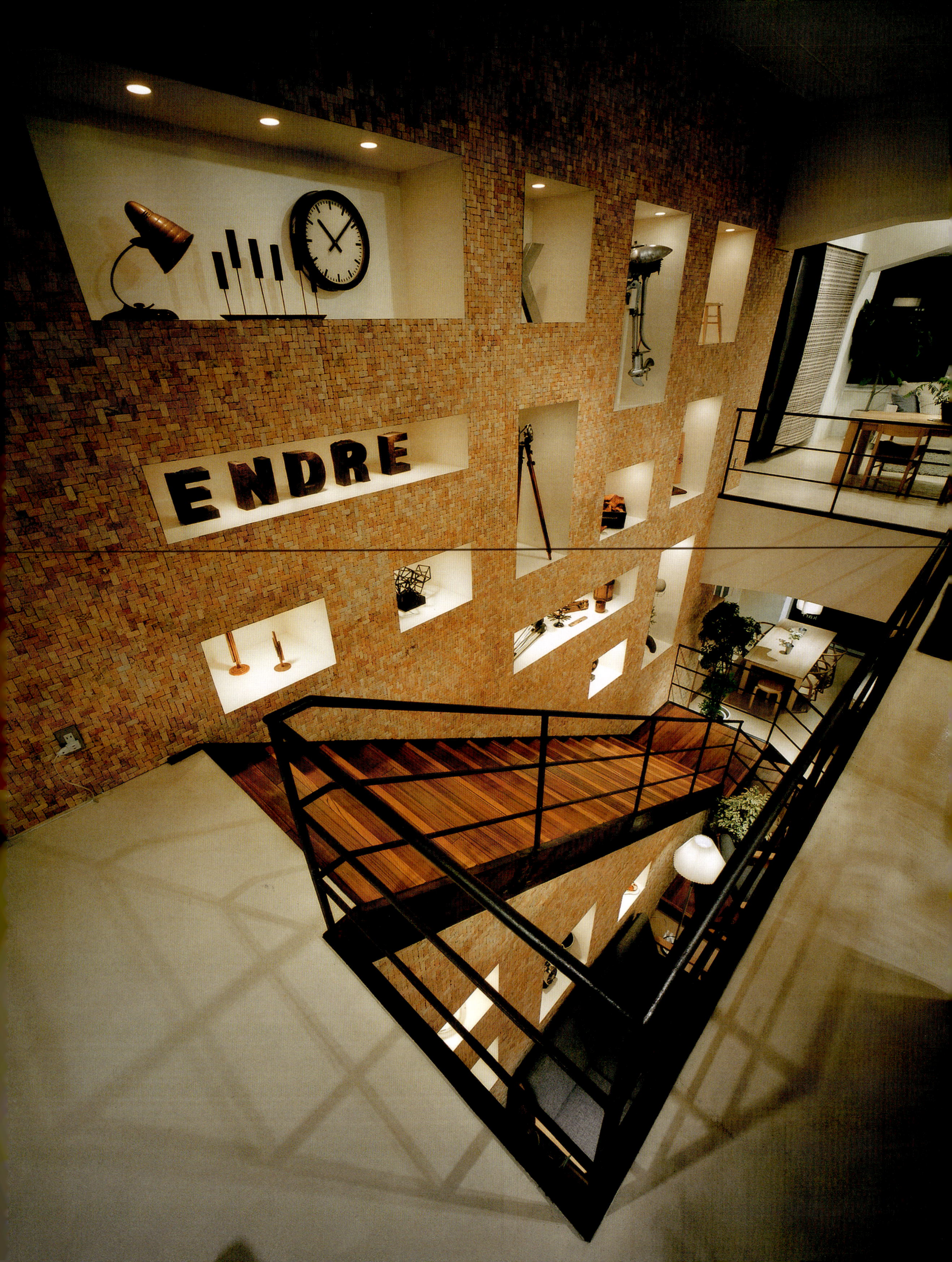
ENDRE

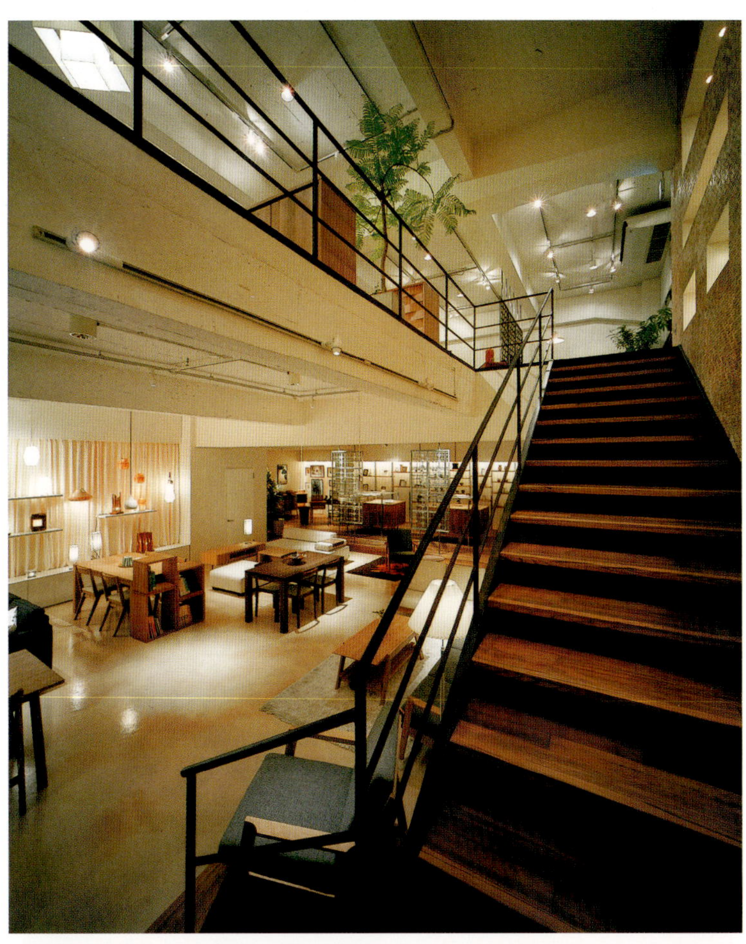
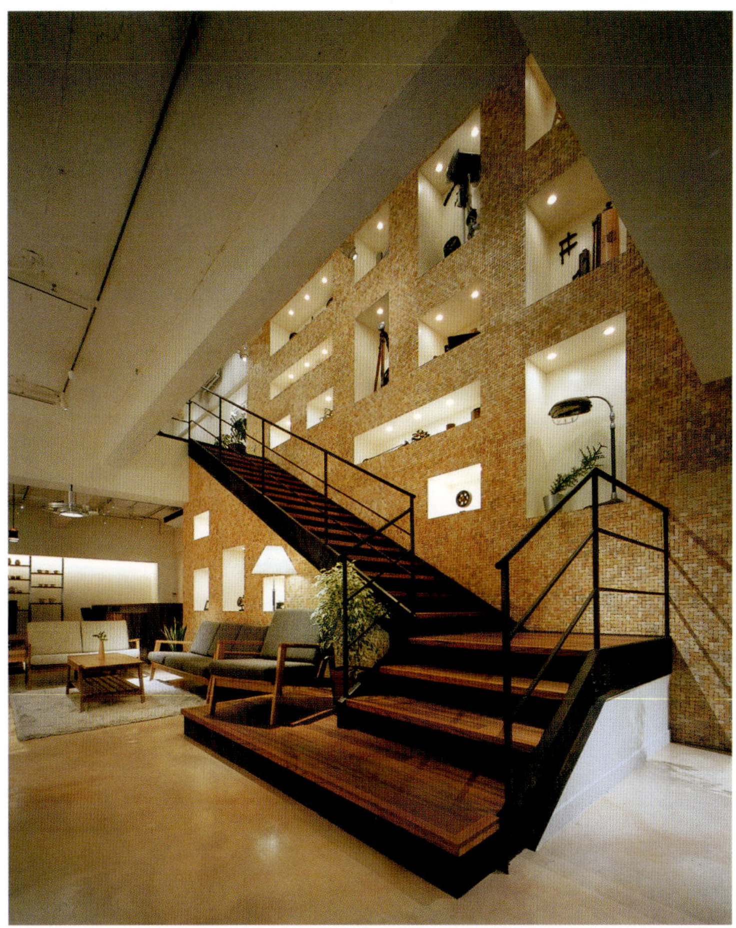

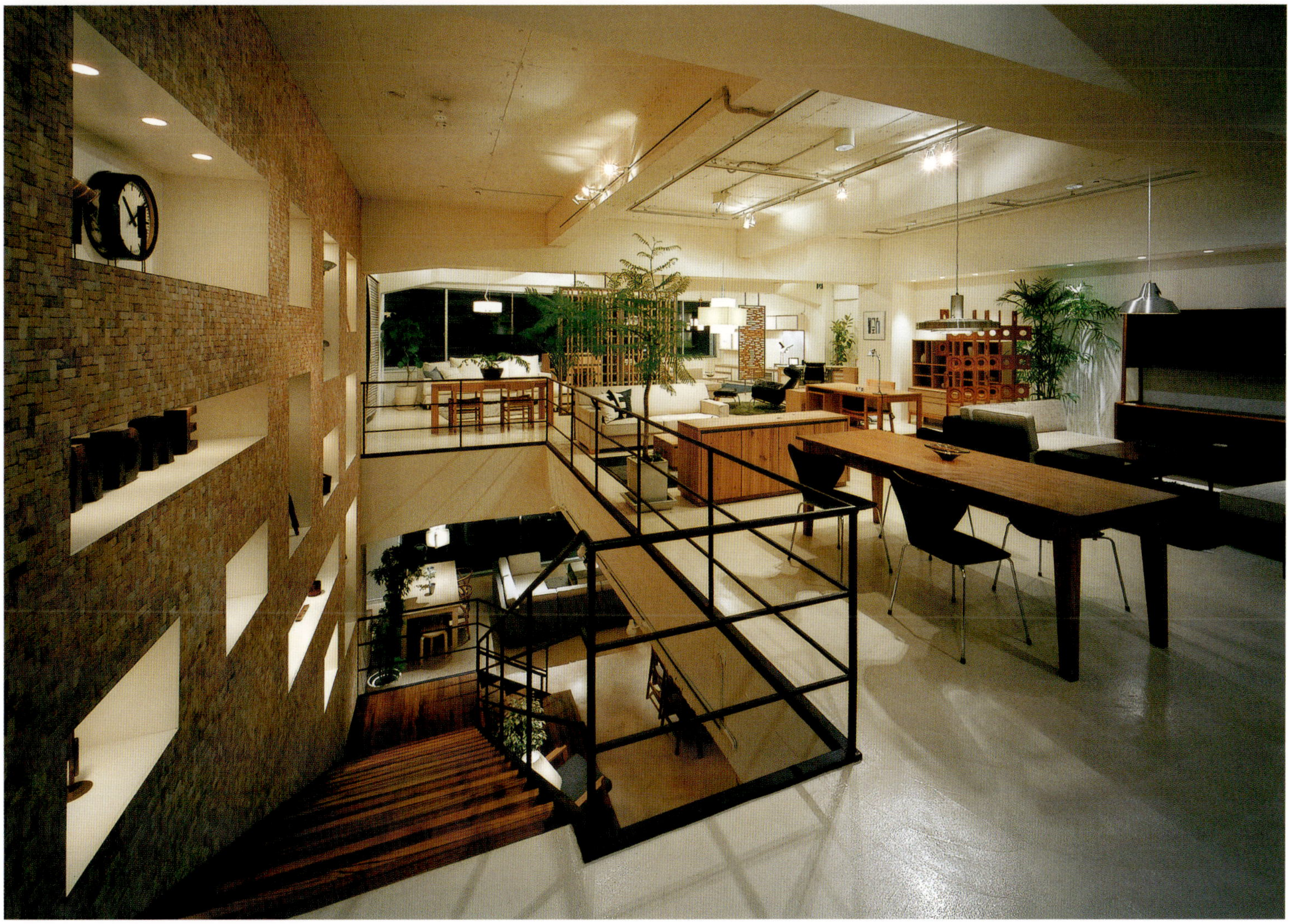

ALLETY
GINZA , TOKYO 2003

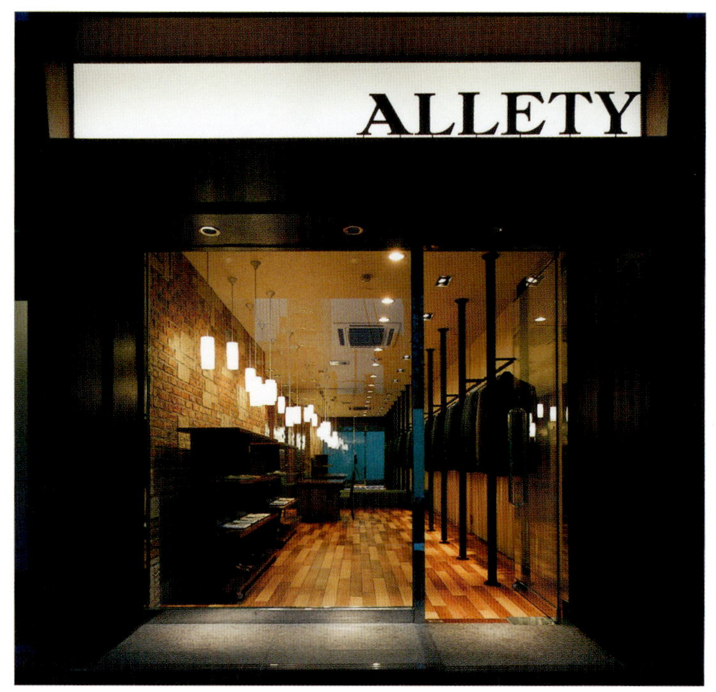

ジャパニーズ ビジネスマン

経済を支える企業戦士たちに、オーナーがセレクトした、こだわりあるモノと、着こなすコトを提供する
ショップです。
　日本の列ら文化をヒントに、人を引き込むデザインを試みました。ランダムに吊られたペンダントがつ
らなって、奥へ奥へと導き、反復するデザインが物量とリーズナブル感を演出します。

Japanese Businessmen

This shop offers items specially chosen by the owner and guidance on looking one's
best to corporate warriors who form the bedrock of the economy.

　Taking a hint from Japan's "Tsurara"(series of overlapping objects) culture, we
aimed at a design that would pull people in. With randomly suspended pendants that
hang down and guide us in deeper and deeper, the repetitive design gives a
performance with volume and a sense of reasonableness.

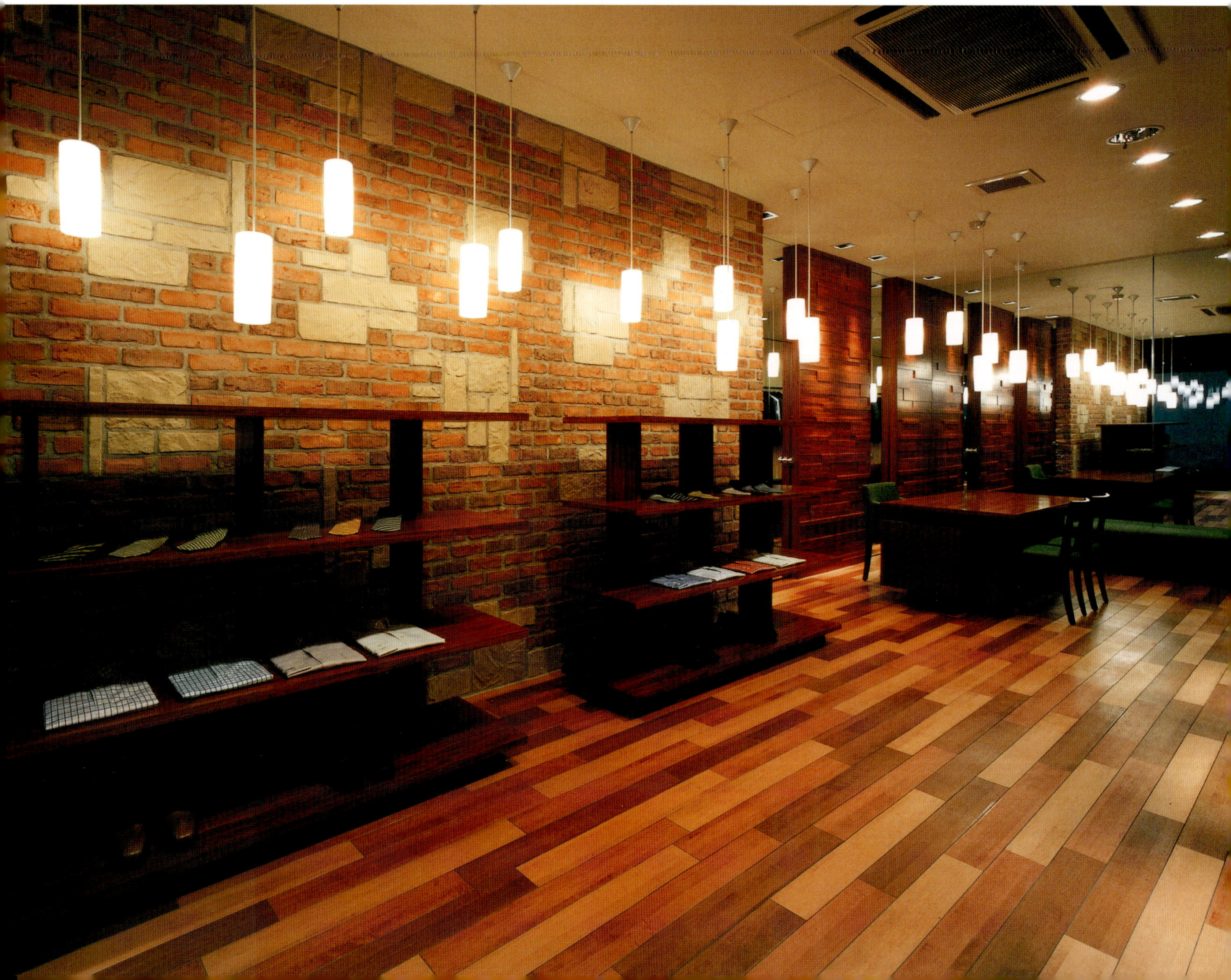

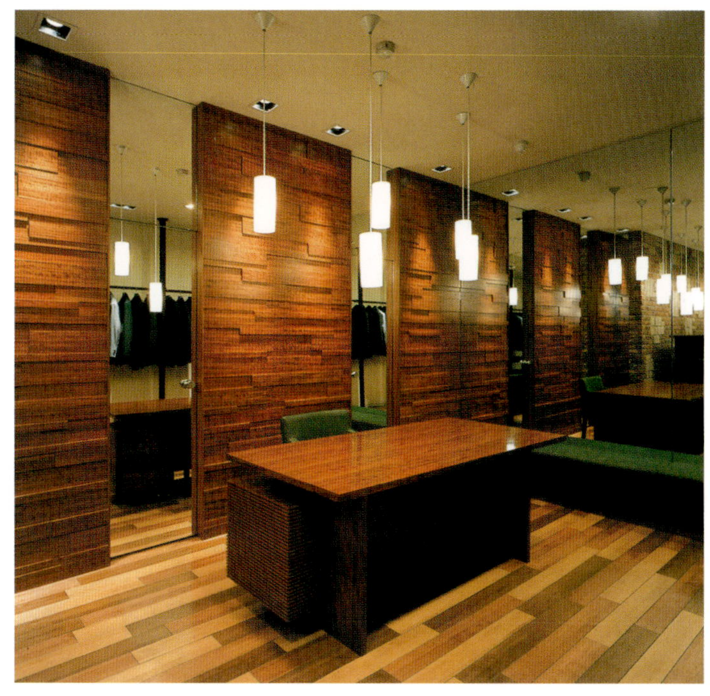

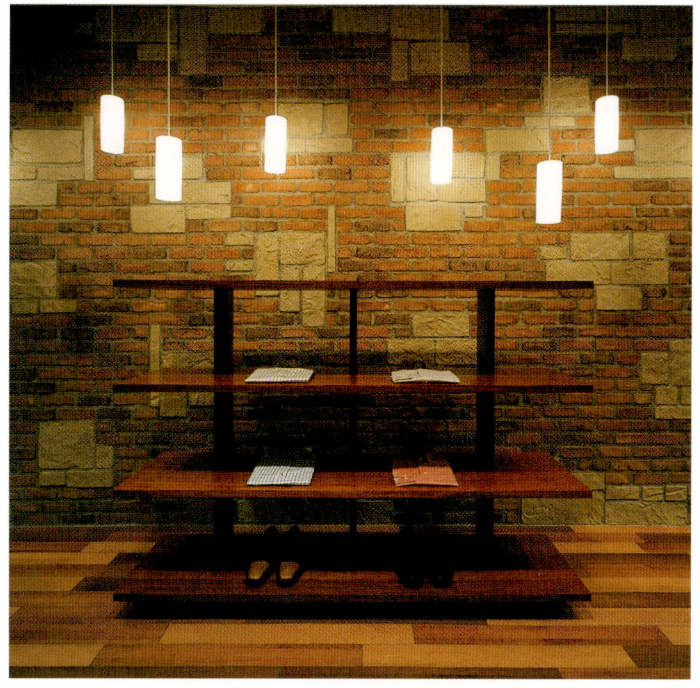

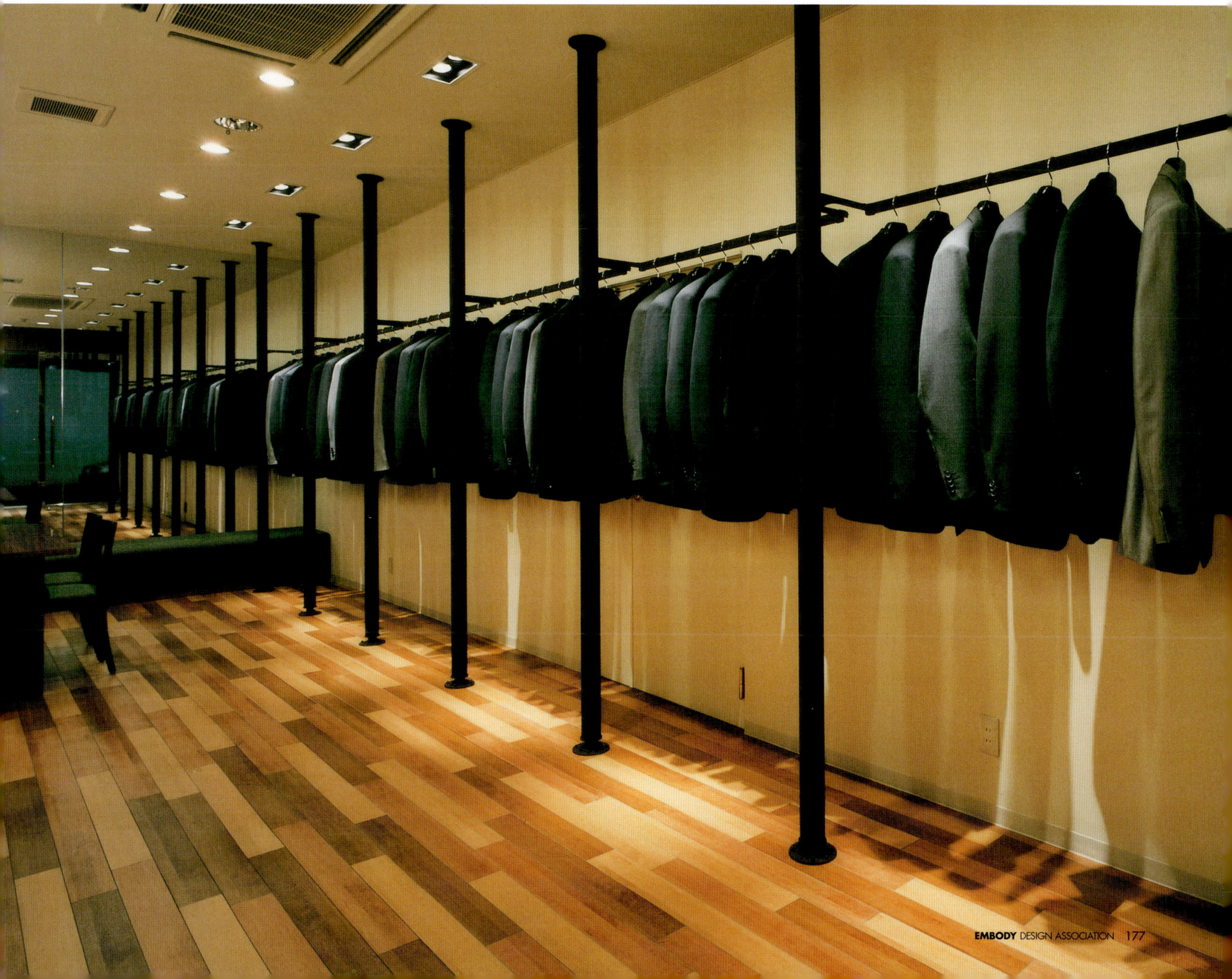

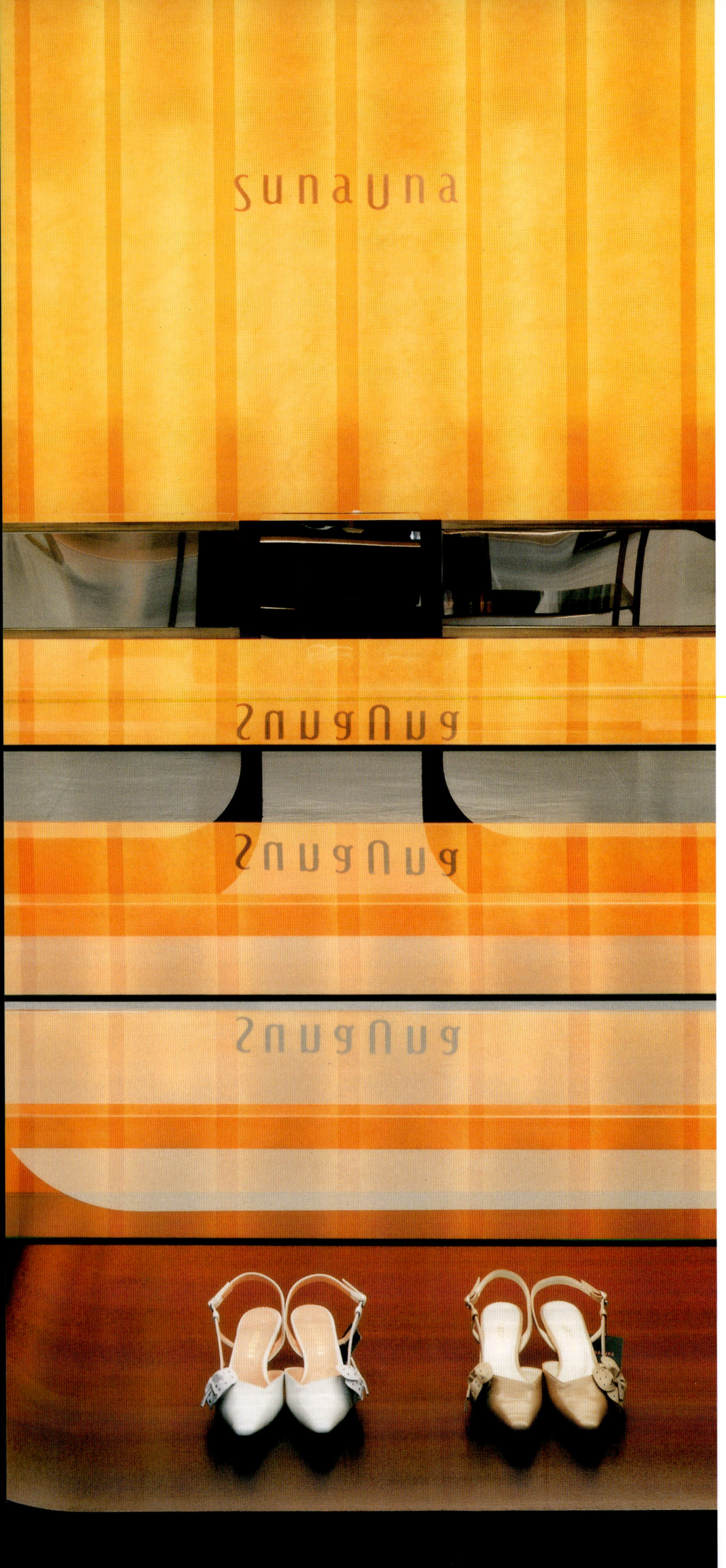

SUNA UNA senri
SENRICYUO , OSAKA 2002

凛とした東洋の香り

ショップデザインにおける、私たちの仕事の一つでもある、ブランディングデザイン。大手SPA（製造小売業）が新ブランドを構成していく上で、生じる様々な問題点をデザインの力で解決し、ブランド構築していくことです。

　それは、単に表層的な箱を創り出すのではなく、服づくりに携わる様々な人々の思いを紐解き、イメージを具体的なカタチに織り込んで行くことだと考えています。

As a Cool Eastern Fragrance

As shop designers, one of our jobs is branding design. We resolve with our design capacity a great number of design problems that arise in creation of new brands by major firm SPA (manufacturing retail business).

　We consider this to be not just a matter of simply creating superficial boxes, but of understanding the thinking processes of the various people involved in garment-making and incorporating these into the concrete shape of the image.

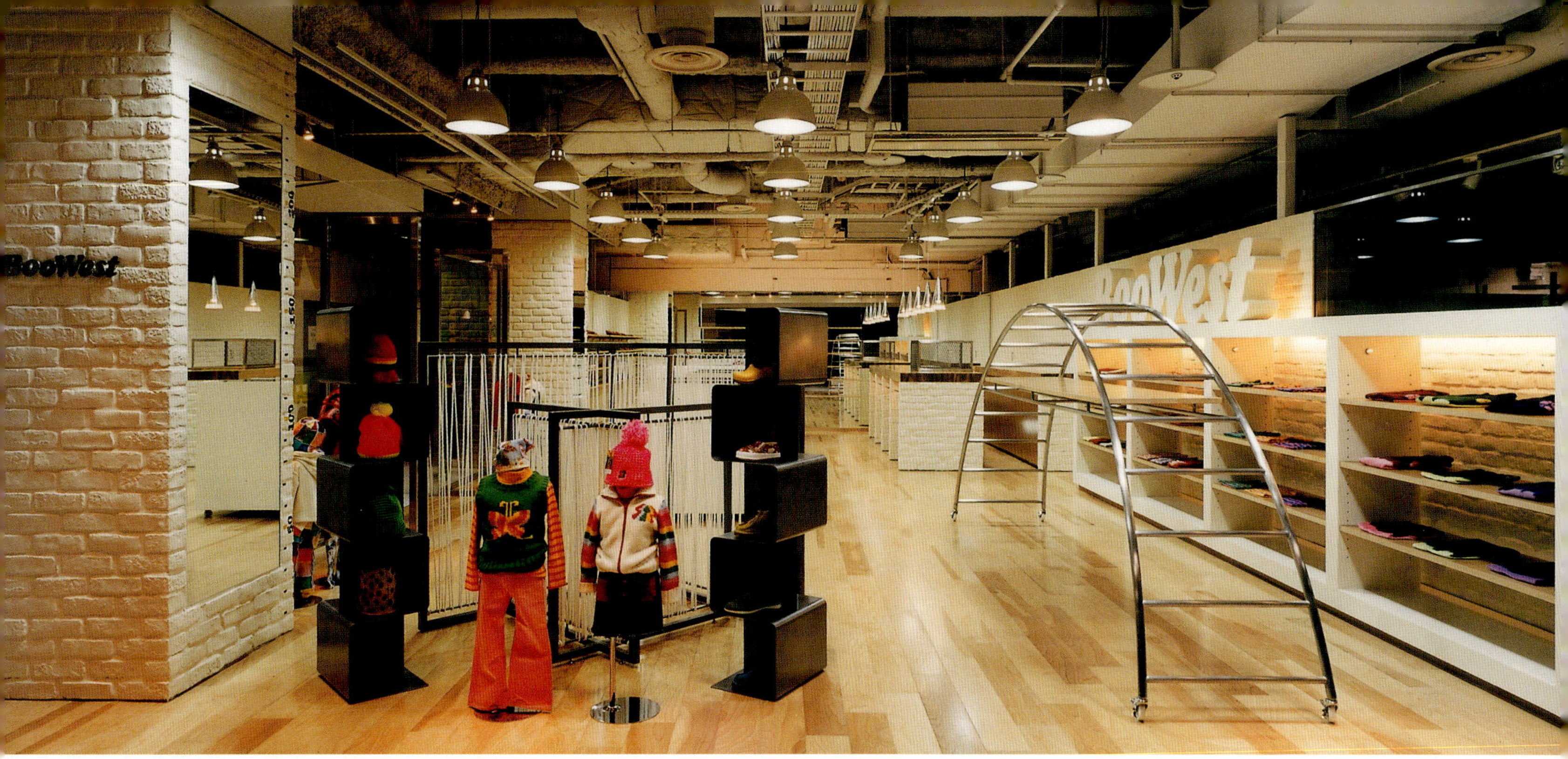

BOO WEST
KOBE , HYOGO 1999

ショップエレメントの記号化

"BOO WEST"は複合施設のキッズフロアに計画された。子供服を通して子供の喜ぶ笑顔を求め、人が訪れるこのフロアの特性を生かし、フロア全体での回遊性をはかり、大きなエントランスを2方向に設けた。このゾーニングは、公園のように、人々にとって心地よい場所になるように、という思いと、通りがかる人に必ず訪れてもらうための仕掛けでもある。

　ショップを構成する様々なエレメントも什器としての機能だけでなく、遊具のように触れたくなるようなフォルムを追求し、「公園」をショップとして記号化した。

Symbolization of shop elements

BOO WEST was planned as a kids' floor in a building complex. To make use of the special character of this floor, where, through children's clothing, people visit expecting to see children's happy faces, in planning circulation for the floor overall, huge entrances were installed bi-directionally. Our idea for zoning was just like that of a pleasant city park, so that it would be a comfortable place for visitors, and this is a device that unfailingly gets passersby to drop in.

As for the various elements making up the shop, we went after playthings in formats that people would want to touch rather than just things that functioned as utensils, and a space that symbolizes a "park" was realized as a shop.

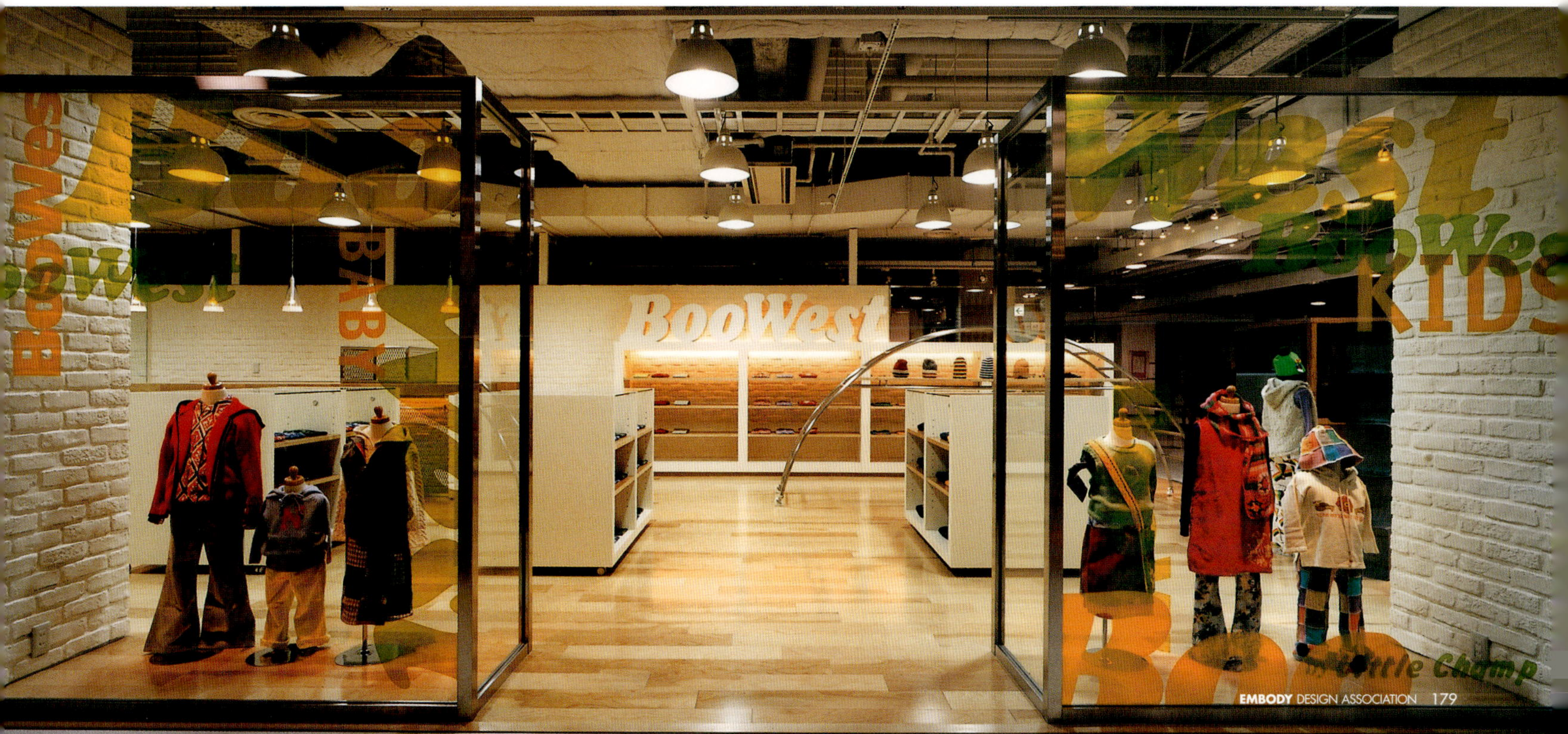

SUNA UNA aoyama
MINAMIAOYAMA , TOKYO 2001

統一と進化の包括

大手SPA（製造小売業）がはかる、新たな流通スタイル。その戦略を理解し、展開を予測して様々な出展エリアやスペースの中で、統一と進化をくり返しながらも、デザインがぶれないようにする。そして、常に外部の人間であるからこそ見える、その進むべき進化の方向性をカタチにする必要がある。

　デザイナーの仕事は、何も、カタチを創るだけではないのだ。

Inclusion of Integration and Evolution

A new distribution style was planned by the major firm SPA (manufacturing retail business). Understanding their strategy, and predicting expansion, we arranged things so that the design would not be spoiled even with repeated reintegration and evolution in the various exhibition areas and spaces. Then, it was necessary to embody the direction the evolution should take, and this could be seen by us only because we were always outsiders.

　The job of the designer is not merely to create shapes for things.

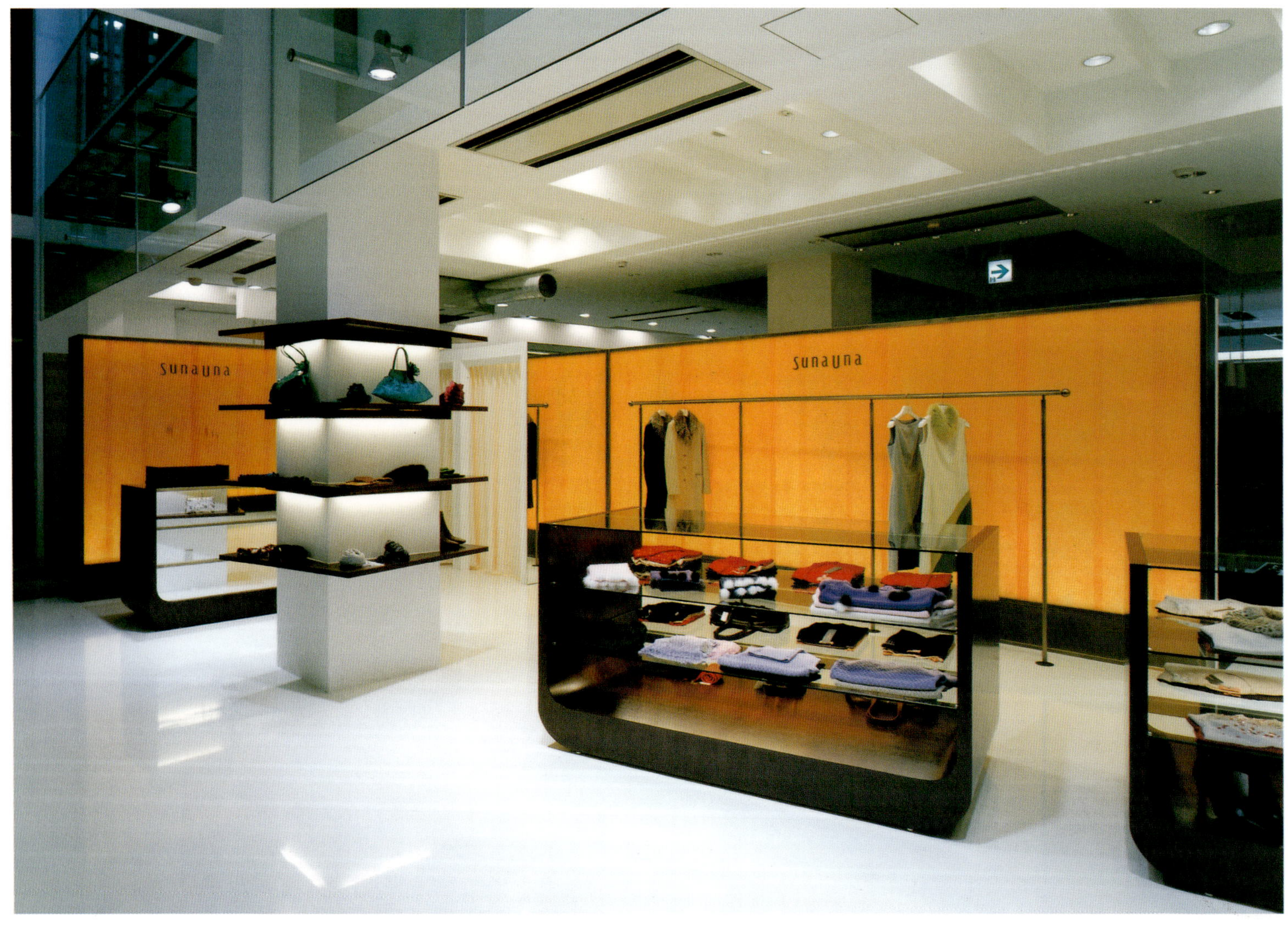

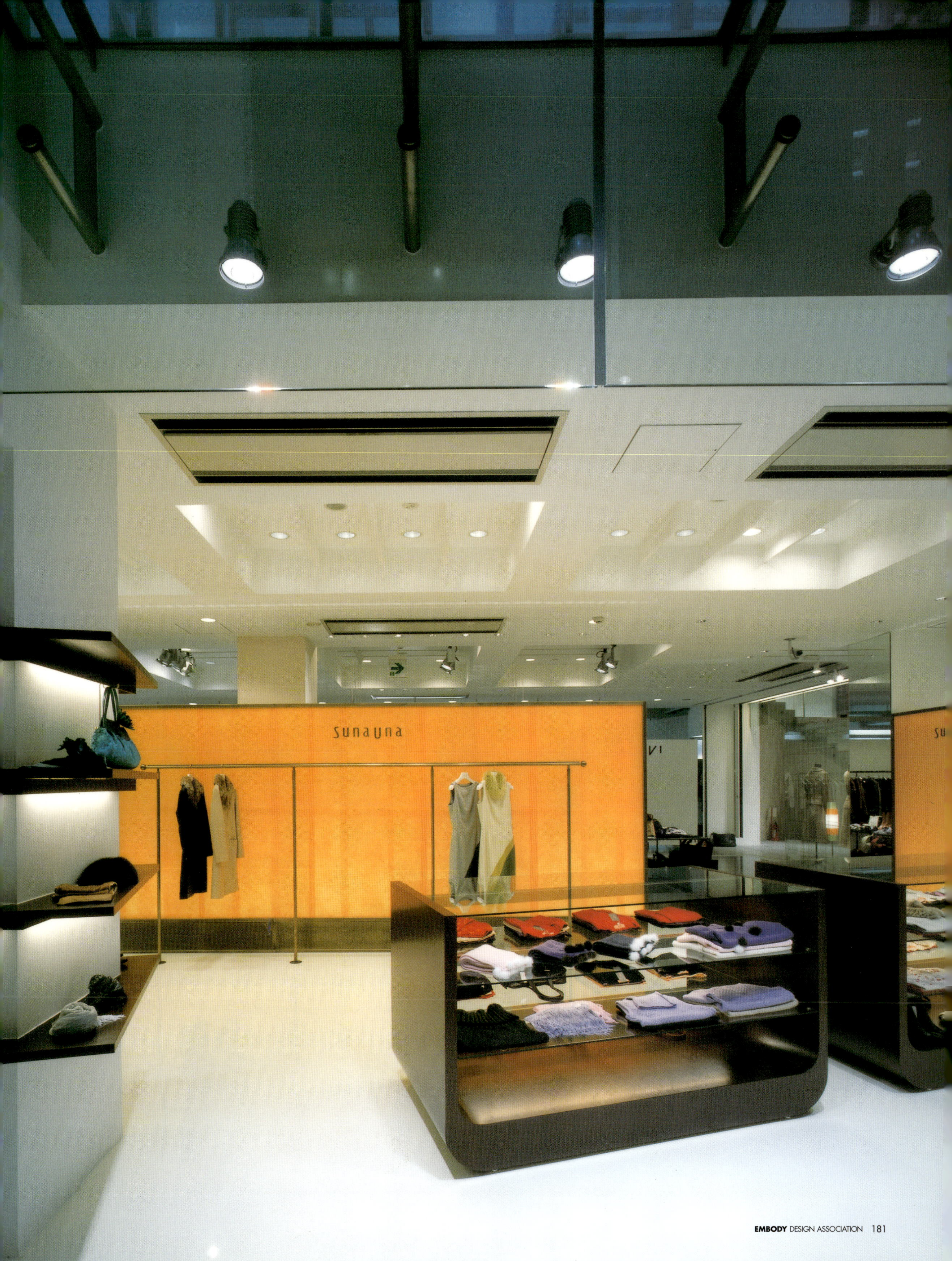

Sunayna

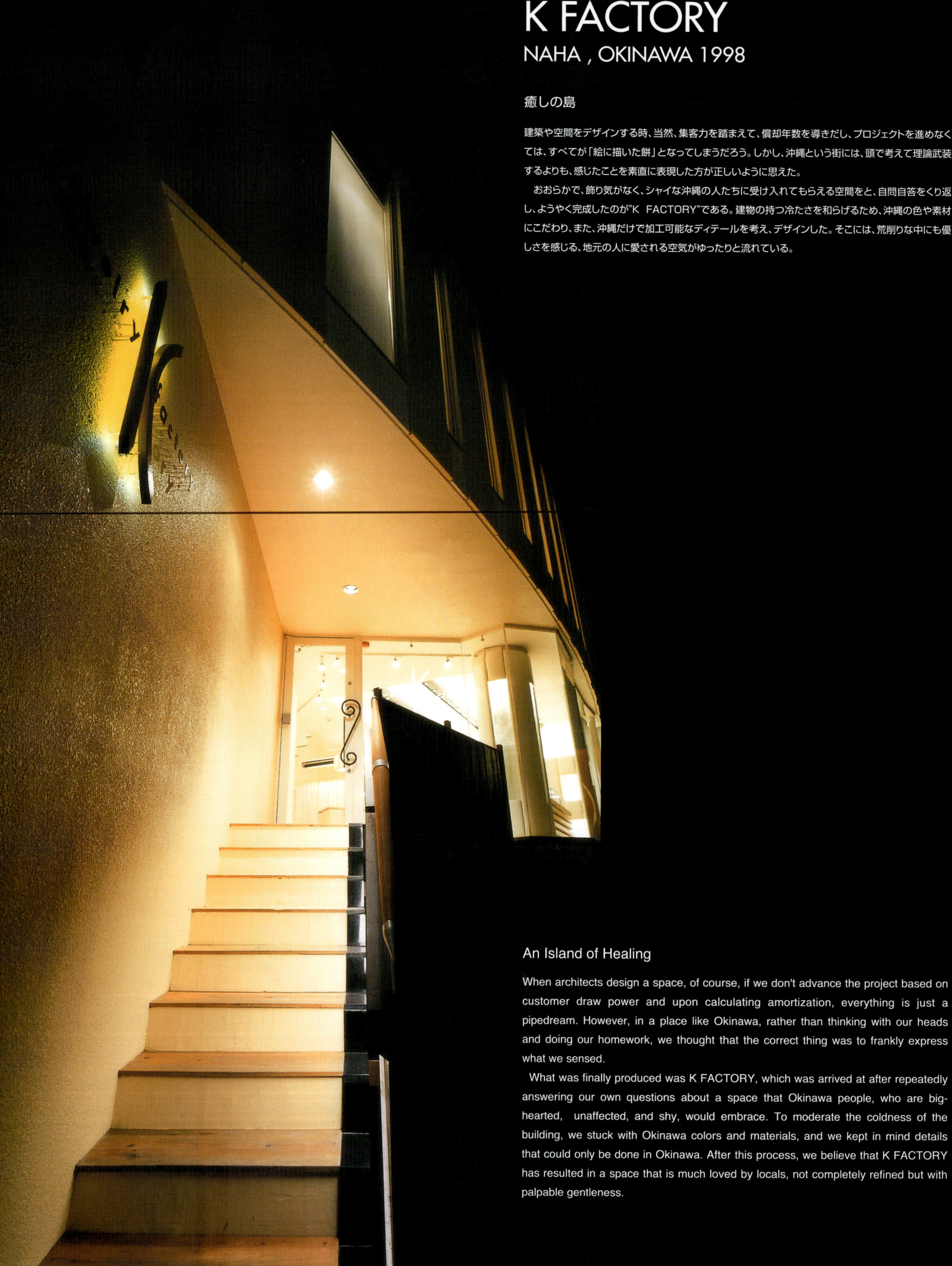

K FACTORY
NAHA , OKINAWA 1998

癒しの島

建築や空間をデザインする時、当然、集客力を踏まえて、償却年数を導きだし、プロジェクトを進めなくては、すべてが「絵に描いた餅」となってしまうだろう。しかし、沖縄という街には、頭で考えて理論武装するよりも、感じたことを素直に表現した方が正しいように思えた。

　おおらかで、飾り気がなく、シャイな沖縄の人たちに受け入れてもらえる空間をと、自問自答をくり返し、ようやく完成したのが"K FACTORY"である。建物の持つ冷たさを和らげるため、沖縄の色や素材にこだわり、また、沖縄だけで加工可能なディテールを考え、デザインした。そこには、荒削りな中にも優しさを感じる、地元の人に愛される空気がゆったりと流れている。

An Island of Healing

When architects design a space, of course, if we don't advance the project based on customer draw power and upon calculating amortization, everything is just a pipedream. However, in a place like Okinawa, rather than thinking with our heads and doing our homework, we thought that the correct thing was to frankly express what we sensed.

　What was finally produced was K FACTORY, which was arrived at after repeatedly answering our own questions about a space that Okinawa people, who are big-hearted, unaffected, and shy, would embrace. To moderate the coldness of the building, we stuck with Okinawa colors and materials, and we kept in mind details that could only be done in Okinawa. After this process, we believe that K FACTORY has resulted in a space that is much loved by locals, not completely refined but with palpable gentleness.

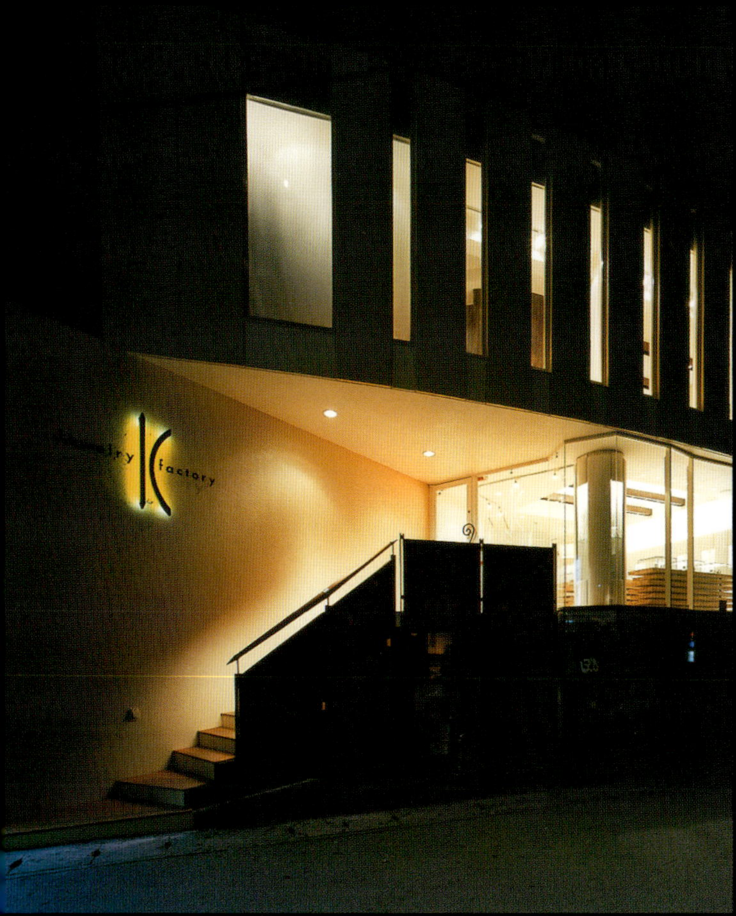

Jewelry K factory

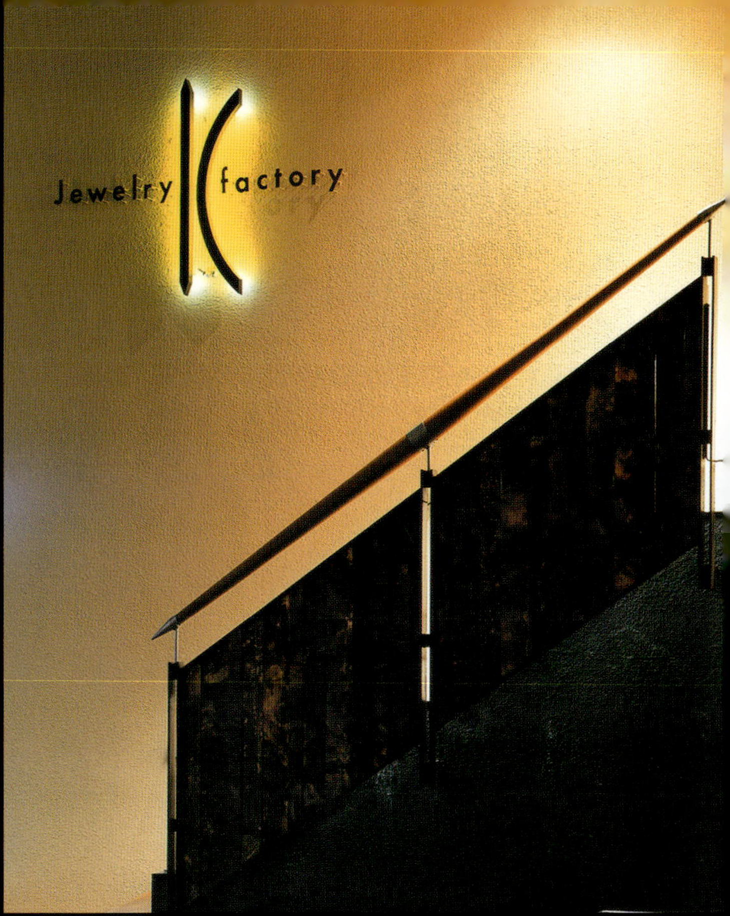

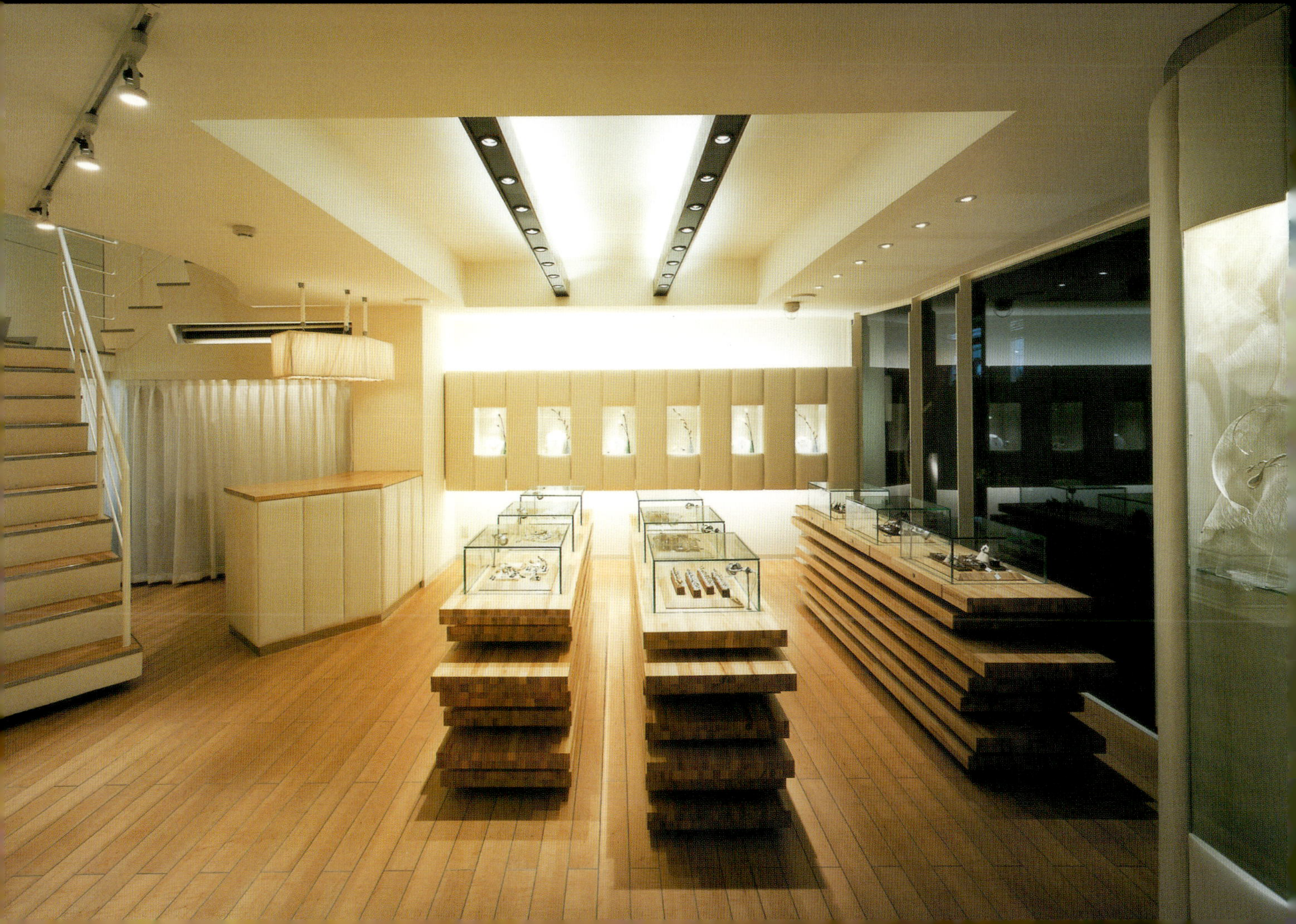

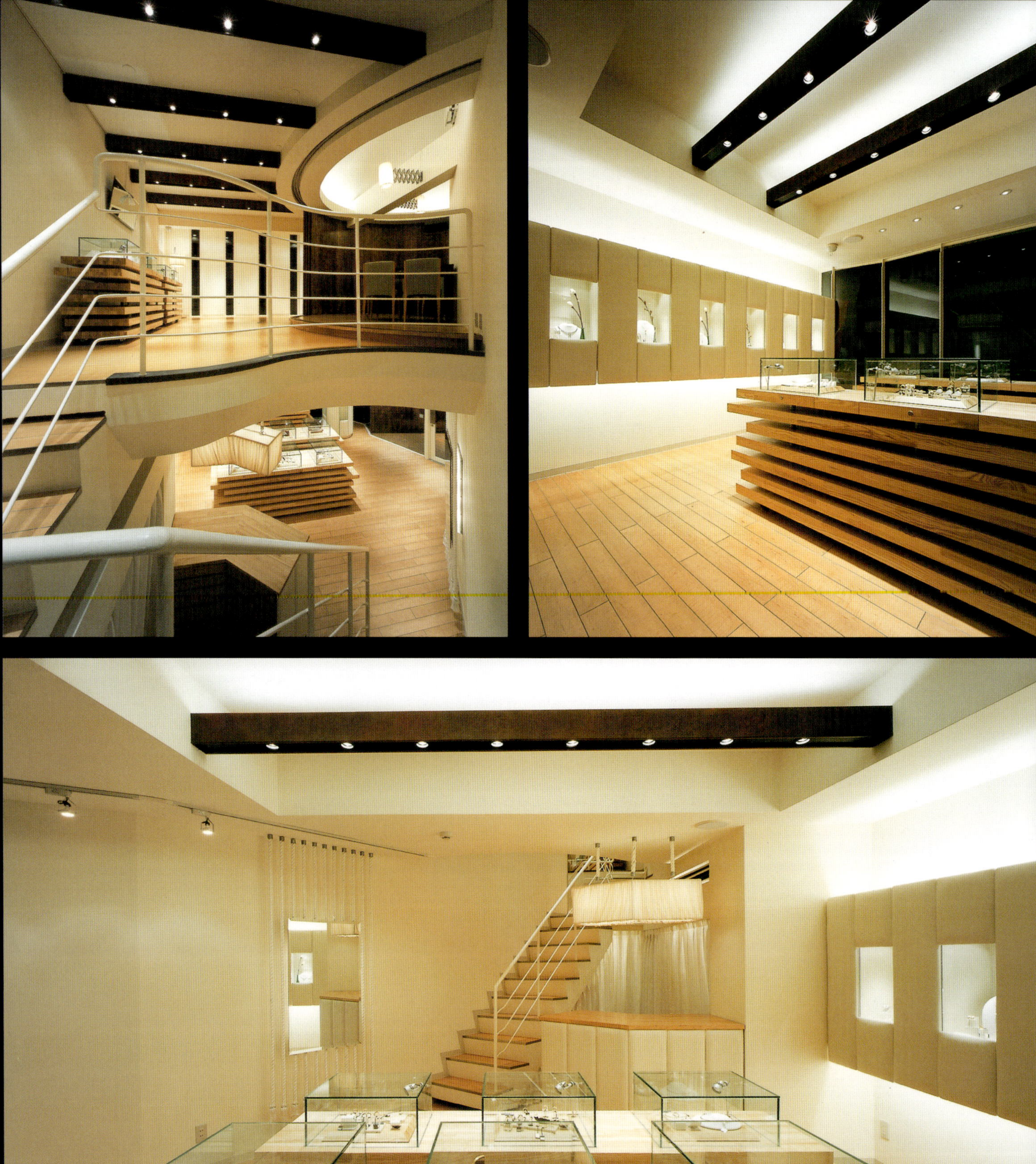

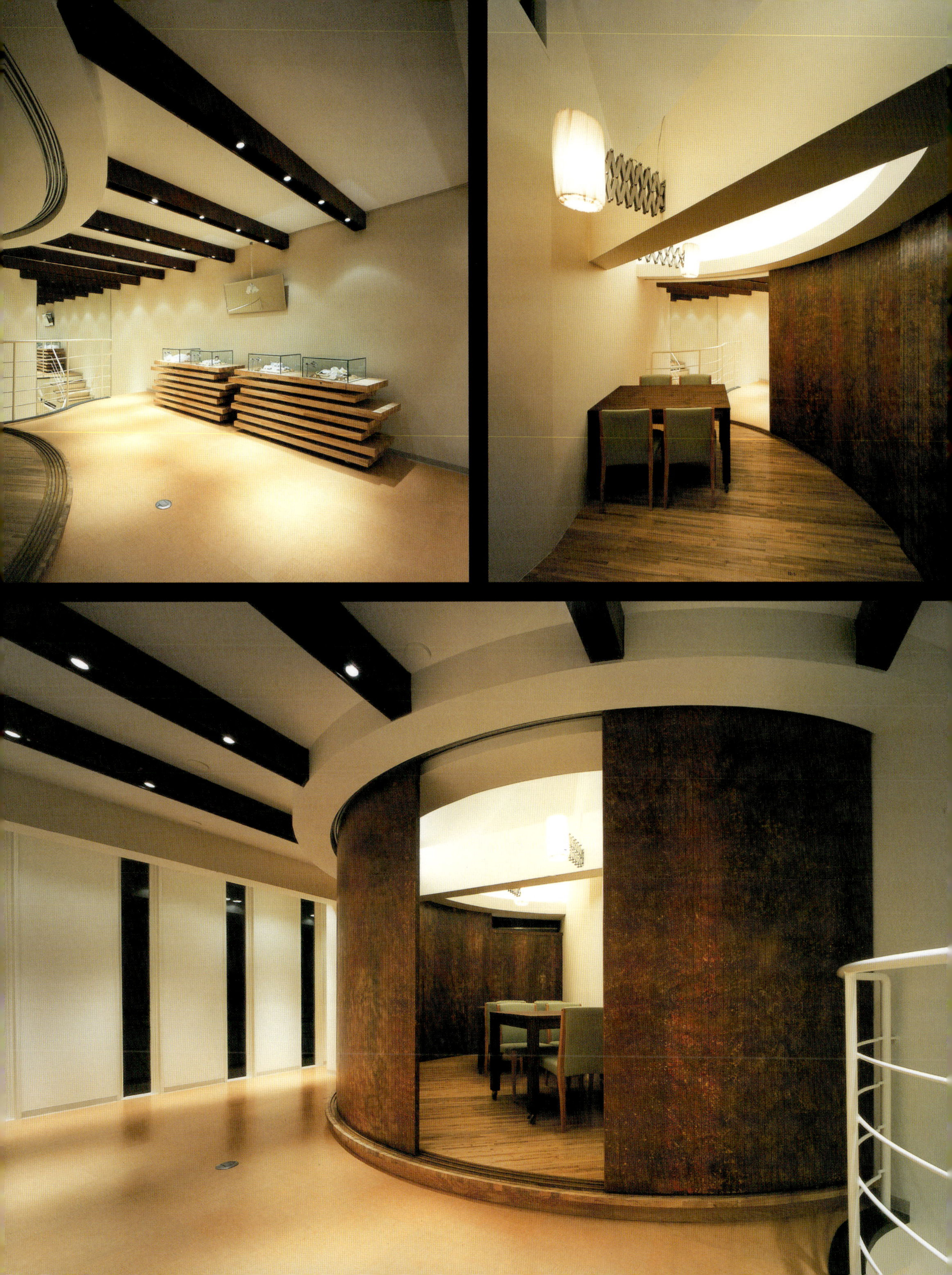

MICKEY & CO
MOMOYAMADAI , OSAKA 1997

主役の魅力を引き出す

アーティスティックで、優しい光が人々を包み迎え入れる、"MICKEY & CO"。大阪桃山台の複合施設の中にある、キャラクターブランドを取り扱うお店です。

　グラフィカルな商品をより美しく浮かび上がらせるため、白を基調とした、ミニマムなデザインを心掛けました。また、「グラフィックアートを着る」をコンセプトに開発された商品を、額縁を通して見せることで、商品のアートの部分を引き出すことにつとめています。

Drawing out the Appeal of the Lead Role.

An artistic and gentle light that envelops and draws people in, MICKEY & CO Located in Osaka's Momoyamadai complex, this shop handles character brands.

For the purpose of making its graphical merchandise seem more beautiful by floating it in the air, we aimed at a minimalist design based on white. In addition, by displaying the products, which are developed under the concept of "wearable graphical art," via picture frames, we tried to highlight the art aspect of the products.

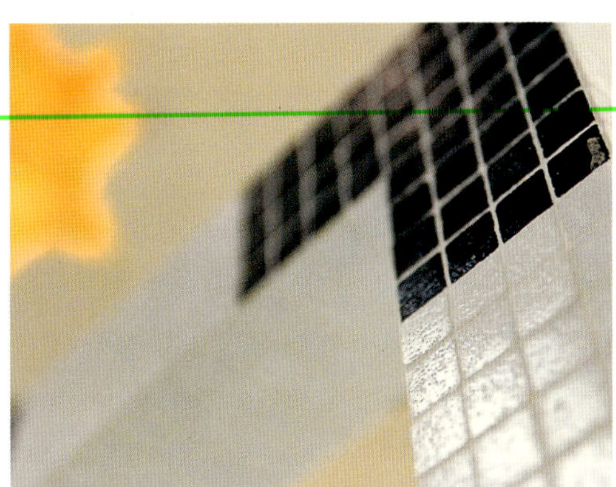

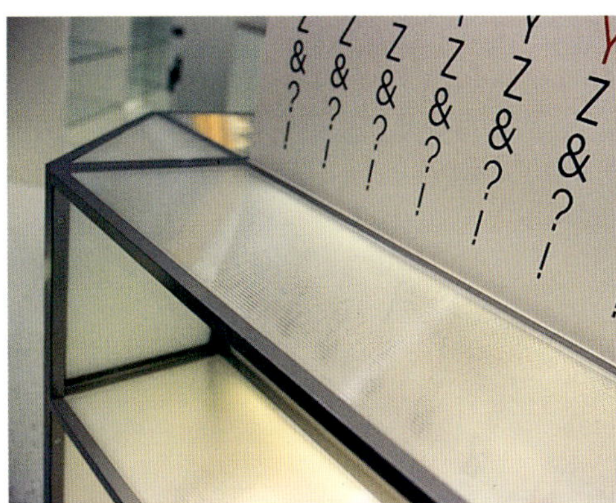

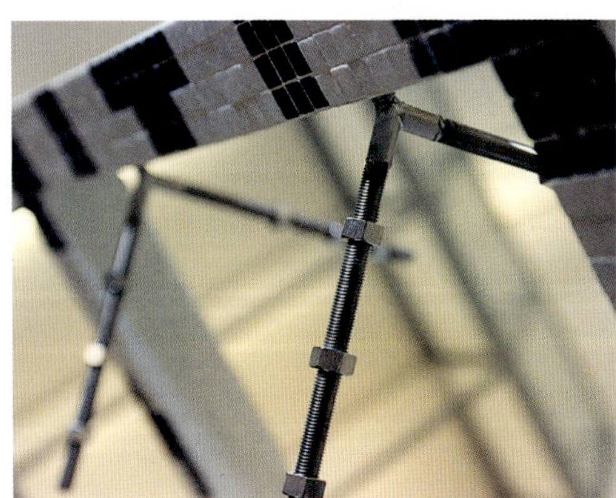

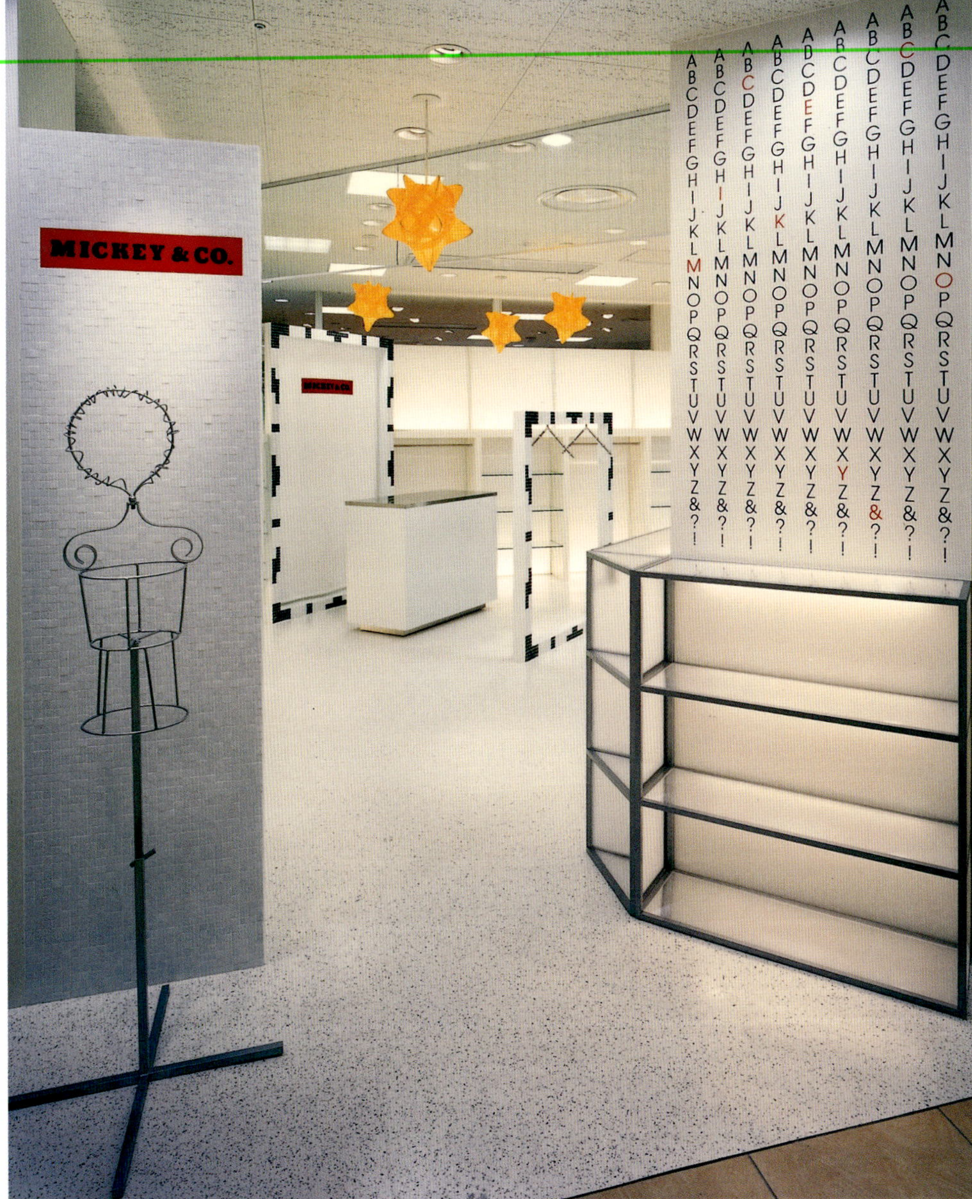

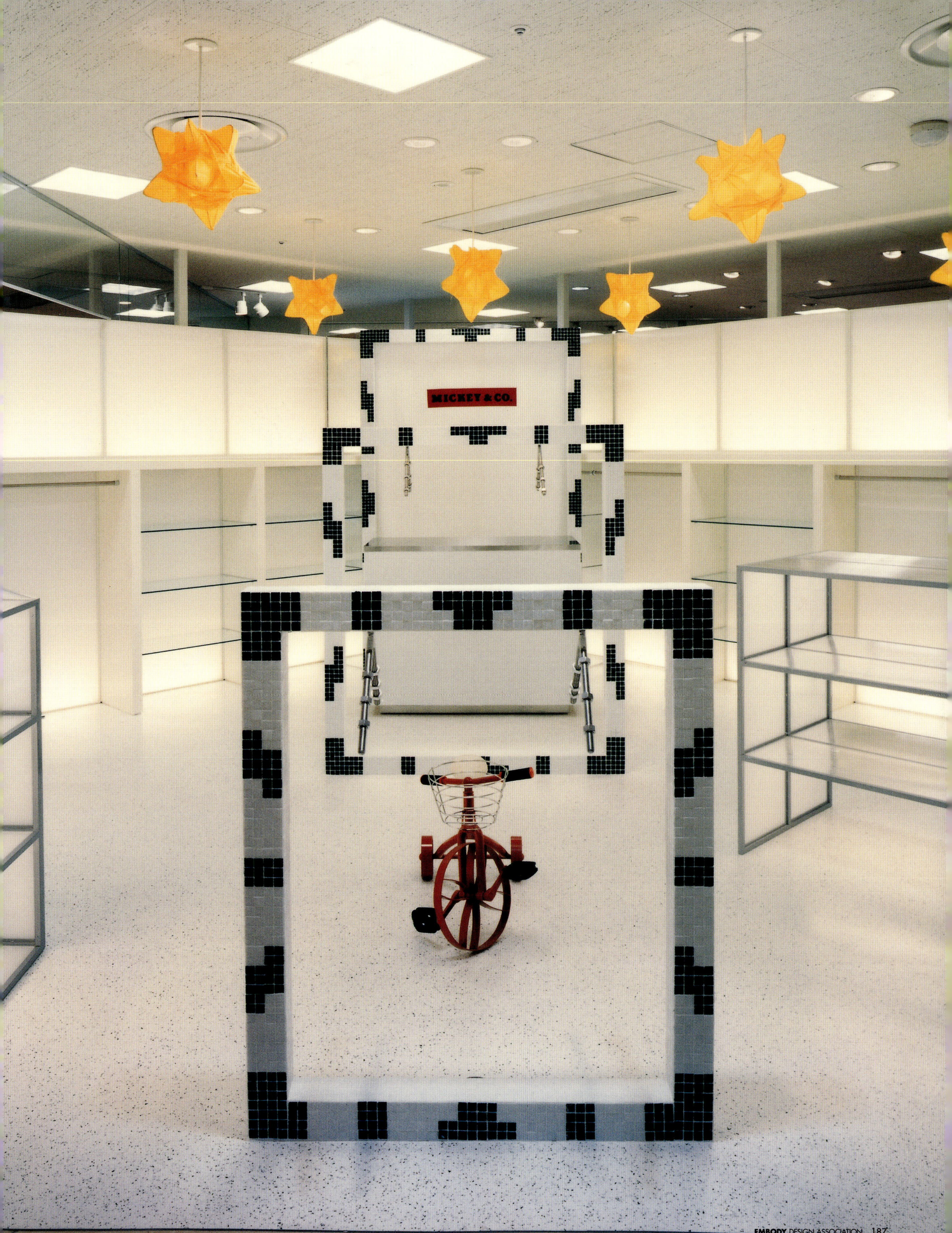

MICKEY & CO.

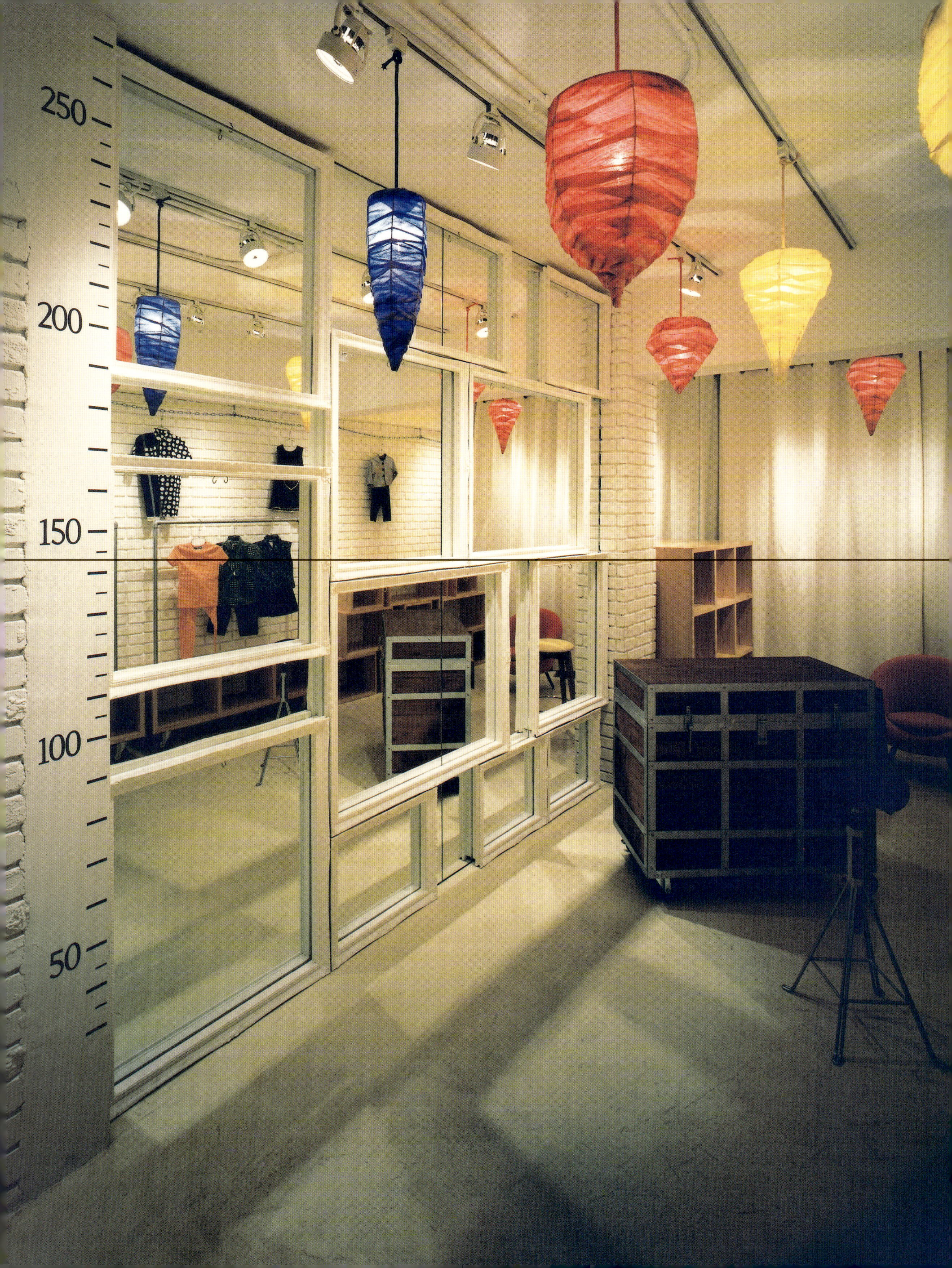

PUSPUS
TOYONAKA , OSAKA 1996

造形をデザインするのではなく、漂う空気をデザインしたい

不思議なもので、お気に入りの服を着ていると気分がいいものです。それは、子供たちだって同じことで、そんなお気に入りの一枚を見つけて欲しい、というオーナーの思いから、"PUS PUS"は生まれました。

　商品をセレクトするオーナーのセンスが生命線とも言えるお店なので、デザイナーが作り込んだというのではなく、彼女のセンスが随所に感じられる空間を目指しました。また、ターゲットとなる地元の主婦たちが、子供連れで公園に遊びに行く感覚で気軽に訪れ、心地よく過ごせるお店となるようにも心掛けています。

Desire to Design not Sculpture, but Drifting Air

It's an odd thing, but wearing clothes you like can make you feel good. In this, children are no different, and, according to the owner, they have that favorite single item that they want you to find--and from this, PUS PUS was born.

Because it's a store that could be said to be totally dependant on the owner's sensibility in selecting merchandise, the aim was at a space in which her sensibility could be felt everywhere, rather than having the designer just build something. What's more, the aim was to have the targeted local housewives drop in casually and pass some time pleasantly--just as they would if they were taking their kids to the park.

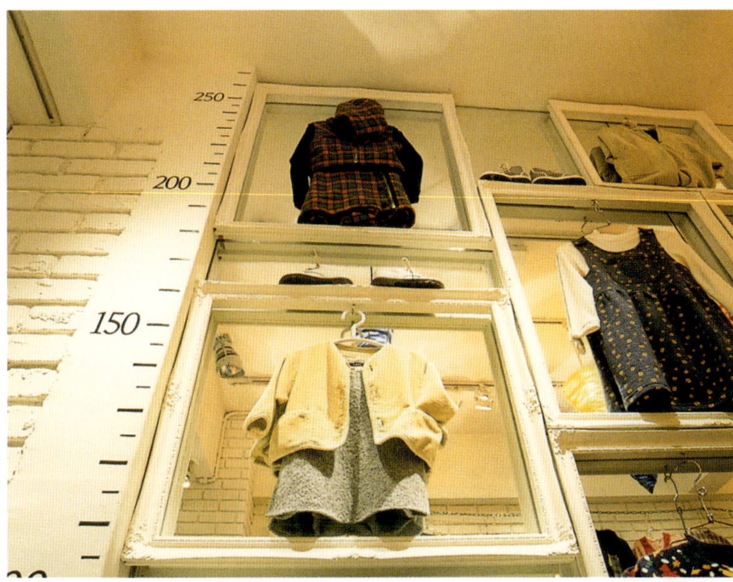

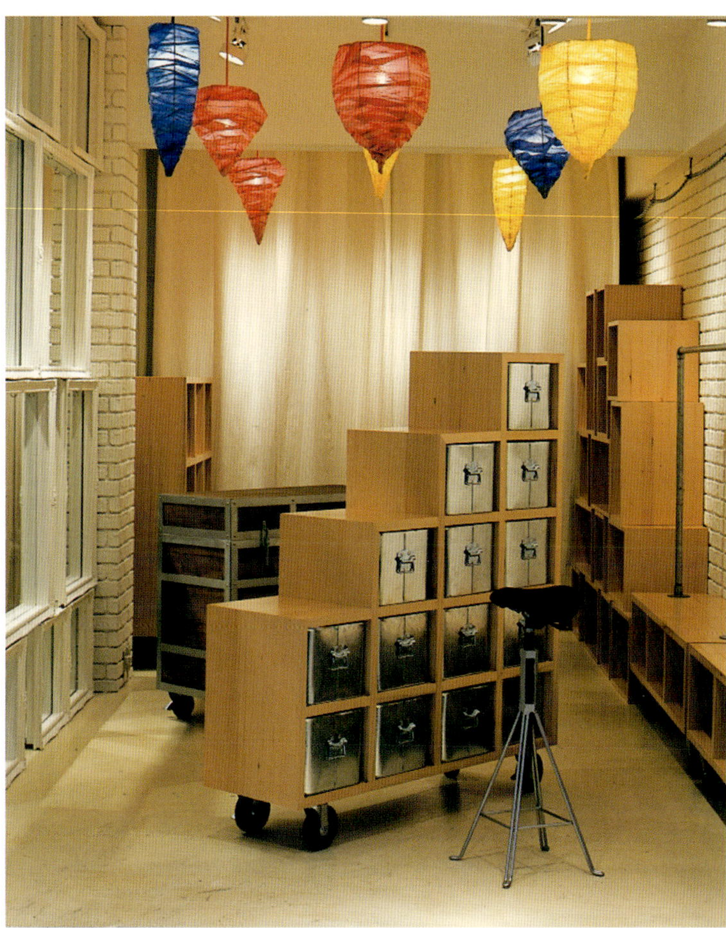

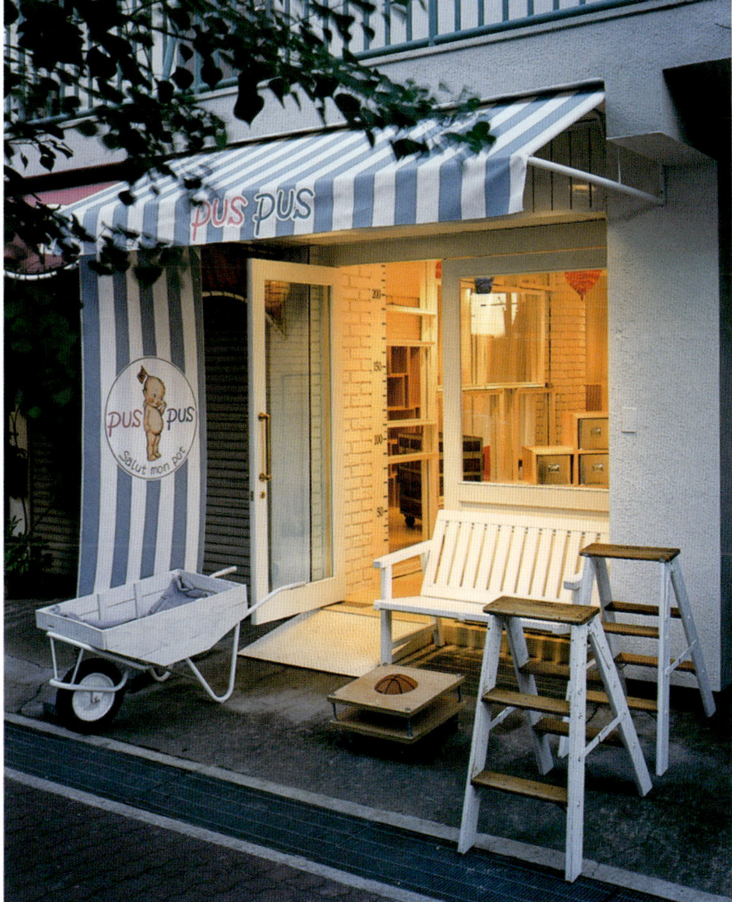

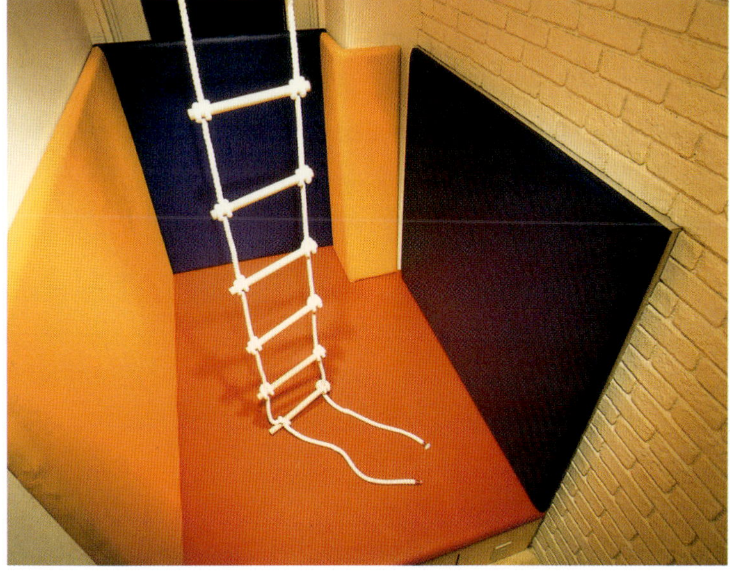

mellow
graceful
flexibility
design the
sharpen the sense
design the sunlight
space to be happy
luxury
subparts
the principal part
make the best use
of surroundings
to do nothing

自然光をデザインする 主役を引き立てる空間
環境を最大限に活かす
品格感覚を研ぎすます フレキシブル 時間をデザインする
幸せになる空間
何もしない 贅沢
大人の艶っぽさ

mellow
graceful
flexibility
design the time
sharpen the sense
sun light
to be happy
luxury
to do nothing
supports
the principal part
make the best
of surroundings
HOTEL
品格感覚を研ぎすます
環境を最大限に活かす何もしない空間
フレキシブル
目然光をデザインする主役を引き立てる空間
幸せになる空間
大人の艶っぽさ
時間をデザインする空間
贅沢

AUBERGE JARDIN

UTSUNOMIYA , TOCHIGI 2002

人を幸せにするための空間

四季を体感できる二万坪の大庭園の中、ホテルのメインダイニングとして"AUBERGE JARDIN"は誕生しました。オーナーの求めるレストランのイメージは、庭園を生かしてレストランウエディングにも使える多目的な大空間。一方、総料理長の求めるイメージは大人の艶っぽさを感じる個室のレストラン。

この相反するような要望を叶えるために考えたのが、額縁型可動パーテーションです。ウィークデーはこのパーテーションが個室をつくり出します。この時、周りのテーブル席は、幾重にも重なりあった額縁を通すことで背景化し、落ち着きと艶やかさを兼ね備えた空間になります。そして、ウィークエンドは額縁が壁面の窓と一体化して大空間が現れ、ウエディングやパーティが華やかに催されることとなるのです。額の向こう側を歩く花嫁の姿は、グリーンをバックにきっと絵のように見えることでしょう。

オーナーとシェフの目的や想いをパーテーションを用いたフレキシブルなデザインで具現化することで、さまざまな人を幸せにするための空間ができたと実感しています。

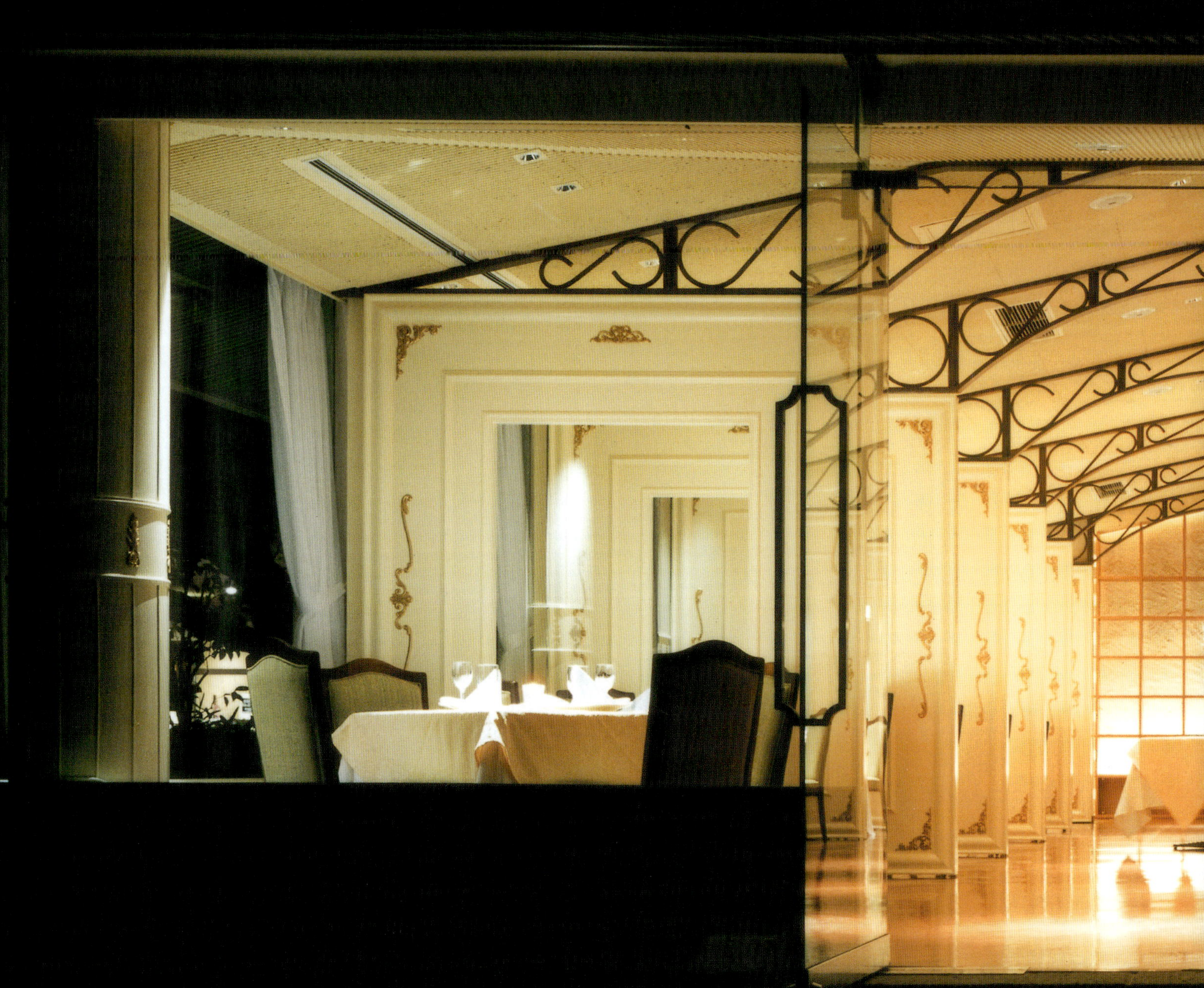

AUBERGE JARDIN was born as the main dining room for a hotel surrounded by a great garden of 70,000 sq. m., where the four seasons can be experienced. The image of the restaurant requested by the owner was of a multi-purpose great space that could be used for restaurant weddings that make use of the garden. On the other hand, the executive chef's desired image was of a restaurant with private rooms where a mature polish could be sensed.

We thought about how to meet these contradictory requests, and the result was partitions with movable frames. During weekdays, these partitions form individual rooms. At these times, when you sit down to one table, the other tables become the background--through layer upon layer of frames--and it becomes a space furnished simultaneously with tranquility and polish. Then, on the weekend, the frames become integrated with the windows at the wall and a great space materializes where gorgeous weddings and parties can be held. Walking on the other side of the frame, against the background of greenery, the figure of the bride assuredly resembles a painting.

By realizing the objectives and ideas of the owner and of the chef through use of a flexible design, we felt that a space was created that would bring happiness to a whole variety of people.

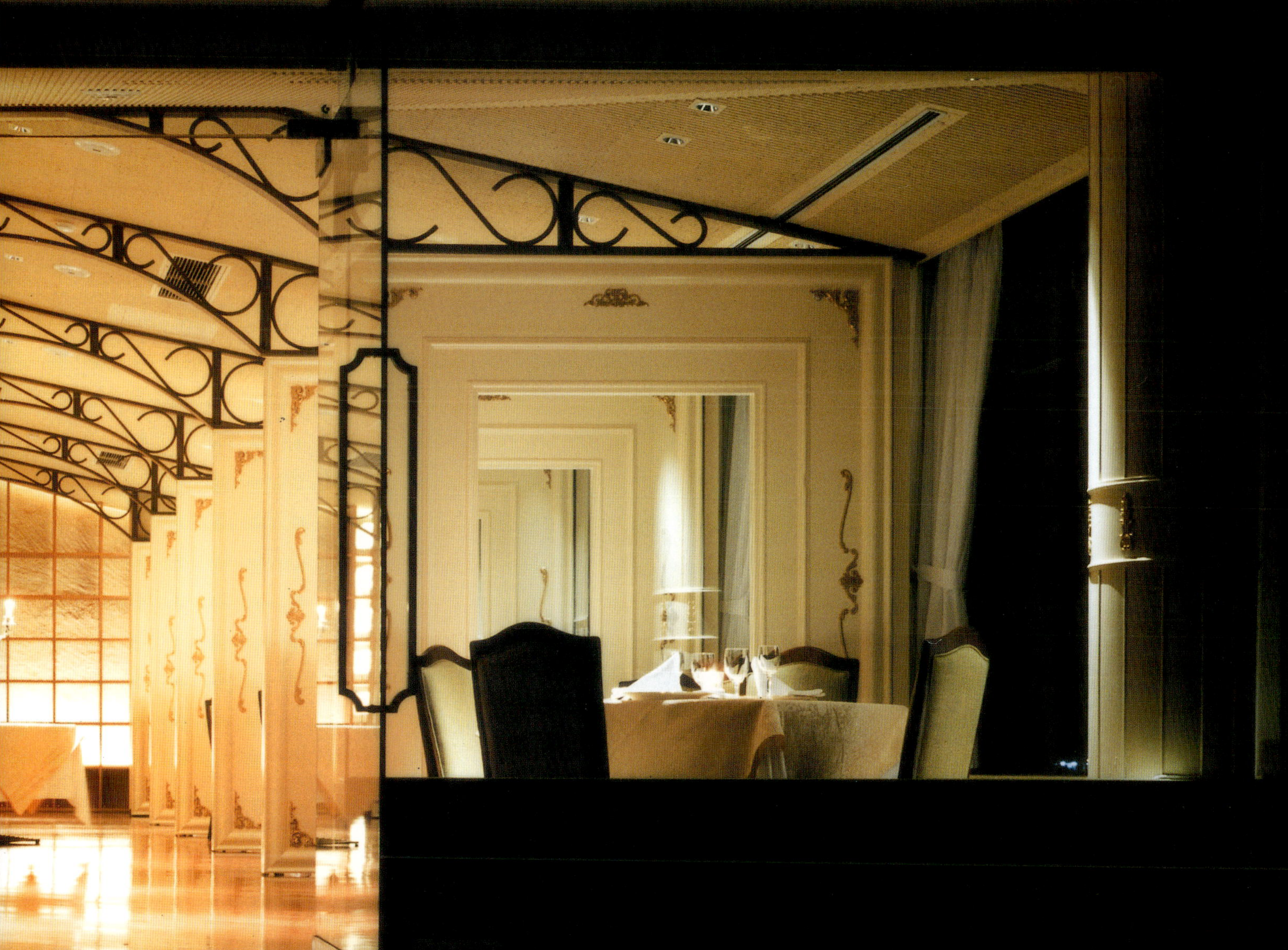

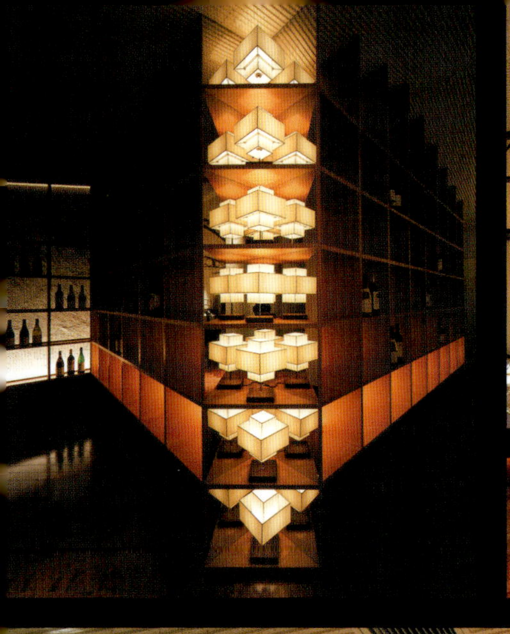
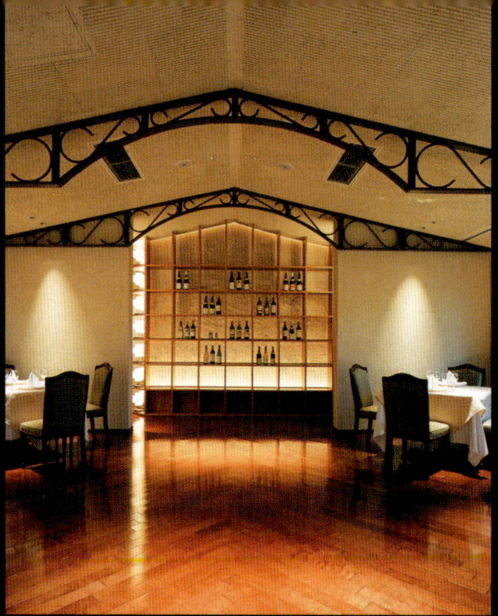
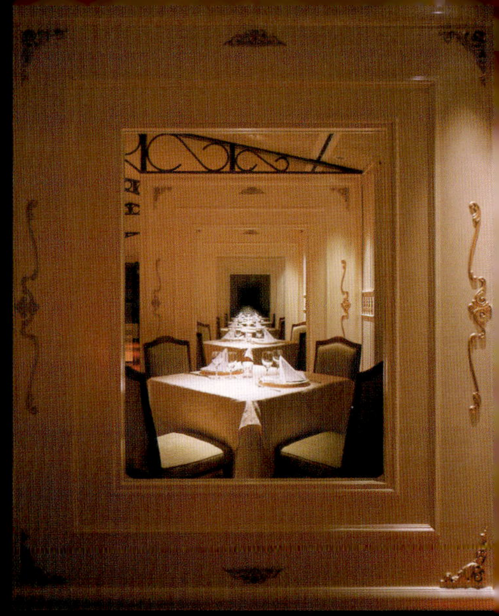

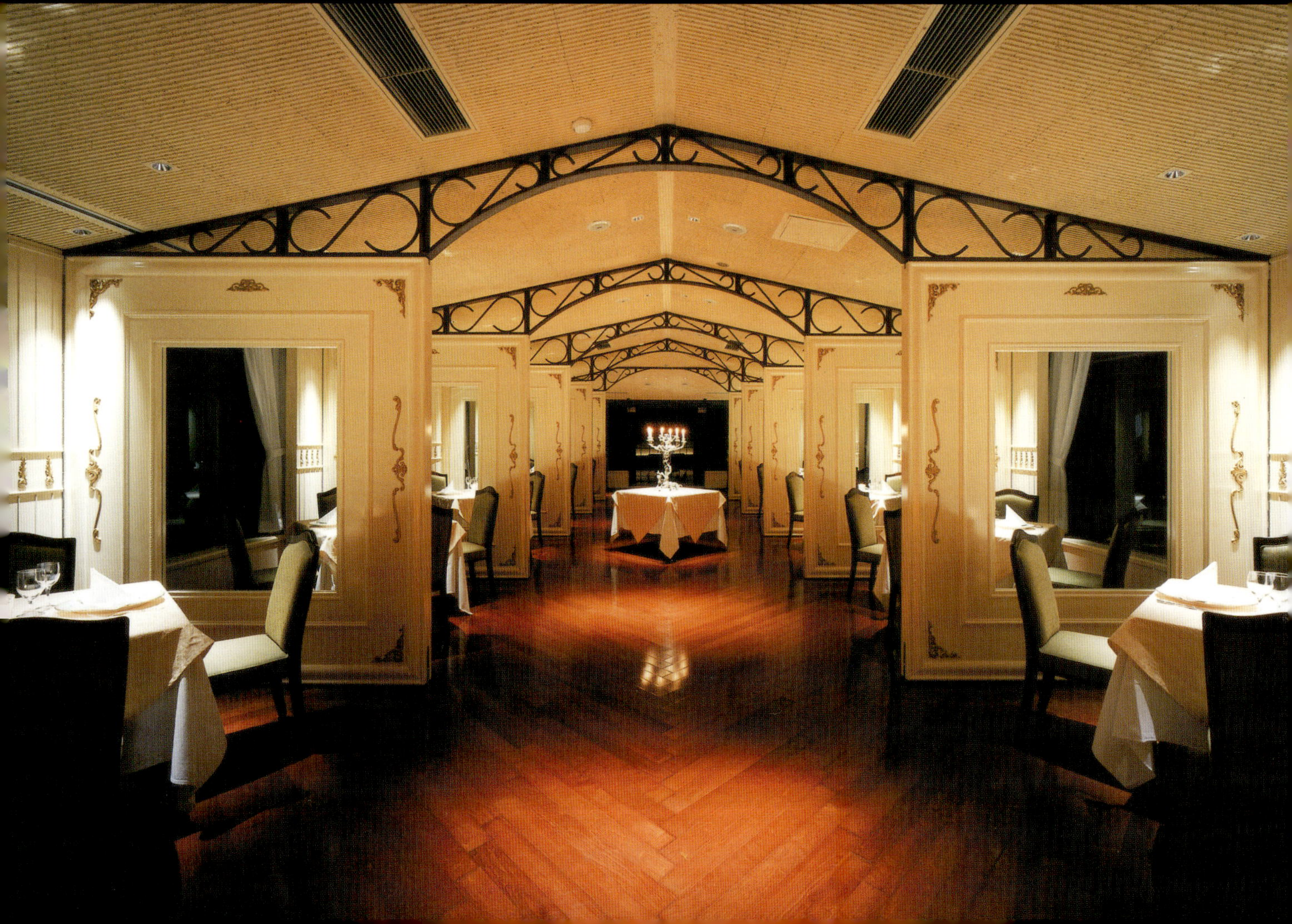

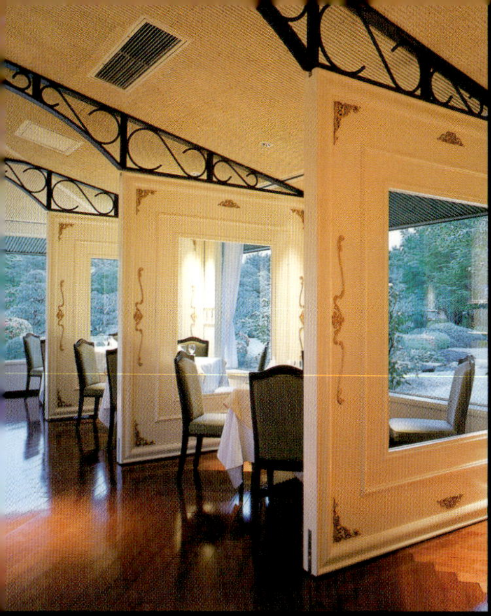

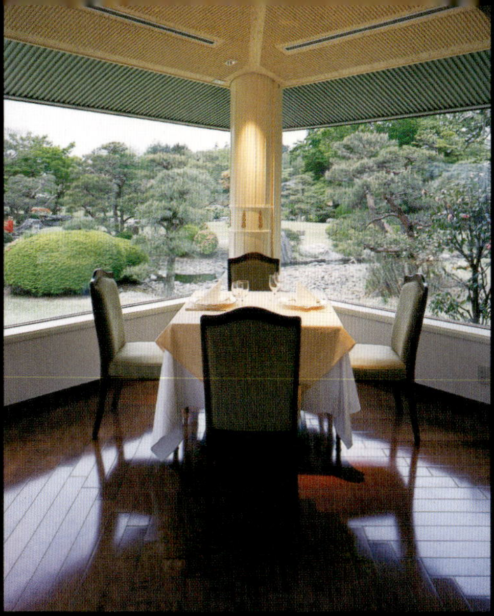

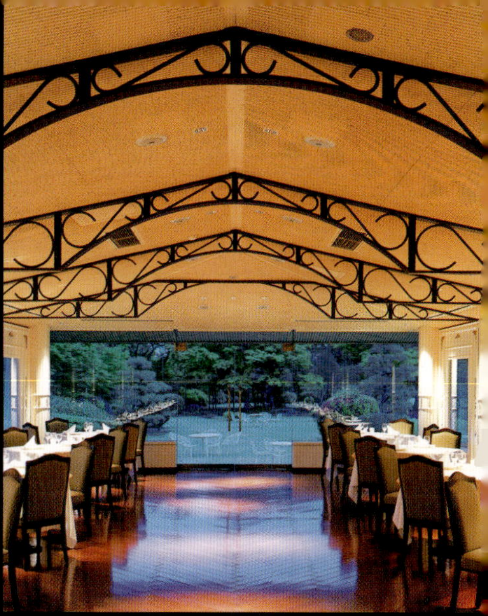

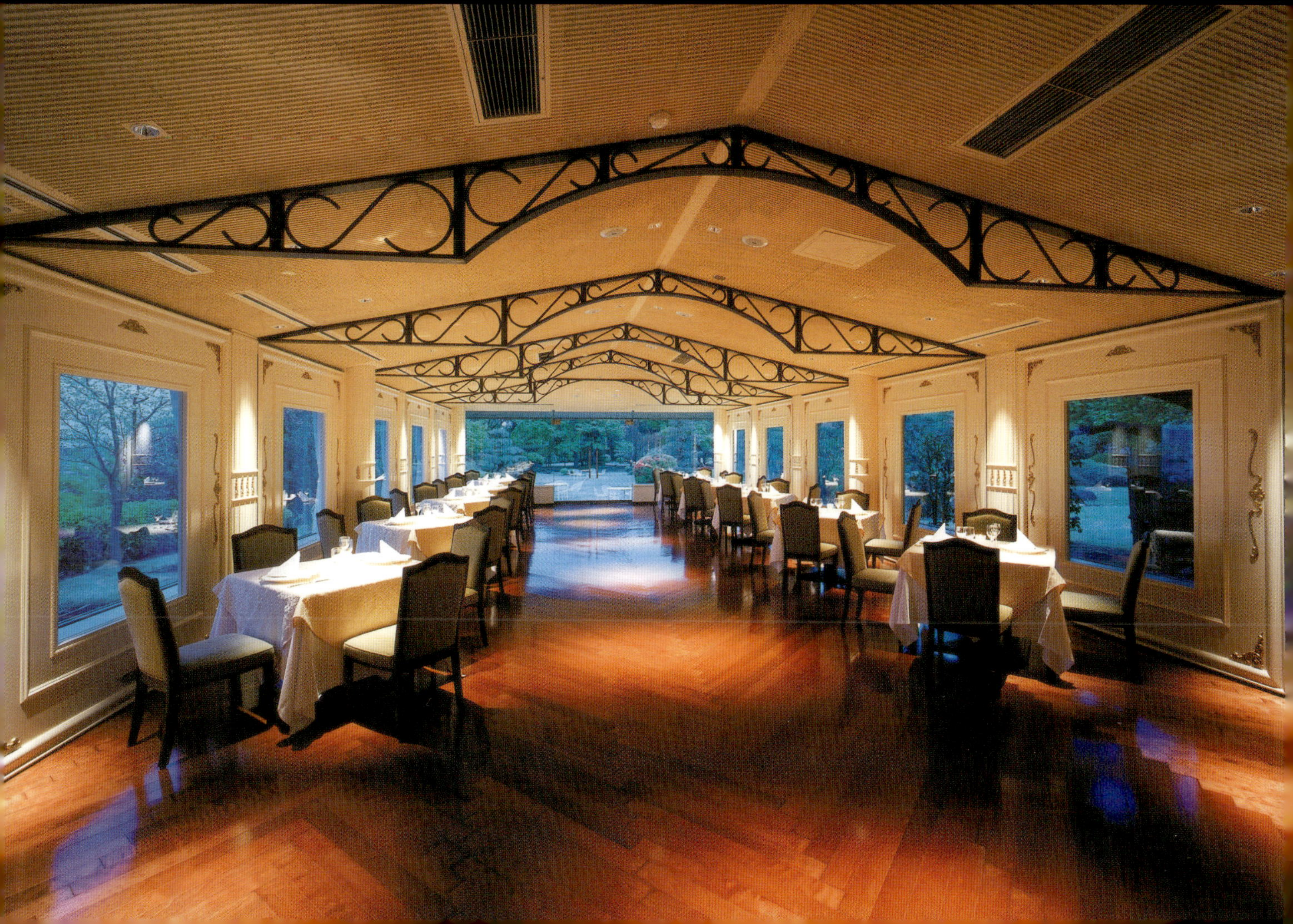

hotel ANAGA

ANAGA , HYOGO 2006

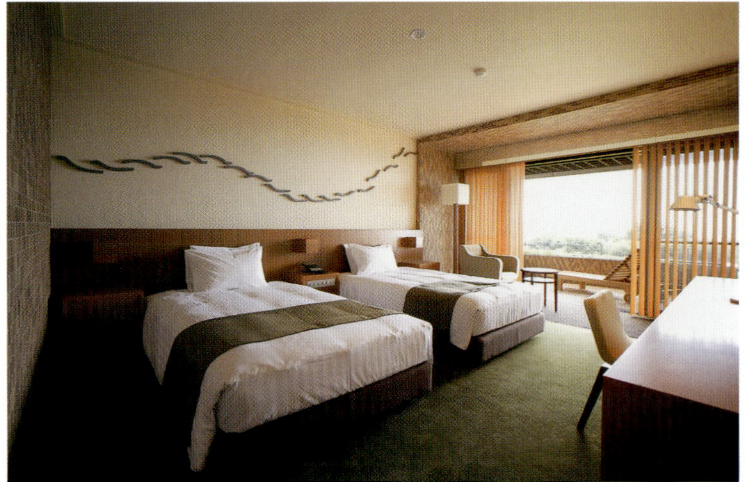

何もしない という贅沢

淡路島。大きな空と広い海、豊かな自然に包まれて、瀬戸内海に浮かぶ島。

　モノに満たされることにだけ幸せを感じる時代が去り、精神の充足や内面を磨くことにも幸せを感じる時代となりつつある、今の日本において「大きな空と広い海、豊かな自然がある」ことはホテルの環境として、大きな武器だと言えます。

　走り続けてきた日本人が、ようやく「なにもしないこと」を「贅沢」と認識できる今、"HOTEL ANAGA"では、その豊かな環境を最大限に活かして、人間本来の感覚を取り戻し、研ぎすます、心豊かで幸福感に溢れる時間をデザインしました。

The luxury of doing nothing

Awaji Island--enveloped in a big sky, a broad ocean and the abundance of nature, an island afloat in the Inland Sea. Leaving behind the era in which we could be content merely with material things, we are at the dawning of an age where happiness is felt through spiritual sufficiency and through working on one's inner self. In today's Japan, being a hotel with "a big sky and a broad ocean and the abundance of nature," could be said to be a major advantage in the hotel environment.

　Japanese people, caught up in the rat race, have now finally recognized "doing nothing" as a "luxury," and, at HOTEL ANAGA, the environment of abundance is utilized to the fullest extent. We have designed for interludes overflowing with feelings of richness and euphoria, when the sensation of truly being human can be recaptured and sharpened.

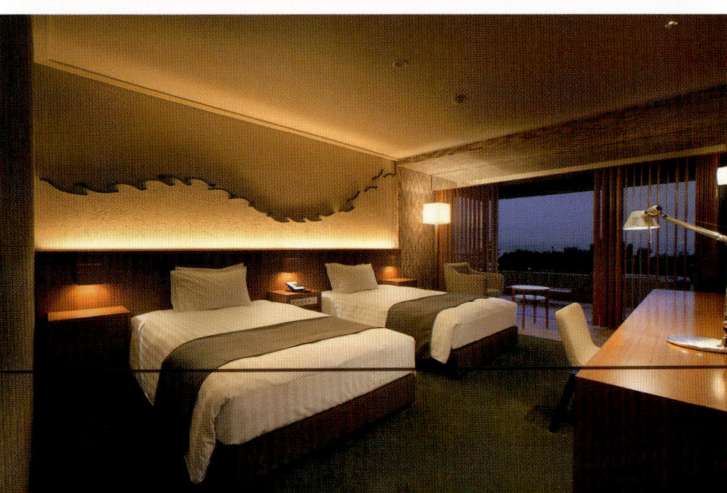

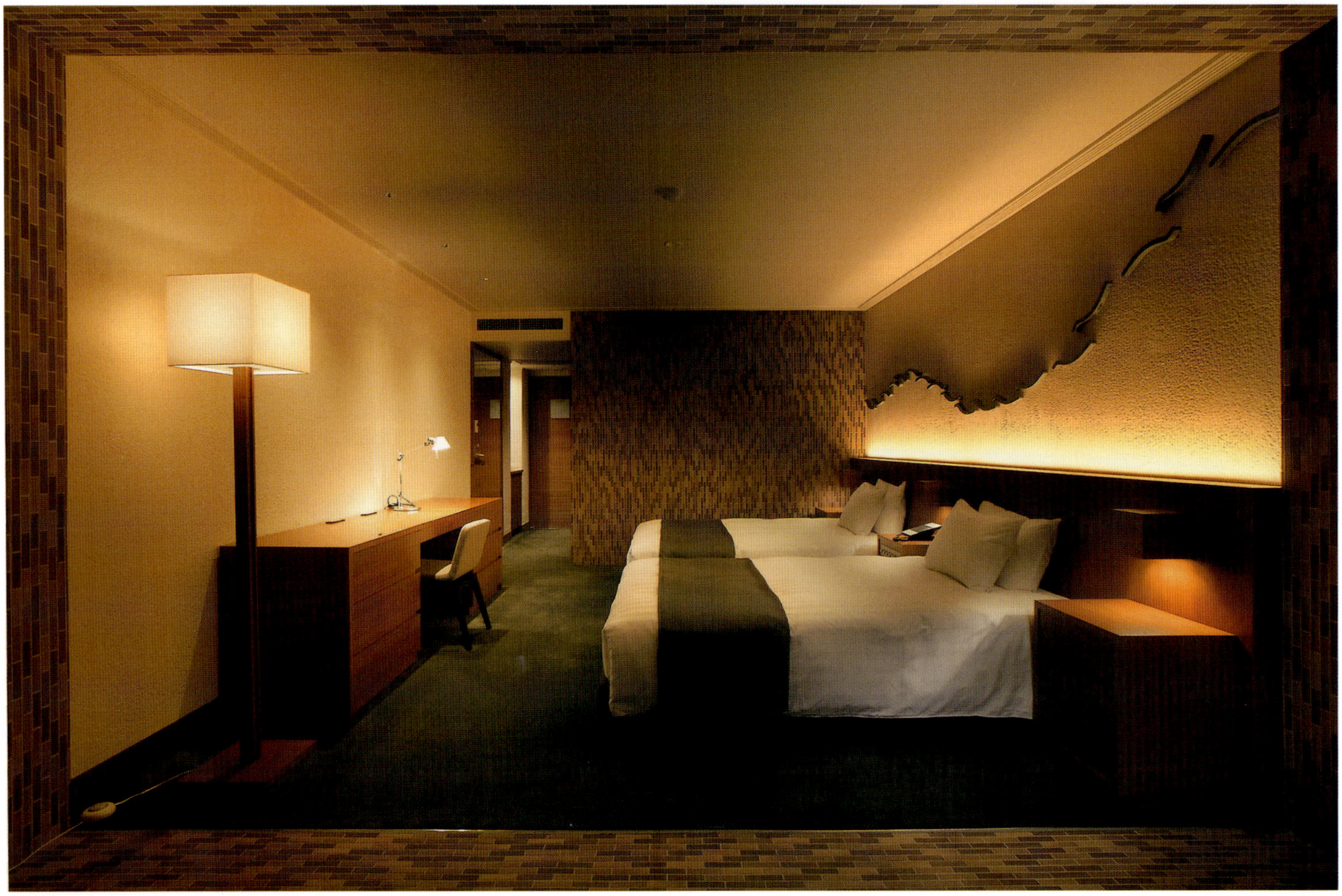

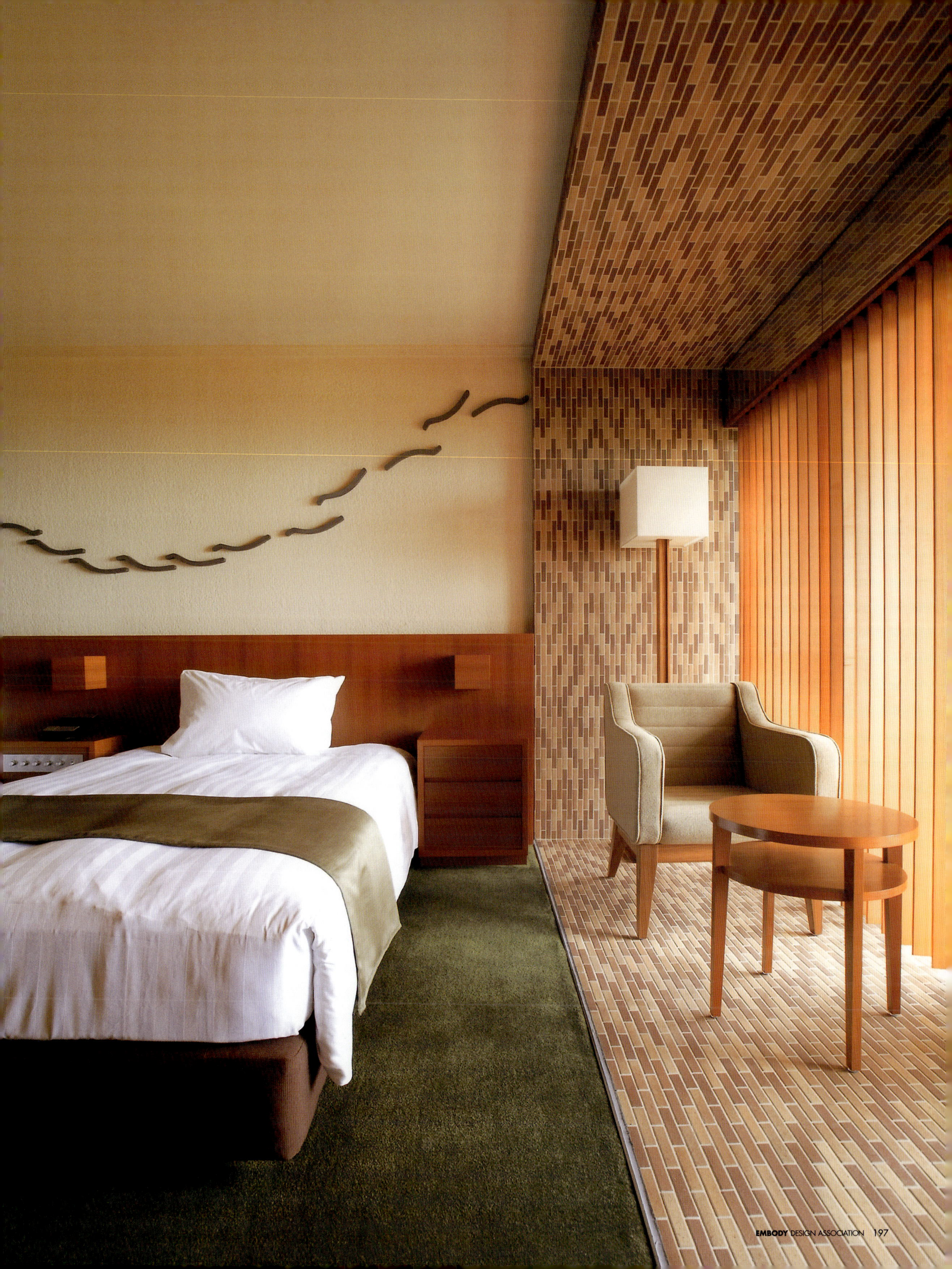

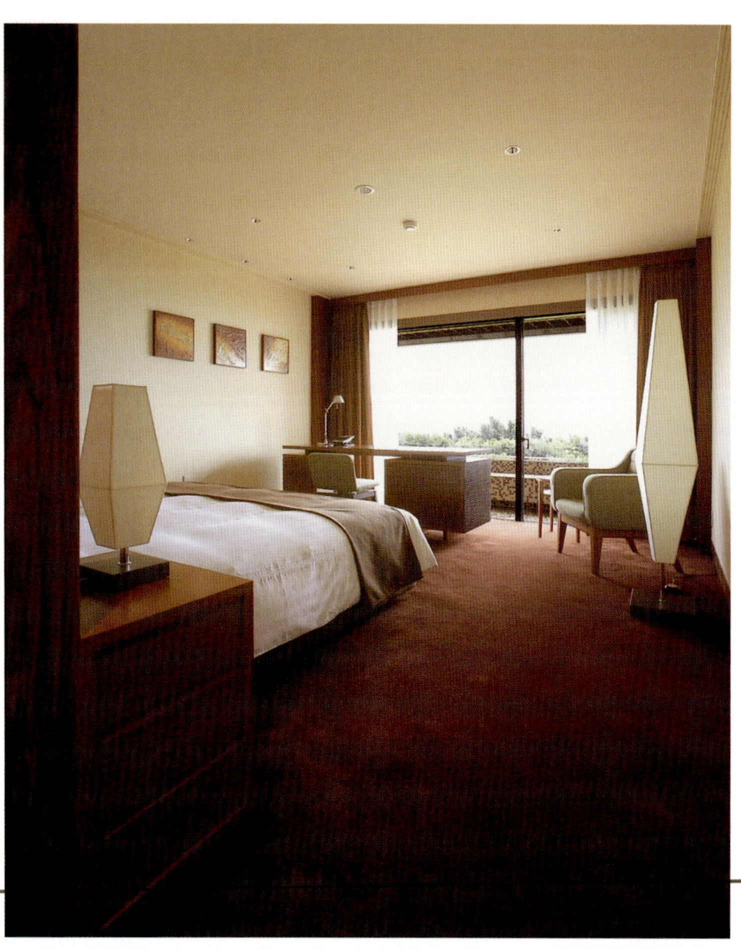
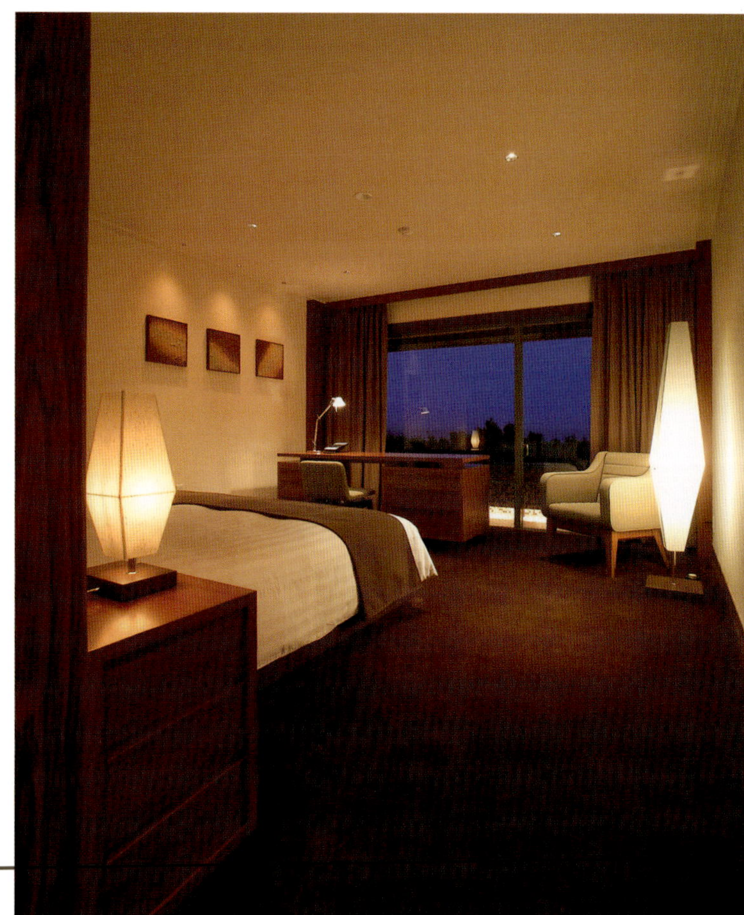

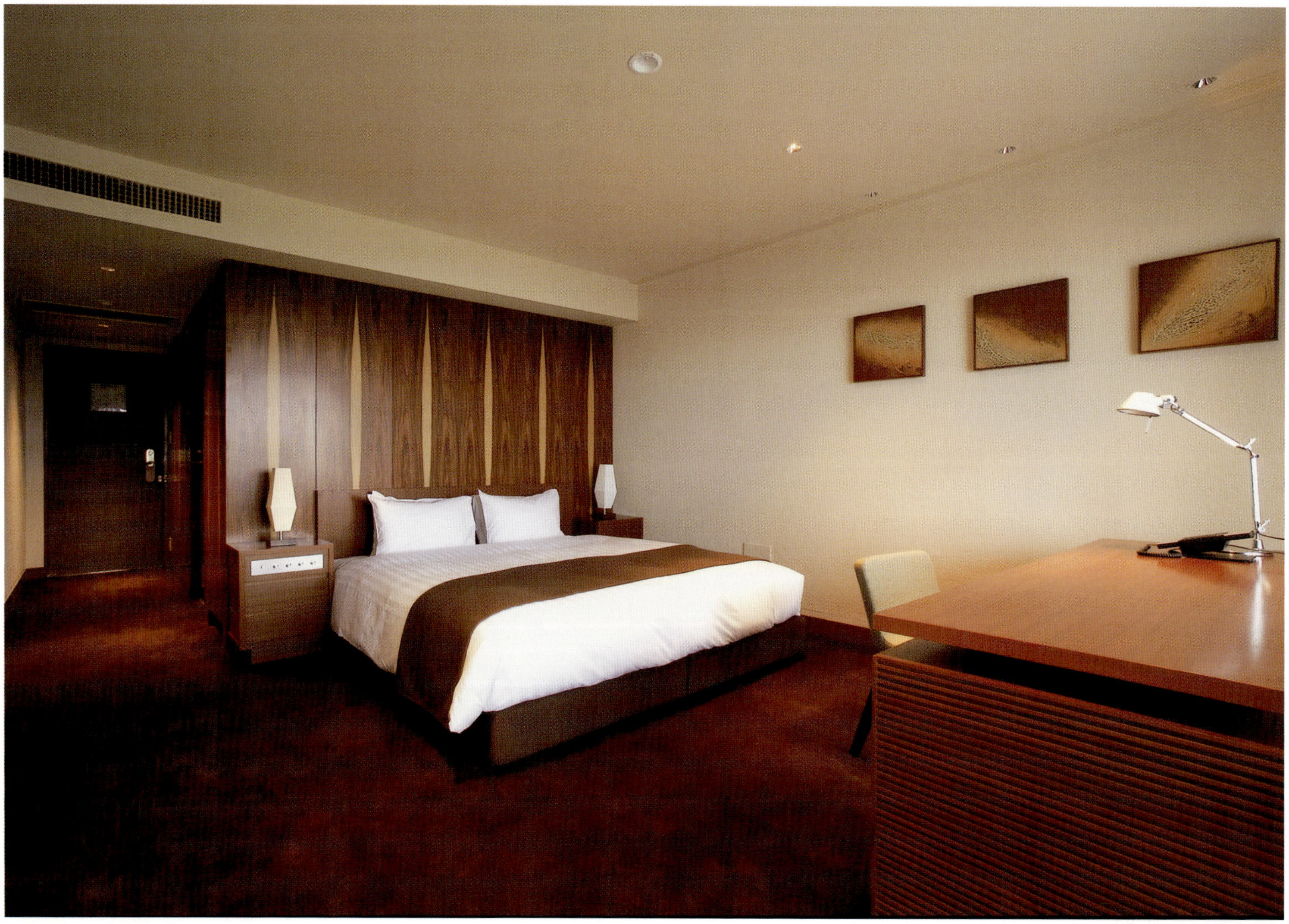

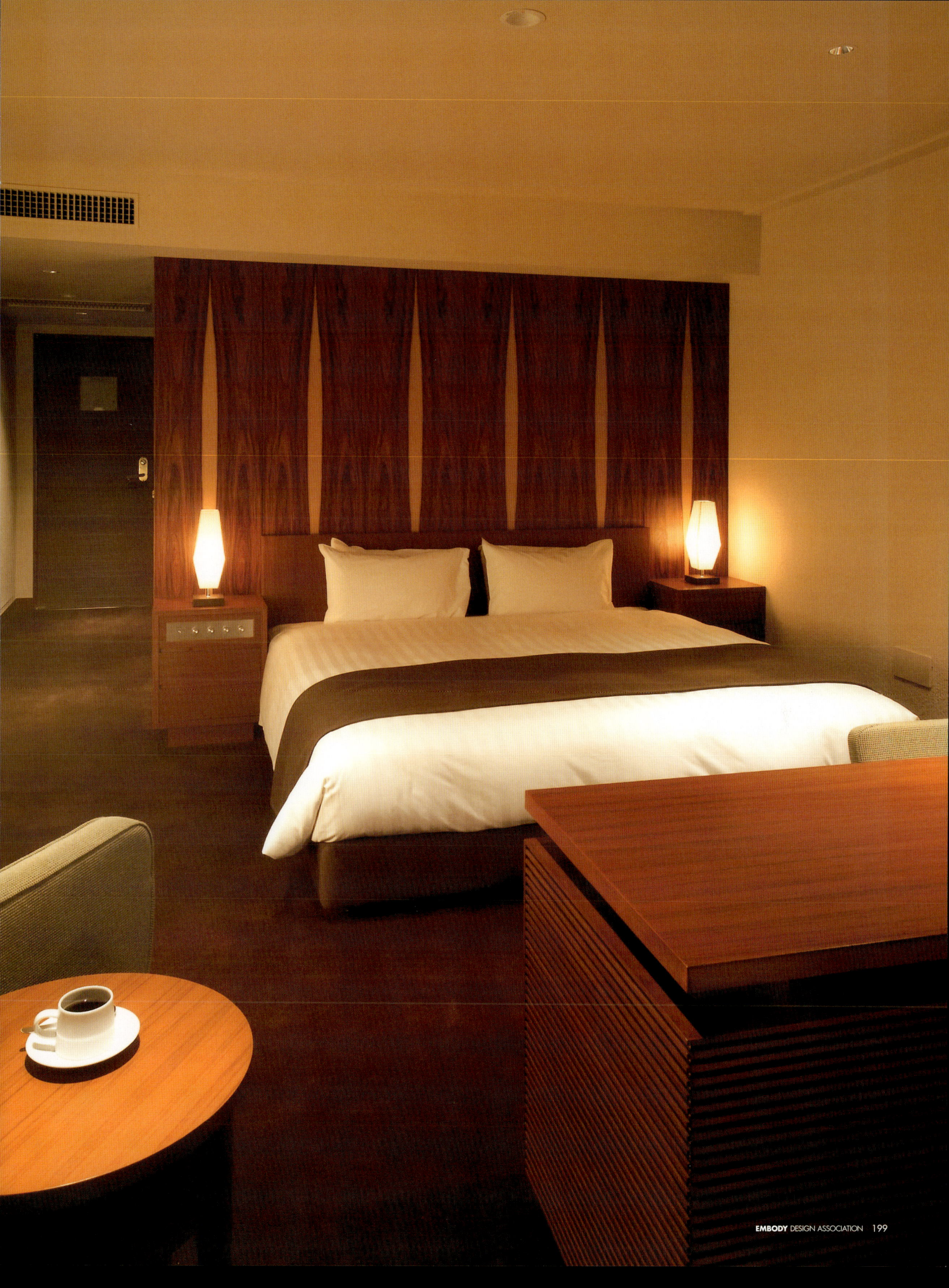

輪廻
transmigration
教育
education
信頼
spontaneous
自然体
reliance

spont
信頼
自信を得る空間
can get the self-confidence
reliance
教育
education
輪廻
自然体
transmigration

リラクゼーション
relaxation
自然治癒力を高める空間
space for the self-healing
open
安心感
開放感
sense of security
satisfy the desire to learn
知識欲を満たす
can get the self-confidence
自信を得る空間
MEDICAL HEALING
リラクゼーション
relaxation
自然治癒力を高める空間
space for the self-healing
安心感
sense of security
開放感 open
知識欲を満たす
satisfy the desire to learn

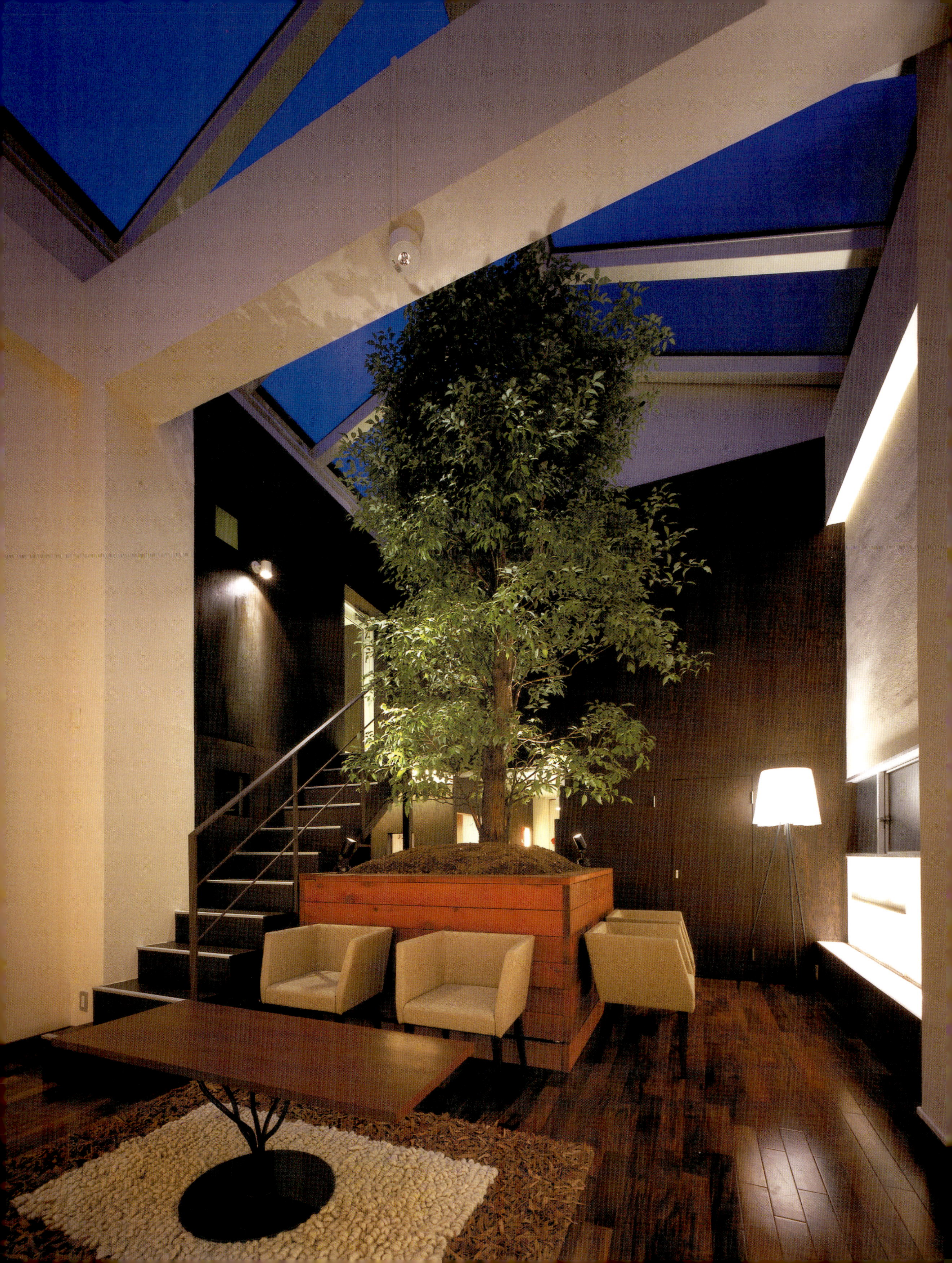

GINZA SHINRYOSYO
GINZA , TOKYO 2005

大都会のオアシス

今、身の回りの何もかもが多様で、複雑に絡み合い、心身共にストレスを感じている人が急増している
と聞きます。そんな現代の、特に大都会で疲れた人々をリラクゼーションへと導くために、"銀座診療所"
は生まれました。

　「癒しから自分磨きへ」をテーマに、癒されるだけではなく、訪れる人々の内面を磨くプログラムのた
めに、空間や環境を整え、自然治癒力を高めるような空間を目指しています。

A Big City Oasis

Nowadays we are surrounded by an overload of things and are ensnared in complexities, and we hear that stressed-out people are increasing rapidly. For just such an era, to guide exhausted people in the big city to relaxation, GINZA SHINRYOSYO (Treatment Center) was born.

　Under the theme of "healing to self-cultivation," for a program of not merely healing visitors but of cultivating their inner selves, space and environment were furnished in an aim at a place to enhance people's natural healing ability.

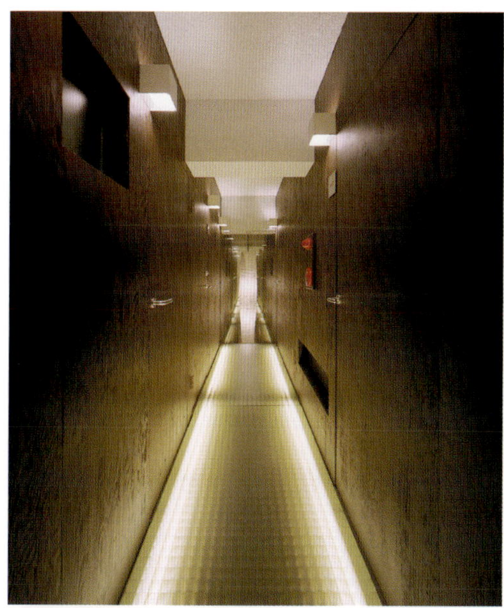

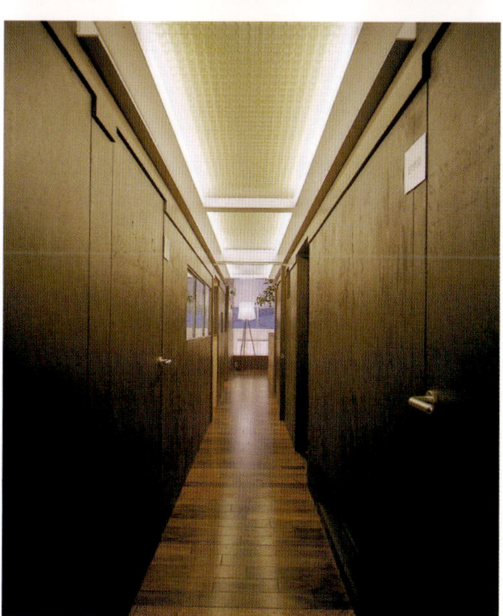

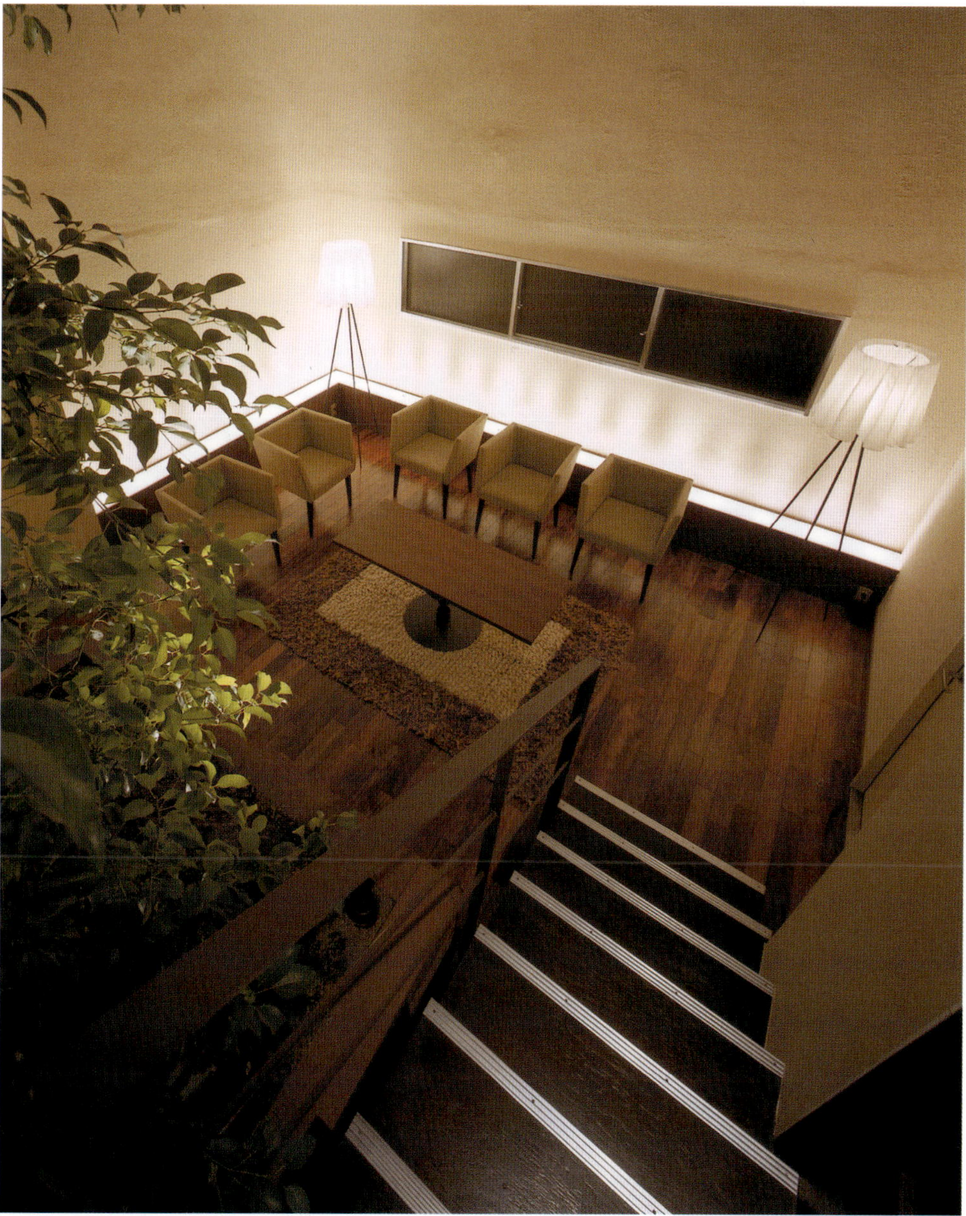

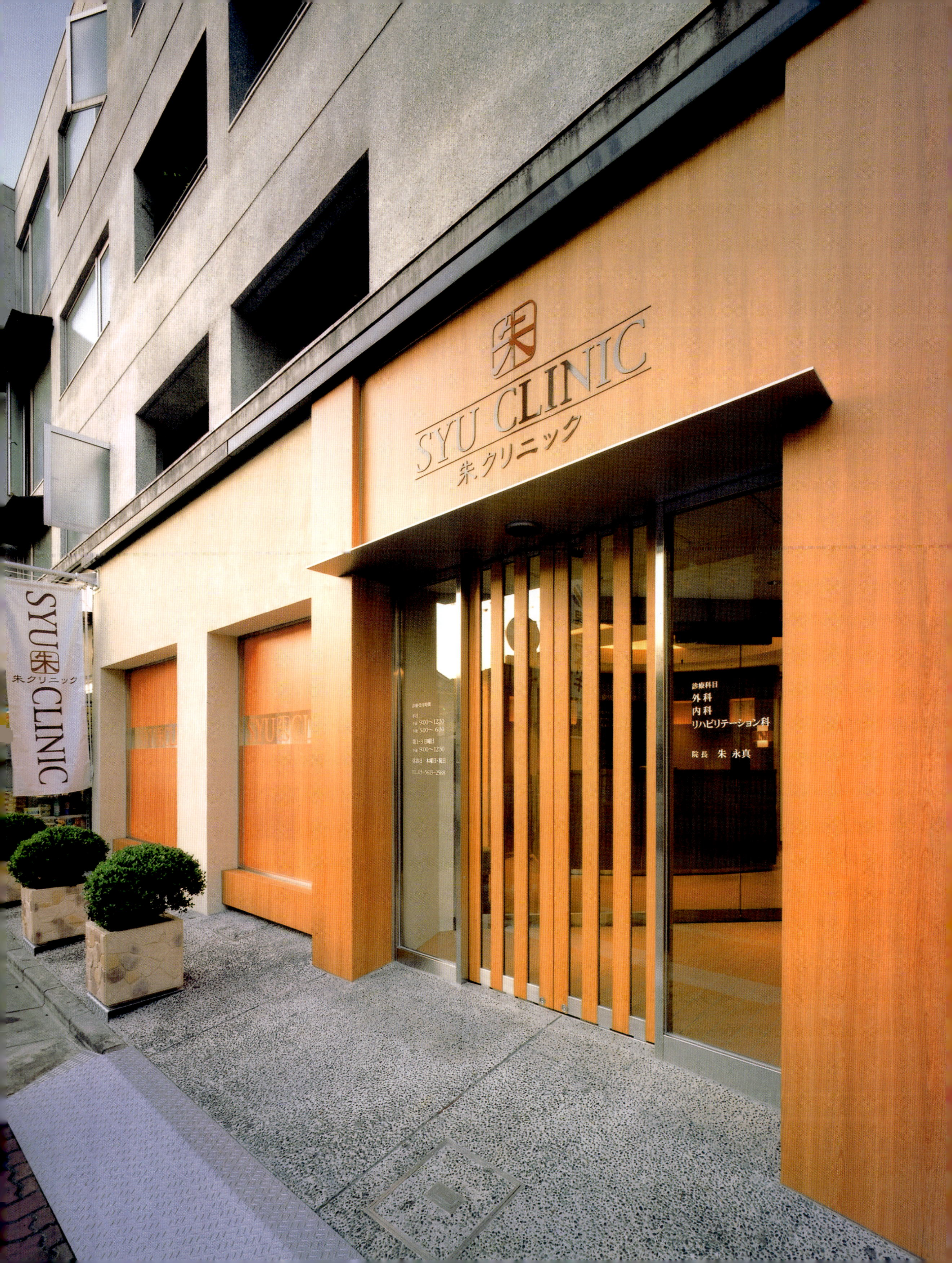
SYU CLINIC
朱クリニック
SYU CLINIC
朱クリニック
診療科目
外科
内科
リハビリテーション科
院長 朱 永真

SYU CLINIC
KAMEARI , TOKYO 1999

癒しの空間

"朱クリニック" の目指す医療とは、西洋医学だけでは満たせない、メンタルな部分に代替医療を取り入れ、人が本来持っている自然治癒力を最大限に引き出し、心身のバランスを整え、健康な身体づくりをサポートする、という一貫した総合医療です。

　その医療を体感する空間は、訪れる人の緊張感をほぐし、安らぎを与える温かさを秘めた「癒しの空間」であるべきだと考えます。マテリアルは自然素材にこだわり、空間は、リラクゼーションをもらたらす開放感と、プライバシーを守る安心感を兼ね備えるなど、これからの医療空間の基本となる部分を提示できたと思います。

A Space for Healing

The treatment at which SYU CLINIC aims is integrated total healthcare, where alternative medical care is incorporated into mental portions that cannot be fulfilled just through western medicine, and by which the natural self-healing power that people originally possess is drawn out to the fullest extent, and a balance of mind and body is achieved, thus aiding in the building of the healthy body.

　We believed that a space for experiencing this treatment would have to a "space of healing" that included warmth to ease the visitors' tensions and give comfort. By limiting the materials to natural things, and by creating a space both of openness that brings relaxation and a sense of security to protect privacy, we believe that we have been able to present elements that will become fundamental to medical spaces of the future.

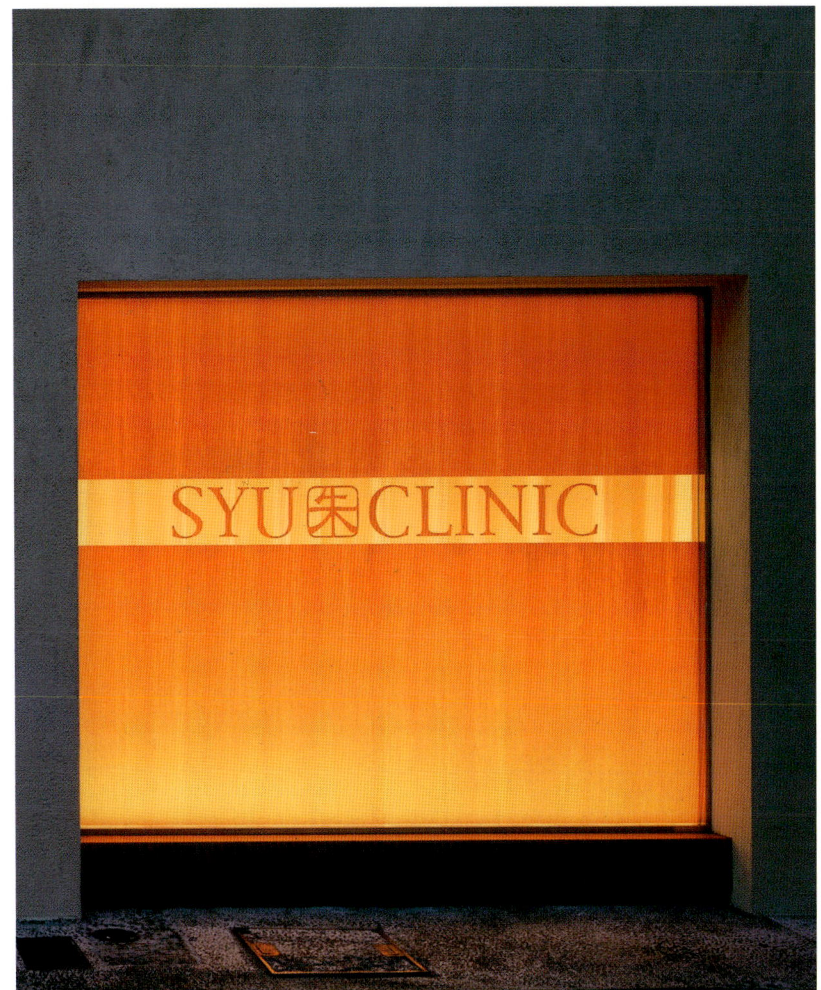

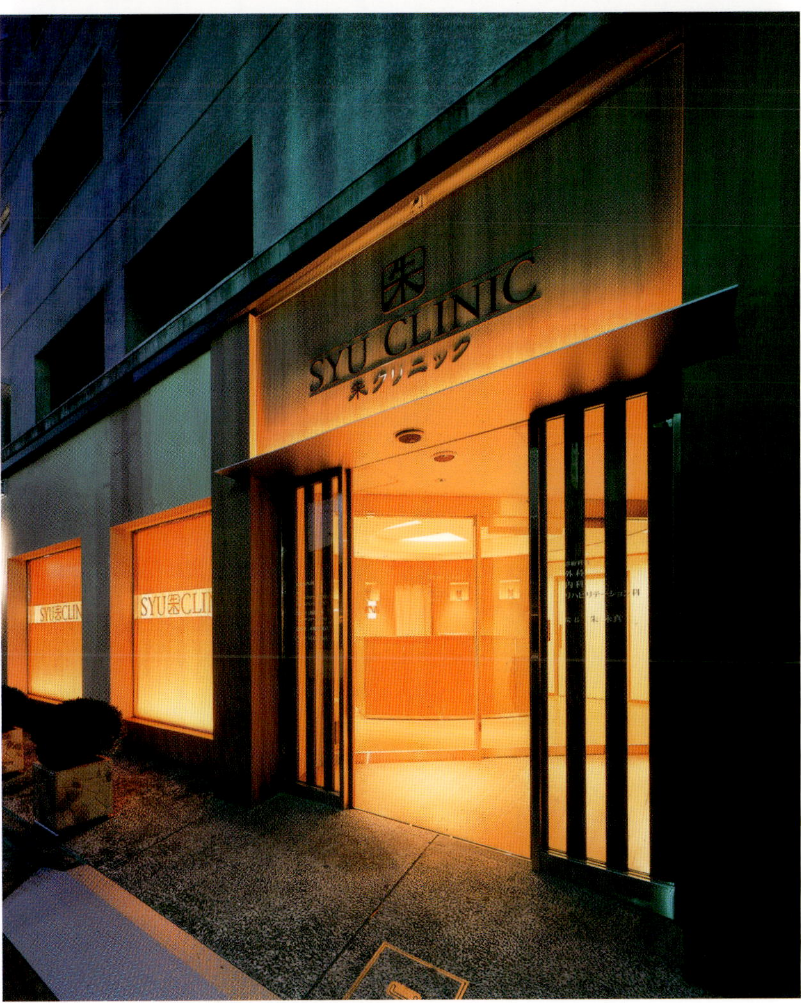

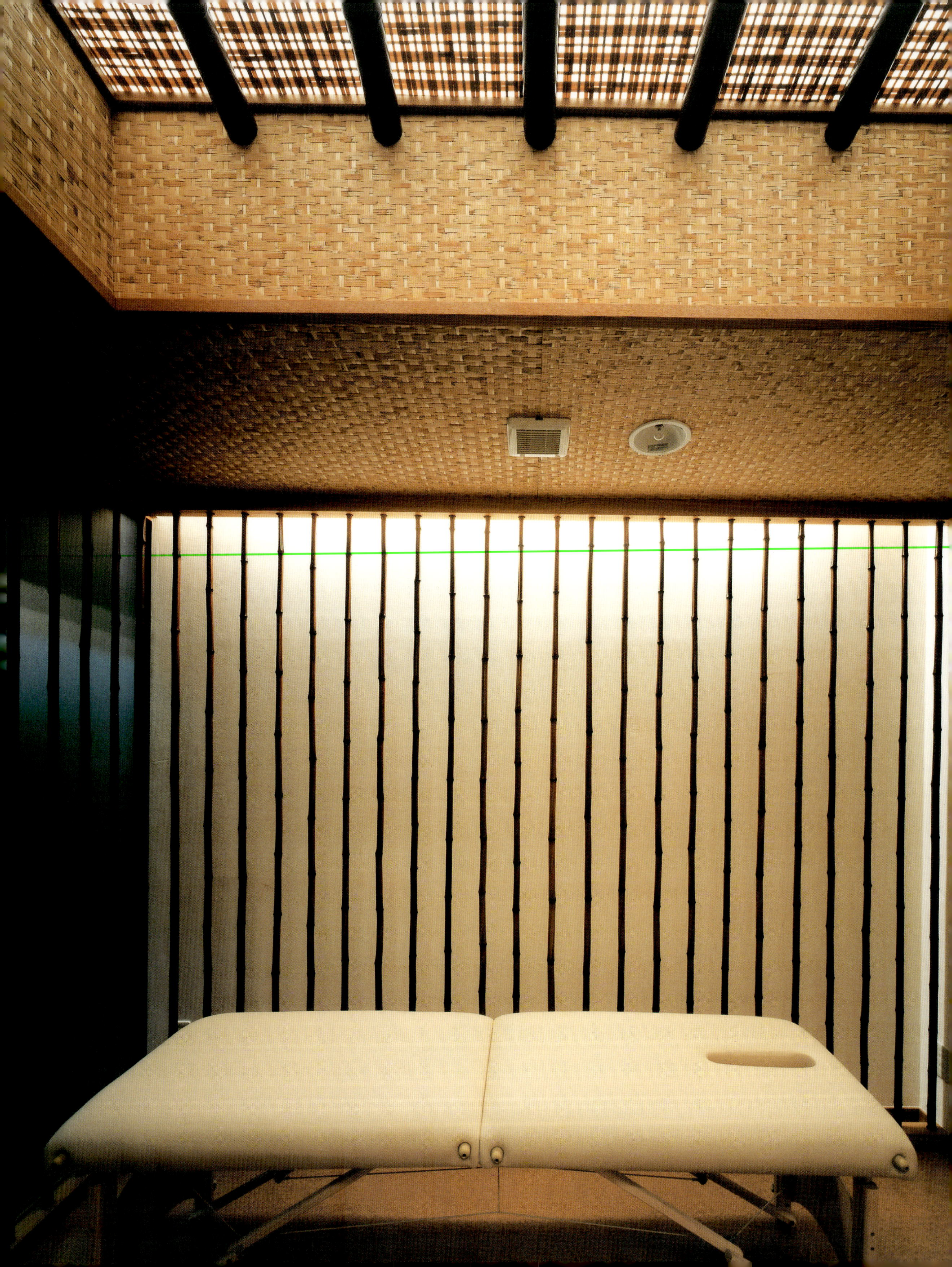

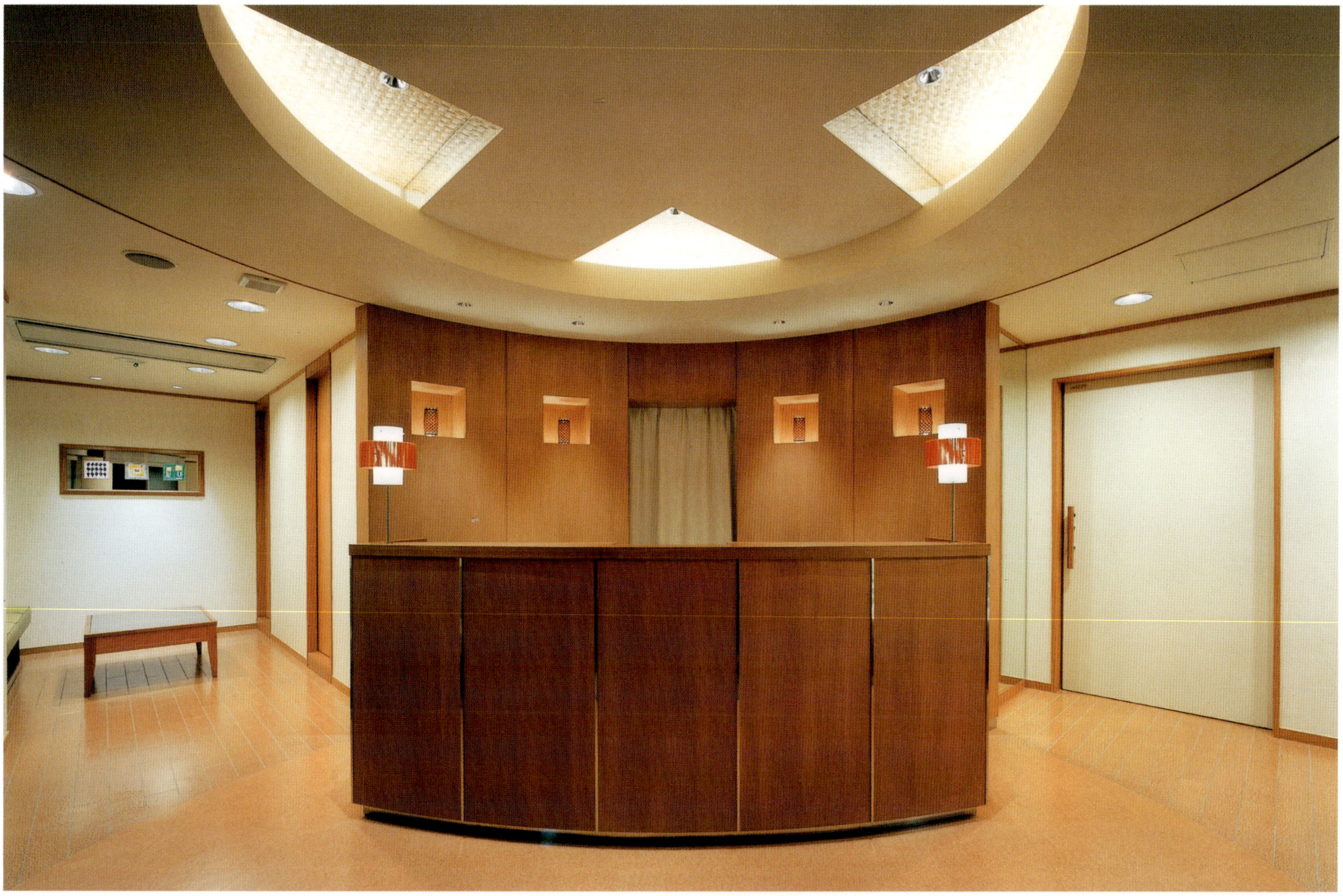

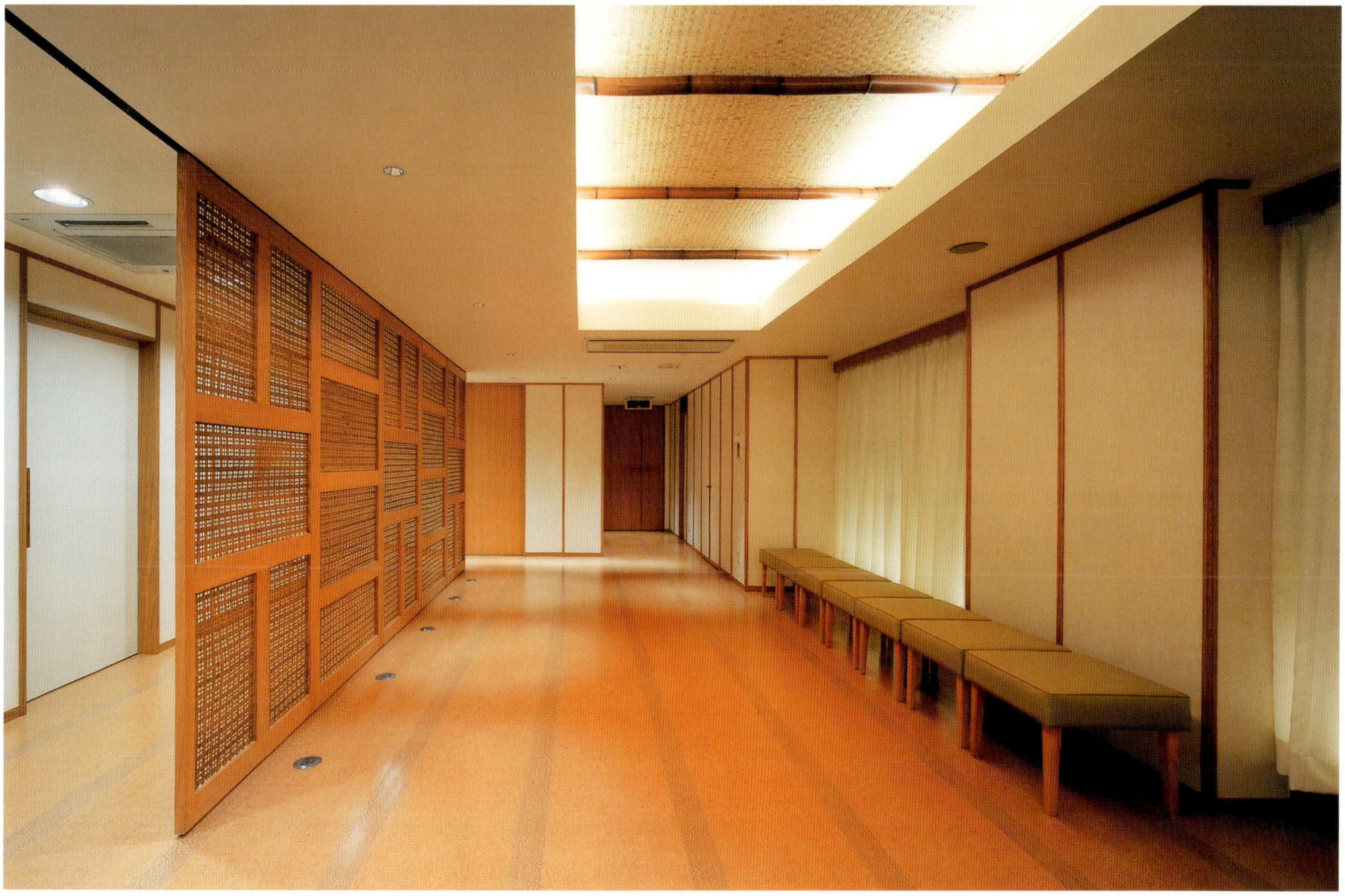

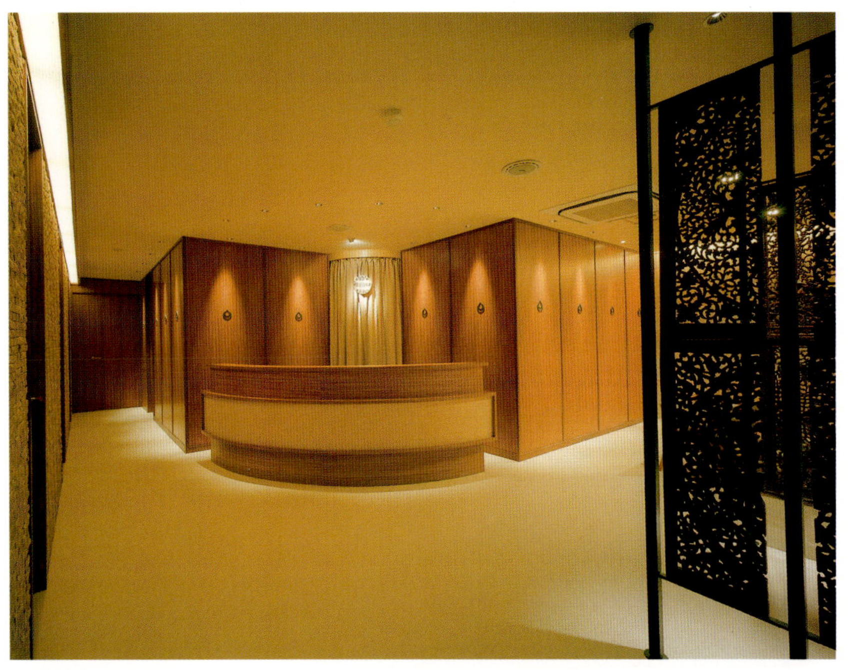

ORIENTAL AROMATHERAPY COLLEGE
SHIBA , TOKYO 2005

医療の未来をデザインする

社会環境や地球環境、時代の変化による人の心身への影響が深刻化する中で、西洋医学と東洋医学、そして、アロマセラピーを融合した新しい医療、メディカルアロマセラピーが脚光を浴びています。

この"O.A.C"は、医療に携わる人たちが、そのメディカルアロマセラピーの本質を学び、現場へと発信、還元、普及していくための、基地として計画されました。そのために空間デザインは、ただ癒すのではなく、治療するアロマセラピーを学ぶ場として、品格があり、また知識欲を満たす空気を創り出すことを目指しました。

Designing the Future of Medical Treatment

While the effects of the social environment, the earth environment, and changes in the times on the bodies and minds of people become more acute, a new medical treatment is in the limelight--one in which there is a blend Western medicine, Eastern medicine and aromatherapy--medical aromatherapy,.

O.A.O was planned as a base where people involved in medical treatment can study the essence of medical aromatherapy, and transmit, restore and spread it to the field. In the spatial design for this purpose, the aim was to create a space with dignity and a place with an atmosphere that satisfies the thirst for knowledge to learn aromatherapy not just for healing, but for medical treatment.

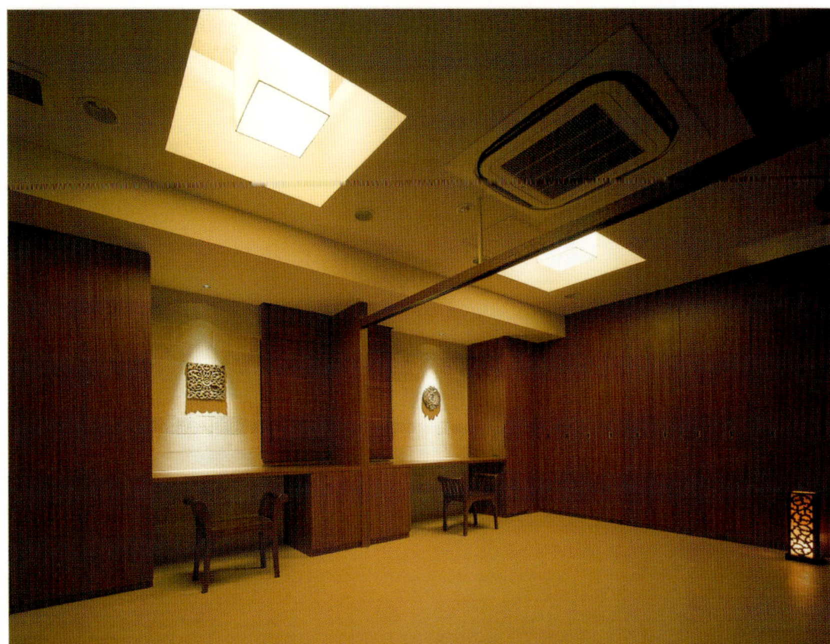

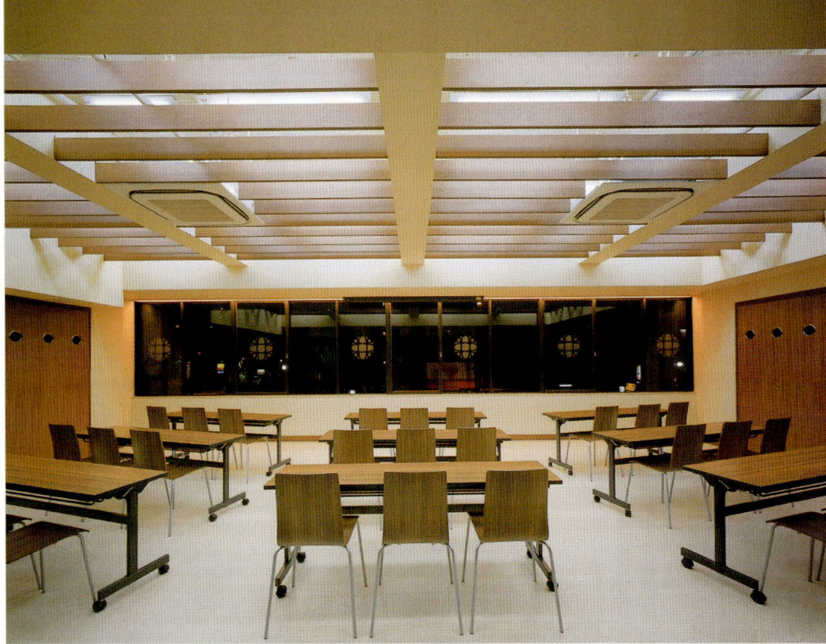

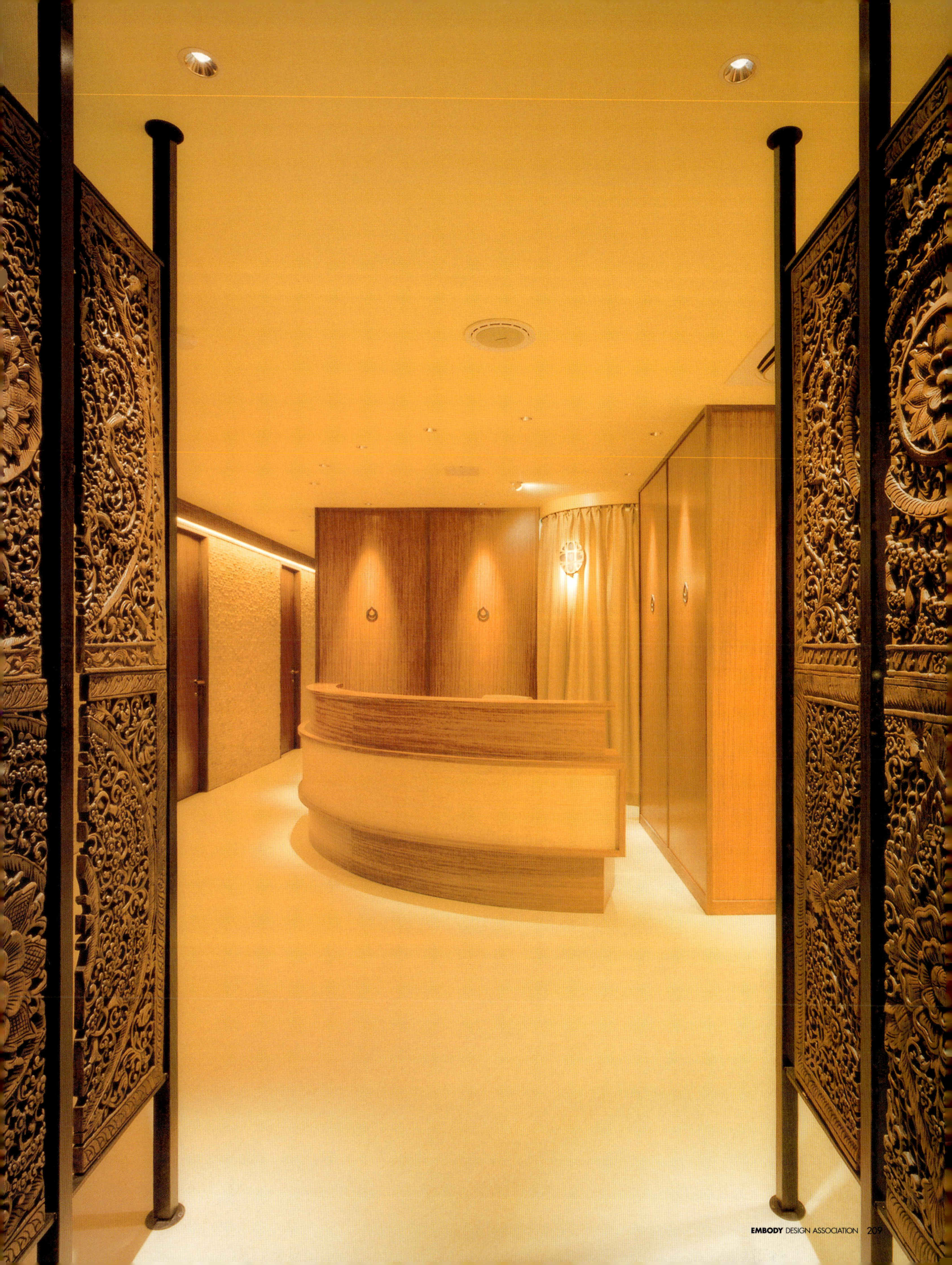

ORIENTAL AROMATHERAPY KAMEARI

KAMEARI , TOKYO 2006

入り口から出口まで

"朱クリニック"（204〜207ページ）の院長は、自らの医師としての経験を踏まえ、安心して医療の現場に送りだすことができる人を育成しようと、"O.A.C"（208〜209ページ）を設立しました。

そして、その卒業生たちが活躍する場の一つとして、新たに創られたのが、この"O.A.K"です。ここは、彼らの知識や技術を世の中へと還元していく場であり、メディカルアロマセラピーと人々の関わりあい方を提案し、発信する場にもなるでしょう。そんな未来を具現化するための空間をデザインしました。

From Entrance to Exit

O.A.C (pp. 208 -209) was set up by the director of the SYU CLINIC (pp. 204-207), based on his experience as a medical practitioner, to train people who can be trusted to be sent into the medical treatment workplace.

Then O.A.K was created as one place where graduates could practice. This is a place where they can spread their knowledge and techniques out into the world, and also to suggest and pass down ways for involvement between medical aromatherapy and people. We designed a space for the purpose of realizing this sort of future.

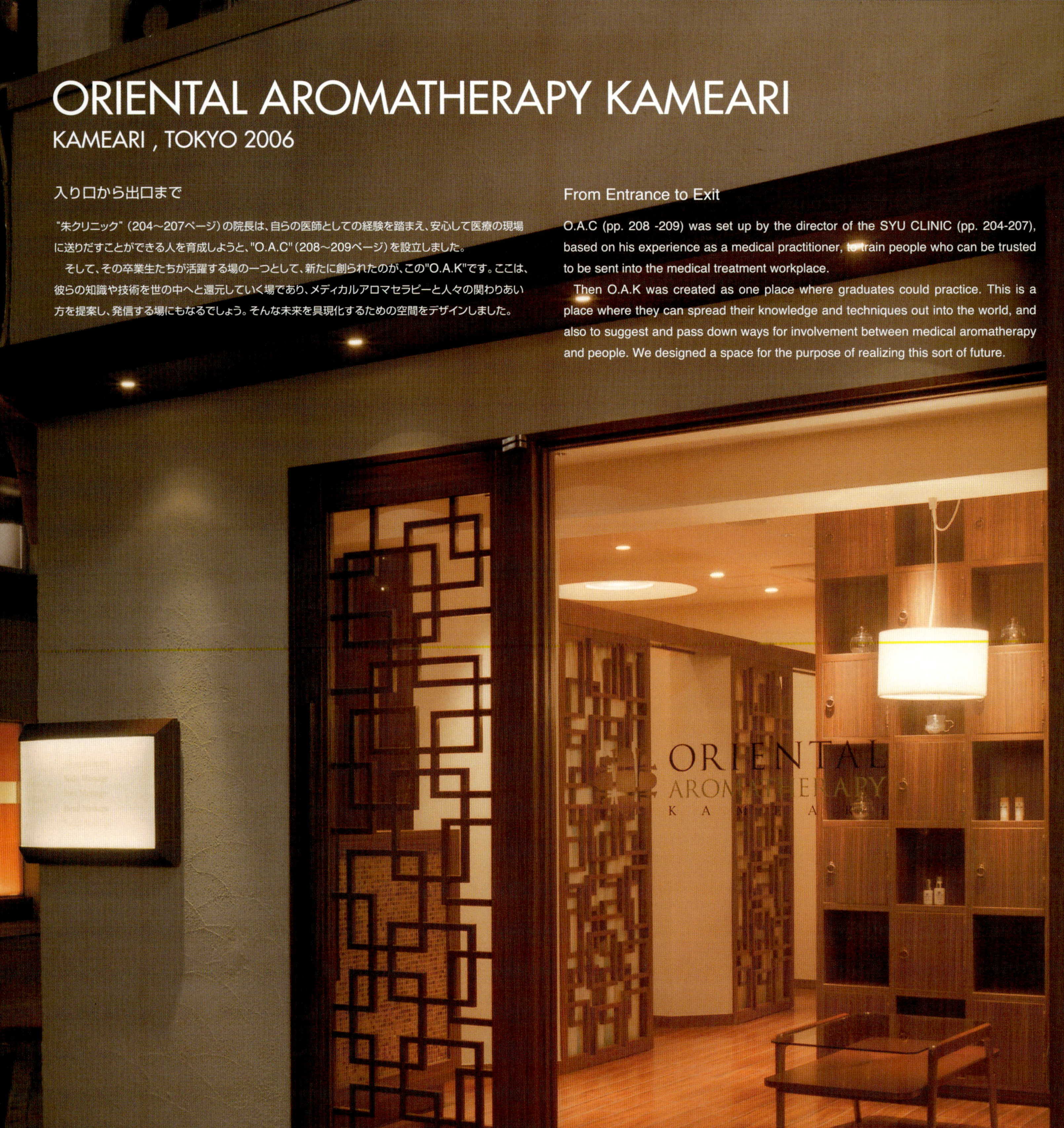

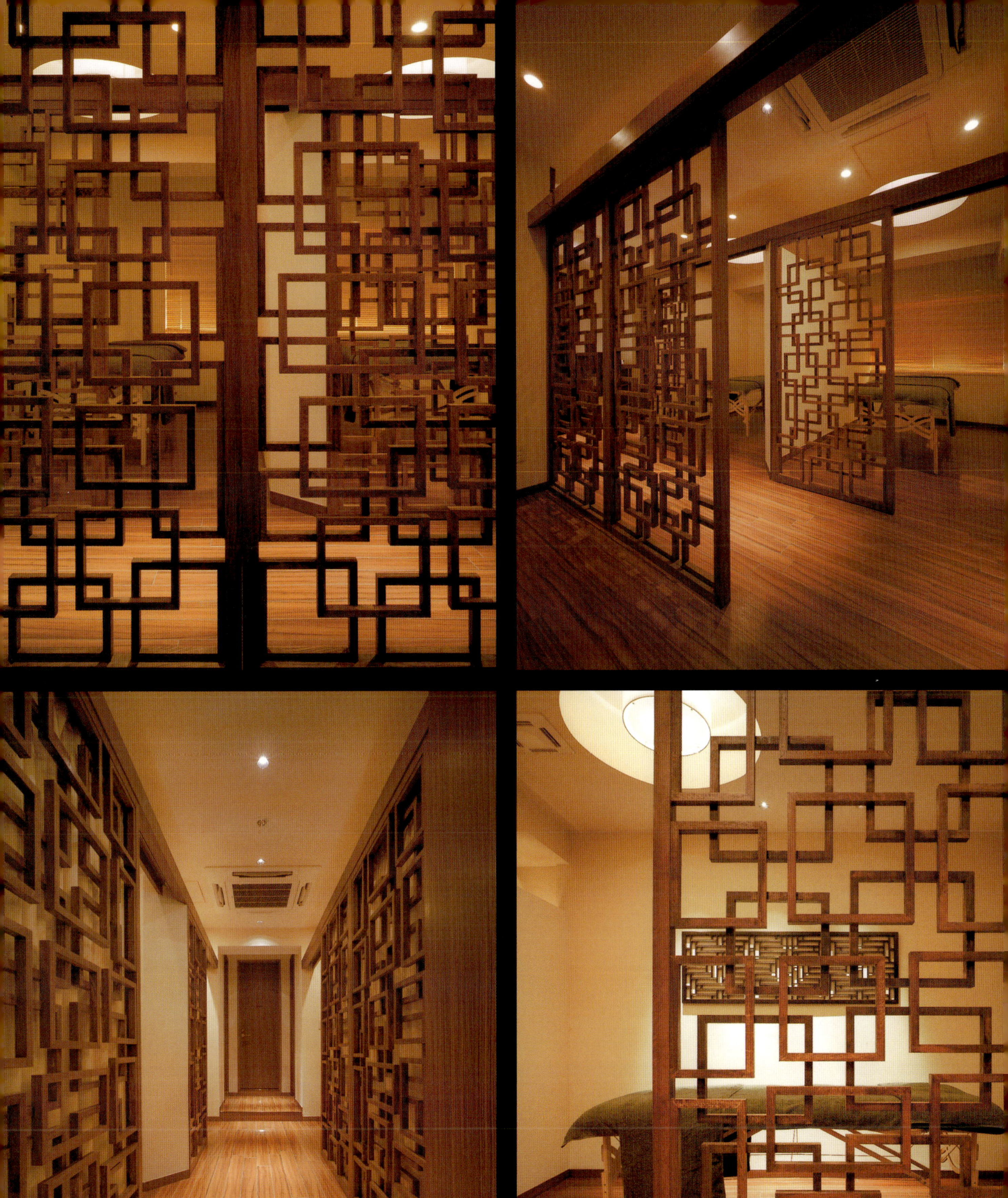

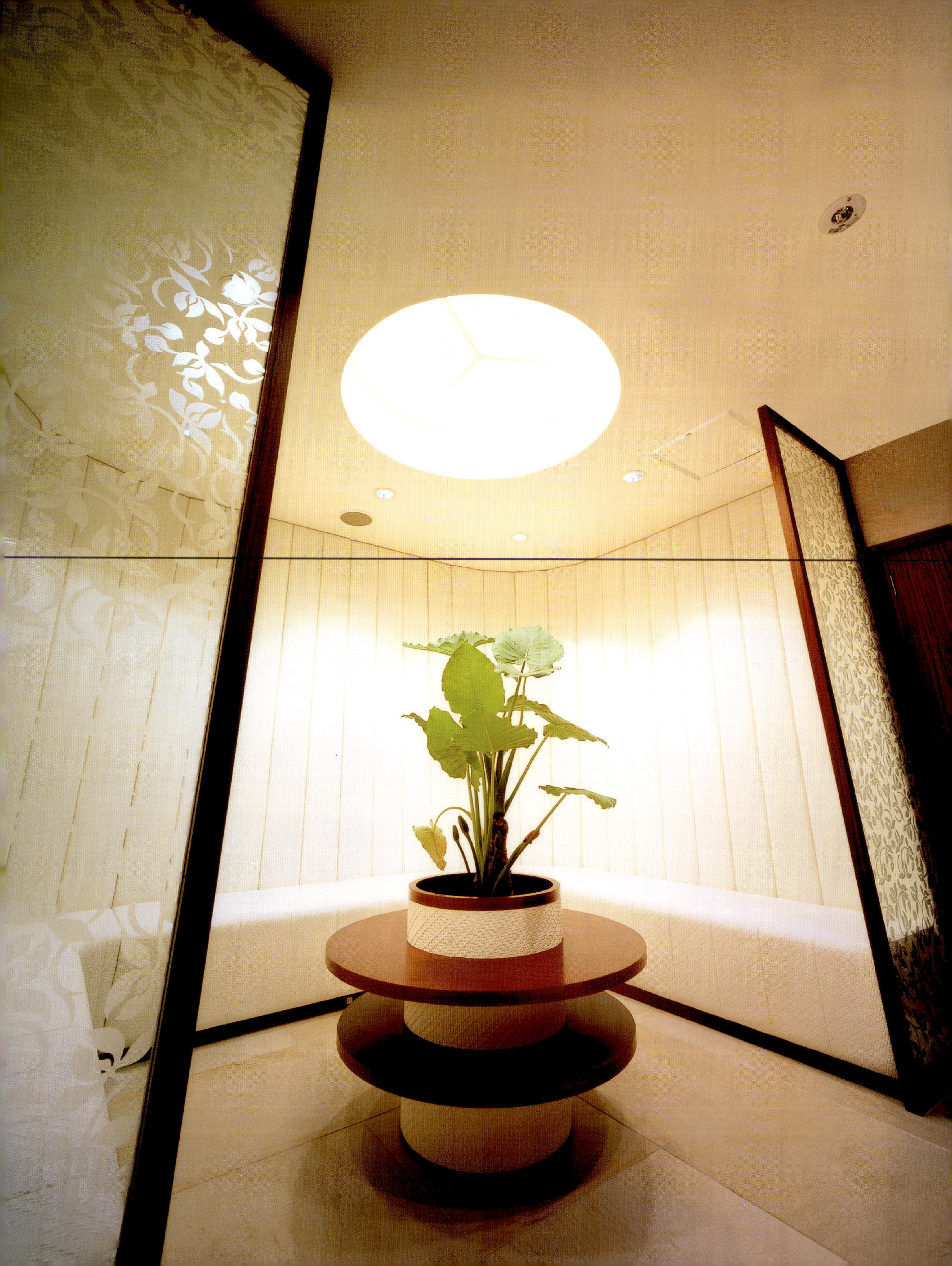

ONISHI MEDICAL LABO
OTSU , SHIGA 2004

訪れる人を幸せにする空間

これからのクリニックは、どうあるべきか。訪れる人は何を求めているのか。

　私がこの課題を踏まえて"大西メディカルラボ"で、コンセプトとしたのは、「peace of mind」です。それは、訪れる人にとっても、働く人にとっても、外見の美しさとともに、自信や内面の美しさをも得、また提供できるような、医療に基づくケアの空間が必要だということです。ゆったりと落ち着いて診療が出来、また、ケアが受けらるように、品格のある空間を目指し、訪れる人たちの心を幸せで満たす空間を具現化しました。

A Space to Make Visitors Happy

The clinic of the future-what should it be like? What do visitors want? Based on this topic, for ONISHI MEDICAL LABO we came up with the concept of "peace of mind."

　This means that a space is needed for care based on medicine, where both visitors and workers can gain confidence and internal beauty, and where these things can be offered. The aim was at a dignified space where treatment could be performed and care received, and, so that a space to fill the visitor's heart with happiness could be realized, the space was embodied with a comfortable and relaxed mood.

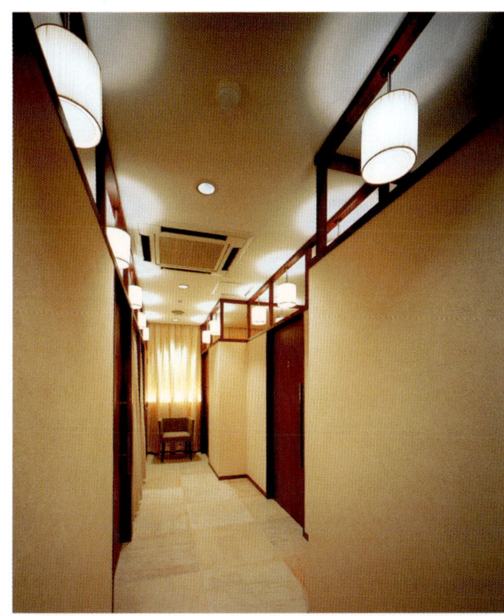

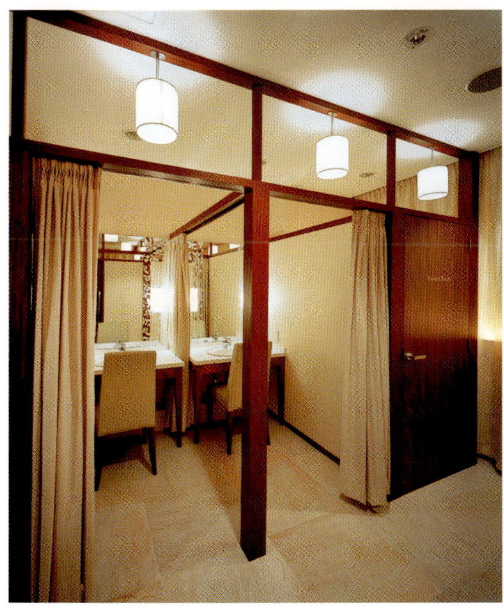

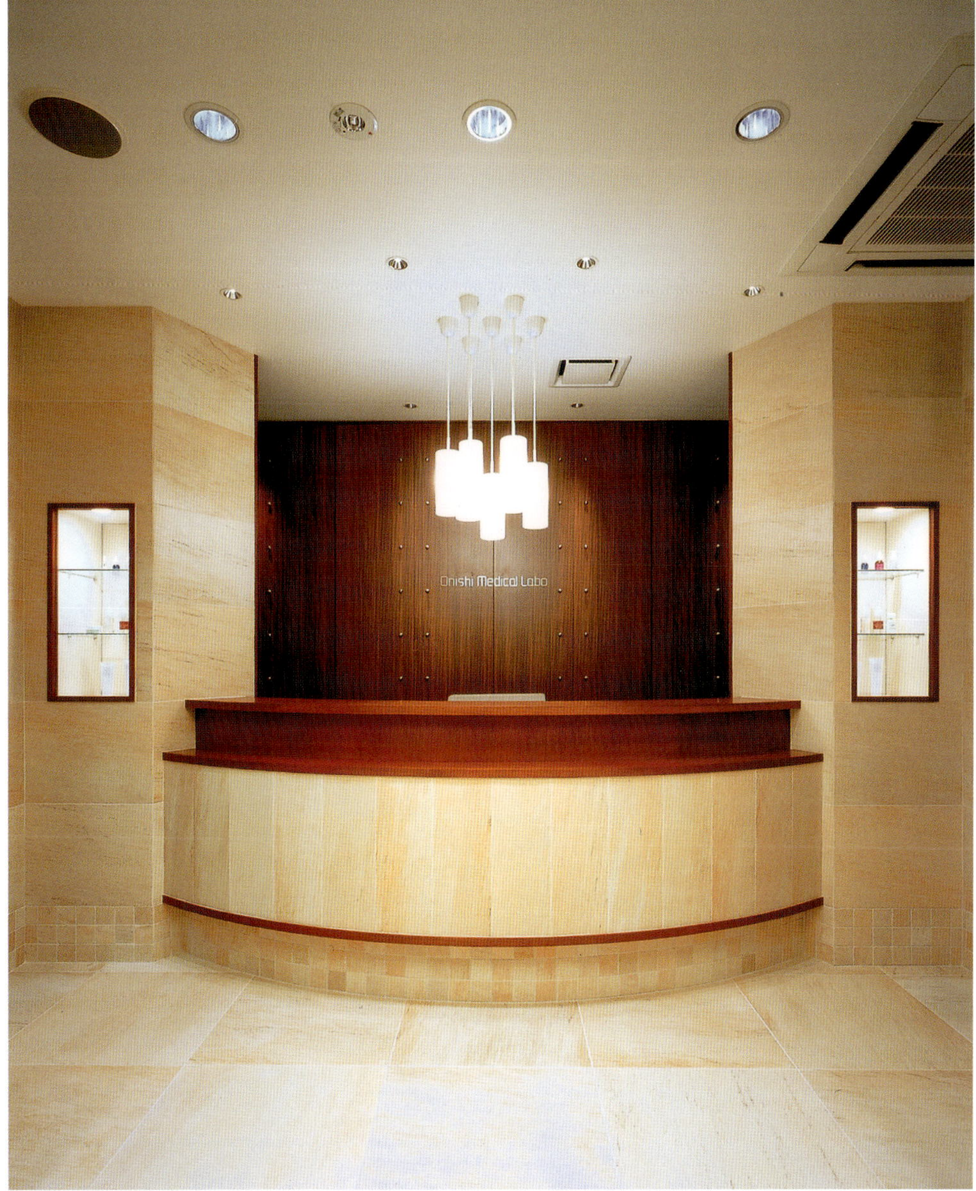

KUSAKABE CLINIC
MURASAKINO , KYOTO 2004

安心と信頼をカタチにする

一般的に、クリニックという場所は、決して居心地の良い場所ではないように思います。"日下部クリニック"を計画するにあたって目指したものは、そんな通説を良い意味で裏切るように、訪れる人に心地よい「時間」を提供できる、自然体のクリニックを具現化することでした。

そこで、計画地である京都という街が持っている環境としての魅力と、建物が持っているポテンシャルを引き出すような空間デザインを心掛け、緊張を解きほぐし、信頼関係が生まれやすいよう、デザインし過ぎず自然体で、安らぎに満ちた空気感を創り出しました。

Giving Shape to Security and Reliability

In general, we believe that clinics are never places of great comfort. In planning KUSAKABE CLINIC, our aim was to undercut the conventional wisdom in a positive way, and to embody a clinic that would make it possible, in a natural way, to offer a comfortable time to visitors.

So, we aimed at designing a space to draw out the appeal of the environment of Kyoto, the planned location, and potential of the building, and created an airy feeling where visitor tensions could be eased and a trust relationship could be born; without going overboard in the design and by leaving things natural, an airy feeling was created filled with relaxation.

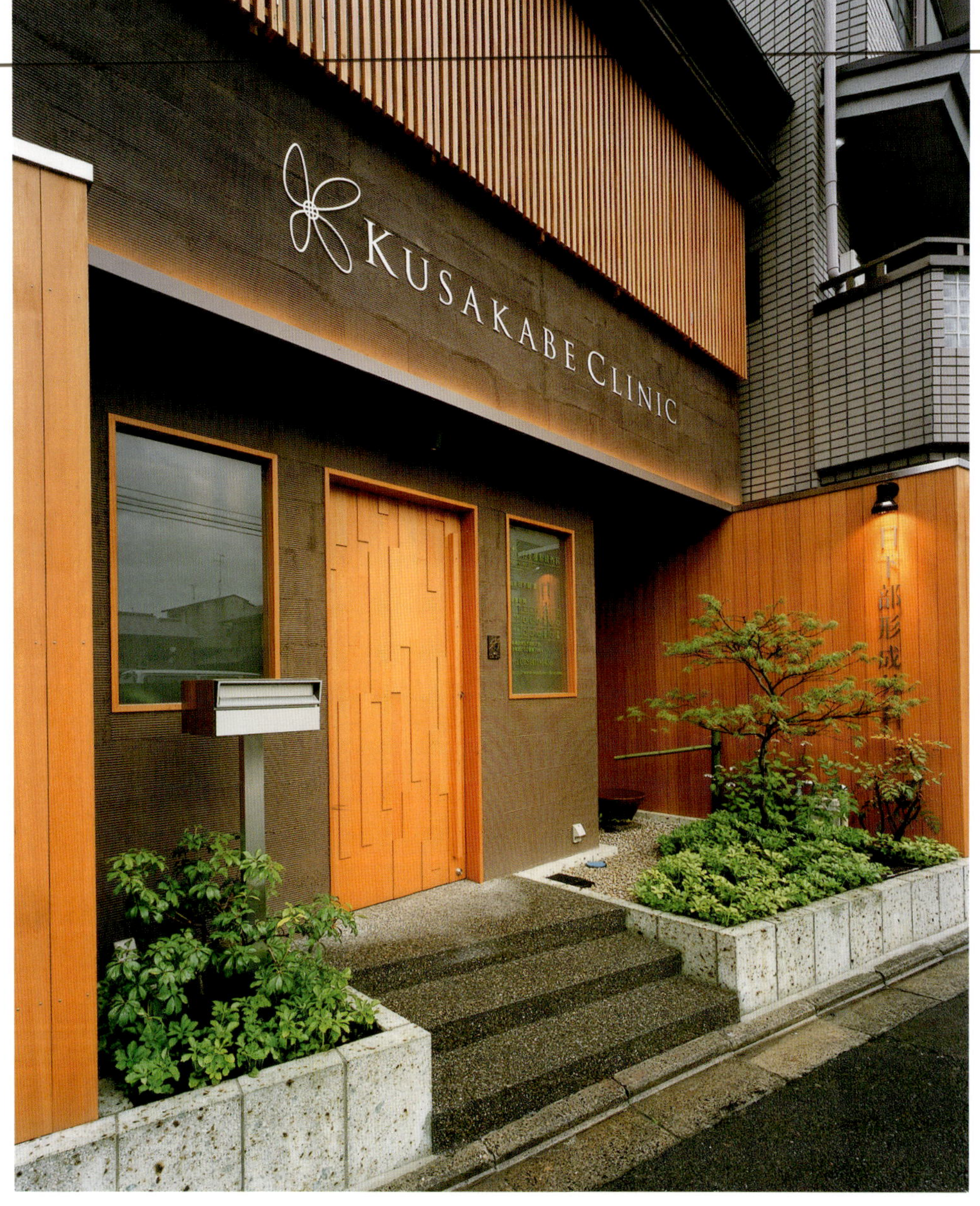

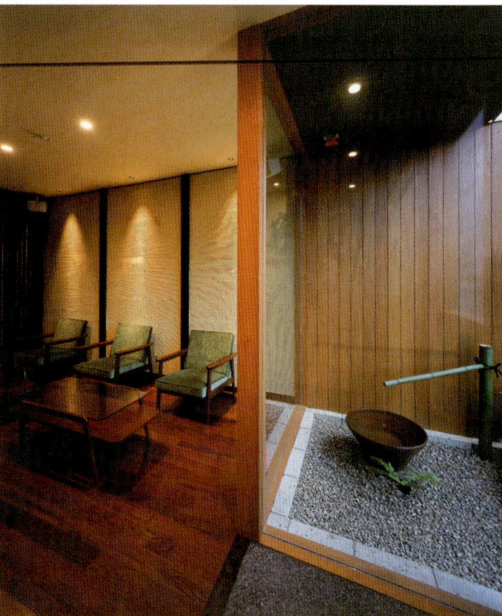

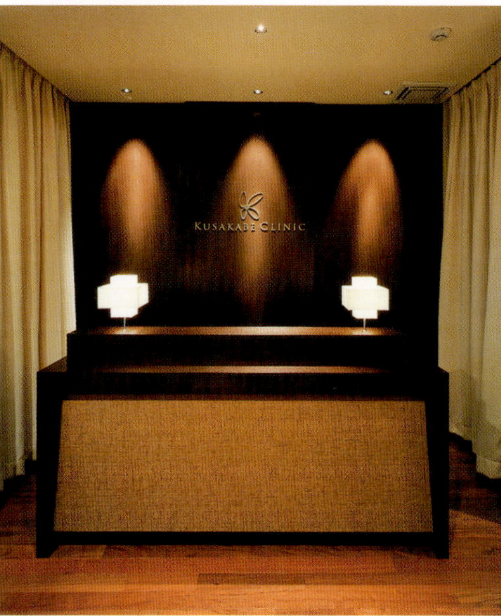

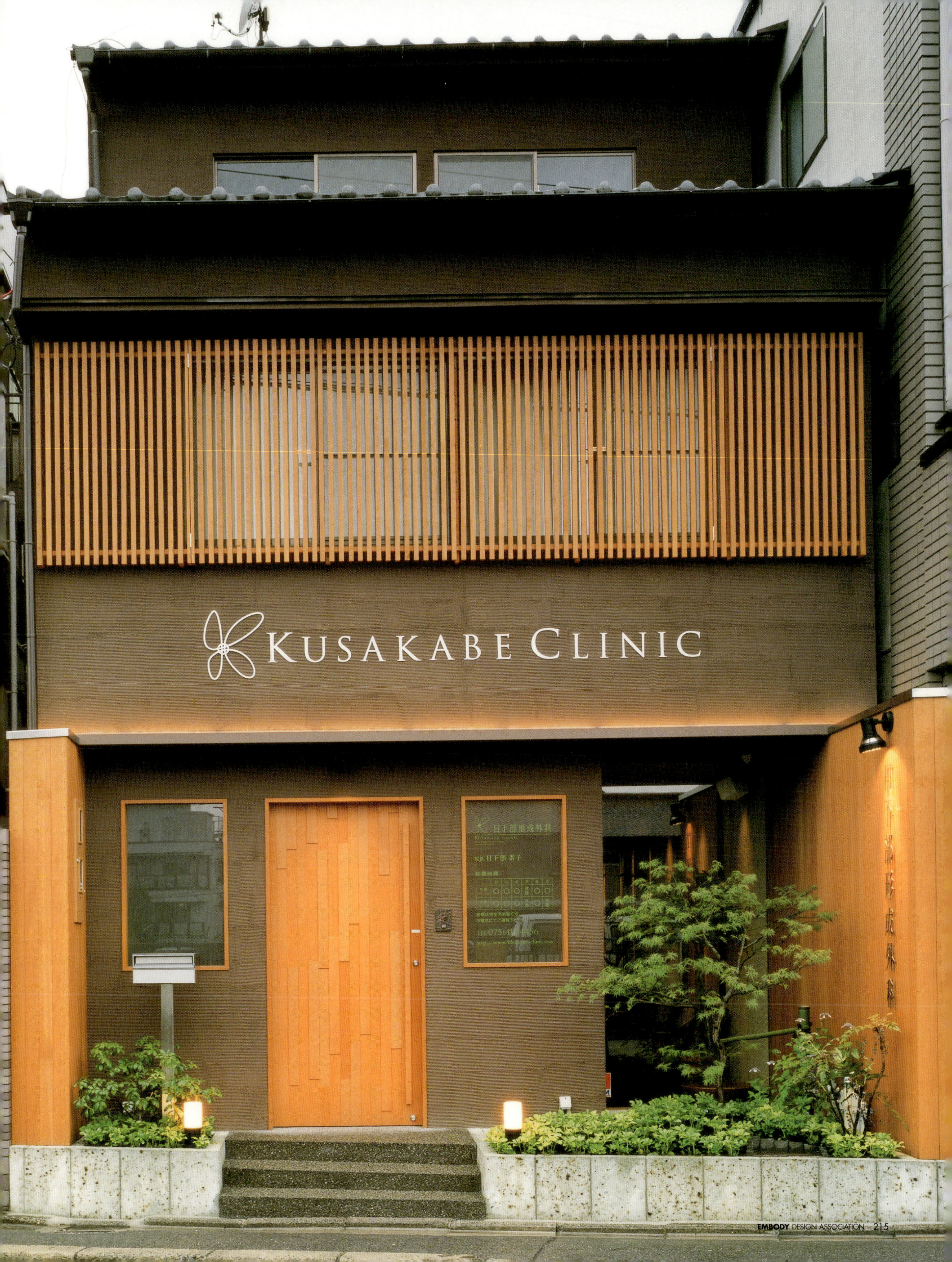

KUSAKABE CLINIC

PROJECTS LIST

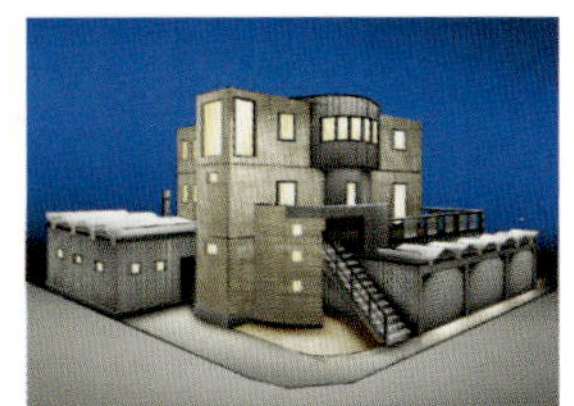

1. M HOUSE
HABIKINO , OSAKA
1992*

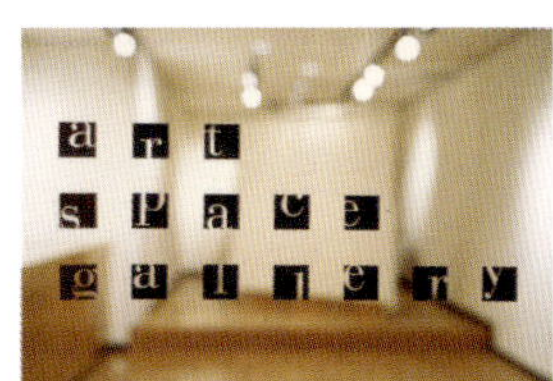

2. ART SPACE GALLERY
NANBA , OSAKA
1992

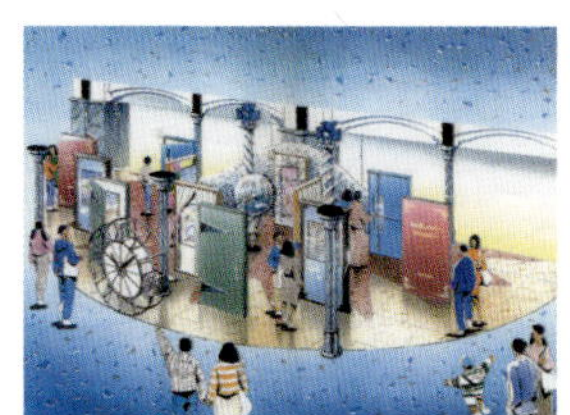

3. LA SERENA GALLERY
TENNOJI , OSAKA
1993*

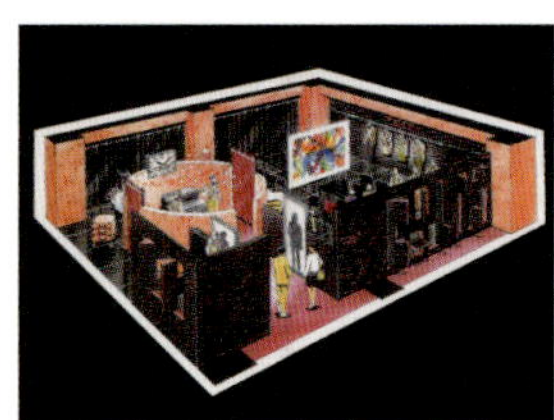

4. BOUTIQUE Ⅰ
AOYAMA , TOKYO
1994*

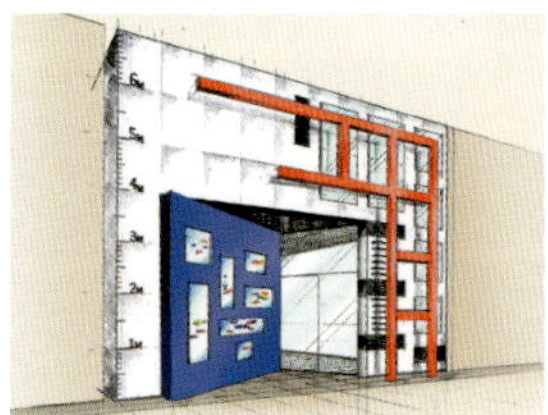

5. PET SHOP
UMEDA , OSAKA
1994*

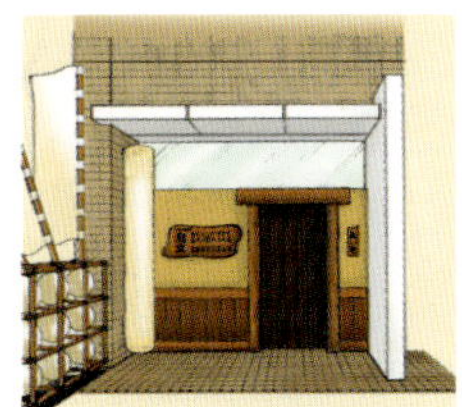

6. TORIBUN
NISHITANABE , OSAKA
1995.04*

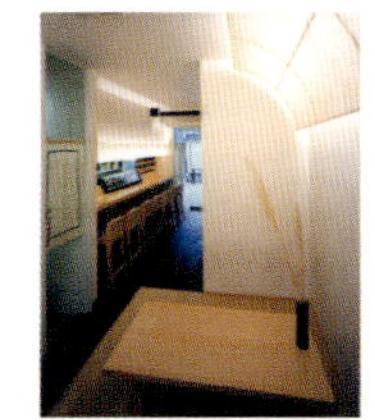

7. ZAKOBA
KYOMACHIBORI , OSAKA
1995.05

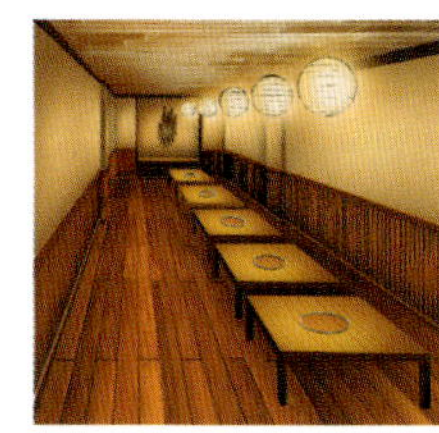

8. JYUBEI
NANBA , OSAKA
1995.06

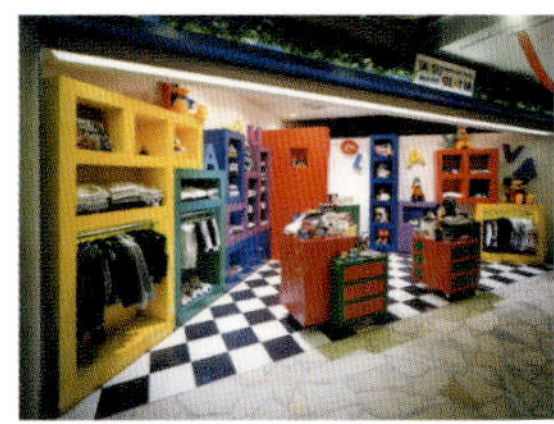

9. TATSU GLAYVA
NANKO , OSAKA
1995.07

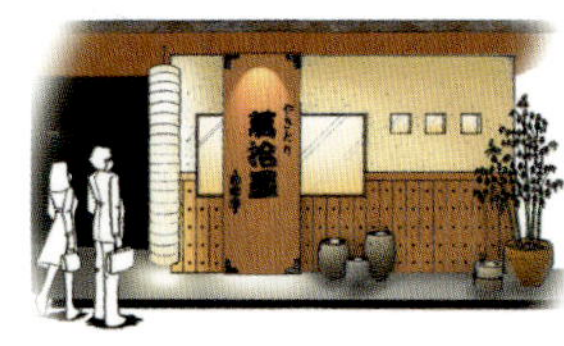

10. MANJYUYA
HIGASHIYODOGAWA , OSAKA
1995.09*

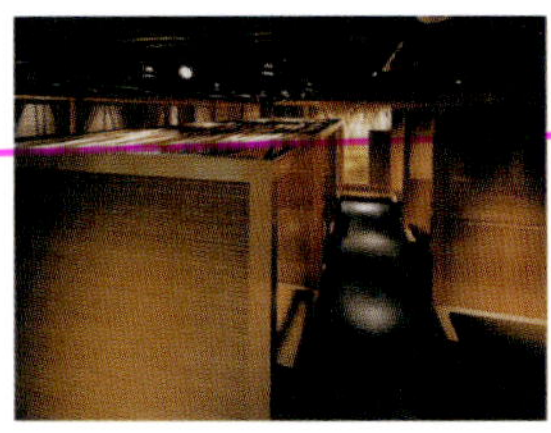

11. IRORIYA kadoma
KADOMA , OSAKA
1995.12

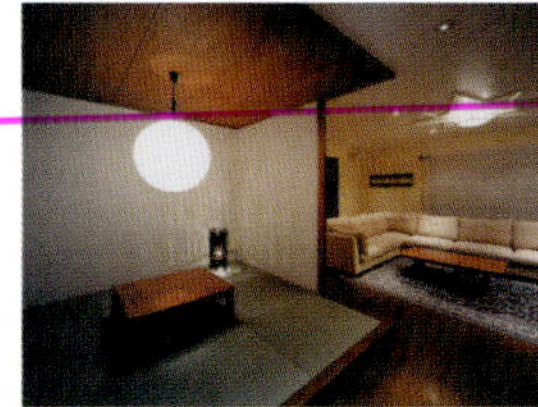

12. I HOUSE REINNOVATION
IBARAKI , OSAKA
1996.03

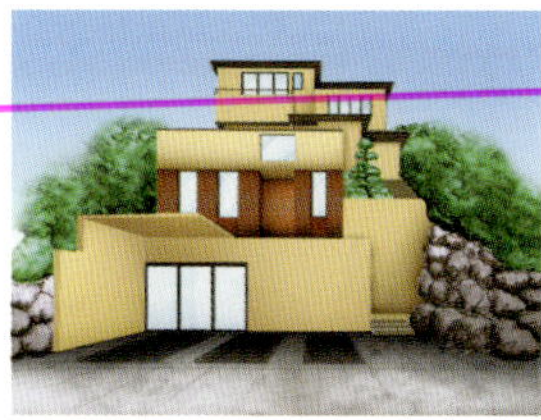

13. I HOUSE LANDSCAPE
IBARAKI , OSAKA
1996.08

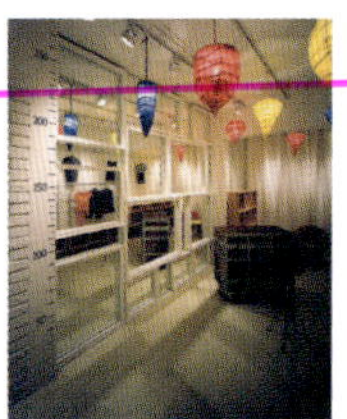

14. PUS PUS
TOYONAKA , OSAKA
1996.08

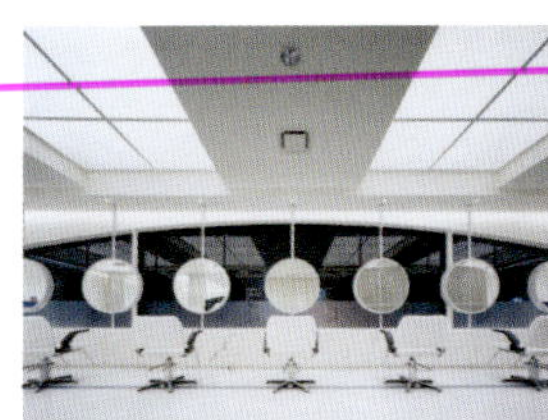

15. CAPELLI
SHINSAIBASHI , OSAKA
1996.12

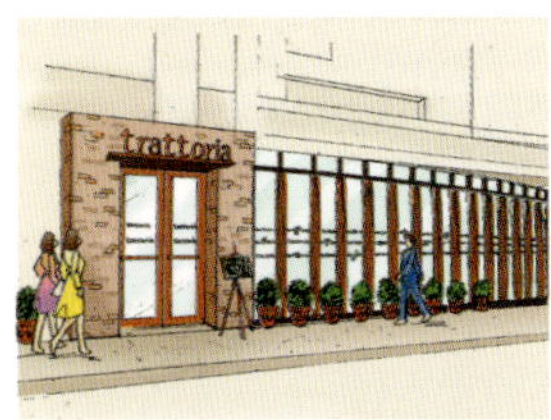

16. RESTAURANT Ⅰ
MINAMISENBA , OSAKA
1997.02*

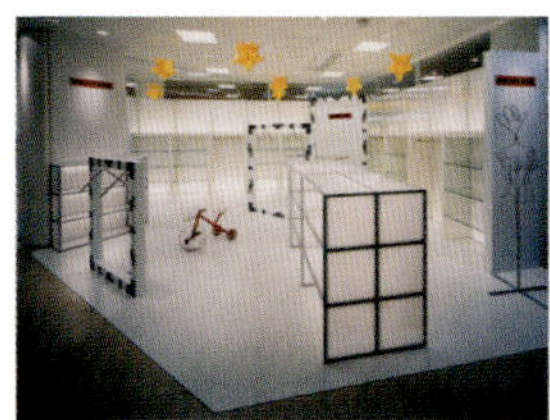

17. MICKEY&CO
MOMOYAMADAI , OSAKA
1997.03

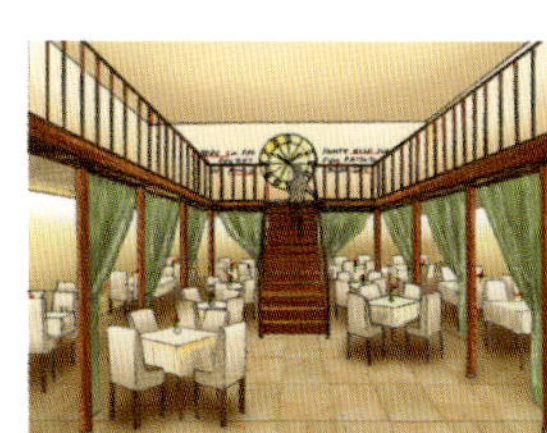

18. RESTAURANT Ⅱ
MINAMISENBA , OSAKA
1997.03*

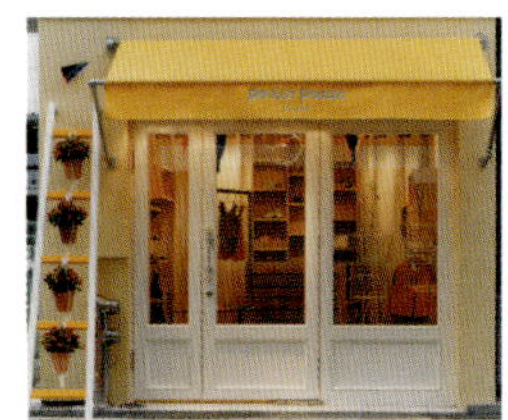

19. POUSSE POUSSE
ESAKA , OSAKA
1997.05

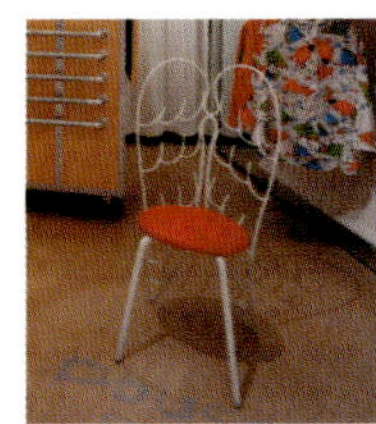

20. ANGEL CHAIR
ESAKA , OSAKA
1997.05

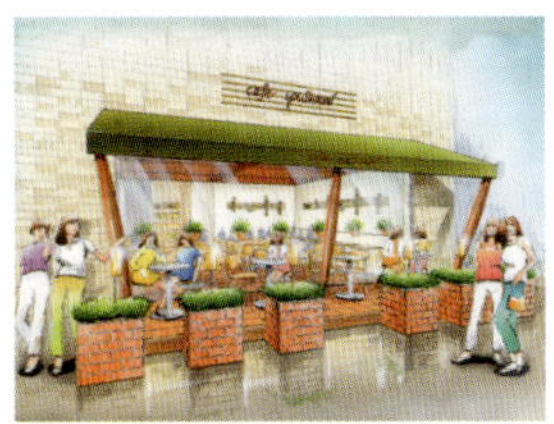

21. UPUSHIRON
HIRAKATA , OSAKA
1997.06*

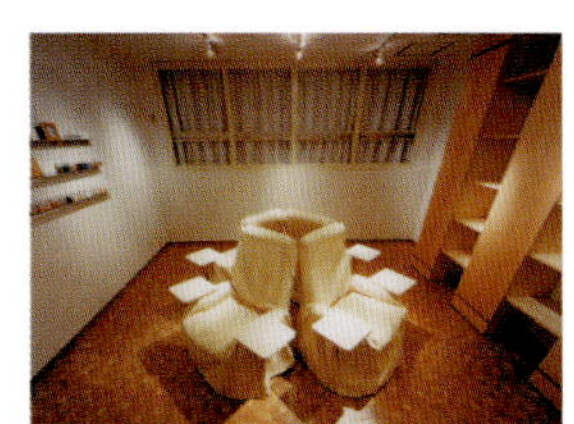

22. L'AMERIC
UMEDA , OSAKA
1997.08

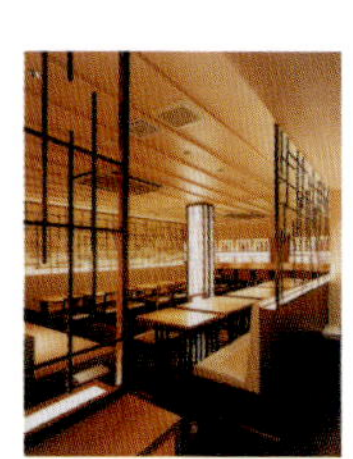

23. RINGOYA honmachi
HONMACHI , OSAKA
1997.08

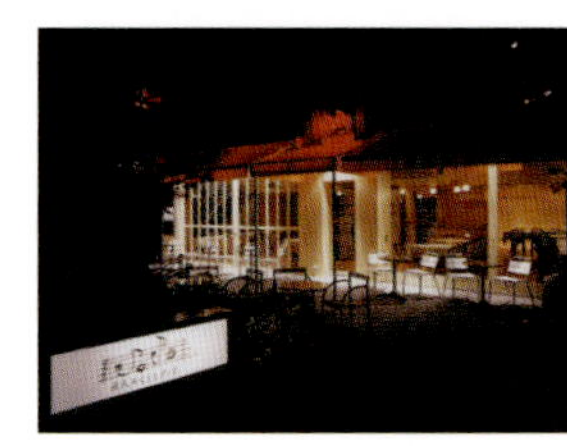

24. JOJO
ASHIYA , HYOGO
1997.09

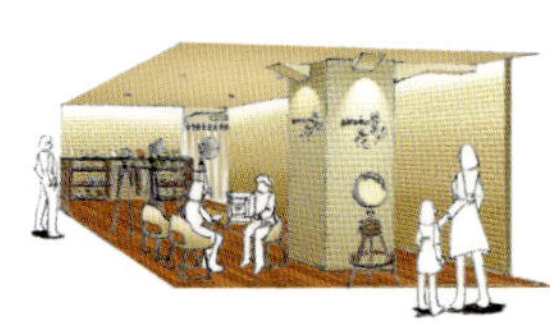

25. BAMBINO
SHIJO , KYOTO
1997.10

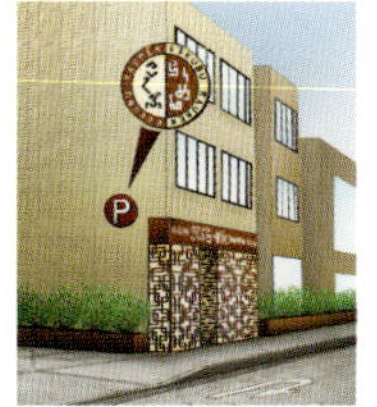

26. KOKUBU RAMEN
MINOH , OSAKA
1998.05*

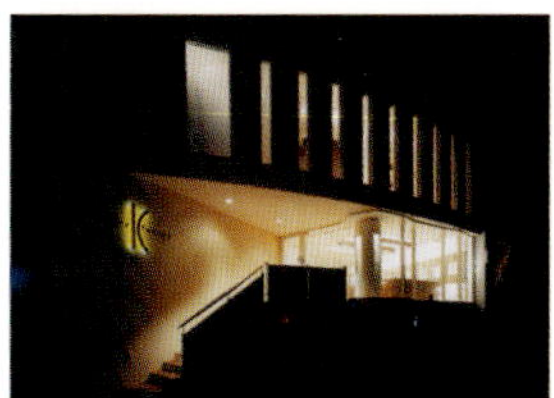

27. JEWELRY K FACTORY
NAHA , OKINAWA
1998.06

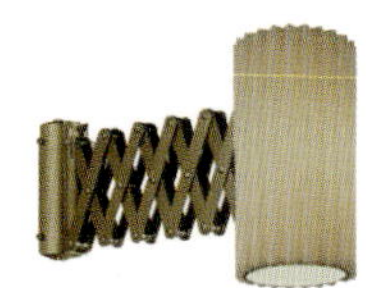

28. FREE STYLE bracket
DAIKO
1998.06

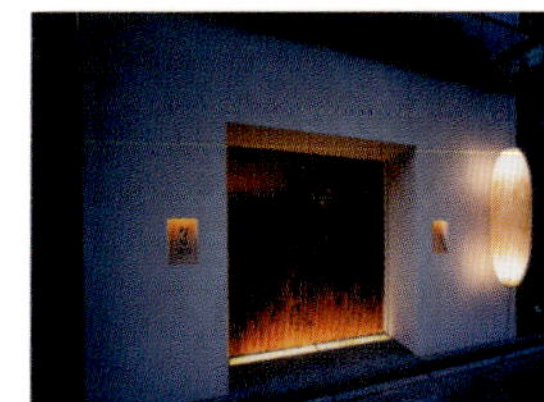

29. NANAYA
SHINSAIBASHI , OSAKA
1998.07

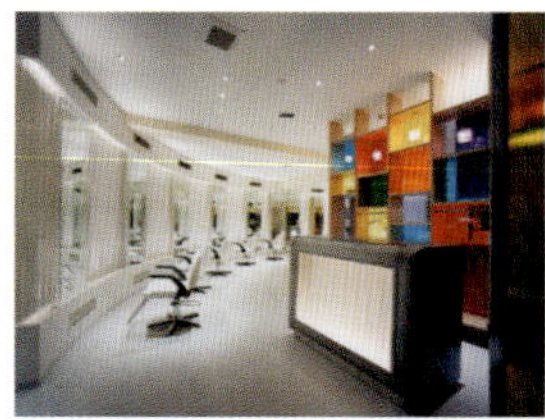

30. BLUE BEAR FACTORY
KAWACHINAGANO , OSAKA
1998.07

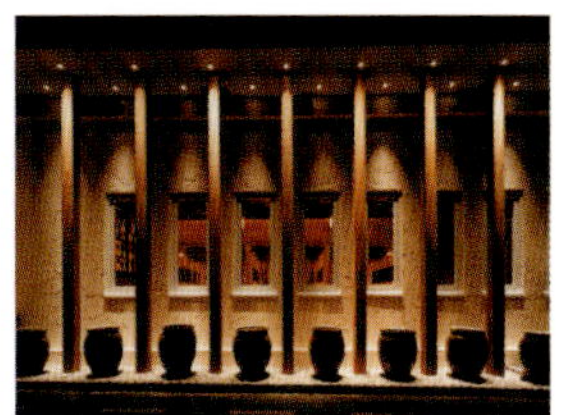

31. IRORIYA neyagawa
NEYAGAWA , OSAKA
1998.11

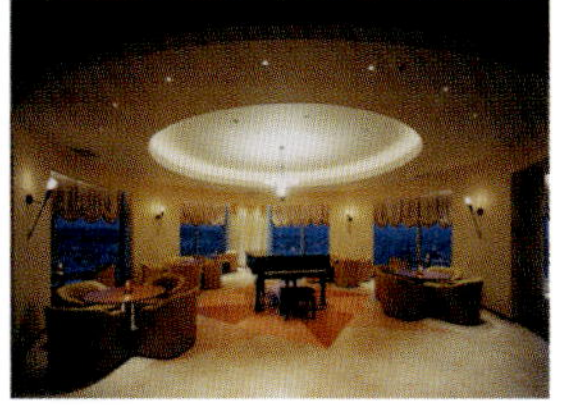

32. HEAVEN
OKAYAMA
1999.02

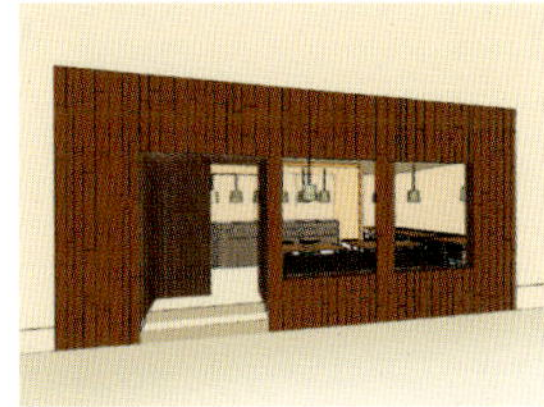

33. KURAICHI
MINOH , OSAKA
1999.03*

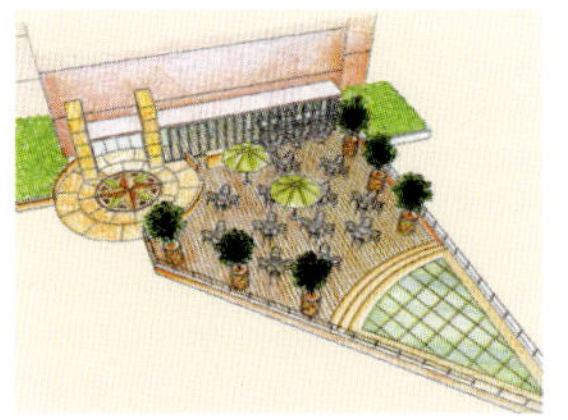

34. CAFE DINING Ⅰ
SHINKOBE , HYOGO
1999.04*

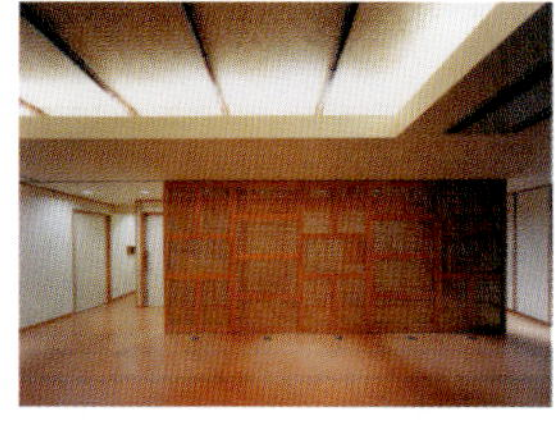

35. SYU CLINIC
KAMEARI , TOKYO
1999.05

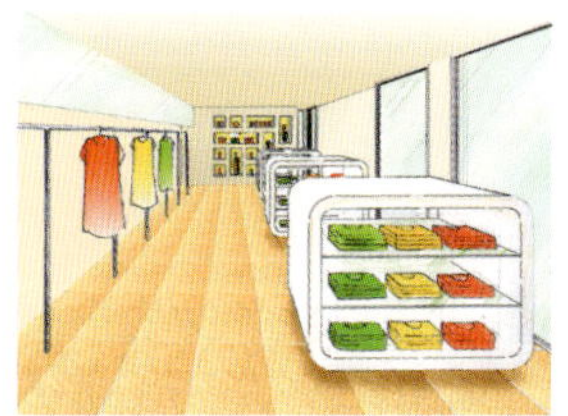

36. BOUTIQUE Ⅱ
NANBA , OSAKA
1999.06*

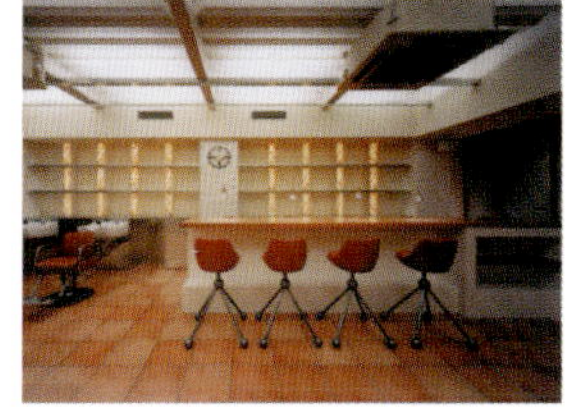

37. MULE MULE HAIR
KITAHORIE , OSAKA
1999.07

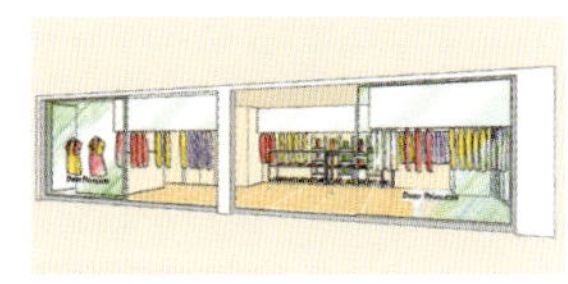

38. BOUTIQUE Ⅲ
NANBA , OSAKA
1999.07*

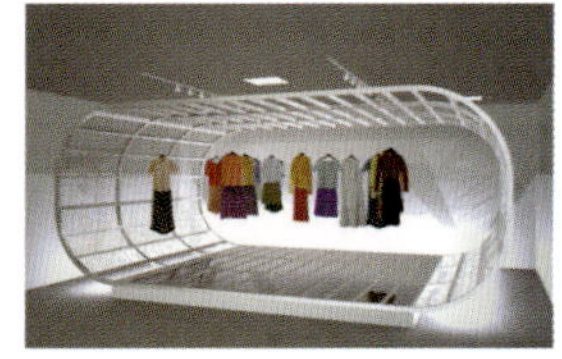

39. ZIP WORKS
SAIIN , KYOTO
1999.08*

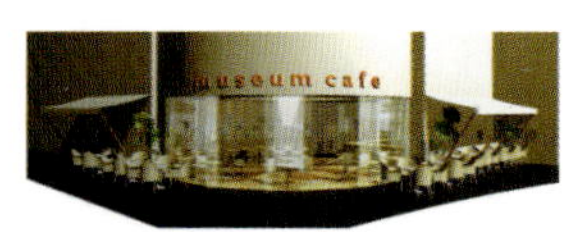

40. MUSEUM CAFE
HIRAKATA , OSAKA
1999.09*

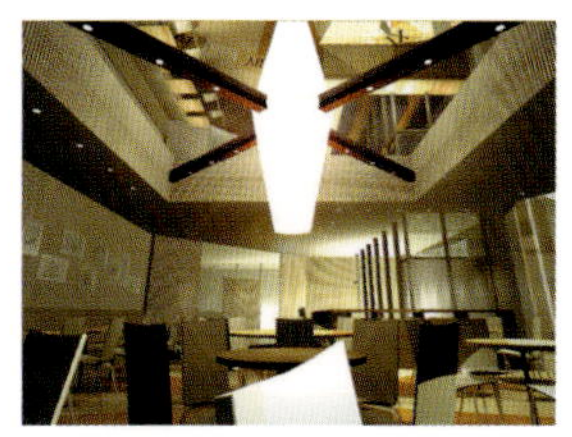

41. CAFE DINING Ⅱ
HIRAKATA , OSAKA
1999.10*

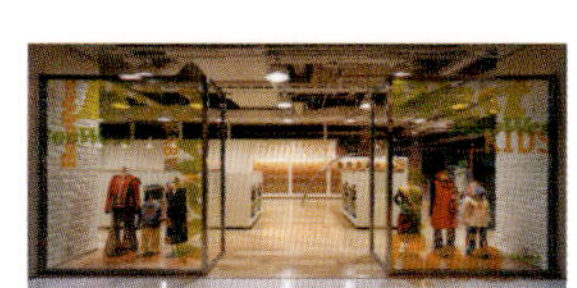

42. BOO WEST
KOBE , HYOGO
1999.10

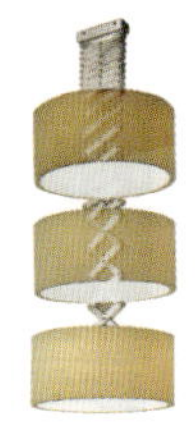

43. FREE STYLE pendant
DAIKO
1999.10

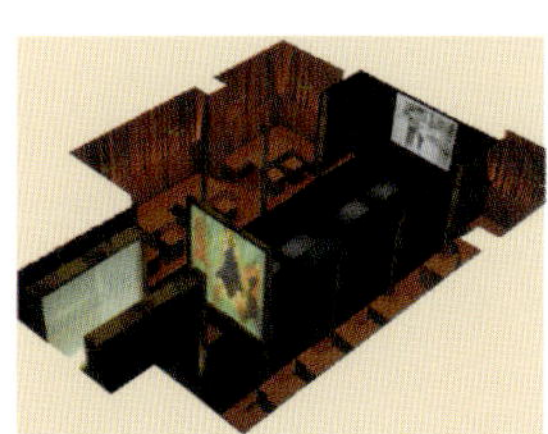

44. CLUB Ⅰ
FUSE , OSAKA
1999.11*

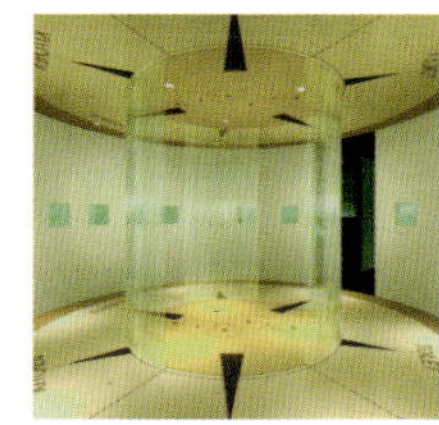

45. CLUB Ⅱ
HIRANO , OSAKA
1999.11*

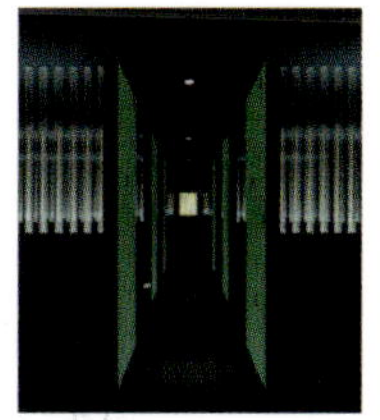

46. CLUB Ⅲ
HIRANO , OSAKA
1999.11*

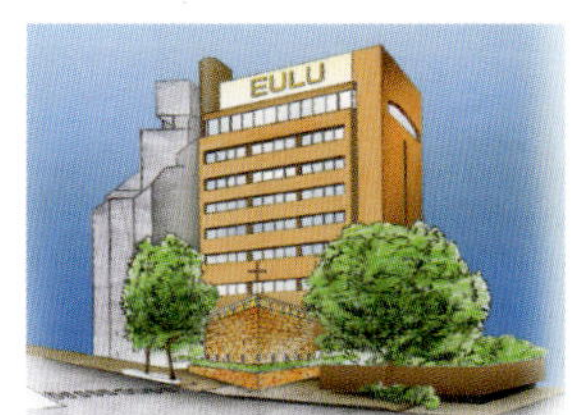

47. EULU OFFICE BUILDING
SHINKOBE , HYOGO
1999.11

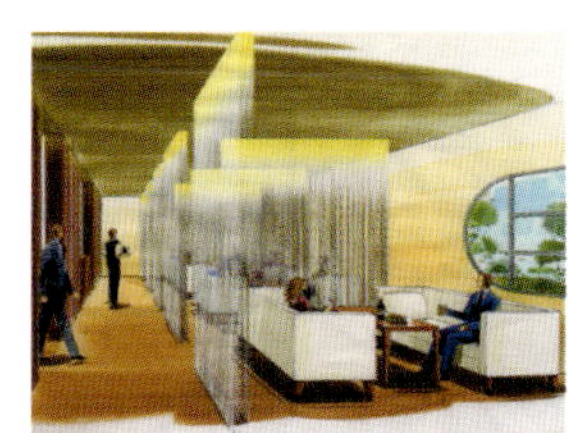

48. USJ SPONSOR LOUNGE Ⅰ
KONOHANA , OSAKA
2000.02*

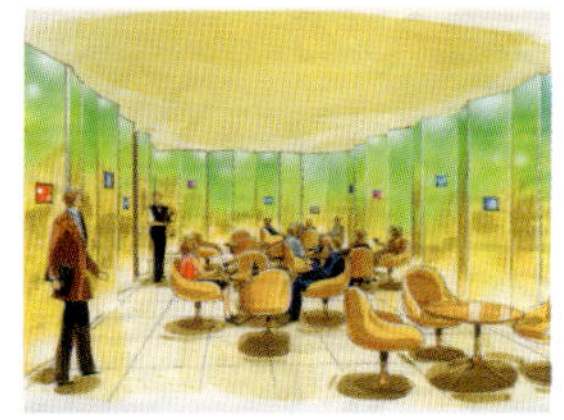

49. USJ SPONSOR LOUNGE Ⅱ
KONOHANA , OSAKA
2000.02*

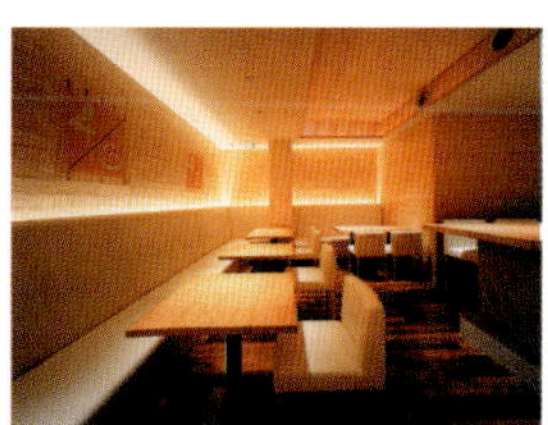

50. AVRIL SIX
KITASHINCHI , OSAKA
2000.03

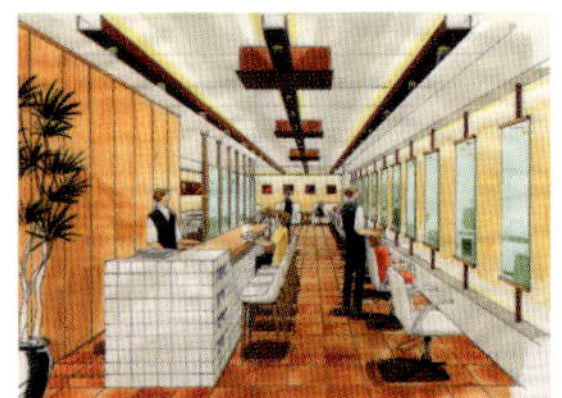

51. HAIR SALON Ⅰ
MULTIPLE SHOP
2000.04*

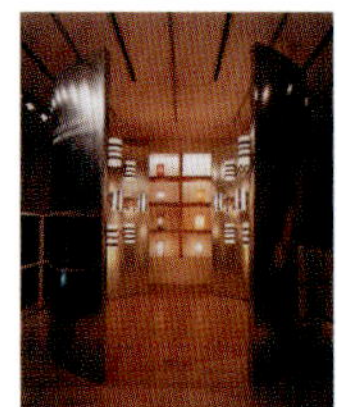

52. KATSUYA IWAMOTO EXHIBITION 2000
MINAMIHORIE , OSAKA
2000.04

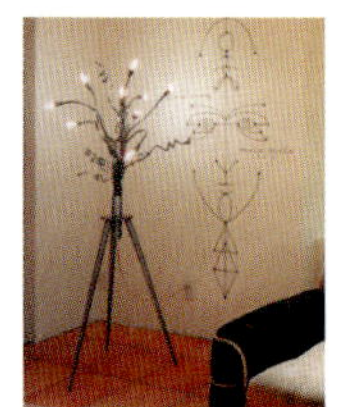

53. CREATORS* CAFE!? 2000
SHINJYUKU , TOKYO
2000.06

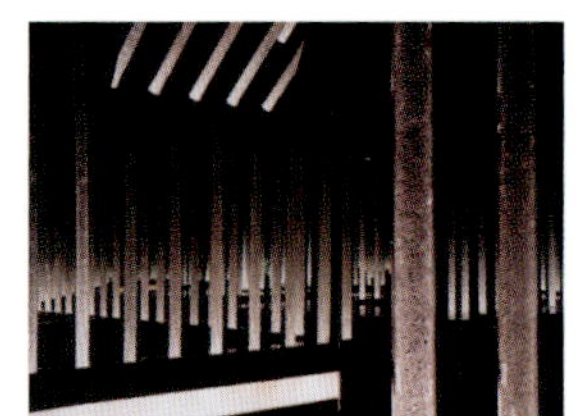

54. RIPPLE
HIRANO , OSAKA
2000.06

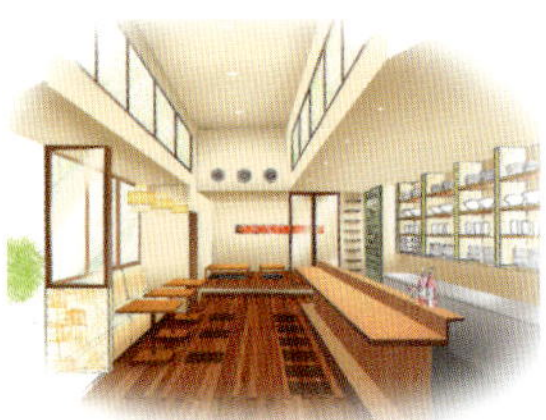

55. NEW LUCY
YAGI , NARA
2000.08

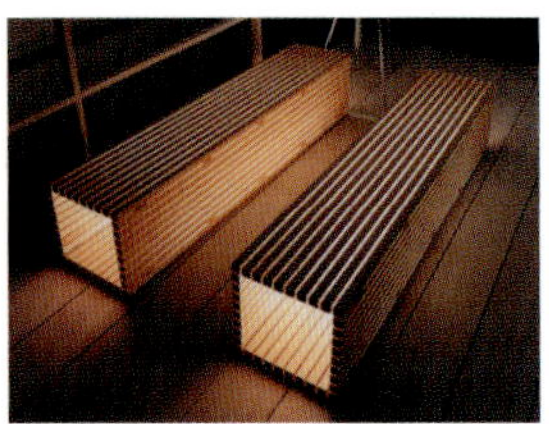

56. PARK ART 2000
MINAMIHORIE , OSAKA
2000.08

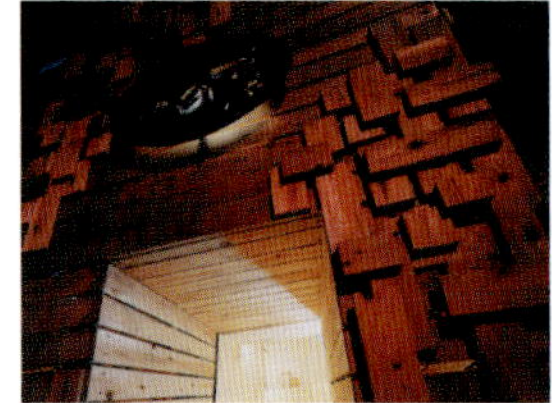

57. HINONA
MINAMIHORIE , OSAKA
2000.08

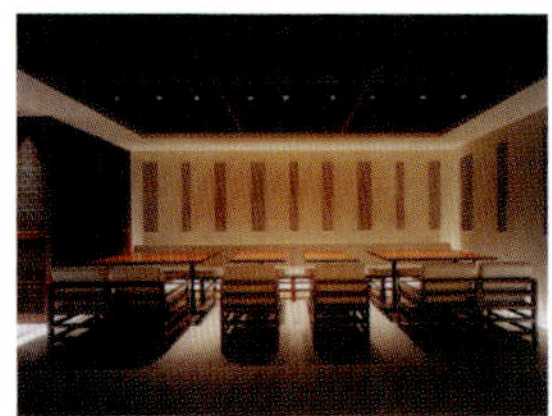

58. FORTUNE COOKIES
KITASHINCHI , OSAKA
2000.09

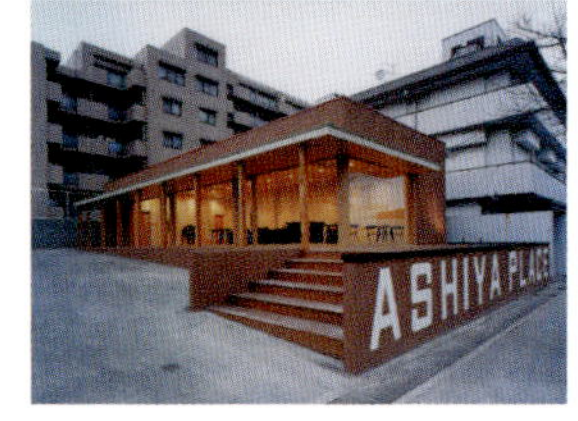

59. ASHIYA PLACE
ASHIYA , HYOGO
2000.10

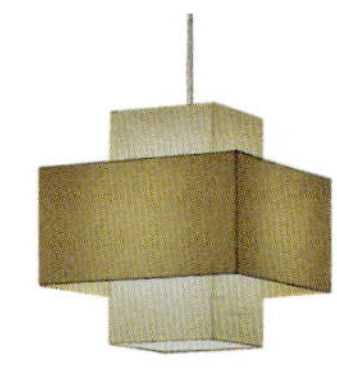

60. CROSS pendant
DAIKO
2000.10

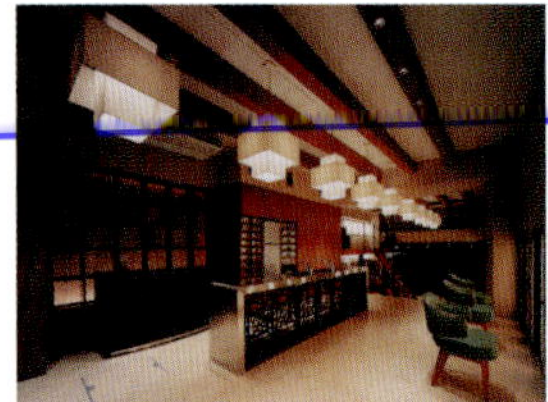

61. STIL STAENS
KITAHORIE , OSAKA
2000.10

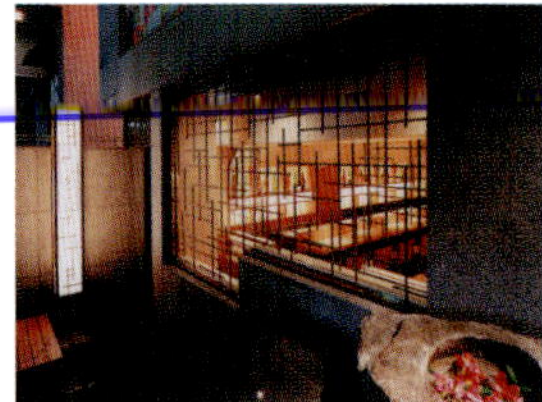

62. RINGOYA shinsaibashi
SHINSAIBASHI , OSAKA
2000.11

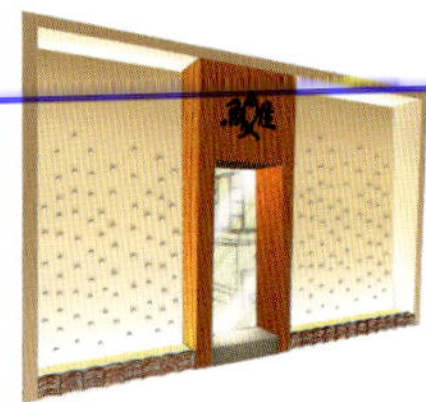

63. UOZUMI
AMAGASAKI , HYOGO
2001.02*

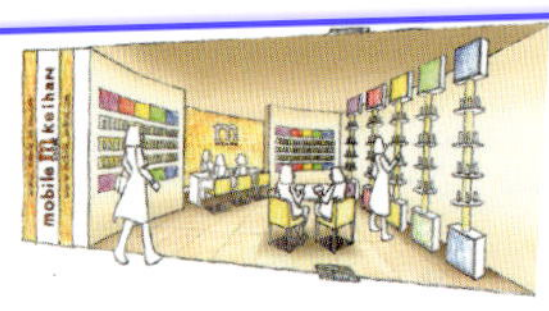

64. SHOP Ⅰ
HIRAKATA , OSAKA
2001.02*

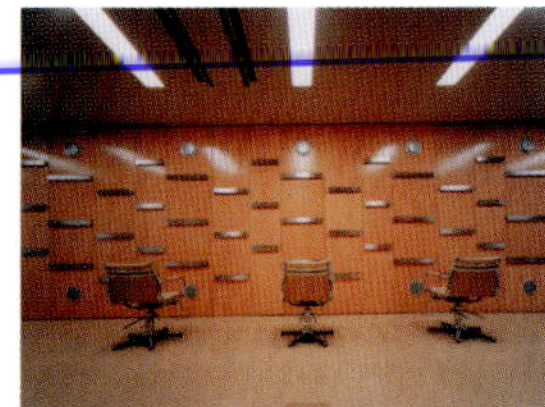

65. DEUX UN
SHINSAIBASHI , OSAKA
2001.03

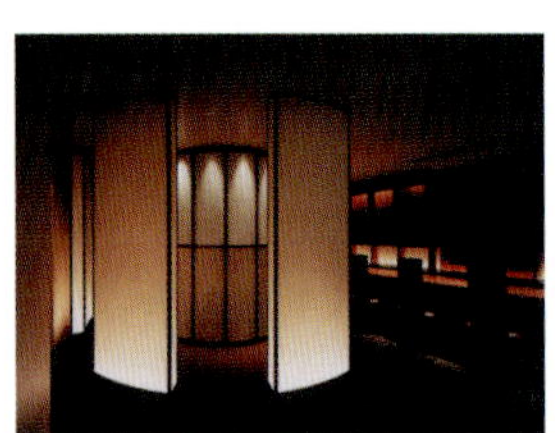

66. CLUB GALAXY
KITASHINCHI , OSAKA
2001.03

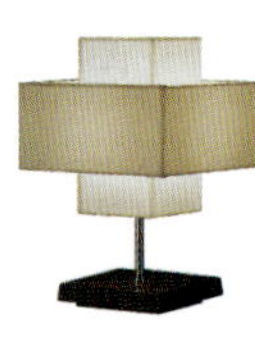

67. CROSS table stand
DAIKO
2001.04

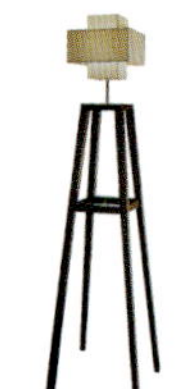

68. CROSS floor stand
DAIKO
2001.04

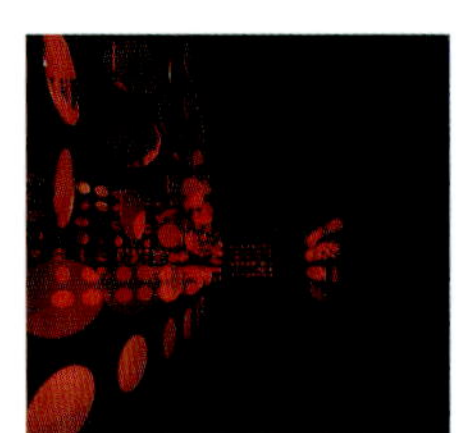

69. CLUB Ⅳ
NANBA , OSAKA
2001.04*

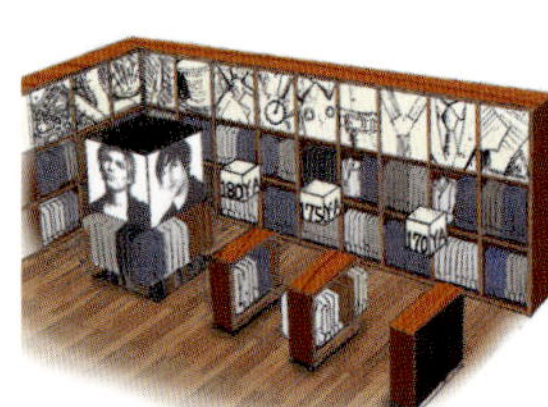

70. ＋AOYAMA
MULTIPLE SHOP
2001.04*

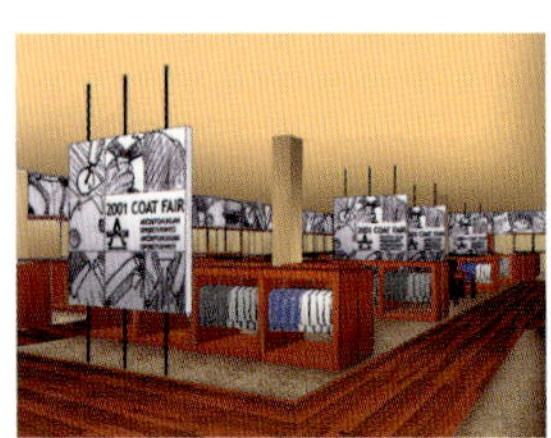

71. AOYAMA STYLE STUDIO
MULTIPLE SHOP
2001.05*

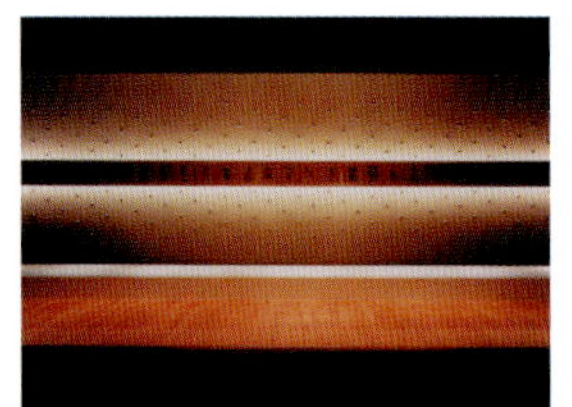

72. MIKAN
KITAHORIE , OSAKA
2001.05

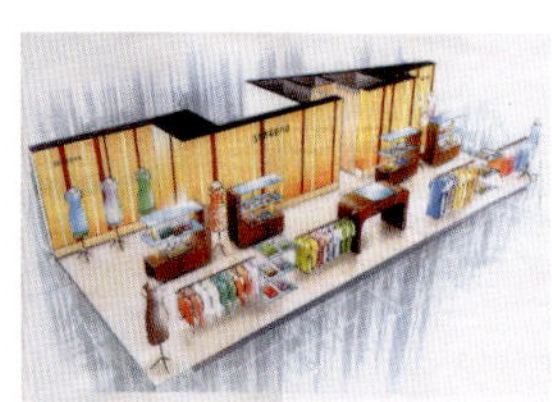

73. SUNA UNA
MULTIPLE SHOP
2001.07

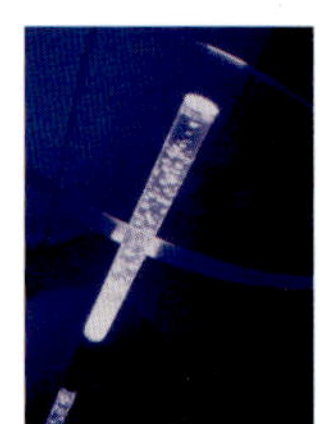

74. WATER PLANET EXHIBITION 2001
UMEDA , OSAKA
2001.08

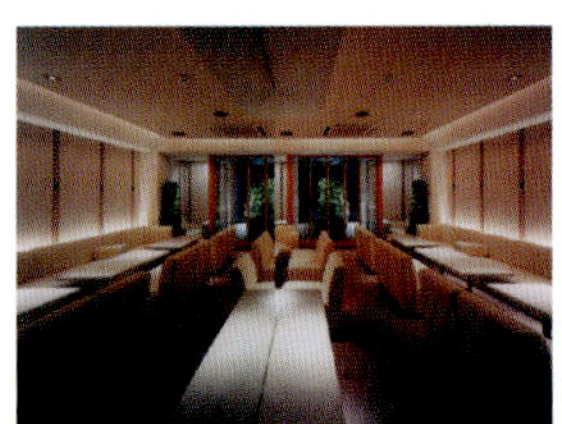

75. KOCHOU
KITASHINCHI , OSAKA
2001.08

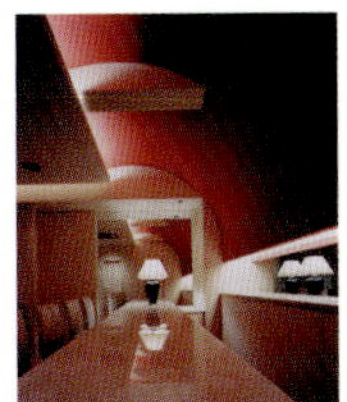

76. SALON DE KOBAYASHI
KITASHINCHI , OSAKA
2001.08

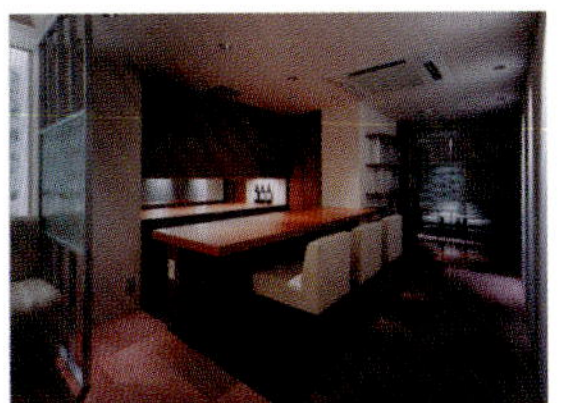

77. PLAY ONE
KITASHINCHI , OSAKA
2001.09

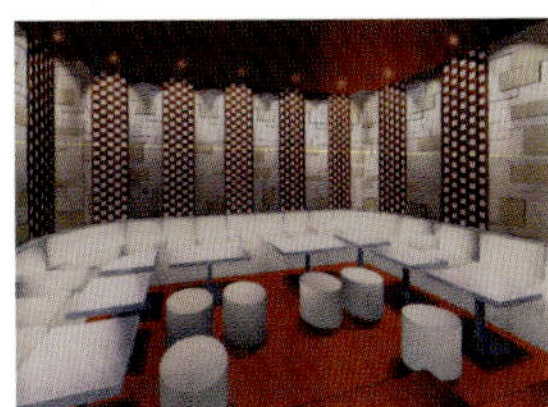

78. ESPACE
KITASHINCHI , OSAKA
2001.10*

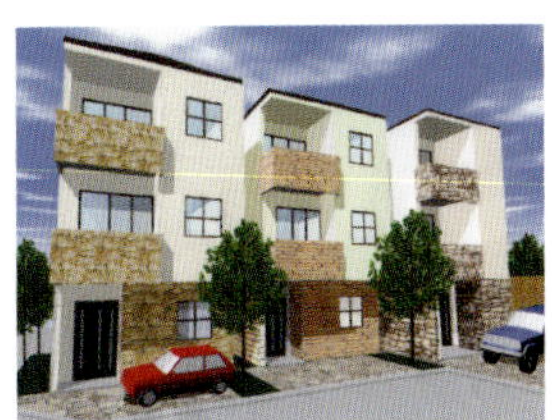

79. CONDOMINIUM PROJECT
HIRANO , OSAKA
2001.10*

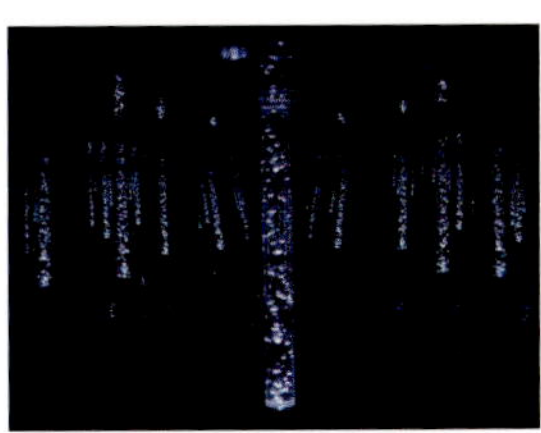

80. TOKYO DESIGNERS BLOCK 2001
DAIKANYAMA , TOKYO
2001.10

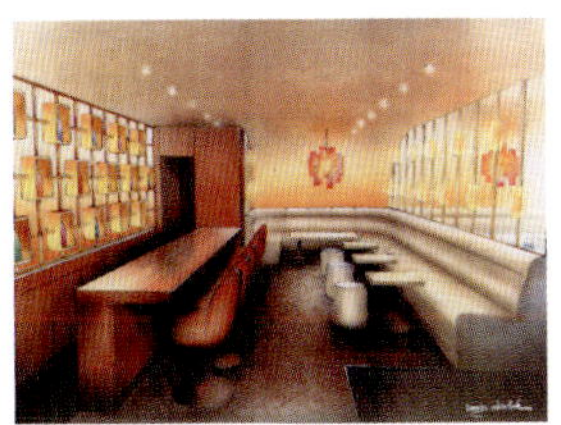

81. LIEBE
YUSHIMA , TOKYO
2001.10

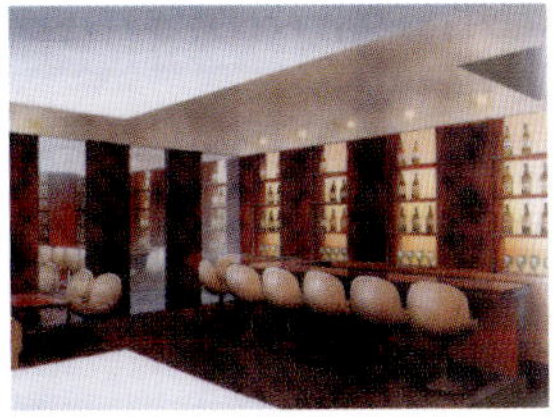

82. BENIR
YUSHIMA , TOKYO
2001.10

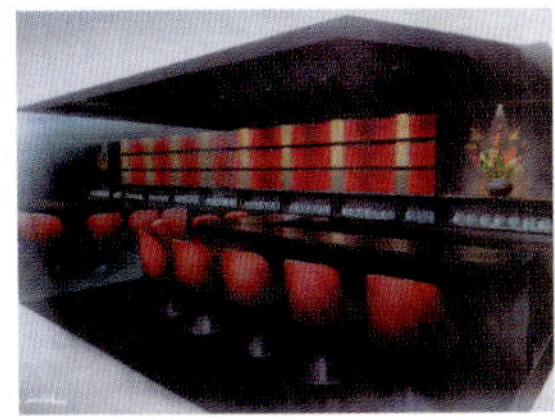

83. TIROLEAN LAMP
YUSHIMA , TOKYO
2001.10

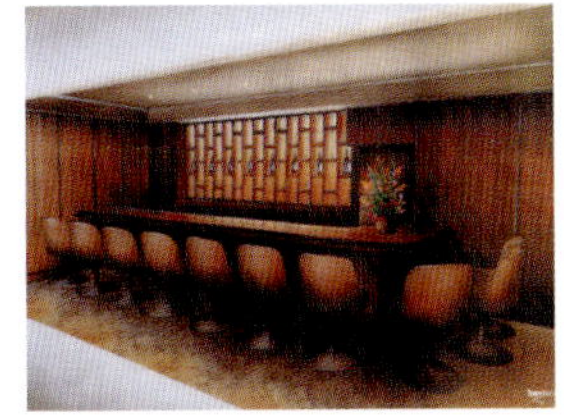

84. SUZURAN
YUSHIMA , TOKYO
2001.10

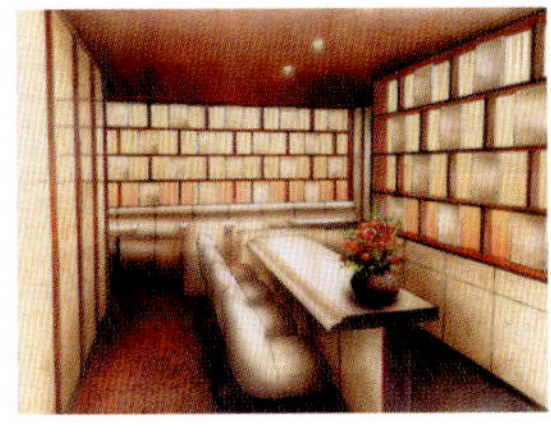

85. NERO
YUSHIMA , TOKYO
2001.10

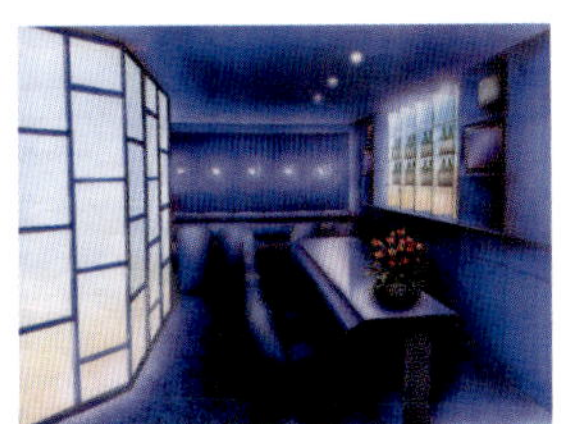

86. MERRY
YUSHIMA , TOKYO
2001.10

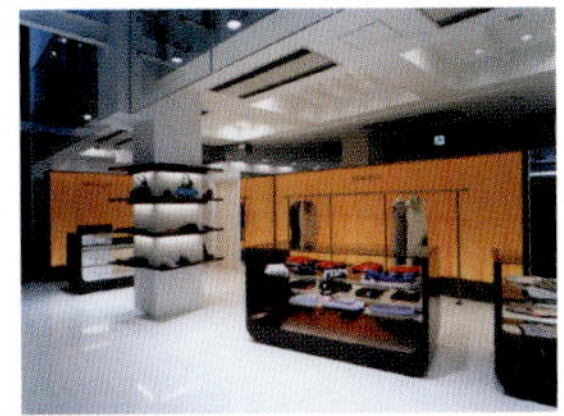

87. SUNA UNA aoyama
MINAMIAOYAMA , TOKYO
2001.10

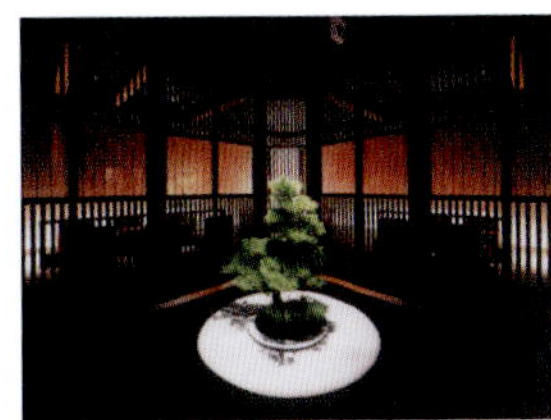

88. KAKEHASHI
FUKUSHIMA , OSAKA
2001.10

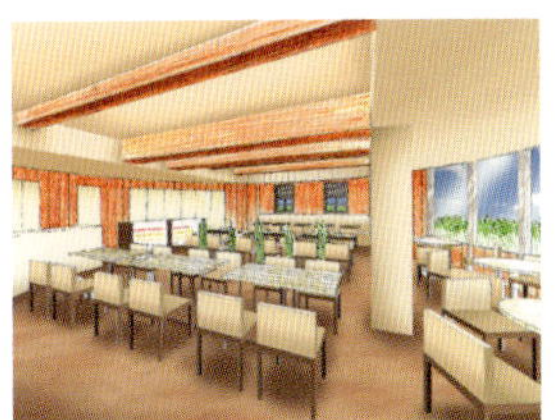

89. CAFE DINNING Ⅲ
SYUKUGAWA , HYOGO
2002.11*

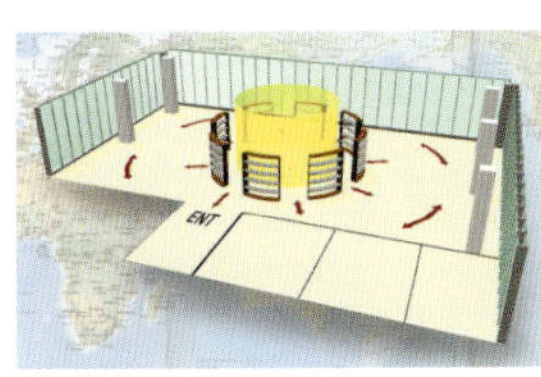

90. ESTATE AGENT OFFICE
YODOYABASHI , OSAKA
2001.12*

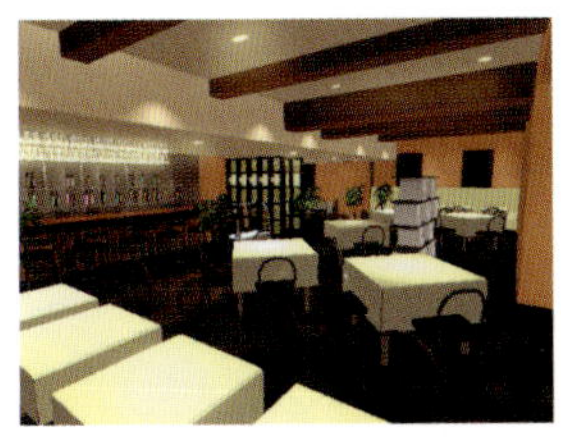

91. RESTAURANT Ⅲ
ASHIYA , HYOGO
2002.01*

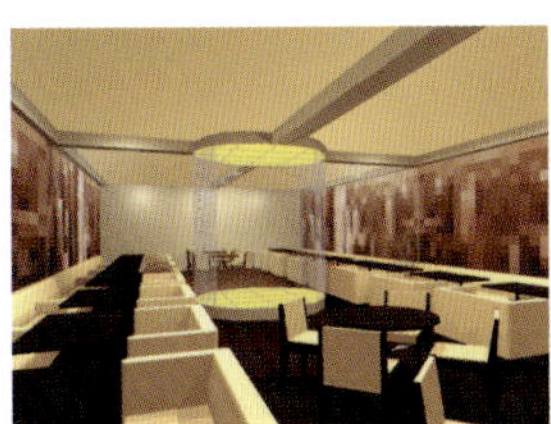

92. PARTY HALL
UTSUNOMIYA , TOCHIGI
2002.02*

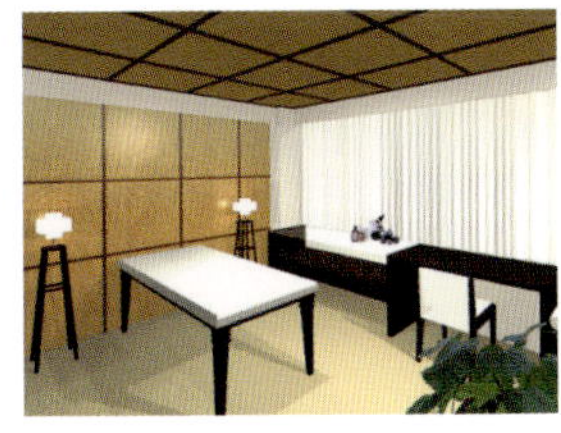

93. ESTHETIC SALON Ⅰ
UTSUNOMIYA , TOCHIGI
2002.02*

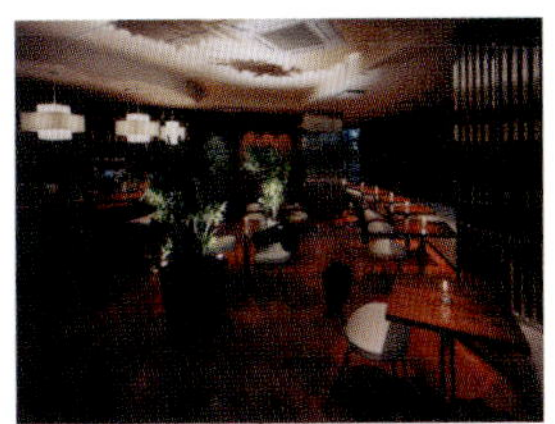

94. EURO CAFE
SYUKUGAWA , HYOGO
2002.02

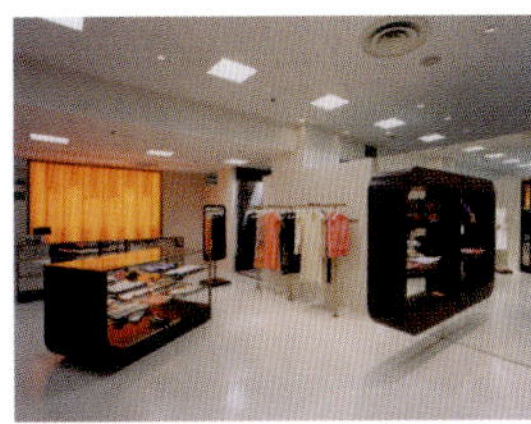

95. SUNA UNA senri
SENRI , OSAKA
2002.02

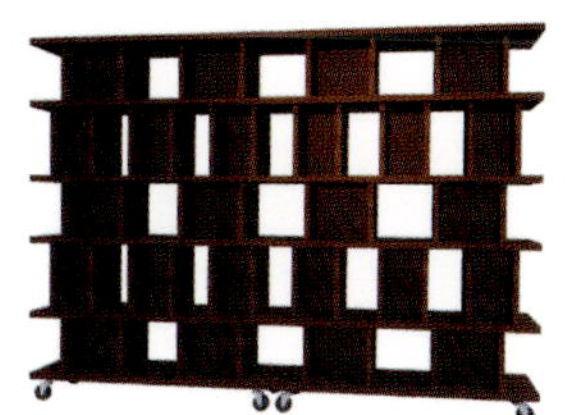

96. G M BOOK SHELF
NISHITENMA , OSAKA
2002.03

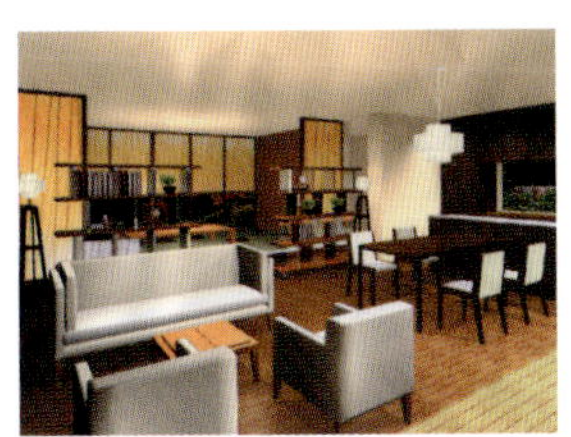

97. MISAWAHOME PROJECT
MULTIPLE SHOP
2002.03*

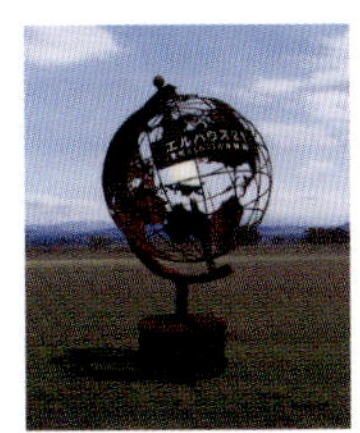

98. ECO BALANCE
JUSO , OSAKA
2002.03*

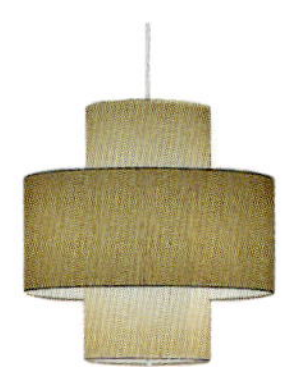

99. LOOP CROSS pendant
DAIKO
2002.04

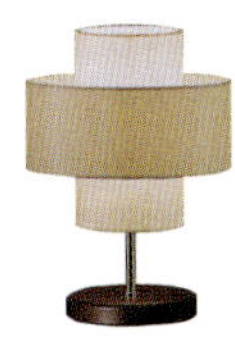

100. LOOP CROSS table stand
DAIKO
2002.04

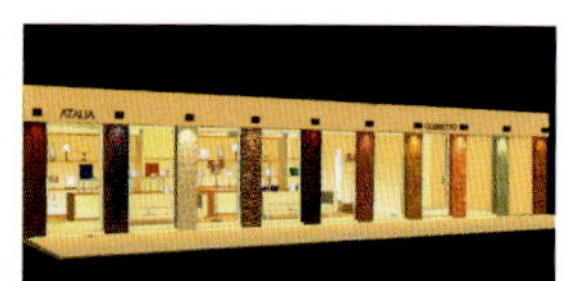

101. ATALIA SHOW ROOM
DOJIMA , OSAKA
2002.04*

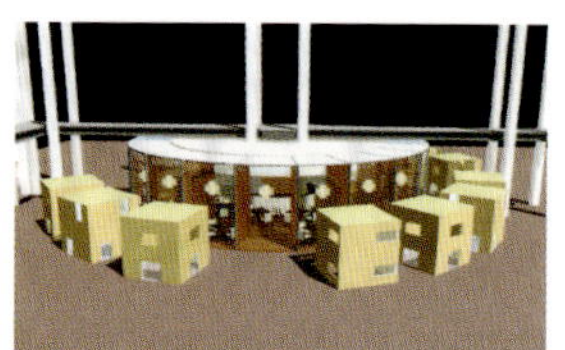

102. RESTAURANT Ⅳ
KISHIWADA , OSAKA
2002.04*

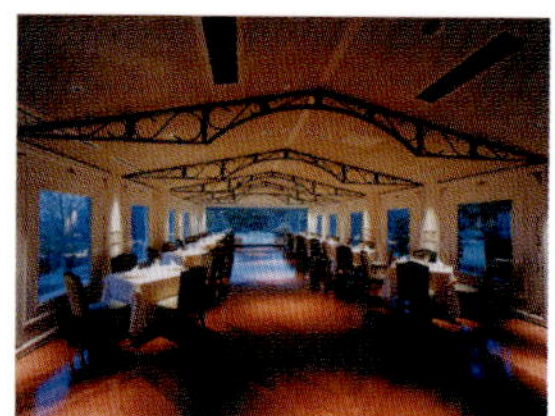

103. AUBERGE JARDIN
UTSUNOMIYA , TOCHIGI
2002.04

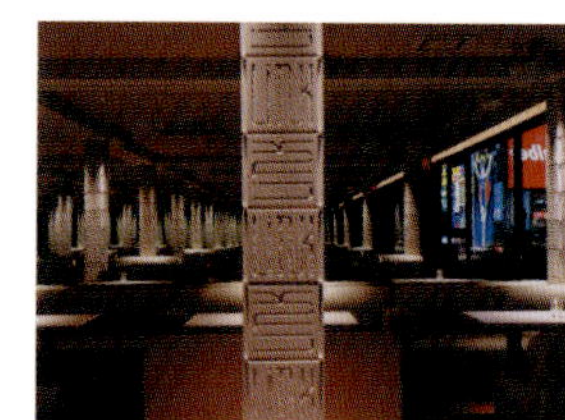

104. LINK
NANBA , OSAKA
2002.05

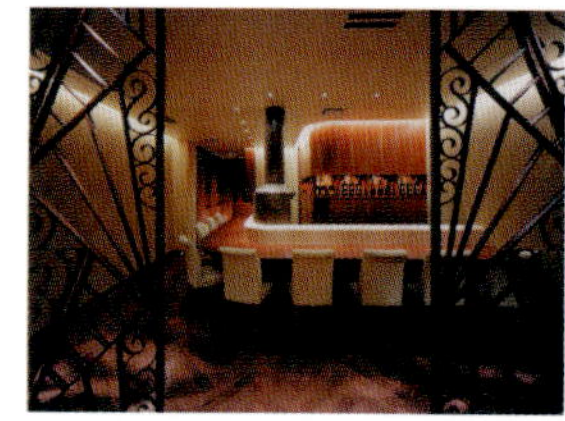

105. LA CENA
KITASHINCHI , OSAKA
2002.05

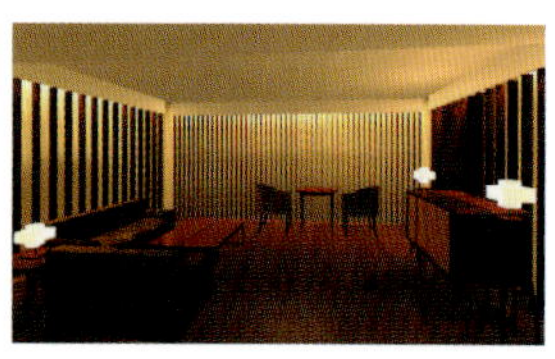

106. GUEST ROOM Ⅰ
UTSUNOMIYA , TOCHIGI
2002.06*

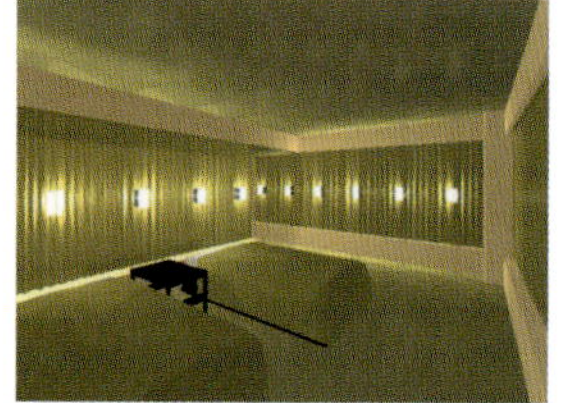

107. GUEST ROOM Ⅱ
UTSUNOMIYA , TOCHIGI
2002.06*

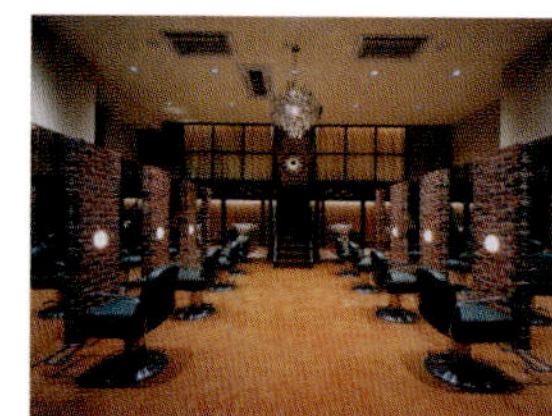

108. TIP TOP machida
MACHIDA , TOKYO
2002.06

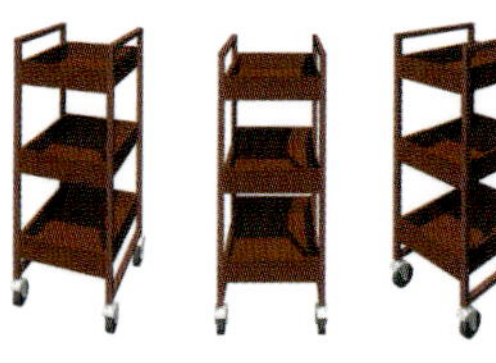

109. WAGON FOR HAIR
SALON Ⅰ
LABEL
2002.06

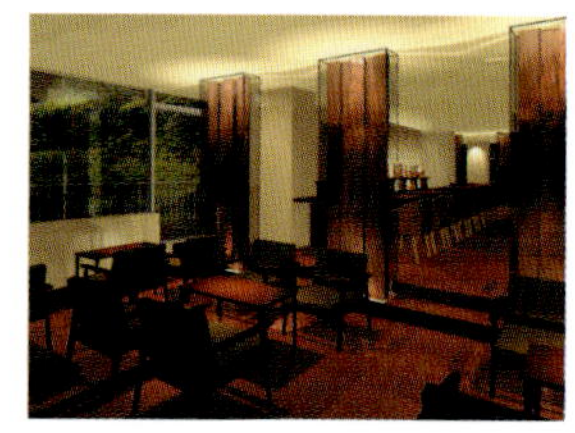

110. LOUNGE Ⅰ
UTSUNOMIYA , TOCHIGI
2002.07*

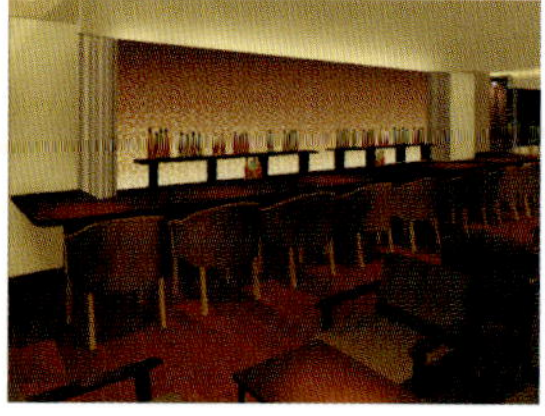

111. BAR Ⅰ
UTSUNOMIYA , TOCHIGI
2002.07*

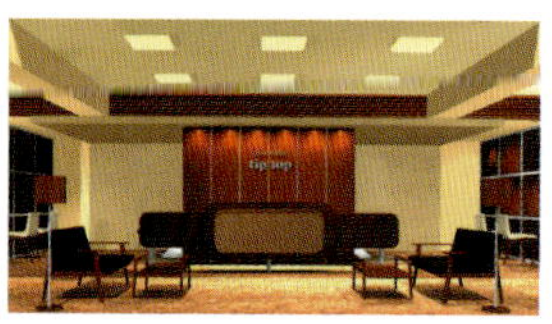

112. HAIR SALON Ⅱ
MULTIPLE SHOP
2002.07*

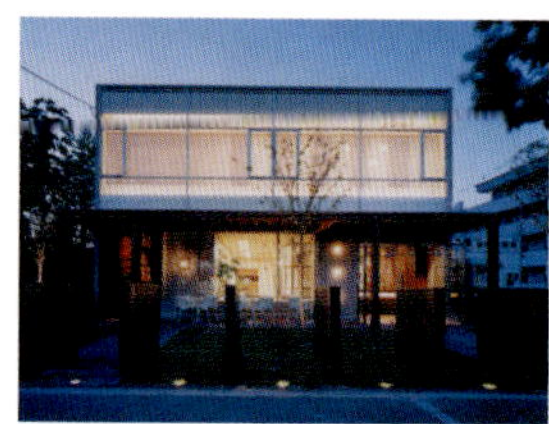

113. JOUR DOUX
KUZUHA , OSAKA
2002.07

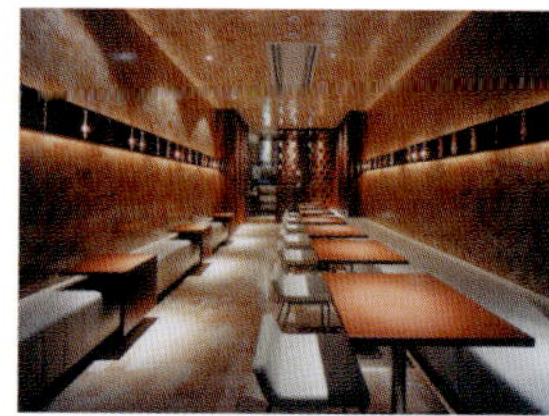

114. JOUR CAFE
KUZUHA , OSAKA
2002.07

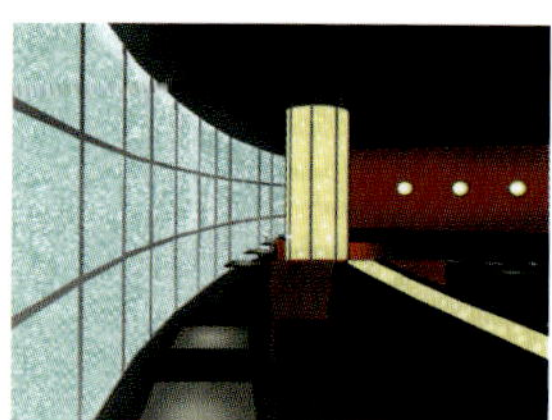

115. CLUB Ⅴ
NANBA , OSAKA
2002.07*

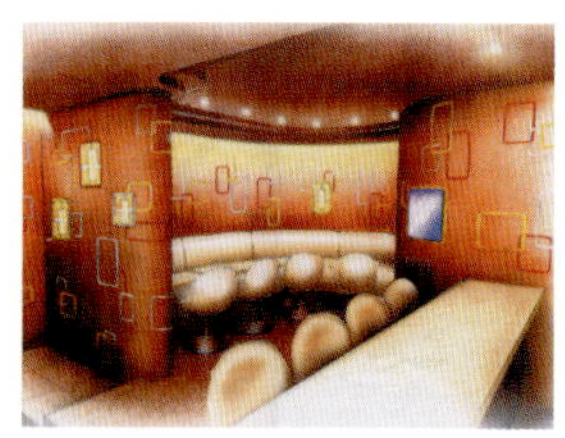

116. BAR Ⅱ
YUSHIMA , TOKYO
2002.08*

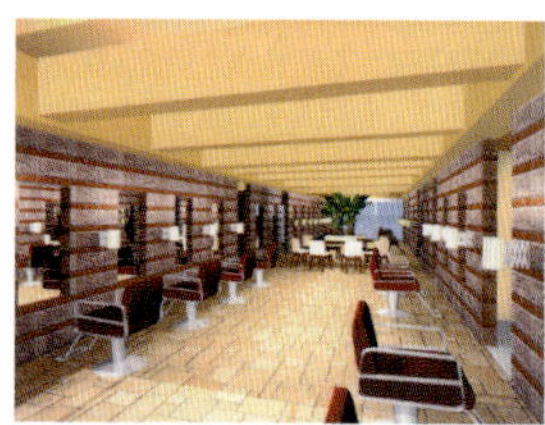

117. HAIR SALON Ⅲ
MULTIPLE SHOP
2002.08*

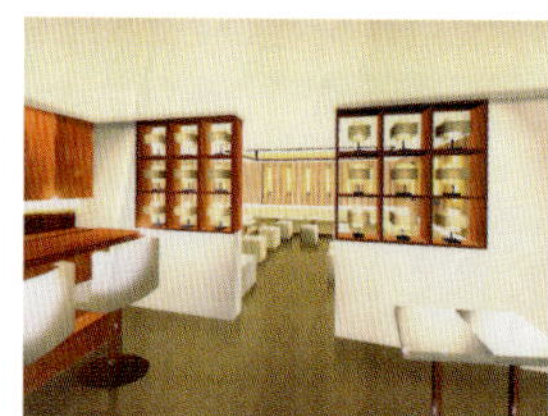

118. DARLING BUILDING
PROJECT
KITASHINCHI , OSAKA
2002.08*

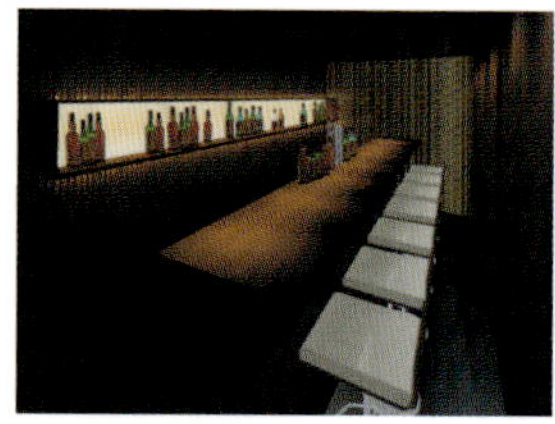

119. BAR Ⅲ
YUSHIMA , TOKYO
2002.08*

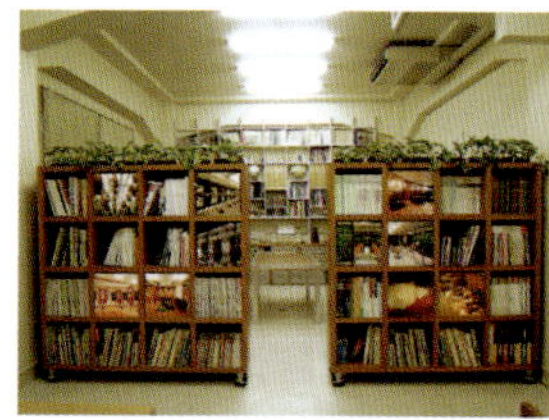

120. EMBODY DESIGN
ASSOCIATION OFFICE
HONMACHI , OSAKA
2002.08

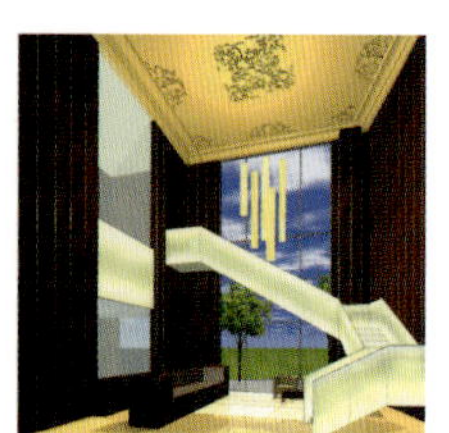

121. RESTAURANT Ⅴ
ROPPONGI , TOKYO
2002.09*

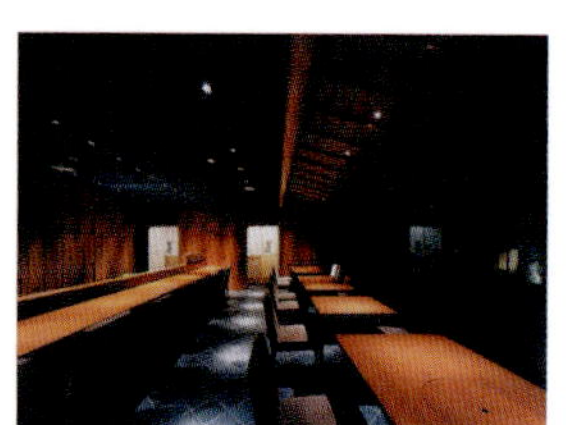

122. KARIN
UTSUNOMIYA , TOCHIGI
2002.09

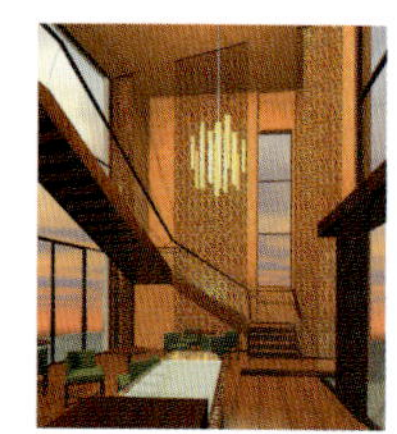

123. CAFE DINING Ⅳ
ROPPONGI , TOKYO
2002.09*

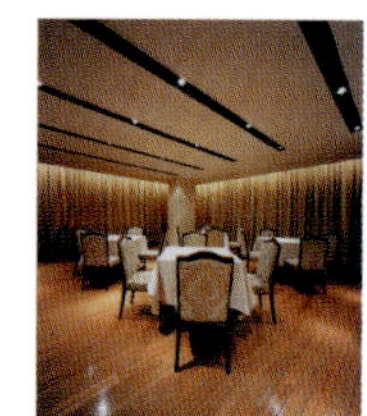

124. UTSUNOMIYA GRAND
HOTEL SALON
UTSUNOMIYA , TOCHIGI
2002.10

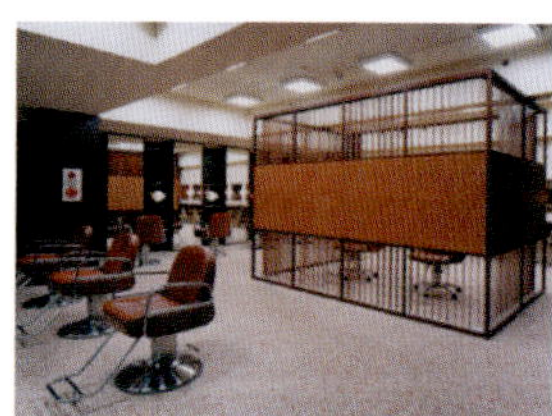

125. TIP TOP tsutsujigaoka
TSUTSUJIGAOKA , TOKYO
2002.10

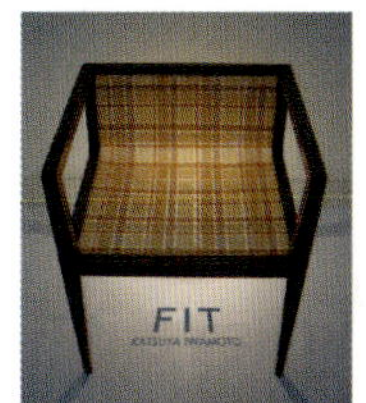

126. TOKYO DESIGNERS WEEK 2002
ROPPONGI , TOKYO
2002.10

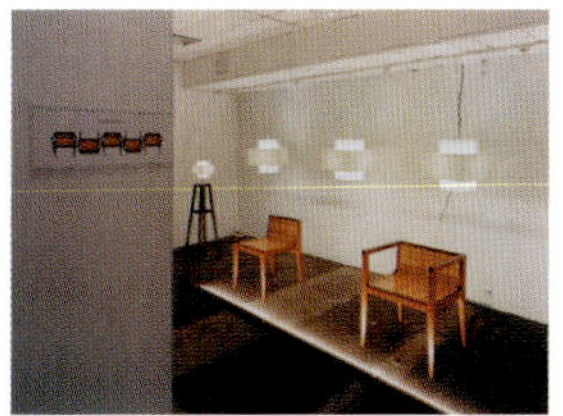

127. TOKYO DESIGNERS BLOCK 2002
AOYAMA , TOKYO
2002.10

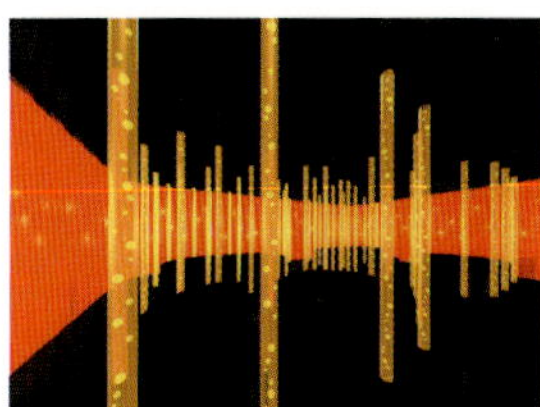

128. CLUB Ⅵ
TOKUSHIMA
2002.11*

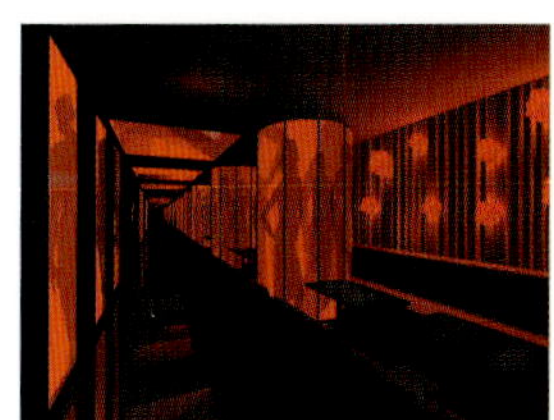

129. CLUB Ⅶ
KOCHI
2002.11*

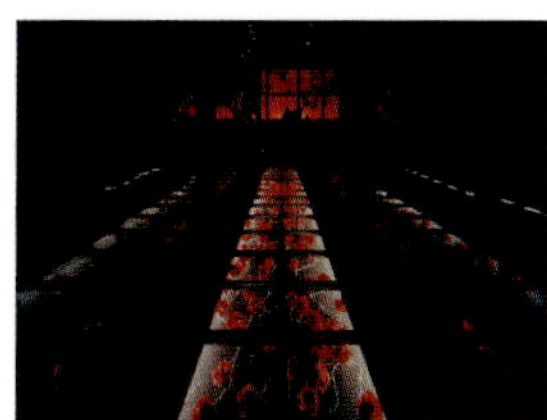

130. ROSA wakayama
WAKAYAMA
2002.11

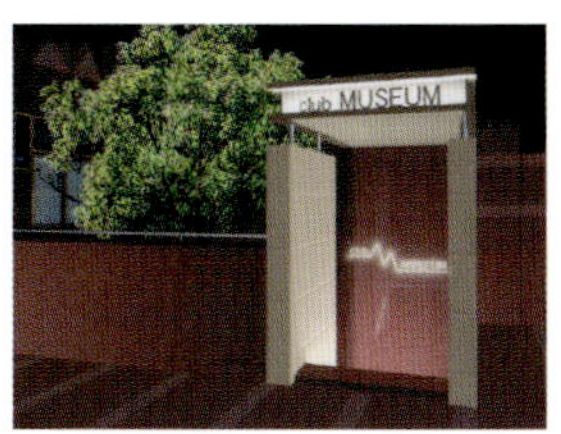

131. CLUB Ⅷ
NANBA , OSAKA
2002.12*

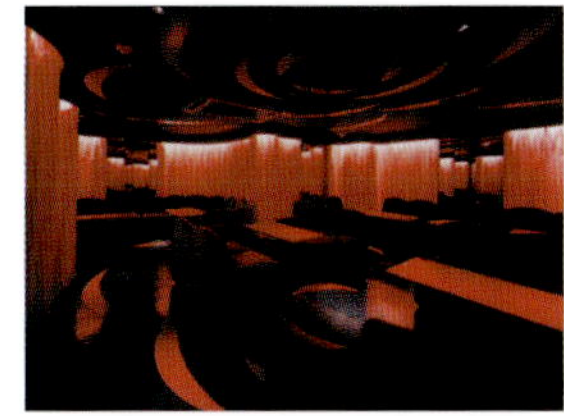

132. ROSA kobe
KOBE , HYOGO
2002.12

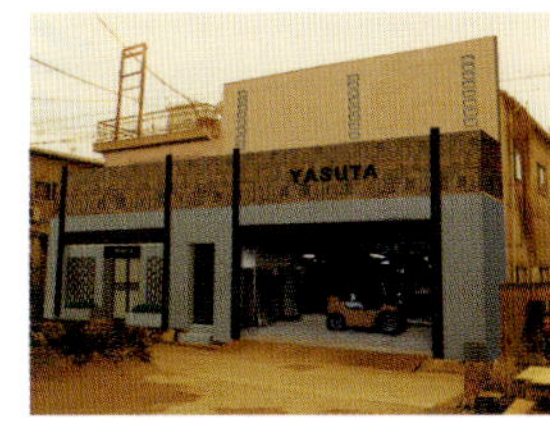

133. YASUTA BUILDING
YAO , OSAKA
2002.12*

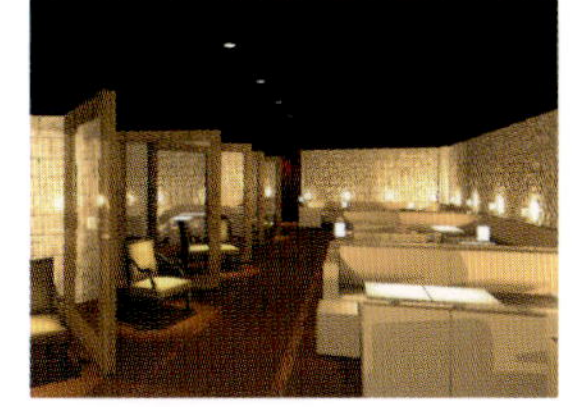

134. LOUNGE Ⅱ
NANBA , OSAKA
2003.01*

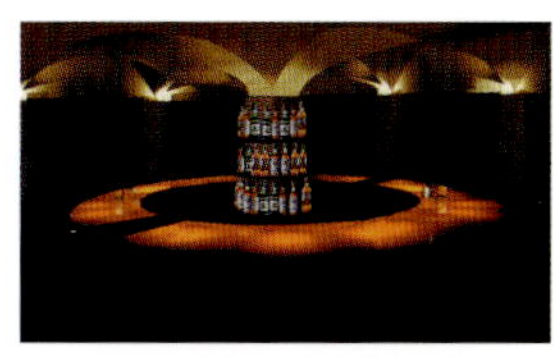

135. BAR Ⅳ
UTSUNOMIYA , TOCHIGI
2003.01*

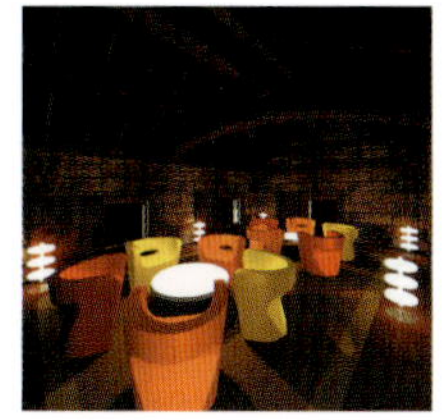

136. LOUNGE Ⅲ
UTSUNOMIYA , TOCHIGI
2003.01*

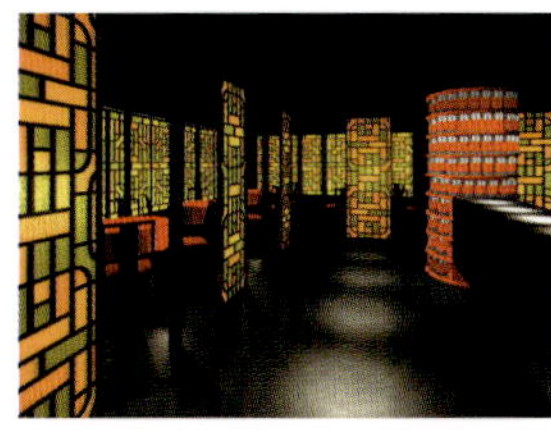

137. CHINESE RESTAURANT Ⅰ
UTSUNOMIYA , TOCHIGI
2003.01*

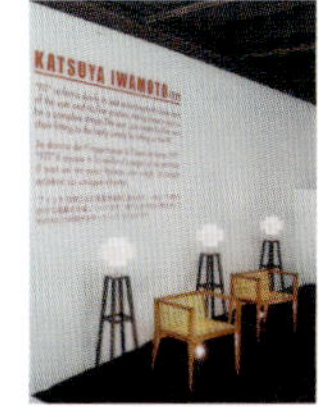

138. SALON DU MEUBLE DE PARIS 2003
PARIS , FRANCE
2003.01

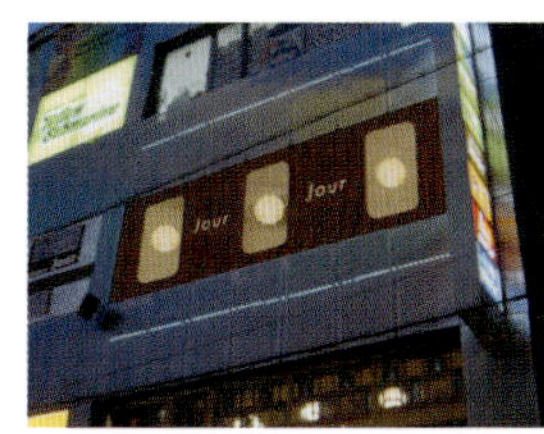

139. JOUR kawaramachi
KAWARAMACHI , KYOTO
2003.02*

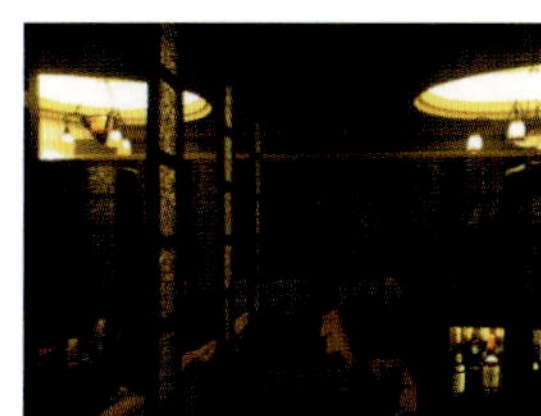

140. CLUB MAMA
KITASHINCHI , OSAKA
2003.02

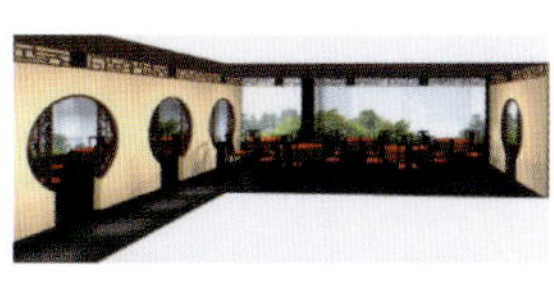

141. CHINESE RESTAURANT Ⅱ
UTSUNOMIYA , TOCHIGI
2003.02*

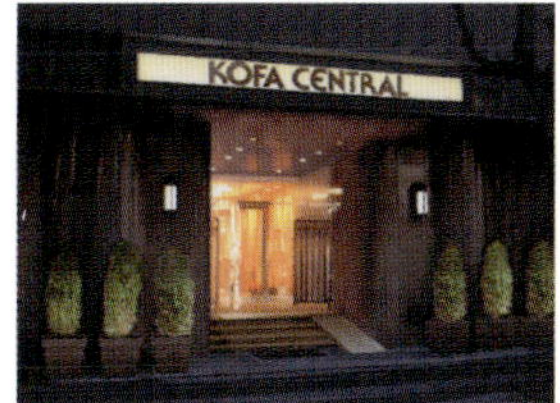

142. CONDOMINIUM REINNOVATION
UEHONMACHI , OSAKA
2003.02

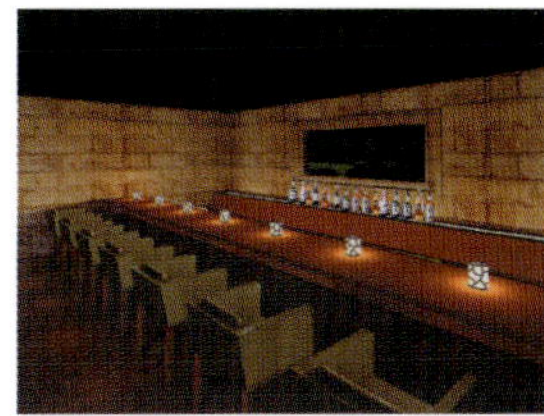

143. BAR Ⅴ
UTSUNOMIYA , TOCHIGI
2003.03*

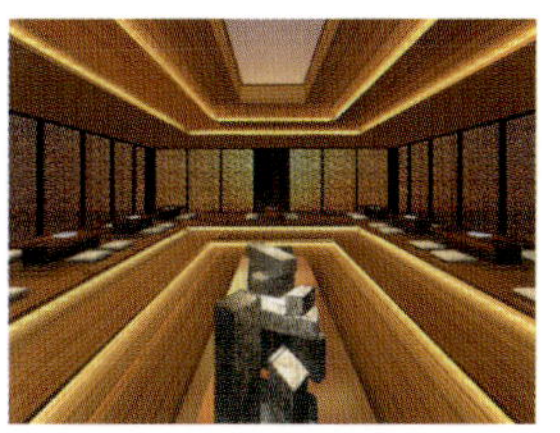

144. GRILL RESTAURANT Ⅰ
NANBA , OSAKA
2003.03*

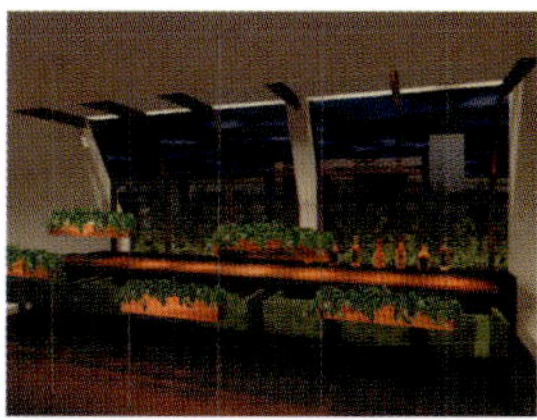

145. CLUB YUKARI
KITASHINCHI , OSAKA
2003.04*

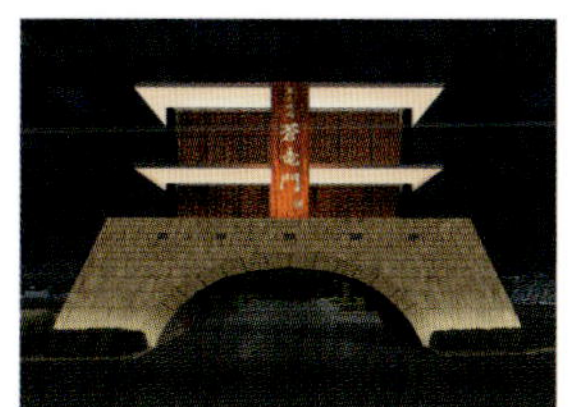

146. GRILL RESTAURANT Ⅱ
KAMAKURA , KANAGAWA
2003.04*

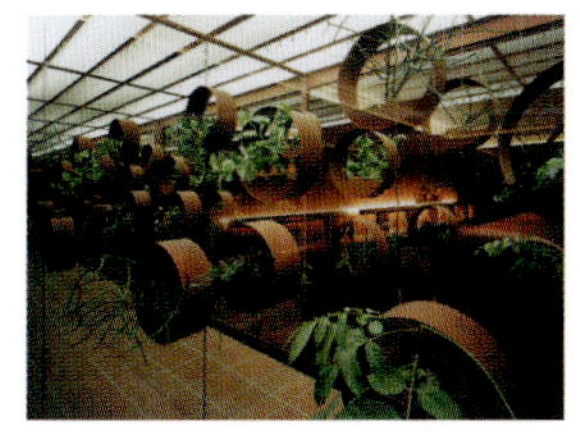

147. ROMI'S BAR
KITASHINCHI , OSAKA
2003.04

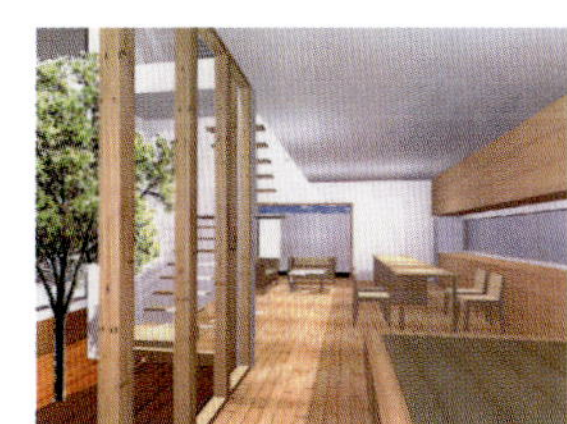

148. I HOUSE
TOSHIMA , TOKYO
2003.04*

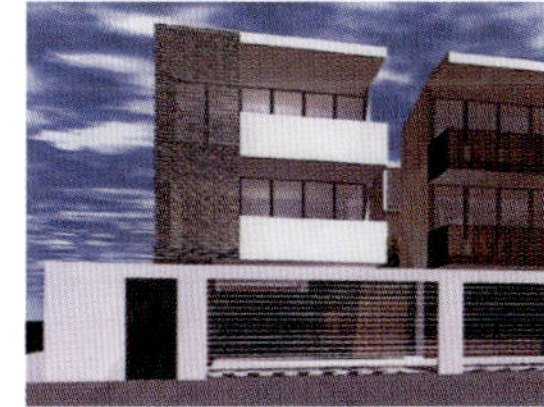

149. E HOUSE
TOSHIMA , TOKYO
2003.04*

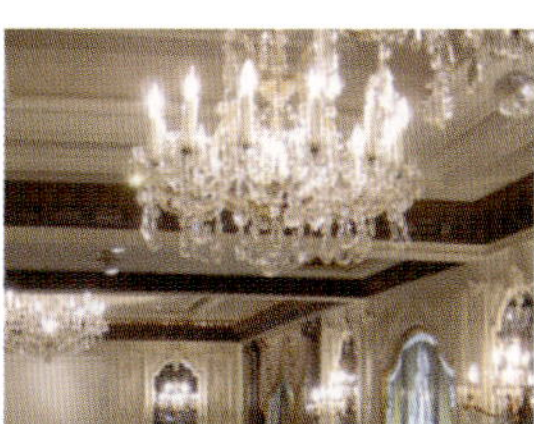

150. CLUB MAHOROBA
KITASHINCHI , OSAKA
2003.05

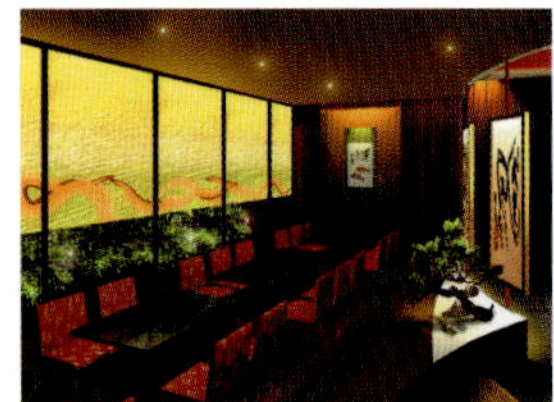

151. JAPANESE DINING Ⅰ
YOKOHAMA , KANAGAWA
2003.05*

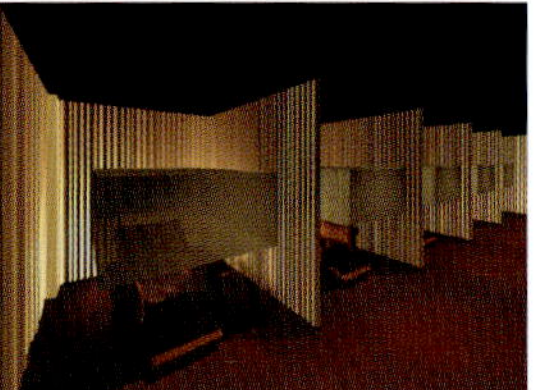

152. FEEL DESSERT
SENNICHIMAE , OSAKA
2003.05

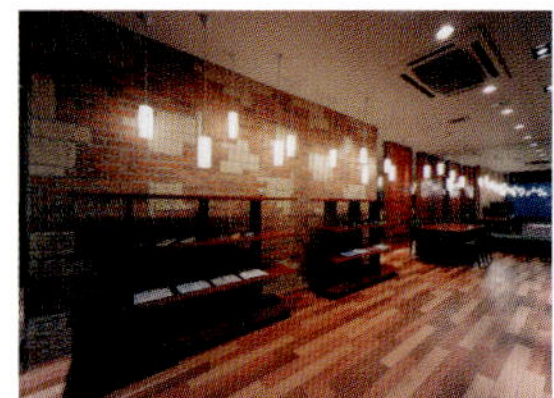

153. ALLETY
GINZA , TOKYO
2003.06

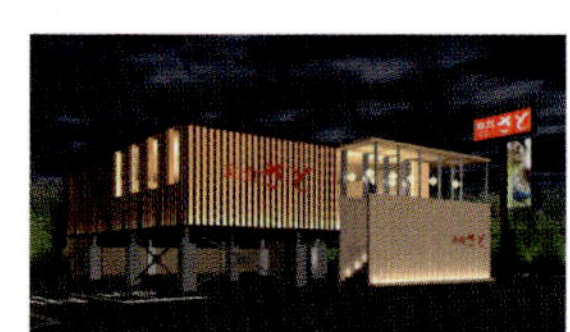

154. SATO
MULTIPLE SHOP
2003.07

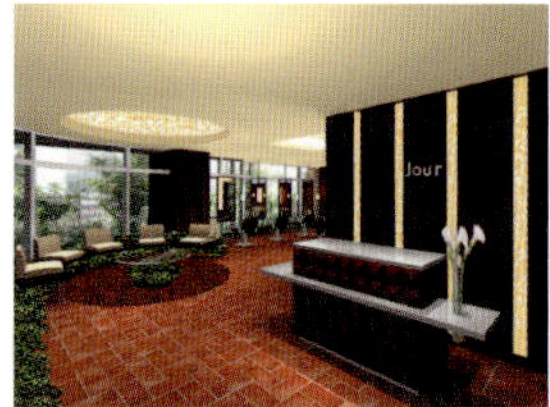

155. JOUR kyotanabe
KYOTANABE, KYOTO
2003.07*

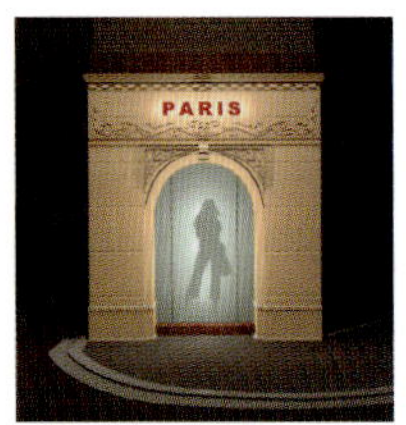

156. LOUNGE Ⅳ
KITASHINCHI , OSAKA
2003.07*

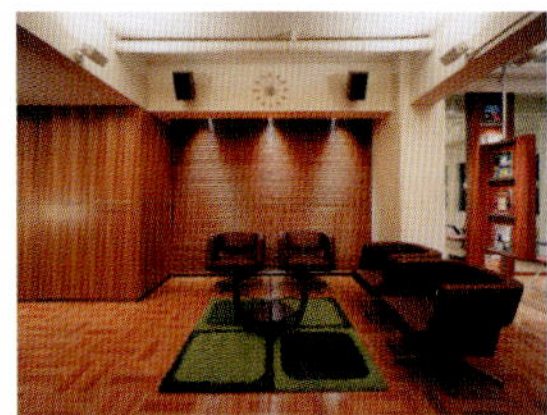

157. SHARE
MINAMISENBA , OSAKA
2003.08

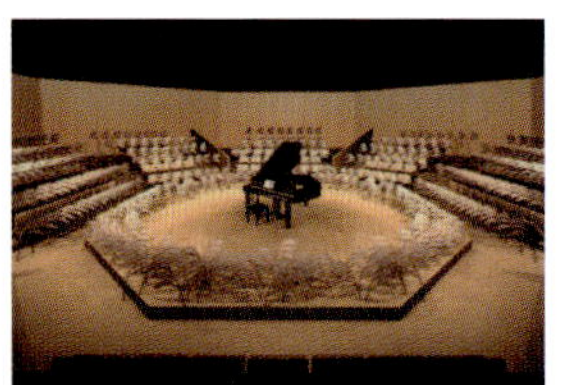

158. PALHASO
NAGOYA , AICHI
2003.09

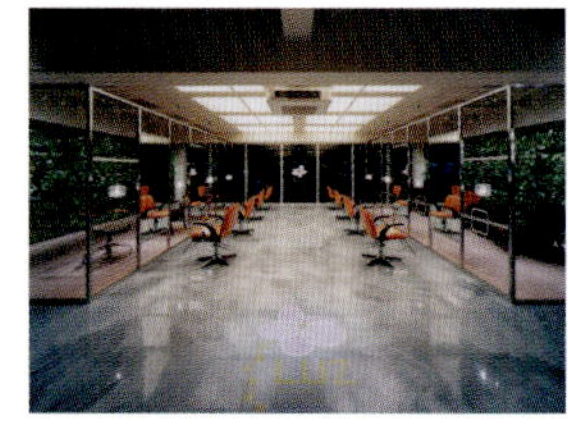

159. LUZ
KITAHORIE , OSAKA
2003.09

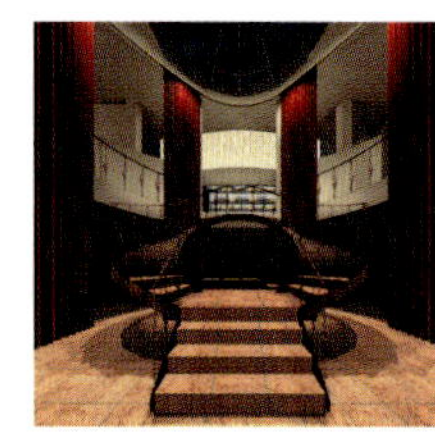

160. FOUR SEASON ashiya
ASHIYA , HYOGO
2003.10*

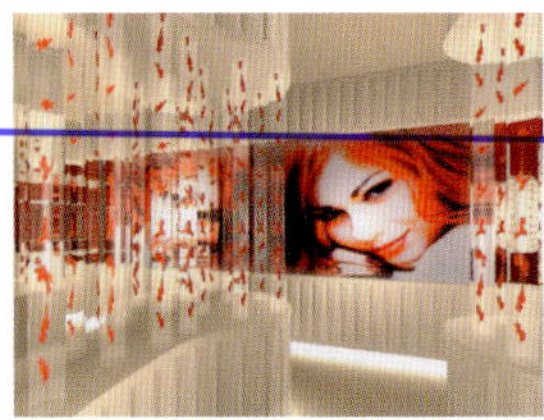

161. CLUB Ⅸ
NARA
2003.10*

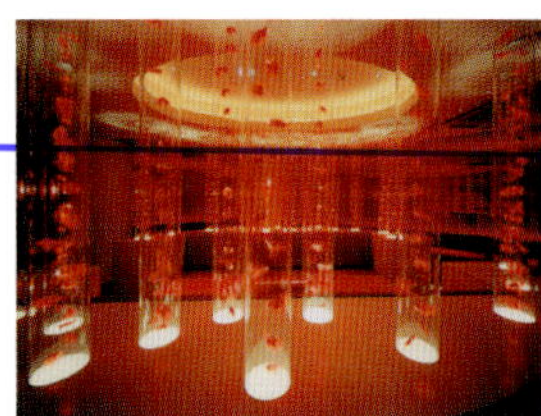

162. RIPPLE okayama
OKAYAMA
2003.10

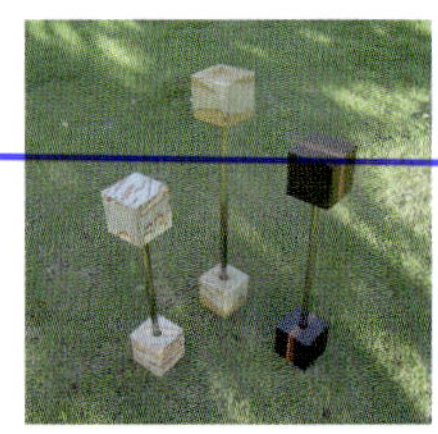

163. TOKYO DESIGNERS WEEK 2003
ROPPONGI , TOKYO
2003.10

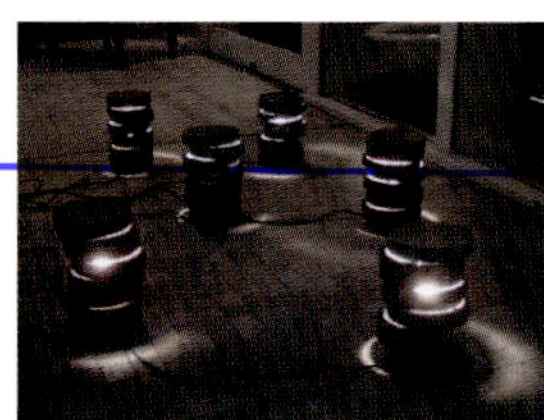

164. TOKYO DESIGNERS BLOCK 2003
AOYAMA , TOKYO
2003.10

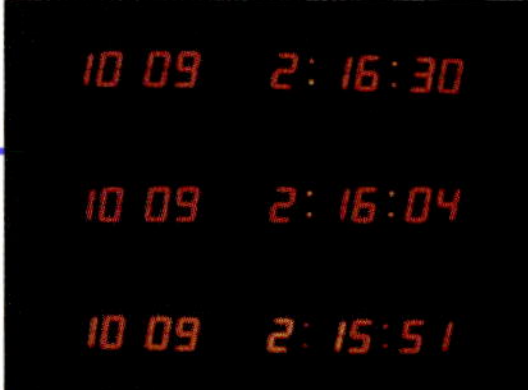

165. CONTAINER EXHIBITION 2003
ODAIBA , TOKYO
2003.10

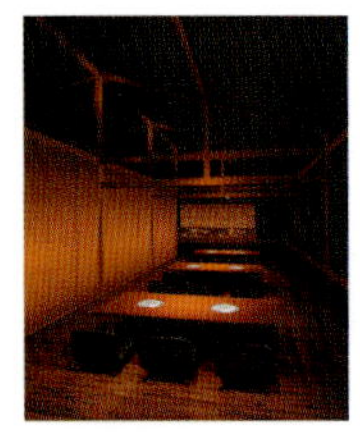

166. JAPANESE DINING Ⅱ
UMEDA , OSAKA
2003.10*

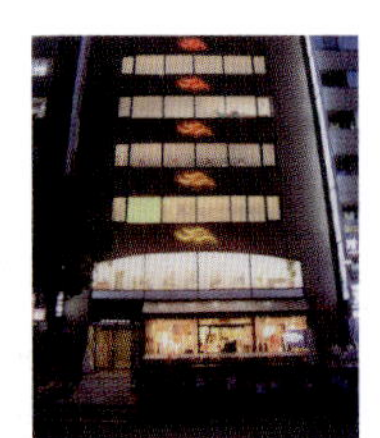

167. ELUNA BUILDING
SHINSAIBASHI , OSAKA
2003.11*

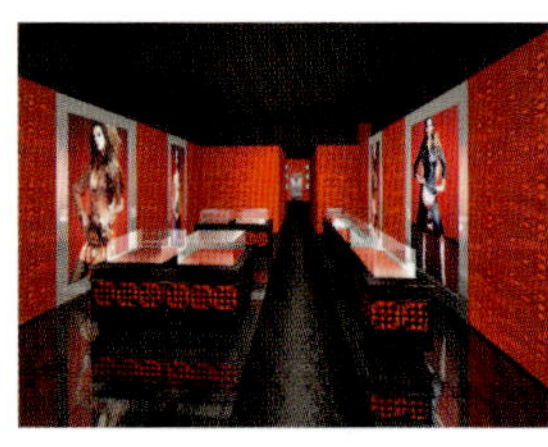

168. ORIENTAL BRAND
SHINSAIBASHI , OSAKA
2003.11*

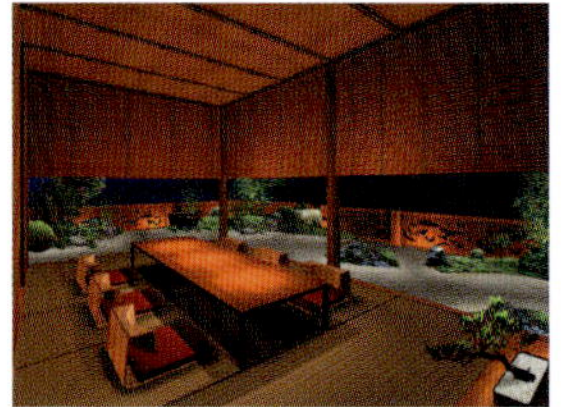

169. JAPANESE DINING Ⅲ
NANBA , OSAKA
2003.11*

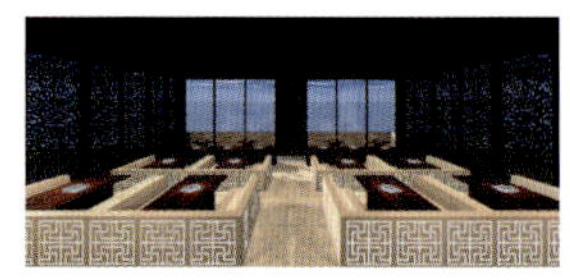

170. GRILL RESTAURANT Ⅲ
ROPPONGI , TOKYO
2003.11*

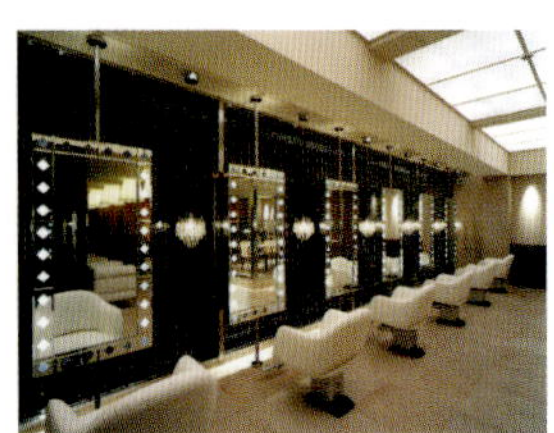

171. TIP TOP mejiro
MEJIRO , TOKYO
2003.11

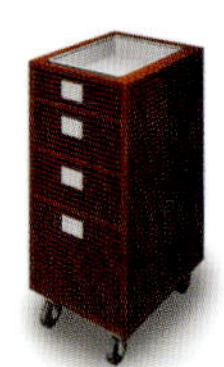

172. WAGON FOR HAIR SALON Ⅱ
LABEL
2003.11

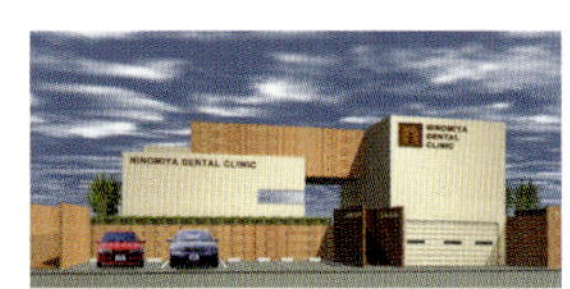

173. N HOUSE
SAKAI , OSAKA
2003.12*

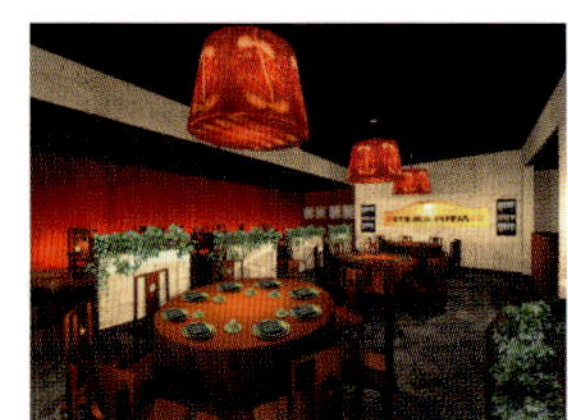

174. MINSEI
UMEDA , OSAKA
2003.12*

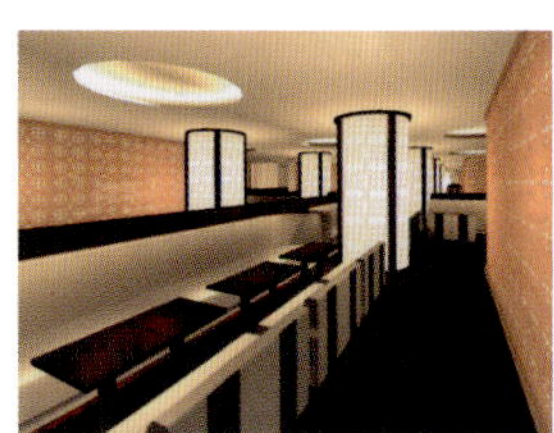

175. LOUNGE Ⅴ
KITASHINCHI , OSAKA
2003.12*

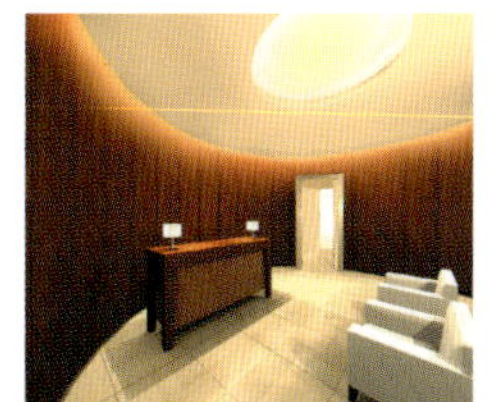

176. CLINIC Ⅰ
SAKAI , OSAKA
2004.03*

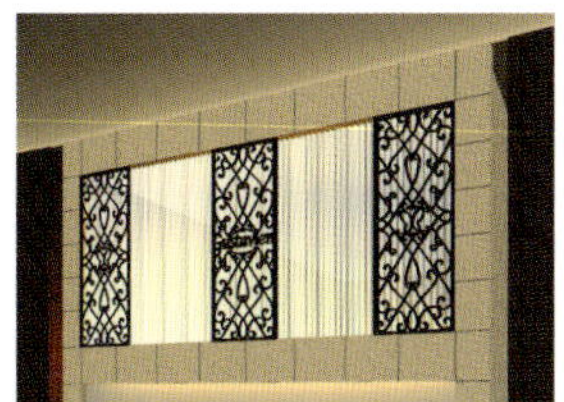

177. GUSTAVIEN
TAKATSUKI , OSAKA
2004.03

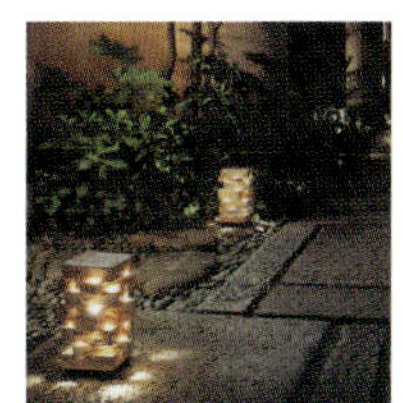

178. KAKU-KAKU
table·floor stand
DAIKO
2004.04

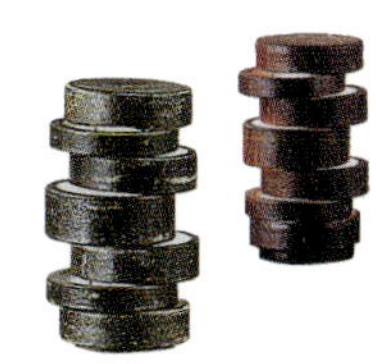

179. MARU-MARU
table·floor stand
DAIKO
2004.04

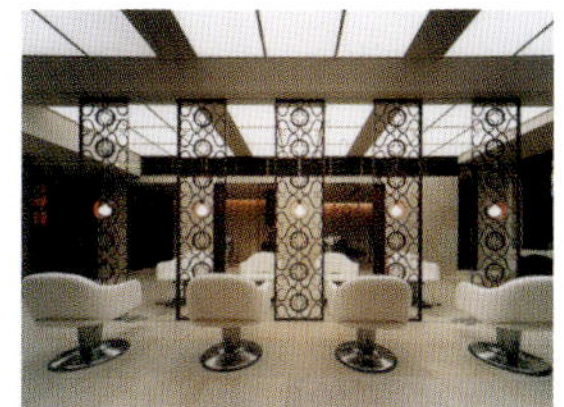

180. TIP TOP ikebukuro west
IKEBUKURO , TOKYO
2004.04

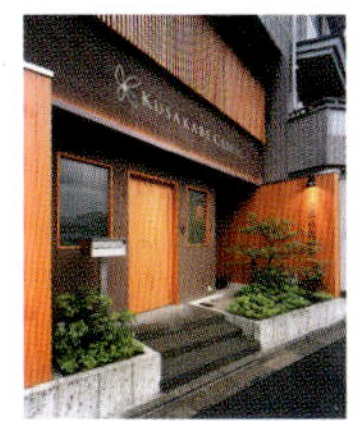

181. KUSAKABE CLINIC
MURASAKINO , KYOTO
2004.05

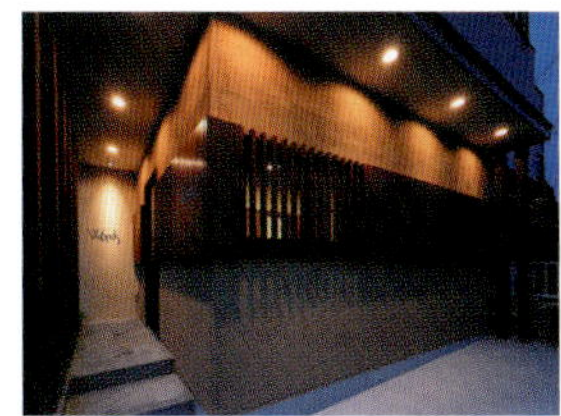

182. WEEDS
HABIKINO , OSAKA
2004.06

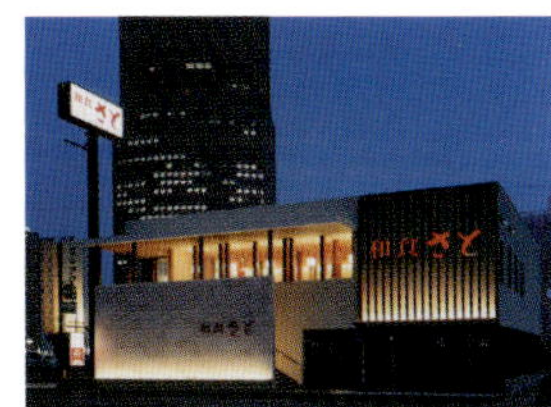

183. SATO hamamatsu
HAMAMATSU , SHIZUOKA
2004.07

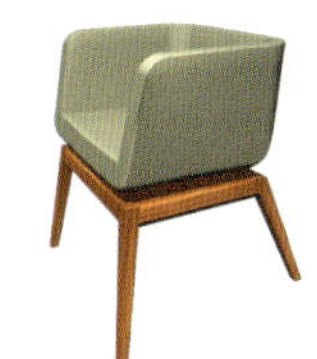

184. KURU-KURU arm chair
KARF
2004.07*

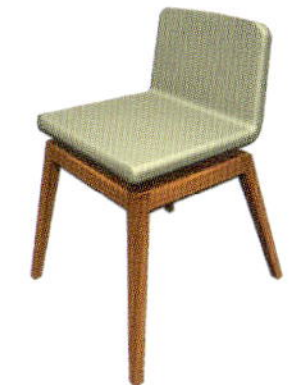

185. KURU-KURU chair
KARF
2004.07

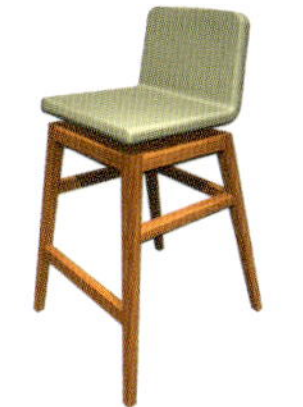

186. KURU-KURU high chair
KARF
2004.07

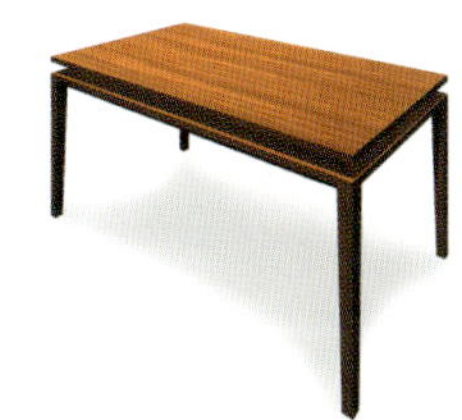

187. DAN-DAN table
KARF
2004.07

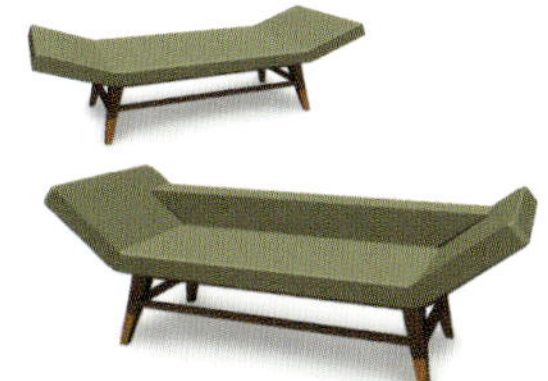

188. GORO-GORO sofa
KARF
2004.07

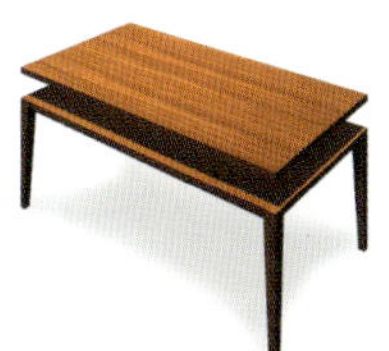

189. DAN-DAN low table
KARF
2004.07

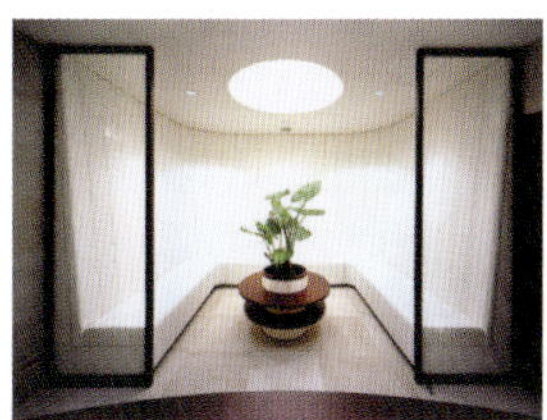

190. ONISHI MEDICAL LABO
OTSU , SHIGA
2004.08

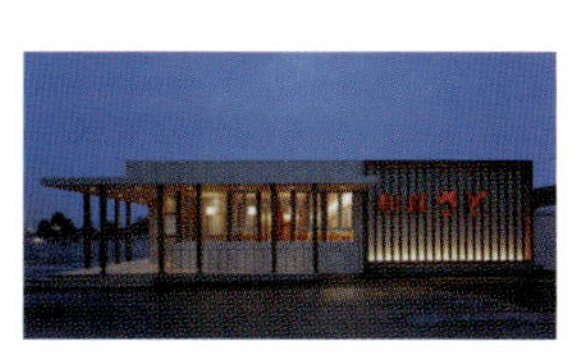

191. SATO yatomi
YATOMI , AICHI
2004.08

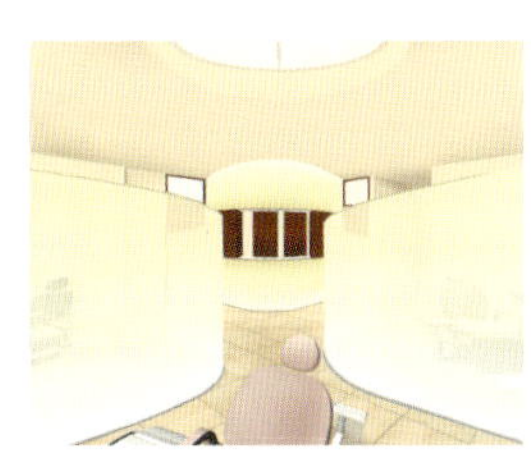

192. CLINIC Ⅱ
SAKAI , OSAKA
2004.09*

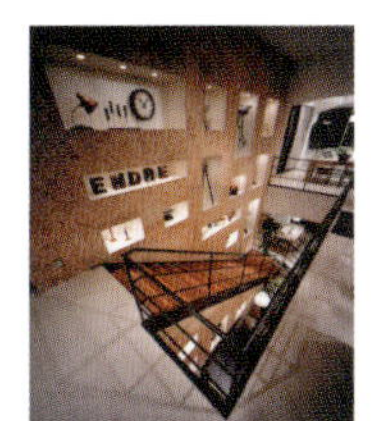

193. KARF
MEGURO , TOKYO
2004.09

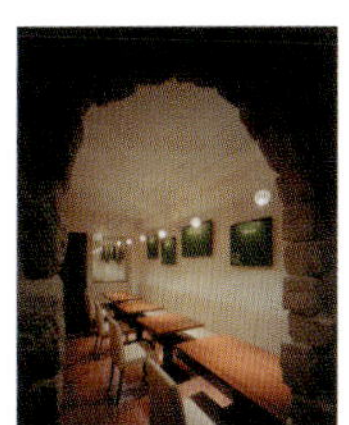

194. BON SOLEIL
KITASHINCHI , OSAKA
2004.09

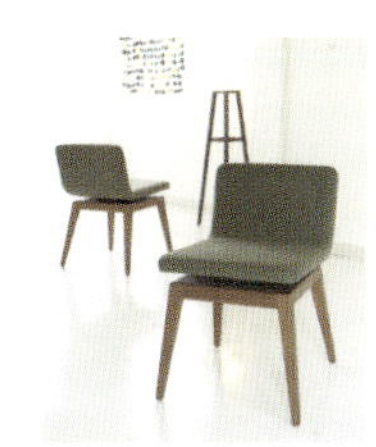

195. MIST 2004
MEGURO , TOKYO
2004.10

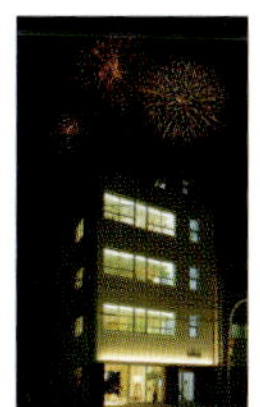

196. LABEL BUILDING
NISHITENMA , OSAKA
2004.10

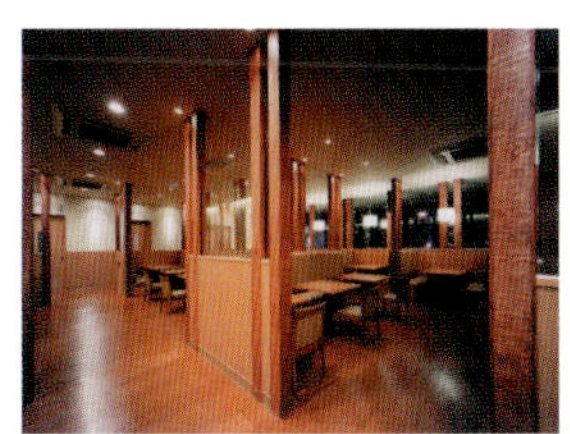

197. SATO horitadori
NAGOYA , AICHI
2004.10

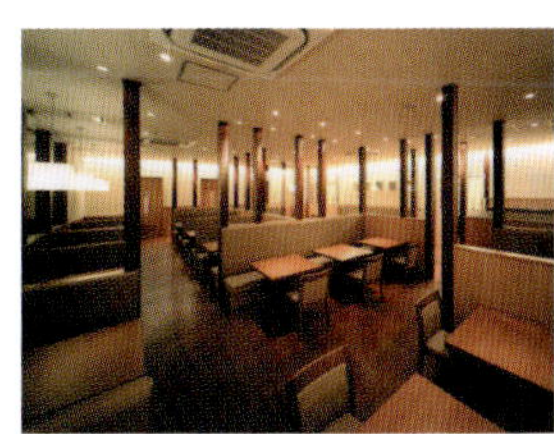

198. SATO sakurajousui
SUGINAMI , TOKYO
2004.10

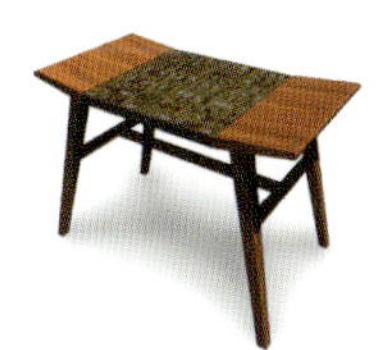

199. TOKYO DESIGNERS WEEK 2004
ROPPONGI , TOKYO
2004.10

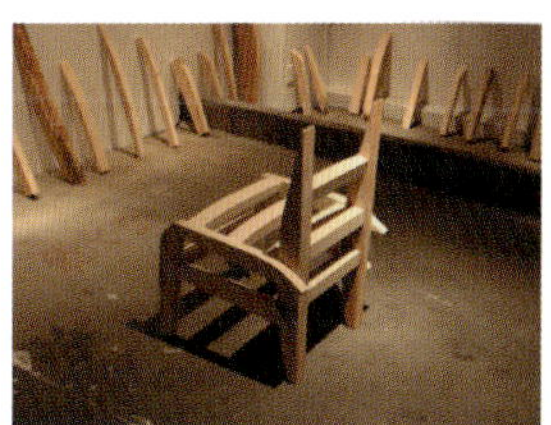

200. MATE-RE-INNO CHAIR
LABEL
2004.11

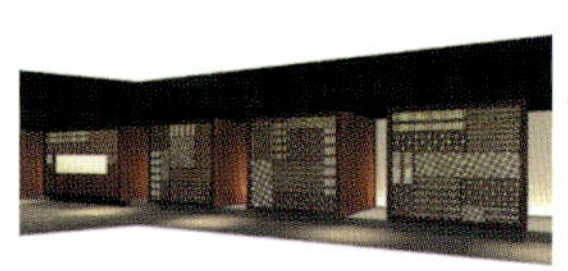

201. HANARE
KITASHINCHI , OSAKA
2004.11*

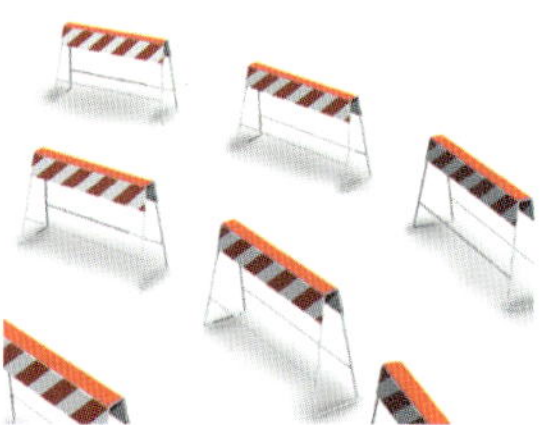

202. OSAKA DESIGNERS WEEK
2004
HONMACHI , OSAKA
2004.11

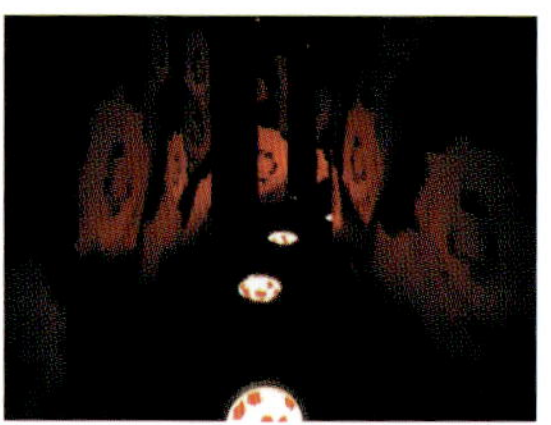

203. ROSA kanazawa
KANAZAWA . ISHIKAWA
2004.11

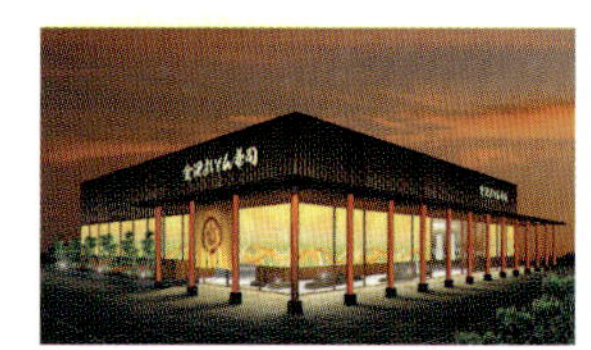

204. JAPANESE DINING Ⅳ
YOKOHAMA , KANAGAWA
2004.12*

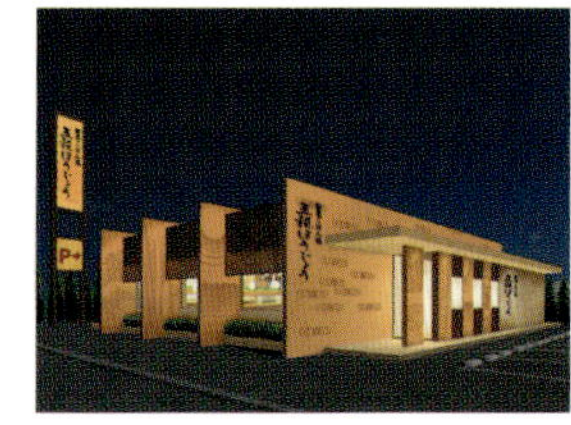

205. GOKOKU HOUJO
MULTIPLE SHOP
2004.12*

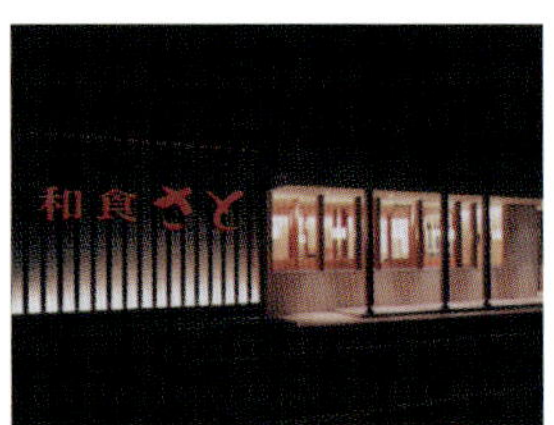

206. SATO shimada
SHIMADA . SHIZUOKA
2004.12

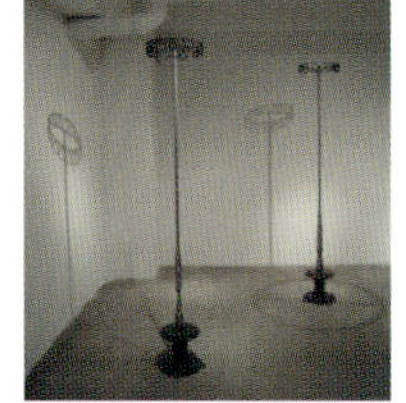

207. MATE-RE-INNO
COAT STAND
LABEL
2005.01

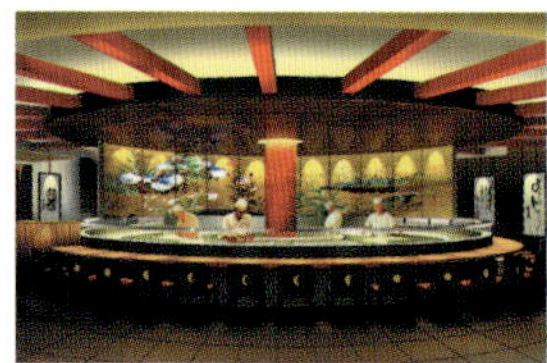

208. JAPANESE DINING Ⅴ
MULTIPLE SHOP
2005.02*

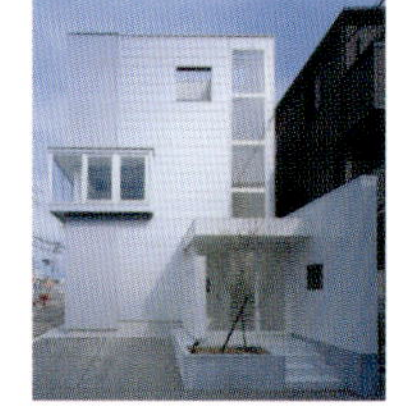

209. K-ART-FACTORY
HIGASHIOSAKA , OSAKA
2005.03

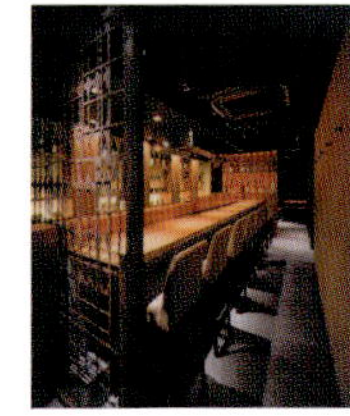

210. BUDOYA
SHINBASHI , TOKYO
2005.03

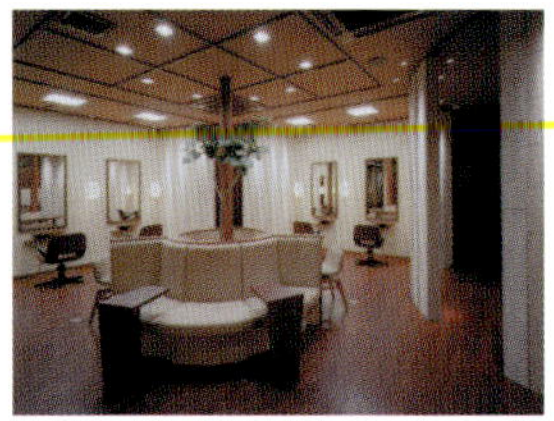

211. M-CLUB
KISAICHO . SAITAMA
2005.03

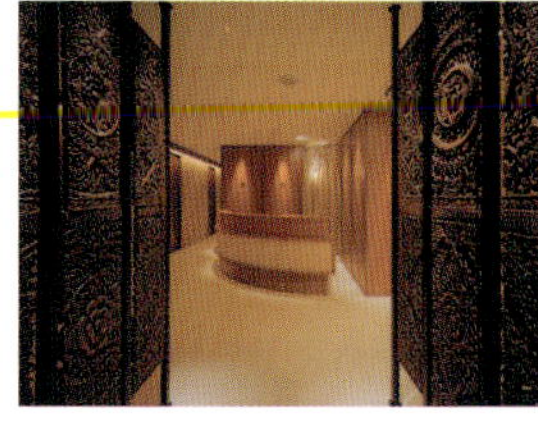

212. ORIENTAL
AROMATHERAPY COLLEGE
SHIBA , TOKYO
2005.03

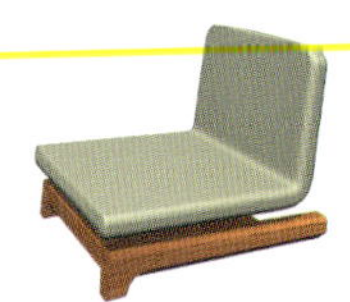

213. KURU-KURU legless chair
LABEL
2005.04*

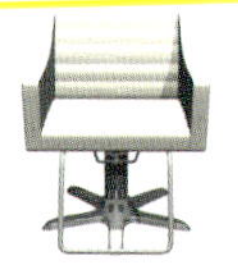

214. EURO CHAIR
ANCC
2005.04

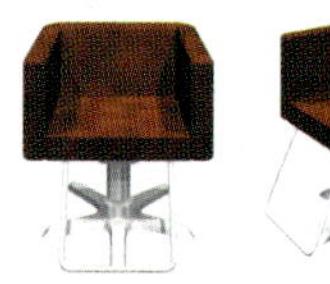

215. ASIAN EURO CHAIR
ANCC
2005.04*

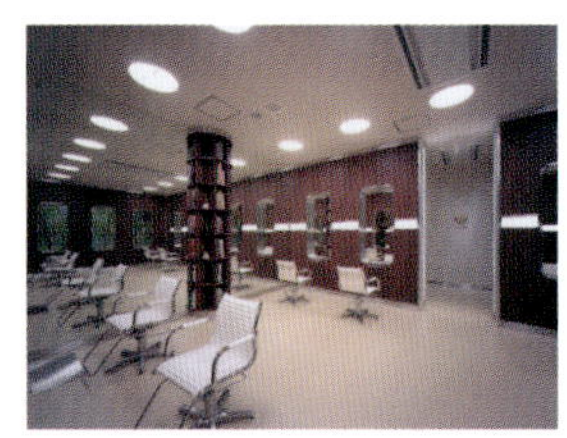

216. CUBIAM
KUZUHA , OSAKA
2005.04

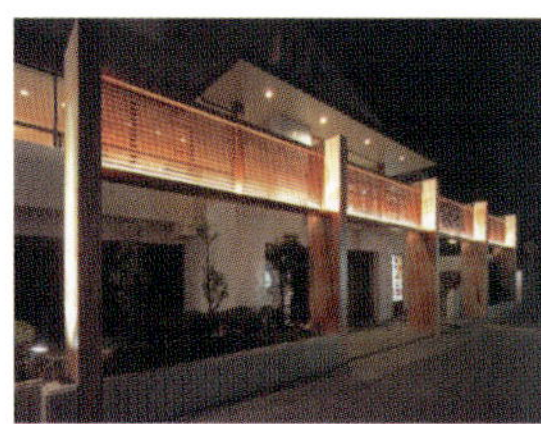

217. TAWAWA hiranobaba
HIRANOBABA , OSAKA
2005.04

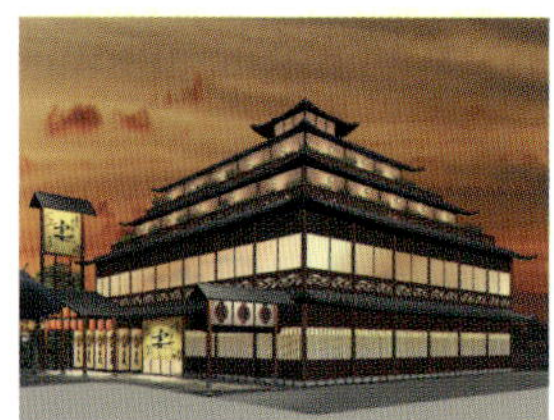

218. UTAGE
NANBA , OSAKA
2005.05*

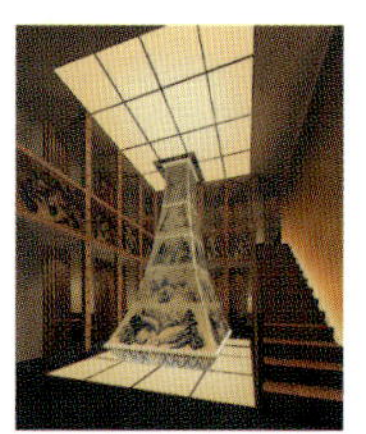

219. JAPANESE DINING Ⅵ
SHINSAIBASHI , OSAKA
2005.05*

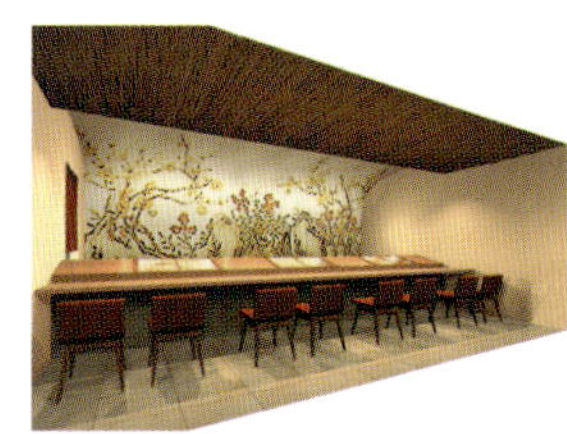

220. JAPANESE DINING Ⅶ
NANBA , OSAKA
2005.05*

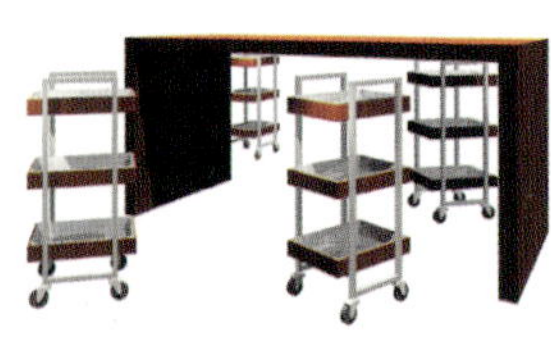

221. WAGON FOR HAIR
SALON Ⅲ
ANCC
2005.05

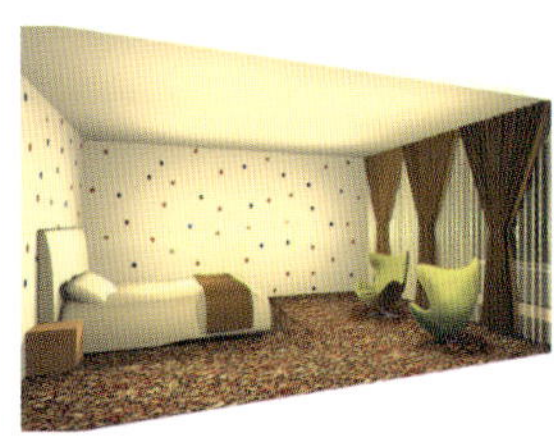

222. GUEST ROOM Ⅲ
ANAGA , HYOGO
2005.05 ~

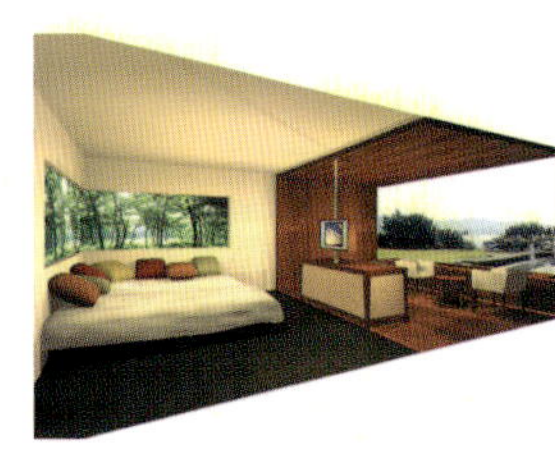

223. GUEST ROOM Ⅳ
ANAGA , HYOGO
2005.05 ~

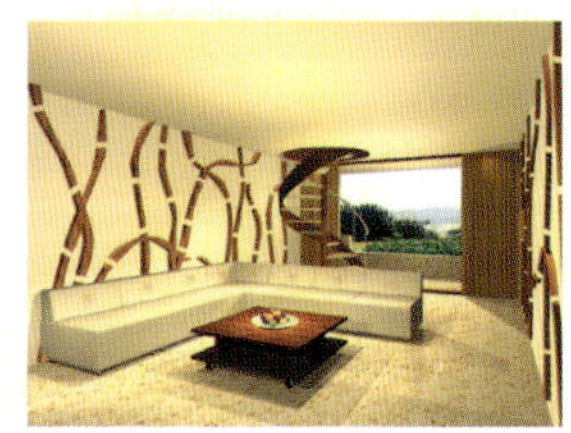

224. GUEST ROOM Ⅴ
ANAGA , HYOGO
2005.05 ~

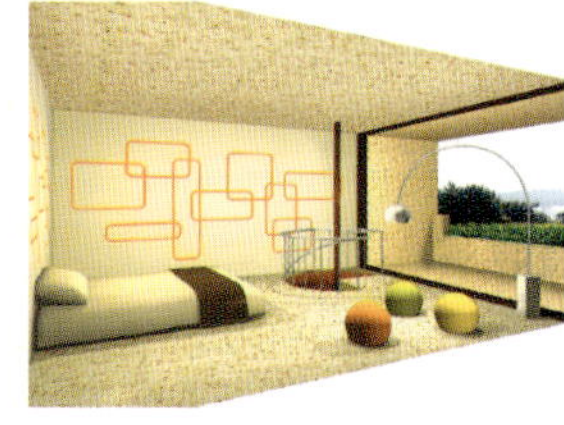

225. GUEST ROOM Ⅵ
ANAGA , HYOGO
2005.05 ~

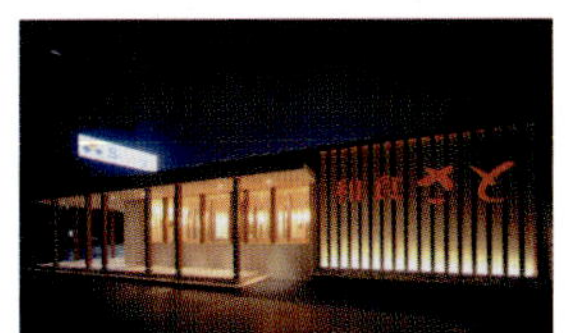

226. SATO toyohashi
TOYOHASHI , AICHI
2005.06

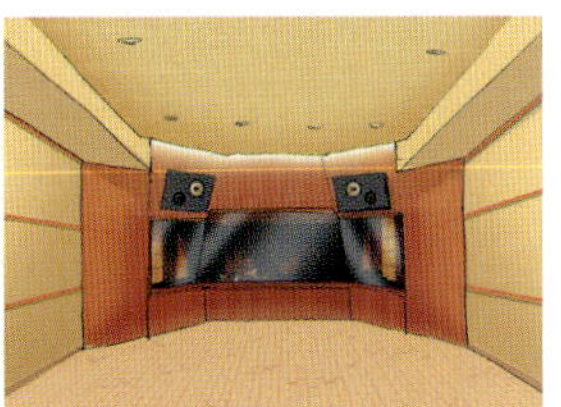

227. FLAVA STUDIO
SHIBUYA , TOKYO
2005.06

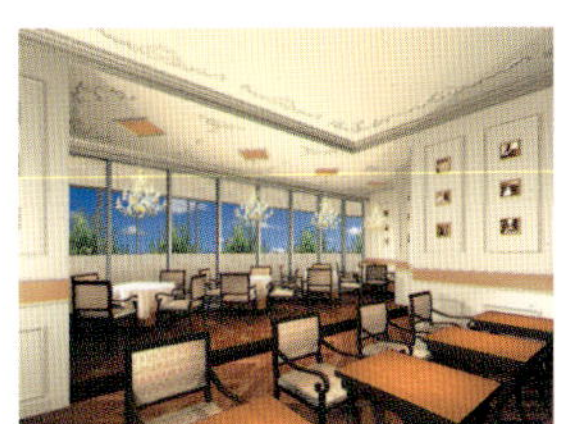

228. WEDGWOOD
SHINSAIBASHI , OSAKA
2005.07*

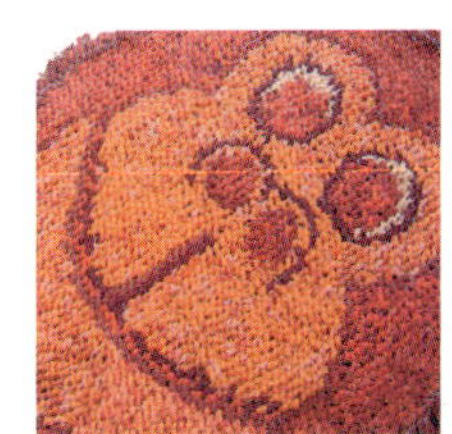

229. MATE-RE-INNO RUG
musubu
LABEL
2005.07

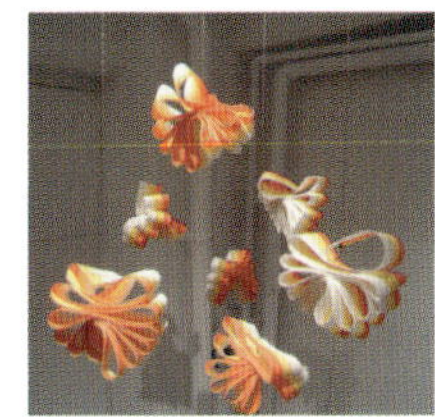

230. MATE-RE-INNO kakeru
LABEL
2005.07

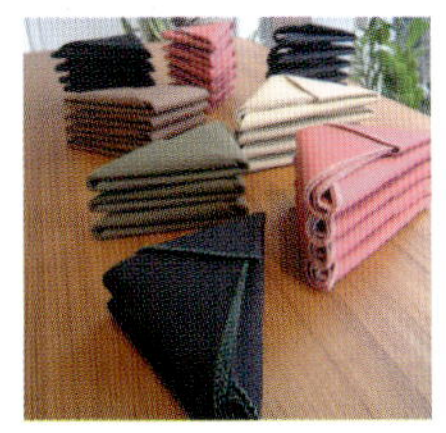

231. MATE-RE-INNO CASE ori
LABEL
2005.07

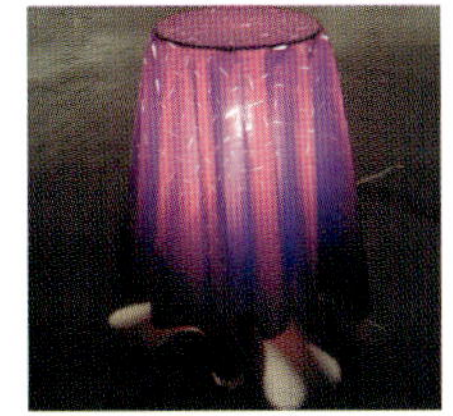

232. MATE-RE-INNO matou
LABEL
2005.07

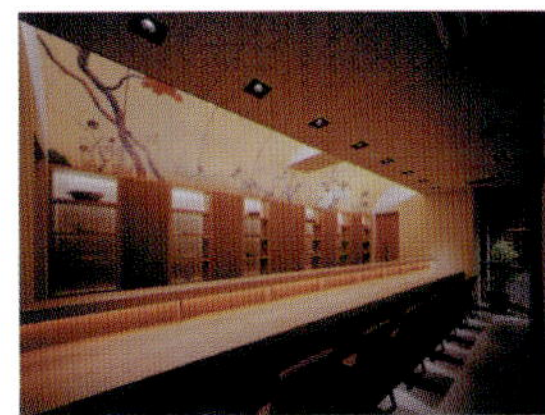

233. TAKENAWA
KITASHINCHI , OSAKA
2005.07

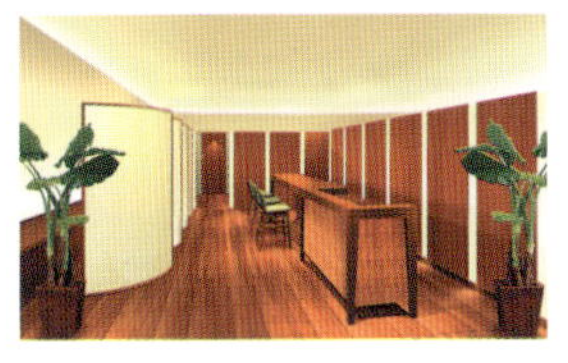

234. ONISHI MEDICAL ESTHETIC
OTSU , SHIGA
2005.10*

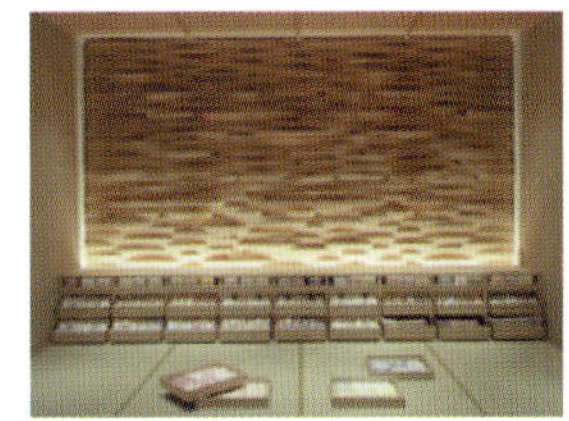

235. SHIRAYUKI FUKIN
MINAMIKIDERACHO , NARA
2005.10

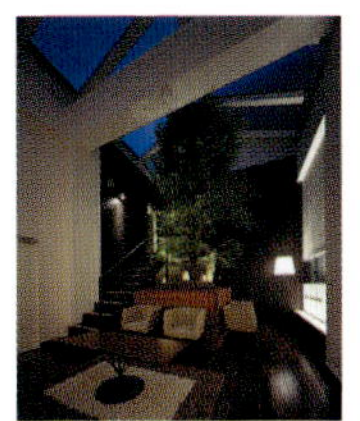

236. GINNZASHINRYOSYO
GINZA , TOKYO
2005.10

237. HALF BALL bracket
DAIKO
2005.10

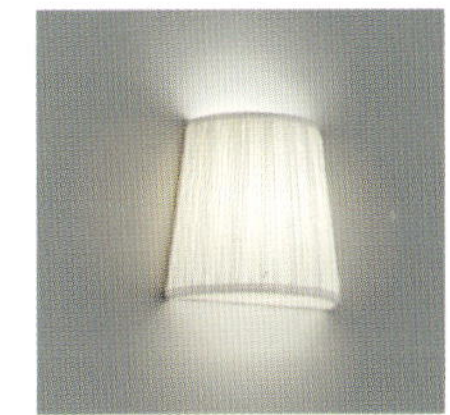

238. HALF BRACKET bracket
DAIKO
2005.10

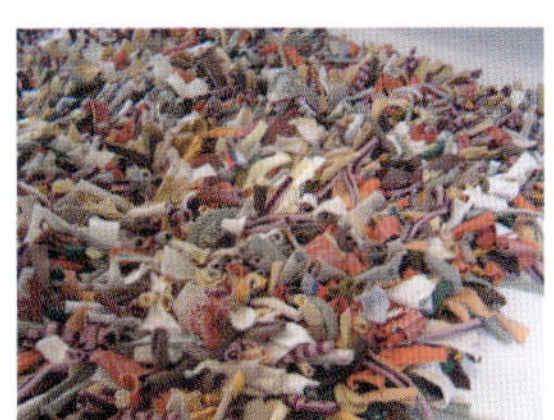

239. TOKYO DESIGNERS WEEK
2005
ROPPONGI , TOKYO
2005.10

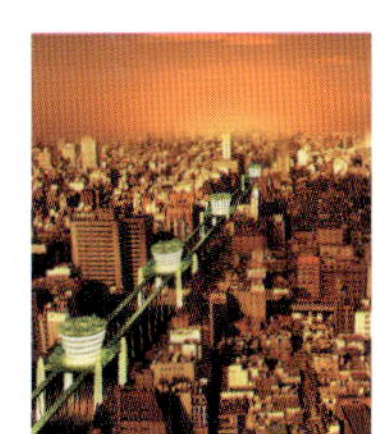

240. SKY CROSS
MIDOSUJI , OSAKA
2005.11*

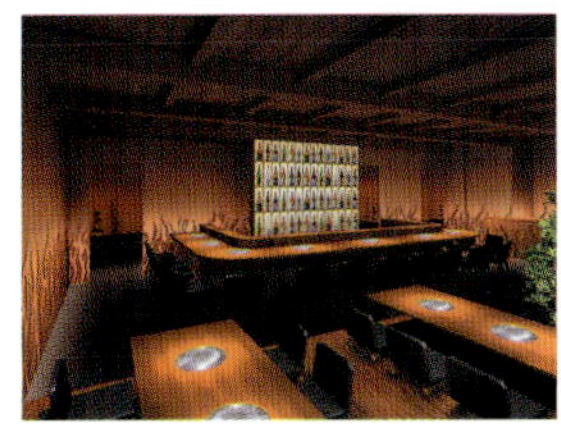

241. GRILL RESTAURANT Ⅳ
DOYAMACHO , OSAKA
2005.12

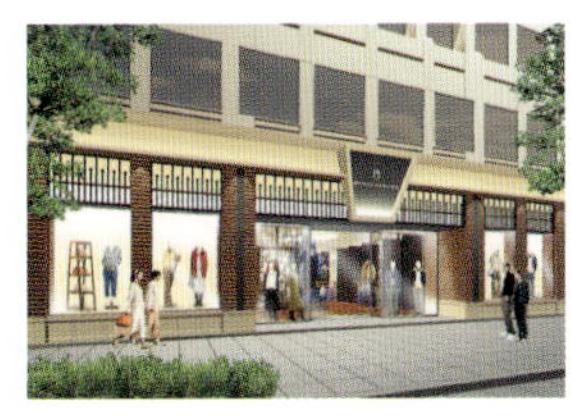

242. SHOP Ⅱ
MULTIPLE SHOP
2006.01*

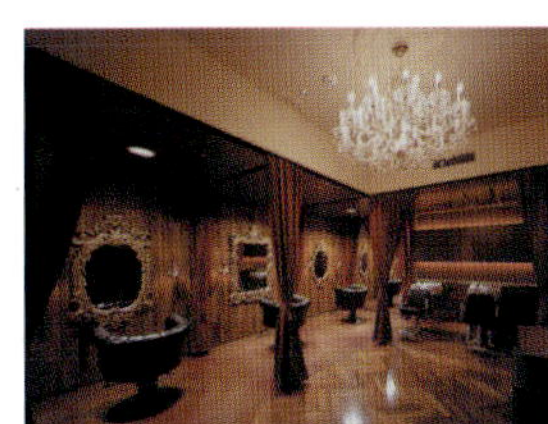

243. BERRY
KUDAN , TOKYO
2006.02

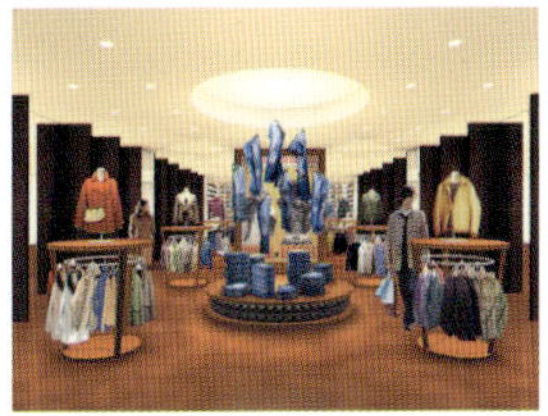

244. SHOP Ⅲ
MULTIPLE SHOP
2006.02*

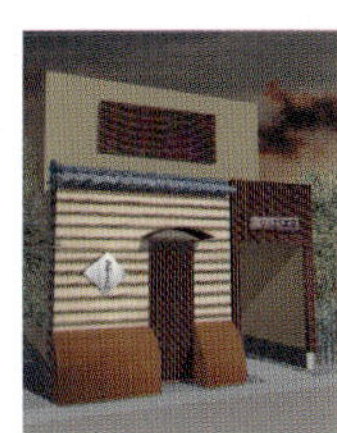

245. SHIRAYUKI FUKIN
naramachi
NARAMACHI , NARA
2006.03*

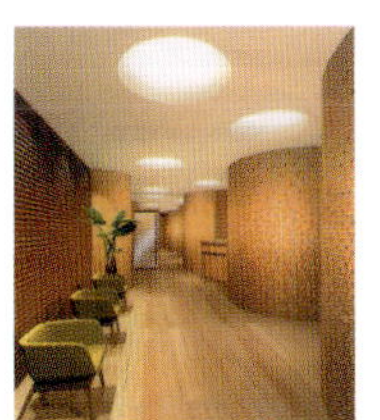

246. BLANC ROUGE
AOYAMA , TOKYO
2006.03*

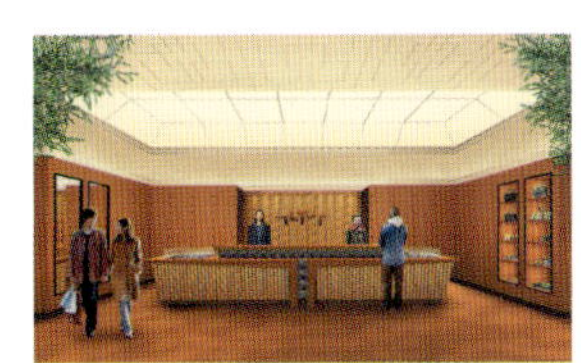

247. SHOP Ⅳ
MULTIPLE SHOP
2006.03*

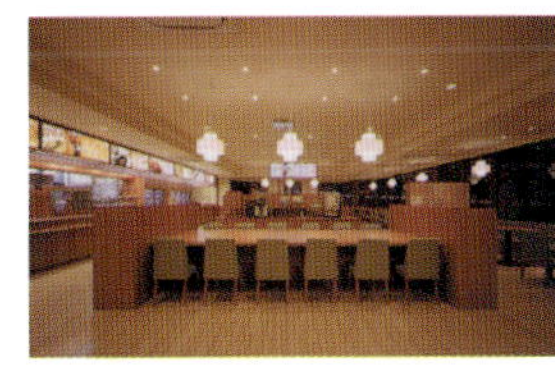

248. TAWAWA tondabayashi
TONDABAYASHI , OSAKA
2006.03

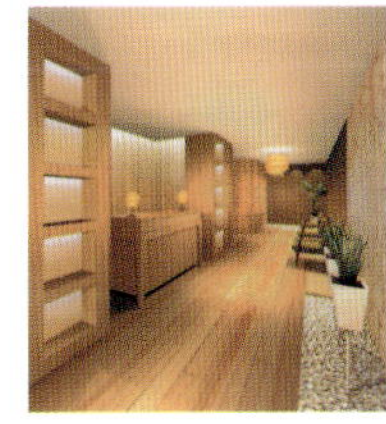

249. ESTHETIC SALON Ⅱ
AOYAMA , TOKYO
2006.03*

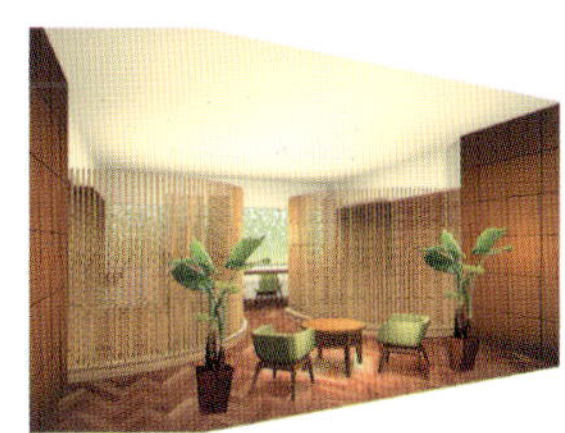

250. NATURAL DESIGN
SHINAGAWA , TOKYO
2006.04*

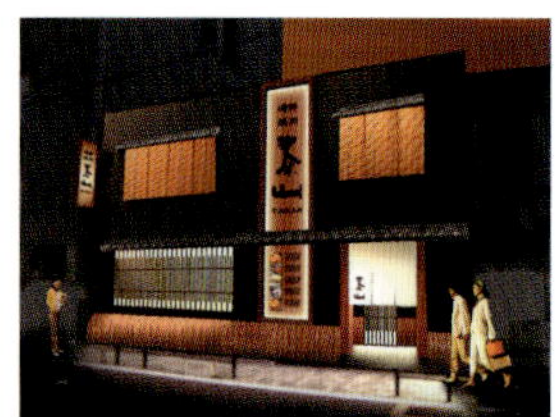

251. GRILL RESTAURANT Ⅴ
DOYAMACHO , OSAKA
2006.04*

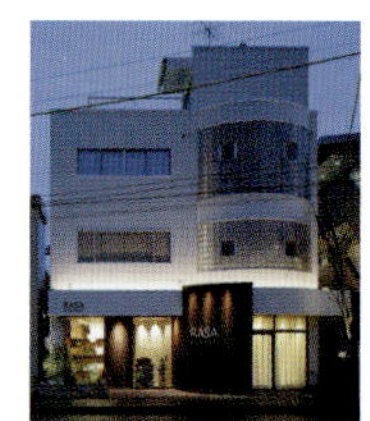

252. RASA
SHIMIZU , SHIZUOKA
2006.04

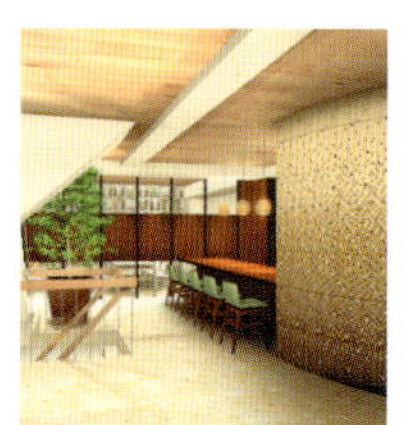

253. CAFE DINING Ⅴ
MUROMACHI , KYOTO
2006.04

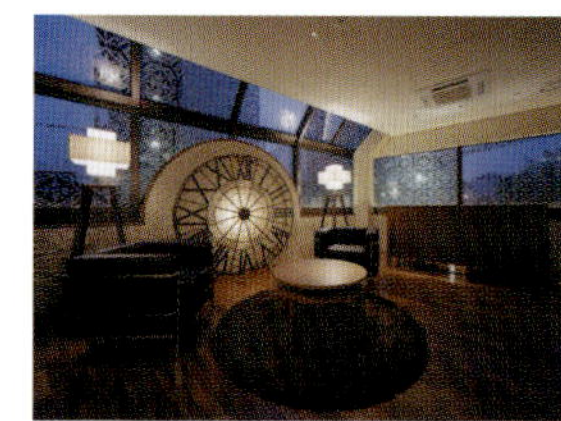

254. DON FUN
MOTOAZABU , TOKYO
2006.04

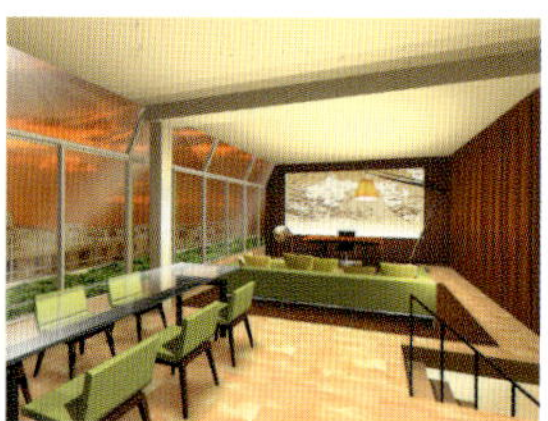

255. ADVERTISEMENT AGENCY
OFFICE
MUROMACHI , KYOTO
2006.04

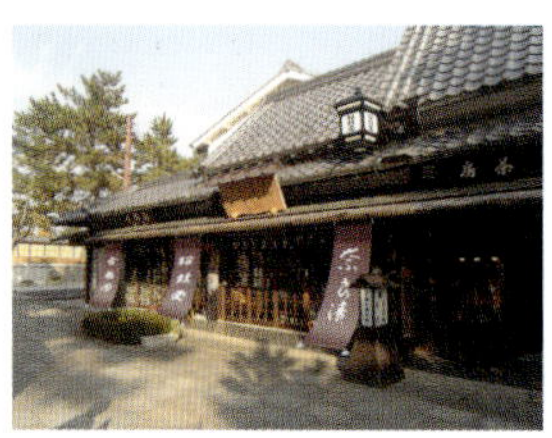

256. SYOKODO
HORYUJI , NARA
2006.04

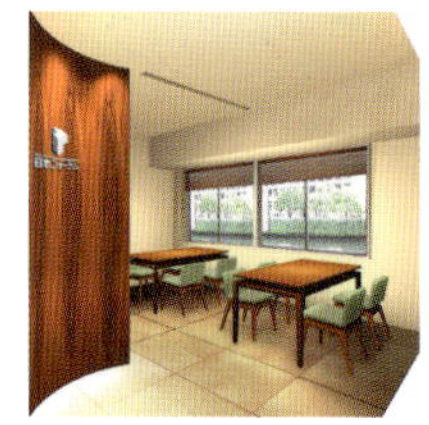

257. NIHON FORUM
NISHITENMA , OSAKA
2006.05

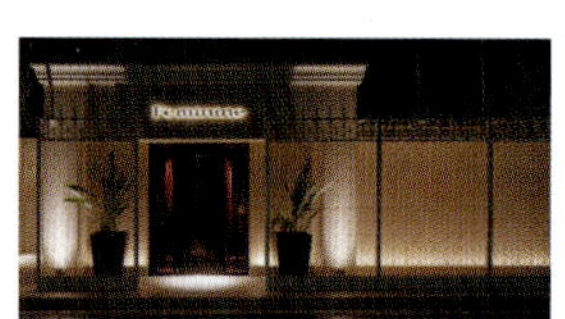

258. FEMININE
IBARAKI , OSAKA
2006.05

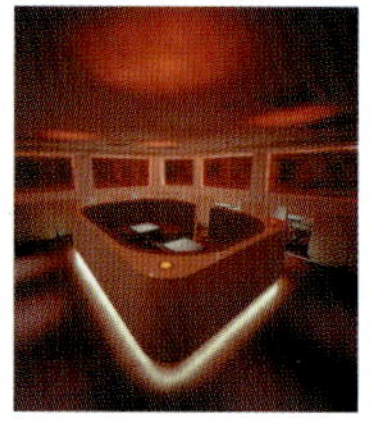

259. REMIX
IBARAKI , OSAKA
2006.05

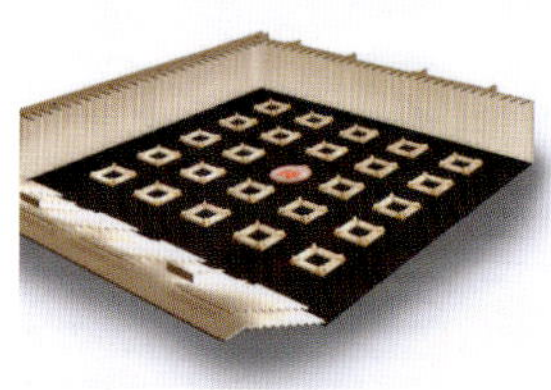

260. IBONOITO
TATSUNO , HYOGO
2006.06

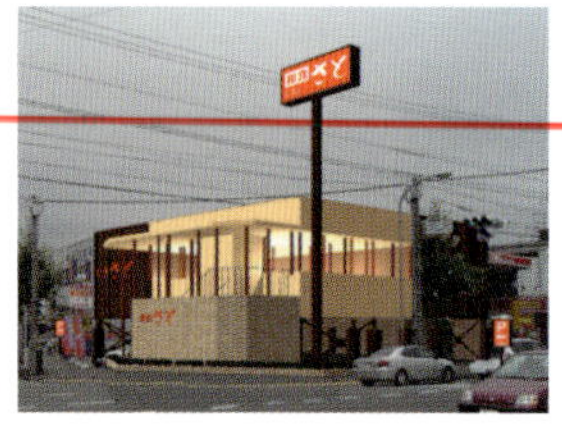

261. SATO shizuoka ikeda
IKEDA , SHIZUOKA
2006.06

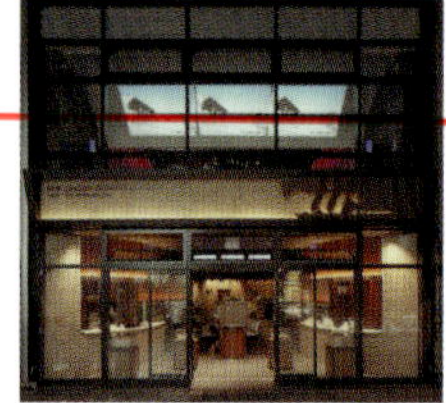

262. AIR
SENNICHIMAE , OSAKA
2006.06

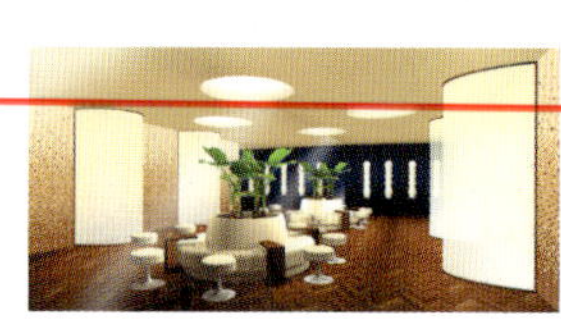

263. AIR CAFE
SENNICHIMAE , OSAKA
2006.06

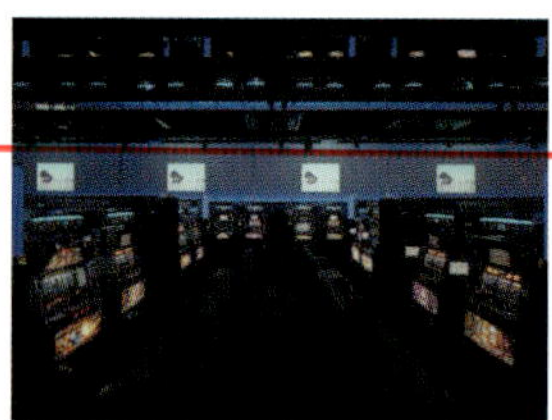

264. AIR LOUNGE
SENNICHIMAE , OSAKA
2006.06

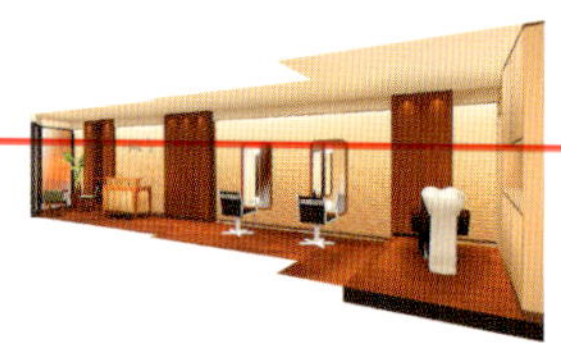

265. ANOKA HAIR
KOBAICHO , OSAKA
2006.06

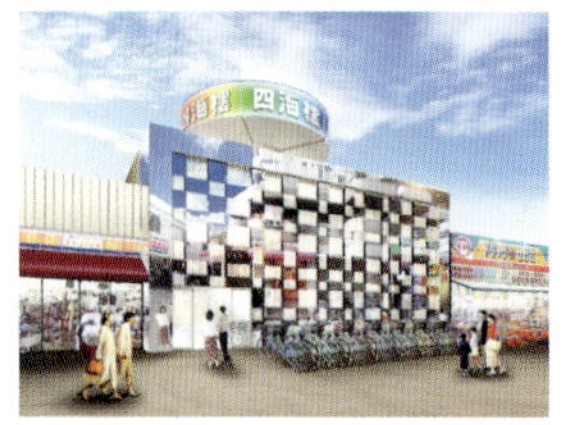

266. SHIKAIRO
SUMIYOSHI , OSAKA
2006.06 ~

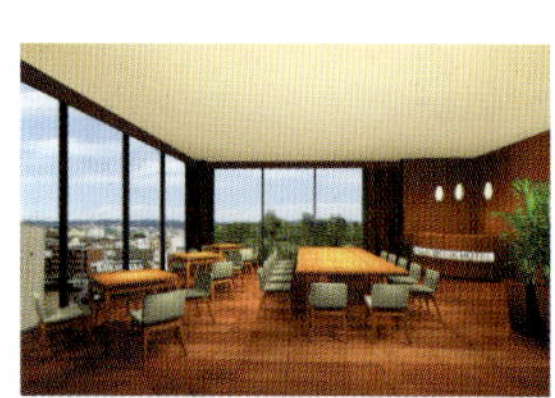

267. FUJI WORK HOTEL
TAKATSUKI , OSAKA
2006.06*

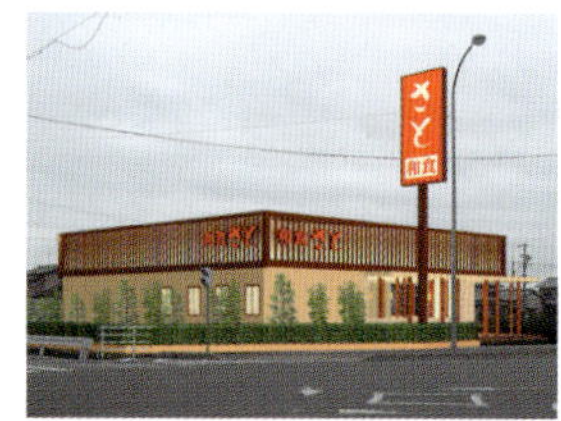

268. SATO yaizu
YAIZU , SHIZUOKA
2006.07

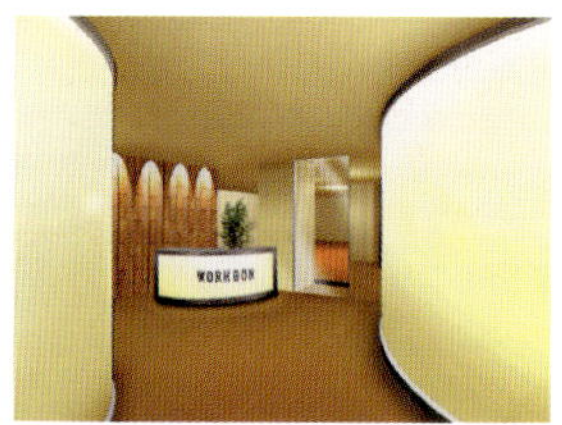

269. KUROKAME HIFUKU
BUILDING
FUCHU , HIROSHIMA
2006.07

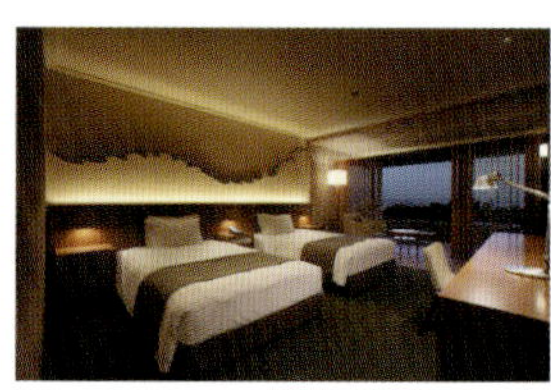

270. ANAGA HOTEL
ANAGA , HYOGO
2006.07

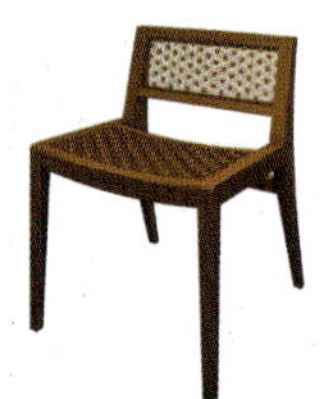

271. KUMIKO CHAIR
ADAL
2006.07

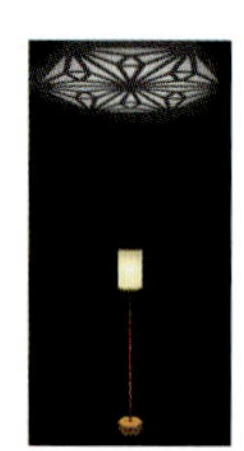

272. KUMIKO LIGHT floor stand
DAIKO
2006.07

273. KUMIKO LIGHT table stand
DAIKO
2006.07

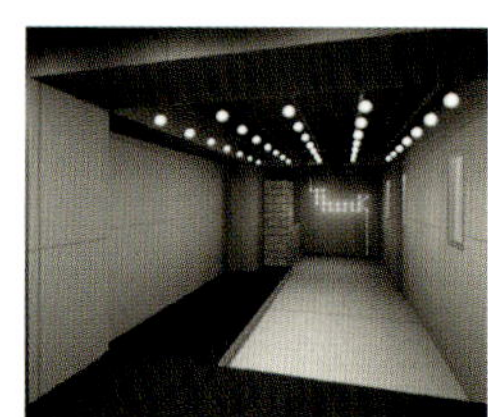

274. THINK GRAPHICS
MINAMIHORIE , OSAKA
2006.08

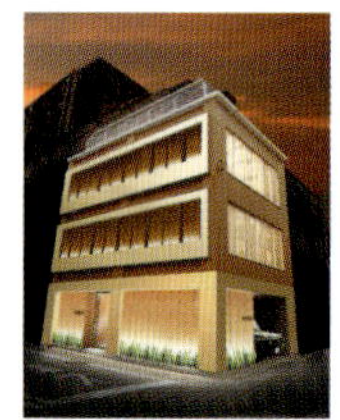

275. INDEN BUILDING
MUROMACHI , KYOTO
2006.08

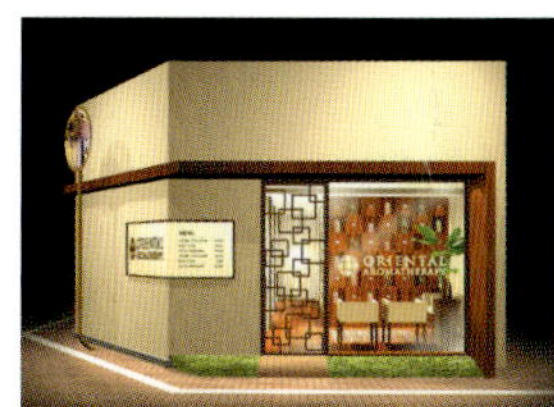

276. ORIENTAL AROMATHERAPY KAMEARI
KAMEARI , TOKYO
2006.08

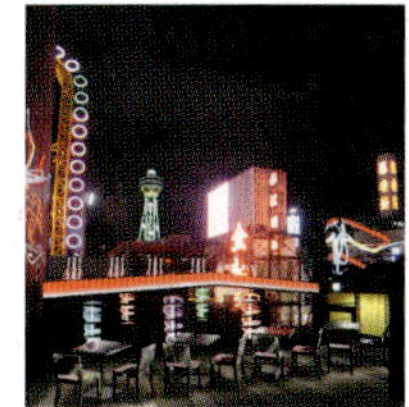

277. NEON BAR dotonbori
DOTONBORI , OSAKA
2006.08 ~

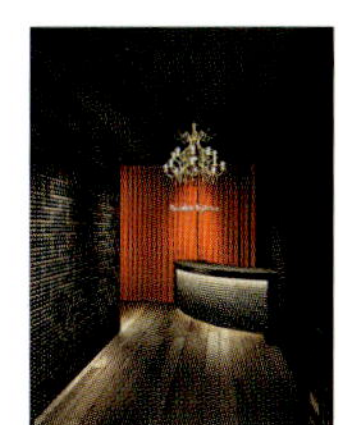

278. HARDEN TIGHTEN
AZABUJYUBAN , TOKYO
2006.09

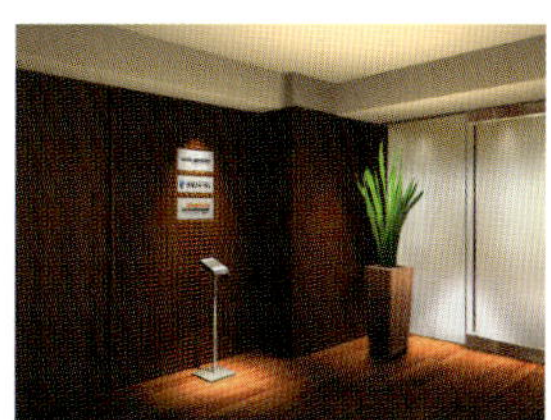

279. GAIA ACCESS
TORANOMON , TOKYO
2006.09

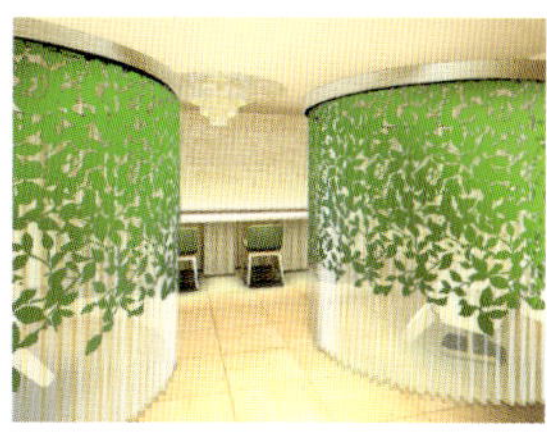

280. ESTHETIC SALON Ⅲ
MINAMIAOYAMA , TOKYO
2006.09 ~

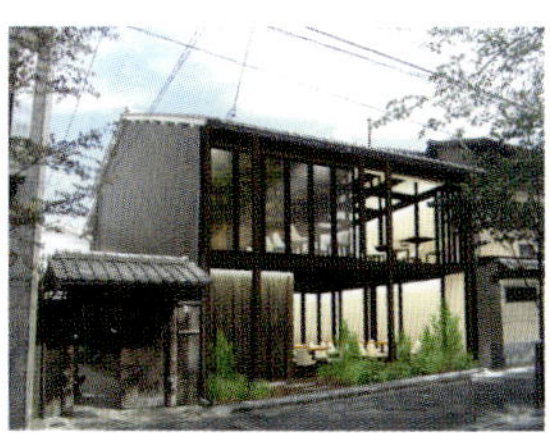

281. INDEN RESTAURANT
KIYAMACHI , KYOTO
2006.09 ~

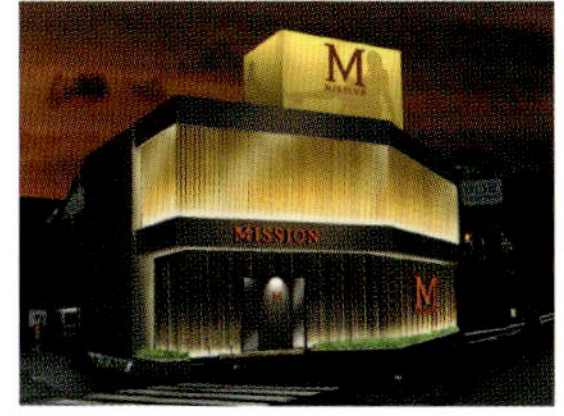

282. MISSION
TAKATSUKI , OSAKA
2006.09 ~

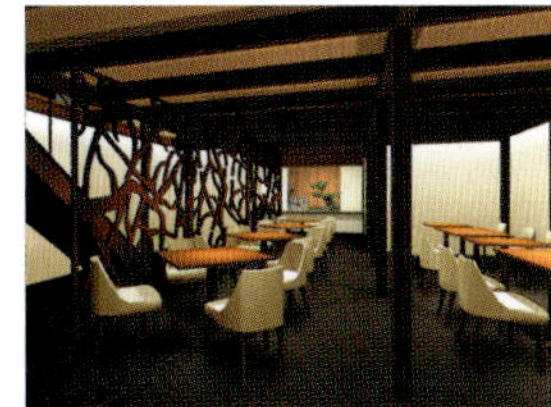

283. INDEN CAFE DINING
KIYAMACHI , KYOTO
2006.09 ~

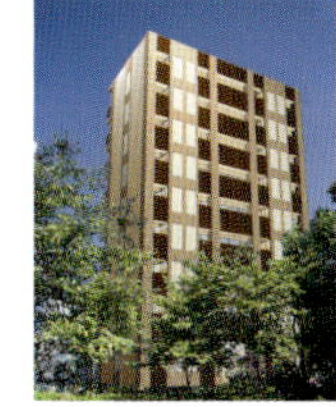

284. CONDOMINIUM sakuranomiya
MIYAKOJIMA , OSAKA
2006.09 ~

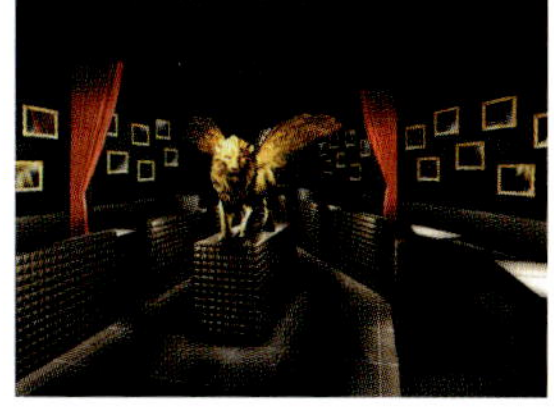

285. MARVELOUS
TAKATSUKI , OSAKA
2006.09 ~

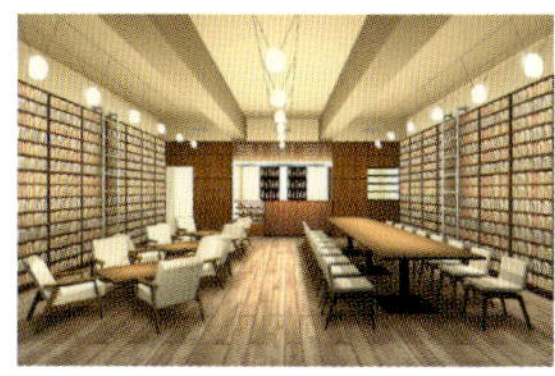

286. KYOTO COMIC MUSEUM CAFE
KARASUMAOIKE , KYOTO
2006.09 ~

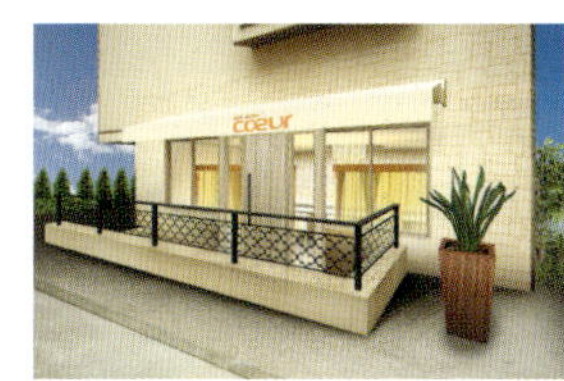

287. COEUR
MINAMIAOYAMA , TOKYO
2006.10 ~

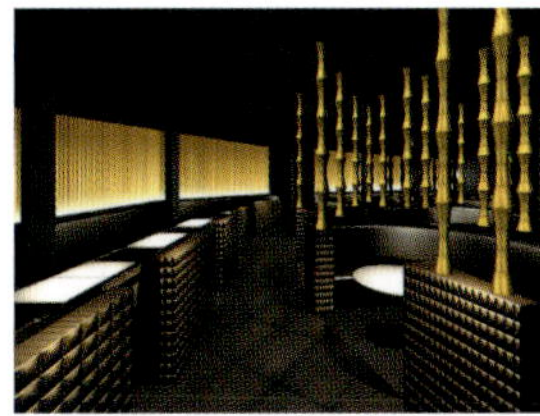

288. GRAN
TAKATSUKI , OSAKA
2006.10 ~

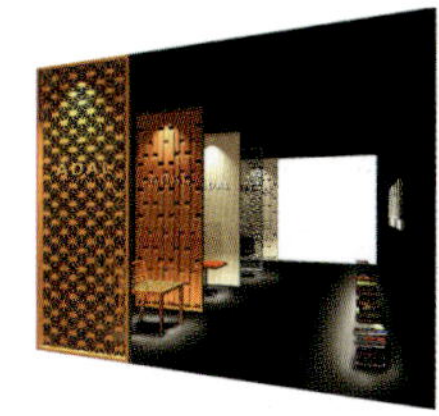

289. 100% DESIGN TOKYO 2006 ADAL BOOTH
AOYAMA , TOKYO
2006.10 ~

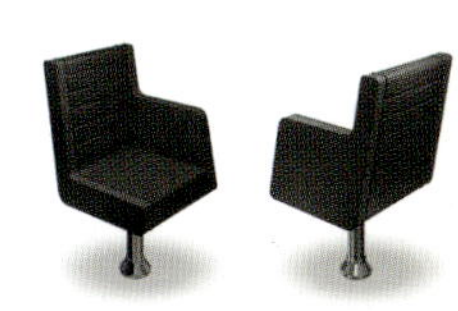

290. CHAIR FOR AMUSEMENT FACILITIES
MULTIPLE SHOP
2006.10~

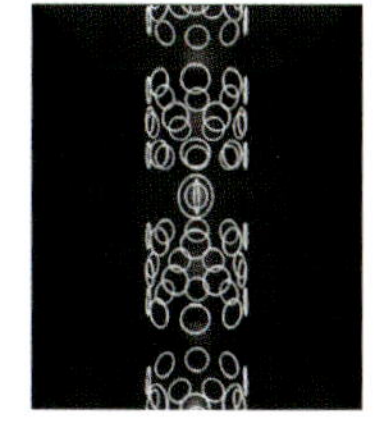

291. 100% DESIGN TOKYO 2006
AOYAMA , TOKYO
2006.10*

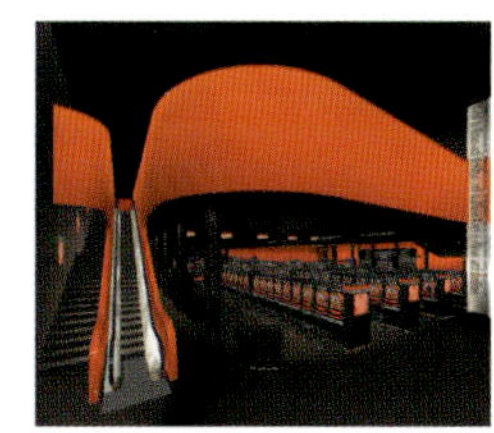

292. ATARIYA
SUMIYOSHI , OSAKA
2006.10~

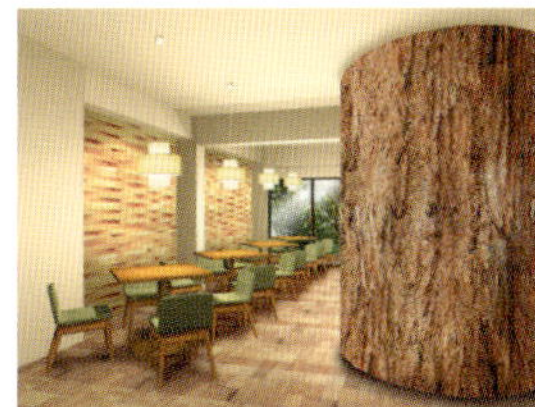

293. LABEL CAFE
NISHITENMA , OSAKA
2006.10~

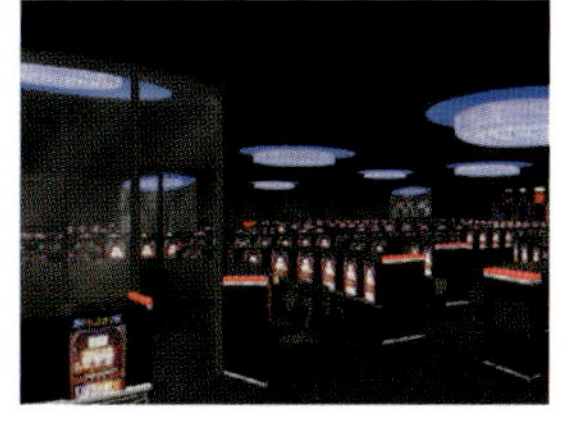

294. AMUSEMENT Ⅰ
MULTIPLE SHOP
2006.10~

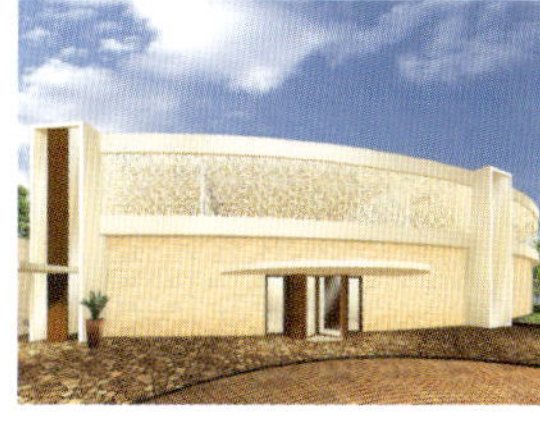

295. BRIDAL BANQUET
YOKKAICHI , MIE
2006.10~

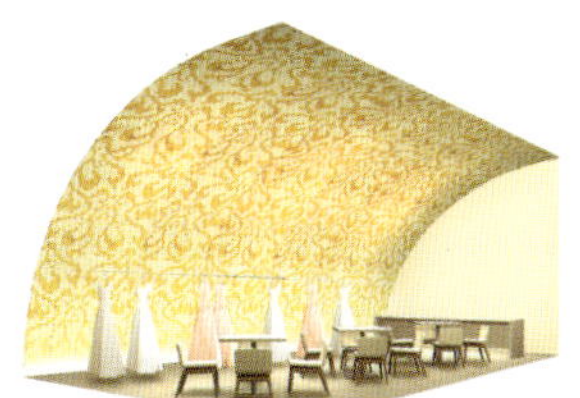

296. BRIDAL SALON
MULTIPLE SHOP
2006.10~

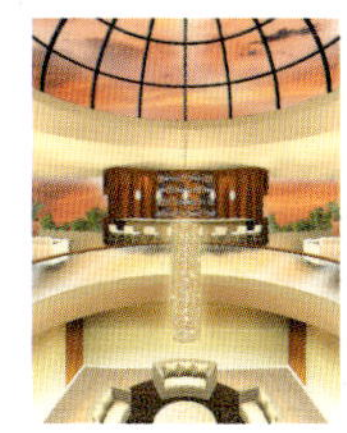

297. LOUNGE VI
YOKKAICHI , MIE
2006.10~

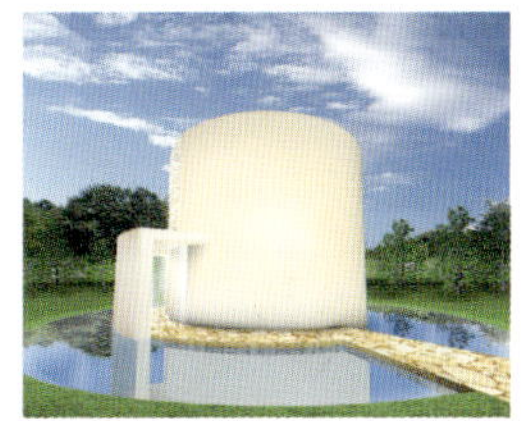

298. CHAPEL
YOKKAICHI , MIE
2006.10~

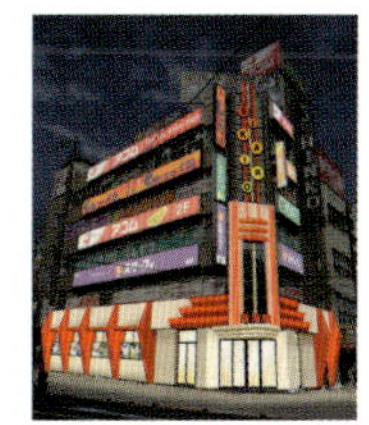

299. AMUSEMENT Ⅱ
MULTIPLE SHOP
2006.10~

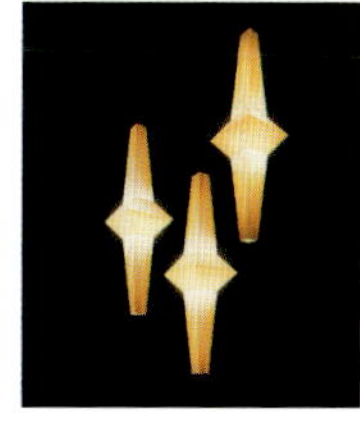

300. STAR LIGHT
DAIKO
2006.10~

「おわりに」と「これから」

商空間デザインは、どちらかというと、オーナーありきのデザインだ。

乱暴な例えかもしれないが、社会や時代としての「水面」に向かう、オーナーの事業計画なる「水滴」があり、

僕ら空間デザイナーが「波紋」となり、様々な現象やコミュニケーションが「水面」に広がって行く。

僕の中では、コトの流れはそんなイメージで、自分は、そのオーナーや現象、コミュニケーションに関わる人達が、

幸せになるコトをずっと追いかけて来た。この本はその軌跡に相違ない。

そんな疾走の中で、デザイナーの僕も一つの水滴となるべく、2004年にLabel（レーベル）という会社を立ち上げた。

これからについて考える時には、このLabelも僕のフィールドの一つとして未来につながっていて、

ここで僕は、デザイナーという肩書きを持つ人間が、社会や時を見て「これが必要だ」というモノやコトを、能動的に創出したいと思っている。

商空間デザインに取り憑かれて約20年。自分のことなどそっちのけで、がむしゃらに走り続けて来た。

これからは、自身のこと、仲間のこと、そして、プロジェクトの意味や目的を共有出来る人たちとの時間を大切に

僕のデザインの道を踏みしめていきたい。

Katsuya Iwamoto

The End and a New Beginning

The design of commercial space is basically the owner's design.

Although the following may seem to be a somewhat crude example, a water droplet,

representing the owner's business plan, falls toward a water surface representing society and an era.

We, the designers become the ripples and a variety of phenomenon and communication results,

spreading out across the water surface.This is how I perceive the flow of things.

It has always been my pursuit to contribute to the happiness of those that interact with the owner,

this phenomenon and the resulting act of communication, and I am sure that this book is no different.

In my pursuit of the above, I established a company known as Label in 2004

in order to facilitate my metamorphosis into the catalytic water drop.

The reason for this was that I wanted to actively create things that designers deemed necessary

through their observations of society and the times.

Label is comprised of designers that do not limit their skills to one particular genre,

working together on a wide variety of projects. There, together with my fellow designers,

we design toys, clothes and fields. Label started out at it's own pace and is creating a future as one of my future fields.

I have spent more or less the last 20 years in the design of commercial space.

Even today, those frantic years remind me of the immense power and possibility of design.

 In conclusion, I would like to sincerely thank the many people who contributed to the publishing of this book. Thank you.

PHOTO CREDIT （アイウエオ順）

荒木 義久	Yoshihisa Araki	018, 019, 072, 073, 208, 209
金村 智久	Tomohisa Kanemura	196~199
ナカサ&パートナーズ	Nacasa & Partners Inc.	028~031, 180, 181
藤谷 伸次	Shinji Fujitani	188, 189
山田 誠良	Seiryo Yamada	010~017, 020~027, 032~065, 068~071, 074~101, 104~119, 122~125, 128~137, 140~165, 168~179, 182~187, 192~195, 202~207, 210~215

KATSUYA IWAMOTO
EMBODY DESIGN

http://www.embodydesign.com

発行日
2006年12月10日　初版第一刷発行

Date of publication
First Paperback Edition, 10/12/2006

著者・アートディレクション
岩本 勝也

Author & Artdirection
KATSUYA IWAMOTO

編集
熊谷 有記（Label Creators Production）
http://www.label-creators.com

Editor
YUUKI KUMAGAI（Label Creators Production）
http://www.label-creators.com

グラフィックデザイン
辻　健（Think Graphics）
http://www.thinkgraphics.jp

Graphic Design
TAKESHI TSUJI（Think Graphics）
http://www.thinkgraphics.jp

翻訳
株式会社ワールドサポート

Translation
World Support Inc.

発行元
株式会社アルファ企画
東京都新宿区三栄町24黒田ビル2F　〒160-0008
TEL. 03-5360-6531　FAX. 03-5360-6544
http://www.e-webpro.jp　info@e-webpro.jp

Publishing House
Alpha Planning Inc.
Kuroda Bldg. 2F,24 Sanei-cho Shinjuku-ku, Tokyo, Japan
TEL. +81-3-5360-6531　FAX. +81-3-5360-6544
http://www.e-webpro.jp　info@e-webpro.jp

発売元
株式会社ワークスコーポレーション
東京都渋谷区道玄坂1-10-8 渋谷野村ビル7F　〒150-0043
TEL. 03-5459-8266　FAX.03-5459-8275
http://www.wgn.co.jp

Distributor
Works Corporation Inc.
Shibuya-Nomura Bldg. 7F
1-10-8 Dogenzaka Shibuya-ku, Tokyo, Japan
TEL. +81-3-5459-8266　FAX.+81-3-5459-8275
http://www.wgn.co.jp

ISBN4-948759-84-8